A Passion for Nature

A Passion for Nature

The Life of

JOHN MUIR

DONALD WORSTER

OXFORD
UNIVERSITY PRESS

2008

OXFORD
UNIVERSITY PRESS

Oxford University Press, Inc., publishes works that further
Oxford University's objective of excellence
in research, scholarship, and education.

Oxford   New York
Auckland   Cape Town   Dar es Salaam   Hong Kong   Karachi
Kuala Lumpur   Madrid   Melbourne   Mexico City   Nairobi
New Delhi   Shanghai   Taipei   Toronto

With offices in
Argentina   Austria   Brazil   Chile   Czech Republic   France   Greece
Guatemala   Hungary   Italy   Japan   Poland   Portugal   Singapore
South Korea   Switzerland   Thailand   Turkey   Ukraine   Vietnam

Copyright © 2008 by Donald Worster

Published by Oxford University Press, Inc.
198 Madison Avenue, New York, NY 10016

www.oup.com

Oxford is a registered trademark of Oxford University Press.

Library of Congress Cataloging-in-Publication Data
Worster, Donald, 1941–
A passion for nature ; the life of John Muir / Donald Worster.
p.   cm.
Includes bibliographical references.
ISBN 978-0-19-516682-8
1. Muir, John, 1838–1914. 2. Naturalists—United States—Biography.
3. Conservationists—United States—Biography. I. Title.
QH31. M9W68 2008
333.72092—dc22   2008001441

9

Printed in the United States of America
on acid-free paper

To my students

Contents

A Passion for Nature

Muir's Trail

I n the summer of 1877, John Muir set out from the irrigated fields of Pasadena, California, where acres of orange trees had recently been planted, on a long and solitary hike. He followed Eaton Creek upstream toward what he called a "little poem of wildness" high in the looming San Gabriel Mountains, along a trail shaded by native oaks and bordered by thick chaparral covering the hillsides like prickly fur. In his pack he carried three freshly baked loaves of bread and a bottle of water, his usual sustenance on the trail.

Although nearly forty years old, he was still relatively unknown to the world. It would be a decade or two before he became celebrated as the nation's most ardent lover of wild places, the founding president of the Sierra Club, and the author of popular articles and books on the mountains of California and the national parks. It would be another century before historians looked to him as the greatest forerunner of modern environmentalism, a powerful influence on people far beyond the West Coast and even beyond America's shores. In 1877 Muir was only an obscure figure, a joyful but unprepossessing hiker into the backcountry.

As he followed the trail up Eaton Canyon, he came upon "a strange, dark man of doubtful parentage" who had built a cabin in a stream-side meadow. "All my conjectures as to his nationality failed," Muir wrote, "and no wonder, since his father was Irish and his mother Spanish, a mixture not often met even in California." Because night was approaching, the stranger invited Muir to share a meal and bed down at his campfire, and the two men fell into a conversation that lasted for hours.

That was vintage Muir. Throughout his life he liked to gab only a little less than he liked to hike. Wherever he went, he started a conversation, and typically it went on and on, Muir doing most of the

John Muir in a photograph by Bradley & Rulofson, San Francisco, about 1872. (H–A, JMP)

talking. Those who knew him well thought he was the most engaging talker they ever knew. Certainly he was the most egalitarian. He talked with everyone he met, from white Anglo farmers, ministers, gold miners, politicians, and bankers, to former African American slaves, women of all ages, hordes of children, and a canoe full of Tlingits paddling along the Alaskan coast. Mostly they talked, and talked passionately, about nature.

So it was with this solitary stranger he met in the foothills. As they sat in the darkening canyon, his host described his dream of creating a vineyard and harvesting honey here in this fertile, beautiful spot. Born in Mexico, he had rambled a great deal—doing a bit of hunting, prospecting, and mining—but was now ready to settle here in his own poem of wildness, to "make money and marry a Spanish woman." Muir was touched by the man's dream and sensed in his fellow camper a shared passion for America's mountains, forests, tumbling streams, and fields of wildflowers filled with feeding bees.

That passion for nature can still draw people together across differences of ethnicity, as it did Muir and his dark-skinned friend. On any sunny weekend they may find themselves walking together up a canyon, watching quail run across the path, sniffing the tang of sagebrush, and looking for stars above the urban haze. For all their differences, nature provides walkers of every sort a common thrill of adventure, a flash of wildness that binds them together.

In his autobiographical *My Boyhood and Youth*, Muir claimed that his passion for nature derived from a "natural inherited wildness in our blood."[1] Although he was writing in 1913, still early days in the science of genetics and evolutionary psychology, he was arguing in genetic terms that everyone is born with an inner bond to nature, drawing us away from civilization, an impulse over which we have little rational control. Meeting people like the man in Eaton Canyon had convinced him of the universality of that "inherited wildness," an equality of passion in which all humans shared.

Muir may have been at least partially right. All the human passions go deeper and are more universal than any fashion or social background. Scientist Edward O. Wilson has suggested, in an echo of Muir, that everyone has an in-born "biophilia," or love of nature and natural things, "the innate tendency to focus on life and life-like processes."[2] Exactly how natural selection could give rise to that passion, however, remains unclear. Someday research may exactly locate a generic feeling for nature in some part of the human brain, making it the product of those complex protein ribbons created by DNA and RNA, but more likely this passion will always remain scientifically elusive and unpredictable. Biology will never fully explain what drove Muir or his Eaton Canyon host into the outdoors. Their shared passion may have derived from a common biological origin, but around that passion twisted strands of personality and ideas.

One should try to understand how culture, as well as biology, shaped John Muir's feelings for the natural world. Culture clothes persistent, universal feelings in ever-changing ideas, policies, and articles of belief. Culture creates those ideas out of specific historical moments, and the ideas encounter critical resistance, go through stages of development and reassessment, and lead people to change their behavior. So Muir's "natural inherited wildness in the blood" became embodied in new ideas with new consequences. The most dramatic of those consequences was the rise of the nature conservation movement.

That movement's deepest cultural origins lie in the late eighteenth- and early nineteenth-century revolution that introduced modern liberal democratic ideals, including the quest for human rights, personal liberty, and social equality. The movement did not stop with the concept of social justice but continued on toward the rediscovery of nature, the appreciation of wildness, and the vision of a green society. Muir was a child of that revolution, and his story helps us see that modern environmentalism, based on a respect for the otherness of nature and an understanding of the emotional and material interdependence of humans and nature, comes out of that challenge to orthodoxy. Muir was a liberal, a democrat, and a conservationist.

A few years before he spent the night talking in Eaton Canyon, he was hiking near his beloved Yosemite Valley when he came upon the carcass of a bear. Immediately, he sat down to mourn, although few, he admitted, would share his grief over the death of a wild animal. Such indifference ran counter to the moral progress the age seemed generally to be making. "We live in an age of liberal principles," he scribbled in his notebook with a note of sarcasm, an age in which "all the human race black brown & yellow are recognized as in some sense brethren capable of Christianity & even admissible to the one Anglo Saxon heaven above." But when it came to bears, the age was not yet liberal enough.[3]

What did he mean by "liberal principles"? He did not seem to have in mind any formal philosophy, nor liberalism confined to politics or economics. What he meant was closer to this definition of liberalism from the *Oxford English Dictionary*: "Free from bigotry or unreasonable prejudice in favor of traditional opinions or established institutions; open to the reception of new ideas or proposals of reform."[4] Particularly he was thinking of liberal ideas in ethics and religion that were challenging orthodox notions of salvation for the few, of innate human corruption, and of a fallen world. Early on he began to strive for a more positive, hopeful view of human nature, along with a more positive view of nature.

The revolutionary movement that challenged those older, more pessimistic attitudes toward nature and human nature emphasized the fused ideals of liberty and equality, or "liberal democracy." Always, they co-existed in tension with one another. Liberty was hailed as the heroic spirit leading the people, but liberty without restraint would lead to chaos, selfishness, and exploitation. Absolute equality of condition, on the other hand, would require a high degree of enforcement and would stifle individuality. To claim freedom of enterprise or speech or belief was good, but not to grind the face of the poor or stifle the voices of others or to allow the rights or beliefs of the majority to become tyrannical. Liberty needed the check of equality, and equality needed the check of liberty.

We associate the rise of liberal democratic ideals with several social reforms that had emerged by Muir's day, reforms that he generally supported throughout his life: the abolition of slavery, emancipation for women, opposition to militarism and war. Liberal principles usually led to political activism for those causes, while Muir tended to avoid politics as a sordid seeking of power for trivial ends. One may criticize him for walking on up the trail and not doing as much as he could have done, say, for women's rights. On the other hand, by not stopping and devoting his full energy to every part of the liberal agenda, he arrived at moral positions more advanced than many of his contemporaries.

For example, he came to believe that government should have the responsibility of setting aside national parks, forests, and wildlife sanctuaries and such places should be open to all citizens, from humble shoemakers to millionaires. But then he pushed well beyond the granting of access to every human being toward granting rights and moral significance to every creature that lives on the earth. Before he had reached the age of twenty, he was asking: "What creature of all that the Lord has taken the pains to make is not essential to the completeness of that unit—the cosmos? . . . They are earth-born companions and our fellow mortals." Not only the higher mammals but also insects, reptiles, and plants were in his view different kinds of "people," and even a "mineral arrangement of matter," he supposed, may be "endowed with sensations that we in our blind exclusive perfection can have no manner of communication with."[5]

Muir was a liberal also in his religious views. Turning from orthodoxy, he "worshipped all Nature, God's works," one of his daughters explained; "the laws of Nature were only another way of saying the laws of God."[6] That fusion of nature and God was not a static order created by a distant Great Mind. "God" for Muir was a deliberately loose and imprecise term referring to an active, creative force dwelling in, above, and around nature. Continuously animated by that divine force, every part of the natural world was in constant flux—the earth moving under foot, glaciers flowing down mountainsides, plants and animals evolving and spreading. Always the flux was purposeful. Always it moved toward beauty. Always and everywhere it was holy.

Nature for Muir, and for other men and women throughout the modern period, was the name given to that part of the world that we humans did not create, that we do not manage, and that can and will survive our extinction. Nature was seldom imagined as a world completely free of human presence or influence—even the phrase "pristine nature" was more relative than absolute. Nature, Muir believed, included humans just as any community includes all of its inhabitants. But he made this critical distinction: while we cannot live without the forces and creatures of the nonhuman world, they can live without us. There is more to the world than humankind and its artifacts.

Well before Muir's day nature had become a source of liberation, a place offering freedom and equality, a necessity for full human development, and, above all, a world independent of people to be defended and respected, even revered. Going into wild country freed one from the repressive hand of authority. Social deference faded in wild places. Economic rank ceased to matter so much. Bags of money were not needed for survival—only one's wits and knowledge. Nature offered a home to the political maverick, the rebellious child, the outlaw or runaway slave, the soldier who refused to fight, and, by the late nineteenth century, the woman who climbed mountains to show her strength and independence.

Conservatives came to fear that more positive and egalitarian relation to nature as a decline into paganism. Alexis de Tocqueville, for example, who in 1835 and 1840 published an English translation of his two-volume work *Democracy in America*, warned his readers to resist this unhealthy tendency within democratic societies. Although a member of the French aristocracy, he tried to come to terms with the "irresistible revolution" that was sweeping people like himself from power, challenging the privileges of high birth. A broad, grassroots movement to work toward a greater "equality of conditions" was what he meant by "democracy." Acknowledging that it could not be stopped, he warned that it carried some dangerous implications.

In a seldom-noticed chapter of the book, Tocqueville noted that the liberal democratic revolution seemed to encourage a strong feeling for nature. Its philosophical tendency, he wrote, is to tear down the traditional doctrines of Christianity and put in their place a new religion of nature, or what he called "pantheism." "It cannot be denied that pantheism has made great progress in our time." For a man raised in the Roman Catholic tradition, that pantheistic tendency was one of the most pernicious threats posed by the new ideas. Tocqueville solemnly urged, "All those who still appreciate the true nature of man's greatness should combine in the struggle against it."

He feared exactly what John Muir hoped would happen—that the barrier between humans and nonhumans might weaken and vanish.[7]

As Tocqueville perceived, democracy was in love with nature, and nature was the natural and logical religion of democracy. Pursuing that religion of nature is the main and persistent theme in Muir's life story. But to place his religion within the context of modern liberalism and democracy is only the first step toward understanding the path he took. His trail had many unforeseen complications.

The America of Muir's old age, compared to the one he first encountered as a youth, was more, not less, economically stratified. Although the average income was comparatively high, the distance separating the social classes had become immense. Every modern nation was similarly divided against itself, as wealth became more concentrated in the hands of a few. Corporations ran the new economies, and a handful of men ran those corporations.

Alexis de Tocqueville had predicted that outcome as he contemplated the enthusiasm that democratic republics showed for industrial development and economic growth. One day, he foresaw, industrialism would give rise to aristocracies based, not on traditional obligations or feudal relations, but on command of capital and expertise. Such a modern aristocracy would feel little responsibility for the people toiling at the bottom; in terms of charity or compassion it would be "one of the hardest that have appeared on the earth."[8]

What that accumulation of wealth meant for nature was as complicated as what it meant for human relations. Just as rich men and women often claimed to be benefactors of humanity, so also they claimed to be lovers of nature. Just as they offered to build libraries for the workingman and to bring cheap consumer goods to the lowliest household, they also offered to help preserve the beauty and integrity of the natural world. In both promises they spoke, with varying degrees of sincerity, the language of liberal democracy. But was the nature conservation they supported the legacy of that revolutionary triad of nature, freedom, and equality, or was their kind of conservation a diminished and distorted shadow of its origins?

How Muir struggled to find his own voice as a rebel against orthodoxy and tradition, how he became part of a struggle for liberal principles that went on across all the world's oceans and political boundaries, is a story that has never been fully told. He met and befriended humble people of every sort but also some of the most powerful men of his day, forcing him to reconcile dreams of economic success with saving the beauty and integrity of the natural world. He explored some of the most remarkable wild places on the planet, always trying to see those places with the eyes of a naturalist but always worrying about falling into the trap of a coldly scientific analysis. He worked hard at becoming a writer who could effectively explain and defend nature to the public, when he would rather be climbing some remote peak. Against the grain of his own desire and temperament, he tried to become a reformer of society. Through all those ordeals, he lived a life constantly driven by intense feelings. The intensity of his feelings made him one of the most celebrated figures of his day, but they also plunged him into conflicts that no man could easily resolve.

A human life, like any mountain trail, winds and twists through a very complicated, ever-changing landscape, taking unexpected turns and ending up in unexpected places. The lay of the land, the physical or natural environment, has some influence over the path one chooses to take—going around rather than over boulders, say, or along the banks of a stream rather than through a tangled wood. Likewise in the course of an individual life, nature helps give shape to the direction a man or woman takes and determines how his or her life unfolds. So also does one's inner self, the drives and emotions that one inherits from ancestors far back in evolutionary time, determine the route. But the trail of any one's life is also shaped by the ideas floating around in the cultural air one breathes. All those influences make it impossible to explain easily why a person's life follows this path rather than another. Muir's case was no exception. He was shaped by an imposing tangle of factors: the physical nature he encountered, the passions he felt, the people he met, and the ideas he encountered along the way.

One thing about him, however, was always simple and predictable: he was never content until he had climbed all the way to the top. Always he pushed his body as far as he could. That summer 1877 excursion into the San Gabriels was no exception. Leaving his immigrant friend behind on Eaton Creek, he sauntered on for several days, sometimes walking in open sunshine, sometimes forced to crawl through dense underbrush, always keeping an eye open for snakes, wolves, bears, and cougars, until at last he stood on the peak of Mount San Antonio. That night he bedded down between two fires for safety from dangerous predators.

After getting back safely to Pasadena, he exclaimed, "I had a glorious view of the valley out to the ocean, which would require a whole book for description. My bread gave out a day before reaching the settlements, but I felt all the fresher and clearer for the fast." That too was vintage Muir—seeing more than he could describe, neglecting his food supply, but returning with a clarified mind and a fresh heart. His moment of regeneration he wanted to share with everyone on earth, and characteristically generous of spirit he became a trusting child of nature and a prophet of hope for humanity.

CHAPTER 1

The Scottish Lowlands

The High Street of Dunbar, a seaport on Scotland's eastern shore, was already by the early nineteenth century a broad modern avenue of business and enterprise. Shoulder to shoulder along its length stood straight rows of solid burgher establishments, with steep red pantile roofs and jutting chimneys. On 21 April 1838, John Muir was born upstairs in one of those places of commerce. It may have been above the small grocer's shop kept by his parents or across the street and over the butcher's shop owned by his maternal grandparents. In either case the first sound of nature the child likely heard was a maritime cry of a sea gull flying overhead, loud and harsh enough to pierce even the thickest walls.

For a man who would become the world's leading advocate of wilderness, who would take as his life mission the preservation of natural beauty, this birthplace may seem a paradoxical origin, so gray and urban. He came forth into a world of dressed stone, cobbled streets, and somber, controlling civilization, where everything green was carefully tucked away in back gardens. Dunbar was compactly built and barricaded out all unruly forces. The town's name came from the Gaelic words for "a fort on a height." Defense was its first reason for existence—defense against dangers that might come from the sea—and wild nature, from whatever direction it came, had long ago been shut out like an invading army.

Seven decades after his birth, when Muir sat down to write his autobiography, he opened with childhood scenes far removed from the sturdy town center and its moneymaking habits. "When I was a boy in Scotland," he began, "I was fond of everything that was wild, and all my life I've been growing fonder and fonder of wild places and wild creatures." He recalled birds cheerily singing in hedgerows, eels and crabs lurking in tide pools, storms crashing against black headlands, all of which he did in fact experience but, in truth, were less a daily part of growing up than the man-made environment of the town. We cannot understand the boy's development into adulthood until we understand the town and society from which he came—the hard-working families living along the High Street and the culture of modernizing Scotland. Some of that wealth-seeking culture he rebelled against, but much of it he absorbed into his core and would never escape.

Muir, regardless of where he traveled, would remain a Lowland Scot all his days. Only secondarily would he become a product or patriot of his adopted United States or a citizen of the world. He spent his first eleven years in Dunbar, and almost all of his formal schooling, before he attended university, was in Scotland. He remained proud of his national origins, of his "mither tongue," and of Scottish history and ballads. He would fill his personal library with the collected works of such Scottish writers as Robert Burns, Hugh Miller, Walter Scott, and Robert Louis Stevenson. To the end of his days Scottish oatmeal porridge would be his preferred breakfast. His native town, along with the culture and society of the Scottish Lowlands, a place with rich tradition but undergoing radical transformation, was the seedbed out of which this "man of nature" would grow.

Dunbar occupied an ancient site of settlement dating back to the second century A.D., when men and women had sat around open hearths grilling meat and tattooing their bodies. Seventeen hundred years on, the undeveloped shoreline along with the islands off shore—The Gripes, The Yetts, Scart Rock, Mackerel Buss—was all that remained of that primitive past, last refuges of primeval wildness. Now and then, to be sure, the sea could still shake the windows of the stone houses. But Dunbar was determined to put that wilder past behind it and craft a modern identity. The town would, after tourism became a new kind of commodity, try to sell itself as the sunniest part of Scotland, cheery, bright, and commodious. In the long, dark winters, however, when the North Sea raged against the protecting sea wall and pummeled the heavy roofs, when the air was thick with salt and chilling to the bone, the town had stern reminders of its old vulnerability to the elements.

The Scottish historian and philosopher Thomas Carlyle visited on a cloudless day in 1843 and painted the place in a beguiling light, his canvas sweeping far out to sea and north toward mountains.

> The small town of Dunbar stands high and windy, looking down over its herring boats, over its grim old castle, now much honeycombed, on one of those projecting promontories, with which that shore of the Firth of Forth is niched and vandyked as far as the eye can reach. A beautiful sea; good land too, now that the plougher understands his trade; a grim niched barrier of whinstone sheltering it from the chafings and tumblings of the big blue German Ocean. Seaward, St. Abb's Head of whinstone bounds your horizon to the east, not very far off; west, close by is the deep bay and little village of Belhaven; the gloomy Bass and other rock islets; and farther the hills of Fife and foreshadows of the highlands are visible as you look seaward.[1]

Broad sea, protected shelter, good soil, and strategic location converged here to give Dunbar a geographic significance, although those advantages would begin to fade with economic changes well underway by the time of Muir's birth.

Down from the High Street sloped a path to the harbor, where fishing was the main work. Here lobster pots were stacked, nets spread to dry, anchors let down behind a massive stone barrier. When Muir was four years old, the town built that barrier with financial help from London, naming it after Queen Victoria, newly seated on the British throne. It replaced an adjacent older harbor built in the time of Oliver Cromwell. Through a narrow gap in the seawall fishing vessels could slip in and out, carrying on an immemorial trade in herring. When the fish began running in July and August, fishermen from all over eastern Scotland arrived here and unloaded their catch where it was salted down and packed in barrels.

A few larger vessels traveled as far as London, Germany, Scandinavia, Russia, and even North America, importing naval stores and wood and exporting whiskey and wheat. The modernized harbor, however, was designed too small for the coming age, and its importance declined as ships grew too large to enter and as railroads came to dominate the national transportation system. In 1846, when Muir was eight years old, the British Railway Company came to town, constructing a yellow-brick station not far from the High Street. A contemporary observer wrote, "A most extraordinary revolution took place . . . by means of this lightning-footed steed[;] the whole host of stage-coaches, from the Royal Mail to the smallest Diligence, were banished from the highway." Fishing boats continued to use the four-year-old harbor, but shipping on the grand scale died. Herring now went out by rail, four thousand tons a year, to Edinburgh and Glasgow in one direction, Newcastle and London in another.[2]

A community of fishermen survived alongside the harbor, living at a wide social distance from the town's bourgeoisie in a labyrinth of narrow, twisting streets and shadowy closes packed with stucco cottages. More than ever, this became the poor, antiquated side of Dunbar, where odors of the sea and sour bedding mingled, where most of the town's pubs stood. In the 1840s the parish counted fifty-three drinking establishments, serving a population of some four thousand souls, most of whom were abstemious members of the Church of Scotland. The maritime side of town more than made up for the drier side, quaffing large drafts from the nearby Belhaven Brewery. The historian T. C. Smout notes that "nowhere else was as sodden" as Dunbar.[3]

On one side of Victoria Harbor, jutting up from the rocks like a finger of doom, was Carlyle's "grim old castle." Once it had been a dark red fortress protecting the Firth of Forth and the heartland of Scotland from English armies. It had many stories to tell of bygone violence. Mary Stuart, Queen of Scots and rival to Elizabeth I, had hidden herself in the castle with her husband's murderer, the Earl of Bothwell, before being caught and hanged. The Scots Parliament, to prevent more such escapades, ordered the structure razed. By Muir's time, three hundred years later, it was a dismal ruin, white-streaked with the guano of noisy gulls, a memento from a bloody past. Muir ironically called it "one of our best playgrounds," where he learned mountain climbing and rock-scrambling skills, taking "chances that no cautious mountaineer would try."[4]

It was the only "mountain" he would know as a lad. Looking inland, Dunbar was part of the rolling agricultural plain of East Lothian, which in turn was part of the Scottish Lowlands, a region that stretched across the country to the River Clyde and down to the Irish Sea. Confined on one side by the Highlands and on the other by a belt of high ground that included the Lammermuir and Cheviot hills, this region was not the Scotland idealized by filmmakers in modern times. No kilted men armed with claymores stole shaggy cattle or marched over heather-covered mountains to the sound of bagpipes. Farming and raising sheep dominated this region. But like the Highlanders, the Lowland Scots were well versed in fighting. They had long engaged in border wars, first with the Gaelic-speaking Catholics to the north, then with the English to the south. Their last great battle had been fought on the outskirts of Dunbar, at Doon Hill, in 1650, against Cromwell's invading army—a battle they lost decisively and ignominiously.

Such conflict had forged the Lowlanders into a single people, "assertive, warlike, resilient, patriotic and freedom-loving."[5] But their history of conflict had also left them a subservient colony. By Muir's time they had come to accept more or less English imperial rule, with its system of class privilege, absentee land ownership, and the presence of occupying armies in towns like Dunbar. They had adopted the English language, although they continued to speak Scots, and they grew accustomed to English tea and clotted cream. Resentment toward the imperialists lurked beneath that surface accommodation, flaring up regularly in fits of nationalism and egalitarianism. Mainly, however, they determined to make the best of their situation by trying to out-English the English. They would become leading agents of the British Empire, showing London how to manage the power and wealth it had amassed around the world.

New economic practices had come flooding in from the powerful empire to the south, especially the rising industrial centers of Manchester and Birmingham. Those practices had taken root all over the Lowlands but particularly in Glasgow, which by 1841 had swelled into a massive industrial metropolis, with a population of 275,000. That city, by far the largest in Scotland, was in the forefront of textile manufacturing and heavy engineering. One of its leading talents, and a shining example of the Scots' ability to emulate and outdo their betters, was James Watt, a self-taught instrument maker at the University of Glasgow. In 1781 he got his hands on a model of the recently invented English steam engine, figured out how to make it work more efficiently, and created a mode of production that dramatically changed the world. With Matthew Boulton, he transformed the steam engine from a water pump into a power supply that could weave cotton, make iron or pottery, or dredge a port. Watt made the modern factory system possible and put Scotland at the center of the new industrial era.[6]

From Dunbar to Ayr the land was filled with men who were adept at inventing machines and making them pay a good dividend. They were attuned to the latest science and technology. They had a strong work ethic. They were quick to innovate. They were close observers, shrewd calculators, and experimental thinkers. Their reward was to gain power and affluence within the framework imposed by their masters, Britain's capitalist class.

No one was more adept at seizing on the invading ideas of economy and society than Adam Smith, who grew up across the Firth of Forth from Dunbar in the seaside village of Kirkaldy. He had been dead for half a century when Muir was born, but he had left behind his magnum opus, *An Inquiry into the Nature and Causes of the Wealth of Nations*, published in 1776 and destined to become the bible of modern capitalism. Freedom in the pursuit of self-interest, he argued, would turn a poor, backward country like Scotland into a rich one. Economic freedom should never override the moral sentiments nor give way to irrationality, he cautioned, but such freedom was the only way to inspire effort and improve the material conditions of the masses. On every High Street like Dunbar's that Smithian logic captured the spirit of the times.

The life of the ordinary Scot, to be sure, often remained desperate and squalid. Peasant farmers still lived in stone-and-earth hovels, many without windows, chimneys, or floors. They existed on herring and potatoes supplemented by gruel and grog. In the towns they found their hard-won skills at weaving superseded by Watt's power looms; over the period 1840–1880 the number of handloom weavers fell from 84,000 to 4,000. Slums populated by the unemployed or underemployed spread through the heart of cities, threatening violence. Their abysmal sanitary conditions gave the lie to Adam Smith's promise of improved public welfare through free-market individualism.[7]

Dunbar had its winners and losers too. The winners would have agreed with Carlyle that their town could offer a beautiful place to stand on a clear day, but commonly they had their eyes on something besides natural grandeur. What the town's leaders had in mind was escaping from a past of material deprivation, which had left them at the bottom of western European rankings. The old tough-minded adaptability in the face of whatever nature could throw their way was giving way to a relentless search for the means by which nature could be turned to profit. Dunbar taught its children to seek opportunities and accumulate fortunes through skill and bold ambition. Be open to change, they were encouraged, make yourself competent, keep your wits about you. Out of this place came John Muir, determined to prove himself and improve the world.

The nearest representative of that Scots ethos of upward mobility, who influenced young Muir more than any other, was his father Daniel. The influence was not all positive. Daniel drove his son toward success but also toward resistance and rebellion against much that the father stood for. They represented warring generations, the older man born thirty-four years earlier, in 1804. Yet at his father's death in 1883 Muir wrote admiringly, "few lives were more restless and eventful than his, few more steadily toilsome and full of enthusiastic endeavor.... Though suffering always under the disadvantage of an imperfect education, he never failed in any important undertaking and never seemed to feel himself over-tasked, but by sheer force of will and continuous effort overcame all difficulties that stood in his way."[8] That generous tribute took a long time to find expression and could have come only after Muir had succeeded in forging his own independent life. He would always, nonetheless, strongly resemble his father and his father's generation.

Daniel was the child of a Scots recruit to the British army, another man named John Muir, who while stationed in Manchester, England, married an English girl, Sarah Higgs. Both parents died before Daniel was one year old, and with his older sister Mary he was taken in by relatives living in the parish of Crawfordjohn, Lanarkshire. He had returned to the home turf of the ancient Muir clan, whose name derived from the surrounding moors where blackface sheep were common and trees were scarce.[9] His sister later married a jobbing stockman, Hamilton Blakley (or Blackley), who took in the little brother too; with young Daniel's assistance, Blakley succeeded in leaving the tending of flocks behind him, acquiring a cart and horse available for hire. Daniel, in his leisure hours when he was not shearing ewes or driving the cart, showed a gift for music. He crafted his own violin and frequently gathered with neighbors to play the old Scots airs. Somewhere along the way he was touched by evangelical Christianity, which soon overwhelmed everything else in his intensely passionate nature.

As soon as he reached his majority, Daniel left the rural life for Glasgow, with only a few shillings in his pocket and a "head full of romantic schemes for the benefit of his sister and all the world besides."[10] Finding little work, he decided to follow his father's career, enlisting in the British Army. Military records do not reveal which regiment he joined; possibly it was the famed Scots Guards, which unlike other regiments recruited soldiers from all over Scotland. Making a favorable impression on his senior officers, Daniel was sent as a recruiting sergeant to Dunbar, where he would soon change his career plans and shift to a civilian line of work.

Tall, bright-eyed, and handsome, Daniel quickly found a wife on the High Street of Dunbar, Helen Kennedy, who had inherited from her mother a small grocery and needed help in running it. But then Helen abruptly died, leaving Daniel a widower with an economic stake in the community and a desire to stay. In 1833 he married Ann Gilrye, the daughter of a "flesher" (butcher) living directly opposite. The register of marriages describes Daniel as "shopkeeper," a label reserved for the lowliest of commercial occupations.[11] He would not remain for long at that level. Over the next fifteen years he would rise to the more exalted status of "merchant," operate a thriving feed and grain business, win a reputation for honesty and intelligence, and become one of the leading citizens of the town. With Ann he would produce eight healthy children, seven of them born in Dunbar, one in the United States, all surviving to adulthood. Despite his humble, forlorn beginnings, he would aspire to be part of the new Scotland, the land of self-made men.

John Muir was the third child of that marriage, coming after his sisters Margaret and Sarah, and before David, Daniel, Jr., the twins Mary and Annie, and Joanna. The small whitewashed rooms above the shop, heated by a single stove, quickly became too crowded, prompting Daniel to buy the much larger building next door at number 130–134. He converted its two stories from the home and office of a physician to the grain business, purveying feed for people and livestock alike, with

Muir grew up in this combination house-store on the High Street of Dunbar, Scotland. After his family left for America it became the Lorne Temperance Hotel. He was born in the building to its left, which is now a museum, the John Muir Birthplace Trust. (H-A, JMP)

a large domestic space upstairs for the growing family. This was the house Muir knew as a child—a stalwart and imposing building, one of the largest in town, now signaling that an outsider had arrived and was making good.

His mother Ann is almost invisible in Muir's autobiography, particularly in the Dunbar years, in contrast to her husband. She appears as one who liked painting and poetry (even writing some herself), was kind and affectionate, conventionally pious, but only vaguely there, never a strong or forceful presence. Apparently she had a tough constitution, for despite all her childbearing, she lived to be eighty-three years old, dying in the United States in 1896. But strength of personality was generally not the quality anyone found in her. Whether because of natural temperament or restrictive schooling in how to be female, she was quiet and undemonstrative to the point of passivity.

Ann's parents David and Margaret Hay Gilrye were not natives of Dunbar but had won a respectable place for themselves on the High Street. David hailed from Wark, Northumberland, and Margaret from Coldstream on the River Tweed. They were married in Dunbar in 1795, when he was twenty-eight and she was twenty-two years old. All but one of their seven children died of infectious diseases. Struck by so much tragedy, the Gilryes doted on their healthy and rambunctious Muir grandchildren living just across the street.

Standing before his shop in a blood-stained butcher's apron, David Gilrye was a popular figure with a reputation for good character and steady work habits. His business prospered so well that he had to hire assistants to help in the slaughtering of cattle, sheep, and pigs kept in pens scattered about town. Behind his shop (and residence) was a small courtyard where his employees, including several household servants, dwelt. Dunbar was quick to acknowledge Gilrye's leadership qualities. When parishioners built a new red sandstone edifice for the Church of Scotland on a rise overlooking the sea, Gilrye was named one of the ruling elders. More worldly affairs in the burgh of Dunbar were managed by a small, self-selected set of magistrates and town councilors; by invitation, Gilrye joined their circle too. As grandson Muir knew him, he was retired from business and politics, devoted to the Kirk, and living off the fruits of a successful life.

Daniel Muir followed his father-in-law's record of achievement and promised to become one of the most powerful men in Dunbar. Reform legislation in 1833 opened the burgh's leadership to wider community participation; under those laws Daniel stood for town council in 1846 and tied for the most votes.[12] He was not of the gentry, to be sure, but others before him—the Falls, the Middlemasses—had climbed to high merchant status from plebeian beginnings and taken over the running of the town as provost or baillie. Daniel's growing business establishment, by now overshadowing the Gilrye butcher shop, his high reputation for probity, and his popularity with the voters in a more open political era all ensured him and his family a prominent future in the community.

As a grain merchant, Daniel shrewdly tied himself to the fortunes of agriculture, and in all of the United Kingdom there was no richer agricultural region than in the environs of Dunbar and East Lothian. The harvest from the sea could not compare with its harvest of roots and cereals from well-drained, loamy soils. For decades those soils had attracted investors. Lothian farming was capitalist farming—farming to make a profit in the marketplace, farming in which economic rationality and a drive for efficiency worked to extract the greatest yield possible. Wheat ("corn" in British parlance) was the chief crop, along with barley, oats, hay, and such root crops as the potato, turnip, and rutabaga.

The scale of individual fields, like the farms themselves, was huge by the standards of traditional Scots or English agriculture. This would facilitate the use of modern machinery in plowing and reaping—Watt's steam engines put to agricultural use, powered by the burning of coal. Local inventors devised and manufactured those machines, attracting attention to Dunbar throughout the empire. Anything natural or irregular in the machines' path had to be removed. "There is but little wood [here]," it was observed as early as the 1790s, "which makes the country look naked. The land is thought too valuable to admit of much planting." Historian Smout describes these fields as "ecological deserts," typified by the Fentonbarns estate outside Dunbar, where the land had been completely transformed into immense rectangles and where nonconforming weeds or wild flowers could not last long.[13]

Riding among the great farms as a buyer, Daniel may have felt cowed by such advanced landownership and production that contrasted starkly with his own rural background. He was, all the same, rising with their profitability. He stood in the position of middleman, retailing that cornucopia to the public with golden opportunities to expand his role in as many directions as he dared. Others in the agricultural economy were not so fortunate. The average farm hired a work force of twenty to thirty laborers, who were often paid in kind rather than cash, and paid poorly. Then there were the itinerant Irish field hands who came each May to weed turnips and stayed on to "lift" potatoes in October, before drifting over the horizon with their meager wages.

A strident critic of this new farming that was spreading throughout the United Kingdom was William Cobbett, who published a series of books called *Rural Rides*, the last of which was based on a tour of Scotland. Seeing the Dunbar countryside, he blasted its tight-fisted owners and operators:

> In this country of the finest land that ever was seen, all the elements seem to have been pressed into the amiable service of sweeping the people from the face of the earth, in order that the whole amount of the product may go into the hands of a small number of persons, that they may squander at London, at Paris, or at Rome.

He watched wheat-laden cart after cart going into Dunbar, "which is a little seaport (though a large town) apparently made for the express purpose of robbing Scotland of all its produce, and of conveying it away to be squandered in scenes of dissipation, of gambling, and of every use tending to vitiate man and enfeeble a nation."[14]

❦

No dissipation or gambling was allowed in the Muir household. Despite their growing wealth, this family sat down to meals that were little better than those of the "hinds" who worked the fields. Breakfast offered a monotonous menu of porridge, milk, and treacle eaten from wooden bowls called "luggies." Lunch was usually vegetable broth and barley scones, evening "tea" was limited to white bread and a little milk mixed with water and sugar, and dinner featured boiled potatoes and scones again. Muir mentioned no meat in his boyhood diet, although as well-to-do relatives of a butcher his family surely could have afforded a leg of lamb or slab of bacon now and then. Perhaps the father was not willing to indulge his children by giving them any expensive protein or fancy meat dishes.

Strict control over the amount and variety of food on the table was part of Daniel's tightly conservative approach to fatherhood. Somewhere along the way this orphan who had never known his own father had decided that he must exercise a strong hand over his wife and offspring lest they fall into evil ways. Placing restrictions on what they ate, where they went, what they did with their time, and even what they thought was his solemn responsibility. If they disobeyed any of his rules, the children must be punished by harsh reproof or whipping. For all his quickness to adopt the new economic freedom, Daniel was determined to adhere within his household to old-fashioned domineering rule.

Muir thus grew up under a daily barrage of stern warnings delivered by a father who tried to make himself as unfeeling as possible. Daniel only partly succeeded in that self-repression; "naturally," his son wrote, "his heart was far from hard, though he devoutly believed in eternal punishment for bad boys both here and hereafter."[15] Whenever he relented from that sense of awful duty, he would get down on his knees and show his children how to carve amusing toys out of turnips or play the violin and sing to them the traditional ballads. The struggle that raged within him between pleasure and self-denial was usually won by the latter, leading him to deny his children the normal pleasures of childhood. Almost anything they wanted to do for fun turned out to be bad.

Despite his popularity and good standing among the townspeople, Daniel perceived that he lived in a dangerous environment that might suck the unwary down into poverty, degradation, or corruption at any moment. Under his own roof he could overcome the dangers by constant vigilance, but away from his protective shield, where so many powerful influences could prey on weak children, he feared the worst might happen. They might learn bad thoughts and bad words from bad company. It was best to keep them close to home and discourage any inclination to ramble about the town or into the countryside.

Not all the dangers were moral; some posed the risk of physical harm. "Father sternly forbade David and me from playing truant in the fields with plundering wanderers like ourselves, fearing we might go on from bad to worse, get hurt in climbing over walls, caught by gamekeepers, or lost by falling over a cliff into the sea."[16] There was genuine solicitude in those prohibitions. But it was mixed with a conviction that children are naturally lawless, prone to theft or violence or wickedness outside of adult supervision. Fathers had no choice but to impose law on their lawless offspring.

Wild nature as much as wild people was a source of danger. Daniel was fearful of cliffs, birds, plants, the ocean—any aspect of nature that was not under his personal command. He was, however, an ardent grower of fruits and vegetables. "Father was proud of his garden," Muir remembered, "and seemed always to be trying to make it as much like Eden as possible."[17] Behind their residence stretched a large garden enclosed by ten-foot walls, and within that space Daniel worked to domesticate nature. He allowed each child a bit of ground, their own property as it were, where they could plant whatever they liked. Aunt Margaret Rae had her special corner assigned within the family garden, which she filled with a luxuriance of lilies. The children stood in awe of those flowers, imagining that each was worth a great deal of money. The lesson was clear: nature belonged in gardens, under man's firm dominion—small private Edens where children could learn the art of management and where flowers signified wealth.

A father struggling to paste hard-faced patriarchy over a softer interior was bound to leave his son confused and aggrieved. Muir felt unjustly treated and became as determined to challenge Daniel's restrictions as Daniel was to impose them. "After I was five or six years old," Muir recalled, "I ran away to the seashore or the fields almost every Saturday, and every day in the school vacations except

Sundays. . . . In spite of the sure sore punishments that followed like shadows, the natural inherited wildness in our blood ran true on its glorious course as invincible and unstoppable as stars."[18]

As Muir attempted late in life to understand where his love of the wild had come from, he exaggerated how much of unreconstructed nature Dunbar offered him. In truth its monotonous fields of wheat or barley could not have afforded much release for that "wildness in our blood." His wildness was more a matter of youthful defiance of rules than bonding with the nonhuman. He went climbing over walls and stealing apples—protecting arms and legs from the broken glass embedded in the tops of those walls by a cushion of pulled grass. In summer he competed with other boys to see who could find the largest number of bird nests. Then in winter they turned to running foot-races, cheering lustily at dogfights, and hoping for a good shipwreck— the usual sporting events of a seacoast town. What he mainly ran away from home to find was an assertive, boyish masculinity rather than any deep experience of nature.

Muir was a quarrelsome little rowdy, just as his father feared. But he was a rowdy of the High Street, not of the maritime neighborhood.

A poor neighborhood in Dunbar, "The Cat's Row," located near the Old Harbor. (H-A, Shone)

He never went out on a fishing boat, nor hung around the wharf, nor poked his head into any of the fishermen's pubs, where he might have seen or heard things his father would have disapproved of. He was walled in even when he thought he was free.

The other adults in his part of town tended to echo father Daniel's view that evil deeds must be overcome by strong punishment. When Muir picked a fistful of common flowers from the apothecary's garden, he was caught and locked into a stable with a dangerous pony that threatened to kick his head in. "Imagine the agony I endured! I did not steal any more of his flowers. He was a good hard judge of boy nature." Even the servant girls tried to scare him into obedience. They warned about ghosts that lurked in the attic and "Dandy Doctors" who nightly prowled the streets and lanes in dark cloaks, seizing wayward children, silencing their mouths with sticking plaster, and choking or selling them. The servants made even the weekly bath a kind of punishment, throwing the little ones naked into frigid tide pools or scrubbing them hard with soap. The Scots in general, Muir observed, had a way of turning every pleasure into duty and then "making every duty dismal."[19]

Schooling was no different—a regimen of rules, discipline, and punishment. It began for him before the age of three, in Mungo Siddons's Infant School at the foot of Davel Brae Street, only a short walk from home. There he was daily drilled in academic subjects, a routine relieved only by lots of schoolyard fights, sometimes six of them a day. "To be a 'gude fecter' [good fighter] was our highest ambition, our dearest aim in life in or out of school." Siddons's lessons were heavily laced with the glorification of war, especially stories of how William Wallace and Robert the Bruce had fought for Scotland's independence. "Of course, we were all going to be soldiers," so the school emphasis on violence, formal and informal, could be justified as teaching the young to defend their country against its dark foes.[20]

At age seven or eight Muir transferred to the recently constructed Woodbush School, located away from the High Street in an open, windy space near the shore. The school was divided into a Grammar and English section and a Mathematical and Navigation section down the hall; there were also a Charity School for the children from the harbor area and a Dame's School for the girls. The academic year began in mid-September and lasted until early May, interrupted by nearly three months of winter vacation. Muir would be a student here for less than four years. Fortunately, he had come to an excellent institution to learn the fundamentals quickly, though the teaching methods were severe.

Woodbush's Master David Lyon taught in Dunbar for nearly three decades, preparing his best students for places in Britain's universities. The son of a teacher in Robert Owen's reform-minded factory school in New Lanark and a graduate of the University of Edinburgh, he had outstanding credentials. Well versed in Greek, Latin, French, and Italian, he also taught his pupils how to write the imperial language of English and to read maps of the Empire. Cursed with squinty eyes and a sour mouth, Lyon had a mean reputation. Like Daniel, he felt compelled to hide any kindness in his disposition behind a rigid show of force. The town magistrates may have been partly responsible for that compulsion after they brought him up on a charge of "inefficiency," that is, of wandering beyond the prescribed program, for which they punished him with poor pay. Lyon responded by applying the "taws," or leather straps, to the backsides of students who did not get their lessons exactly right. He had made that "grand, simple, all-sufficing Scotch discovery...that there was a close connection between the skin and memory."[21]

The one male adult in Muir's life who offered an alternative to heavy-handed patriarchy was his grandfather Gilrye. Oddly, it was this butcher who encouraged the boy's tender feelings toward other creatures and his desire to explore the natural margins. "My earliest recollections of the country," wrote Muir, "were gained on short walks with my grandfather when I was perhaps not over three years old." They strolled out to Lord Lauderdale's gardens, where the boy filled his pockets with figs and apples. On one occasion, while sitting with the older man on a haycock, Muir discovered the nest of a field mouse and her babies; "no hunter could have been more excited on discovering a bear and her cubs in a wilderness den." Grandfather also was the first to teach him his letters from shop signs on the High Street, and, when the children reached school age, he "took pleasure in seeing us and hearing us recite our next day's lessons." That this gentle, nurturing man also performed the "horrid red work" of slaughtering pigs may seem incongruous, but for Muir that side was fun too, and he ran eagerly toward the sound of "desperately earnest squealing," hoping to see the dead pig's guts or get its bladder to blow up for a football.[22]

Growing up in Dunbar gave Muir a complicated set of ideas and feelings: a conviction that life must be vividly, intensely felt though strongly bounded, a high level of literacy and a roving imagination, a feeling of security yet an unsatisfied hunger for freedom, a willingness to endure pain or hardship for the sake of forbidden pleasure.

<hr/>

Whether Muir's passion for nature was part of a common genetic endowment or was peculiar to his make-up was a question on which he wavered. But he had no doubt that it was "inherited wildness" that set him apart as a child from most of the adults he knew and made his early life difficult. It put him at odds with his father's attitudes toward life, his teacher's methods of education, and his society's drive to make money. He felt that he must defy their impulse to repress and extinguish nature, within and without.

But the culture of Scotland, northern Britain, and indeed western civilization was undergoing profound change, and change could go in more than one direction. One direction would encourage youths like Muir to put a new value on wildness in outdoor nature and inner temperament. That movement came to be known as Romanticism. A confusing tangle of ideas, one of Romanticism's core convictions was that nature—the wildness that lies beyond human technology and culture—is essential to the psychological and spiritual well-being of people. The need could not be satisfied by the utilitarian approach to nature exemplified in industrial capitalism nor by older Christian teachings nor within traditional patriarchy. They all lumped nature with the "useless," the "pagan," and the "female"—inferior qualities to be subdued rather than honored. Romanticism sought to liberate nature and the natural human instincts from that history of cultural repression. It sought to bring culture into closer harmony with the wild.

The Romantic Movement began in the eighteenth century with the French philosopher Jean-Jacques Rousseau and others spreading anti-civilization ideas into the everyday lives of thousands on both sides of the Atlantic. Muir may have absorbed some of its spirit through his mother's efforts at poetry or from other informal sources difficult to determine; his sisters and brothers all grew up sharing to some extent that desire to get back, at least occasionally, to nature. For all of them, but Muir especially, it was the popular Scottish poet Robert Burns (1759–1796) who was the most decisive Romantic influence on their youth. As Muir wrote in a late tribute, "On my lonely walks I have often thought how fine it would be to have the company of Burns. And indeed he was always with me, for I had him by heart. . . . Wherever a Scotsman goes, there goes Burns."[23]

Born in a simple clay cottage in Alloway, the son of a tenant farmer and his ballad-singing wife, Burns learned to read and write at his father's table after working long hours at plowing and threshing. He felt his social inferiority keenly and, in reaction, wrote poems that celebrated the common people of Scotland. He boldly dismissed the courtly English language, the language of conquest, and wrote poetry in the old Scots dialect. More than anyone else, he gave legitimacy to the vernacular ballads of his countrymen, saving over three hundred of them from neglect. A man of strong appetites, he left behind him a trail of illegitimate children and empty bottles, yet amazingly the church-going Scots came to regard him as their greatest poet and a national hero.

Muir had many favorites among Burns's poems: "The Cotter's Saturday Night," "Tam O'Shanter," "My Heart's in the Highlands," "Sweet Afton," and "Auld Lang Syne." The most important in shaping his moral outlook were those that assumed the perspective of other creatures in their relationship with humans. In "The Twa Dogs," Burns tells of a well-bred English dog, wearing a fine brass collar, comparing notes with "a ploughman's collie" on their respective masters, "the lords o' the creation." The gentry, seen from the dogs' view, are a sad, immoral, and worthless lot. In the poem "To a Louse," Burns watches with mock horror as a tiny insect crawls up a fine lady's bonnet in church, forgetting its rightful place on the bodies of the poor and unwashed. In a less satiric mood, Burns pens an apology to a panicked mother mouse, "poor, earth-born companion / 'An fellow mortal," whose nest has been disturbed by his plow, a symbol of "man's dominion." The poem upsets all the moral hierarchies that civilization has declared, portraying humans as a destructive force on earth and, just as radically, the simple plowman as the person most likely to regret that destruction.[24]

Burns's gift to his culture, and particularly to young readers like Muir, was an exuberant embrace of liberty, fraternity, and equality, the ideals of the French Revolution and modern liberal democracy. He made such ideals seem natural to Scotland by translating them into the language and lore of its past. And, true to Rousseau's legacy, he identified them with the natural world.[25]

Another northern lad besides Muir had been deeply touched by Burns's passion for nature and the egalitarian feelings that accompanied it: William Wordsworth (1770–1850). A child of the sublime but economically backward Lake District just over the English border, young Wordsworth was inspired by Burns to make poetry his vocation too. With the publication of *Lyrical Ballads* (co-authored with Samuel Taylor Coleridge in 1798) and his autobiographical poem *The Excursion* (1814–15), Wordsworth became the Romantic Movement's most powerful muse. Although Muir was far less apt to quote him than Burns, there can be no understanding of the Dunbar boy's indebtedness to Romanticism without seeing the force of the Wordsworthian tidal wave that washed over his time and place.

Whatever privileges it had brought him and others, Wordsworth called for a rebellion against imperial civilization. When political revolution failed in France on the grand scale, dashing his hopes, he came home to work for it in the realm of the individual mind and feelings. He would start by recovering his childhood love of water, woods, and mountains, "and of all that we behold from this green earth." In his poem "The Tables Turned" (1798) he named "Nature" as his most important teacher, confident that "one impulse from a vernal wood" may teach more of "moral evil and of good / Than all the sages can."

Revolution must begin by pulling down the rule of "meddling intellect," whether science or art, freeing the natural impulses of the heart.[26]

In the final month of the eighteenth century Wordsworth and his sister Dorothy came home to their native region, moving into a former coaching inn and pub in the vale of Grasmere. Here they lived amid a wild profusion of flowers, with views across green meadows to shining lake waters, the mounts Hevellyn and Fairfield at their backs. They made long excursions by day and night, slept whenever it suited them, read William's poems aloud under the apple trees, and though poor and often hungry, felt at peace with themselves and the creation. A wife for William, babies, and several friends likewise fleeing the city came along to share their paradise. In return, from this out-of-the-way place came a flow of radical thoughts that would suffuse and subvert English-speaking society for decades to come.

What Wordsworth put in simple, accessible, and moving words was a new religion that made nature the source of revelation. Put aside your old creeds and dogmas, your theories and libraries, he invited, and go to the mountains. There you will find answers to your most fundamental questions: what is good or evil? How should humans live? Does God exist? Nature says yes to the last question, but no to a deity conceived in the Judeo-Christian tradition. Instead, nature gives "a sense sublime / Of something far more deeply interfused . . . a spirit, that impels / All thinking things, all objects of thought / And rolls through all things." Was that spirit located above and beyond, or was it located within nature, Wordsworth asked himself, but it was a question he never resolved. In "Home in Grasmere," the opening to his unfinished narrative poem *The Recluse*, he came as close as anywhere to stating his core belief: "The external World is fitted to the Mind; / And the creation (by no lower name / Can it be called) which they with blended might / Accomplish." Nature and mind co-exist in a seamless harmony that humans can call divine.[27]

Coming home to the Lake District and redefining his faith made Wordsworth one of the greatest religious figures of his day and, indeed, of the modern era. While many found his enthusiasm for the all-sufficing light of Creation too radical, footloose, and self-reliant, others heeded his call, throwing aside their written scriptures or disregarding pulpit authorities and going outdoors to find their own direct insights. To be sure, orthodox Christians had already begun to allow that nature is a "book" in which one can find "evidence" for religious beliefs. Wordsworth was not alone in opening wide the doors to the natural environment and inviting believers to go for a walk and reinvigorate their senses. But orthodoxy, even when it was lured into the green world to read the "book of nature," still insisted on finding in the natural world the evidence to support traditional religious doctrines.

The Scottish evangelist Thomas Dick, for example, in *The Christian Philosopher*, published in 1823 (a book young Muir read), broke with his society's traditions and sought in nature a confirmation of his faith. He bought a telescope and, contemplating the heavens, "where moral evil has never shed its malign influence," found evidence of "Divine Beneficence." The terrestrial world offered scenes of beauty and order, to be sure, but in the old Christian way he found that nature on earth was "disfigured" by sin. Others, impressed as Dick was by natural science, were more hopeful that terrestrial nature could afford proof of God's existence; they found such proof in the intricate, efficient relations displayed among plants and animals—evidences of "design." They spoke of a "divine watchmaker" who had invented an organic machine, an artifact of Divine Intelligence.[28]

Wordsworth, in contrast, did not think of nature as a well-contrived machine but rather as a living organism. And he went further than any of those Christian naturalists to the point of embracing nature as a wholly sufficient foundation for faith. He did not need the Bible or church instruction in his rambles over the fells; he had confidence in his own spontaneous perceptions. He left behind all established doctrines—the atoning death of Christ, the supreme authority of the written Word, the "Fatherhood" of a distant and all-powerful God—so that "Christian" no longer accurately described his religion. None of Christianity's principal beliefs could be found written among the daffodils he saw waving along the shores of Ullswater or in the clouds of moisture drifting over Skiddaw or Scafell Pike. Yet religion—his own personal religion—was there, freely given and freely accepted.

If a Romantic love of nature did not lead Wordsworth to affirm the Judeo-Christian idea of God, it did lead him to a love of humankind. Democracy was the social expression of his Romanticism. He had almost lost that fellow feeling in the centers of civilization, marred by "the deformities of crowded life," but back on the land, among farmers and shepherds, he regained it. "Intent on little but substantial needs," those rural people represented human nature at its best; he found them sensitive to natural beauty, generous toward others, and humble before the unnamed Power that lurked in the mountains. The lone herder of sheep on the hillside became Wordsworth's ideal man or woman. His ideal society became a republic made up of such people, where none outranked the others and none had any illusions about dominating nature. Once glimpsed in their essential goodness, people everywhere, even "among the multitudes of that huge city," seemed more worthy of hope.[29]

Robert Burns had been dead nine years when Wordsworth, in 1803, paid homage in a visit to his grave. He joined the broad flow of mourners but felt more deeply grieved than others, for Burns had profoundly touched his life, showing "my youth / How Verse may build a princely throne / On humble truth." He had added his burred Cumbrian voice to the Scotsman's brogue. Their common search, on the northern margins of British civilization and empire, for a Romantic, liberal, democratic view of nature and humanity, and for a more harmonious relationship between the two, set up an influential counterforce to Watt, Smith, and industrial expansion, which would inspire Muir his whole life.

On 29 January 1849 Daniel resigned his seat on Dunbar's town council, dashing any expectations that he might become the community's next "big man." Nearly three weeks later, as his son recalled, on the very eve of their departure, the children learned that they were going to North America. The news hit them like a providential thunderbolt. Quickly, they ran into the streets, telling everyone that they were leaving for that far hemisphere where no one they knew had ever been but where everything must seem an earthly paradise.

No more grammar, but boundless woods full of mysterious good things; trees full of sugar, growing in ground full of gold; hawks, eagles, pigeons, filling the sky; millions of birds' nests, and no gamekeepers to stop us in the wild, happy land. We were utterly, blindly glorious.

Muir's schoolbooks had given him exotic descriptions of America by the Scottish ornithologist Alexander Wilson and by John Audubon, the wildlife artist. That was about all he knew of the other side of the Atlantic, but it was enough to make him giddy with anticipation. Now their father had decided, for reasons that were unclear but appealing to their imaginations, to take them there.[30]

It is unlikely that Daniel cared about his children's fantasies or his wife Ann's desires or the opinions of anyone else on the High Street as he arrived at his startling decision. He consulted only his own mind, where neither the prospect of wild pigeons, the desires of family, the ties of friendship or community had much influence. Nor did his business interests enter into the decision, for he was putting at risk all his accumulated capital and future prospects by leaping into the unknown. What compelled him to take such a gamble with so many lives was a religious worm that had long been gnawing at his vitals.

When he first came to town, Daniel refused to join the established Church of Scotland. Instead, he went over to a local dissenting congregation, the Secession Church, attending services in their building at the end of the High Street. In 1831 he appears on that congregation's list of building subscribers, indeed was one of the largest contributors. Other names on the list were a cross-section of the population: common workmen, lawyers, merchants, schoolmaster Siddons, a publican, and even gentry—a group fully as respectable as those worshipping in the Kirk. In 1837 Daniel appeared on the congregation's list of "managers" and was made collector of seat rents (a kind of treasurer). This dissident but respectable church affiliation put him at odds with the Gilryes but did not impair his standing in Dunbar.

Over the preceding three centuries the Scots had grown used to religious wars, beginning with a hard knot of Protestants, the Covenanters, who had broken with the Roman Catholic Church in 1557. Their spiritual leader was John Knox, a former Catholic priest who, exiled to Switzerland, had become a fierce, implacable disciple of John Calvin. Through Knox, Calvinism became entrenched in the Church of Scotland, an institution based on Presbyterian rather than Anglican doctrine. Calvinism put people in a tough place: on the one hand, it taught that everyone is born corrupt and sinful, predestined for hell, with no hope of redemption except that given by God to a select, undeserving few; on the other hand, it urged them to join the new economy of capitalism, work hard, save money, accumulate as much wealth as possible, and avoid self-indulgence, with the faint hope that God might save the more successful. Sharing that difficult and conflicted set of precepts, Scots proceeded to argue about everything else.

Daniel's fellow communicants were followers of Ebenezer Erskine, who in 1733 had broken away from the mainstream over the issue of selecting ministers. They disagreed with the policy of giving landowners only the right to decide who should be hired as minister in the Kirk. The Reverend Erskine had argued that the right should belong to all members of the congregation, the poor and propertyless included, a conviction that got him thrown out of the establishment. His flock became the Secession Church; although eventually it broke apart over several issues, during Daniel's time in Dunbar it remained united against powerful landlords in the countryside.

The seeker Daniel, however, grew more and more critical of all organized religion, despairing that any group was true to the gospel of Jesus. Catholics, Covenanters, or Erskinians, they all allowed too much human authority, usually looking toward an educated clergy to intervene between a man and his God. Daniel was determined to free himself from every form of earthly power and to get back to the pure, unpolluted biblical truth. He would become his own clergyman. His decision to emigrate was driven by that desire for liberation. It was in a spirit of religious rebellion that he turned toward North America as the land of freedom.

Even anarchists may seek or need leaders, and Daniel found one in Alexander Campbell, a voice calling to him from a distant wilderness. Campbell was a Scot born in Ulster, educated at the University of Glasgow, the son of a minister in the Secession Church, Thomas Campbell, who had immigrated to Pennsylvania with his family. Father and son had stirred up a following along the American frontier, and through a series of widely publicized debates, Alexander had won a reputation as a formidable intellect and speaker. In 1847 he returned to Britain on a preaching tour, passing through Dunbar and on to Edinburgh, where on 9 August he spoke for three solid hours to a large, sweating, attentive crowd. The audience probably included Daniel Muir and two friends, the brothers Philip and William Gray. Campbell's message shook Daniel so hard that he, along with the Grays, decided over the next few months to forsake Scotland for Campbell's greener pastures.[31]

Thus, hearing the Campbellite gospel radically changed the destinies of the Muir family as it changed the mental world of the father and, in ways that will become clear, that of his oldest son. In some ways this extreme form of egalitarian Protestantism reinforced, while in other ways it opposed, the democratic and Romantic influences of Burns and Wordsworth, and Muir would spend his early adulthood trying to sort out the tangle. Where the Romantic poets tried to escape the "meddling intellects" of civilization, encouraging each individual to consult his own heart, Campbell tried to overturn a power-seeking "priesthood" that claimed authoritative insight into religious truth. As church historian Robert Frederick West writes, Campbell's mission was "to unmask the clergy and their kingdom." He denounced them as corrupt, conceited about their academic degrees, self-promoting, and tyrannical. He would abolish the whole profession, relying on laymen to preach or oversee each congregation, independent of outside control. This, in Campbell's view, was how Christianity had originally functioned, without much structure, a loose and fluid gathering of believers. Every man should be his own priest in a pure and primitive democracy.[32]

Like the Romantics, Campbell found God in the woods and mountains, wherever the landscape reached sublime proportions. His adopted home was the Appalachian uplands where he liked to wander in a worshipful mood, inspired by the visual splendor of their forested ridges. "The voice of nature," he declared, "will never contradict the voice of revelation."[33] Unlike the Romantics, however, he always carried his Bible with him, for nature in his opinion was an insufficient guide to spirituality. Nature could be misread, he warned, as the ancient Greeks and Romans had done, setting up many false gods instead of the one true God. Nature *could* betray the heart that loved her. Only the Bible spoke clearly, without ambiguity or confusion, to the human mind.

Although he criticized Calvinism as another set of man-made dogmas, Campbell remained, unlike the Romantics, a moderate Calvinist in his view of human nature. Children do not come into this world evil by nature, he allowed, but neither are they Wordsworth's little angels of light. They must develop a capacity to read, reason, and discover truth for themselves. As they do so, they will discover in the Bible what they cannot derive from nature: an understanding of how evil has originated through disobedience to God's law. It never crossed Campbell's mind that the Bible, like nature, might be susceptible to more than one reading.

Daniel the seeker absorbed this volatile mix of rebellion and authority and marched straight out of the Erskine congregation and into the parlor gatherings of the Campbellites, who were organizing still another breakaway denomination, the Disciples of Christ. More than that, he drank in greedily his hero's encomium to American independence. "I would not sell my political rights and privileges of American citizenship," Campbell declared on his return home from Britain, "for all the emoluments that cluster around the stateliest and most aristocratic subject of any European or Asiatic crown ever worn on earth."[34] How then could Daniel sell his soul for a seat on the Dunbar town council or a prosperous business?

Grandfather Gilrye had witnessed his son-in-law's drift away from Scottish orthodoxy with increasing dismay. Now, after so much disagreement with Daniel over where one should go to church, he was about to be completely deserted by the whole Muir tribe. All he could manage to say was, "Ah, poor laddies, . . . you'll find plenty of hard, hard work." With sober face, he gave each of the children a gold piece. He managed to persuade Daniel to start off with only three children, Sarah, John, and David, leaving Ann and the other children behind until a home had been prepared for them somewhere in the New World. After that second departure, the Gilryes would never see their daughter or any of their grandchildren again. Within four years, they would both be dead and buried in the Kirk's graveyard.[35]

On the morning of 19 February a determined Daniel led his little vassals to the railroad station, where they caught the train to Glasgow. They departed only two months after the close of one of the most tumultuous years in European history, 1848. It had marked a time of famine, not only in Ireland, where millions had been threatened by starvation due to the potato blight, but also along the entire west coast of Scotland. Severe economic depression had simultaneously struck the industrial centers of Great Britain, provoking massive demonstrations in the streets, including one on Glasgow Green. The urban working class expressed its demands in the People's Charter for universal male suffrage, vote by secret ballot, and annual parliamentary elections. This Chartist movement had gathered over a million signatories but been repulsed by legislators; now, in the midst of so much suffering, they called for a huge popular demonstration against the government and threatened to take it over by force if necessary. On the continent of Europe as well 1848 was the "year of revolution" in almost every national capital. Angry commoners took up the cry for democracy and relief, bringing back memories of Parisian mobs storming the Bastille prison and the Tuileries palace, of revolutionaries dropping the guillotine blade again and again during the Reign of Terror.[36]

Three hundred thousand Scots, most of them poor, dispossessed, and hungry, emigrated that year, seeking a less confrontational way out of their troubles. Among them were the Carnegies of Dunfermline, who like the Muirs had come to Glasgow looking for boat passage. They had lost their weaving business to the new power looms, a shock that had transformed the father from artisan-proprietor to Chartist rebel. They were on their way to Pittsburgh, Pennsylvania, taking the British government's advice that immigration was the best cure for Scotland's ills. Their enterprising son Andrew, three years older than Muir, would find work as a telegraph messenger boy and, rising quickly to steelmaker, eventually amass one of the greatest fortunes in the world.[37]

Daniel Muir was no Chartist, nor was he emigrating out of economic desperation or as a protest against class oppression. Quite the contrary, he had every reason financially to stay and would end up poorer than he had been in Dunbar. But he did share the common yearning for freedom and opportunity that was coursing through his fellow countrymen crowding the docks. For him the key desire was for spiritual freedom—freedom to read the Bible for himself and preach its truth without hindrance. Buying passage on the good ship *Warren*, he and his children were taken aboard with seventy-two other Scots, and on 3 March, with a full cargo below the decks, they set sail with hope in their eyes.[38]

CHAPTER 2

"That Glorious Wisconsin Wilderness"

Crossing the Atlantic Ocean in the days of sail was an ordeal that migrants seldom wanted to repeat. Once on the other side, most were there for good. Even with the best of weather, the voyage took about six weeks—long days and nights of enforced idleness, with little room to walk and little to do. The tarred rigging creaked and groaned, the sails billowed and luffed, the view never seemed to change, and in all directions the depths were dark and inscrutable. Cholera or typhus often came aboard and left many dead at sea. Below deck the air was thick with the smell of closely packed people—unwashed bodies, musty blankets, the vomit of seasick passengers.

For Muir, however, a light-hearted boy of eleven, "the auld rockin' creel" offered the stimulus of endless novelties and an escape from the confinements of home and school. He and brother David showed off their classroom English, French, and Latin to the captain, who in turn showed them his cabin. During rough seas, while father and sister stayed in their bunks, the boys went on deck to watch the waves crashing against the bow. Muir boasted that he never had a touch of nausea, on this trip or any other—he was a natural-born sailor. Nearing New York harbor, he spotted dolphins and whales, then the stone and brick piles of America's first metropolis. They arrived on 10 April, when springtime was just popping out. Once ashore, they would have still another arduous journey to make.

In those days of less regulated international movement immigrant ships stopped briefly at Staten Island, where passengers were cursorily checked for disease (inspectors asked simply, could they walk?), then crossed the estuary to disembark at Manhattan's waterfront. Hawkers, porters, and swindlers clustered around the gangway, pressing their services on the bewildered passengers. No St. Andrew's Society was yet organized to help the Scots newcomer, nor was any railway company or state immigrant bureau on hand to suggest where to settle. Every man must fend for himself in this land of push and grab. Daniel wasted no time in hustling his family from one ship to another going up the Hudson River to Albany. There they bought train tickets to Buffalo, where a former neighbor awaited whose advice they would seek on where to go next.

When the Muirs arrived in 1849, the United States was merely sixty years old yet already beginning to lurch toward civil war and disintegration. Its population stood at twenty-three million, more than three million of them slaves. Its twelfth president, Zachary Taylor ("Old Rough and Ready"), had just been inaugurated, adding to the confusion about where the country was headed politically, geographically, and morally. A wealthy plantation and slave owner from Kentucky, he deserted his caste to oppose the forced extension of slavery westward, throwing his influence behind a policy of letting new states determine for themselves whether they would allow slaves or not. An opponent of territorial acquisition, he had nonetheless commanded troops along the Rio Grande and emerged a hero from the Mexican War, which led to the annexation of California and the entire Southwest. The unpredictable Taylor would die of an infection the following year, and the nation would continue on its downward spiral of sectional hostility that would end in a bloodbath.

News of a gold strike had come from the California foothills in the previous year, and thousands of natives and newcomers—the "Argonauts" or "49ers"—were on their way west to strike it rich. Others were taking the Oregon Trail to the Willamette Valley or the Mormon Trail to the Great Salt Lake where a small band of Latter-Day Saints, led by Brigham Young, had declared the new state of Deseret. Later as a man John Muir would travel to all those destinations too, but as a boy they were only vague, faraway abstractions on the immense map of the new continent.

As they rode through upstate New York's forests and fields, Daniel and his family had more personal, immediate matters in mind than the state of the nation or the glitter of gold or the fate of the West. They were looking for a home but also for a new identity; neither would be easy to establish, but the latter would be especially hard. What would be their relation to all those contending national forces? What would this continent allow them to do or become? Where would they live, and would they then still be Scots or something else? Young Muir was naively exhilarated by the adventure of migration, but such questions of forging a new identity would plague him for at least three decades. Unlike William Wordsworth, he was not coming home to a familiar place but confronting what seemed like a vast unexplored wilderness. He would wander erratically for years, uncertain about who he was and what he should do with himself—a perpetual newcomer who would find it difficult to put down new roots.

Daniel was forty-five years old—more economically secure, but also less flexible and energetic, than the average immigrant. He had been a successful merchant and, from the sale of his High Street business, possessed substantial capital. That advantage gave him plenty of career choices and opportunities. He had lugged from home a heavy chest containing the beam scale used in his grain store, with a full array of cast-iron weights and a set of carpenter's tools. Apparently, he was ready for anything—trade or construction if necessary. But what he really wanted, perhaps foolishly at his stage of life, was a radical change of livelihood; he had decided to try the challenge of backwoods farming. The simple, independent life on the land, he imagined, might be in harmony with his search for a more primitive, self-reliant Christianity.

In Buffalo the Muirs stayed with fellow Campbellite William Gray, who had probably arrived only a few months earlier himself. Once a grocer in Dunbar, he had set up as a grain dealer in this strategically located depot of inland transportation. He may have corresponded with Daniel about making the journey, as fellow immigrants commonly did, and now he served as their territorial scout. Daniel asked him about farming possibilities. The family had set out with the intention of going to the United Province of Canada (later, Ontario), a loyal colony in the

A portrait of Daniel Muir painted by his daughter Mary after his death. (H-A, JMP)

British Empire and a destination for many of Alexander Campbell's followers coming out of Scotland. Aboard ship, after long conversations with the other passengers, Daniel had shifted his plans to the United States, maybe to Michigan or Wisconsin, when he realized how much hard work would be involved in clearing the Canadian bush. Now Gray told him that most of the good wheat he saw was coming from the brand-new state of Wisconsin, and that fact clinched the decision: they would go there and raise wheat.

Getting to Wisconsin required taking a steamer through the Great Lakes to the port of Milwaukee, a four-day trip that was frequently plagued by shipwreck, collision, and thievery. The Muirs' luck held and they arrived safely, coming ashore with a motley crowd of opportunity seekers—Germans, Norwegians, Swedes, Swiss, and Britons of every sort—all of them arriving, in the words of the Transcendentalist writer Margaret Fuller, "in their national dresses all travel-soiled and worn."[1] The Muirs found Milwaukee an eager, bustling town, with a population of over twenty-five thousand and growing fast, a good place, it might seem, for a transplanted grain dealer to set up in

An undated photograph of Ann Gilrye Muir. (H-A, JMP)

business. Beyond the city, however, stretched a still more inviting prospect: over thirty-two million acres of woodlands and savannahs, lightly settled by a population of three hundred thousand. Less than a year earlier Wisconsin voters had ratified a new constitution and been admitted as a state to the federal union. They were avid for more settlers who would turn those undeveloped acres into a prosperous civilization.

Like most of his fellow travelers, Daniel had developed a powerful hunger for his own piece of land. A desire to escape every personal or institutional constraint on his spiritual life was the main force driving him to America, but he was not immune to the pervasive feeling that a man could never be completely free and independent until he owned his own farm. He felt the itch of secular as well as religious freedom. Such land ownership he had never achieved in the old country, but here at last was an opportunity to become master of his universe. Possessing one's own land was a dream that transcended language barriers and crossed oceans, luring people all the way to the western frontier, where land was cheap enough for almost anyone to acquire. The erstwhile Dunbar merchant, therefore, did not tarry in the city but went looking for a way into the hinterland, where he hoped to become as free and virtuous as one could manage on this sinful planet.

The frontier line of settlement, which marked a density of fewer than two white settlers per square mile, ran in a diagonal from Green Bay to Portage, and it was toward the latter end of the line that they headed. A farmer returning home with an empty wagon agreed to carry their household goods (including an iron stove, pots and pans, a scythe, and a cradle for harvesting wheat that Daniel had acquired in Milwaukee) over a makeshift road. One hundred miles of mud and potholes later, they fetched up in the village of Kingston, where Daniel rented a room for the children while he went looking for land to buy. Days later, he returned with good news: he had found "fine land for a farm in sunny open woods on the side of a lake."[2]

The property was located near the Fox River, in the recently surveyed township of Buffalo, county of Marquette, and belonged to the Fox and Wisconsin Improvement Company. The company had acquired the land as part of a state grant to finance the digging of a canal between the Fox and Wisconsin rivers. A short ways from the Muir property those rivers nearly collided—only a low, swampy patch of land little more than a mile wide separated them, which looked easy to breach with a man-made ditch and locks. In 1673 the French explorers Jacques Marquette and Louis Jolliet had passed through here on their way to discovering the upper Mississippi, portaging their birch bark canoes and blazing a route for future fur traders, soldiers, and capitalists. The latter dreamed of making a fortune in this place.[3] Daniel, who relied on a local farmer named Sandy Gray (another fellow Scotsman) as his guide and advisor, was quick to see what a farm located so near a future canal might mean financially. His hunger for autonomy was not so great that he would eschew all trade with the world left behind.

Daniel purchased the maximum allowed under the land grant's rules, 160 acres at $1.25 per acre. The best Wisconsin soil it was not; mostly it was sandy outwash from ancient glaciers. But it was a lovely spot to look upon, with a spring-fed lake fringed by white lilies, dark sedges, and flowery green meadows edged by low hills and thick deciduous woods. A year later Daniel acquired directly from the state another 160 acres, giving him a substantial domain by East Lothian standards, although the land was neither as productive nor as ready to produce crops as in the old country. Over the summer he put up a log cabin hewed from the oak groves, and in the fall he was ready to receive wife Ann and the remaining children into their bucolic haven, four miles from the nearest neighbor. Soon, with the addition to their litter of a new baby, Joanna, they would require more space. Daniel would construct a more proper house, which they called their Fountain Lake farm.[4]

On 9 May, before the Marquette County court clerk, Daniel swore that he intended to become a citizen of the United States and renounced all allegiance to foreign powers, naming in particular Queen Victoria, whose subject he had been. Although happily a new American, he would recognize no true sovereign but God and pay no attention to the politics of his adopted country. But temporarily he put Heaven and religion aside to concentrate on struggling with nature.[5]

⚬══✦══⚬

Muir's lifelong memories of Wisconsin fastened on that first pioneer home more than anything else. It gave him his first, and one of his most intense ever, encounters with a wild and fecund nature. "This sudden plash into pure wildness," he wrote, "[this] baptism into Nature's warm heart—how utterly happy it made us. . . . Oh, that glorious Wisconsin wilderness!"[6]

But the happiness that a wild natural landscape provided a sensitive lad came with a woeful sense of loss. Everywhere one looked on that frontier the plow and axe were at work to destroy nature, and often to destroy with a ruthlessness that left Muir, as it left many of his contemporaries, with emotional scars that would never heal. They witnessed what few Europeans ever saw—both an abundance of wildness and the sheer violence with which emigrants went out to colonize the lands of North America, Africa, Australia, or New Zealand. Living on a wild frontier could awaken in those settlers long-hidden passions toward the natural world, some of them positive and restorative, others negative and destructive. For Muir, the passion was all of the positive sort, but even within his own family's experience he could see both what had been missing in their Dunbar life and what was being lost all over again in this new place. Wildness, old and precious but also vulnerable and endangered, was almost a daily theme of his years in rural Wisconsin, and a feeling of new openings mixed with immense loss would haunt him the rest of his days.

That first American summer and fall he lived much of the time out of doors, forgetting all the tedious hours spent in Dunbar's bleak, severe classrooms. Here were no schools, no garden walls, and for a while no fences—no warnings of terrible dangers lurking in back alleys, no places he should not go. Daniel's own quest for independence had the unforeseen but joyful consequence of opening his son's eyes to more freedom than he had ever known before, more freedom than any city life in Dunbar or Milwaukee could ever have afforded, more freedom for children than Daniel thought was altogether right. That freedom would not last, but initially it seemed without limit.

Was this place truly a wilderness? By the most extreme definition, meaning an absolutely pristine place where no human had ever passed or left any trace (a definition that Muir never used), the land around Fountain Lake was no wilderness. An Indian trail, for example, crossed the Muir property. For a few thousand years, this part of Wisconsin had been home to the Winnebagoes (today known as the Ho-Chunk nation), before being displaced by the white man. In 1837, under some duress, the natives had sold their lands east of the Mississippi River to the U.S. government. They agreed to vacate the territory within four years, but then were forcibly removed in the summer of 1840, less than a decade before the Muirs arrived.

Some of the aboriginal owners had managed to evade the soldiers and could still be spotted in the neighborhood. One winter young Muir spied an Indian spearing a muskrat a half mile from the family home. They lost a piglet to another indigenous hunter, and their horse Nob to an Indian who tried to sell her to a farmer over at Green Lake. Other natives came through, occasionally stopping at their house to ask for food or use their grindstone. Indians, thus, had long been here, were still around, and would never altogether disappear.

But their obvious and persistent presence did not negate all wildness, no more than did Daniel's preliminary efforts at cultivation. The land on which the Muirs settled had been a lightly inhabited wilderness, never having seen an iron plow or wagon. And for the wide-eyed boy that was wilderness enough. Powerful, unconquered nature confronted them here on all sides, a nature that could overwhelm human effort and defeat ambition. It was wild when the Muirs arrived and it was still partially wild when they left, so wild that it defied Daniel's prodigious will and even helped bring about his failure as would-be squire and patriarch.

What made Wisconsin especially wild and glorious in Muir's eyes was the abundance of undomesticated, nonhuman inhabitants filling the sky and water. They were everywhere around him. Above all, he wrote, here was "a paradise of birds." The blue jay, with its loud, raucous call, aggressive habits, and spectacular plumage, early greeted his eyes; his "first memorable discovery" was a nest of its enchanting green eggs. There followed a profusion of woodpeckers, hawks, partridges, snipes, chickadees, nuthatches, red-winged blackbirds, meadowlarks, prairie chickens, wood ducks, Canada geese, bobwhites, nighthawks, and loons. No species seemed more wonderful than the passenger pigeon, which migrated through the state in flocks of millions, "like a mighty river in the sky." Each spring they arrived after the ground was clear of snow, and each fall they passed through again, stopping only to harvest acorns. Then the Muir children discovered flying squirrels, croaking frogs, snapping turtles, black bears, and a cacophony of insects thrumming in the air.[7]

The conventions of autobiography usually feature a tale of family events and personalities, the doings of self or friends, the achievements of an illustrious career. By that norm Muir's account of his Wisconsin childhood is very odd: those wild creatures and their natural history, not people, dominate the story. He gives more space to "the plucky kingbird" defending her nest against marauders than to his own mother's adjustment to her unaccustomed social isolation, more to the whippoorwill's monotonous singsong than to conversations with his sisters or brothers. This unusual perspective may reflect

Muir's adult aesthetic and scientific interests rather than his youthful feelings about family, which on the whole were warm and positive. But in slanting his story thus he meant to show that human life includes more than humans; in a sense his most important neighbors were the pasqueflowers, cinnamon ferns, sugar maples, and hickories, all of which he describes with scrupulous detail, even putting in their Latin names. Those facts of natural history came to him later, for as a child he was ignorant of science. But he wants us to know the *full* community of which he was a part and to see how the wildness of this place awakened his senses, stimulated his mind, and stirred passions that the family circle could not fully satisfy.

Not all of those passions Muir felt in encountering the Wisconsin wilderness were benign. In retrospect, he regretted how far he had regressed to a savage state—becoming wild enough to kill. In frontier Wisconsin boys were allowed to carry guns and aim at whatever came into their sights. He did so like the rest, roaming over Observatory Hill or down along the river, looking for something to shoot. While he never went on organized sweeps of the countryside as other men and boys did, practicing a kind of biotic cleansing, he did hunt deer, muskrats, raccoons, foxes, hares, and gophers. He tasted, as everyone did, pigeon pie. In adulthood he became more tender-minded, a severe critic of sport hunting. It was painful then to recall how his beloved wilderness had briefly turned him into an avid hunter, before he matured and learned to practice a higher ethic toward other creatures.

> All hale, red-blooded boys are savage, the best and boldest [himself included], the savagest, fond of hunting and fishing. But when thoughtless childhood is past, the best rise the highest above all this bloody flesh and sport business, the wild foundational animal dying out day by day, as divine uplifting, transfiguring charity grows in.

In this particular, at least, it was his view that nature should be subdued—the dark side of *human* nature, that is, the predatory animal within the boy that must be suppressed.[8]

A harsh climate was also part of Wisconsin's savage nature, overpowering in its dramatic swings and extremes, more violent in its ups and downs than the gently rolling terrain might suggest. Summers came with almost tropical force, making Scotland seem mild and temperate by comparison. Muir's first sight of their new home occurred on a sultry evening when the meadows were lit up by "millions of lightning bugs throbbing with light." On such nights huge thunderstorms could suddenly erupt, "marching in awful grandeur across the landscape, trailing broad gray sheets of hail and rain like vast cataracts, and ever and anon flashing down vivid zigzag lightning followed by terrible crashing thunder." He witnessed a lightning bolt shatter an old, decaying bur oak and learned that this was the way that fires began in the forest, creating wide prairie openings in the canopy, a process of landscape modification that the Indians learned to imitate with their own burning techniques.[9]

In winter Muir's ardent feelings for the outdoors grew fainter and nearly froze to death. They had come to a land that, on average, lies blanketed under snow for three whole months of the year, very different from the drizzly winters along the North Sea. The heavy snow was a grim reminder that this place once had been covered with mile-thick glaciers. Arctic air masses still regularly flowed down from the poles, dropping temperatures far below zero Fahrenheit. The Muirs could get plenty of fuel from the surrounding forests, but their father was chary with that supply, forcing an unnecessarily strict economy that left them shivering around an underfed stove. In later years brother David remembered how the three boys had huddled in their bed to stay warm,

> the quilts all frozen about our faces in the morning & how awful cold it was to get up in the morning & dress & go down to the kitchen barefooted. Oo-oo-ooo. It makes me shiver to think of it. And going to Portage with loads of corn—running behind the wagon to keep warm & having to cut frozen bread for our lunch. I don't want & have not had any of that kind of diet since.[10]

Such severe, long-lasting cold, endured in starkly furnished cabins and farmhouses with drafty windows, was not what Muir had in mind when he enthused about Wisconsin's wild glories.

Yet on an icy winter night, when the stars sparkled in the heavens and the aurora borealis began to flicker and pulse in the northern sky, the whole family would troop outside to watch the show. Even Bible-reading, nature-indifferent Daniel could get excited: "Come, mother! Come, bairns! and see the glory of God," he called to them. "Hush and wonder and adore, for surely this is the clothing of the Lord Himself."[11]

The occasionally ecstatic father was nonetheless determined to transform the wildness of nature into a productive farming estate that would guarantee their economic and moral independence. In the beginning he knew nothing about the natural environment around him, and whatever he knew about the craft of farming he had learned in a far-away place. Twenty years earlier he had worked as a farm laborer in Lanarkshire, but that had been under someone else's direction and on pastures and tilled fields that had been won from nature through many toiling generations. Now he had 320 wild acres to subdue as quickly as possible. At the rate of ten acres cleared per year, he would be old and broken down long before he got the property fully under control. Unlike the East Lothian landlords, he had no army of employees to do the brutal work for him, although he hired people for such demanding seasonal chores as harvesting. His main, year-round labor force, therefore, would have to be his offspring. They would have to make the conquest of the wilderness their work too.

Daniel's battle with nature soon became a battle with his eldest son. Their relation in Dunbar had been tense enough, but now an aging father, desperate to succeed in his high-risk gamble, was pitted against an adolescent boy who saw no personal stake in the outcome. One had capital, the other had labor, but they would never negotiate on equal terms. The father expected the son to yield all of his labor unquestioningly in a project that had no end in sight. Eventually Daniel would lose interest in agriculture but perversely expect his son to continue working harder than ever.

On their arrival, the boy of eleven or twelve was set the task of hauling and burning brush, clearing land for the plow. Then he learned how to hoe the planted fields, ridding them of every invading weed, until a horse-drawn cultivator could be bought. By his teenage years, he, like his brothers David and Dan, was breaking prairie sod, swinging a scythe through the ripe wheat, thrashing grain, grinding axes, chopping firewood, and splitting oak logs into rails for fences. He learned how to "corduroy" the swamps (laying down a roadbed of logs), to track a honeybee to its hive, to restore fertility to depleted soils, and to frame a barn. Some of those skills came from Daniel, but the father was not always good with his hands and was ill informed on how to make a living here. Other skills were picked up from work crews that the boy joined as part of the rural proletariat. Thereby he gained knowledge of the land different from that of hunters or naturalists, endowing him with competencies that no city person could acquire. But the heavy farm work also stunted his physical growth, he claimed, and left him "the runt of the family."[12]

Daniel enforced his son's work regime, not through inducements or praise, but through thrashings and sermons. A burning brush pile became a reminder that an everlasting hell was waiting for bad boys who disobeyed God (or withheld their labor). "The old Scotch fashion of whipping for every act of disobedience or of simple, playful forgetfulness" continued on the frontier, but now it had become part of rural work-force discipline. Most of the beatings, Muir wrote, "were outrageously severe" and most of them fell on him, not on his sisters or younger brothers. Eventually, Daniel hoped, his eldest son would internalize all the rules so that punishment would become self-inflicted. Something like that did in fact happen, as Muir drove himself to overcome all bodily weakness, fear, or sloth. He learned a "grim self-denial" that he could don all his life, like a heavy coat that made him immune to the elements and privation. But he also came to understand that his father's motive was not purely the denial of self that religion taught all men and women; on the contrary, Daniel was out not to deny himself but to further his patriarchal ambitions. He would try to gain possession of the wilderness by driving his son relentlessly.

Rarely were there holidays and moments of leisure from that perpetual round of toil. On New Year's Day and the Fourth of July and after sunset in summer when the seventeen-hour workday was done or on Sundays, when Bible lessons and church meetings were over and no physical labor was allowed, the children were permitted a few moments of pleasure—looking for birds' nests or swimming in the lake. But those were exceptions, carefully and grudgingly doled out.

"We were all made slaves," Muir complained, "through the vice of over-industry." Their master was none other than insatiable land hunger that derived from a desire to escape all the restraints and injustices that immigrants felt they had endured in the Old World. Among the people they knew in Marquette County that anxiety ran strongest in Daniel, but their Scotch, English, and Irish neighbors and the many Germans who came to farm elsewhere in the state all showed a similar drive to work and win their independence. In contrast, according to Muir, the native-born American settlers took life more casually and were contented with "less of everything." Their fields were smaller, their work hours more easily interrupted for fishing and hunting or for gathering nuts and berries. In general, "they tranquilly accepted all the good things the fertile wilderness offered," which was precisely what the boy thought he should be doing as well.[13]

Before the Fountain Hill farm was fully established, Daniel decided to buy still more land, another half-section of 320 acres, lying about five miles away. There he would recommence the whole process of agricultural conquest, trying to wrest an even greater return from nature. For two growing seasons he daily walked the distance over to the new farm. Then when Muir was nineteen years old, they set up residence there, building a house on the place they named Hickory Hill (or sometimes Hickory Dale). Daniel sited the house grandly on a high ridge overlooking a valley, like a baronial seat. But he miscalculated badly in one particular and nearly lost his chief worker. There was no water on the ridge, so the son was put to work digging a well, which went deeper and deeper into the hard shale until it was ninety feet down. Where Muir crouched with hammer and chisel at the bottom of the well, a layer of "choke damp," or carbonic acid gas, had collected, and it nearly killed him before Daniel pulled him up. After a neighbor showed them how to eliminate the suffocating gas by throwing down a bundle of burning hay, Muir returned to the job but was more resentful than ever toward a father whose ignorance had nearly cost him his life—a father who "never spent an hour in that well."[14]

The laboring son began to identify, not so much with the hired help, for they were relatively free to do as they pleased, as with the farm animals that Daniel bought and sometimes overworked and abused. He acquired five yoke of oxen for the plowing, logging, and hauling, and added to them pigs, horses, a dog and cat. Fellow victims of man's land hunger, they were remembered fondly well into Muir's old age: the pony Jack (sold by Daniel to a man who wanted him to ride to California), the dog Watch (shot by Daniel for killing chickens), the ox Buck (who learned how to open a pumpkin with his head). Muir came to think of them, as Robert Burns had taught him, as "fellow mortals" or "kin," part of a common "humanity." He rejected the notion that they had neither minds nor rights or had been made merely "to be petted, spoiled, slaughtered, or enslaved." Like their wilder cousins, they deserved love and respect. But unlike creatures of the wilderness, they were mere workers in the eyes of Daniel and his fellow agriculturists. Although valued as investments, too often they were exploited, just as Muir himself was.[15]

Father Daniel wore out his body and his iron will on the Wisconsin hills. Within ten years of their arrival he began to lose interest in acquiring land, putting in crops, or building barns for the cattle. He began to withdraw from farming as a way of life. Part of his first farm he unloaded on daughter Sarah and her husband David Galloway; then in his fifties he began a wholesale retreat from the project of wresting a grand estate from nature. More and more he turned his energies to preaching the Gospel, as he understood it, and for a long preparatory period stayed indoors with his Bible while others in the family went on sweating in the fields. That change in his life's purpose came too late for his family to indulge or accept; in the end he ended up alienating permanently his oldest son and losing almost all control over the rest of the family. None of the boys would follow in his farming or preaching footsteps, and only Sarah and Margaret among the girls would choose to live a farmer's life. Every acre of the Muirs' rural property eventually would have to be sold. Much of the profit from that sale went to support Daniel's evangelical mission, which drove him out of the countryside and into town and city, until finally he was left living alone, separated from his wife and children, half-demented and emotionally isolated. In the end the man who had started off so well in Dunbar, with so much promise of power and wealth, left only a small financial inheritance—and left no one to carry on his wishes, and only a passing impact on the land.

His son John repudiated, on the whole, the tradition of agrarian patriarchy from which he had suffered so grievously, although later he would face its demands once again as a married man. The times, he sensed, as well as his own desires, were running against such patriarchy and toward a more liberal ideal. He rejected the domineering relationship it taught between parents and children, between men and women, between husband and wife, and between humans and nature. For a long time Muir would avoid marriage altogether, unsure of what being an adult or father should mean, with no role models that he could follow. The most telling lesson of his days in rural Wisconsin was that the old idea of patriarchy and the society that it created, or tried to create, rested on an antagonistic stance toward the natural world, and he would have nothing to do with it.

❦

A dozen years after the Muirs arrived, Frederick Jackson Turner was born to a newspaper-owning family in the town of Portage, Wisconsin, just ten miles away from the Fountain Lake farm. He would grow up to become one of the most influential historians of the United States, famous for his argument that the American frontier was the seedbed of world democracy. He maintained that the frontier had promoted individual freedom by dissolving the bonds of complex society. Confining institutions fell away, at least temporarily, he explained, restoring "a kind of primitive organization based on the family. The tendency is anti-social. It produces antipathy to control, and particularly to any direct control." That antipathy had spread back toward the older settlements, affecting civilization on many levels, but especially political attitudes and practices, and eventually had spread to Europe as well.[16]

If Turner had interviewed the Muir family, he might have revised his theories somewhat. In the first place, that particular family brought a boatload of egalitarian ideas with them from Scotland to the American frontier—critical attitudes about imperialism, positive attitudes about democracy, social justice and mobility, and economic and religious freedom, attitudes that had long been clashing with old established hierarchies on the other side of the Atlantic. Second, the shrinking of social context down to their nuclear family level did not restore any primitive democracy. Daniel made sure of that, acknowledging no contradiction between his personal antipathy toward outside control and his urge to control others, specifically his wife and children. Patriarchy characterized the Muir experience on the frontier. Third, it was the *end* of the frontier, the growth of settlement, that restored a set of checks and balances on the power of fathers like Daniel. His son felt freedom expand precisely as the neighborhood filled up with more adults, more diversity of thought, and more encouragement for his struggling efforts to dissent.

Within three or four years of their arrival, the Muirs witnessed a community beginning to flourish around them, with farmers on almost every quarter section of land. Most of the local newcomers were immigrants from the British Isles—English, Scotch, and Irish—which was unusual in Wisconsin experience. Generally, it was the more numerous Germans and Scandinavians who carved out thickly settled enclaves, while the Yankees, coming mainly from New England, New York, and Ohio, scattered across the map and dominated most counties. In 1850 there were only 3,527 Scots in the whole state, or less than one percent of the population. Although nearly every county had a few Scotch families, some in agriculture, others in business or the professions, in no place were they a large group or a majority. Marquette County, in contrast, attracted a lot of Scots, ranging from rebellious Campbellites to old-line Presbyterians, and through church attendance the Muirs knew them all.[17]

Philip Gray, for example, formerly of Edinburgh and brother of William Gray, settled down the road. He too was an ardent disciple of Alexander Campbell's "back to the Bible" brand of Christianity. Gray arrived with family in tow the same year as the Muirs did and the next year bought land immediately to the south of their Fountain Lake place. Philip's son David was two years older than Muir—one of a pair of boys known as "the twa Davies," who became John's close friends. The other David in that pair was surnamed Taylor, and his family, also from Scotland, settled just to the northeast of the original Muir homestead. In contrast to Daniel, their fathers permitted books besides the Bible, including books of Romantic poetry. The first David later moved away and became editor of the Buffalo (N.Y.) *Courier*, while the second lived out his life on the old place, unmarried to the end, a Wordsworthian poet and nature lover.

Other neighbors included Daniel's sister Mary Blakley, now a widow, who followed their trek to Marquette County and lived there until her death in 1867. Families named McReath, Galloway, Duncan, Reid, and Whitehead also settled nearby, making possible a real congregation at last—"a wee white kirk" in the country, where the preaching was done in a brogue they could understand. But religious sectarianism, even among the Muirs, became more muted and indeterminate than back home in Scotland, as families went from church to church comparing notes on the Baptist, Methodist, Presbyterian, or Disciples preachers, and the Old World religious wars seemed less significant here.

William Duncan had been an ironworker and stonemason in Lanarkshire. He and his wife befriended young John, reproved Daniel for feeding his children poorly and for nearly killing John in the well digging, and (most important) loaned books from their substantial library. Jean Galloway not only blessed the marriage of her son David to Sarah Muir but also became a second mother to John, furnishing sympathy and advice that did not always echo his father's. The Reid boys, Charles and William, became his good friends, very religious but fun loving.

> We were swift to see the way [the neighbors] behaved, the
> differences in their religion and morals, and in their way
> of drawing a living from the same kind of soil under the
> same general conditions; how they protected themselves
> from the weather; how they were influenced by new doc-
> trines and old ones seen in new lights in preaching, lec-
> turing, debating, bringing up children, etc., and how
> they regarded the Indians, those first settlers and owners
> of the ground that was being made into farms.

Muir learned from those neighbors that there were other ways of
being Scottish, or being American, besides Daniel's overbearing and
idiosyncratic version.[18]

Even the right to possess Wisconsin lands had more than one angle
of seeing, as Muir learned in listening to his father converse with a
neighbor. George Mair, another immigrant from Scotland, felt sympathetic toward the indigenous people who had been displaced, a view
that Daniel did not share. Mair called the displacement of the Indians
"robbery" and a "ruthless" destruction of their means of livelihood.
Daniel replied that it was God's will that another race take command;
the Indians had failed to turn so fertile a country to good use, so they
must give way to "industrious, God-fearing farmers" who would make it
support "ten or a hundred times more people in a far worthier manner,
while at the same time helping to spread the gospel." Neighbor Mair
retorted that, in fact, the Scottish and English farmers were inexperi-
enced agriculturists, many of them (now he was cutting close to Daniel's
own story) having been "merchants and mechanics and servants" in the
old country, and that they would feel sorely abused were they to be displaced by more skilled, scientific farmers, "who could raise five or ten
times as much on each acre as we did." For the listening son, the lesson
was clear, and it was not favorable to parental authority: his father did
not occupy the high ground or pursue moral consistency. Rather, he
advocated "the rule of might with but little or no thought for the right
or welfare of the other fellow if he were the weaker."[19]

The growing community liberated more than Muir's ethical awareness; it offered him books, ideas, schooling, a few girls to moon over,

greater recognition for useful work that was not farming, and finally the encouragement to leave home. Around age fifteen a hunger for knowledge began to stir in the boy, but there was little to feed on in his household, nor were there any schools in the district. The family had brought only a few religious texts from Scotland, and Daniel set himself up as censor over any other material that came into the house. He allowed home instruction on the basics of mathematics and grammar, but not Walter Scott's novels or even Thomas Dick's pious *Christian Philosopher*, on the theory that the Bible furnished all the philosophy anyone needed. So Muir had to learn the arts of deception if he was to satisfy his intellectual hunger, acquiring and guarding a small private library with titles by Shakespeare and the poets John Milton, William Cowper, and Mark Akenside.

Two authors in particular fired him with zeal for traveling to exotic foreign places: Mungo Park and Alexander von Humboldt, both of whom were household names among the more literate families. Park was a native of Selkirk, Scotland, and (perhaps reassuring for Daniel) a member of the Secession Church. He had studied medicine with a local doctor, then been sent by London philanthropists to search for the headwaters of the River Niger in West Africa. His *Travels in the Interior of Africa* was published in 1799, six years before he drowned in the Niger; the book, which is loaded with hair-raising adventures among roaring lions, exotic Muslim villages, and nasty slave traders, became a classic account of the so-called Dark Continent. The German traveler Humboldt was even more popular—indeed, he was the greatest name in nineteenth-century natural history and adventurous travel before Charles Darwin. With his French companion Aimé Bonpland, he explored the Latin American tropics, describing the rivers, people, flora, and fauna of Venezuela and Brazil with irresistible brilliance and endlessly colorful anecdotes. His river eels could kill a horse with a single electric jolt; his gaudily painted Indians ate roasted monkeys, ants, and one another; his forests teemed with crocodiles, macaws, jaguars, and vampire bats; his floods raged with unstoppable violence; his missionaries fought each other viciously for territorial control.[20]

Aware of her son's absorption in those narratives, Ann predicted that he would "travel like Park and Humboldt some day." Daniel upbraided her for such nonsense: "Dinna put sic notions in the lad-die's head."[21] But such notions were already stirring, although incho-ate and dreamy and with no clear means of realization. Muir had begun to imagine becoming a doctor like Park or a naturalist like Humboldt, although he had no money to pursue either calling. Moreover, at this point he had only eight years of formal schooling. He had not been in a classroom with a teacher since Dunbar days—nine years earlier.

In the winter of 1858 a school finally opened in the district, housed in a log cabin one mile from Hickory Hill. Forgetting all his former distaste for schoolmasters, Muir briefly became a pupil again. He was nearly twenty years old! But he had done a considerable amount of reading on his own, so that his teacher, George Branch, likely knew little more than his gangling student. Mostly Muir came to school for the ballad singing and other amusements. His academic performance did not really matter, and anyway he was now too old to whip if he didn't get his lessons. Ever the prankster when the authorities were not looking, he and a friend one night stuffed sod down the school's chimney, driving everybody out into the cold to escape the smoke. He ogled the females who sat near him in class and felt a rising lust that the old Scottish schoolmasters had tried so hard to squelch. Known among his classmates as "the bashful gentleman," Muir penned a pri-vate ode to a young beauty with "exquisite ears" and golden hair falling over her shoulders, taking keen notice of her "bust half maidenly half womanly in its undulating graces."[22]

Notwithstanding those high jinks and erotic impulses, religious piety kept a strong hold over Muir's libido, so much that he often preached to others with as much solemnity as he heard at home. In his first extant letter, written to Bradley Brown in 1856, he pictures being poor and alone on a stormy night, then seeing a light from a rich man's mansion and getting a warm welcome from its propri-etor, who brings the wanderer in to the fireside. "Would you ever forget such a man?" he asks. "How much more has Jesus done for you." Again, he warns a friend that Satan is always lurking about, and the faithful must protect themselves by concentrating on the next life and fighting a constant war against sin in this one. Neither his friends nor anyone else in their faith-based community would have found anything unusual in those sentiments; they were common-places, although for most in the community they did not exclude pleasure or the good life.[23]

One widely approved way of serving God and humankind in the Scottish and Scottish American mind was to invent labor-saving machines, much as James Watt had done back in Glasgow. Muir dis-covered he had a talent for inventing that could win applause from the community, albeit not from Daniel, who regarded physical labor as divinely ordained and devices for evading that labor as the devil's playthings. Pride in one's ingenuity was for the father a form of sin, and his son seemed stuffed with pride—"a contumacious quibbler too fond of disputation."[24] But most other Scots made heroes out of their inventors and engineers, for their achievements were the basis of economic and social progress. Certainly the majority thought so on this frontier, where there was more work to do than they could manage without mechanical assistance.

Muir's first invention was a self-setting sawmill, built as a small-scale model in their icy-cold Hickory Hill cellar one winter (right under the parents' bedroom). Lacking a proper workshop, he had to make some of his tools from scratch in order to construct the model. By automating the sawing of logs into lumber, his machine would speed up the conversion of wild forests into useful commodities. Others approved and, over the next two decades, they would give him plenty of opportunities for perfecting his original design.

Children, it is often noted, are born with a desire to take things apart, find out how they work, and put them back together in new forms. They tear off a butterfly's wing to watch it struggle to fly, or they get curious about what makes a clock tick. But the adult inventor goes beyond that childhood curiosity and makes a career of thinking up new and better ways to do things, to improve the world, whether for personal profit or social approval. He sees inefficiencies or imperfections in nature's ways or in people's ways, and he wants to make what is flawed flawless. That impulse emerged in young Muir as a defining characteristic and stayed with him through his entire life. He would always try to overcome the flaws in the world around him, either by rationalizing them—that is, by seeking the true perfection in the Creator's design—or by offering practical remedies and mechanical devices, becoming an assistant to the Creator.

Inventing new machines soon became an obsession, driving him to sacrifice sleep and put his health at risk. Rising every morning at 1 a.m. so that he would not interfere with his regular farm jobs, he headed straight to the cellar where he launched a one-man technological revolution—"water wheels, curious door locks and latches, thermometers, hygrometers, pyrometers, clocks, a barometer, an automatic contrivance for feeding the horses at any required hour, a lamp-lighter and fire-lighter, an early-or-late rising machine."[25] All of these were whittled out of scraps of wood and fastened together with pegs and rope, and many were more remarkable for their ingenuity than their practicality.

Above all, he was obsessed with devices that could help discipline the lazy human body and turn it into a more time-efficient machine in a work-driven society. His own laziness was often the target for his devices. Even as he rejected Daniel's control over his time and labor, he sought to create father-substitutes in the form of outlandish contraptions. They became his task master, unrelenting and unforgiving. Often they featured a ticking clock, like the bedstead that woke him in the morning by dropping him with a thud and setting him upright on his feet, ready for the day's work. Commonly they had less to do with factory production or rural mechanization than with self-improvement and self-redemption.

His obsessed mind dreamed of machines all the time, even when he was not whittling—machines that often had no obvious function or would not work if they were ever built. Many were more symbolic than practical, existing only on paper or in his imagination, suspended in a mental twilight zone where nature and technology merged into one another, or more ominously where all of nature had been turned into a machine. He mounted some of those drawings (they are undated but probably were done around 1859–60) on coarse linen and tinted them with sepia or pastels, suggesting works of art rather than blueprints. One shows a female doll harnessed to a rope and beam that rhythmically rises and falls, forcing her arms up and down, transforming her into an automaton in a long gown. Another depicts a dead stump jutting from a lone clump of flowers. Hanging in the fork of the tree is Father Time's scythe, the symbol of death; its blade is stuck all over with gears, while suspended from the blade's tip hangs an arrow that bristles with still more arrows pointing in all directions of the compass. Its motto reads like a biblical proverb: "All Flesh is Grass." A third drawing shows a barren landscape of stumps, rail fences, and log cabins lying beneath a naked, bulbous hill. Over the scene hovers the dial of a great clock; it is a little after 8 p.m., and the setting sun is shooting its last rays down to earth.[26]

Muir, these drawings suggest, was caught between a passion for the wild, uncontrolled flow of nature and a drive to control, discipline, and invent. The contradiction was felt throughout Great Britain and the United States—it was perhaps the dominant contradiction of those modernizing societies. Muir, like so many of his contemporaries, was torn between a desire to master and yet to liberate nature and human nature. He felt compelled to invent new ways to harness nature's energies (and his own and other people's energies too). Yet he wanted

Muir's illustration (circa 1862) of a means to record time by use of a star, entitled "The star hand rising and setting with the sun all the year." The nearly treeless landscape suggests the environmental impact of frontier agriculture. (Wisconsin Historical Society, WHS Image ID 32870)

to break free of that urge to invent, fearing where it might take him. Even as he invented his strange machines, he was troubled by apocalyptic fears of runaway mechanistic forces. Yet he went on inventing and devising, satisfying his creative impulses and winning approval, while resisting the outcome.

The good folks of Marquette County likely knew little of those ambivalent, troubled drawings; what they saw were the homemade thermometers and sawmills, evidence in their minds of uncommon ingenuity, practicality, and cleverness. While his mother hoped he would become a minister, and Daniel gave him no encouragement to do anything but farm, the community told him he might become a promising businessman or inventor, careers that had high standing in the Scottish mind.

His own early career plan, even while he was dreaming of running off to South America or Africa, was somehow to get a job in a large factory and to use that as a financial stepping-stone to a career in medicine or engineering. For that to happen, however, he would have to leave home and the countryside, no matter how unsure he felt about his ability to succeed. Caught between so many conflicting emotions, he dithered and worried, until finally a friendly neighbor pushed him forward, urging him to enter his inventions at the state fair in Madison. "There's nothing like them in the world," the friend said and predicted a great reception for the backwoods boy genius.

So in the late summer of 1860, Muir left home, feeling very much alone and full of trepidation, with no blessing or financial aid from his father. He was setting out on his first real trip since coming to the United States, breaking family ties and getting free of paternal control. He could not have imagined where, or how far, that step would take him.

CHAPTER 3

Climbing the Ice Mountain

No lurching wagon rides this time: Muir bought a ticket on the new railroad that ran from Pardeeville to Madison, a distance of about forty miles, and rode on the forged-iron tracks of progress. He carried aboard a bundle of two clocks and a thermometer made of an old washboard and whittled-down hickory sticks that drew curious onlookers along the way. One wag at the station said the bundle looked like a gadget for extracting bones from fish. Amateur phrenologists wanted to examine the bumps on the inventor's skull. The train's engineer and conductor were so impressed with their clever passenger that they allowed him to ride out front on the cowcatcher, where he could feel the full brute force of the locomotive rushing through the peaceful countryside.

This would be one of the longest excursions Muir would ever make, not in miles but in self-discovery. Twenty-two years old, he had left off being a dependent seated at his father's table and was headed toward independence and manhood. The price of leaving home, however, was an aching loneliness that hit him hard in Madison and would trouble him on nearly every solitary trip he would take throughout the rest of his life. Soon he would discover that being independent was not enough; he needed other people—neighbors and family, mother and siblings. He would ease the loneliness by making plenty of new friends, for friendship came easily to him and he held on to his friends with great tenacity. Above all he would seek and find many women friends, some of them his own age while others were considerably older, who would fulfill his persistent need for home, nurture, and companionship.

The rail line to Madison was also the first leg of a journey that would take him far from Daniel's rigid, if idiosyncratic, doctrines of evangelical Protestantism and toward a more liberal, free-form faith and piety. It would require a decade or so to get there. A scientific and secular education would contribute much along the way, beginning with formal studies at the University of Wisconsin and informal studies on his own for years to come. Over that period Muir would wrestle hard with his inherited Calvinist, Presbyterian, and Campbellite background, never escaping altogether its language or temperament. But eventually he would break free from its constraining set of ideas and embrace the Romantic and democratic religion of nature espoused by women and men on both sides of the Atlantic Ocean.

Among the most difficult challenges facing him as he set out on his own was to decide what kind of citizen he wanted to be, or what polity, if any, he wanted to join. Unlike Daniel, he never signed an official declaration of allegiance to the U.S. government; no one required him to do so as an immigrant child, and the concept of national identity had never crossed his mind. So far he had lived rather insulated from American life and politics in his Scottish frontier enclave. Now he would have to become more intimate with Wisconsin's Yankees, many of them fiercely nationalistic, proud of their country, and determined to hold it together even if it meant shedding blood. They were sure that the United States was mankind's last best hope, a notion that Muir had never really thought about. He would not find the boast very compelling; in the classic pattern of children growing up in an immigrant family, who had not made the decision to migrate or sworn a new allegiance, he would find it difficult to identify with American nationalism or so-called manifest destiny.

The year he left home, 1860, saw a presidential election campaign of unprecedented bitterness and with profound consequences for the United States. The Illinois lawyer Abraham Lincoln, who won the Republican nomination that summer, vowed to stop the spread of human slavery, confining it to the South until it faded away as an outmoded and immoral institution. Although he would win the presidency (with less than 40 percent of the vote) and win Wisconsin (barely), his election almost brought an end to the United States as a thriving nation, its dreams of empire, and its sense of mission. Before Lincoln's inauguration, seven slave-owning states seceded from the union and formed the Confederate States of America. Four more states joined them after he issued a call to arms to put down the rebellion. By the next April the country would be engaged in a civil war that would last four terrible years.

Thus, when Muir came flying into Madison on his iron horse, wide-eyed and expectant, he was descending into a maelstrom of contention from which there would be no easy escape. The nation's politics, colleges, religious groups, cities, and rural communities were all in turmoil, and no barometer he could devise—no mechanism of any sort—could tell a young man what was coming or how to prepare for it.

∞━━━∞

Each year Madison, as the capital city, staged a fair to show off the state's crops, livestock, and inventions, and to demonstrate its high level of intelligence and advances in civilization. The year 1860 saw the best fair ever, with more than two thousand exhibits. Muir entered his bundle of machines as an exhibitor and set them up in the building called the Temple of Art, where they immediately drew attention. On 25 September the front page of the *Wisconsin State Journal* reported that "some very ingenious specimens of mechanism" were catching the public's eye: clocks without cases, their wheels moving "with beautiful evenness," and a thermometer made in the form of a scythe "hung in a dwarf burr [sic] oak very tastefully ornamented with moss about its roots." The *Wisconsin Evening Patriot* likewise praised Muir's scythe-thermometer (labeled "Old Time") and added that it "could only have been executed by genuine genius." The judges gave him a special cash prize. Afraid of too much praise leading to vanity, he lowered his eyes and tried to stay humble, although he sent an exulting letter to brother David.[1]

No one had told him what to do next, when the fair was over, so he hung about the town for a few days, knowing nary a soul, lacking bread money, and feeling homesick after all his brave talk about setting out on his own. To his sister Sarah Galloway he wrote that he would gladly give up "Madison's pretty ice mountains" to be home again and reassured her that he was still thinking of his Savior despite all the distractions. He hiked up the hill overlooking Lake Mendota where the state university, founded only thirteen years earlier, had laid out a campus consisting of three buildings—University, North, and South halls—amidst a hundred park-like acres. Daunted like any country bumpkin, he poked fun at it as a great place for breaking steers. It would prove to be the prettiest, coldest, most enticing, and most difficult of the city's "mountains" that he would try to climb.[2]

A local entrepreneur, John Varnel, offered room and board and promised a contract to manufacture Muir's woodsy thermometer if they could get a patent on it. But when nothing immediately came of the idea, Muir was compelled to throw in with another inventor, stern-faced Norman Wiard, who at the fair had exhibited a steam-powered iceboat intended for winter travel. Wiard offered to take him on as unpaid assistant in the Mississippi River town of Prairie du Chien, where he had set up his foundry and machine shop. The boat was no success, and its maker was hardly ever home, leaving Muir to fend for himself. Fortunately, the protégé gained access to a shelf of books on technical design and a good set of drafting tools—aids, he hoped, that might prepare him to move on to some eastern city where his chances for long-term employment might be better. He wrote to a Philadelphia factory about work, but they had nothing to offer.

Faithfully every week, Muir sent a letter home, and back came a barrage of news, gossip, questions, and prayers. The folks were surprised that he had ended up in Prairie du Chien and were anxious about his living in what they heard was a fever-ridden place. Father, now in a more forgiving mood, packed off a trunk filled with clothes, papers, and books, inadvertently leaving out a silk necktie Muir had requested. They wanted to know which church he was attending. On his side he worried that his absentee boss might be a Catholic and complained that he had ended up in a miserable place.

In a long and lofty letter of advice to Daniel, Jr., on how to become a machinist or inventor, Muir offered a veiled, and pessimistic, assessment of his own career plans. Gloomily sitting at a window as a funeral procession went by, he reflected that before long they both "must die" and that, whatever ambition raged within, one must always be sure that "God has you by the hand." In retrospect, he was glad that he had stayed home so long, getting a strong spiritual grounding, which was more vital for success than any time spent in monotonous labor at a factory workbench.

> It is certainly a dreary thing to file in a great smoky shop among devilish men on two piece[s] of iron for two or three days to make them fit closely . . . and even suppose you got so far as manufacturing engines (steam ones I mean) and made a hundred a day every bolt and bar and rod and screw in each would be alike likely and soon there would be but precious *little* more fun in the business or romance either than there would be in the wonderful manufacture of everduring [*sic*] fencing material from the mighty and majestic ever young everlasting and God made oaks.

He pictures the poor machinist (his projected self!) with blackened face coughing up "sooty and brassy and irony" phlegm from his lungs. Far better than such a life would be getting to know God and, "as joined by fathers will," reading books on philosophy and engineering. Perhaps it came as a relief then that no factory wanted his talents.[3]

Muir remained in Prairie du Chien for several months, while the iceboat project foundered, and instead of getting a start in a flourishing workshop he was forced to depend on the unexpected generosity of strangers. He moved into the Mondell Hotel, owned by a couple named Pelton, where he could live free in exchange for keeping the fires burning. All three of the females in the family, the wife Frances, her baby daughter Fannie, and her mature niece Emily, opened their hearts to him, and on that chance encounter he quickly built an intimate friendship. They may have seen in his large guileless eyes a confused and vulnerable boy needing affection or (in the case of Emily) even a potential husband; but Muir turned to them as a source of "Christian love" that he desperately needed to keep him on the right path. Temptation was already laying siege to his puritanical defenses, and he was grateful for their steadying support.

The other hotel boarders were a spirited group of unmarried men and women, "all mannerly and educated," but in Muir's stiff-necked view too fond of salacious parlor games like blind man's bluff and fox and geese. On Thanksgiving they were in a flirtatious and frolicking mood, while he stolidly sat at table, consenting to try the turkey but not to join their fun. "They are great kissers," he wrote to Sarah, "but they don't kiss me." He threw Solomon's words at them: "My son, if sinners entice thee, consent thou not." That dash of cold water ended the festivities, and the next day they apologized for their offensive conduct. "I have a great character for sobriety," he reassured the home folks, and "there is much here to lead me away from God."[4]

By winter Muir was tentatively back in Madison, making and selling a few of his tilting bedsteads, ordering an uncased time piece from a Connecticut clockmaker to investigate, addressing insurance circulars, and working as a lowly carriage driver and errand boy in exchange for board. To Mrs. Pelton he wrote that he had been used as a "humble stool" by pretentious socialites in the capital but had broken free of them. Once again he was lonely and gloomy but reassured her that "I am always happy in the center."[5] Finding no work prospects in the East, and uncertain they were really what he wanted anyway, he began looking for opportunities closer to hand.

On his near horizon loomed the university, still seeming distant, icy, and unaffordable but undeniably attractive. He ran across one of its students whom he had met at the state fair and complained that, because he was poor, he could not become a student there. But it would not be so expensive, he learned, if one lived simply on bread and milk. Taking heart, he applied for admission. Somehow he would find a way to finance a real, advanced education. He would storm the ice mountain and claim his diploma. That at least was how Muir remembered his college career beginning and ending, but that was not quite the way it happened. In truth, he depended on his father's largesse to get a start, and his college years, which were often interrupted by the need to work and earn money, did not end with a degree.[6]

The university estimated that a student required $75–110 per year, including $10.50 per term (the academic year was divided into three terms) for tuition, room, and heat. Food was extra, and students commonly arranged to board with local families or cooked for themselves. Hard, crusty Daniel, who had refused to give any pocket money on Muir's leaving the farm, now repented and gave him $50, enough to finance at least half a year at university. Hoping to deliver his gift in person, Daniel apologized that he could not come because of bad winter roads and sent the money in a letter. In April he sent $10 more, and in May another $10, with a promise of another $20, all with his usual exhortations attached: save much, borrow little, live temperately, but don't starve yourself. "I should like you to have the real necessaries of life," he wrote, "& if you want the luxuries of life I would not feel vexed about it." With that unexpected paternal kindness, the son was able to enter college.[7]

Muir applied to be admitted for the third term, which ran from late March to late June. The dean of faculty and professor of mathematics and natural philosophy, John Stanley, M.A., interviewed him for admission and allowed him into the preparatory, or pre-college, department until he could demonstrate that he was capable of doing advanced studies. By the end of the term he had met the test, and the next August he was back in school, promoted to freshman standing despite the skimpiness of his formal educational background.

Most of his classmates had come from urban places like Madison, not the rural sticks, had more schoolroom time than he, and were younger. He enrolled with about ninety of them in the scientific curriculum, which was far more popular than the classical one, although the distinction was small. Three recitations or lectures a day, following morning chapel, was the established schedule, with conduct and attendance records regularly sent to parents. The prescribed subjects for freshman science students included algebra and trigonometry, mensuration and navigation, Latin (the poet Horace and historian Livy, whom he had read in the original language in Dunbar days), Greek (Xenophon's *Anabasis* and *Memorabilia*), and U.S. and "general" history. The science part would not come until the last term of their final year.[8]

That first spring at university Muir sent home to younger sisters Mary, Annie, and Joanna a sketch of his new surroundings. On the positive side his room on the first floor of North Hall, the men's dormitory, overlooked Lake Mendota, where he often went for a swim or a walk, gathering shells, pebbles, and flowers. Or he liked to sit under a large basswood tree, reading a book and watching a hummingbird. On the negative side were the morning sounds of a hundred roosters crowing and train engines whistling in the city below, adding to the noise of student feet pounding on wooden stairs. He kept his window open, hoping to hear thrushes singing above the din, reminding him of quieter days at Hickory Hill. From the upper floors of University Hall one could look across Madison's rooftops toward two great windmills turning in the wind nearly seven miles away (he had carefully calculated the distance). He was not sure whether they would like living in such an overpopulated place, or come to that whether he wanted to be there either.[9]

Feeling a lingering doubt about where he belonged and a persistent embarrassment about his countrified ways, Muir cultivated an image of eccentricity. He grew a long, shaggy beard that attracted a few jeers, one fellow threatening to light it with a match. With the administration's permission he set up his alarm-clock bed and other machines, turning his room into a little chamber of wonders, open at all hours to the curious. At a formal reception where they wheeled out a large piano, he took off his shoes and climbed into the piano case to see how it worked, setting tongues clacking. Then another student, Milton Griswold, who, like Muir, was often laughed at for an overly earnest desire to instruct or impress, introduced him to botany; and botany, he decided, was ideally suited for the eccentric but serious mind.

Griswold found him lounging idly on the dormitory steps one day and directed his attention to a locust tree arching overhead. Did Muir know what kind of tree it was? Not at all, but he thought it looked like an overgrown member of the pea family. It was a good guess, Griswold said, and a good place to begin. The classmate had taught himself plant taxonomy with the use of analytical tables in Alphonso Wood's *Class Book of Botany*; he plucked stems, leaves, and flowers, tried to identify them, affixed labels where he could, and stuck them in his herbarium for future reference. One could discern through such study, he explained, the unity and harmony of nature, and ultimately the wisdom of the Creator. There was nothing arbitrary or chaotic in the plant kingdom, if one knew its principles of classification. Now Muir too saw for the first time the inner beauty of flowers, and through them "glorious traces of the thoughts of God, and leading on and on into the infinite cosmos." He purchased his own copy of Wood and began rambling with Griswold around lakes and fields. Soon every jar, bottle, or washbasin in his room contained a sprig or branch of some botanical specimen.[10]

When his first term ended, Muir went home to work on the family farm for the summer, cutting wheat and doing other familiar chores in the daytime while in the evenings trying, sometimes past midnight, to identify the plants that grew in the vicinity and that he had known since youth. Disappointing news came that his patent application for the alarm-clock bed had failed, so becoming a famous inventor seemed to recede further as a career. Letters from school friends brought reports of bombastic Fourth of July celebrations and of distant battles waging between Union and Confederate forces in Virginia. Still, when the summer ended he was ready to leave again the bucolic life for the city.

Thanks to the wages paid by his father, he could afford the next term at school. To save railroad fare, he walked the whole way with David, who had decided to become a student too, in the preparatory department. Both found that they could stand such strenuous physical exercise; indeed, it felt good walking across the quiet and peaceful prairie. Their whole family seemed ready to troop after them; with the two older boys leaving, the farm had lost the core of its labor pool, so Daniel proposed abandoning farming altogether and moving to Madison. Instead, he was persuaded by Ann to settle in the town of Portage, putting Hickory Hill in the hands of his son-in-law John Reid and daughter Margaret, and devoting himself to preaching the Gospel.

In Madison the air was noisier than ever with fierce martial talk. To Sarah and her husband, who had become his main family confidants, Muir wrote, "How warlike things are here." A local regiment was preparing to leave for the front, making an imposing appearance but prompting him to ask, "How can all the great and showy coverings of war hide its real hideousness?"[11]

⁕

Perhaps because of his reputation for scientific aptitude, the school allowed Muir to depart from the prescribed curriculum and, in his second term, attend the lectures of Ezra Carr, M.D., professor of chemistry and natural history. It marked the beginning of what would become Muir's near-professional, lifelong interest in the sciences and of a long and significant friendship with the doctor and his wife Jeanne. They were an eloquent and talented pair; each would leave an impact on the freshman student, Jeanne especially.

The Carrs had arrived in Madison in 1855, and Ezra was immediately and characteristically embroiled in controversy. Thirty-six years old, he had been a professor in medical colleges in Castleton, Vermont, and Albany, New York, a veteran of state geological surveys, a former vice-president of the American Medical Association, and president of a temperance society. Science, in those days, was not a very specialized profession. In his inaugural address delivered in the Wisconsin senate chamber he warned that "our learned institutions are losing their hold upon the popular mind" because they fail to address the needs of the farmer, mechanic, and manufacturer. Sounding a theme he would repeat often over the next few years, he declared that it was time to replace an outmoded curriculum with "useful knowledge." Students should learn to observe the "plan and purposes of God as expressed in the natural world," spending at least as much time on science as on the study of rhetoric and mathematics. Training in the practical sciences would promote economic development and democracy; "it is science," he reminded the legislators, regents, and professors before him, "which is making this great west the garden of the world."[12]

Carr soon ran into a wall of resistance, mainly from indifferent administrators at the university but also from professors who did not share his vision of relevance. Four years after joining the faculty, he

Photograph of Professor Ezra Carr, University of Wisconsin, taken before 1860. (Wisconsin Historical Society, WHS Image ID 3401)

angrily denounced a "curriculum of fossil usages...filled with fossil men who are subject to hydrophobic spasms at the mere mention of the word science." In an age when other schools were beginning to accept the natural sciences as an important part of their educational mission, he remained the university's only science instructor. Worse yet, he felt treated like a mere boy "governed by a master." His persistent refusal to attend chapel became another bone of contention.[13]

Oblivious to such faculty politics, Muir was an eager student in Professor Carr's class that fall of 1861 and assiduously saved the notes he took. "Nature," he scribbled down, is the "name for an effect whose cause is God." Experimental science is "the only road to a true acquaintance with nature." Atoms are indivisible, inconceivably minute forms of matter, and their combination makes everything we see around us. The microscope reveals a world of animals so small that millions of them would not weigh as much as a grain of sand. The wings of insects are as thin as $1/200,000^{th}$ inch. The optic nerve carries signals to the brain, which turns them into ideas. A miscellany of facts and aperçus, the course stimulated Muir's growing interest in nature, more for its philosophical than utilitarian value.[14]

Carr reported to his wife that he had a promising new student who wanted to study science, and geology in particular. Then one winter morning that same student rang her doorbell on Gilman Street—"a stranger with a scriptural quotation and request to see the lady of the house." She admitted that she was that lady, invited him into their library-conservatory where a wood fire was burning, and offered a tray of coffee and refreshments, "which we enjoyed together in a serious mood." She was struck by his "most cordial and beneficent" countenance. Muir had brought along a violin and was soon playing and crooning a lovely old hymn "such as the covenanters of Scotland may have been comforted with." Then he sang songs of a livelier tempo and ended their interview with a brief prayer, blessing the house and its inmates. He left with an invitation to return, which he did often during the rest of his Madison days.[15]

Jeanne Carr shared her husband's confidence that natural science was a positive guide to the mind, offering strong support to religious

Undated photograph of Jeanne Carr. (H-A, JMP)

faith and good works as well as improving material conditions. But her preferred science was botany, especially the mosses and wild orchids, a science that seemed in that age more suitable than geology for women. Botany was the feminine science, geology the masculine. By the age of nine she had collected nearly 700 species of plants, and her house and garden in Madison were filled with greenery. She combined genuine scientific interest with a keen sense of the beauty lurking in the most delicate leaf, the most inconspicuous blossom. Plants brought out her nurturing instincts. "The first thing I learned," she wrote, "was—*to love,* and most blessed experience, to love *best,* creatures smaller, weaker and more helpless than myself."[16]

Born of old New England stock in the early 1820s, Jeanne had grown up in the Berkshires of Massachusetts and the Green Mountains of Vermont. Her father had been a medical doctor in Castleton, a graduate of the same college where Ezra came to teach. Kept out of college by her sex, she educated herself through a mixture of books from the family library and field study in the swamps and woods near her home. Her unpublished essay of 1850, "A Day among the Hubbardton Lakes," describing a buckboard ride through the autumn tinted hills of Vermont, was dedicated to Harriet Martineau, the English freethinker, abolitionist, and critic of American manners. Although raised in a Bible-oriented household, Jeanne, like others of her generation, tried to free herself from orthodoxy and looked to nature more than ancient written texts for spiritual enlightenment. Like Ezra, she considered herself a liberal in theology, a follower not only of Martineau but of such fellow New Englanders as Ralph Waldo Emerson, the Transcendental sage of Concord, Massachusetts, and Louis Agassiz, the Swiss American naturalist at Harvard. She likely knew Henry David Thoreau's work too (*Walden* appeared in 1854), although there is no evidence that she ever mentioned his name to Muir. Altogether, her home library was by far the most extensive and progressive that the countrified student had ever seen.

Intelligent, well read, and talented, Jeanne was also an attractive woman, with large, soft eyes, long brown curls, and a petite figure. Clearly, Muir was immediately drawn to her, though their relationship deepened and became more intimate later on, after he had left Madison, than while he lived there. His feelings toward her at this early point are impossible to read reliably: was she a mother figure, a more forceful woman than his own mother and one who offered more guidance than she had done? Or was she the older sister type, like a more educated Sarah or Margaret, who offered him sympathy and companionship? Or was she sexually attractive to him, stirring the kind of erotic passions that he had resisted in Prairie du Chien but shyly expressed back in his schoolboy days? Most likely, Jeanne Carr represented a combination of all those female possibilities. On the other hand, it is even more difficult to say what attraction she might have felt toward the much younger Muir (he was in his early twenties, she was nearly forty when they first met), or how those feelings may have conflicted with her devotion to husband Ezra.

A third adult who helped thaw the university's ice mountain for Muir was a professor of ancient languages and literature, James Davie Butler, LL.D. He had come the same year as the Carrs and, like Jeanne, was a native of Vermont. After graduating from Middlebury College and Andover Theological Seminary, he occupied various Congregationalist pastorates and, before the school went bankrupt and stopped paying his salary, professed the classics at Wabash College in Indiana. The state university of Wisconsin offered him a position—but only after taking twelve faculty ballots, which may have reflected the faculty's confusion over its academic direction more than his lack of intellectual merit. The professors may not have adequately appreciated natural science, as Carr charged, but neither did many of them see any value in teaching "dead" classical languages. Butler was, to be sure, no great scholar, although he read widely and had a scholar's contempt for material cares. He compiled a huge book of commonplaces, consisting of page after page of tiny, handwritten notes on his eclectic reading; and an eclectic writer he was too, turning out scores of articles for newspapers and magazines, many of them on contemporary themes. Like Ezra Carr he was a maverick, which is why he loved the quirky, fervent young man from Marquette County. Muir in turn grew to love him and his whole family, although he did not love Butler's academic subjects; botany was far more exciting than "grave tangled Greek and Latin."[17]

In 1867 the university, after much contention, dismissed both Ezra Carr and James Butler, forcing the latter into premature retirement.

Butler tried his hand as a railroad colonization agent for a while and then turned back to writing occasional pieces for *The Nation* magazine. The Carrs, feeling badly used in their struggle for educational reform, left for greener pastures in California. Their transitory presence in Madison was lucky for Muir, who needed liberal-minded, educated adults willing to share their knowledge, encourage his inclinations, appreciate his talents, and help him find a way—his own way—out of his constricted past.

⌒══╪══⌒

During the winter of 1861–62 the Muir brothers, lacking money after the fall term and expecting no more from Daniel, took a temporary leave from studies. Even a few months at college was enough to qualify one for a job teaching in a rural district. Muir accepted a post at a one-room school named Oak Hall for its rough-hewn walls, located south of Madison and west of Oregon, Wisconsin. He was paid $20 a month to teach fifty students of all ages and offered free board in their homes. On Saturday evenings he gave public lectures on chemistry and natural philosophy, making good use of his notes from Professor Carr's class. As a teacher or lecturer, he was a complete novice, not knowing what to say nor what to do and as bashful as a child. To Sarah he confessed that he felt like "a mud turtle upside down on a velvet sofa." One student declared that the teacher "didn't seem to know bran," and Muir could only agree.[18]

Discipline was the first subject that parents expected their schoolmaster to instill, and for Muir it was the hardest of all. Although he adored small children, he found his pupils were no angels, no more than he had been back in Dunbar days, and needed many doses of discipline. Their parents, who believed in using the rod as much as the Scots did, complained angrily that the new teacher "don't half whip." For all his own whippings as a child, he found it difficult to "skelp the little chaps" even when they deserved it. He wished there were a machine that could take over the responsibility of boxing ears. In the end he did what he was required to do, although his voice "would shake for hours after each hazel application."[19]

Much of his success with students came from showing off his mechanical genius, winning their attention and respect. He had left his peculiar clocks behind in Madison and, having no pocket watch, set about making a device to keep time in the classroom by shooting a fine jet of water through a coin. Another contraption was a big wheel set up on the front table that told each grade when and how long to recite. Most astonishing was his morning fire-starter, which demonstrated the practical value of chemistry in cold, biting weather. A small wooden clock was made, precisely at 8 a.m., to drop sulfuric acid on a mixture of potassium chlorate and sugar, causing a small explosion that ignited a stove full of oak wood. By the time teacher and pupils came in the door, shaking their snowy boots, the schoolhouse was summery warm.

Those three months confirmed Muir's view that he was not cut out to be a schoolteacher. Although he got on exceptionally well with the children, several of whom wrote grateful letters after he left, he had trouble controlling himself, let alone others. In a poem written on the quality of rural schooling he complained that Plato, Milton, and Shakespeare were being murdered: "Torn limb from limb in analytic puzzles, / And wondrous parsing passing comprehension. / The poetry and meaning blown to atoms, / Sad sacrifices in the glorious cause / Of higher all-embracing education."[20]

Happily, the final term at university saw him back in North Hall, enrolled once more in classes. David, however, did not rejoin him; a poor student, he would never return to Madison; and of the other siblings only Daniel, Jr., and Mary would ever go to college. Muir gained a new roommate that spring of 1862, a fourteen-year-old boy from Stoner's Prairie, Charles Vroman, whom the officials figured needed an older student's steadying influence. Muir was sawing boards when the boy came to his corner room and found more of a museum than a living space. The boards were intended for shelves, plenty of which already ranged along the walls and up to the ceiling, filled with retorts, glass tubes and jars, botanical and geological specimens, and mechanical gadgets. Larger machines stood about on the floor, including the alarm clock bed that woke its owner up every morning at 5 a.m. with a shower of stones and falling frame—and woke everyone else in that part of the dormitory too.

Drawing of John Muir's student desk clock. (Wisconsin Historical Society, WHS Image ID 26482)

Among the machines was a new study desk, baroque in detail and heavy in symbolism. Whittled out of wood like the rest, it represented the flowering of Muir's technological imagination. Its front legs were long calipers, its rear legs were stacks of imitation books, its desktop a great wheel with gear teeth and spokes surmounted by an ornate clock tower. He arranged a shelf of his textbooks above the wheel, and as the clock advanced, the books dropped down one by one, each opening to a page for the student to scan before it closed and another took its place. An astonishing vision of automated learning, it was meant for the lazy minded (Muir in particular) who could not keep their attention fixed on task. Vroman pictured him "sitting at that desk as if chained, working like a beaver against the clock and desk," determined to become more orderly and regular in his studies.[21] That he felt it necessary to lock the book delivery mechanism, once in motion, and put the key out of reach suggests how hard it was for him to resist the overpowering temptation to stop, dawdle, and look out the window at the lake.

To the roommate, Muir was an amazing figure—brilliant, generous, unpretentious, "the most cheerful, happy-hearted man I ever knew." He told stories of his severe youth in a heart-wrenching way and, dropping into a rich Scots brogue, recounted the dark legends of Dunbar Castle. He read aloud the poems of Robert Burns, which were, with the Bible and schoolbooks, his only reading material. His diet was simple and plain—bread, molasses, graham mush, an occasional potato baked in the basement furnace. For exercise he walked, swam, and played the college sport of wicket, a version of English cricket. Every morning and evening he said his prayers, asking divine help to avoid all temptation and put each moment to the best possible use. "A high-minded Christian gentleman, clean in thought and action," and "of a most gentle and loving disposition," he seemed the perfect mentor for a green country lad.[22]

❦

Older than the average student though he was, Muir was nonetheless wracked by adolescent self-doubt and confusion. During the next school year ('62–'63) those doubts doubled and quadrupled, until in the end he drifted away from the university, never to return. The problem was not financial; summer work on the Galloway farm earned him enough money to continue his studies toward the degree without interruption. The problem was painful indecision over questions of career, religious faith, and life's purpose. In the college catalog for that year he is described as an "Irregular."[23] The label meant that he did not follow the established curriculum path, but it might be read also as an indicator of his mental state of indecision. The wartime atmosphere did not help that mental state; everything was in an uproar as the national political struggle unsettled Madison, pulling classmates away from their recitations to go fight on a distant battleground and provoking endless debate over the wisdom or justice of the Union cause. Muir wanted to find peace in his own mind and peace in his surroundings; finding neither, he began to look for a way to escape.

By this point the eastern front of the Civil War had bogged down in a deadly stalemate that would not be broken until the battle of Gettysburg in early July 1863. Meanwhile, Lincoln's commander on the western front, Ulysses Grant, was winning victories at Shiloh, Vicksburg, and New Orleans, all at an enormous cost in lives but shifting the momentum in favor of the North. The president, midway in Muir's second school year, issued a proclamation emancipating slaves in most parts of the Confederacy and a few weeks later signed the nation's first conscription law, touching off anti-draft riots among the Irish in New York City and angry resistance everywhere else, including among the German communities of Wisconsin. By the final term of the year Muir, an able-bodied male for whom there would be no exemption, faced the dreadful prospect of being drafted to fight in a terrible war that seemed, to him, to violate the most basic Christian ideals.

Back in March news had come that his younger brother Dan had left for Canada to avoid being drafted by the state governor, who was assigned a quota of over 40,000 troops to raise that year by a Congress that was as yet unwilling to establish a conscription policy of its own. All Wisconsin men between the ages of 18 and 45 were required to sign up with their county sheriff or draft commissioners for possible duty.

Muir's father, once a recruiting officer in the British Army, took no stand on the question of how his sons should respond to the state's draft; he refused to give any travel money to Dan but allowed his wife to do so. Ann wrote to John about the anguish she was going through, as her youngest son was preparing to leave. She worried about her older sons being forced to fight. "Have you thought anything about [the draft]," she asked, "I would like to know." In her view those who had initiated the war should do the fighting and not force the unwilling to do it for them. Rich men were commonly evading the call-up by buying replacements, while poorer men could not.[24]

Muir was as worried as his mother; in fact, he was doing little else but thinking about the war and finding it hard to concentrate on botany or even on his inventions while his dormitory mates were talking endlessly about guns, cannons, and armies on the march. Some of them were hot to kill southerners, southern sympathizers, and all traitors to the Union. They wanted to start by attacking opponents of the war on campus or within the state. As one of those anti-war opponents, although no advocate for slavery or the South, Muir was bound to come in for harsh criticism. That fall he wrote to the Galloways:

> Our university has reached a crisis in its history, and if not passed successfully, the doors will be closed, when of course I should have to leave Madison for some institution which has not yet been wounded to the death by our war-demon.... How strange that a country with so many schools and churches should be desolated by so unsightly a monster.[25]

The war was drying up state educational funding and turning student against student, professor against professor, destroying the intellectual life that had drawn him to campus, throwing a dark shadow here as it was over every corner of the nation.

The city of Madison as a whole seemed to be losing its moral tone as thousands of randy young men milled through the streets, thrilled by the adventure of going off to war. Where the state fair once had its grounds now sprawled Camp Randall, a place for training military recruits who dwelt here by the thousands in cotton tents, cooked their meals over outdoor campfires, and shelled out money to peddlers of liquor and sex. Muir took to visiting the tent city regularly to see his friends and encourage them to hold fast to virtue. Among those he met were two acquaintances from Prairie du Chien, splendidly decked out in new blue uniforms and ready for gore. He admonished them to develop firm principles and remember what their mothers expected of them. After spending an evening in their tent, he sent a shocked report to Frances Pelton—"such conversation," he complained, such coarse language. They needed the "holy influences of home" to prevent vice from undermining their good character. But Muir was even more profoundly disturbed by their happy faces and loud laughter as they prepared to "murder" their fellow humans. Such slaughter, he felt, should at least be performed in a solemn way, full of awareness that some day one might meet in heaven the enemy soldier beheaded on a sunshiny day at Bull Run.[26]

So moved was Muir by fear of violence and moral disorder that, in spring 1863, he joined a local chapter of the Young Men's Christian Association. Soon, he became its president, with the mission of improving the mental, spiritual, and physical condition of young men wandering loose and disoriented in the city. George Williams, a Protestant evangelical in London, had founded the "Y" in 1844. Like Muir, Williams came from a rural background and, finding urban life demoralizing, had rallied others for Bible study and prayer. Outside the shops and factories where he worked roamed a dangerous mob of beggars, thieves, drunks, and prostitutes; to counter their bad influence the "Y" offered nonsectarian religion, open and free to all. By the 1850s branches had formed in cities across Canada and the United States. During the Civil War the "Y" sent volunteers (including the Brooklyn poet Walt Whitman) to the battlefront to comfort the sick and wounded and pass out Bibles. Muir was uninterested in going to the war zone, but he felt the Y's call to do what he could on the home front.[27]

Meanwhile, there was the powerful call of natural science and the conundrum of what kind of scientific career he should follow. Going to university had preempted his earlier scheme of becoming an inventor or engineer by working his way up from the factory floor; he had not, however, given up the idea of becoming a physician. Ezra Carr encouraged him to get a medical degree, as he had done. He also suggested that Muir might start as an apprentice with a local doctor before going off to medical school, a strategy that seemed financially attractive. Then Muir decided he would not linger in Madison but go straight to the University of Michigan in the fall. All through the summer of 1863, right up until August, he was telling friends that they should send their future letters to Ann Arbor. Then abruptly, only weeks before the school term began, he changed his mind, partly out of fear that the draft might catch him in Michigan as easily as in Wisconsin, partly out of a nagging doubt about what to do with his life.

In late September 1862 Muir wrote an astonishing letter to Mrs. Pelton, revealing just how erratic his thinking had become. She expressed a yearning to go back to her New England hills and suggested that he might find those hills a good substitute for the Scottish Highlands. "Nonsense," he had replied; there could never be a substitute for Scotland for him. Forgetting that he had never actually seen the Highlands, he waxed nostalgic about them. His love of Scotland (he circled the name in the letter) was growing stronger "with every pulse so that I cannot see the name or hear it but a thrill goes to every fiber of all my body. One of the more prominent of my future hopes is that I shall one day visit SCOTLAND."[28]

In time stolen from his schoolwork, Muir had begun to make notes on Scotland's history and geography. He collected information about its main physiographic divisions, its mountains and major river basins, the lands lying along the Tweed and Clyde, and so forth, trying to get a picture in his mind of the country he had left fourteen years earlier. From a gazetteer he laboriously transcribed details of minor and major Scottish towns and landmarks, listing them alphabetically—beginning with Abbey Craig and Walter Scott's Abbotsford, and going through Dunbar and Gilmerton before he ceased. For all his longing, he had no money to travel overseas or to try to reclaim his early national identity, if that was truly what he wanted to do.

Instead of going to Scotland Muir decided to make a cheaper excursion closer to home. After classes and examinations were over, he and two college friends took off in late June on a geological and botanical excursion that they hoped would last all summer. On their backs they carried a cotton tent, a hatchet, blankets, spoons, books, and plant-collecting equipment. They were bound for the Blue Mound west of the city and thence down the Wisconsin River to the Mississippi. The rest of their plan involved crossing into Iowa and traveling up the Mississippi to St. Anthony Falls, then going north to Lake Superior, where they proposed to hike along its southern shore, turning south along Lake Michigan to Green Bay, and from there down the Fox River to home. Nothing quite worked the way they planned; the trip ended within three weeks and they never got farther than Iowa. But Muir was now bitten by the bug of going deep into North America's wilds, leaving all personal, social, and national turmoil behind. In that sense the summer excursion of '63 proved to be a turning point in his life.

The sentimental piety he displayed in so many of his letters, the gnawing anxiety about the rapid passing of time that shadowed his life in town, fell away during the brief time of this excursion. Out in nature Muir began to relax and have fun. He carried along his Bible, of course, and periodically knelt in the woods to pray. He slept on the hard ground, arising in the morning with every bone aching. Their food was usually bad—purchased from some German families along the way, "a little dutch gray bread and dutch gray butter." Some days they ate only once, other days as many as five times. They came upon a plethora of shabby pioneer farms, with turned-up stump fences, dooryards ankle-deep in filth, odorous hog pens, and fierce little curs snapping at their heels. Yet along the way he found release, adventure, companionship, and the joy of new plants to identify. And he no longer needed any alarm clock.

Above all on this excursion Muir rediscovered the spontaneous beauty of wild nature, which had become almost obscured by his worries about the draft, career, and the growing violence of a wartime society. He allowed his feelings to flow with the organic tides around him. He gazed "in ecstasy over miles and miles of beauty all aglow with the morning sunlight." But he was also prepared to penetrate and find order in that wildness with the aid of the science he had been studying. Now he understood how rugged valleys had been formed over the earth's long geological history: "What waters have deposited these naked strata—what strange animals people those ancient seas which once flowed in calm or storm above the peak on which we stand." Nature, he realized, was written in hieroglyphics that science could help him read, decipher, and appreciate in new ways.[29]

By early July the party was encamped near McGregor, Iowa, on a bluff overlooking the broad upper Mississippi. Muir later recounted a carefree adventure filled with comic moments: the picturesque glen filled with fossils that they went fruitlessly seeking, their mad scrambles up and down steep river bluffs, the rustic log house they came upon and its well-dressed male and female inhabitants lined up like gothic spirits in the front yard, the mysterious travel directions they were given, their quick retreat in comic alarm.[30] But then came a letter recalling one of the hiking party home, and unwilling to carry on alone, the two remaining hikers decided that the trip must come to an end. Still in high spirits, they purchased a little boat with the idea of rowing up the Wisconsin, until the strong current beat them back. Putting a few "postage stamps" (an inscription) on the boat, they "mailed" it downstream and walked on home.

Back in Madison once more, Muir began packing up his possessions and preparing to leave. Years later he concluded the autobiographical *My Boyhood and Youth* with a dramatic scene of farewell to the university. Claiming that he had spent four years there (when actually he had spent only six terms), he recalled how he took a last view from the north side of Lake Mendota of his ice mountain. Then, "with streaming eyes," he turned around and headed for "the University of the Wilderness." Much of that account was self-dramatization. It was true that he left Madison for good that summer, for reasons that he never explained but included dissatisfaction with his college studies, except for natural science, and distaste for the wartime atmosphere. Neither the YMCA, the Carrs, Professor Butler, nor other personal or intellectual attachments could hold him any longer.

Whatever his reasons for leaving, he did not head, as he later claimed, directly to "the University of the Wilderness." Instead, he moved in once more with his sister Sarah and brother-in-law David living at the beloved Fountain Lake farm and remained there for seven months, through the fall and winter of 1863 and 1864. Relations between son and father had deteriorated once more, so that they could hardly spend a week together without quarreling. Brother Dan was still in Canada, while brother Dave had married his local sweetheart and begun working in a Portage haberdashery, where eventually he would become a partner. That was a good life for Dave but not for them, Muir wrote to Dan: "You and I must not on any account permit ourselves to think of marriage for five or six years yet . . . for if you permit yourself to fall in love adieu to study." If he was sure about nothing else, he was convinced that he needed further intellectual development. While trying to make up his mind about how to achieve that, he took up manual labor again, plowing fields, cutting cordwood, and splitting rails. In the evenings he studied French, Latin, anatomy, and Scottish history and manners. Perhaps he would have to become his own teacher.

"War is now casting its terrible harvest through all this unhappy land," Muir wrote to Dan late in 1863. "Drafting is becoming more and more severe[.] [W]e sometimes wish that we could all be with you. I have not money enough to stay long in Scotland[.] I hardly know what to do[.] War seems to spread everywhere. It seems difficult for a peaceable man to find a place to rest."[31]

By the first of March he had arrived at a momentous decision: he would leave the United States, but he would not go to Scotland. He would cross the border into Canada, where he would join Dan in seeking a refuge from the threat of war and army life. He would, as the common lingo put it, "skedaddle," although he was in no immediate danger of being drafted. In a note to Emily Pelton, he announced, with a great deal of melancholic flare, "I am to take the cars in about half an hour[.] I really do not know where I shall 'halt'[.] I feel like Miltons Adam and Eve 'The world was before them where to choose their place of rest.' . . . Goodbye I feel lonely again."[32]

CHAPTER 4

Border Crossings

T he line separating the American Republic from British North America was not open and undefended in 1864. For nearly a century the colonials living north of the line, subjects of the Queen, had feared invasion by the aggressive and fast-growing empire to the south. On more than one occasion they had protected themselves with arms. Now in a time of U.S. civil war, when a large part of the British North American press was anti-Lincoln and anti-Northern, it was the Yankees' turn to become fearful that they might be invaded or infiltrated by Confederate sympathizers or spies sneaking across the border. Muir had to sense the tension along the border, perhaps even feared that he might encounter some hostility, but feeling no particular loyalty to the United States, he trustingly stepped across the line and became a resident of Canada. During the time of his stay, about two years in all, this pacifist man without a country found a tolerant, even warm and generous, reception.[1]

He crossed early in March, just a few months before delegates gathered in Quebec to discuss the formation of a new federation in the north that could protect them from the rising American colossus. It was the most momentous time in their lives and one of the most important in the history of the continent. Before that meeting the name "Canada" referred only to the United Province of Canada, a marriage of Canada West (formerly Upper Canada, later Ontario) and Canada East (Lower Canada, or Quebec). Afterward, the name would refer to an immense nation that stretched from the Atlantic to the Pacific, from the Great Lakes to the Arctic Ocean. Such nation building did not impress Muir. He was not interested in the speeches of John Macdonald, who would serve as the first prime minister of the new nation, or those of his fellow nationalists. Their vision of competitive imperialism was not what drew Muir northward. He was there because he was an outsider, a man who would not fight for any nation or empire, a man without any fixed identity or ambitions of his own.

Also he was there because he loved green plants and was keen to see what the Canadian wilds might offer to the roving naturalist. What he had not figured out was what he would do in winter, when the plants go dormant and the woods are full of snow. Fortunately, he found indoor work that brought him back to his early notion of a career in mills and factories, a life among machines. Canada gave him that opportunity where Philadelphia or Prairie du Chien had not. It was a very limited opportunity, however, and did not last. Looking for better chances, he would return to the United States in the spring of 1866 and try his hand at working in an American factory. In the midst of immense geopolitical forces and events that would profoundly influence the course of modern history, he would experience a great deal of trouble in taking command of his personal destiny. The continent was going through large changes in political alignments and modes of production. They bounced Muir around like a chip at sea. He was at their mercy and felt completely adrift.

Muir's second big excursion (after the one to the Mississippi River) began where the first one had aimed but failed to reach: the point where Lake Michigan, Superior, and Huron touch, far removed from the more tensely watched stretch of the international border. After botanizing along the shores of Huron, collecting plants from the offshore St. Joseph and Manitoulin islands, he swung southward.[2] That circuitous route brought him at last into Canada West, a ruggedly beautiful landscape of dense forests, lofty limestone ridges, tumbling rapids, and dark, mysterious wetlands, a place that, fifteen years earlier, had nearly become his home, before Daniel shrewdly chose an easier place to settle. This colony sprawled from Lake Ontario to the Ottawa River—some of it flat and fertile, but much of it bisected by a rocky escarpment that ran northwestward from Niagara Falls to the Bruce Peninsula. Neither wheat nor corn would ever make outstanding crops here, by the standards of America's prairie states; it would become more a pastoral than a grain country. Two intrepid sisters, Susanna Moodie and Catharine Parr Traill, had experienced the hardness of the place in its frontier stage, the 1830s, as they pioneered with their husbands in the lake district near Peterborough. It was then covered by "bush"—"interminable forests, through which the eye can only penetrate a few yards."[3] When Muir arrived three decades later, much of the territory was still bush, with only scattered, fragile openings of farms, fields, and towns.

Arriving in the spring, when wildflowers were beginning to poke through the brown forest duff, he headed toward the Holland River north of Toronto. Now drained and intensively farmed, it was then a vast—and in the eyes of pioneers, a useless—swamp punctuated by thickets of tamarack, white cedar, balsam fir, pine, hemlock, beech, birch, and maple, crossable only by wading or by jumping from exposed root to root. For days in June Muir plodded along, feeling more and more weary and discouraged. Then one warm afternoon he came upon the orchid *Calypso borealis* blooming on a barren hillside. Suddenly he was lifted up, thrilled to the point of tears by its unexpected beauty, "so perfectly spiritual, it seemed pure enough for the throne of its Creator." The Bible taught that the world was cursed with weeds and that they must be cleared away by human sweat, but Muir rejected that view. "Are not all plants beautiful? or in some way useful? . . . The curse must be within ourselves."[4]

Inspired by that discovery and hoping that there would be many more, he kept on walking. He trudged for weeks, making a sweeping circuit through Simcoe, Dufferin, and Grey counties. He carried a compass but no blankets, sleeping in the open air, and packed no food, stopping whenever he came upon a house where he asked for a loaf of bread. When he ran out of money, he asked for work. Most of the people he met were fellow immigrants—Scots like himself, or English or Irish, here to find the same independence that Daniel had sought, but in this case under the protection of the British flag. Muir learned that large numbers of them had come from the Highlands, where they had been tenant farmers until they had been put off the land for sheep.

One such family were the Campbells, a mother, daughter, and two grown sons who lived on the edge of the Holland swamps. Muir stayed with them for a month, sleeping in their house overnight while exploring the surrounding wilds by day. They laughingly called him "Botany," for they had no idea why anyone would want to wade around in the muck collecting plants when there was productive work to be done in clearing forests. But he found sympathy among them, and a mother-like care on those days when he felt ill and had to stay in bed. For a practical joke, the sons reported him to the authorities as an army deserter, which he nearly was but from a different army. And they told uproarious stories, well lubricated with whiskey, a beverage he likely did not share. They allowed him his purity, but no one on that tough and demanding frontier was allowed to feel any other kind of superiority.

The pioneers of Canada West, relying on one another like those south of the border for mutual aid, organized various "bees" for raising houses or barns or for removing forests. Muir witnessed such a "logging bee" during his rambles. With heavy axes the men slashed down every tree shading the ground, dragged the tall, slender logs into great piles, and when the logs were dry set them afire. "Those beautiful trees," he lamented, so ruthlessly destroyed. To be sure, he had helped do the same thing to Wisconsin's forests and understood that there was no other practical way to establish agriculture in the backcountry. Once the trees were gone, the thickly matted roots remained, allowing very little room for a plow, and late or early frosts often destroyed crops and left many families hungry. It was a frontier life he knew quite well, enough so that he could lend a hand and win a meal, but it was not to be his life. Quickly he went back to exploring for plants.

Younger brother Dan, who had earlier dodged the draft and crossed into Canada, continued to wander independently through this bushy hinterland. Late that summer they did join up to trek along the southern shore of Lake Ontario and see Niagara Falls. Muir wrote to sister Annie that they were stunned by their first glimpse of the Falls and had to return several times before they could absorb it as "the greatest sight in all the world."[5] Less thrilling was the night a pack of wolves began howling around the campsite, keeping the brothers nervously awake and busy stoking a huge fire to hold the beasts at bay. Then they split off once more, Dan heading far north to Georgian Bay and the sedate village of Meaford, located where the Bighead River empties into the bay.

Late on an August afternoon Dan wandered into a mill site three miles upstream from the village. His clothes were shabby, and clearly he needed a meal. When the mill owners, a family named Trout, learned that he was a member of their religious group, the Disciples of Christ (the Campbellites), they took him in as a brother. A couple of months later they did the same for John, who, feeling the winter coming on, was eager to find a warm nest for the season.

The Trouts were a large brood like the Muirs—literate, generous, enterprising, and intensely religious. The parents William and Margaret Trout had migrated to Meaford nearly twenty years earlier and established a small farm on the Georgian Bay and the first Disciples church in the town. With his sons, William built houses on contract and then set up a mill to make harvest tools. When the Muir brothers arrived, son William Jr. and his partner Charles Jay were in charge of the mill and hired them as laborers. Hardwood needed for making hay rakes came from the thick forest surrounding the mill site. Where the Bighead River came rushing down between low hogbacks, they constructed a dam for waterpower, and across the millpond on the right bank they built a log shanty where the two managers and two other Trout siblings, Mary and Peter, lived. Here Muir settled for the rest of his Canadian sojourn, spending a year and a half working in "Trout Hollow." After Dan moved on to a machine shop in Buffalo, New York, they were only somewhat less crowded than before: five unmarried adults in a small cabin with no windows and a single plank door. Only a person of considerable sociability could have endured two long winters shut up like that. A loner in many ways, Muir was also remarkable for his capacity for intimate social life (although he got a little peevish as the months went on).[6]

Short on amusements, he had fun with their surnames—Trouts and Jays, he wrote to his sister Mary, now ruled over "two scotch

Muir drawing of Trout House, Mill Hollow, near Meaford, Ontario, circa 1865. (H-A, JMP)

heather Muirs." One of the Trout women who regularly visited, Harriet, a school teacher, he described as "a very happy and sportive fish" prone to fits of giggling; the other, Mary, who was their "house-keeper," seemed fated to mate with a Jaybird. Together they lived happily, with other Trouts and Jays occasionally dropping in, and frequent journeys to town where they sat through sermons preached by Father Trout.[7]

Once more the alarm-clock bed was reassembled, waking Muir at five each morning to face an eighteen-hour workday. There was much to be done. A year after his arrival he signed an agreement with the owners to build an addition to their sawmill where he would produce 12,000 rake handles and 30,000 broom handles. No more jack knives and hand-whittled gears; for the first time in his life he used serious industrial tools to make large machines and create a whole production system—tasks at which he was a complete novice. Driven by the magnitude of the job, he was forced to put botany aside, allowing himself only one brief excursion along Owen Sound during the duration of his contract. After spending long days in the mill, he studied in his room until late at night. On average, he allowed himself a mere four or five hours of sleep. To his sisters he complained, "I sometimes almost forget where I am, what I am doing, or what my name is."[8]

He did find time to send a few letters to friends and family in the United States, and they show that he was still agitated by uncertainty and ambivalence, which the intense work pace only partially relieved. "I am at times touched with melancholy and lonesomeness," he admitted to Emily Pelton, although he added that he was fortunately living in a "retired and romantic hollow, . . . so comfortably separated from the worlds noisy dust." Walking down river to church, he looked about him with gratitude on the landscape "so fraught with the glory of the creator." He added that the forest towering over the mill had taken on an industrial look, rising "like the thick smoke from a factory chimney."[9] The metaphor reflected his obsession with industry, yet he still believed that the world of nature was not some lowly man-made mechanism, like a mill, but showed evidence of higher, divine skill and creativity. In contrast, he portrayed himself as a simple, flawed, human creator, applying skills that could bring more efficiency and order to the work environment. It was a life he enjoyed immensely, but he missed faraway friends and family—and he had begun to miss the university and its atmosphere of learning for which he had found no satisfactory substitute.

Two years after saying goodbye to the University of Wisconsin, he had not been forgotten on campus. The professors sent a message that he could come back as a free student, relieved of all tuition. Their offer got lost in the mails, but then came a letter from Jeanne Carr informing him of the decision. He replied that he was in a quandary: he wanted to finish his degree, but he also wanted to study medicine and help lessen human misery, invent useful machines, return to Scotland, and study nature there and in "all the other less important parts of our world." That last idea of world travel was gaining prominence: "How intensely I desire to be a Humboldt!" he declared.[10] It would take a million years to achieve all those goals. Where should he start?

Despite the long hours spent indoors working on machines, he still saw himself as a lover of nature, one of the privileged few who appreciated the natural beauty around them. None of his Canadian acquaintances, he told Mrs. Carr, shared that love: "They grub away amid the smoke of magnificent forest trees, black as demons and material as the soil they move upon." Not one of them seemed to know or care anything about the wild plants. Their indifference to a higher, spiritual relationship with nature might be explained, he supposed, by the difficulty of the environment they faced and the elemental needs they had to satisfy. It did not occur to him that he was complicit in their aggressive materialism as he turned trees into hay rakes and broom handles. It was as though his brain had compartmentalized his own tangled desires into a set of incompatible demands—there was his job and there was the outdoors—and he could find no way to balance or integrate them.

The Carrs now stood out as his most important adult mentors. It was Ezra who had "first laid before me the great book of Nature." That the student (so far) had been unproductive as a scientific explorer should not obscure the fact that he now knew where and how to seek knowledge. Jeanne, however, was really the important Carr in his pantheon; she had become his ideal of intelligent, sensitive femininity, a kind of womanhood he had never fully discovered in his own family circle or in the many frontier shanties he had visited. She represented at once intellectual and erotic companionship. How often, he confessed to her, had he wanted to creep "like some hungry worm . . . into that delightful kernel of your house—your library," with its shelves of books, portraits of scientific men, glass cases filled with mosses and ferns, and her soft womanly presence.[11] Her sexuality he could hardly separate from her books, her botany, or her moral refinement. She had opened his whole being to a physical and spiritual relationship with nature. In a sense she was that ideal nature, and every flower he came upon reminded him of her.

Psycho-biographer Steven Holmes suggests that the erotic feelings Muir felt toward Jeanne were not narrowly or exclusively sexual. According to the psychoanalytical theory on which Holmes draws, erotic feelings (or "Eros") can refer to any self-preserving, as opposed to self-destructive, instincts, including the attraction of a child to its mother's body or an adult's sense of comfort, physical health, or wellbeing. By this interpretation Muir's erotic feelings could be aroused by women young and old, but also by men, and above all by the natural world, by the sense of God dwelling in the forest. This is a plausible reading of a man who seems so intensely passionate about nature and life, so burning with a desire to experience the world around him, so irresistibly moved by his feelings, yet was so inexpressive of and seemingly indifferent toward his own or others' sexuality. Victorian social norms discouraged men or women from expressing openly their sexual appetites, or, at an extreme, even admitting that they existed. Muir, who was generally so free and unembarrassed in his feelings, was always reticent about sex. For him sex was not the beginning and end of all deep feeling. His passion for nature transcended and sublimated the coupling of men and women. He was aroused through his whole body by the beauty and spirituality he found in wild natural places.[12]

Jeanne did not respond with any erotic invitations into her kernel of a library. Instead, she answered his long letter of mid-September 1865, the first of many that he would send to her, by talking about doing good work. She offered encouragement that "a great mechanical genius is a wonderful gift," exemplified by Charles Goodyear, who while in debtor's prison discovered the process of rubber vulcanization and then was forced to sell his patent rights at a fraction of their value. Goodyear was a benefactor of the species who sought nothing for himself. His was a better kind of materialism, she reminded Muir, than the ordinary drive to escape poverty. Anyone who helped others secure a better economic life, who transcended that gnawing and corrupting desire for improving one's social status, was God's instrument. Perhaps such might be Muir's divinely appointed role—to become another Goodyear who would unselfishly bring great material benefits to all humanity.[13]

He waited a few months to reply, but then sent her eight full pages, pouring out his ardent thoughts on a cold January night. All the mosses and ferns (her favorites, his too) that he had collected from Canada's hills and glens he listed at length. He described the machines that he had been working on—a self-feeding lathe, for example, that could turn out eight handles a minute, lowering their cost to the consumer. Cheap brooms meant improved cleanliness, and wasn't cleanliness one of the cardinal virtues? Might he already qualify as a disinterested benefactor of humanity like Goodyear? His other machines produced more and better hay rakes, making it possible for farmers to produce cheaper grain and for the poor to get more bread to eat. Here, he seemed to be arguing, was a calling worthy of her respect, and of his own self-esteem. By learning the arts of the millwright he was working for the good of society.

The most difficult problem troubling his mind, however, was how far he could trust "the page of nature" to guide his religious feelings. Alexander Campbell had taught, and the Trout Hollow housemates surely agreed as good Disciples, that nature reflected divine truth; one could find in the forest all the character and attributes of God, even though they might be spending little time looking in that direction. Campbell had added that nature was silent on the question of the fall of man and his need for redemption; only revelation could explain that central historical fact. But Muir was losing faith in traditional doctrines and was less and less convinced that humans were born depraved or unequipped to find ultimate answers in nature. "I take more internal delight from reading the power & *goodness* of God," he confessed, "from the things which are made than from the bible." The hidden difficulty in that more positive reading from nature was the old conundrum: if God is so good and nature is so good, how can his human creatures be so weak or evil? Are they as innately evil as orthodoxy teaches? Such heretical questions, he admitted to brother Dan, were creating a split between him and the Trouts.[14]

The split with his father was also widening, for Daniel did not approve of the rake-making contract or of any secular career his son was contemplating. He feared that the kingdom of heaven was becoming less important to John than the kingdom of earth. Man, he wrote in a letter, "naturally is productive of nothing but evil."[15] He confessed himself to be the very embodiment of corruption, the filthiest creature in the world, the worst sinner of all. Increasingly, that was his uncompromising message, an intensification of old Calvinist doctrines, which he was now carrying far from home on evangelical missions, the last of which would soon lead him—following his two sons—across the

Canadian border to the city of Hamilton, where he would preach on street corners, trying perversely to save the souls of people who were, according to his Calvinist logic, beyond redemption.

On a stormy night in late February 1866, misfortune struck Trout Hollow and put an end to Muir's winter evening meditations. A spark from the mill's chimney landed on the roof and set the building ablaze. Across the millpond the cabin's inhabitants saw the fire and ran across the bridge to put it out. They were too late; the mill burned to the ground. All the new machines and all the rakes and brooms produced so far were destroyed. There was no insurance and no money in the treasury to pay the millwright, who was owed some three hundred dollars for work performed to date. Muir reduced his bill to two hundred dollars and then left the river, trusting the proprietors Trout and Jay to pay him whenever they could get back on their feet.[16] With only a small amount of cash in pocket, he recrossed the border into the United States. After stopping to search for a job in Buffalo, he went on searching through the urban Midwest. By mid-March 1866 he was writing to tell his mother that he had found his next stopping point—Indianapolis, Indiana.

⚬━✦━⚬

The Civil War had ended almost a year earlier, with the surrender of Confederate armies in Virginia. President Lincoln had died of an assassin's bullet, and his successor Andrew Johnson was already feuding with Congress over what to do with the defeated South. Because of those terrible distractions and because so many Americans had evaded or resisted the draft, Muir could quietly reenter the country. He might have stayed in Canada and sought work in Hamilton or Toronto, but economic prospects in those cities were dimmer than in the victorious U.S. North, while the full realization of the new Dominion, with all that it might bring in material expansion, was still in the future. The United States boasted ten times more people than its colonial neighbor and a more advanced industrial system. So despite the prospect of continuing national turmoil, Muir recrossed the border to find a job.

Now twenty-eight years old, he had managed to impress everyone with his mechanical genius but so far had little to show for his efforts.

Indianapolis was a well-tamed, heavily settled flatland compared to the Bighead River tumbling off the Niagara Escarpment, but also a good deal less peaceful than Trout Hollow. Inspired by Charles L'Enfant's design for Washington, D.C., it was a city of blocks and squares and radiating avenues laid out on the banks of the White River. The serenity of that orderly, civilized vision had been severely disrupted by the coming of railroads, linking Indianapolis to Pittsburgh, Cincinnati, Cleveland, and Chicago. On the south side of the Union Depot a crowded district of factories and workingmen's boarding houses had sprung up, well stocked with smoky, beery saloons. It had a bad reputation for ague and cholera, but it offered decent wages, if one could stand the dusty mayhem. This became Muir's abode for the next sixteen months.

"Nature and the railroads," explained a guidebook, had made Indianapolis "the leading market of the country for desirable grades of hard lumber—walnut, oak, ash, etc., and for poplar."[17] Remnants of the continent's magnificent deciduous forests could still be found on its fringes, and from them came an abundant, cheap supply of the wood products on which the nation's economy depended. Within an hour or two of stepping off the train, Muir found work in a steam-powered factory that turned out wooden hubs and spokes for wagon wheels. Located one block south of the depot, at 230 South Illinois Street, the firm of Osgood, Smith, and Company had been in existence since the late 1840s and proudly advertised itself as the manufacturer of Sarven's Patent Wheel, with a sideline in plow handles. Woodworking was their business, and as his employers soon discovered, woodworking was Muir's craft. He made $10 his first week, $18 his second week, and then $22 after his promotion to sawyer.

Much of his income that spring and summer was paid out to a succession of boarding-house proprietors—he tried five different places before settling with the Sutherlands, good Scots and Disciples, on McCarty Street—and to his fellow workers in the form of loans. To one sick man he gave $50, to another $10, to his brother Dan in Buffalo $25, with an offer of more if needed. Everywhere around him were men who had been injured at work, who fell ill and could not keep a job, who drank too much, or who faced heavy debts and needed his help. For Dan in particular he felt an elder brother's responsibility, giving frequent advice along with cash, even finding a job for him at Osgood, Smith, until Dan hurt his hand and, after recovering, left to seek work in Michigan.

Accumulating wealth was not Muir's chief goal, although in the back of his mind he harbored the dream of saving enough money to return to college some day. Again, he felt compelled by his technical

Photograph of John Muir, 1863, Madison, Wisconsin. (H-A, JMP)

gifts as well as by some mysterious fate to find a useful career in the world of machines. "I suppose," he wrote to Sarah, "that I am doomed to live in some of these noisy commercial centres." He reassured them that he was not saddened by that prospect, but he felt "*utterly homeless*" in the world of transient urban workmen. He feared that he had become a "wandering star," with no fixed orbit or trajectory.[18]

Dan became a frequent confidant, since he too had rejoined America as a member of the industrial proletariat and was going through a similar quandary over where he belonged. "I am determined," Muir declared to him, "not to leave [Indianapolis] until I have made my *invention mark*."[19] This time it was do-or-die. Reviving the curious scythe-clock idea, he constructed a model to submit to the U.S. Patent Office, but then changed his mind about the ethics of patenting useful inventions, which he decided (following the influence of Jeanne Carr) should be given free to society. Once more he built a variation of the alarm-clock bed, this time with a pan of cold water installed underneath to jolt him awake in the morning. Meanwhile, Osgood, Smith, and Co. encouraged him to experiment with their saws and lathes to increase output, and even offered to make him foreman with authority to bring it to a peak of productivity. Muir turned down that offer but tinkered away with the same obsessive energy he had shown in Trout Hollow.

He justified his factory work in grandiose and ethnocentric terms: by succeeding in industry he would show all humankind that "the Scotch are the salt of the earth—and the salt of *machines*." On one hot, humid August day, he went even further, admonishing Dan to "remember the nation to whom you belong, and the age in which you live—its streets must be trodden not by "black Gentoos [Hindus] & pagan Turks" but by "the white & fixin loving people of the sons of Japheth [Noah's third son], and its squares and avenues must be shone upon by the sun of the nineteenth century." What was that "nation" to which they belonged? "White people" more than Scotland or America, it would appear; the brothers were the vanguard for the entire Indo-European race locked in a competition with backward Asians. It was an unusually racialist moment in Muir's effort to find a sense of purpose, when he tried to define himself as nothing less than an Aryan instrument of modern civilization fighting against the dark-skinned forces of alien paganism.[20]

The cause of promoting modernity and progress, at least in this passing moment, had become his personal cause. He was part of a struggle for global industrial development. Besides a few letters, three documents from that Indianapolis interlude survive, and they suggest how far he had gone toward embracing industrialism as a worldview. They show too how intensely his mind had become trained on problems of human management as well as machinery. Two documents deal with the "sawyers end" of the factory, in which he outlines a more efficient system of reducing rough logs to graded lumber and earning higher profits. The third and most revealing is a "chart of one days labor," which aims at harmonizing all human behavior in the factory with the rhythm of machines. He graphs the typical worker's activity curve before and after noon. On a cold morning a man arrives on the job disinclined to get started, especially when no supervisor is around to increase motivation. The pace spikes up whenever "the masters pass through the shop," then falls as lunchtime approaches and again as lamps are lighted in the late afternoon. "Lamplight labor," notes Muir, "is not worth more than two-thirds daylight labor." But the "great central difficulty" in achieving a more efficient workforce is that people do not see the process as a whole; every worker is left free to work out his own methods and his individual task is uncoordinated with others. "In all good communities 'no man liveth to himself,' and in the departments of good factories no man or machine worketh to itself." Better management requires a more organized flow of materials, more careful supervision of workers, and more coordination by those in charge.[21]

The intention behind those documents was not necessarily unfeeling toward labor or exploitative. Muir had plunged fully into a world that he had long imagined and half-dreaded, where workers could be dehumanized as well as endangered in life and limb. Dozens of factories like Osgood, Smith lined the back streets, as close as they could get to railroad tracks for loading and unloading materials; and each was a deafening pandemonium of shrieking saws, clattering machines, men shouting and swearing, timbers falling and banging heads, wagons coming and going. A coal-burning steam engine provided the motive power, while a cat's cradle of long leather belts, spliced together from bison or cowhides and slapping overhead and underfoot, transferred that power to all departments of the establishment. Raw wood came in the back entry, finished wheels rolled out the front. Ten hours or more of working in that constant hubbub could leave a man deafened and dulled—or missing a finger or arm, or with little sense of peace or harmony. Muir sought to improve that chaotic, dangerous environment for himself and for men like his brother and the other workers with whom he toiled on the factory floor.

Sundays offered a day of respite from that wearying, monotonous assault on body and senses. Muir divided the Sabbath day more or less equally between the religion of Campbellism and the religion of nature. He began with indoor worship, "generally," he reassured Harriet Trout, meeting with the Disciples of Christ, who had formed a large congregation in Indianapolis. Then he taught a "mission" Sunday school class—teaching "the beauty & *grandeur* of the Christian religion" to working-class children. On Sabbath afternoons, however, he lit out for the surrounding oak and hickory forests, adding to his botanical collections and worshipping at the altar of nature. With pen and ink he drew pictures, not of ear-piercing machines but of ferns and mosses he found in serene landscapes far from the city's din. Sometimes his private botanizing and drawing expeditions lasted longer than a day and necessitated finding a substitute teacher for the mission. His boarding-house hosts, the Sutherlands, filled in for him and promised, in a letter on one such occasion, to keep "the Robbers and little Boys out of your room"; they also cautioned him not to go "away down south in the lonly woods whare something may gather you."[22]

The last phrase suggests that, within five months of resettling in Indianapolis, and despite his professed ambition to become a great inventor, spiritual son of James Watt or Adam Smith, defender of Scottish honor, leader of the white man's civilization, and missionary to the unchurched, Muir was subversively dreaming of escaping into deep, untrodden woods.

His anxious mentors in Madison, who could not really imagine or accept their prized nature-loving student being imprisoned by cities or machines, deliberately stoked his rebellious desire to escape. Addressing him for the first time as "John" rather than "Mr. Muir,"

Jeanne Carr asked, "Did you not feel more at home with the nature there [in Canada], than in the human element now surrounding you?" Rather than praising the likes of Charles Goodyear, she reminded Muir of his "power of insight into Nature, & the simplicity of your love for her."[23] Nature promised spiritual truth, a value beyond industrial profit.

To fire up that love of nature, she recommended the French poet and statesman Alphonse de Lamartine, whose 1851 novel *The Stonemason of Saint-Point* she sent in the mail. Lamartine represented the spirit of free, self-defined religion. He had broken the bonds of his native Catholicism to become one of the leading figures in Romantic literature. His novel, reminiscent of Rousseau's reveries or Wordsworth's poetry, tells the story of a rustic countryman who finds God, not in formal theology or churches, but in the awful presence of Switzerland's mountains and through dwelling simply with rural animals and rural people. Accused of atheism, Lamartine denied the charge, but his concept of the divine was completely his own; it expressed that liberal religion of nature that Carr cherished and encouraged Muir to follow too.

The student heeded carefully his feminine advisor and repeated her advice to others. When his younger sisters asked for his comments on their efforts at poetry, he told them to put down their pens and go into the natural world. Confessing that all the Muirs had an itch to write poetry (himself, Mother, Father, even David), he "never saw a rhyme that a Muir had made that was worth half a reading." They should give more time to the poetry of botany, as he longed to do, for through botany "a pure & intelligent love for the Creator will become more and more intense." Nature spread for them a "table of beauty," far from the world's fever and wickedness, which they should taste and savor. "In all my wide journeys," he wrote, "I have never seen a place or section of country so rich in sweet wild flower wealth as your own. . . . I would not spend much time in verse making but you can scarce spend too much on cultivating a taste for the beauties & sublimities of nature."[24]

In contrast to Jeanne Carr's advice to renew his ties to nature, Muir heard a more class-conscious sermon from Professor James Butler. In Butler's view, Muir needed rescuing from the lower-class coarseness of his factory life; he needed the improving influence of genteel people who knew the importance of books and refined conversation. In particular, he recommended his friends the Merrills of Indianapolis, who were transplanted Vermonters, highly civilized, well read, and well to do. Reluctant and inveterately shy, the protégé screwed up his courage and called on them in their brick home. He may have met the father Samuel Merrill, a banker and railroad president, bookstore owner and publisher (the Bobbs-Merrill Company descended from him). But most important Muir found a warm and empathizing reception from daughter Catharine, who was fourteen years older than he, a writer and traveler, women's club member, and eventually professor of English literature at what became Butler University—the second woman to become a professor in the United States. She was not only like Jeanne Carr in age and education but also in physical appearance: a petite, fine-boned woman with wide-set eyes and gentle manners. Muir later called her "the first friend I found in Indiana, and one of the kindest, wisest and most helpful of my life."[25]

A benevolent soul with many civic projects always in motion, Catharine added him to her list of causes. She represented the high-minded life, much as those other New England Yankees, the Butlers and Carrs, had done in Madison, a different social class from Muir's blue-collar companions. Although religiously liberal, she was more conventionally Protestant than Jeanne Carr. She and Muir would have many intense discussions on the subject of religion, with Muir listing toward unorthodoxy while she kept pulling him back toward her Presbyterian creed. Other Merrill siblings included Julia Moores, whose son Merrill Moores became one of Muir's young admirers (and much later a prosperous lawyer and Republican member of Congress), and niece Katharine Merrill Graydon, who followed her aunt into a teaching career. All of them, despite his initial trepidation, became his friends for life.

Merrill Moores later recalled that early summer evening in 1866 when Muir first came to their door. The child had been only ten years old, but his memory stayed sharp for more than sixty years. He remembered the man they saw as tall and sturdy, "with blue eyes and a clear, ruddy complexion as well as handsome hair and beard. . . . He had a marked Scottish accent and was obviously a working man, but was plainly and neatly dressed; and he at once impressed me as the handsomest man I had ever met."[26]

Despite his pleasing outward appearance and charming bashfulness, however, the inside of Muir's skull was looking a lot like a disorganized and dissonant factory where no one was fully in charge. He was certainly not able to draw up a clear blueprint for his life, in contrast to what he was achieving on the work floor, or to manage the conflicting advice he was getting from so many strong-minded women and men, or even to see what his end product ought to be. Inventing machines or organizing them into a coherent system of production was much easier than inventing a life or finding coherence in what one thought or believed. In fact, the noise inside his head was getting to be deafening. At one hour he was wearing his leather work apron and wielding a wrench, at another he was sipping tea with the Merrills. On one day he sounded like a faithful Campbellite, on another he left Christianity behind and went looking for divinity in the sinuous leaves of an oak. Indianapolis of the long straight avenues was turning out to be the most confusing place he had ever lived.

<hr />

For a while it looked like Messrs. Osgood and Smith might resolve some of Muir's inner conflict simply by picking a quarrel and forcing him to quit. Miffed by their frequent criticisms, he went so far as to offer an employer in another city a contract to turn out three thousand broom handles a day. Then his bosses calmed down and "were as good as pie again."[27] Come winter, he was making for them a thorough inventory of the factory's belt system, finding many that were loose, badly joined, or worn to the breaking point. "Gentlemen," he lectured in a little essay called "Beltology," "belting is at once the nerves & sinews of factory life" and requires a careful investment of cash, not a false economy.[28] Ironically, his advice led to their installing many new belts, and it was precisely that wave of improvement that led to a second, and pivotal, tragedy in Muir's factory career.

On 6 March 1867, as he was setting up a new circular saw, he noted that the looped belt bringing power to it from the main shaft had stretched during its breaking-in period and needed to be shortened. To do that he had first to unlace it, severing the closed loop so that he could trim a piece from one end—a routine job. The lacing was tight, and he began prying hard at the stitches with the sharp end of a file. The file slipped in his hand and flew upward into his right eye, piercing the edge of the cornea. When he opened the eyelid, the liquid filling the space between the lens and the cornea dripped into his hand. In a few minutes the injured eye turned sightless. His whole body trembling, he walked out of the factory and home to Sutherlands' boarding house, where he climbed into bed. Within hours the left eye temporarily went dark too, out of sympathetic shock, and he feared that he had been completely blinded.[29]

A few days later the Indianapolis newspaper reported "a sad accident" to "Mr. Muir." "The loss is a serious one to more than the sufferer himself," the paper said, "as he has formed quite a class of the lads in his vicinity whom he instructed at night, gratuitously, in drawing, in which he was quite a proficient, and who are now deprived of their pleasant amusement and their generous teacher and companion."[30]

Others received the news quickly and directly from Muir himself. Within hours of the accident, he sent a message to the Merrills, telling them what had happened and fearing a loss darker than any "pleasant amusement," darker than any loss heretofore in his life. His right eye, he mourned, would never again look upon "a single flower, no more of lovely scenery, not any more of beauty."[31] Lately, he told them, he had been studying maps and planning a walking tour through the American South, the West Indies, South America, and Europe—a grandiose botanical expedition that he had contemplated for years, ever since he had read Humboldt's captivating visions of tropical flora. He expected such a journey to satisfy his insatiable craving for natural beauty, after which he could shrink away into some obscure corner. It was a dream that had begun to emerge out of the din in his head, promising to bring purpose and clarity. Suddenly it seemed hopeless to pursue. He was left weary, pained, unable to work, and prostrated by sorrow.

Right away Muir let his mother know about the accident, adding that the Sutherlands were taking good care of him. Jeanne Carr got the news too and rushed a long letter, written lovingly "as your sister," reminding her "precious soldier boy" of the many thousands who had endured even worse injuries in the late war. Trust in God, she advised, for in allowing such calamities to strike down "one of His Beloved" He must have a benevolent purpose.

What that purpose might be she could not fully say. What she did understand was that God had given him "the eye within the eye, to see in natural objects the realized ideas of His mind." This trial of pain and loss must somehow be intended to strengthen that gift of perception. Whether he would ever use his physical eyes or not, he was destined to become a seer, a man of uncommon vision, one who would lead men and women to find God in nature. Such was her dream for him, and such he would surely do, accident or not. The Andean mountains, the River Amazon, and all the other holy places on earth would still be there when he had recovered. She passed on her doctor-husband's advice that he should consult the best possible medical authority before deciding that the eye was permanently damaged. Above all, he must restore his serene confidence that everything was for the best in this divinely organized world. Out of adversity would come clarification and renewal.[32]

Nothing that anyone said, however, could brighten his mood of suicidal despair and discouragement, for he felt robbed of his most vital organ for intense living and for religious experience. What good was "the eye within the eye" if he was physically blind? How could one see into the ideas of God without being able to see nature? Seeing was everything; seeing was the basis of vision. His and Jeanne's religion depended on seeing for oneself and seeing (not hearing from any written text) the truth and beauty inherent in the world.

> The sunshine and the winds are working in all the gardens of God, but I—I am lost. . . . When I received my blow I could not feel any pain or faintness because the

tremendous thought glared full on me that my *right eye* was lost. I could gladly have died on the spot, because I did not feel that I could have heart to look at any flower again.[33]

But within a month of the accident he had reason to hope that his eyesight was not dead, and therefore he had reason to live.

Catharine Merrill came over to cheer him up, bringing an oculist to examine the injury. His worst fears had been groundless, the expert said, for the injured eye would heal within a few months and Muir's sight would be restored. The good lady also brought along her small nieces and nephews with arms full of wild flowers and stories they could read him. Little Merrill proposed reading Washington Irving's biography of Christopher Columbus or William Prescott's *Conquest of Mexico*, but Muir had already read the first and was not interested in hearing more about the brutality of the conquistadors, so the patient and visitor settled on Irving's comic *History of New York*, as told by the eccentric character Dietrich Knickerbocker. The gloom had begun to lift.

Weeks later, Jeanne wrote again with encouraging words: "Who knows but we shall see South America yet?" She prophesied that one day he would recover both his sight and vision and would return to Madison as professor of botany (perhaps as a distinguished Fellow of the Royal Botanical Society) and keeper of the campus grounds, would dwell in a plant-filled greenhouse, and would spend his days in close touch with growing things like the famous Swedish naturalist Carl Linnaeus. She recommended the study of Spanish to aid him on his travels. And then she added a new destination to his world list—the Yosemite Valley of California, whose description she had recently read in a magazine. "Oh this home of our Father!" she ended, "I would like to know all its mansions—and often to meet and compare notes with you, who love it with the same fervent love."[34]

Revealing as much about her own desires as Muir's prospects, Carr's words did prove prophetic in many details. Muir did rise up from his tragedy a new man. Eventually the injured eye recovered completely, leaving only a small scar on the cornea. Within a month of the accident he began to read on his own, walk the streets and visit the factory, and even saunter again into the healing woods. His spirits recovered so much that he picked up his pocketknife and began whittling a miniature windmill with wooden butterflies fluttering around its vanes. A stream of children and adults came to admire his handiwork, and they helped revive his pride and determination.

And he did put the Yosemite Valley on his travel list. In fact, it had been there already, after he too had read a description of it the previous year. He had "thought of it most every day since. You know my tastes," he wrote back to Jeanne, "better than anyone else."[35] In the not far off future he would try to see the famed valley—indeed, he and Jeanne would see it together.

In the meanwhile, the old perplexity over choosing a career briefly resurfaced. His bosses promised to put him in charge of the new shop they were building, so that he would have to do less manual labor and could concentrate on management. To his friends in Meaford he wrote that, while at the time of the accident "I could gladly have died on the spot," after weeks of partial recuperation he was contemplating going back to work. "Now that our factory has marked me I feel like making a good Scottish mark upon it."[36] But those weeks of darkness had wrought a permanent change in his thinking, and that change would gather force during the spring and ensuing summer. He would never go back to Osgood, Smith. He would throw down his tools, abandon forever any career in industry or invention, and seek his own independent way on earth.

⌒═✦═⌒

When his sight was virtually restored, Muir determined to see as much of wild nature as he could before it passed him by forever. He had earned enough money to take a long sabbatical, leaving behind the cities, factories, churches, even well-meaning personal ties that had pulled him this way and that. His destination would be South America and the world beyond, with no final end in sight. First, however, he wanted to return to Wisconsin, make his farewells, and assign a few personal assets to his heirs, for what he contemplated doing next was risky to the point of death. In that darkened room he had glimpsed death. It was not something he feared, but he wanted to be ready for the possibility that he might never return.

When summer rolled around, he was ready to go on what he called a preliminary "walk with Nature," avoiding railroads much of the way. He would walk across Indiana and Illinois, with his final destination Madison and the old homestead at Fountain Lake, taking along as companion eleven-year-old Merrill, with the permission of the child's trusting parents. Man and boy strolled across prairies, admiring the last of that soon to be displaced biome, brilliant with flowers before the devastating plows arrived. They filled their pockets with fossils and minerals and stopped to make little dams on prairie streams and to shear a farmer's sheep. They hiked along the banks of the Vermillion River, passed through the pleasant town of Bloomington, Illinois, home of Illinois Wesleyan College (and the future explorer of the Grand Canyon, Professor John Wesley Powell), and rambled on north to Rockford, where they rested their weary feet by catching a train to Wisconsin.

His parents offered nothing but discouragement for his plans of world travel. Daniel and Ann were back living temporarily at Fountain Lake (the Galloways having moved to another farm at Mound Hill), where Muir went to see them for possibly, in his mind, one last time. Merrill formed an unflattering impression of the declining patriarch: tall, slender, looking much older than his sixty-three years, "a narrow and bigoted fundamentalist, who made no secret of his belief that the study of geology was blasphemous and with his pious wife was accustomed to rebuke John unceasingly for his study of geology." Botany was for them no better pursuit, "although they were unable to give me any reasons for this belief." Daniel sat sternly in a rocking chair under one of his planted Lombardy poplars, copying out portions of Foxe's *Book of Martyrs* (all but the Latin portions), railing against the Catholics but professing ecumenical acceptance of all Protestant denominations. What Merrill did not witness was the cold, bitter moment when Muir bid his parents goodbye. Daniel, according to family legend, insisted that John pay for his room and board during the stay and refused to give his blessing to any fool-headed expedition into the wilderness. If the story is true, then perhaps it was because Daniel, despite his blinding religious obsession, was still shrewd enough to sense that his son, in setting out for distant places, was forsaking him and all he stood for, indeed was ready to forsake almost all entanglements to family and place. Mentally he was prepared to cut free of everything—family, friends, the Middle West, North America.[37]

On the way back to Indianapolis Muir and his young companion digressed to the Dells of the Wisconsin River, where the stream abruptly narrows between sandstone walls before widening out on its way to Portage. Tributary streams came tumbling in from both sides of the stony passage, flowing out of dark, green jungles of plants. "Those ravines," Muir had earlier written, "are the most perfect—the most heavenly plant conservatories I ever saw. Thousands of happy flowers are there but ferns & mosses are the favored ones no human language will ever describe them. . . . [W]ho can describe a greenhouse planned & made & planted by the great creator himself." Recovering that reverential mood, he bid a decisive farewell to the glorious Wisconsin of his youth.[38]

They stopped over in Madison for a week, while Merrill made friends with the Butler and Carr boys and Muir laid out his plans to their parents, seeking more encouragement than Daniel or Ann had given for the indeterminate adventure ahead. This time he found enthusiasm aplenty, especially from Jeanne, who had become so intent on rescuing him from a life in cities and factories and turning him toward the life of a prophet who would go into the world and preach the gospel (her gospel) of nature. Promising to write from wherever he went, although offering no assurance that he would ever see them again, Muir said another farewell and headed back to Indianapolis by train. They stopped for five hours in Chicago to do some botanizing before deciding that its polluted air and mobs of heavily shod feet had killed off everything interesting. Back at his room with the Sutherlands he packed up his inventions, books, and extra clothes, storing them with his landlord but prepared to leave them forever if necessary.

On the last day of August he sent a letter of thanks to Jeanne, confessing that he wished he had a better sense of where he was going, knowing only that he was "doomed" to be carried into the wilderness. "I wish I could be more moderate in my desires," he wrote, "but I cannot, & so there is no rest." The following day he sent a note to Dan about his travels: "I mean to start for the south tomorrow." The old sadness came on him as he contemplated leaving so many good people, not knowing when or whether he would see them again. In the event of his death, the money owed him by Trout and Jay should be given to his three unmarried sisters. His other siblings Sarah and Dan should divide up his clocks, machinery, and tools; other members of the family should get his books and pictures. Mother should have first choice of everything—but father nothing. He was anticipating great pleasure from this journey, along with much fatigue, but did not worry about any great danger. "My warmest love to all," he ended, "goodbye John Muir."[39]

CHAPTER 5

The Long Walk

Visions of warm, dark jungles where tangled lianas hung in the green shadows and brilliantly colored birds called from the high canopies drew many nineteenth-century travelers to South America. The Hudson River painter Frederick Church came with his brushes, and the young British naturalist Charles Darwin came with his collecting boxes and specimen labels. They came because, like Muir, they had read Alexander von Humboldt's multivolume work *Personal Narrative of Travels in the Equinoctial Regions of America during the Years 1799–1804*. They came to lose themselves in the wildness of Humboldt's Rio Negro or Amazon rainforests. Darwin, whose travels occurred just before Muir's birth, was more impressed by those sublime forests than any other place on his round-the-world voyage. They were, he wrote in an unusually pious mood, "temples filled with the varied productions of the God of Nature. No one can stand in these solitudes unmoved, and not feel that there is more in man than the mere breath of his body."[1]

Humboldt himself was more ambivalent about the rainforest. Nothing human, he noted, contained or impeded the vigorous growth of vegetation there or could protect one from a thousand dangers to life and limb. Crocodiles and boa constrictors ruled the rivers. Jaguars and monkeys lived without fear of or interference from people. Strange tropical diseases festered in the midst of botanical grandeur. "Here in a fertile country, adorned with eternal verdure," he wrote, "we seek in vain the traces of the power of man; we seem to be transported into a world different from the one that gave us birth." That nonhumanized land was never one that he, a highly civilized and elite European, could completely accept. "One may almost accustom one self to regard men as not being essential to the order of nature," but not quite. Humboldt inspired a generation or two to come and experience the superhuman force of the greatest expanse of forest on earth, while he kept looking for reassuring evidence that civilization was beginning to make an impact.[2]

A world without trace of human power, however, was precisely what Muir now wanted to immerse himself in. The fastest way to get to South America's tropical paradise from the man-dominated urban-industrial Midwest was to go by steamboat down the Ohio and Mississippi rivers to New Orleans, the leading southern port, and then across the Gulf of Mexico to the mouth of the Orinoco. Yet Muir never gave that direct route a serious thought. Arriving on 2 September 1867 at Louisville, Kentucky, he strode past all the boats tied up along the waterfront and marched straight through the city in search of the first green space he could find. On the outskirts, under a canopy of oaks, he spread his pocket map on the ground and plotted a path that would take him first through the great primeval forest of the Appalachian Mountains. Botany was his intellectual calling, wild nature his heart's desire, and wherever those could be satisfied most quickly was his true destination.

Now twenty-nine years old, he was setting out in a joyful mood of freedom, shaking off all the constraints that had been pressing him down into a mold of conformity. A factory job that had nearly blinded him for life was only one of those constraints. Conventional religion was another—the duties of regular church attendance and the authority of established doctrines in which he no longer believed. Then there was the social pressure to become a "so-called pillar or something": a financially comfortable, married adult male with children, orthodox in all his opinions, living like the Merrills in an upright brick box in the city furnished in the best "parlor taste," and helping others make their way up the same ladder toward bourgeois standing. That was the ideal marked out for anyone like him who had a modicum of college education and technological skills, to become "a useful, practical man."[3] He rejected that ideal, and indeed rejected the whole theory of civilization on which it was based—a theory that measured success by the size of one's property, income, or progeny. A life in nature was his alternative, vaguely defined though it might be, and he was now ready to seek it. He would live among trees and flowers, whether on this continent or another did not matter much, as a pilgrim seeking an independent relation to society but dependent on the universe.

Strangely, in his newfound freedom Muir felt he had no control over his choices or destination. Something mysterious was pulling him away from bourgeois respectability and driving him into the forest. Freedom was irresistible, compulsive. He could not explain that inner compulsion to others, but likened himself to Shakespeare's Brutus, who defended his own actions in stoic terms: "There is a tide in the affairs of men / Which, taken at the flood, leads on to fortune; / Omitted, all the voyage of their life / Is bound in shallows and in miseries."[4] Brutus, however, ran on his own sword and died, offering no promise of a happy outcome. Muir's joyful sense of release was mingled with fear that he too might be risking suicide, dying socially in the eyes of the world and perhaps even dying a literal death.

He felt driven to lead the life of an outlaw toward society, at least for the moment—to become a wild instead of a proper, cultivated plant. Someday he might want to change course and cease his wanderings. But doing so would require a radical conversion from the rambling life for which he seemed predestined. He would have to learn, like Methodist converts at a revival, "to love what I hate & to hate what I most intensely & devoutly love."[5] For now he would happily remain an unrepentant, free-ranging sinner in the eyes of the world.

Turning his back on social conformity did not mean repudiating everything produced by civilization. What he carried with him suggests how much of society's goods he still deemed necessary. He wore a flat-brimmed hat over his long hair and a single suit of outward garments—tough shoes, gray trousers, shirt, and jacket with a supply of money concealed in a pocket. Over his shoulder he carried a black rubbery bag filled with a single change of underwear, a bar of soap, a towel, comb and brush. Maintaining a high standard of cleanliness was important wherever he was heading. There were also three small books in the bag—a collection of Robert Burns's poems, John Milton's *Paradise Lost*, and the New Testament—and a fat, heavy one, weighing in at some five pounds, Alphonso Wood's *A Class Book of Botany, being Outlines of the Structure, Physiology, and Classification of Plants; with a Flora of the United States and Canada*, probably the 1862 edition he had acquired as a student in Madison. Wood's was the only American book (no Emerson or Thoreau in his traveling library); the other volumes were all tokens of his Old World upbringing as a Scot, a student of British literature, and a Protestant Christian.[6] On his back he strapped a homemade plant press for drying specimens collected along the way. Wood gave instructions for making such a gadget: two sheets of wire gauze held together by three or four leather straps, each a yard in length, with buckles; and a dozen quires of ordinary blotting paper for extracting moisture from the plants he collected. Thus, he was only a semiliberated man, pursuing the simple life yet unwilling to abandon his books, science, or hairbrush, while depending on American dollars to buy food along the road.

Muir began his journey out of a desire to escape some of the snares of society, but his overland route, which followed established arteries of travel and commerce, would necessarily take him through a human community that even a single-minded, plant-collecting botanist would have to acknowledge. Ahead lay the South, a region that had just been through a devastating war that had ended two years earlier, leaving 600,000 Americans dead, the southern economy bankrupt and dislocated, and millions of African Americans emancipated from slavery.

It was not Muir's intention to discover what the Civil War had meant to the losers or winners. He remained opposed to war of any kind or for any purpose. He had been against slavery too, but pacifism more than abolitionism had dominated his thoughts in the run-up to the war. Now, inevitably along his trail he would encounter both black and white southerners, would eat at their tables, sleep in their beds, listen to the dominant race's views about the future of the South, as they writhed under a federal policy of military occupation and reconstruction, and encounter for the first time in his life a minority people who had long been oppressed by Euro-American civilization. He would find white southerners bitter, obsessive, and reactionary about such matters. Blacks he would get to know less well, as they guarded their speech carefully and he recorded little of whatever conversations he had with them, but on the whole his experiences with them left a positive impression. Having extricated himself from one entangling society, he was not eager to become entangled in another whose problems were enormous and beyond easy understanding or resolution. Yet, as it turned out, his very life would depend on those people, white or black, he met along the way.

This lean, bearded stranger, in contrast to all the Yankee troops that had recently come and gone, was a harmless if peculiar figure for nearly everyone he met. In fact his handsome face, his wide-open blue eyes, so innocent and sparkling with excitement, endeared him to many. They took him into their houses, quizzed him about his aims, had trouble understanding what he was after or where he was going, and then let him pass on. A runaway from civilization mainly preoccupied with his own needs, most of which he found satisfied best in solitary rambling, he learned that freedom from human affairs could never be absolute.

◦━━✦━━◦

The traveling satchel included, as a final significant item, a blank notebook bound in dark covers, with some two hundred ruled pages four by six inches in size. Its owner inscribed his name and address on the inside cover: "John Muir, Earth-planet, Universe." It was an announcement that he had cut all ties to a local or national identity, claiming as his home place the whole planet. Nothing merely human could define who he was or could draw a line around his loyalties. He was the ultimate cosmopolitan, not merely a citizen of the known world, as the ancient Greeks understood citizenship, but a part of the greater community of nature that had no boundaries.[7]

Filling the pages of that journal became Muir's nearly daily task on his travels through the South. The journal was his first extended piece of writing and eventually became the core of his posthumously published book, *A Thousand-Mile Walk to the Gulf*. Words crowd the margins in the original journal, many of them crossed out or written along the edges as he searched for the right choice, and the prose is more colloquial, immediate, and sharp-edged. He included sketches of himself and of the plants, landscapes, and people he saw. The published version divides the daily flow into chapters with titles, softens a few of his more caustic remarks, and throws in episodes calculated to amuse an audience—as later in life he learned to play the role of popular raconteur rather than outsider. Fifty years would change him, but both the first and last version reveal a young man who is trying to find answers for life's ultimate questions regarding the meaning of death, fear of the unknown, a sense of belonging, a meaningful occupation, and humanity's place in the natural world.

The journal breaks down into three roughly equal sections. The first three weeks, lasting from 2 to 22 September, took him through Kentucky and Tennessee, where the contrast between nature's splendor and man's degradation became increasingly stark. Then came three weeks wandering through Georgia and camping on the fringes of Savannah, from 23 September to 14 October, a tense and doubt-filled interlude. He finished his travels with a longer period, mid-October to early January, spent walking across Florida from Fernandina to Cedar Key, but mostly spent stricken by illness and lying at death's door. Each of those places took him farther away from middle-class conventions and deeper into rebellion. Yet it was a rebellion frequently mixed with other moods—loneliness, hope, sociability, gratitude, scientific detachment, and moments of pure delight.

For the most part his route took him down dusty, man-made roads cut through forest and field, along which he could find farmhouses or taverns where he could put up for the night. Tiring of bad accommodations, he slept once on a student bench in a schoolhouse, and more often in the outdoors under bushes, which he had promised his mother he would never do. He first struck south from Louisville, heading toward the famed Mammoth Cave, whose hundreds of miles of underground passages carved by water from the bedrock limestone had attracted tourists for half a century. If he explored any of those amazing passages, he did not record it, but stayed completely above ground in his descriptions, drawing comparisons between the artificial and paltry gardens of the site's tourist hotel and the surrounding natural grandeur of Kentucky's black oaks, ferns, walnuts,

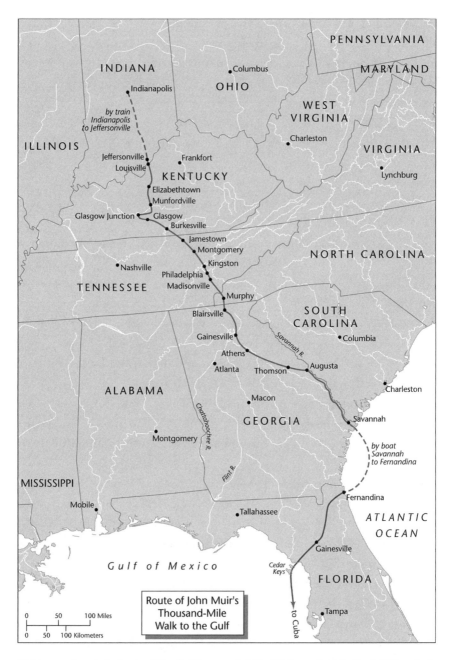

Muir's route through the South, 1867. (A Thousand-Mile Walk to the Gulf, *ed. William Badè,* *1916)*

and hickories. "Kentucky," he scribbled, is "the greenest state I have seen. . . . Here is the Eden, the paradise of oaks."[8]

Next, he swung southeastward, trudging through an uninspiring mosaic of corn, cotton, and tobacco fields, with forests hovering on the horizon; he was following a trail from Glasgow to Burkesville (today, Kentucky's state route 90, the John Muir Highway). In one of the few letters he wrote during his trek to the Gulf, addressed to the Carrs, he described his preferred kind of in-transit bedroom: a wooded hilltop furnished with a moss-clad log against which he reclines. He complained of sore feet, not surprisingly since he had just hiked 170 miles, but added, "I am paid for all my toil a thousand times over."[9]

Crossing the Tennessee state border, he entered the realm of the fallen Confederacy, albeit far to the east of the blood-drenched battlegrounds of Shiloh and Nashville. After scaling the Cumberland Plateau, he began his ascent of the Appalachian Mountains south of what is now the Great Smoky Mountains National Park. In all directions he could gaze on spectacular forests crowning ridge after ridge, with mountain mists drifting through the valleys, the most sublime picture his eyes had ever beheld. "Such an ocean of wooded, waving, swelling mountain beauty and grandeur . . . Oh, these forest gardens of our Father! What perfection, what divinity, in their architecture! What simplicity and mysterious complexity of detail!"[10] Now his blotting papers were filled with drying leaves and flowers: cinnamon fern, sensitive brier, milkwort, goldenrod, aster, magnolia, laurel, azalea, and rhododendron. Autumn was approaching in the mountains, summer green was beginning to fade to fall browns and yellows, the air was cold at night, and Muir was in heaven.

If southern nature was overflowing with so much beauty, diversity, and harmony, why were the human traces on the land so often repellent? The small towns of eastern Tennessee were a blot on the earth: Jamestown, "an incredibly dreary place"; Montgomery, "shabby"; Philadelphia, "a very filthy village in a beautiful situation."[11] Those were all relatively prosperous valley settlements. The higher he climbed, the more backward and benighted the people became, and the more dangerous. It was in the delightsome mountains that Muir met a roving band of outlaw whites who lived by marauding and plundering. They let him pass because he looked like a poor, hapless collector of herbal remedies. Never before in the Midwest or Canada had he known real danger in his travels, but the South was a land where men regularly carried guns and where officers of the law were often far away, a condition that seemed to increase with the grandeur of the surroundings.

One old peaceful and nonthreatening mountaineer offered to put him up if he would stay for a few days to enjoy the natural splendors of the country and come to know its people better. Muir gladly agreed to the offer but was unimpressed by the humans he saw and even shocked by their barbarism. He witnessed wild, unshorn, and uncombed men carrying bags of corn out of the hollows to be ground at a gristmill. They looked a lot like he must have looked by this point, except for their uncombed hair, but in their way of life he could see a huge difference from his own. They were so pathetically uncivilized! They were unlettered, lacked technological sophistication, and showed "not the faintest sign of that restless spirit of speculation and invention so characteristic of the North." Archaic ways were best, they asserted, and making improvements was nearly a crime. "This is the most primitive country I have seen," complained the former clock and lathe inventor, "primitive in all things."[12] Even their farming was shiftless: they skinned the hillsides, setting in motion a cycle of soil erosion, declining productivity, and abandoned fields—bad agricultural practices they tolerated in the hope that one day gold and copper mines would materialize, making them rich enough to buy their food from someplace else.

Mountain women were as uncouth as their menfolk, lacking vital energy, showing pale and sickly faces, and poking snuff up their gums. One farmer's wife, whom Muir found unusually smart and neat in appearance, was nonetheless as crude as the rest; she had developed a talent for spitting farther than any man could do. In a passage left out of the published version, probably because he feared it would give offense to middle-class readers, he describes how she ejaculated "superabundant saliva" from the left corner of her mouth, accompanied by "a sudden jerk of the head, but without any apparent uneasiness or disordering of the lips."[13] So different from the respectable women he had known in Wisconsin and Indiana, she both amused and offended Muir's sensibilities. Such mountaineers were, like himself, of old English, Scots, or Scots-Irish stock, but in their coarseness of manners, their negative attitudes toward work and innovation, and their superstitious mentality, they were nearly another species.

A few blacks lived in these mountains, although Muir had met many more in the Kentucky and Tennessee lowlands. Previously he had had little experience with black people; now he frequently found himself in close contact with them. He forded a stream on the back of an old horse with his arms around its owner, a small, chubby black boy, whose woolly head grazed Muir's long whiskers. He accepted a ride in the wagon box of a black farmer who shared his anti-war views— which in Muir's eyes made him a shrewd and eloquent observer. He ate string beans, buttermilk, and corn bread at the table of a black family. One night he stayed with a black teamster, who offered a surplus of information on his craft along with simple lodging. Compared to the sometimes suspicious or close-minded whites, these African Americans seemed consistently courteous and generous. Nor apparently did they find his botanizing a suspicious pursuit, in contrast to at least one white fellow who hinted that a real, hard-working man should be able to find something better to do with his time than go along effeminately picking flowers. Whatever Muir may have missed about the deeper turmoil of southern blacks' lives, he met them more or less as equals and shared the intimacy of their homes to an extent that few white northerners, or white southerners, ever did.

⚓

Georgia was one of the core states of the late Rebellion, the fifth to secede from the Union and one of the last to feel the sting of defeat. Late in the war General William Tecumseh Sherman had burned the capital Atlanta to the ground and, in his infamous march from Atlanta to the sea, had set fire to fields and farmhouses and demolished fences and mills, a destructive onslaught whose traces one could still find.[14]

Coming down from the mountains into that former war zone, Muir first entered a piedmont of knobby hills and small shady towns, staying briefly with a former fellow worker from Indianapolis in one. Here primeval nature had largely given way to cotton plantations created by the labor of generations of slaves and now tended by ex-slaves working for subsistence wages. Lacking broad white support for postwar land reform, the freedmen had little prospect of acquiring any property of their own. Muir appreciated the politeness they showed him but harshly noted, "The negroes are very lazy [revised to 'easy-going' in the published version] and merry. . . . One energetic white man, working with a will, would easily pick as much cotton as half a dozen sambos and sallies."[15] He, of course, was not volunteering to do any of that picking himself. Instead, he saw himself as running away from an overindustrious past and getting free of any steady employment—getting free to ramble in a way that no black person could safely do.

In contrast to blacks, white men had made plenty of money in the prewar era out of the rich Georgia soil, and as they recovered from Sherman's invasion, they hoped to make still more. The profits from their antebellum enterprise they had invested in great houses and aristocratic towns like Athens. That city was the most beautiful Muir had seen on his journey, "and the only one in the South that I would like to revisit."[16] It offered a pleasing contrast to the rickety cabins and broken-down fences of eastern Tennessee. Yet here in the midst of a more advanced agriculture, he began to feel an "indescribable loneliness" gripping his heart. More than ever he felt like an alien in a strange land. Most of the whites, for all their easy affluence, proved less hospitable than elsewhere. On one day he walked forty miles because no one would give him shelter. Deep South polish and wealth often meant Deep South coldness and prejudice.

Below the piedmont stretched a wide, subtropical, sedimentary plain drained by long, muddy rivers, much of which was still either undeveloped for agriculture or had been reverting to a more feral condition during and after the war. That recovering wildness was hard for a naturalist to ignore in order to dwell on the plight of a defeated civilization. As he walked across that plain, he passed through the "pine barrens," where long-leafed pines still grew in vast numbers, and then across prairies of magnificent tall grasses and around aromatic cypress swamps. Following the Savannah River downstream, he encountered once more a plantation landscape, this time growing rice wherever the soil was still being cultivated, but even here nature was everywhere in evidence, contesting the rule of man.

On 8 October he arrived at the historic port city of Savannah. Here as in Athens the profits of commercial agriculture had built up a graceful way of life that was still surviving. Numbering 36,000 residents, it was the largest urban center in the state. An elegant city of imposing squares named after eighteenth-century generals and statesmen—Washington, Franklin, Oglethorpe, Pulaski, Lafayette, each square embellished with stone monuments, palms, live oaks, and elegant townhouses—it had come through the war unscathed. Down on the river level, among the wharves, shipping offices, rice mills, and machinist shops, trade was picking up again. Savannah was surging ahead of its rivals, Mobile and New Orleans, in commodity receipts, boasting that it would soon become the New York City of the South. The boosters were too optimistic, but after a long debacle they were beginning to do well again.

Politically, however, the white people of Savannah and, indeed, the whole state of Georgia were in a vicious mood over changes in race relations. Because Georgians had refused to ratify the Fourteenth Amendment to the Constitution, which gave equal protection of the law to all citizens, black or white, and prohibited any Confederate rebels from holding political office, the state had been put under federal military rule. The troops were there to see that blacks were allowed to vote without harassment; within a year of Muir's visit thirty-two of them would take seats in the state legislature, assuring the ratification of the amendment. To restore white supremacy a secret militia organization, the Ku Klux Klan, was organizing across the state. One of its principal targets was the "carpetbagger," any northerner who had come south for political or financial advantage and who favored equality between the races.[17]

For Muir, Savannah turned out to be a most threatening place, but not because he carried a northern carpetbag or openly advocated black civil rights. He was silent, even in his private journal, on some of the most hotly fought political issues of the day.[18] His thoughts focused on the fact that he was nearly broke. After his first night at the Planters Hotel, where he slept under mosquito netting, he had only a dollar and a half left. Back in Kingston, Tennessee, he had shipped his plant collections home to brother David in Portage, Wisconsin, with a request that a draft on his bank account be sent to an express office in Savannah, but the next day he learned that the money had not yet arrived. How long would he have to wait? Despite boasting ten lumber mills and bustling with commerce, the city had nothing to offer him in the way of temporary employment. The second night he went to the shabbiest hotel he could find, worrying about how he might get by until the long overdue draft came through.

The "indescribable loneliness" he had felt over the preceding days now gave way to a fear of "downright starvation."[19] It looked like he might be reduced to stealing corn or rice from the fields, as Yankee troops had done. He had to find a place to camp while waiting. Here the journal gets confusing as he later amended and inserted text, breaking the narrative flow and creating some repetition and back-tracking. What is clear is that he left the central streets and squares to look for a campsite among the tidal marshes and sand dunes that lay to the east of the city, anxious to avoid "miasmas" that he feared might give him malaria or poisonous snakes or roving ex-slaves who might do him violence.

It was nearly dark when, three miles from town, he came upon the Bonaventure cemetery sited on the banks of a placid tributary, the Wilmington River. Once part of a former governor's plantation, it had been set off as a cemetery in 1847—not a graveyard crowded behind a church but a more picturesque, spacious style fashionable in antebellum America. Its designers had laid out a mirror image of Savannah's squares and avenues; a central thoroughfare ran through the cemetery, lined with great spreading live oaks draped with silvery-gray moss swaying from the branches. Each square was devoted to the marble tomb of a deceased member of the city's elite, planted with camellias, wisteria, yellow jasmine, and dogwood, and protected by wrought-iron fences and gates. Surrounding this ordered core of graves lay an undisturbed native forest running down to the river.

Muir, hoping that this would be a sanctuary where no one would molest him, stretched out on the ground and fell sleep.

The next morning, awakening to the screams of a bald eagle, he discovered that he had been sleeping on an unfenced grave. Nonetheless, he arose refreshed by the sylvan sights and sounds around him—"by far the most impressive assemblage of animal and plant creatures

Muir drawing of himself sleeping on a grave in the Bonaventure cemetery. (H-A, JMP)

I ever met."[20] After breakfasting on a few crackers, he walked back to the express office to check on his package—and still it had not arrived. In fact it would not appear for five days, during which time he had to survive on a mere twenty-five cents. Back he went to the cemetery, this time to build a sleeping bower in the underbrush and to try to live on birdsong and imagination.

No matter how botanically interesting, a cemetery was a difficult place to endure for a man condemned to a starvation diet. Muir's head began to grow faint and his thoughts turned morbid. He put aside plant collecting and began to dwell on the possibility of dying in this place. Death was an event that he had been taught to fear as an "Eve made" curse, a punishment for Adam's giving way to temptation, always to be resisted and avoided as fiercely as possible. Death had come wrapped in denial or anxiety or drenched in tears. The "civilized swarm of Christians so called" could, on the one hand, tolerate the murder of thousands in a war and call it heroism, while on the other hand an ordinary death in the family brought on the burial companies, somber black clothes, desperate hopes of the resurrection of the body, a corpse encased in a box and lowered into a deep hole in the ground, a cemetery "full of all kinds of glooms & ghosts."[21]

That "death orthodoxy" (which he called "the grimmest body to be found in the whole catalogue of civilized Christian manufactures") he tried to confront head on and break its hold over his mind. He rebelled against the bleak teaching that we live in a cursed, fallen world and that death is the punishment we must all suffer for ancient disobedience. What Bonaventure revealed to him, in contrast to the old pessimism, was that death is not a form of punishment. Death and life are forever and inextricably blended together in a positive whole. The animal or plant dies, or the human being dies, and others take their place in the ever-renewing circle of nature. All is "harmony divine."[22]

Even in romantic, bosky Bonaventure cemetery, Muir found evidence that humans tried to resist death and to deny their place in the natural order. The cemetery's marble tombs and wrought-iron fences stood as an "art blunder" that nature was slowly working to erase. Already the iron and marble were corroding, the grave mounds eroding, and competing weeds drifting in to reclaim the plots from the rose bushes and showy flowerbeds planted to memorialize the dead. Eventually those funerary artifacts would be wiped away and forgotten. "Life is at work everywhere," he approved, "obliterating all memory of the confusion of man."[23]

Fortunately for posterity, Muir did not die in this spot or yield his body to the cosmos. Eventually, a package of seventy-five dollars arrived at the express office and, despite a lack of written identification, he was able to claim it. Immediately, he bought a hunk of gingerbread from a black woman on the street and, stuffing food into his undernourished body, rushed to the waterfront, where on 14 October he boarded a coastal steamer, the *Sylvan Shore*, bound for Florida. Now his mood shifted to a more serene, sunny contemplation of life rather than death. As he sat on deck watching the famed Sea Islands pass before his eyes, he overlooked all the cold receptions he had received and decided that the people of Georgia were the most charming and impressive of all the southerners he had met. No longer on the edge of starvation, he happily (if inconsistently) admired the costly homes that the more prosperous whites inhabited with so little effort or pretense, the blacks' obliging and cheerful dispositions. Above all, he ticked off with pleasure the many new species of trees he had added to his knowledge since leaving home.

The last day in Savannah had brought him long overdue letters from his mother, brothers Dan and David, and the Galloways. In a reply written aboard ship he recalled their sailing to America two decades earlier and childhood memories of the sea around Dunbar. But the desire to enter new domains and cut free of his past was still strong. He could not tell them where to write next, or even where exactly he was going, but admonished them to take "the extremest care of my specimens."[24]

❦

Forty-five days out from Indiana, Muir reached the state of Florida, radically unlike any place he had ever been and unlike even the several states he had just traversed; it was a natural, subtropical bridge to Humboldt's tropics. Its name promised, with a Spanish accent, that here he would find a flowery garden where old men would grow young again and young men find romance. Nothing, however, could have been further from reality. But under Florida's broad, brilliant skies, he reached a state of moral clarification that would become the foundation for his life's philosophy. Here he discovered at last where, intellectually, he was heading.

Fernandina, just over the Georgia line, was the terminus of the Florida Railroad and the main portal to this state. Completed six years earlier, it ran as straight as it could over one of the flattest places on earth to the other side of the peninsula, the Gulf port of Cedar Key. Disrupted by the war, the railroad had recommenced operations shortly before Muir arrived. Examining the prospect of its steel rails heading inland, he found "not a mark of friendly recognition, not a breath, not a spirit whisper of sympathy, and of course I was lonely." On either side of the track stretched a monotonous vista: a hot, sandy, waterlogged, vine-entangled plain, designed more for alligators and cottonmouth snakes than rambling botanists. He felt like a spider trapped in a web. He trembled at the thought of big reptilian jaws closing around him. Then, ashamed and astonished at his own cowardice, he decided to take the safe and practical way and continue on. Instead of forging his own path through the wilds, he set out along the railroad tracks, making brief side excursions here and there to inspect the unfamiliar vegetation that rose like a wooden palisade around him.

His first sighting of a member of the palm family, the cabbage palmetto (*Sabal palmetto*), caused him to throw down his plant press and bag and, disregarding all fears, to splash through the brown water for a closer inspection. After all, no less an authority than Carl Linnaeus had lauded palms as the princes of the plant world. This one stood almost alone in a grassy spot, its gray shaft rising like a broom handle, its broad fan-shaped leaves sprouting like ten-foot feathers from the end of the shaft. Its leaves rustled loudly in the wind, giving it a higher "power of expression" than any plant so far met in his journey. Plain and simple it might have been, but it seemed incredibly alive, individualistic, and human-like, telling him of "grander things than I ever got from [a] human priest."[25] Mainly it told him that he had stumbled upon a cheery fellow creature, who (for all he knew) was no more imperishable or soulless than any human being. With that discovery of a heavily anthropomorphized plant companion Florida became a friendlier place, but only barely.

Muir drawing of the cabbage palmetto, near Fernandina, Florida. (H-A, JMP)

Not until Gainesville, the midpoint of his transit, would Muir reach a town where he could sleep in a bed. Before that, finding a spot of dry ground to lie down on was difficult. The first couple of mornings he awakened cold and wet with dew, his bread supply again rapidly depleting. He needed to secure a meal to keep going. Yet the first people he met were not very encouraging company. A party of backwoods loggers cutting out pine near the track surpassed even the long-haired Tennesseans for "downright barbarism," although they were ready to share their pork and hominy with him. Other people began to appear down the line, many of them renegades from society like himself—a young black man who tried to rob him, a white family stricken by malaria and living in squalor, and shaggy hunters looking for alligators to kill. Wherever there was enough dry land to support timber, make a hunting camp, or plow a farm, people collected like seeds looking for soil. But here as elsewhere they offered an unappealing contrast to other forms of life—so often certain of their moral superiority to nature but so far from living a clean, disciplined life.

By far the most humble people he met along the tracks were a dirt-poor African American family camped at night in the open, with a blazing log fire but hardly any possessions. He asked for a drink, which they readily gave in a gourd. "Seen anywhere but in the Negroid South," he wrote, "the glossy pair would have been taken for twin devils, but here it was only a negro and his wife at their supper." Fevered superstition, he was saying, might make them seem menacing, when in fact they were quite harmless, generous to a stranger, and loving to one another, if appallingly poor. So dark-complexioned were these people that he did not at first notice that they had a child sleeping on the ground, as black as his own shoulder bag and as "naked as to the earth he came." The woman "bent wooingly over the black object and said with motherly kindness, 'Come, honey, eat yo' hominy.'" What he saw in these people's faces was not, by his standards, beauty, but neither were they wholly repellent or alien. In the original journal he wondered what this family might reveal about the then much-disputed origins of humankind—whether the different races had a common ancestry or not. In the published version, however, he rejected any notion of separate racial origins and imagined them coming out of the "black muck of the marsh" just as God had "manufactured . . . Adam direct from the earth." Unflattering though his descriptions were, Muir accepted blacks as part of the family of man and did not come down on the side of southern or northern racists or white supremacists.[26]

Accepting the humanity of blacks, no matter how primitive or ugly some of them seemed, was one lesson of Muir's travels through the South and Florida. Another, related conclusion was that all creatures great or small, nonhuman or human, no matter how useless or ugly they might seem ("devils" of another sort), had a moral claim on humans. All should be free to enjoy their own place on earth. Humans looked at predators like the alligator with little sympathy or understanding. But this animal, which at first had struck fear in his mind, now appeared in a different light. "Doubtless these creatures are happy," he wrote, "and fill the place assigned them by the great Creator of all. Fierce and cruel they appear to us, but beautiful in the eyes of God."[27] They were part of a plan that carefully and wisely organized all beings into a marvelous whole. They were all His children, even those He had given dangerous teeth.

For the first time in his writing Muir introduced the modern liberal, democratic language of "rights" to explain the moral claims that other creatures make on humans. Everything in the creation, he asserted, has a right to live. Because alligators, by virtue of their divine origin, have that right, they also have a right to eat whatever they catch—including an occasional human being. Muir went so far as to wish them a "mouthful of terror-stricken man by way of a dainty."[28] Presumably in that wish, he was allowing that alligators had a moral right to eat *him*, although he was not willing to make it easy for them and continued to watch where he put his feet.

One might suppose, by Muir's moral logic, that human hunters had as much right to kill a deer as alligators to kill their prey. He certainly did not question the right to hunt or eat venison; indeed, he dined on a fresh supply at the house of a Captain Simmons, formerly an officer in the Confederate army, an avid hunter, and, despite his prejudices against blacks and Yankees, a genial host to the traveling botanist. Muir even went hunting with Simmons and a local judge, but he soon regretted it. Their kind of hunting was not the same as an alligator catching a meal. The captain and the judge were not after sustenance but sport and smugly assumed that deer were put in the woods to give pleasure to such important fellows as themselves.

Quietly in his private thoughts Muir dismissed that sort of reasoning as contemptible. He did not point an accusing finger at the poorer class of humans who hunted to have food on their table but did at "the creation's braggart lords," who were usually white men of property and standing.

> Let a Christian hunter go to the Lord's woods and kill his well-kept beasts, or wild Indians, and it is well; but let an enterprising specimen of these proper, predestined victims go to houses and fields and kill the most worthless person of the vertical godlike killers—oh! that is horribly unorthodox, and on the part of the Indians atrocious murder! Well, I have precious little sympathy for the selfish propriety of civilized man, and if a war of races should occur between the wild beasts and Lord Man, I would be tempted to sympathize with the bears.

It was the attitude of elite sport hunters that was most objectionable. They claimed to be pious but had little respect for the Creation. Strikingly, Muir criticized not "man" in general, but "Lord Man," a figure of high social standing and "propriety" who took for granted his God-given right to seize and use the land any way he saw fit.

Linking the right of nonhuman species to exist and the right of Native Americans to defend their homelands, as Muir did in that quoted passage, was a bold, original stroke. What Indian resistance was he thinking about? Nowhere along the route had he directly encountered any indigenous people, although near Murphy, North Carolina, he had visited a site where the Cherokee had been rounded up in the 1830s and sent on their long, deadly "trail of tears." Perhaps he was remembering the argument he had heard as a child between his father and a neighbor over whether whites had a right to dispossess the Indians or not. Or it may have been the Seminoles of Florida he had in mind; their long-running resistance to the U.S. government had come to an end less than a decade earlier, when three thousand of them had been removed beyond the Mississippi River, leaving a few hundred behind, hidden in the swamps. Scarcely hidden in the coils of Muir's moral imagination was the assumption that Indians everywhere were part of the divine Creation and, as such, had a right to live free and defend themselves from intruders.

Those radical thoughts against white imperialism were broken off by his arrival at the Gulf Coast on 23 October, at the small seaside village of Cedar Key, the end of the rail line. The village name came from a cluster of low islands, or keys, on which southern red cedar grew among the palms, slash pines, and cypress. Nationally, redcedar was a sought-after wood for the making of pencils; before and after the war, the Faber Pencil Company had begun to strip out the trees and ship them to its northern factory. The local economy was more inclined toward the sea, where the local fishermen harvested mullet, turtles, clams, and oysters. The smell of the sea was strong in the air, and slow-flying platoons of cormorants and pelicans coming in at dusk were a daily ritual. Unfortunately for a footsore traveler hoping for a quick passage from there to South American ports, the harbor was empty on the day of Muir's arrival.

The proprietor of the local general store promised that a schooner would appear in a couple of weeks to pick up a load of milled wood. Although destined for Galveston, Texas, not South America, that boat would offer Muir his best transportation hope, and he rushed off to see the mill's owner for work in the interim. The mill was over on Way Key and belonged in part to R. W. Hodgson, a native of Delaware who had brought his North Carolina–born wife Sarah to live here on the eve of the war. All milling had ceased for repairs. A new pulley cover needed fitting, Hodgson was unsure how to do the job, and fortuitously here was Muir, a veteran millwright and sawyer. Soon, he had the saws buzzing again and a job cutting up cedar and pine for as long as needed.

He would not work there long. The very next day his head began to hurt, he broke out in a cold sweat, his limbs turned leaden and numb. Hours later, he collapsed on the path leading from the workers' bunkhouse to the mill, lying there unconscious until dark came and he staggered back to his lodging. The watchman thought he was drunk, as Muir crawled up the stairs to his bed. When he awoke, it was days later and he was lying in the Hodgsons' house. Sarah Hodgson was pouring quinine into him, for she had seen malaria before. She realized that Muir was in no condition to carry on his journey and became his Florence Nightingale, attending him through a two-month bout of paroxysmal depths alternating with periods of recovery. The busy mother of six children, she opened her heart to this fevered stranger and earned his life-long gratitude.

Bad air (or "mal aria" in Italian) had long been identified as the source of this common disease of the tropics, so that Muir would have assumed that some miasma rising from putrefying vegetation had struck him. Not until 1880 would scientists discover that the real cause of the disease is the group of microscopic organisms named *Plasmodium*, and not until the turn of the century would they identify biting mosquitoes as the vector. Most likely the species that attacked Muir was the more common and less dangerous *Plasmodium vivax*, a species that seldom kills but can leave its victim debilitated and listless for years. This parasite is transmitted by mosquitoes of the genus *Anopheles*, which thrive in swamps or the sluggish backwaters of rivers, and it enters the victim's bloodstream, where it attacks the red blood cells. Symptoms appear some ten to sixteen days after the bite, so Muir was probably bitten in early to mid-October, perhaps while in the Bonaventure cemetery. The only cure in his day, before the modern drug chloroquine, was the bitter alkaloid quinine, derived from the bark of the cinchona tree, which can have many undesirable side effects.[29]

Except for his eye accident, he had lived a remarkably healthy life before this moment and had seemed often careless about his body's well-being in his intense, workaholic approach to everything. For example, he had set out at a grueling pace on his walk to the Gulf, had gone hungry for days on end, and had put himself at risk repeatedly. Nature, he assumed, could never harm him, for it was the primal source of health, the remedy for all ailments. Sickness belonged to places like Indianapolis. However, it was nature now that made him sick, not cities or factories or other people, and he had to come to grips with that fact.

Malaria forced him to slow down and rest his overstressed body. He could look about him more deliberately and take up at more leisure those complicated feelings toward nature that had been churning in his mind. Sarah proved to share his love for flowers and gardens; likely, she made plants a part of her therapeutic program. For long periods of time Muir lay looking at flowers or convalescing under a massive live oak on the Hodgsons' little hill or listening to the wind and lifting his gaze from time to time toward the uninhabited keys across the water. He sketched those beckoning isles in his journal and then was able to sail a skiff over to study them more closely. Mangroves grew there, he learned, and tall, dignified white herons fished among their stilt-like roots, while on the shell-laden island sands grew Spanish bayonet and impenetrable thickets of cactus. Questions came back to be resolved in his journal: what was the value of those beautiful things? Why had nature made him sick? What did his individual life or death matter in the full scheme of things?

Like hurricanes cutting gaps in the forests, he observed, diseases regularly swept through the South's human population, striking down blacks and whites alike. Malaria was only one of those diseases; there were also yellow fever and cholera. Muir believed that both kinds of disaster, devastating winds and devastating fevers, must be part of God's plan for the universe; they had ultimately to be purposeful, intentional events. Believe otherwise, and he must conclude that the world is without purpose or plan, that there is no Creator. Religiously unorthodox though he might be, he would not accept that nihilistic conclusion. The difficulty was to discover divine intentions, for they lay above and beyond the human mind.

So most of the world's religions have taught, not least the Calvinism that had formed so much a part of Scottish spiritual heritage. Muir had enough of the old Calvinism still in him to resist some of the modern trends toward demystifying the divine. He recoiled from a rising confidence in post-Calvinist, Anglo-American theology that divine intentions could be read in minute detail. Such a confidence, he feared, led to putting human reason at the center of the cosmos. It undermined traditional religious humility and eventually led to the heretical confidence that everything in nature exists for the purpose of satisfying human need and advancing the cause of human progress.

The world, we are told, was made especially for man—a presumption not supported by all the facts. A numerous class of men are painfully astonished whenever they find anything, living or dead, in all God's universe, which they cannot eat or render in some way what they call useful to themselves. They have precise dogmatic insight of the intentions of the Creator, and it is hardly possible to be guilty of irreverence in speaking of their God any more than of heathen idols. He is regarded as a civilized, law-abiding gentleman in favor either of a republican form of government or of a limited monarchy; believes in the literature and language of England; is a warm supporter of the English constitution and Sunday schools and missionary societies; and is as purely a manufactured article as any puppet of a half-penny theater.[30]

Such thinking was more than erroneous. It was presumptuous, arrogant, and irreligious; it transformed even God into a mere artifact of the human mind.

Muir had walked away from his father's Bible fundamentalism, which demanded chapter and verse for every belief. He was losing faith in the Christian story of a supernatural messiah come down from Heaven to live and die among mortals and offer them redemption in another world. But he had not lost his capacity for reverence. Nature had come to supplant written revelation as a source of truth and as the only heaven he needed, and before that nature, an old-fashioned humble, unquestioning reverence remained the only acceptable stance.

To a point, he had converted to natural theology, which since the eighteenth century had taught that reason and science offered a foundation for faith equal or superior to the tradition of written texts. Yet his version of natural theology was overflowing with piety and a sense of mystery, not pride in human understanding. As it was commonly taught, natural theology seemed to him too rationalistic, too conservative, and too anthropocentric.

When he opened Wood's *Botany*, he found the gospel of natural theology represented, with its insistence that the phenomena of nature instruct us in ultimate truths. The field study of plants familiarizes the botanist with the "thoughts of the intelligent Creator." In Wood's opening pages he could read that there is nothing inscrutable or accidental or valueless in the natural world: "Each species is created and established to answer some worthy end in the vast plan; and hence, no individual, animal, or plant is to be regarded by science as insignificant."[31] That much he too believed. But for Wood, the principal of a girls' school in Brooklyn, New York, the study of botany promised to reinforce traditional Christianity. Muir had arrived at a different reading of the evidence. Human salvation is not the central theme of life on earth. The true plot is God's slow, inscrutable unveiling of a natural world that existed before and will exist long after the human species.

Common attitudes on both sides of the Atlantic held that God had created nature for man's use. Sheep existed to provide clothes for people and whales to provide illuminating oil. Animals that had no obvious utility, like noxious insects or alligators, must owe their existence to the Devil, who had gained a foothold in nature through human disobedience in the Garden of Eden, and they could be exterminated.

New geological evidence (not to mention Charles Darwin's theory of evolution, which had appeared less than a decade earlier) had put the age of the earth far back in time and challenged that traditional anthropocentrism. If the history of the universe was much older than humans, how could one conclude that everything had been specially created for that one species? Whales and deep-sea organisms had lived long before humans did and must have their own reasons to exist. Men and women were latecomers, playing small, marginal parts in the cosmic drama.

New perspectives in geology and biology were only one source of Muir's discontent with the conventional religious ideas of his day. Another was his Rousseauist view that piety and humility were giving way to the self-importance of civilized man. Still another was his long-festering resentment of class hierarchies associated mainly with English society. Muir saw the upper classes of England as the enemy, for they had manufactured God in their own image and assumed that their institutions, language, and culture were the acme of civilization. It was they who had turned nature into a storehouse of commodities.

Growing up in Scotland, learning through severe discipline to speak a foreign tongue and ape foreign ways, Muir had early been made aware of the claims of the British Empire and its ruling classes to moral superiority. Undoubtedly he absorbed some of his countrymen's resentment, expressed in the nationalistic and egalitarian poetry of Robert Burns. Now, recovering from illness down on the coast of Florida, he felt all over again what it meant to be a Scot in an Englishman's world. Twenty years in the United States had not erased his feelings of inferiority.

True, his travels through the South had not always evoked a strong egalitarian identification with poor, backcountry folks struggling to survive on the fringes of empire, nor had it evoked a persistent hostility toward the rich and successful. Often he was shocked by the degraded lives of the poor, particularly the "mudsill," or bottommost, class of white southerners. As he wrote of one such family in Florida, the dirt did not so much cover as envelop them, "the most diseased and incurable dirt that I ever saw, evidently desperately chronic and hereditary."[32] He had created his own social hierarchy, based on the standards he had been taught from Dunbar days on, for judging others: the best people were those of any class or nationality who pursued cleanliness, industry, thrift, mechanical aptitude, and literacy. He measured rich and poor alike by those standards. Anyone who fell short, or had never tried to achieve them, Muir tended to regard as an inferior human being.

In his darkest, most misanthropic moments when neither rich nor poor seemed to be worthy inhabitants of nature, all class sympathies (or antipathies) could fly out the door. "Not the world," he wrote to the Merrills and Mooreses on one of his final days in Florida, "but the people who are in it, need to be burned and reconstructed." Surely he did not mean to rain fire and brimstone on those dear friends who had been so kind to him in Indianapolis, or on Sarah Hodgson, who had nursed him so faithfully, or on the many others whom he had befriended along the way. He was lapsing from his more usual benevolent view of the human species. Generally, his sharpest and most fulsome invective was directed not at "people," not even at the most slovenly individuals, but at those who saw themselves as "Lord Man," placed by God above all others and treating the earth as their footstool.[33]

Together, those religious and political sentiments pushed him toward a revolutionary moral position: the Creation was of divine origin, and its purpose, as best he could understand it, was to provide life and happiness for all God's creatures, "not the creation of all for the happiness of one." "Why," he asked himself, "should man value himself as more than a small part of the one great unit of creation?" Every species, plant or animal, had been made in the same way as humans from the dust of the earth. "They are," he wrote, echoing Burns, "earth-born companions and our fellow mortals."[34]

It had taken more than four months of traveling through the South (and a lot of deep thinking while immobilized in Cedar Key) to reach that clarification. Now he could understand why he was nearly killed by malaria. The enemy was not the nature of the South, to be purged and defeated by draining its swamps and burning its vegetation. The cause of illness lay in his own obtuseness; he had not understood that he was never intended to live in such a malaria-inclined climate. He had rambled into a place for which he was not suited, and instead of blaming nature for his illness, he must blame himself.

Admitting that he was unsuited for where he was and for where he was heading in South America threw his whole scheme of travel into a quandary. Although he still hoped to see the lands of Humboldt, which had kept him going for many months, he feared that he might run into other diseases or a recurrence of malaria. Evidently, nature put limits on his movements. The grandiose motto on the flyleaf of his journal ("John Muir, Earth-planet, Universe") had failed to antici-pate those limits. He had started off in a spirit of world exploring, arms outspread as though he could claim the whole globe, but through sad experience had come to believe that every species and every man has an assigned place beyond which he ventures at his peril.

Nonetheless, he decided to continue what he had set out to do. "I suppose these fevers are the price of my walk," he wrote to David, "but I am willing to pay it."[35]

❦

A strong wind from the north carried Muir away from Florida, from the generous Hodgsons, and from his long confinement among the keys. The injury to his eye and the malaria in his blood had each left him lying in sick bed, fearing that his body might never recover from its injuries, learning his vulnerability. Yet in the midst of those trials he had also advanced a thousand miles toward at least an external, spatial independence, most of it by relying on a pair of healthy, sturdy feet. He had shipped back a wonderful array of plants, the proof of scientific self-education. Now things were looking up once more, as he traveled to Cuba on a little timber schooner, the *Island Belle*. Before leaving Florida he had made a new round of teary goodbyes, and, his face lifting toward the Caribbean, hoped to see soon the snow-capped Andes.

The ship plunged and pitched through high seas, with Muir staying on deck for the whole voyage, exulting in the power of the waves. Early the next morning they sailed past the imposing stone ramparts of Morro Castle and into Havana's harbor. The ship's captain persuaded his passenger to accompany him to see the grand flowery plazas and quaint, narrow streets of the city; on that Sunday morning the cathedral bells were ringing, and in the afternoon the bulls were bellowing in the bullfight arena. Muir watched elegant equipages filled with Cuba's beautiful elite classes circle the plazas while pigs and chickens, tied by their legs and slung over the back of a mule, suffered on their way to market. The moral contrast between Catholic piety and genteel wealth, on the one hand, and cruelty to animals, on the other, disturbed him here as much as a similar dissonance had among the Protestant upper classes. By nightfall, thankfully back on ship, Muir was wondering how he could escape this "fearful Spanish confusion."[36]

He spent an entire month on the island, but little of that was devoted to the city, except for visits to its fine botanical garden. Almost every day he was rowed to the less peopled side, where he collected along a ten-mile strip of coast rich in vines, cacti, composites, legumes, and grasses. The indigenous vegetation there seemed to have survived ecological invasion better than the natives of more temperate, northern climates. They seemed better armed with spines and other defenses and more resistant to the trampling hooves and "enslavable plants" introduced by Spanish farmers and stock growers. Here, he was pleased to believe, "Lord Man" had met his match.[37]

The climate, however, was relentlessly hot and humid, and he was not over his malaria. He often felt tired and enervated. He wanted to leave this island quickly, but there were no ships bound for South America and none expected. Even if one had been available, he might not have taken it. More heat, more fever, more torpor lay ahead if he continued toward that destination. It was difficult for him to accept the fact that his body had failed him and that he had lost a capacity for strenuous effort.

His energy revived when he saw a New York newspaper advertising cheap fares to California, where there were cooler forests and mountains and where his health and high spirits might revive. He would have to get to New York first—sailing far north to come back even farther south, to Panama, and from there by ship to San Francisco—but he was in no hurry. He had his whole life ahead of him; no job was pulling on his shirttail, and he felt no aversion to the sea. A detour into winter seemed exactly the medicine he needed. His own body-nature was telling him, against the ambitions he had long formulated in his mind, to abandon course and seek a healthier environment.

It was mid-February when he left Havana on a "fruiter" loaded with a cargo of loose oranges. He sailed as an illegal passenger for he had no formal consular papers and his name was kept off the captain's list. As they beat along the U.S. eastern seaboard, Muir fantasized about hiking across the watery hills made by the waves, across a glassy waterscape without trees or human traces where flocks of flying fishes played. Here was another forbidden country that humans were never designed to walk across or possess. That might change, he allowed in an amendment to his earlier views. "In view of the rapid advancement of our time, no one can tell how far our star may finally be subdued to man's will." As his vessel was tossed about by the ocean's power, he was feeling once more his personal limits and the depths of his ignorance before the planet's vastness; yet he was also feeling uncertain about whether any limits could be placed on the human drive for conquest. "None can tell how far man's knowledge may yet reach."[38]

They sailed into New York harbor on a frosty day late in February, with a cold wind sweeping across their bow. He stood shivering and gaping at the city's snow-covered ground and leafless trees, but the cold felt strangely delicious to his fever-wracked body. Venturing ashore to unlimber his bones, he quickly felt lost in the immense metropolis. The ten-year-old Central Park, designed by Frederick Law Olmsted and Calvert Vaux, beckoned, but he did not dare to go see it for fear of losing his way back. For ten days he hovered about the waterfront, until his next vessel was ready to leave. Forty dollars sent from his home account got him a cheap steerage ticket and the company of a "barbarous mob" on their way to California. Twenty dollars more got him a dozen large maps on rollers that he was persuaded he might sell for a profit (a foolish investment he later thought). Gathering up his gear, he was on his way once more through glittering phosphorescent seas, back to a tropical clime, but this time skirting Cuba for the coast of Central America.

He got only brief glimpses of dense emerald rainforest from the open cars of the Panama Railroad puffing across the narrow isthmus. Responding to the California gold rush, work gangs had built a railroad from Aspinwall (Colón) following the Chagres River most of the way. For ten dollars Muir could buy a second-class ticket. A "riotous exuberance" of vegetation sheltering populations of toucans, howler monkeys, sloths, and jaguars flashed before his eyes, but all too soon he was stepping down from the train at the Plaza Cinco Mayo, looking for another wharf and the steamer *Nebraska* bound for San Francisco.

On 29 March 1868, he passed through the portals of the Golden Gate, a place he had not envisioned as his destination eight months earlier when he had set out from Indianapolis. Nor did he realize that this time he had arrived home. California would prove to suit him so well, body and soul, that he would never live anywhere else.

CHAPTER 6

Paradise Found

In the heyday of the Spanish Empire the lands of Florida and California had attracted conquistadors, missionaries, and other explorers as fabulous and mythic destinations, but they were worlds apart. Although each was a warm, sunny place cooled by ocean breezes, the long peninsula of Florida was a wet green pancake located near the main currents of transatlantic commerce and open to all the storms and currents of the Gulf of Mexico. California, in contrast, stood far off as an isolated and mysterious rampart, sheltering under its high mountain walls a string of arid, sun-drenched, low-lying basins. In the track of those old conquistadors came the explorer Muir, looking for exotic plants. Florida, a state in the Union since 1845, had proved to be an ordeal for him, a place of near-death rather than Ponce de Léon's fountain of youth. Still recovering from malaria, he approached the coast of California, which had been admitted as a state in 1850, in a still hopeful mood.

This time he found a genuine, health-filled paradise on earth, but one that offered far more than health or mythology, far more than he expected. In California he discovered a place that laid such a hold on his affections that he could never leave. It became his true and only home, however much he would travel during the rest of his life. Yosemite Valley was the spiritual center of that home, a place he knew he would love even before he left Indiana, for its unique qualities of shelter, light, and soaring grandeur of rock. But the whole state held out an irresistible appeal, and for more than aesthetic reasons. Here was a place he had found all on his own, with no connection to his family or his past life, where he could start anew. He had been looking for somewhere to put down roots, but they had to be his own roots and nobody else's. California was a home he did not inherit from his ancestors, and that fact made it all the more precious to him.

As soon as he landed in San Francisco, he abruptly departed in the company of a young cockney immigrant named Chilwell, whom he met aboard ship. The famed city by the bay held no interest for Muir; he startled a workman on the waterfront by declaring that they were seeking not a job or opportunity, but anyplace that was wild. Straightaway the two companions sauntered southward along the lower of those stony walls, the Coastal Range. Once again, Muir took an indirect route toward his destination. He was heading for the famed Yosemite Valley in the Sierra Nevada, the standard route to which was by steamship through the Delta and up the San Joaquin River to Stockton, thence by stagecoach and horseback. Instead, they decided to walk down the state to a point where they could cross the coastal mountains and then follow upstream the Merced River, which flowed out of the Sierra like a river flowing out of Eden.

Muir later described the air he breathed along the way as a "flavor" to be savored—"a *taste*, that thrilled through the lungs [and] throughout every tissue of the body." Good life-giving medicine, the air seemed to get better and better as they crossed the Coastal Range at Pacheco Pass, a series of smooth, swelling hills still green from the winter rains. They descended cool ravines crowded with ferns and rushing streams, climbed grassy slopes dotted with live oaks, hiking up and down and up again. At last they stood looking eastward across the sun-filled Central Valley, which ran four hundred miles north to south and almost a hundred miles across—a vast plain of rivers, sloughs, and grasslands. The distant Sierra rose like a smooth, unbroken wall of dark-green forests and granite peaks, shutting out America and the rest of the world. It was, recalled Muir, "a scene of peerless grandeur."[1]

What footprints had humans left on this place by 1868, the year Muir arrived? California had been the home of Indians for millennia, of Spanish-speaking padres and ranchers for a century, and of Anglo-Americans mainly since the gold rush days of '49. Once several hundred thousand natives had lived in the state, but due to disease, enslavement, and violence their numbers had dwindled to seven thousand. It would take a keen-eyed botanist or archeologist to find their traces below in the valley—no Yokuts or Miwok settlements were visible. As for the Hispanics, the very name Pacheco Pass betokened their presence, but beyond putting such names on a map their impact mainly lay behind him, closer to the coast and in the vicinity of their surviving missions, not in the inland valley.

California counted more than a half million residents, but mostly they clustered around San Francisco Bay, in the capital city of Sacramento, in mine-rich Nevada County, with a small portion living to the south in Los Angeles (a mere 15,000 out of the total). Below him in the Central Valley a good telescope might have spotted cattle grazing along the streams or scattered fields of wheat planted in virgin soil. But the Anglo footprint was still faint over much of the state. Only six million acres, out of nearly a hundred million, were improved farmland.

That footprint would soon get much larger and heavier. Already Chinese and Irish laborers were laying down a transcontinental railroad line that would be finished by May 1869, opening a flood of trade and travel from the east. Over the next half century California would gain another three million inhabitants, and Los Angeles would become its largest metropolis. The Central Valley would be transformed by irrigation into the world's largest and most profitable fruit and vegetable patch.

Descending from the pass, the travelers plunged into an unfenced prairie of bunch grasses and wildflowers that stretched away like a knee-deep living carpet. At Hill's Ferry on the San Joaquin, Muir marked off a square yard and, mixing science with wonder, sat down to inventory its vegetation. He carefully counted a total of 7,260 flower heads in that space (or 165,912 if the multiple heads of the predominant *Compositae* were counted separately), representing 16 species, in addition to thousands of grass panicles and a million tiny mosses. The dominant color in the tapestry was solar gold, with a purple and green woof running through it. Here, he wrote to Indianapolis friends, is the true Florida, the true land of flowers. "Here it is not as in our great western prairie, flowers sprinkled in the grass, but grass in the flowers."[2] But, alas, those flowers were, compared to Cuba's or

Florida's hot, thorny gardens, unarmed and unable to defend themselves against man and his livestock.

California instantly appealed to Muir as a world where primeval innocence still could be found, despite its long human history, a world long protected by its mountain ramparts from modern destructive forces and offering peace, beauty, and independence. On his long walk through the South he had carried Milton's "Paradise Lost" and found in Adam and Eve's exit from the Garden of Eden a story of personal psychological meaning more than religious significance; so too had he left his Wisconsin-based family security and had felt anxious as he entered a more dangerous and uncertain state of self-reliance. Entering the unspoiled Central Valley, however, he could feel the tension and fear leaving him. He might well have cited the companion volume, "Paradise Regained," with its opening words so appropriate to his sense of new beginnings: "I who erewhile the happy garden sung, / By one man's disobedience lost, now sing / Recovered Paradise to all mankind, / . . . And Eden raised in the waste wilderness." The blind Puritan poet, however, never imagined such a place actually surviving on earth, with real flowers, real plains, or real mountains. For Muir, California immediately seemed like the real thing—a this-worldly paradise that could be breathed, measured, and slept on, as he did on the valley floor.[3]

He and Chilwell followed their plan of ascending the Merced, passing by Coulterville and arriving, after a month of walking, at Yosemite Valley in early May. Along the route Muir's semi-dormant malaria briefly flared up, slowing them down for several days. They picked up an army shotgun to protect themselves against bears, and Muir, testing the gun at a target fixed on a shanty, accidentally shot his companion, who had thought himself safe inside the building. It was not a serious wound—merely a bit of birdshot in Chilwell's shoulder—but it was the closest they came to true danger. The only bear they saw was in Yosemite, where they camped for more than a week; it shambled off, leaving them unharmed but fearful it might return in the night. They bought a piece of bear meat, which Chilwell, starved for protein, nearly devoured. So much for Muir's first experience with the incomparable valley and the nearby Mariposa Grove of giant sequoias—natural wonders that would come to be linked to his name above anyone else's. He came, he trembled at the sight of a bear, and he left again, writing little about any of it.[4]

After touring Yosemite they went looking for work. Muir accepted, if only barely, that to live in nature he must also live in an economy that required cash to purchase food—hard cash that must come from selling one's labor. The only jobs readily available were in that narrow settlement belt where the Central Valley met the foothills, and most of those jobs were in small-scale mining or a nascent agriculture. So he became a farm laborer, earning his bread as Adam did by the sweat of his brow. A farmer hired him to drive a wagon alongside a newfangled "header," which clipped the heads of wheat and tossed them into the wagon box. After harvest, Muir tried his hand at breaking wild horses, piloting a ferry over the Merced, and shearing sheep with a multiracial gang of men. In the fall an Irish immigrant, John Connel, commonly known as Smoky Jack, offered him a dollar a day and board to look after a flock of sheep through the coming winter. The sheep were folded in a place called Twenty Hill Hollow, a cluster of grassy knobs between Snelling and LaGrange, and Muir went off to take charge.

An unusual heavy rain was falling when he arrived at the dingy black cabin with leaking roof that would be his hermitage for many months. A ring of old shoes, stove ashes, and sheep carcasses circled the cabin, and wild pigs roamed the yard looking for food. His meals consisted of tea, beans, flapjacks, and sourdough bread that he had to learn through trial and error how to make. In the mornings the sheep, eighteen hundred of them, went streaming out of their corral and over the hills, accompanied by a couple of sheep dogs and the shepherd; amazingly, they docilely came back in the evening, minus those that were lost to eagles or coyotes. Despite the poor accommodations, this job was not so onerous after all, he decided, and would allow him ample time to carry on his studies of the wild flora and fauna. The native pronghorns had been driven off, but there were still plenty of jackrabbits, ground squirrels, and bears, although all of them were diminishing fast from the poison baits and traps set out by the sheep men.

Muir, ever the scholar, carried a few books and a journal with him as he kept an occasional eye on the flocks. Sheep, he wrote, were

Muir entitled this drawing, "View of the Sierra from Twenty Hill Hollow Feb 18/69. Connecting link of year flower circle in foreground." (H-A, JMP)

"unhappy creatures, dirty & wretched, miserably misshappen [*sic*] & misbegotten & I am hardly sorry to see them eaten by those superior beings, the wolves." During a night of winter storm, he lost a hundred of his charges. "Poor unfriended creatures," he wrote; "Man has injured every animal that he has touched."[5]

The job of foothills pastoralist stuck him in the middle of two contrasting realities: on the one hand, the squalid cabin, bleating sheep, and white bones littering the ground, and on the other, songs of meadowlarks, a great arching sky, the spreading grasslands. He struggled to ignore the former, dismal side and concentrate on the latter, joyful side, to keep alive that first impression of a California unmarred by human degradation. He reveled in this still open country that could satisfy his hunger for freedom from "the tyranny of man," whose cities, factories, clocks, and calendars had all been left behind. In his long daily walks, he wrote, "there has been no human method—no law—no rule."[6] Man's efforts to dominate nature through technology, to domesticate and civilize, had too often turned out flawed, ugly, and disorderly. But so far little of that disappointing outcome had reached this place; here were unfenced plains, here were unconquered mountains at his back. Here he could pretend that, unlike the sheep commodity, he was a native butterfly flitting from flower to flower.

No one in the Muir family knew exactly where he was until midsummer, months after his ship had landed. They had sent letters to San Francisco, all of which came back unopened. The first to learn his whereabouts were the Galloways, who passed on the news to the others. On 14 July Muir let them know where he was and sent brother David a full account of California, this "splendid country . . . [flowing] with more of milk and more of honey than ever did old Canaan in its happiest prime." He had come at last to the best part of his travels, he declared, and was feeling completely mended. On 1 January 1869 he sent New Year's greetings from Twenty Hill Hollow to Maggie and John Reid, complaining about his "great mutton family" but predicting that he would not be a herder for long.[7] Exactly what he would do next, or where he would go, he did not say, because he did not know.

Whatever he decided would have to depend on the local prospects for employment. Work, although necessary for survival, would require too much attention and teach him too little about nature. Mainly, the available jobs taught the laborer how to operate a machine or use an axe; they did not open one's eyes to natural beauty or teach one how nature works. Knowing the natural world required hours of close observation. This was Muir's most difficult dilemma: he must find manual work to survive, often hard, bone-wearying work, but he also had to find enough freedom from that toil to study, observe, and understand truly and well how nature in this California wonderland created a harmony out of diversity.

Sharpening the dilemma was the fact that, in this half-wild, half-barbaric country, work, like society in general, was commonly violent, destructive, unregulated, or lawless. He would have to work in a state of near anarchy. Many had come there to escape the rule of law; in a sense, he had done the same, reveling in a state of "no law—nor rule." But there was a difference: he carried within him a set of moral restraints acquired from Dunbar days on, while many of his neighbors, who had arrived during the gold rush, did not always possess those inner checks. For them work often meant the unrestrained exploitation of fellow human beings and the natural world.

Such was the critical view of California foothill life offered by Frederick Law Olmsted, the architect-in-chief of Central Park, head of the U.S. Sanitary Commission during the first part of the Civil War, and manager of the Mariposa gold-mining estate at Bear Valley, just twenty miles east of Muir's sheepherder cabin. Olmsted did not succeed in putting the estate on a sound financial footing but during his two-year stay accomplished much. He played a crucial role in the preservation of Yosemite Valley and, less well known, gathered notes for a book that was never published on "The Pioneer Condition and the Drift of Civilization in America." Reading it would have given Muir plenty of insight into the society for which he was laboring.

The California foothills witnessed a pattern that had unfolded in thousands of raw, new settlements on the frontier of American expansion. At the pattern's center stood the pioneer, celebrated in legend and art for his (and her) fortitude, independence, and egalitarianism. More often than not, the pioneer had come from the most restless, marginalized classes of Europe or the eastern seaboard and brought an antisocial attitude with him. Along the way he acquired racial prejudices against African Americans, Indians, Chinese, and Mexicans, his immediate competitors in the struggle to acquire land. Olmsted recorded lynching and shooting in the Bear Valley vicinity that went unpunished, since most of the victims were not white. The pioneers were a conquering horde that had never been wholly civilized and had regressed even further on the edges of settlement.

Civilization, Olmsted argued, was not the exclusive property of the rich or well born, or of the white race. It belonged to whoever showed a quality of "communitiveness," a capacity for living with others, for honesty, civility, temperance, and self-discipline. By that definition California seemed wanting. "I find not merely less of a community but less possibility of community, . . . here among my neighbors of all kinds than in any other equal body of men, I ever saw."[8] The human species, Olmsted concluded, was divided into wanderers, those who rejected the bonds of community, and settlers, those who worked to strengthen them.

On which side of that divide did Muir stand? On neither exclusively, for he was both a wanderer *and* a would-be settler. He had a high capacity for "communitiveness," yet Muir resented the galling pressures to conform, the restrictions on radical thoughts and feelings, the power of hierarchy to separate people from one another and from nature that civilization also represented. How to straddle that divide between freedom and civilization, how to belong here without losing a sense of independence, would worry his mind over the next decade, until finally he would find a permanent home in the state.

If Muir needed further tutoring in the communitarian spirit, he could turn above all others he had known in his youth to the pair of Carrs, especially Jeanne, who had been at once sister, mother, friend, fellow nature lover, and spiritual guide. Suddenly she and her husband showed up to share his life in California, making it more than ever an appealing home for him. In August 1868 she wrote that Ezra had resigned from the Wisconsin State University and was looking for a position somewhere in the East, Argentina, or California. She was presently sojourning in her girlhood home of Vermont, dreaming idealistically as ever of a day when "there will be one great nationality, *one great family*, where so lately were many opposed and conflicting nations." Muir did all he could to persuade the Carrs to move west and explore with him the marvelous variety of California landscapes. "I doubt if in all the world mans comforts & necessities can be more easily & abundantly supplied than in Cal[iforni]a," he promised; but then he warned, for Professor Carr's sake, that "pure science is a most unmarketable commodity in California—conspicuous energetic unmixed materialism rules supreme in all classes."[9]

Ignoring that warning, the Carrs decided to move west the next February, taking a big risk, for they came without the offer of a teaching position (although one materialized soon at the state university, then located in Oakland but relocated to Berkeley in 1872). After they arrived Muir would not see them for several more years, but letters flew back and forth with increasing regularity. Over a hundred letters would pass between Muir and Jeanne over the next decade or so, a quarter of them during the year 1872 alone. Far from being private love letters filled with tender intimacies and expressions of undying love, they were open, public documents, for Jeanne showed them around to her husband and friends, urging everyone to get to know this remarkable young man.[10]

She resumed her project of turning her protégé into a cultural force, a prophet leading people to value nature and to worship the spirit behind it. She wanted him nearby in Oakland, not in the mountains or foothills but down the street from her as he had been in Madison days. A worthy cause as much as a friend, Muir appeared, in her mind, as an unfinished man who needed her encouraging, directing hand. She must get him reunited to society. "You must be social," she wrote, "you *must make friends among the materialists*, lest your highest pleasures taken selfishly become impure. I could envy you your solitude, but there may be too much of it."[11]

As he had done before, Muir poured out his feelings to her, but often he ignored her advice. He found her the most sympathetic person he had ever met, but still he tried to keep his distance from the society she offered and did not feel ready for the role that she wanted him to assume. When she sent him some of her poems inspired by the nature-loving Baptist preacher Walter R. Brooks, he returned enthusiastic praise. "[I] am beginning to know how fully congenial you are," he wrote. "Would that you could share my mountain enjoyments! In all my wanderings through Nature's beauty, . . . you are the first to meet me, and I often speak to you as verily present in the flesh."[12] But tellingly, she was not actually present, which is the way he wanted their relationship to be—close in spirit but not confined to her parlor.

In July 1869 she came looking for him in Yosemite, but by then he was miles above her in forests and meadows, trailing sheep; an opportunity to see the place together would have to wait until four summers later. When his contract with "Smoky Jack" Connel ended, Muir found a job with another sheep man, Pat Delaney, a former Catholic seminarian and Forty-niner—a tall, bony figure whom Muir called "Don Quixote." He was by many lights a good, generous man, and he glimpsed in his employee a creative talent worth nurturing. The new job was to help drive 2,050 sheep to the headwaters of the Merced and Tuolumne rivers, an area of open range and free grass located nine thousand feet above sea level and to the north of Yosemite Valley. Delaney needed someone to watch his hired watcher, a loutish and unreliable shepherd named Billy. Muir would have little responsibility, he promised, except keeping Billy and the St. Bernard guard dog Carlo on the job, leaving plenty of time to gather plants and climb mountains.

They left the Delaney ranch at LaGrange on 3 June, with the boss leading the way, and a Chinese and an Indian hired hand along to drive the sheep to the high country. If Muir carried any books on this excursion, he did not record their titles; most likely, he had shed his New Testament and Milton by this point, while *Wood's Botany* was useless on this far side of the continent and Burns's poetry he knew by heart. He and the flock would not come down until 22 September, minus twenty-five head lost to bears, rattlesnakes, various other mishaps, and the camp menu.

Summer transhumance was new among California sheep men, and routes were still being worked out. Pushing the sheep at a rate of one mile per day, they arrived at their first central camp at the foot of Pilot Peak Ridge. Here Delaney and his extra hands turned back home, leaving Billy and Muir alone, but promising to return with food provisions in mid-summer. After a couple of weeks, they managed to get the flock up to Tamarack Flat, and then, after another lull, they struck the Mono Trail, which crossed the Sierra to Mono Lake and the Great Basin. Along the way they passed between Mount Hoffman and Lake Tenaya and forded the Yosemite Creek above the point where it plunges spectacularly over the Yosemite Valley rim. Muir spent the latter part of July making daily jaunts to the edge of the great gorge, looking down on its sheltered gardens from the height of North Dome and sketching the ring of icy peaks rising to the east— the Cathedral Range and, towering beyond, the 13,000-foot summits of Mount Lyell and Mount Dana. Their end of trail was the lush Tuolumne Meadows, where they pitched camp in early August at Soda Springs.

Muir kept to his journal-writing habit during that summer excursion, but this was one journal he did not preserve in its original form. Nearly twenty years later he revised it and threw the original away. Then, in 1910 he made a further and final revision, which became one of his most engaging books, *My First Summer in the Sierra*, published the next year. For all its seeming spontaneity and immediacy, the printed version was a much-labored over and retrospective account. The record of actual events did not change through all the permutations, but what was going through Muir's mind as he recalled those events may have been heavily filtered through time.[13]

What seems clear is that his Sierra summer awakened the deepest and most intense passion of his life, a long moment of ecstasy that he would try to remember and relive to the end of his days. His whole body, not his eyes alone, felt the beauty around him. Every sense became intensely alive. He bounded over rocks and up mountain sides, hung over the edge of terrifying precipices, his face drenched in the spray of waterfalls, waded through meadows deep in lilies, laughed at the exuberant antics of grasshoppers and chipmunks, stroked the bark of towering incense cedars and sugar pines, and slept each night on an aromatic mattress of spruce boughs. Each thing he saw or felt seemed joined to the rest in exquisite harmony. "When we try to pick out anything by itself," he wrote, "we find it hitched to everything else in the universe."[14] Nature was all one body, beating with a heart like his own, and more intensely than ever before in his life he felt his own heart beating in unison. He experienced, in the fullest sense yet, a profound conversion to the religion of nature.

The closest equivalent to Muir's summer of bliss was William Wordsworth's first years in the Lake District. Muir was thirty-one years old in 1869; Wordsworth was twenty-nine when he moved into Dove Cottage and, from its doorway, began daily walks across the meadows and mountains. Both had left behind a society that seemed severely flawed in morality and aesthetics. Both discovered in the high country a renewal of faith, optimism, and joy. Conventional faith had ceased to move them, but in the presence of a wilder nature they felt spiritually renewed, recovering a piety that cold, bookish church doctrines had almost succeeded in stifling. Wordsworth called it "natural piety," a faith without doctrines or theology that unmediated nature alone could evoke or satisfy. In 1802 he wrote these lines that anticipated completely Muir's own experience: "My heart leaps up when I behold / A rainbow in the sky: So was it when my life began; / So is it now I am a man . . . I could wish my days to be / Bound each to each by natural piety." For Muir a similar wish came true that summer as he drifted "about these love-monument mountains, glad to be a servant of servants in so holy a wilderness."[15]

Muir had undoubtedly read Wordsworth in Dunbar, in frontier Wisconsin, and during his college period in Madison. The two men shared a common faith, as expressed by Muir: "Everything turns into religion, all the world seems a church and the mountains altars."[16] There were, however, bound to be differences separating the two men—differences in era, experience, as well as literary talent. Muir was not the great philosophical poet that Wordsworth was. He found his Wordsworthian faith nearly two decades after the poet was dead. Moreover, his Sierra was radically unlike the Lake District. The Sierra Nevada was a far wilder country, with prowling grizzlies, magnificent natural forests that had never been logged, and alpine meadows that had never, until recently, known the teeth or hooves of domestic grazers. For Wordsworth, on the other hand, sheep and shepherds belonged in nature and had lived together for hundreds of years, forming a pastoral tradition out of which he drew his poetic shepherd Michael, a man of virtue, feeling, and intelligence. No one like that appeared in Muir's California. There, shepherds, like their flocks, were a gang of vandals laying waste to beauty.

Billy, for example, was hopelessly incapable of any appreciation of the natural world. The profusion of flowers that sheep destroyed was, in his view, simply fodder, and Yosemite Valley was "a d—d good place to keep away from." Compared to the clean-living animals of the forest, he was, as Muir described him, a perambulating garbage dump: his pockets were filled with cooked mutton that dripped grease over his whole body, his shooting iron, and his garments; to his rancid trousers clung ancient bits of rotted wood, bark, hair, wool, insect wings, mineral grains, pollen, and miscellaneous plants. Then, he was far from a faithful shepherd; as Delaney feared, Billy decided to quit after a dispute over herding methods, temporarily leaving only Muir and the dog in charge of the flock.[17]

Muir's dislike of sheep intensified that summer, and for their destructive effect on the native vegetation he called them "hoofed locusts."[18] Two thousand of them massed together and driven through any territory would leave only the trees unscathed; everything at ground level would be chewed, digested, and stomped to dust. Even if plant life recovered, it was irrevocably changed, and the land was cut up by criss-crossing trails and corrugated hillsides. Here was no soft, smooth greensward shaped by generations of flocks watched over by careful stewardship. The Sierra was highly vulnerable to ecological assault.

Muir understood that he could not hold the wooly animals responsible for their destructiveness, nor even shepherds like Billy hired to watch over them. This was a profit-seeking industry far more exploitative of men and land than the more traditional sheep farming of northern Britain. In Scotland, he pointed out, the shepherd was as well trained for his work as his collie. He watched over his own small flock, was never far from home, and often carried books along to read. In contrast, "the California sheep owner is in haste to get rich, and often does," Muir noted, and wealth quickly acquired created a lust for more, "dimming or shutting out almost everything worth seeing."[19] The flocks were too large, the hired work force was unhappy, and the food was bad, and sometimes too scanty to live on. That summer in fact, while Muir was trying to feast on nature's splendor, their mundane food supply nearly ran out; they had no flour or bread for weeks and were forced to eat a nauseating diet of mutton and tea until Delaney showed up with provisions. Muir held no grudge against that particular owner, indeed liked and appreciated him, but the economy of sheep raising on this frontier was not to be compared with Scots or English traditions.

Another distinguishing feature of this California pastoral life was the occasional appearance of Indian bands. The Delaney crew first encountered a group of Miwoks (or "Diggers," as they were called for their supposed root-grubbing habits) at Browns Flat. Muir observed that, in contrast to the white man, "the Indians walk softly and hurt the landscape hardly more than the birds and squirrels." Their main effect, he went on, was through burning the vegetation, a practice that kept the landscape more open than it otherwise would have been. So far Muir was being complimentary to the Indians. Then an old woman with a basket on her back walked silently into their camp. Dressed in dirty calico rags acquired from white men rather than her native garb, she was a repellent figure and as "unnatural" in his eyes as the beribboned tourists riding their ponies into Yosemite Valley.[20]

Weeks later, as he hiked down Bloody Canyon to see Mono Lake, Muir came upon a party of Monos. Their base lay east of the mountains, but they were on their way westward to harvest acorns in Yosemite, now that their old rivals the Miwoks were in decline and could not keep them out. They surrounded Muir on the trail, begging for whiskey or tobacco, their hands and faces lined with dirt, clutching at his garments, filling him with disgust. They seemed a blot on the wild beauty of the canyon, but for Muir the cause of their hideousness was not their race, for they were no more repellent than the white shepherd Billy, but rather their all-too-human dissonance with nature. "Perhaps if I knew them better I should like them better," he wrote. "The worst thing about them is their uncleanliness. Nothing truly wild is unclean."[21]

Muir struggled with his feelings about California's Indians, the first he had ever met up close or witnessed making their way through the land. He was saddened by their low condition and embarrassed by his feelings of repulsion. They were part of humankind, he acknowledged, but people in general often depressed him by their frequent inability to harmonize with the rest of nature. Hard as it was to summon any feelings of brotherhood toward the natives he encountered, he proceeded on his way, repeating to himself Robert Burns's hopeful egalitarianism: "It's coming yet, for a' that, that man to man, the warld o'er, shall brothers be for a' that."[22]

California, even in its purest, most unspoiled reaches, could be a darker place for Muir than the Lake District was for Wordsworth—darker in its message about human beings. Wordsworth found it easier to idealize local, indigenous, rural society. His disillusionment came from within as he fought off the fear that the glory in the earth must diminish with age. Muir, on the other hand, was not worried about hanging on to his faith in nature, which remained strong the rest of his life, but rather about finding enough reason to hope that mankind, however local or simple or in direct contact with nature, could ever match the grandeur of the mountains. Both men had seen "the light." The English poet had had glimpses of a nature "appareled in celestial light," but it was a light that dimmed as he grew older. The Scots American naturalist had discovered what he called "the range of light," the High Sierra, a light that would never go out for him, but it was a light dimmed by a human shadow.

⚬━◆━⚬

Summer over, Muir announced that he would resume his botanical expedition to South America via Cuba. He wrote David that he would leave in a few weeks and offered a loan of five hundred dollars, or nearly two years' worth of earnings, money he would not need for the journey. His pockets were flush and overflowing. When the time of departure came, however, Muir realized that the summer in the Sierra highlands had changed his outlook and altered his priorities. Instead of going to the Amazon, he decided to move into Yosemite Valley for the winter, for he was eager to experience it through a season of snow and cold. The tourists, he knew, would all be gone then, leaving him and the few year-round residents in peaceful silence. Over one thousand tourists had entered the Valley in 1869; double that number would come annually within another ten years, but they came for the dry, sunny days of summer. In their absence he could get to know this heart of the Sierra far better, and then next spring perhaps he could take up the Humboldt trail at last.

Soon after coming into the valley in November, in the company of an orphaned lad named Harry Randall whom Muir had befriended at Delaney's ranch, Muir was offered employment by hotel proprietor James Hutchings. The job would last almost two years. Unexpectedly, the valley gave him a home to call his own, introduced him to some of the nation's most interesting minds, and drove South America indefinitely out of his head. As he explained to David, he was now "locked up in an house not made with hands whose walls are a mile in height & beautiful as those of the New Jerusalem." Yosemite appealed as a natural house to live in that was also the house of God. Since leaving the Midwest, Muir had not been at church a single time, "yet this glorious valley might well be called a church."[23]

Compared to the plains below and the highlands where he had spent the summer, Yosemite Valley offered a more enclosed, domestic-like nature—a sense of peaceful refuge. In that quality it epitomized what so many people wanted out of California as a whole: a home in nature that had clearly defined boundaries, a wild grandeur that paradoxically sheltered and nurtured, a sense of the sublime mixed with a more rustic kind of lived-in beauty.

One entered the secluded valley through a well-forested threshold and then descended to a broad, level floor where the Merced River meandered gently through soft green meadows. It was like one great room six miles deep and a mile or so across. Near the entrance stood the massive buttress of El Capitan with Cathedral Rocks and Bridalveil Fall on the other side, framing a doorway made for gods. Next along the north wall stood Three Brothers, the 2,400-foot cascade of Yosemite Falls, Indian Canyon, Royal Arches, and North Dome. Along the south wall ranged Sentinel Rock, Glacier Point, Vernal Falls, Nevada Falls, and the straight vertical face of Half Dome (or in the Indian language, Tissiack) rising nearly a mile above the floor. Far in the back, behind a curtain of trees, lay the stillness of Mirror Lake, a reminder that this valley had once been entirely under water, when the sound of plashing falls echoed even more loudly through the chamber.

The first careful plat of the valley floor, made a few years before Muir arrived, categorized 745 acres as meadowland, or a fifth of the whole. The rest was forested lands of three types: old-growth stands of Ponderosa pine, incense cedar, white fir, Douglas fir, and black oak, most of them dating before 1600 A.D.; younger stands of pine and cedar that had taken root around 1800, when the resident Indians had temporarily fled to avoid an epidemic; and clumps of conifers that had been growing only since 1860, marking the coming of the white man.

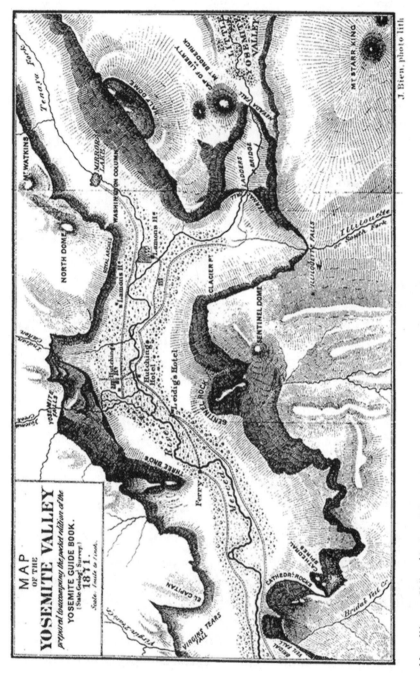

Map of Yosemite Valley. (Geological Survey of California, The Yosemite Guide-Book, 1870)

Before that invasion the natives had set grass fires to keep down the coniferous competition and encourage the oaks, which were a crucial food source. Heavy natural flooding and high winds during the winter of 1867–68 had opened up vistas too. In this great airy room humans and nature alike had been rearranging the furnishings for a long while, yet the chamber itself stood imposing and intact.[24]

The Indians who had long made this valley a home were a branch of the Miwoks called the Ahwahneeches, or people of the gaping mouth. Over thirty historic villages and campsites would one day be identified, most of them shifting clusters of cedar-bark huts sheltering a population that at one time may have totaled as much as a thousand. There was no gold to attract miners and, if there had been, no easy way into its hidden haven. But when some of the Miwoks made the mistake of raiding gold mining camps down in the foothills, whether out of desperation or opportunism, the state authorized a militia, the Mariposa Battalion, under the successive command of James Savage and John Boling, to threaten, punish, and bring all Miwoks, the innocent and guilty alike, down to a common reservation on the Fresno River. With that purpose in mind whites first entered Yosemite in 1851. They chased the Ahwahneeches out of the place, only to have them quietly filter back in again. In the end it was not the whites who delivered the coup de grace to the Ahwahneeches, but the Monos, who raided the valley two years later and crushed the skulls of the chief Tenaya and many of his men, leaving only a dispirited remnant to carry on the culture.[25]

Maps showed a single "Indian village" surviving in Yosemite decades after those brutal years, but quickly whites began to move in, take control, and stake claims. A large, taciturn giant named James Lamon was the first to build a log cabin and lay out a small farm, in 1859 in the upper end of the valley. Far more conspicuous a presence was James Hutchings, a short, bald-headed, and temperamental entrepreneur who, born in England in 1820, had found his way to the gold fields, led the first tourist party into Yosemite, founded *Hutchings' California Magazine*, which helped make the valley known to the public, and, in 1864, bought the Upper Hotel, a ramshackle, two-story wooden structure not far from the base of Yosemite Falls. His wife

Elvira Sproat Hutchings and her mother came along to help manage the business. Their daughter Florence (Floy, or Squirrel) was the first white child born in the valley, and a younger daughter named Gertrude (Cosie) and a handicapped son William completed the family. Downstream stood two more hotels, Black's and Leidig's, with assorted bridges, ladders for viewing the falls, dusty roads, hay meadows for feeding livestock, rickety fences, and a canvas-sided saloon. Already the valley floor had begun to acquire a familiar American frontier look.

Muir's task, as he settled in for the winter, was to embellish that look by cutting up logs for further construction. The hotel needed extensive repairs and additions, and there were cottages to build. First he must get Hutchings's new sawmill to work, a familiar chore for this veteran millwright, although it took several months. Choosing a shady location a quarter of a mile from the hotel, at the base of Yosemite Falls, he dammed the creek and dug a mill race to a water wheel, powering the saw, and then borrowed Lamon's oxen to drag logs to the site. The logs were pines that had been leveled in the previous winter's storm. By spring the sawdust began to fly and clean new boards to stack up. Among the first uses for the boards was a handsome little

Muir drawing of his Yosemite Valley cabin, 1869. (H-A, JMP)

cabin Muir built for himself near his work, at a cost of three dollars. Here he slept in a hammock suspended from the rafters, above a stream running through the room like a miniature Yosemite and ferns poking up through the flooring.

Hutchings assigned other work to Muir and Randall, including milking the cows, tending a flock of turkeys, and installing wooden partitions in the hotel (replacing thin muslin curtains that gave little privacy to guests). Then he assigned the small workforce to "take charge of the ladies" while he went off to Washington, D.C., to press his claim to ownership. He thought he was entitled by right of preemption to 320 acres squarely in the valley's center.[26] Elsewhere, pioneers had done what he had done: broken out new ground in advance of the land surveyors, or purchased someone else's improvements, and squatted there until they could file for ownership. The bachelor Lamon was filing a claim on 378 acres. Thus the accumulation of wealth was supposed to proceed in this magical valley as elsewhere in the nation, turning Yosemite by a little labor into private property.

If Muir had any opinions on his boss's claim, he kept them to himself, but his correspondent Jeanne Carr was all in favor of giving the center of the valley to Hutchings if it meant keeping roads and tourist masses out. She had stayed in his hotel and felt that he cared deeply about the beauty outside his door and would be passionate about preserving it. The valley was in good hands. Others were not so eager, however, to give Hutchings such a monopoly over so spectacular a national treasure. According to Josiah Dwight Whitney, director of the state geological survey, privatizing the valley would create another Niagara Falls debacle, where runaway development had turned a place of uncommon natural grandeur into tawdry commercialism, "a gigantic institution for fleecing the public." The valley, he wrote in *The Yosemite Book* (1864), a handsome and eloquent travel guide, had been designated "a National public park" and should be kept as such. Fortunately, Whitney's view prevailed, and in 1872 the U.S. Supreme Court turned Hutchings's land claim down. Legislators then appropriated a generous $24,000 to buy out his investments, with another $12,000 for Lamon and $22,000 for Black of Black's Hotel, and the valley remained forever the property of the American people.[27]

In 1864, Abraham Lincoln had signed a bill giving Yosemite Valley (the floor, walls, and land running one mile back from the rims) and the Mariposa Grove of sequoias, together an area of nearly 40,000 acres, to the state of California to preserve for public use and recreation. Some have argued, as Whitney's words above suggest, that this was the nation's first national park, predating the establishment of Yellowstone National Park by eight years. It was indeed set aside as a park, but it was not a national one in the sense of being owned or managed by the federal government. Henceforth it was to be state property under the control of Sacramento politicians; a Yosemite Commission was appointed by the governor to act as stewards—eight men in all, including Whitney, Israel Raymond of the Pacific Steamship Company, and Frederick Law Olmsted of the Mariposa Estate.

Only slightly before the Yosemite grant a wasteland on Manhattan Island had been turned into Central Park, also a publicly owned piece of nature, however much enhanced and restored by art. The two places had a lot in common. Like Central Park, Yosemite was seen as a quiet, bounded sanctuary set apart from the bustle of modern life. Each was meant to be a place where anyone should be free to enter and enjoy the beauty of nature. That a need for such beauty existed in all people, whatever their economic class or ethnic origins, and that access to beauty should be a common right, was an underlying assumption wherever the word "park" was used. Parks were not to be the exclusive property of any tribe, group, or individual, nor should the extraction of resource commodities take place within them. The purpose of parks was to stimulate both the mind and emotions in a positive way, invigorating the whole person. They would improve virtue, expand the imagination, and civilize the more violent, antisocial impulses. Parks were to advance the cause of democratic civilization, and in that movement Yosemite became, after Central Park, the next step forward.

Frederick Law Olmsted did not play a major role in getting Yosemite Valley deeded to the state of California, but he served as "First Commissioner" on the Yosemite Commission and wrote a "Preliminary Report upon the Yosemite and Big Tree Grove" in August 1865, just before he returned to New York. He argued that the main principle to be followed in the park should be "the preservation and maintenance as exactly as is possible of the natural scenery." Future generations would debate that principle endlessly, disputing what it meant or how closely it should be followed. For Olmsted, the most immediate threats came from those who would throw up inharmonious accommodations for tourists, but he also singled out the painting on walls and rocks of advertisements for patent medicines and the hacking and burning down of trees. He noted approvingly that the state had forbidden any forest destruction in the park, supposedly precluding a sawmill, but warned that without supervision people were liable to disobey. One of the commission members, Galen Clark, had been hired as park guardian, but he lived thirty miles from the valley, at Wawona near the Mariposa Grove where he ran an inn and ranch. The people's park needed closer vigilance, then and forever after.[28]

Muir had come to live in Yosemite at a pivotal moment, when far-reaching decisions were being made about its future, and indeed about the future of the American West and how to preserve its wonderful natural assets from unregulated self-interest. A nobody in the eyes of the world, he paid little attention to the politics or philosophy of conservation. Instead, he concentrated on his own life, trying to find a personal balance between the sacred and the profane. To Jeanne he wrote soon after arriving that "I am dead & gone to heaven." Yet he admitted to brother Daniel that "it seems most sacriligeous [sic] to mar the harmonies of these divine waterfalls with the screeching of a mill—to set the white waters of Yosemite to work ere it is tranquil in its passage from the sky."[29]

As snow began to blanket the valley, he could walk out his door in the mornings, before the sun was high overhead, into a phalanx of trees dark against the whiteness of the ground and saunter along the obsidian luster of the creek. Lifting his eyes, he could see, not a flat or blank wall, but jeweled cliffs with more facets than any diamond, cliffs soaring thousands of feet overhead with clouds of vapor drifting back and forth across them, catching the first gleams of golden light. This place was privately and intimately his own, more so than it was for the litigious, deed-hungry Hutchings or for the summer tourists who passed through the park on a three- or four-day stopover.

Americans who lacked the time or money to visit the park in the early years could experience it vicariously through the photographs of Carleton Watkins or the oil paintings of Albert Bierstadt, whose work had been pivotal in persuading distant legislators to save it from homesteaders and speculators. Watkins had come to the valley in 1861, a self-taught expert in the new wet-plate process of photography, with twelve mules to carry his fragile glass plates and his enormous Dallmeyer lens. He was not the only camera artist to come along, but he was the best, rivaled only by the younger Eadweard Muybridge. The landscape painter Bierstadt, who brought his German Romantic training to the valley in 1862, gave the world an even larger portrait, and one in extravagant color, that photographers could not match on any scale. Over the next decade he produced fifteen large oils that transformed the valley into a dreamland unlike anything that ever met mortal eye. Different as they were, both Watkins and Bierstadt shared Muir's natural piety. None was interested in social realism—pictures of Indians grinding acorns, carpenters nailing together a bridge, cows being milked for the tourists' breakfast. That mundane, humanized world could be easily found in this place too, but to discover it was not what drew them to Yosemite. The artists came to find not man-made beauty or man-made ugliness, but an other-than-human beauty. This they sought to capture and take away. Muir, in contrast, sought to make that beauty part of his daily, lived experience—letting it capture him.[30]

Winter nonetheless could put him in a lonely and sentimental mood, as he remembered the good women and men he had left behind. By post he reestablished ties with some of them, not only the Carrs but also the Trouts in Meaford, Ontario, Emily Pelton in Prairie du Chien, Wisconsin, and Sarah Hodgson in Cedar Key. To the Canadians, he wrote that he was putting to use the skills he had developed in their hollow. "The folks here think that a crazy flower gatherer cant build mills & that this one will never run but I will show them whether it will or not." To Emily he apologized for his intolerance on matters of religion and morality when they had first met; what an orthodox prig he had been and how much he had changed. "I do not think you will recognize me," he declared, "like John the baptist I dwell in the wilderness & have a leathern girdle about my loins & I wear sackcloth & when I camp out I have ashes on my head & on my whole body." He invited her to spend "a week of naked, unoccupied time" with him in his wilderness. Emily, reading that invitation—which to modern eyes looks astonishingly carnal—with equal innocence, declined to come for fear of encountering rough men and crude ways. Muir reassured her that "I am not in *contact* with them; I do not live with them, I live alone, or, rather, with the rocks and flowers and snows and blessed storms." Sarah Hodgson, who as his nurse had seen him more intimately than anyone else, joked that she might be in love with him, but she was not free to leave home and head to the mountains, as he had done. "I '*am but a* woman' [;] I cannot make the animal part keep pace with the mental or spiritual existence."[31]

Whenever he wrote to the most important woman in his life, Jeanne Carr, he could throw off all reserve and become a wild-eyed enthusiast again, confident that she would always be the understanding friend who would never find him too silly or extravagant or unorthodox. "I'm in the woods woods woods, & they are in *me-ee-ee*," he exulted after visiting a sequoia grove in autumn.

> The King tree & me have sworn eternal love—sworn it without swearing & Ive taken the sacrament with Douglass Squirrels drank Sequoia wine, Sequoia blood, & with its rosy purple drips I am writing this woody gospel letter. I never before knew the virtues of Sequoia juice. Seen with sunbeams in it, its color is the most royal of all royal purples[.] No wonder the Indians instinctively drink it for they know not what. I wish I was so drunk & sequoical that I could preach the green brown woods to all the juiceless world, descending from this divine wilderness like a John Baptist eating Douglass squirrels & wild honey or wild anything, crying, Repent for the Kingdom of Sequoia is at hand.[32]

Muir would never have written such impetuous, paganistic words to another man, or to a woman whom he was seriously courting, trying to impress with his manliness or maturity, or to an orthodox believer in the Gospel, or to any of his family. Jeanne, on the other hand, was seen as his trusted, like-minded confidante—whose heart vibrated as his did in the presence of great forests.

When the 1870 tourist season rolled around, once again he postponed his plan to go to South America and decided to continue on with Hutchings, mixing sawing and carpentering with long hikes down the valley and into the high country. The more adventuresome visitors sought him as a naturalist-guide and he accepted, disregarding Jeanne's indignation that he was demeaning himself by becoming a servant to the fashionable hordes. "All sorts of human stuff is being poured into the valley this year," he agreed, "& the blank fleshly apathy with which most of it comes in contact with the rock & water spirits of the place is most amazing." He compared the average tourist climbing into a saddle to a plump frog struggling up a stream bank. They showed as much emotion before Yosemite's splendors as their horses and were satisfied after a few hours that they had "done it all." Many never got far from the hotel or saloon. They floated "slowly about the *bottom* of the valley as a harmless scum." But their indifference did not touch him.[33]

That "scum" was by no means poor in pocketbook or reputation or fortitude. The majority came from the northeastern part of the United States, with a substantial minority from Great Britain, and once they had completed a long railroad journey to San Francisco Bay, they still had 250 miles ahead of them to reach the valley. However fashionable their dress, they arrived sore, tired, and dirty. Among them were businessmen, politicians, former military generals, scientists, professors, and philanthropists. They included Dorothea Dix, the New England advocate for the mentally ill, and Phineas T. Barnum, showman and circus entrepreneur (Muir called him "a lively eccentric old fellow").[34] Many of the tourists found Muir to be an uncommonly interesting fellow, so horny-handed with manual toil but so able to explain the secrets of nature. For his part, Muir had to admit that not all of them were mere frogs or pond scum.

During the previous summer, when he was tending sheep a couple of miles from the rim, the tourist horde had included a Madison friend and mentor, James Butler, erstwhile professor of classics. He had sent a letter that he was coming to the valley, but the date was left uncertain. Muir had already missed connecting with Jeanne Carr and was anxious not to miss Butler as well. As he gazed down into the valley from North Dome, a premonition that the professor must be down there somewhere seized him, and he scrambled down the wall to discover he was right: there was the professor crawling hot and exhausted along the slopes above the Vernal Fall. It was an astonishing reunion, one that Muir could not stop thinking about or trying to explain. Such telepathy "seems supernatural," he admitted, "but only because it is not understood." He always resisted any occult theories, including extra-scientific explanations for this remarkable case of strange intuition. Whatever mysterious electric bond the two men shared was broken the next morning, when Butler's traveling companion, an army man, marched them back to civilization, rejecting Muir's pleas to stay and see what the visitors so often missed.[35]

Also impressive and congenial among the tourists was Maria Theresa Longworth, also known as Theresa Yelverton or the Viscountess Avonmore, a thirty-four-year-old Englishwoman who came fleeing a star-crossed past. Born to wealthy but estranged parents, she had married an impoverished Irish viscount named Yelverton—or thought she had, until he abandoned her in a state of pregnancy, claiming their wedding was never legal, and married another. She showed up at the Hutchings hotel in spring 1870 and stayed for three months, enraptured by its beauty. She impressed the locals with her notoriety, pedigree, regal bearing, and witty tongue. Soon she was writing a novel featuring the valley and its white inhabitants: *Zanita: a Tale of the Yo-semite*, published in 1872.[36]

Theresa Yelverton's novel is mainly the story of a geology professor's wife who leaves him to his science in the city while she goes on summer holiday in the valley. There she meets a hotel-keeping couple, the Naughtons, whose daughters Zanita and Rosie become the center of an improbable romance. After her mother dies, wild, dark, and mysterious Zanita (short for the manzanita shrub and modeled after Floy Hutchings) goes to live with the professor's wife in San Francisco, where she falls in love with a roving Englishman named Egremont, but Egremont decides he loves Rosie (modeled after Cosie) better. The tangled story crashes to an end when Zanita and Egremont die in a fall from Yosemite's cliffs.

What saved the novel from well-deserved obscurity was the fact that the opening chapter, entitled "Kenmuir," is about a quaint and reclusive mountaineer who looks a lot like John Muir. That he had become an intriguing figure for tourists, women in particular, was a minor theme of the book. "His open blue eyes of honest questioning, and glorious auburn hair might have stood as a portrait of the angel Raphael," the author writes of her character. Despite a belt made of grass, a long sedge in his buttonhole, and a pair of worn-out shoes, he speaks educated English and knows his science. The professor's wife finds him too much the sermonizer but is titillated by traveling alone with him in the wilderness, feeling his strong arms around her as he lifts her over streams. Kenmuir soon vanishes from the story, although in the final chapter the narrator finds him again, now dressed in a good tweed suit and enjoying his honeymoon with Rosie/Cosie in the Swiss Alps.[37]

Yelverton's imagination overheated at times, but she was smart and animated and grateful to Muir for his help with her descriptions. Above all, she helped spread an image of him that was very much to his liking (except for the honeymoon part): the wild but eloquent mountain man. He proudly told his family that he was now a character in a novel, even if the story took liberties with the truth and the racier parts had to be repressed by the publisher. The Naughtons, he explained to Sarah and David Galloway, were indeed patterned on his employers, but only loosely; for example, contrary to the novel, Mrs. Hutchings was always kind while Mr. Hutchings was not.

> As for Kenmuir I dont think [Yelverton] knew enough of wild Nature to pen him well, but I have often worn shirts sailed ragged & buttonless but with a spray like what I sent you stuck somewhere or a carex or chance flower it is about all the vanity I persistently indulge in at least in bodily adornments. I have had to wash shirts—& sew buttons etc since I came to Cal[.] It is terribly irksome to me. [A]s for socks I have at this minute seven or seven and a half pairs all out at toes to a terrible extent & at heels also although all were new a few mos ago. I wish you or Maggie would knit

me a pair [of] strong ones & send by mail. They would cost letter postage but would save my feet this summer. Mtn' walking is severe on feet.[38]

Compared to his sisters, Yelverton was not the sock-knitting kind, but she introduced Muir to a more free-spirited, adventurous womanhood than he had ever known before. On her way out of the valley, she nearly died in a snowstorm. A year later she was beckoning him to join her in Hong Kong, before going on to South Africa, where she died at an early age.

Muir gained a great deal more from the cosmopolitan horde of tourists than he wanted to admit, and they may have been a reason that he stayed on with Hutchings during the summer of 1870 and through the next winter and summer as well. Certainly it was not because of Hutchings's charm or friendship. There was a lot more tension between Muir and his employer than Yelverton had realized. Some of it can be explained as jealousy on Hutchings's part, a jealousy that grew as he watched his employee win over the tourists' hearts and replace him as their voice of authority on Yosemite matters. Then there was the matter of Mrs. Elvira Hutchings, whose "kindness" toward Muir may have gone beyond what an oversensitive husband would have approved.

Elvira was an immature girl, more than two decades younger than her husband and a decade younger than Muir. She resented her marriage, which she felt had been forced on her in a state of innocence, and after having three children she found Hutchings's sexual embraces increasingly repugnant. Longing to be free of him, she spent her days dreamily strumming on a guitar, writing poetry, and wandering alone in the out of doors while her mother ran the hotel. She nearly starved her children on various cockeyed diets but otherwise paid little attention to them. So unhappy was she that finally she left her children behind and went back to the city, moving in with her sister's family, and eventually marrying another man.

Through all this *sturm und drang* Muir proved to be a sympathetic listener, so much so that she fancied she was in love with him. She lent him books and went on flower-picking rambles by his side. To Jeanne Carr, whom she had met during Carr's stay at the Hutchings hotel, she wrote that, happily, into her life had come "one whom you know, and . . . he walked down into the very depths of my soul." Carr, however, was appalled to think that her protégé might be encouraging Elvira's irresponsibility as a mother and wife. "It will disappoint the best and dearest hopes I have had for you," she wrote to Muir, "if you are indeed too blind to see *righteously* where her duty is and what must be while those children live. . . . The eternal laws are wholly against any relating between Mrs. Hutchings and yourself except one of friendship. I believe the very spirituality of your love has blinded your judgments and dulled your conscience, and made you see both her and yourself, so to speak, above the laws of duty to one's neighbors."[39]

What Muir actually did and said to encourage Elvira's dislike of her husband or her decision to run away from home lies beyond the written record. After Jeanne's death, he tried to get eight of his letters of this period destroyed or expurgated—succeeding with four—letters that presumably put him in a bad light in his relations with Elvira. Likely he was truly guilty of aiding in the break-up of her marriage and family, but not of reciprocating her love or of getting into Hutchings's bed. He was too much of a spiritual prude and too sensible a man to return the desperate affections of such a sad case, and anyway there was the mother nearby standing guard all the while. He did listen patiently to Elvira's laments and may even have helped her leave the valley. Whatever his guilt, Hutchings blamed him for ruining his marriage, although he would realize a few years later that Elvira would have left him regardless of what Muir said or did.[40]

The two men went through a secondary clash during the fall and winter of 1870–71, when Muir took an extended leave of absence to accompany Harry Randall back to the Delaney ranch and stayed away for several months. Perhaps he thought it was better to get away for a while. Part of that time he spent exploring the remote and seldom seen Hetch Hetchy valley, a twin to Yosemite. Winter storms, an injured hand, and a near case of snow-blindness slowed his getting back to work, and Hutchings, growing impatient with his peregrinations and delays, fired Muir and let another take over the ferny cabin. When Muir finally showed up, he quickly got his sawmill job back (there was no one else around to hire) but had to construct a sleeping box high up in the mill, like a chicken coop reached by a cleated ramp, for his lodging.

The two men sparred and spatted until July 1871, when Muir, raring to get back to the mountains, abruptly quit his job in the sawmill, complaining to correspondents about Hutchings's meanness and failure to pay him what was owed. Yet he had done well enough. He still had five hundred dollars in savings, even after sending his brothers and sisters over one thousand dollars, enough wealth to let him walk free of all employment if necessary. "You know that the Scotch do not like to spend their cash dollar," he wrote to Jeanne; "some of my friends are badgering me to write for some of the magazines & I am almost tempted to try it, only I am afraid that this would distract my mind from my main work more than the distasteful & depressing labor of the mill or of guiding. What do you think about it?"[41]

Carr advised him, as his troubles with Hutchings intensified, to join her sons John and Ned in a colonization project in northern Bolivia, where he could get 320 acres of undeveloped land free of charge. Perhaps the good lady wanted to protect his honor or keep him away from other women if she could not have him. Or perhaps she did not always understand what her protégé wanted or provide consistent advice. "Mrs. Carr," he replied, "why do you wish to cut me from California & graft me among the groves of the Purus. Please write the reason[.] This Pacific sunshine is hard to leave." Not only did she not comprehend his ambitions, he complained, but also, by urging him to emigrate and become a landowning colonist, she was saying that she could bear to see him move away to another continent. Perhaps she was being more subtle than he realized and was simply trying to force him to say that he would never again leave her.[42]

If Jeanne was simply testing his loyalty, Muir met the test successfully in part. He was not interested in uprooting himself to grab land in South America. On the other hand he was not quite ready to become her model of a new-era religious prophet, preaching to or writing for an urban congregation of nature lovers. By his "main work" he meant breaking free of manual labor and launching a thorough scientific investigation of the mountains above and beyond the valley. It would take a couple of years and would mean shifting his attention from Jeanne's favorite science, botany, to rocks, ice, and glaciation. He sought a deeper knowledge of California's high mountain landscape, he testily informed her; and if she could only see that, "you would not think of calling me to make machines or a home, or of rubbing me against other minds, or of setting me up for measurement."[43]

Three years' residence had left him with some big questions about the deep past of California: "How did the Lord make it? What tools did he use? How did he apply them & when?" For a long while he had thought about those questions within the confines of Yosemite Valley and in terms only of present-day processes, before he realized that his approach was wrong:

> Yosemite is the *end* of a grand chapter—if you would learn to read it—go commence at the beginning. . . . The grandeur of these forces & their glorious results overpower me & inhabit my whole being, waking or sleeping I have no rest[.] In dreams I read blurred sheets of glacial writing or follow lines of cleavage or struggle with the difficulties of some extraordinary rock form. Now it is clear that woe is me if I do not drown this tendency towards nervous prostration by constant labor in working up the details of this whole question. . . . [N]ow that you see my whole position I think that you would not call me to the excitements & distracting novelties of civilization.[44]

The "bread question," he confessed, was still "very trouble-some." To support his research he would have to continue irksome guide work. But his days as a manual laborer in the state's budding agricultural, pastoral, or tourist economy were coming to an end. Winters he would still spend in Yosemite Valley, boarding at Black's Hotel, reading books of science and writing papers for the journals. But henceforth summers would find him far from the valley's touristy din, taking the full measure of the great California ramparts.

CHAPTER 7

The Higher Peaks

"I am hopelessly and forever a mountaineer. . . . Civilization and fever and all the morbidness that has been hooted at me has not dimmed my glacial eye, and I care to live only to entice people to look at Nature's loveliness. My own special self is nothing. My feet have recovered their cunning. I feel myself again."[1]

Muir had been in California six years when he made that pronouncement to his friend and counselor Jeanne Carr. He had just returned to the Sierra from a long visit to her Oakland home, where he had felt trapped by straight-edged streets and china-clinking dinner parties, and by at least one nauseating experience of a room full of spiritualists trying to communicate with their dead relatives. Back in the mountains, he was relieved to find his head clearing and his feet as sure-footed as ever. But the contrast with the urban lowlands had clarified his life's mission—to "entice people to look at Nature's loveliness." More than ever, he saw that his method of opening others' eyes must be through scientific exploration and scientific explanation. The beauty of the natural world would be revealed through an immersion in facts and mechanics. If he had a social purpose, it was to become a mountain naturalist—particularly adept in the history of glaciation—and to publish his findings to the public.

As part of that mission he went out to climb several of the highest peaks in the state until he almost forgot what it was like to live with level horizons. He acquired an ice axe, a felt hat, and hobnailed shoes, the standard equipment of the sport of mountaineering in those early days. Often climbing alone, he discovered a new way to feel self-confident around his fellow humans, who seldom could match his poise or skill in bounding from rock to rock or inching along a granite cliff with a cold, stiff wind in his face. But mountaineering for him was more than physical challenge; it was also a way of gathering knowledge about the history of the earth, a pathway to revelation and worship.

Knowing mountains became an all-consuming preoccupation after Muir left the Hutchings saw mill, a career to be financed by his savings and whatever he could earn by his pen. To come to know mountains, he must read as well as walk and climb. He commenced to read widely in science, mountaineering, art, and philosophy, buying or borrowing books written by leading intellects of the day, some of whom showed up in Yosemite Valley; such visitors mixed among the other tourists and made the park an outdoor college unlike any in the world. But books could not substitute for real, lived experience. He must get to know the mountains as well as he knew himself, until they become one with his bone, flesh, and spirit.

Pushing himself harder and harder, pushing beyond the limits of prudence, became part of his quest for knowledge. He took risks that few others would take, risks that might have left him dead or maimed. In early April 1871, for example, on a night when the moon was turning Yosemite Falls into a ribbon of glowing silver, he climbed to Fern Ledge at the foot of the upper falls, intending to camp there with a blanket and chunk of bread—and then he rashly decided to edge behind the falls to see the moonlight through a gauzy curtain of spray. Suddenly the wind shifted, and a 1,430-foot column of water pounded down on his head and shoulders. "I crouched low, holding my breath," he wrote to Jeanne only a few minutes later as he sat shivering under a blanket, "and anchored to some angular flakes of rock, took my baptism with moderately good faith." No amount of faith could save him from a concussion or plunge over the cliff, but quick body reflexes and good luck came to his rescue, leaving him only soaked and bruised. Shaken by that "adventure," he admitted to Sarah that it had "nearly cost all." News of his mishap could hardly have been reassuring to friends or family, but he was by no means done with pushing himself to the very edge of disaster.[2]

His first big feat of mountaineering was climbing to the top of Mt. Ritter, rising 13,156 feet above sea level on the eastern flank of the Sierra, a peak that no records said had ever been climbed. He set out in October 1872, a time of stunning fall colors in the high meadows, but of dangerous early ice and snowfall above timberline. Two artists (one of whom was William Keith, a Scots immigrant and landscape painter who would become one of Muir's closest friends) went along as far as the meadows to set up their easels; then Muir proceeded on alone, carrying no blankets and little food, to scale the summit. Crossing an ice field, he came to the base of a sheer cliff that he began to climb, until halfway up he panicked and a slip and a drop seemed certain. It was his most fearful moment ever in the mountains. As he clung by his fingers to the rough wall a "preternatural clearness" came over him—whether a guardian angel or an ancient intuition he could not say—and his "limbs moved with a positiveness and precision with which I seemed to have nothing to do at all." Normal, conscious reason failed, but something beyond reason (perhaps the self-preserving instincts of the body) showed him the way forward, and he went on sure-footedly to the topmost crag, where he stood gazing joyfully at a pristine wilderness that reached all the way south to Mt. Whitney.[3]

Ritter gave him confidence to attempt his next, higher climb, that same Mt. Whitney, named after the eminent geologist Josiah Dwight Whitney, director of the state geological survey. At 14,494 feet, the mountain was the highest in California and the second highest in U.S. territory. In mid-October 1873 Muir left another set of companions encamped among dry grasses and followed a dung-splattered mule trail up the east side of the mountain. The climb turned out to be easy and the peak unimpressive. Mt. Ritter far surpassed it in "commanding individuality" and "colossal grandeur." The invidious comparison was aimed at the mountain's namesake, Professor Whitney, whom Muir had begun to challenge on scientific matters. He also poked a bit of fun at others on the survey crew who had beaten him to the top but only barely. The vaunted mountaineer Clarence King had mistakenly climbed the wrong peak two years earlier and had rectified his error only a few weeks before Muir arrived, on 19 September (after a party of farmers and stockmen had become the first to scale it the previous summer). Then Muir copied down a misspelled note left on the summit by the survey's cook: "however is the looky finder of this half a Dollar is wellkom to it." The coin was missing, leaving only unintended humor behind. Still, for all his smugness toward his competing mountaineers and his dismissal of Whitney's big mountain, Muir did not have an altogether easy time. He spent a bitterly cold night on the barren crest, dancing to keep warm, and came down the next morning feeble and hungry.[4]

His third extreme climb was Mt. Shasta, a volcanic cone rising to 14,162 feet in the far north of the state, part of the Cascade Range. In early November 1874 he left the hotel-tavern run by Justin and Lydia Sisson on the stage road, heading for the summit ten miles to the east. He and his companions were not discouraged by the more experienced Sisson's warnings about snowstorms they might encounter. They drove their packhorses laden with plenty of blankets, bread, and venison up the mountain until packed snow blocked their advance. Muir went on alone and set up camp in the lee of a lava ridge, collecting logs and branches to feed a fire. The next morning a storm was raging across the mountain, leaving his campsite drifted over—a storm that lasted a full week. Muir was ready to stay hunkered down to the end, "snug, bug, rug," but Sisson sent up a rescue party and

Mount Shasta, California. (William Cullen Bryant, ed., Picturesque America)

brought him back to the hotel. Neither chastened nor daunted, Muir would return three more times to climb Shasta, his favorite among all the state's mountains. Its solitary majesty, intense weather, and remoteness from the beaten path appealed to him strongly as an ideal of life.[5]

Californians referred to the Sierra Nevada as their "alps," suggesting that they could boast a local grandeur equivalent to the mountainous parts of Austria, France, Italy, and Switzerland. The Coastal Range they compared to the low, gentle Appalachians of the eastern United States, but the Sierra thrust them into world-class status: a high range of sharp-edged granite with flanks of metamorphic slates covered here and there by basaltic caps or blackish lava that had spewed from once fiery craters, all carved and scraped by glacial ice. If the forbidding mountains of Switzerland could become the destination of civilized travelers in Europe, argued Professor Whitney, then California's highest range could offer a similar destiny for Americans. That outcome was still far off; he estimated that ten times as many Californians had seen the Swiss Alps as the Sierra. But one day the world's mountaineers were sure to discover these spectacular alps of North America.

Recreational mountain climbing, in contrast to more passive mountain contemplation, was a new thing under the sun. The highest peak in Europe, Mount Blanc (15,782 feet), was climbed for the first time in 1786, by a Chamonix physician paired with a peasant guide. The first British mountaineer, the Edinburgh professor of natural philosophy James Douglas Forbes, trekked every Swiss mountain district between 1827 and 1844, and after him came a flood of climbers. In 1857 they established the Alpine Club, whose most prominent members included John Ball, Leslie Stephen, John Tyndall, the Reverend Charles Hudson, and Edward Whymper. It was Hudson and Whymper who led the first successful assault on the Matterhorn in 1865, a triumph that turned to tragedy on the way down, when a broken rope sent four of the party to their death. Dangers notwithstanding, climbers continued to flock to the Pennine Alps, the Bernese Oberland, the Engadine, and Dolomites. They bought guidebooks and maps, marked routes for degrees of difficulty, and transformed poor mountain villages into international resorts crowded with posh hotels and spas. For some a stroll across flowery pastures echoing with cowbells was enough exercise, but for others only the most strenuous climbs with the best equipment could get the blood flowing and the spirits soaring.[6]

Switzerland had become what Leslie Stephen called the "Playground of Europe," where newly affluent, urban dwellers could test their mettle and escape summer heat. The Sierra Nevada presented a different but potentially equally attractive source of recreation and inspiration. Compared to Switzerland, California offered "sublimity and grandeur, rather than beauty and variety," wrote Whitney, "[it] should be studied by all who wish to see nature in all her variety of mountain gloom and mountain glory."[7]

Whitney was voicing distinctions that had become well established among outdoor enthusiasts in Victorian England: nature sublime vs. nature beautiful, mountain gloom vs. mountain glory. The source of those distinctions was the Victorians' leading tutor in landscape appreciation, John Ruskin, the anonymous "Graduate of Oxford" who authored the multivolume *Modern Painters* (1843–60). He taught Britons and Americans how to approach and evaluate mountains. That first distinction, between the beautiful and the sublime in nature, which dated back to the eighteenth century's philosopher-statesman Edmund Burke, he revived but then tried to brush away: the sublime, Ruskin pronounced, was simply another, higher form of beauty. The second distinction between mountain gloom and mountain glory he proposed as a check and balance on uncritical popular enthusiasms.

Raised like Muir from Scottish evangelical roots, Ruskin sought spiritual meaning in the natural world rather than traditional creeds. Throughout his writings he argued that man-made beauty, whether in painting or in architecture, should always conform to the beauty of nature, for nature's beauty is one with truth and virtue. Nature shows humans the way to moral goodness and light, and artists should do the same. Among the varied aspects of nature it was mountains that represented the most beautiful, truthful, uplifting forms. They were at once beautiful and sublime. "Sublimity is found wherever anything elevates the mind," Ruskin wrote, "wherever it contemplates anything above itself, and perceives it to be so." The Jungfrau or the Matterhorn could have precisely that elevating effect on the human imagination.[8]

Those were not merely fashionable notions, Ruskin believed, apt to change with the whims of rich, easily bored consumers. For him a reverence for nature had a fixed, enduring place in the human heart and transcended passing fashions in aesthetics or philosophy. "Mountains have always possessed the power, first, of exciting religious enthusiasm; secondly, of purifying religious faith." They had been the people's cathedrals before the Middle Ages erected their soaring arches of stone, before the Israelites' Mount Sinai and the Greeks' Mount Olympus were identified as the dwelling places of gods. Even the most primitive cultures had their sacred hills or peaks. But if a reverential feeling toward mountains was ancient and universal, it could also be uncritical or naïve. Ruskin feared that an "excessive love" for mountains might produce a "too favorable interpretation of their influences over the human heart." He added, therefore, a balancing concept—"mountain gloom" contrasting with "mountain glory." Even in happy, bucolic Switzerland one could find reminders of the dark side of nature. Its jagged peaks were the scene of such destructive powers as earthquakes, landslides, glaciers, floods, and other natural disasters, calamities that had made the indigenous people's lives precarious and impoverished. "No good or lovely thing exists in this world," he reminded himself as much as others, "without its correspondent darkness; . . . the universe presents itself continually to mankind under the stern aspect of warning, or of choice, the good and the evil set on the right hand and left."[9]

Such ambivalence about mountains, and indeed all of nature, was unacceptable to the Sierra devotee Muir. Right after his battering under Yosemite Falls, he challenged Ruskin's admission that nature could be foul or in any way hostile or threatening to humans. Nature never betrayed the heart that loved her. "How cordially I disbelieve him tonight," he wrote to Jeanne, "and were he to dwell a while amongst the powers of these mountains he would forget all dictionary differences betwixt the clean and the unclean, and he would lose all memory and meaning of the diabolical sin-begotten term *foulness*." Avalanches, earthquakes, windstorms were all for Muir positive manifestations of the essential goodness of nature. Off and on he and Jeanne continued debating the merits of Ruskinism. In the end she agreed "there is a great deal of morbidness in Ruskin's writings, the traces of terrible anguish, which he has seen reflected in the tortured rocks. God has been so loving, so gentle to thee, my bairn, you cannot realize that other side, the terrors of wrath under which in natural and spiritual things some souls abide."[10]

Muir saw only glory, and never any gloom, in his mountains, even when they nearly killed him. But he agreed with Ruskin that a love of mountains was instilled in every person; it was a mark of enduring human equality and was not the exclusive, acquired property of the rich, well-educated classes or modern individuals. In defense of that theory he took on the distinguished Irish physicist and Alpine enthusiast, John Tyndall, who in his classic *Hours of Exercise in the Alps*, had tried to explain his own strong personal attraction to mountain scenery as an acquired human characteristic. Muir countered that the passion was in-born: "I think that one of the *properties* of that compound wh[ich] we call man is that when exposed to the rays of mountain beauty it glows *with joy*."[11]

He found glory, to be sure, in whatever natural environment he encountered. Some of his most affecting memories were of the grand horizons of the North Sea off Dunbar, the green prairies of Wisconsin, and California's Central Valley in springtime bloom. "Visions of holiness are pure & abundant in vales as on mtns," he noted in a journal, "only the holiness is of a less conspicuous palpable kind." The dullest minds could not miss the sublimities of the Sierra, while the lowlands spoke only to the more sensitive, subtle souls. By the mid-1870s, as tourists had begun making their way into the high country, they sought "like children . . . the emphasized mountains," or they gushed over waterfalls "because they are as yet the only por-tions of river beauty plainly visible to all." The day would come, he predicted, when "the lowlands will be loved more than alps, and lakes and level rivers more than water-falls." It was a confession that he too was still in a childish state of development, for he was inclined as much as the ordinary "sticks and stones of humanity" to seek nature in its most dramatic and stirring expressions.[12]

Mountain elevation produces intellectual and spiritual elevation. All mountain lovers of the Victorian era, on both sides of the Atlantic Ocean, believed in and pursued that proposition. Nature as a whole (and on the whole) is inspirational, they felt, but the highest peaks are the most inspirational of all. It seemed a simple enough faith, but in fact it concealed deep philosophical questions that proved difficult to resolve. Were mountains themselves imbued with the power to inspire? Did beauty and goodness actually reside in granite or basalt, or were mountains only a blurred, imperfect reflection of the glory of God? Or was it humans who brought those higher qualities to the mountains through their imaginations? What role did science play in these matters of the soul?

Clarence King gave decisive answers to these questions near the end of his book *Mountaineering in the Sierra Nevada*, published in 1872. After successfully climbing Mt. Whitney, he stretched out on the desert sands to contemplate the massive peak and felt himself trembling on "the edge of myth-making." The mountain seemed alive with power and consciousness, a notion that he repressed as some primitive urge welling up from within his own mind, like magma pushing against layers of civilization and science. "A gaunt, gray old Indian" crouched beside him and softly explained that the mountain was his people's guardian spirit who would shake the country with earthquakes "to punish the whites for injustice toward his tribe." King shook off that native perspective as "superstition." Then he went farther to reject John Ruskin's landscape descriptions as a similar kind of primitive myth-making in which beauty and morality were seen to inhere in nature—intrinsic qualities revealed through science and art working together. Only science, King reminded himself, could truly reveal the mountain, and what science revealed was "hard, materialistic reality." The archaic imagination invested nature with mood and emotion. Modern science, in contrast, dissolved myth and liberated the mind. Reasoning along those lines, his myth-making mood vanished, and "I saw the great peak only as it really is, a splendid mass of granite."[13]

Yet it was not that simple. King, after all, was an orthodox Christian who always carried a Bible in his field kit; he was not ready to give up that particular mythic account of nature and ultimate causes.

Nor could he give up the scientist's faith that beautiful order can be found in the physical world. One of his heroes was John Tyndall, who declared that what seems chaotic and confusing in nature is "merely the unknown intermixture of laws, and becomes order and beauty when we rise to their comprehension," a stance that was surely an expression of faith that went beyond "hard, materialistic reality."[14] Muir, like King and Tyndall, believed that "order and beauty" are inherent in nature, as revealed by science. Like so many other scientists, artists, and philosophers of the age, he was sure that seeing the mountain "as it really is" meant seeing more than what could be measured: seeing granite, but seeing more than granite—seeing qualities that demanded reverence.

❦

The scientists of the California State Geological Survey (King, Whitney, William Brewer, James Gardner, and Charles Hoffmann) had been given a mandate by the legislature to find useful minerals, promote industrial development, catalog plants, assess agricultural potential, and make topographic maps. Along the way they affixed to the highest peaks the names of leading scientists of the day, and a few of their own number, including Mt. Lyell, Mt. Dana, Mt. Tyndall, Mt. King, and Mt. Hoffmann. Such names represented a new voice of authority in matters temporal and spiritual. According to the survey director, the ultimate purpose of science was "to trace out all the steps by which our planet has passed from chaotic desolation up to order, life and beauty as at present exhibited on its surface." Science had the power to reveal the "infinite progression" in nature that led to man himself, the noblest work of God, to explain the very "plan of creation."[15]

All over the American West in the post–Civil War years geologists and biologists in the pay of government were busy scaling mountains, following rivers through canyons, and collecting plant specimens. The expansion of American empire was part of their mission but so was the discovery of "order, life and beauty." In 1869, at the very moment when Muir was trailing sheep up to Tuolumne Meadows, the one-armed Illinois scientist John Wesley Powell was leading a small band of men on an exploring expedition down the Colorado River and through the Grand Canyon. Over the next decade the Powell Survey would gain federal status and propel its ambitious leader into the directorship of the newly established U.S. Geological Survey in Washington. Clarence King would gain federal sponsorship of a survey of the fortieth parallel from California to Colorado's Front Range. Then there was Ferdinand Hayden's government survey of the western territories and, after 1871, Lieutenant George Wheeler's survey of lands west of the hundredth meridian.[16]

Muir had arrived in the West at precisely the moment when new careers in scientific exploration were being made. Sick of manual labor, he dreamed of joining the ranks of those scientists in this great new era of landscape investigation. Needing better credentials, he inquired of his alma mater what it would take to finish the science curriculum and get his degree; the answer came that a year would suffice, but two years would be even better, and they could hire him to supervise a boarding school for boys. The offer of financial aid was less appealing than herding sheep. Enthralled by California scenery, he could not tear himself away or see how going back to college would fit him for a professional career. In this regard he was not altogether alone. Powell, for example, had no more formal education than he. Somehow, both men hoped, they could acquire more expertise on their own than a college could give.

In August 1871 a query came from the Smithsonian Institution in Washington, D.C., about Muir's willingness to send in reports on his mountain rambles. Gladly, he would do so. "If I could give my whole time to science I should be happy indeed, and no amount of hardship and labor could crush or outweary me." Since Madison days he had studied, all on his own, the science of botany and could boast a fair degree of competence in identifying species, finding rare or new ones, and preserving them in a herbarium. But the science of mountain geology presented a fresh and different challenge: what was the history of those immense rocks, and what forces had given them their intricate shape? Those were questions that even the best-credentialed scientists had trouble answering.

His first substantive encounter with mountain geology came on a field trip with Professor Joseph LeConte and eight male students in the summer just before receiving the Smithsonian letter. LeConte, the son of a pre-Civil War plantation owner and student of the Swiss émigré scientist Louis Agassiz, had joined (with his brother John) the faculty at the University of California in 1869. Muir guided the LeConte party to Lake Tenaya, Tuolumne Meadows, and Mono Lake and, in turn, learned much about new theories of glaciology and what Agassiz had termed "the Ice Age," a time when much of Europe, North America, and even Brazil (claimed Agassiz) had lain under massive sheets of ice. The balding LeConte and the shaggy Muir became good friends that summer, for they shared a common natural piety as well as intellectual interests. LeConte might have been quoting Muir when he scribbled in his trip notes, "Natural beauty is but the type of spiritual beauty. . . . I lifted my heart in humble worship to the great God of *Nature*."[17]

Returned home to Yosemite Valley, Muir incessantly talked ice to everyone he met. That summer made him a proselytizer of Agassiz's revelations of a cold, deep past.[18] Then, in October 1871, shortly after leaving Hutchings, he made a most remarkable discovery: the Ice Age was not finished and buried in old glacial till, erratic boulders, and moraines—there were glaciers still surviving in the Sierra Nevada! At the headwaters of the Merced River he came upon a trickle of muddy melt water flowing out of a huge snow bank and knew immediately that here was more than snow—here was an active, moving body of ice grinding against mountain rock. In fact there were dozens of true glaciers extant on Mounts Lyell and McClure, as well as on distant Shasta. The next summer he set up wooden stakes in order to measure glacial movement (he calculated a speed of one inch per day). Thus, he set out to gather scientific proof of "the common, measured, arithmetical kind."[19]

Finding active glaciers was common enough in Switzerland, but not in the United States. Thanks to his sharp eyes and native intelligence, Muir had made a significant finding and, in that act, established himself as a bona fide scientist in training. He had leapt from piles of sawdust and sheep manure into an important field of inquiry,

Muir drawing of himself ascending a glacier toward California's Matterhorn Peak, circa 1873. (H-A, JMP)

vaulting over other, more established names in the field. Immediately he sent news to Professor LeConte, who began spreading the word of living glaciers to his university classes and evening lecture audiences, sometimes apparently with little acknowledgement of his source. Muir did not mind the borrowing, pointing out that the professor "seems to have drawn all he knows of Sierra glaciers & new theories concerning them so directly from *here* that I cannot think he will claim discovery etc. If he does I will not be made poorer." When the great Agassiz showed up in Berkeley on a visit to his former student, LeConte managed to give full credit to his noncredentialed mountain guide, impressing Agassiz so much that the Harvard scientist declared, "Muir was studying to greater purpose & with greater results than any one else had done."[20]

Muir followed Agassiz's theory that once upon a time, and only once, a vast kingdom of ice had covered much of the continent. In California, Muir argued, a single frozen mass made up of many tributary sheets had buried all but the highest peaks and advanced all the way down to the Sierra foothills. In September 1871 he sent off his first essay on the subject, "Yosemite Glaciers," which was published in Horace Greeley's New York *Daily Tribune*, Muir's first appearance as an author in print. The mountains, he began, present an open book whose outer pages may seem storm-beaten, crumbling, and hard to read but whose inner pages are still intact and easily read. They tell a story of glaciers pouring into Yosemite Valley "by every one of its cañons," cascading over the edge like a never-ending frozen waterfall, filling the entire valley. Everywhere the ice marked its track with striations etched on granite. "The great valley itself...was brought forth and fashioned by a grand combination of glaciers....All of the rocks and mountains and lakes and meadows of the whole upper Merced basin received their specific forms and carvings almost entirely from this same agency of ice." Against this frigid picture he portrayed himself now sitting quietly by an outdoor campfire, surrounded by silver firs and pines that grew where the ice had once ruled.[21]

The ruling potentate of California rocks, Josiah Whitney, was far less impressed than LeConte or Agassiz by Muir's campfire science. Son of a wealthy New England banker, graduate of Yale College, formerly an advanced student of German academic mineralogy, and the state's most prominent scientist for more than a decade, he soon got wind of this new theory of Yosemite's glacial origin and sneered that it was the absurd notion of a mere "sheep herder." Whitney's men had turned up plenty of evidence of glacial history in the Sierra, including Yosemite Valley; the evidence would have been hard to miss. But the director had already considered and rejected any glacial origin for the valley. Ice could never have displaced so much rock, he was sure, nor could running water. The valley must be the result of an underlying fault in the bedrock that abruptly opened one day, letting the floor collapse. Only such a catastrophic subsidence could explain, he went on, why there was so little detritus—piles of fallen rock normally found in abundance at the foot of cliffs—on the valley floor; it had all been swallowed up in the abyss.[22]

Clarence King, ever quick to put himself in good favor with those in authority, followed Whitney's lead. In his book *Systematic Geology* (1878) he archly declared that "Mr. Muir's vagaries will not deceive geologists who are personally acquainted with California" and hoped that "the ambitious amateur himself may divert his evident enthusiastic love of nature into a channel, if there is one, in which his attainments would save him from hopeless floundering." In other words, go back to your hiking and leave serious matters to the experts. Even more generous-minded scientists were skeptical. Dr. Samuel Kneeland, secretary of the Boston Society of Natural History and author of a much-reprinted travel guide, agreed that Muir was out of his depth. Although he printed, without authorization, several letters that Muir had sent him describing the winter pleasures of the valley, and even introduced his glacial origin theory at a meeting of the Society, he agreed with Whitney. LeConte, on the other hand, in the beginning swung quickly to Muir's side, presenting a synopsis of his ideas and data before the California Academy of Sciences in September 1872. But two and a half decades later, he recanted and went back to Whitney's theory of a great catastrophe.[23]

By the early twentieth century, however, science had begun to tilt toward Muir's way of thinking, thanks to investigations undertaken by François Matthes of the U.S. Geological Survey, who at the end of his studies pronounced that Muir "was more nearly right . . . than any professional geologist of his time."[24] The amateur, to be sure, had made a few mistakes. He had not realized (nor had anyone else before the Scots glaciologist James Geikie) that there had been not one but several ice ages, punctuated by warm periods, or that Yosemite Valley had been substantially eroded by river action long before any ice had come along to hollow out its V-shape into the classic U-shape of a glaciated valley.

Dismissed as "wrong" and incompetent, Muir resented those who considered themselves his "superiors." A nobody, he was determined to be accepted but uncertain how it was done. Needing advice, he turned to John D. Runkle, president of the Massachusetts Institute of Technology, whom he had guided on an eye-opening expedition to high-mountain ice fields, where he had laid out his glacial theories. Runkle encouraged him to work them up into formal papers, but Muir was not trained in that kind of performance. Instead, he sent back a rambling essay on Hetch Hetchy valley, based on an excursion he made in fall 1871, his first journey into that handsome gorge carved by the Tuolumne River and glaciers; Runkle liked it so well he got it published in the Boston *Weekly Transcript*. Here was another ice-carved valley, Muir enthused, "over twenty miles in length, abounding in falls and cascades, and glacial rock forms." By this point more than a thousand Americans had seen the original Yosemite, but only a few had ventured into its twin. Tourists, he urged, should ride out of their way a few miles to learn that "the world is so rich as to possess at least two Yosemites instead of one."[25] Writing such encomia for the traveling public, however, would not win any recognition from the scientific community, and Muir had yet to publish solid data and arguments for the mountain-shaping power of ice.

A full professional treatise was needed to wave before the world, and such he meant to produce. "I have commenced the work of making a book for the Boston Academy of Science on the ancient glacial system of the Merced," he wrote Daniel, "wh[ich] will occupy my time for several years." The plan was formed by November 1871, but, novice that he was, he could not have imagined how difficult it was going to be. Four months later he was thanking Dan for sending his Indianapolis trunk full of those marvelous hand-made clocks, a few blank notebooks, and a dictionary and was half-boasting, "I am making a great many friends among men of science. You know how people used to say that I was a genius in mechanics, well they say the same about my readings of Nature, but it yet remains to be proven." To Oxford University acquaintance James Cross, he wrote that same spring, "I hope to see your Tyndall this year who is one of the very greatest of Englishmen. So is [Thomas] Huxley. The Scientific Association will meet at San Fran in Aug this yr"—and apparently he intended to be there, shaking hands with the scientific nobility. (Unfortunately, the venue was switched to Dubuque, Iowa, and he never met either man.)[26]

With far less confidence, he wrote Jeanne that he was approaching "a fruiting time. . . . All say *write*, but I dont know how or what." The project began to grow and grow, so that he did not know how or where to commence or how long it would take to finish. First he must visit the alpine landscapes of Europe and then the massive glaciers of Greenland, "before I write the book we have been speaking of. & all this will require a dozen yrs or twenty, & money[.] The question is what will I write now etc. I have learned the alphabet of ice & mtn structure here & I think I can read fast in other countries. I would let others write what I have read here but that they make so damnable a hash of it & ruin so glorious a unit." Sending ideas for Kneeland or Runkle to translate into proper scientific discourse had been a mere beginning, not altogether successful, and he was uncertain about where he should put his foot next. In this kind of mountain scaling the most finely tuned bodily instincts were not of much use.[27]

While the "big book" was stretching away before him like an endless wall of ice, he managed to hew out a few intermediate steps. First he undertook to write a series of seven articles on mountain glaciers for the San Francisco magazine *The Overland Monthly* under the common title of "Studies in the Sierra." They followed an earlier series of miscellaneous pieces, beginning in April 1872, on such diverse topics as Yosemite waterfalls, his sojourn at Twenty-Hill Hollow, his "Living Glaciers" discovery, "The Geologist's Winter Walk," "Hetch Hetchy," "Tuolumne Cañon," and "Wild Sheep." Then, as the "Studies" series was making its way into print, he sent an abstract to the American Association for the Advancement of Science, which appeared, devoid of his many field sketches, in the society's proceedings for 1874 and was widely distributed as reprints.

The AAAS abstract covers nine pages of small print and demonstrates an astonishing grasp of mountain sculpting acquired in a mere three or four years of intense study, sufficient perhaps to have won him a doctorate in any university of the day. It demonstrates a comprehensive and yet finely detailed understanding of the interaction of ice and rock over hundreds of square miles that far exceeded what the Whitney survey, which had mainly produced a good set of maps, had achieved in glaciology. (Muir declared, with some exaggeration, that the Sierra range was "almost wholly unexplored" by the survey except for "a few nervous raids" made from random points along established trails.[28])

His analysis, based on knowledge strenuously acquired through long, solitary expeditions into the most remote backcountry, was all embracing. His gaze swept from the fine scratching and polishing of rock surfaces by slow-moving ice to the piling up of long terminal and lateral moraines of glacial till to the carving of valleys, ridges, lake basins, and the whole jagged skyline of the Sierra. On the whole, and in contrast to the tone of much of his private correspondence, his language was cool and dispassionate, his tone explanatory. All the talents he had brought to the organizing of mills and machinery he now turned to laying bare the mechanics of the landscape. He saw the multiplicity of parts and yet grasped their coherence into a whole.

The magazine series "Studies in the Sierra" laid out those landscape mechanics in far greater detail, enough to furnish a small book, but now the language became more imaginative and the story more literary. Muir pictured a "Master Builder" choosing a sculpting tool—not earthquakes or lightning or rain in this case but "the tender snow-flowers, noiselessly falling through unnumbered seasons, the offspring of the sun and sea."[29] In the beginning there was the rock, hard, simple and seemingly undifferentiated, and there was the ice, likewise hard, plain, unadorned, but ironically made of softest flakes that could melt at a touch. Together, they fashioned a "sublime landscape," an incomparable work of art on a global scale. Antarctica and Greenland were still works in progress, whereas California, undergoing a warming climate, had been all but completed. How it was done in material specifics the mind could readily grasp, leaving the greater questions of why and wherefore to more daring leaps of the imagination.

What Jeanne Carr once termed Muir's "eye within the eye, to see in natural objects the realized ideas of His mind," took on a new meaning: a capacity to discern in the original, uplifted block of Sierra granite or sedimentary shale the final artistic product. Mountains he had come to see as intricate structures of brick-like blocks hidden deep into the earth, far from ordinary human sight. The blocks were bound together by differing qualities of adhesion and along differing planes of cleavage. Bring heavy layers of moving ice in contact with those blocks and they began to fracture, divide, and peel away in variegated shapes. Here glaciers rounded the solid rock into sheep-like forms (*roche moutonnée*), while over there a rock face had been cut along the vertical like a piece of cake; and yet farther on a great dome stood out along a roofline of spires and pinnacles. Cones, eggs, cirques, concentric seams, knife-edges, wedges, diagonals, floors, bumps, all lay waiting in the underlying structure of the rock. There was a grain to this earth, or rather a multitude of grains, which the ice had laid bare. "Every carpenter knows that only a dull tool will follow the grain of wood. Such a tool is the glacier.... Mighty as its effects appear to us, it has only developed the predestined forms of mountain beauty which were ready and waiting to receive the baptism of light."[30]

A subsequent article challenged Professor Whitney's hypothesis of sudden subsidence for the origin of Yosemite Valley. Muir objected because it made nature seem chaotic, violent, and destructive. That the earth could open suddenly into a yawning hell seemed an idea belonging to the dark ages, defying rational explanation and encouraging superstitious fear. His own science was based on uniformitarian logic first proposed by the eighteenth-century founder of modern geology and fellow Scot, James Hutton, author of *The Theory of the Earth* (1795), and carried down into the nineteenth century by England's Charles Lyell, whose influential *Principles of Geology* appeared in 1830–33. Earth's history, they argued, shows a steady, uniform pattern of change over immense periods of time, a pattern observable in ordinary forces at work in the present.[31]

Signing on to uniformitarianism meant rejecting any literal reading of the biblical story of creation. There could have been no actual, historical Adam or Eve, nor an exact moment when God—say, at a time 4,004 years before Jesus, according to the calculations of Archbishop James Ussher—called the world forth out of the void. Muir accepted the new scientific timescale stretching over millions of years and redefining "creation" as a slow unfolding of earth's potential. We must give nature "time enough for her larger operations," he wrote, "or for the erosion of a mere cañon furrow, without resorting to sensational cataclysms." With sufficient time and sufficient periods of coldness, mere water vapor taken up by the sun from the Pacific Ocean and transported inland could carve a valley a thousand feet deep. Since the retreat of the ice many millennia ago, Muir estimated, the Sierra surface had been eroded by only a few inches. "Atmospheric weathering has... done more to blur and degrade the glacier features of the Sierra than all other agents combined."[32]

The payoff for humans from the work of California's glaciers was a garden of unsurpassed beauty and productivity. The glaciers had created soils, and on those soils vegetable life had flourished, and so had people. Outwash from the mountains had created a "magnificent belt of soil on which all the majestic forests of the Sierra are growing." Foothills and lower slopes constituted one vast moraine, in some places more than a hundred feet deep and twenty miles wide. At first the new soils had been fit only for sedges and willows, but then came grasses and pines and hundreds of other species. In some places the glaciers had left bogs, but these were slowly aging according to "beautiful laws," becoming alpine meadows supporting a dazzling array of blooms. On a more practical level, the glaciers had made broad, level valleys possible where people could grow wheat and apples. Always and everywhere, nature testified to benevolent order: "Every soil-atom seems to yield enthusiastic obedience to law—bowlders and mudgrains moving to music as harmoniously as the farewhirling planets."[33]

Muir kept Jeanne regularly informed of his studies in letters that were, as ever, edged with more flowery extravagance than he put in print. "Glaciers," he sang to her, "are paper manufacturers & they pulped these mountains & made the meadowy sheets on wh[ich] this leafmusic is written." She needed such poetic inspiration, he felt, for the notion of an Ice Age left her, a lover of cultivated plants, cold and bored. In turn, he was disappointed by her indifference, and increasingly a note of tension crept into their correspondence. You have encouraged me to read the mountains, he reminded her, and now you will not listen. Come visit the high peaks, and "you will be iced then."[34]

In July 1873 she agreed to go on a camping trip to the High Sierra— long postponed and overdue. Her son John came too as did Albert Kellogg, a botanist with the California Academy of Science. Now, with Muir as their guide, she was sure to learn about ice. They headed with loaded packhorses to Tuolumne Canyon. Gallantly, Muir chopped down a pine tree four feet in diameter to enable her to cross the river dry-shod; it snapped in two and floated downstream. Then her heroic mountaineer ate too many stewed plums and fell sick, while she remained hale and hearty. To save his eyes from snow-blindness, she brought along a pair of green-tinted spectacles, and together they went sauntering on a glacier, she barefoot and gloveless, and he in shades. Returning to camp, they found her stockings and their food supply chewed up by bears. Nothing in that exuberant and crazy reunion, however, could overcome her aversion to his beloved ice fields. It was, she reported in a speech to the Oakland Farming Club, an "affection for trees & plants" that had united the party in the end.[35]

Muir tried as hard to get his family in Wisconsin to see the intellectual and moral worth of his glacial studies and the scope of his scientific ambition. He sent copies of his magazine pieces, which his mother puzzled over, finally admitting that they were beyond her ability to understand. To a more sympathetic Sarah, he wrote, "The Scotch are slow but some day I will have the results of my mountain studies in a form in wh[ich] you all will be able to read & judge of them. In the mean time I write occaisonally [sic] for the Overland Monthly but neither these magazine articles nor my first book will form any finished part of the scientific contribution that I hope to make."[36]

Father Daniel, on the other hand, was quick to denounce the articles, whether he read them or not, and his son's ambition to become a glacial scientist he derided as worthless, godless, and unnecessary. As demonstrated in a religious tract he was sending by return mail, nature was obviously the handiwork of God, as any believer could see. Yet the study of nature was a dangerous distraction from the worship of God, who was unseen and eternal. "You cannot warm the heart of the saint of God with your cold icy-topped mountains," he ranted. Come back to the church and God's Holy Word—leave glaciers and nature behind. Burn your writings so that they will do no more harm to you or others. Signed, "your affectionate father in Christ."[37]

Daniel was not defending Genesis against geology, pitting one account of the Creation against another, the supernatural against the natural, but rather was defending the supreme authority of the literal written word on which his religious fundamentalism rested. He would not trust "words" inscribed on the face of nature that science could help decipher. Muir thoroughly grasped the difference between them and chose science. Reading the landscape through the aid of science was a great deal more difficult, he supposed, than reading First Corinthians or the Book of Revelation, but it was a more reliable basis for faith.

It would require years of enthusiastic study to master the English alphabet if it were carved upon the flank of the Sierra in letters sixty or seventy miles long, their bases set in the foothills, their tops leaning back among the glaciers and shattered peaks of the summit, often veiled with forests and thickets, and their continuity often broken by cross-gorges and hills.

Gradually, as one learned to decipher the blurry fragments, a "comprehension of their unity and of the poised harmony of their general relations" emerged, but always it was subject to revision. The struggle between father and son was between two kinds of faith: one based on the liberal mindset of empirical science and the other on the authoritarian rigidity of fundamentalism.[38]

Yet Muir's rejection of Christian fundamentalism did not imply atheism or even doubt about the moral ideals he had been raised on. Before he undertook his glacial studies, while camping at the base of Mt. Ritter, he jotted in his journal his view of the relation of science to faith and morality: "I never found the devil in the Survey," he wrote, "or any evil[,] but God in clearness [sic] & the religion of Jesus Christ."[39] Every mountain seemed to testify to the ethical principles taught in the Sermon on the Mount. A few more years of mountain science would diminish such admiring references to Jesus or the Christian religion, but he never would renounce a belief in God (or some god-like force flowing through the natural world, flowing through the ice, and creating a world fit for life). Nor would he ever repudiate the simple, universal ethics of the Beatitudes taught by nature better than any written testament.

⊂━✦━⊃

The knowledge that Muir sought was historical but went far deeper into the past than the chronicles of kings or political regimes. His century was the first to discover deep time, stretching beyond the origins of humankind or even the appearance of life. It was a perspective that suited well his feeling of man's insignificance in the sum of things.

After geology, the science of biology began to assume leadership in exploring that deep past and demonstrating that, to understand nature, one must approach it historically. Every species of organism, scientists discovered, came from some earlier species, by a process of natural evolution that was open-ended and endlessly creative. The naturalist Charles Darwin, in his book *On the Origin of Species*, presented the most convincing argument for that theory to the public in 1859, an argument he expanded to cover human beings in *The Descent of Man* (1871). Together, and in a remarkably short time, those books demolished longstanding theological notions that every species, and particularly *Homo sapiens,* had been specially crafted by God and placed in a habitat fully prepared in the beginning of time for its needs.

Muir's personal tutor in the science of evolution was none other than Asa Gray, the botanist who was Darwin's most prestigious defender in North America. From obscure origins as a farmer's son and small-town medical doctor, Gray had risen to become an internationally famous plant taxonomist. In an era when botany mainly meant the identifying, naming, and cataloguing of plants collected from the wild, Gray stood supreme. His taxonomic skill earned him a faculty position at Harvard in 1842, and his *Manual of Botany* became the standard text. Gray's most famous moment came when, two years before *Origin of Species* appeared, Darwin chose the American to confess that he had come to "the heterodox conclusion that there are no such things as independently created species—that species are only strongly defined varieties. I know that this will make you despise me." Far from it, Gray proved to be a highly cautious but loyal, committed supporter of evolution through natural selection and the leading advocate of evolution in the United States.[40]

Religious beliefs must always give way to well-argued scientific theory buttressed by facts—on that principle Gray was firm. Although a faithful Congregationalist, he came to believe that evolution was God's method of bringing new species forth. In that belief he found himself at loggerheads with his equally theistic colleague Louis Agassiz. They disagreed over the latter's notion that each and every species must have been first an idea in the divine mind, or that its exact distribution across the continents must have been decreed in Heaven. By the 1870s the weight of opinion swung to Gray's side, throwing a permanent shadow across the reputation of the Ice Age theorist who had so inspired Muir as he had a slew of scientists, philosophers, poets, and Harvard trustees.

Muir went over to Darwinism with the rest and formed a lasting friendship with Gray. It began as a distant collaboration, after the Harvard scientist sought his help in field collecting. "What a splendid *plant-finder* you are," enthused Gray in a letter, "and I envy, while I shudder over your walk." On his high-country rambles Muir became another member of Gray's army of collectors, plucking leaves, stems, and seeds to pack off to the laboratory. Gray was grateful for this assistance and held out the promise of immortality. "Pray find a new *genus,* or at least a new *species,* that I may have satisfaction of embalming your name, not in glacier-ice, but in spicy wild perfume." Not long after, he received from Muir that very thing—a hitherto unknown perennial forb with pale yellow blooms that he dubbed *Ivesia muirii,* or granite mousetail.[41]

Word came in July 1872 that Professor Gray was on his way to Oakland and then Yosemite Valley, hoping to meet his mountain collaborator. "I feel [him] to be a great progressive unlimited man like Darwin & Huxley & Tyndall," Muir wrote in anticipation.[42] Gray and the others named had come to comprise a new pantheon of "progressives," displacing not only Agassiz but also the once much-admired Alexander von Humboldt, whose popular natural history, for all its brilliant descriptions and holistic vision, never really explained anything. In volume after volume Humboldt had promised to show a "unity in diversity," but in the end he could not even show how the Sierra had been formed or how the Sequoia tree had arrived there. The four evolutionists, in contrast, exemplified a better science that boldly took on the big questions—the origins of Earth and mountains, of species and humankind—and gave stunning, revolutionary answers.

When Gray showed up in Yosemite, Muir hailed him as "the first botanist in the world." Nonetheless he turned out to be in some ways disappointing as a personality. "He is a most cordial lover of purity and truth, but the angular factiness of his pursuits have kept him at too cold a distance from the spirit world."[43] Gray's cold, reserved response to mountain glory was not due to any requirement of scientific objectivity, but was only the mark of an overly guarded imagination and a repressed upbringing.

Still, the stone-faced Gray would have another chance to warm up over a Muir campfire in California mountains. Five years after his first trip to the West Coast, he came back with England's leading botanist, Joseph Hooker: a Glaswegian of irritable temper, a world traveler and student of plant biogeography, a close friend of Darwin's (the first confidant in fact to hear, in 1844, the long and well-kept secret of evolutionary theory), and director of the Kew Botanical Gardens in London. Gray and Hooker joined Muir on a climb up Mt. Shasta in September 1877. All three were lean, vigorous hikers, two of them were sexagenarians and internationally famous, while the least known among them was full of youthful self-confidence. "We had a fine rare time together," Muir wrote Sarah, "discussing the botanical characters of the grandest coniferous trees in the world camping out & enjoying ourselves in pure freedom." They recorded the first sighting of *Linnea borealis* in those parts and filled their plant presses with other high-altitude species. Muir relished the opportunity to talk science at length with "Natures noblemen." Gray and Hooker were, however, little moved by grand alpine vistas or the sight of firelight reflecting off lofty silver firs. They refused to join him as he danced about, shouting, "Look at the glory! Look at the glory!" Yes, it was a beautiful scene, they admitted later, but "Muir is so eternally enthusiastic, we like to tease him."[44]

Gray and Hooker were more openly enthusiastic about Darwin, their acknowledged leader in science and a man of high personal integrity. Muir heard the Darwinian worldview expounded around the campfire and read Professor Gray's published endorsements in the journals. Already he had discovered Darwin before he knew either of Darwin's defenders. In fall 1871 John Runkle had sent him the *Origin of Species*, which he read during the ensuing winter in his Yosemite cabin. Perhaps even earlier he read Darwin's extraordinary account of his voyage as ship's naturalist aboard the H.M.S. *Beagle,* around South America and across the southern Pacific Ocean, first published in 1839 and in subsequent editions as *The Journal of Researches, Naturalist's Voyage Round the World,* or *The Voyage of the Beagle.* Darwin's most Humboldtian work in its descriptions of exotic peoples and places, it enjoyed a large, popular audience, but also showed the author, particularly during his stay in the volcanic Galápagos Islands, brooding over the explosive question of why species varied from place to place and what that revealed about the origins of life.[45]

Muir went beyond reading and accepting the controversial theory of evolution. He too became a defender of Darwin. He did not, to be sure, defend everyone who spoke in the name of scientific evolution. In 1878 came a letter from a woman friend who had been troubled by a popular science lecturer, William Gunning, author of *Life-History of Our Planet.*[46] Gunning enjoyed shocking his audiences by insisting that the Bible was a fraud, that evolution proved blacks were superior to whites, and that humans had descended from "lower" animals. Muir chose not to refute any of those specific arguments but rather questioned Gunning's overall motives and effect. "I know very little about him nor will I be likely to know much more, because I fear he belongs to a class of 'Profs' who are animated less by love of truth than by a vulgar appetite for notoriety & money." He was a "hum-bug," Muir charged, after meeting the "professor" and sparring with him. "Not that I would in anyway oppose the discovered truths of evolution for I embrace them most cordially, but it is terribly aggravating to hear one claiming the office of teaching discoursing so well & so heartlessly on the glorious creation, of God." Gunning's chief failing, it would seem, lay in his self-aggrandizement and his repudiation of nature as a moral universe.[47]

Darwin, in contrast, was a man devoted wholly to truth and not sensationalism, and his theory must be accepted, on the whole, as based on good evidence. Muir defended the embattled naturalist against his anti-evolution critics:

> I wish too that you would read some of Darwin's writings if for no other purpose than to learn how pure

& good a man he is. His noble character has suffered from silly, ignorant, unbelieving men who say much about Darwinism without really knowing anything about it. A more devout & indefatigable seeker after truth than Darwin never lived. . . . If you do not care or have not time to examine his heavy plodding scientific works, at least read his 'Voyage of a Naturalist 'round the World.'[48]

Such a glowing endorsement reveals how far Muir had traveled from evangelical Christian orthodoxy and toward a more liberal, science-based view of the world.

All the same, he was never comfortable with any implication, whether made by reputable scientists like Darwin or charlatans like Gunning, that nature was characteristically bloody or ruthless in its methods. Victorians were often apt to read the facts falsely, to Muir's mind, besmirching the essential goodness he found all around him. Alfred Tennyson's sinister line, "Nature, red in tooth and claw," from the poem *In Memoriam,* had crept even into Darwin's understanding of evolutionary processes. Such false reading distorted the truth and made nature into a mirror image of mankind's often selfish, violent, and competitive behavior. In one of his early field journals Muir admitted that the alpine plants he saw fighting to survive against extremes of cold and wind might seem like "the pinched blinking dwarfs wh[ich] almost justify Darwins ungodly word struggle."[49] But just as he had survived those altitudes, and even flourished there, so they were surviving and flourishing. So all manner of living things were thriving, finding secure homes in the most challenging places, and adding to the harmony and beauty of the earth.

Perhaps Jeanne Carr was right that circumstances had been so kind and gentle for Muir that he had lost any capacity to feel the terrors that haunted so many of his contemporaries. Yet he had passed through his share of dark nights of the soul. He had often gone hungry, skimping by on a meager diet of bread and tea, had endured bone-chilling nights and rough accommodations, and on more than one occasion in California had nearly lost his life. Over and over he had tested nature's benevolence, and always he had come away reassured that there was nothing truly or deeply hostile to him or anyone else in the universe. "I never saw one drop of blood, one red stain on all this wilderness. Even death is in harmony here."[50] Those who found tragedy in the workings of nature had lost any sense of fitness or any instinct for survival. Fearing bogeymen and disasters lurking in the wilderness, they had found them. For those who had overcome such irrational fear, however, the terror and gloom disappeared (as Muir had discovered even in mosquito- and alligator-infested Florida).

That species were the product of natural evolution, not direct supernatural creation, was a science he could live with, and even find uplifting, for it bonded him to all other creatures. What he could not accept was a gloomy interpretation of nature or nature's laws. Evolution need not undermine faith or hope. Just as the glaciers had produced fertile soil and a richness of life, so evolution worked to produce a more productive and more beautiful home for all creatures.

Ultimately, beauty more than productivity was the basis of Muir's faith. The natural world was so utterly, inexpressibly beautiful that it must be the result of an underlying principle of divine goodness—call it God or call it something else. His thesaurus offered many synonyms. Beauty, however, was the most common word he substituted for God. On an excursion down the Tuolumne Canyon he scribbled, "Beauty is God, what shall we say of God that we may not say of Beauty."[51] Despite a thorough absorption of Darwinian science, he continued to feel a surge of piety whenever he rambled in the wild outdoors, whether far above timberline, or in low forests, or on the desert. All was beauty. All was God.

Was Muir a Transcendentalist? The great oracle of that philosophy in the United States, Ralph Waldo Emerson, included Muir as "one of my men" in a list of nearly twenty names entered in his journal of 1871. Subsequently, many have followed that designation, sometimes even reducing the core list of great Transcendentalists to a bare threesome:

Emerson, Thoreau, and Muir—all poets of nature seeing with a common eye. The difficulty in that labeling is that it ignores all the other, earlier influences, scientific and cultural, that made Muir what he was well before he sat down to read thoroughly the New England philosophers.

Muir grew out of the soil of Protestant Christianity, but also out of Robert Burns's revolutionary democracy, Wordsworth's piety that pervaded North British culture, and natural science's approach to truth. Emerson came out of rather different soil. He was the child of Unitarian Boston, which emphasized human significance, and of Harvard and its classical education; moreover, he had no scientific training.[52] Thoreau comes closer to the mindset of Muir; they rejected bourgeois society, needed solitude, felt a visceral love of material nature, and inherited a mechanical and scientific aptitude. But Thoreau was a prickly sort of man who found friendship difficult, whereas Muir was an intensely social being who made friends easily and kept them for life. There were many similarities among the three, but there were also telling differences.

Transcendentalism was, to be sure, more than a New England invention. That movement began with nineteenth-century German idealists (Johann Wolfgang von Goethe and others), the poetry of England's Samuel Taylor Coleridge, and the essays of Scotland's Thomas Carlyle, all inspirational for the Massachusetts poet and seer Emerson and his disciple Thoreau. Transcendentalists were a radically individualistic lot, but they shared a conviction that the world is constituted of both matter and mind, each reflecting the other in perfect correspondence. They also were convinced that mind "transcends" matter and is more powerful and important. Mind created matter, not the other way around. To be sure, they welcomed science and conceded that any modern system of thought must never posit any beliefs that contradict scientific evidence. But ultimately for every transcendentalist it was the poet or artist, not the scientist, who could perceive the mind dwelling behind nature. Poets alone had the vision required to penetrate the material veil. A poet lurked in every human being, said Emerson, but some men were great poets and others were not.[53]

Early in 1871, while he was still in Hutchings's employ as sawyer and carpenter, Muir received news from Jeanne Carr that Emerson had arrived on the West Coast and was on his way to Yosemite Valley. She was eager to have her protégé and the sage of Concord meet; perhaps she envisioned her Muir as Emerson's successor, for the latter was now sixty-eight years old and his best days were behind him. The great one was traveling in the watchful company of a Boston lawyer who fended off the crowds of admirers. On the morning of 9 March the pair came by invitation to Muir's workplace and were charmed by what they found. They climbed to his bird-nest room in the rafters, admired his plant collections and pencil sketches, and were surprised by his enthusiasm and knowledge. Emerson had just come from telling the Harvard community (in an address entitled "The Natural History of Intellect") that answers to the big questions of life were not likely to come from egotistical, complacent university professors but rather from obscure corners of native, untutored genius. Here was such a man. Muir may not have read widely or cultivated the best taste in literary matters. Nonetheless, the big-nosed and big-hearted Emerson took to him like a friend and father and left a warm, powerful impression.

Ralph W. Emerson. (H-A, JMP)

Over several days they rode together, touring the Mariposa red-woods and staying overnight in Galen Clark's hotel. Muir thought Emerson should sleep on the ground among the giant trees, but the lawyer-guardian vetoed it. Muir invited his famous guest to "a month's worship with Nature in the high temples of the great Sierra Crown," seeing glacial lakes and cascades that the "barbarous tourists never see." That too was vetoed. After naming one of the sequoias "Samisen" (or Samoset), honoring the Indian ally of the Plymouth Colony, Emerson departed for home, pausing only briefly to wave his hat in farewell and leaving Muir sorely disappointed. The party, "full of indoor philosophy, failed to see the natural beauty and fullness of promise of my wild plan," he was still complaining nearly thirty years later, "and held Mr. Emerson to the hotels and trails."[54]

Although he would never again see America's famed philosopher, Muir was so moved by the older man's wise and benevolent aura that he wrote several letters to keep their friendship alive. "I would will-ingly walk all the way to your Concord if so I could have you for a companion—the indians & hot plains would be nothing." Then this invitation went out the following spring: "You cannot be content with last year's baptism 'Twas only a sprinkle, Come be immersed. . . . I do not beckon you because mountains are more glorious than plains, but because they are less glorious, because they are simple & absorbable. Here we may most easily see God." More inducements gushed forth but to no effect; Emerson never came back. He died in 1882, content that he had added a far-western man, one with the bark still on, to his circle of sympathetic, like-minded souls. "I have everywhere testified to my friends," he gave as a benediction, "who should also be yours, my happiness in finding you—the right man in the right place—in your mountain tabernacle."[55]

After their poignant encounter, Muir began to read Emerson in earnest. Undoubtedly he had heard many endorsements from Jeanne Carr and Professor Butler, both vibrating to the same idealist philos-ophy. Back in Madison days Jeanne had read him Emerson's two-part poem "Woodnotes," a wispy celebration of the "forest seer," and more recently sent the "Song of Nature." But it was only now that Muir began to read as many poems as he could lay his hands on. "I had not seen any of your poems before," he confessed to Emerson. He studied the essay, "Society and Solitude," with its difficult warning to a man in his position: "Solitude is impracticable, and society fatal." Emerson helped his reading by posting a full set of his essays, which Muir happily accepted as "the two brown books, like loaves of bread."[56]

Likewise in those early California years Thoreau's writings too began to find their way into his program of self-education. In May 1870 Muir secured a copy of *The Maine Woods,* a posthumously published account of several trips Thoreau made to the northern backcountry. Reading those chapters brought back memories of his own refuge in the Canadian forest, among white pines and hemlocks, but he did not share the chill that Thoreau felt on the stark summit of Mt. Ktaadn, where the Concordian struggled to connect his spirit with the material universe. In his Boston *Weekly Transcript* sketch of the Hetch Hetchy valley Muir echoed a few of the other man's phrases from that pivotal moment on Ktaadn—"the unhandselled globe," for example, and "matter, vast, terrific"—but he did not share the New Englander's fear that wild nature might not be "bound to be kind to man." Back home in Yosemite, he paid homage to "the pure soul of Thoreau," who "would have been content with my log house."[57]

The main figure behind Muir's interest, at around age thirty-four, in Thoreau's writings was not Emerson or the relentless mentor Jeanne Carr. It was another strong-minded woman, Abba Woolson, a Maine-born teacher and suffragist who had met him on the trail. She and her husband Moses had moved to Boston in 1868, where she became a popular lecturer on social issues, English literature, and, on the basis of her one-time visit, Yosemite Valley. An enthusiastic hiker, she became particularly famous for her campaign to free women from the awkward clothing fashions of the day. She was no advocate of the widely-ridiculed Bloomer outfits but called for garments that would permit women to pursue healthy exercise and yet remain feminine.[58]

For all her social activism, Woolson admired the arch-loner Thoreau's nature writings and pushed Muir to read them. In February 1872 she mailed her own copies of *Walden* and Thoreau's collected essays, *Excursions.* Decades later Muir would add the 1906 comprehensive edition of Thoreau's journals and writings to his library, but those two original volumes from Woolson remained in his collection and were well marked with his own penciling. Apparently, the entire chapter "Higher Laws" in *Walden,* with its celebration of both human transcendence and animal health, resonated with him, for it is heavily marked. Muir approved too of the poet-naturalist's distaste for self-righteous philanthropic reformers who failed to look first to correcting their own faults. He marked vigorously the line "There are a thousand hacking at the branches of evil to one who is striking at the root," that is, at the corrupt and selfish human heart.[59]

Abba Woolson accepted that her friend Muir was never going to join the active ranks of her reform movement, any more than Thoreau would have done. "Such things as social reforms seem to you needless botherations," she acknowledged. "But it is one thing to live in a happy wilderness, and another to live amid a struggling, suffering community of human beings, one half of whom oppress the other half because they are too stupid to know that it is oppression." She reminded him that gender prejudices restricted her from pursuing the kind of free, outdoor life he lived. "But though nature and not man makes your world, and you can live almost independent of human institutions, I do not forget that you told me once that I had convinced you of the right of woman suffrage. I still claim you as a convert."[60]

Muir sympathized with Woolson's cause probably because women had done much to shape his own thinking and he had no reason to fear their equality with men. Nonetheless, he tended to be insensitive to the social pressures on women that kept them from leaving their families and confining roles as easily as he had done and the dangers they would face in rambling alone on the frontiers of civilization. Like Thoreau (and Emerson), he tended to think that men and women were not so much oppressed as ensnared by their own inclination to conform, stifling their better natures.

Soon, with Woolson's gifts in his possession, he began sounding more and more like Thoreau the campaigner for self-liberation. "I have yet to see the man who has caught the rhythm of the big slow pulse beats of Nature," he wrote in one journal. In another entry, he declared, "Our forefathers have forged chains of duty & habit wh[ich] bind us notwithstanding our boasted freedom, & we ourselves add link to link." "How hard to pull or shake people out of town. Earthquakes cannot do it nor even plagues[.] These only cause the civilized to pray & ring bells & cower in corners of bedrooms & churches." "How infinitely superior to our physical sense are those of the mind.... Imagination usually regarded as synonym for unreal[.] Yet this is true imagination healthful & real—less likely to mislead than the coarser senses." "Talk of immortality. After a whole day in the woods we are already immortal. When is the end of such a day?"[61] The cadence and substance in those aphorisms would have sounded familiar around Walden Pond.

If Transcendentalism is reduced to be the proposition that self-reliance is the key to personal development or that mind creates and pervades the natural order, then Muir was one with Emerson and Thoreau. So too were other naturalists, and so too were plenty of nonscientists. Transcendentalism, pantheism, and related ideas were all in the air, asserting the unity of spirit and matter and each claiming that it offered the best marriage of science and the imagination. To borrow a metaphor from evolutionary biology, the intellectual landscape of Britain and America in the nineteenth century was scattered with species, near-species, and assorted varieties of a common transcendentalist or pantheistic genus. They dispersed from common points of origin into all manner of habitats, or they sprang up on their own, responding to independent but converging pressures to bring new spiritual ideas into being, ideas compatible with natural science. It was not only an age of science but also an age proliferating nature-based religions and philosophies.

Muir was one of those independent varieties of a widespread species, nourished by a distinctive cultural soil and flourishing in the unique California habitat. He was no clone of a New England philosophical movement. Instead, he should be catalogued as that hitherto unknown species *Pantheism muirii* var. *sierra*. A fair description of key beliefs that had emerged by his mid to late thirties would include the following: behind the beautiful material face of nature breathes a world-controlling power called "God," "Beauty," or "Love." Humankind is out of synchrony with that power—an alienation that must be healed by direct experience of wild, natural beauty. Humans are not naturally corrupt or fallen but only strayed away from the true source of happiness and virtue. Science was his mode of reestablishing contact with the world spirit. With its assistance, "I will fuse in spirit skies. . . . I will touch naked God."[62]

Once this peculiar seed had found its mountain niche, it would not be uprooted and transplanted to someone else's soil. Muir resisted all pressure to go to Boston to further his intellectual development. Such advice came from President Runkle, who urged his guide to come away with him to study science professionally at MIT. "He thinks that if the damp mosses & lichens were scraped off I might make a teacher—a professor faggot to burn beneath their technological furnaces," Muir wrote Jeanne. "All in kindness but I'd rather grow green in the sky."[63]

Then came a letter from Emerson, who, ignoring his own advice about self-reliance or being "in the right place at the right time," tried to persuade the talented young millwright-naturalist to abandon Yosemite for New England. "There are drawbacks," he wrote, "to solitude, who is a sublime mistress, but an intolerable wife. So I pray you to bring to an early close your absolute contracts with any yet unvisited glaciers or volcanoes, roll up your herbariums and poems, and come to the Atlantic Coast." After he had tired of the "dwarf surroundings" offered by Concord, he could find teachers like Asa Gray and Louis Agassiz in nearby Cambridge. Although flattered by the invitation, Muir disagreed that he needed different soil, "the *better men* in New England." One day he supposed that he would make that trip eastward, but only to pay Emerson and other luminaries a visit and not to study or live in their elite circle. "I have been too long wild," he protested. He was not ready to live in one of their glass hothouses.[64]

CHAPTER 8

Coming in from the Cold

After five and a half years of high-country rambling Muir came down to dwell in the city, in November 1873, hanging his stained and battered hat in a house overlooking San Francisco Bay. He would do so for seven winters in a row, while continuing to ramble into the hinterland during the warm, dry summer months. The move came as the snow-bound winters in Yosemite Valley began increasingly to seem confining and monotonous, offering little discovery or intellectual excitement. Where once he had scorned the city, he was now irresistibly drawn to it. The city promised not only an outlet for his writing talents but also a home place, a circle of friendship, and a richness of culture that the Valley in the off-tourist season lacked. Although he would always call the Sierra his "true home," he deceived himself a bit. When his period of deep, daily immersion in nature's wildness came to an end, he chose to settle in or near the metropolis, where he remained for the rest of his life.

Those Sierra years of near-total immersion in the wild, far from towns, farming communities, roads, and modern technology, had transformed him into a new man. He had been born again into a higher relation with the natural world—liberated from religious orthodoxy, family pressures, and industrial labor. So strong was the memory of that experience that thereafter, no matter where he dwelt, he could easily slip away in his mind to that former life and imagine that he had never left it. He stretched those Sierra years into a myth of eternal youth, so that in all of his subsequent writings it would seem that he had never left the mountains. For the next four decades, although embedded in civilization most of the time, in his imaginary eye he was always on a trail somewhere in the high country. So too his readers would tend to believe that he had just come down from the summits for a brief spell and would return tomorrow.

His first winter in the lowlands was spent in the household of J. B. McChesney, superintendent of schools in Oakland, as civilized a place as one could find in America. Here on the east side of San Francisco Bay also lived the Carrs, and it was through them and their highbrow dinners and coffees that Muir first came to meet many of the city's intelligentsia. Besides McChesney, the Carrs introduced him to local stars like Ina Coolbrith, poet and librarian, the painter William Keith, and educator John Swett and his wife Mary.

The next winter he moved across the water to San Francisco, where the Swetts became his landlords. They lived in a three-story house on Taylor Street near the top of a steep hill, from the crest of which one could see a fleet of fishing boats tied up at the waterfront, with Alcatraz and Angel islands looming offshore and the distant Golden Gate half-obscured by the morning fog. The long climb to the house from the Embarcadero, where the ferry from Oakland docked, was no challenge for a mountaineer. But this trail led through a world far removed from forests and meadows—through the crime-ridden Barbary Coast, through crowded, bustling Chinatown with its out-door fruit and vegetable stands, through a variety of neighborhoods opulent and squalid, and alongside the new cable car tracks installed just a few years earlier.

The Swetts had recently moved from Sacramento, after John became principal of a San Francisco school. Earlier during the 1860s he had served as state superintendent of public instruction, after trying his hand in the gold business and failing. An idealistic reformer from New Hampshire, he stood for free, universal public education and led the state to create one of the nation's finest school systems. Mary was, like John, politically and culturally liberal and an activist for women's suffrage.[1] To help meet expenses, they took in artists and writers as boarders, but Muir became their favorite, indeed a friend for life. He stayed under their roof until the winter of 1878, when the sickness of their infant daughter Helen drove him over to Valencia Street, in the flatlands of the Mission District, where he took up lodgings with the bookseller Isaac Upham.

As he became more acclimated to urban life, Muir, observed a friend, seemed "more interested in those about you, in people generally, than you used to be." That greater interest did not necessarily lead to a more accepting disposition. He enjoyed contesting others' ideas—engaging in long conversations about politics, literature, educational theories, science, and social inequalities. Mary Swett, after years of his company, knew him as well as his own sisters and warned about his contentious ways.

> Five times today has he vanquished me. Not that I admitted it to him—no, never! He not only excels in argument, but always takes the highest ground—is always on the right side. He told Colonel Boyce the other night that his position was that of champion for a mean, brutal policy. It was with regard to Indian extermination, and that he (Boyce) would be ashamed to carry it with one Indian in personal conflict. I thought the Colonel would be mad, but they walked off arm in arm. Further, he is so truthful that he not only will never embellish sketch or word-picture by any imaginary addition, but even retains every unsightly feature lest his picture should not be true. . . . I must tell you that I have been trying all day to soften his hard heart of an old animosity and he won't yield an inch. It is sometimes impossible to please him.

Yet she kept on trying, for like all of Muir's friends she wanted him at her table, entertaining with his amusing stories, provoking with his opinions. She wanted him for her children's sake, for they adored this unusual boarder who gave them so much lively, affectionate attention.[2]

Yet Muir shut himself away in his room for painfully long periods, working to turn his mountain experiences into publishable books and articles. If he was to pay the rent or buy his bread without going back to the drudgery of manual labor, he must learn to craft words into paragraphs and paragraphs into chapters and find an audience for them. That was the most immediate practical reason that he was in the city—to

pursue a writing career. Above all, he aimed to turn his years of mountain research into a book on the Ice Age that would be comprehensive,
authoritative, and path breaking. If he succeeded, it would make him
world-famous as a scientific writer and open up further doors.

The first rainy winter he spent as a city-based writer proved highly
successful, as he managed to sell his glacial series, "Studies in the
Sierra," to the San Francisco–based *Overland Monthly* at a steady rate.
That larger book project, however, never materialized. After three
years of grinding away he wrote Sarah that the book was finished and
in the hands of a New York publisher. He sent her the goose quill used
in its writing: "The book that has flown from its whittled nib is . . . as
wild as any that has ever appeared in these tame civilized days."[3] But
the manuscript was not accepted, probably because it was altogether
too wild a mix of the scientific and the spiritual. He could not find a
market for it. Another projected book, a more general description of
Sierra natural history, did not even get finished, let alone find a publisher. As a writer of books, Muir, for all his proud determination,
was failing. Competition in the publishing world back east was fierce,
and he could not strike the tone or summon the steady discipline that
would make him a success.

Magazine articles were easier for him to produce, and fortunately
there was a thriving local market for such writing through the medium
of the *Overland Monthly* and its subscribers. Founded in 1868, the magazine presented itself as a West Coast version of Boston's *Atlantic Monthly*.
Its first editor was Bret Harte, who helped build circulation by publishing his own short story, "The Luck of Roaring Camp," which told
the story of a child born to a prostitute on the gold mining frontier.
Other early authors in the magazine's pages included Mark Twain,
Charles Warren Stoddard, Ina Coolbrith, and Ambrose Bierce.[4] By
the time Muir arrived on the scene, Harte and Twain had left, and a
new editor was looking for more refined subjects than whiskey drinking, frog-jumping contests, and gunfights. In April 1871 the *Overland*
eagerly bought Muir's "Yosemite Valley in Flood" and asked for more.
In all, before the magazine ceased operations in 1875 (temporarily
as it proved), it published eighteen of his articles, all on California's
high-elevation scenery.

Magazine writing was tough, demanding work that paid modestly, earning enough to pay for his room and board but affording little surplus. To sister Sarah Galloway he confessed that he lacked fluency and vocabulary, writing at an agonizingly slow pace. Yet he had come to "rather enjoy it and the public do me the credit of reading all I write, and paying me for it, which is some satisfaction."[5] Pride and self-confidence were never altogether lacking. He had met so many challenges in life that this one could not daunt him for long.

The *Overland Monthly* saw itself as the center of San Francisco's budding literary community and shared that community's yearning for a more refined urbanity. Muir's contribution was to bring home to readers the humbling, inspiring grandeur of the natural world. His articles helped the editors promote a post-frontier, post-materialist identity for San Francisco that could redeem it from the chaotic decades of the gold rush era. The distant mountains, they hoped, could come to stand for more than quick, easy wealth; they could provide the richness of beauty, a fund of knowledge, and magnificent hiking. They could remind San Francisco that, for all its bumptious affluence, it was still tied to and dependent on greater forces in nature. Muir's last essay for the magazine poked at the "soft hypocrisies" of those who congratulated themselves on having vanquished nature and all its dangers. "Man's control," he wrote, "is being steadily extended over the forces of nature, but it is well, at least for the present, that storms can still make themselves heard through the thickest walls."[6]

Despite the push for higher values the polyglot streets of this city were animated as much as ever by insatiable lust for wealth and power. During the 1870s San Francisco's population increased from 149,000 to 234,000, making it one of the ten largest cities in the United States and by far the largest west of Chicago and St. Louis. The driving figures behind that growth were the banker William Ralston, the captain of mining George Hearst, the railroad syndicate headed by Collis Huntington, and the de Young brothers, who used their newspaper, the *Chronicle*, to promote the unshackled pursuit of money. The biggest sources of wealth were the Comstock silver lode of Nevada, the sawmills of lumber companies, and the foundries and machine shops clustered south of Market Street.

No city in America surpassed this one in avidity, or in violence. The lower ranks of society were often no less violent than the well-to-do, for there was a general spirit of lawlessness rampant throughout the city. Among the more controversial figures was Denis Kearney, an Irish-born labor agitator who organized the Workingman's Party in 1878 to drive the Chinese out of the state. Illegal vigilantes, hired by rich employers who wanted cheap labor from Asia, met that vicious campaign of intimidation armed with pick-handles to enforce law and order. In 1879, editor de Young shot and wounded a popular Baptist minister for insulting his prostitute mother, then in revenge was killed by the minister's son. As historian Kevin Starr writes, "most of California in the decade of the 1870s seemed to be falling apart," and the epicenter of that social disintegration was San Francisco.[7]

The Swetts counted themselves among the party of peace, order, and virtue locked in a struggle against greed and aggression. Among their allies in the city was the radical journalist Henry George, whose 1879 book *Progress and Poverty* would sell millions of copies and start a national movement to gain control over the capitalists. The "great enigma of our times," George wrote, was why, in the midst of so much techno-logical progress, so many people were impoverished.[8] He diagnosed the inequality around him as the result of land monopoly. No man, he argued, produced the earth itself or any of its natural resources—God created it for all. But then a few people had appropriated it as their exclusive property, leaving the rest poor, hungry, and with no access to nature's abundance. In the name of justice George would impose a single, heavy tax on private property.

John Swett was one of George's key advisors and, as he did with all his liberal and radical friends, introduced him to Muir. If the dispu-tatious lodger had any opinions on the single-tax notion as a cure for poverty, he never put them on paper. An open, democratic society, he made clear all his life, was part of his principles; he was opposed to entrenched hierarchies of any kind. He sympathized with the home-less poor that he saw huddling in doorways and felt alienated from the "metallic money-clinking crowd" who ran the city. But, although himself a poor, property-less man, he did not resent his landlord Swett's better standing in the real estate market. In his eyes the greatest need in society was not a forced redistribution of wealth or a program of punitive taxation but an individual, spiritual reconnection with the natural world. Nature meant more to him than it did to the utilitarian George; it meant more than "land," more than a potential source of income. It was the source of Muir's religious feelings, and looking beyond politics and economics, he asserted that society needed such a religion to redeem the human spirit from base materialism.

"Alack! there seems to be a hook or two of civilization in me that I would fain pull out, yet *would not pull out*—O, O, O!!!" The city was one of those hooks. But its hold left Muir morose and conflicted. No amount of liberal reformism, no amount of magazine writing, no amount of urban planning could remedy the most serious flaw in the city—its lack of wild mountain beauty. On one dreary January day, he showed how unreconciled he was to the aesthetically impoverished cityscape.

> The streets here are barren & beeless & ineffably mud[d]y & mean looking. How people can keep hold of the conceptions of New Jerusalem & immortality of souls with so much mud & gutter, is to me admirably strange. A eucalyptus bush on every other corner, standing tied to a painted stick, & a geranium sprout in a pot on every tenth window sill may help heavenward a little, but how little amid so muckle downdragging mud.

Each winter he sweated over his writing, buoyed up by the proximity of his friends. But always he dreamed of that summer day when the mountains would be free of snow and he could be among them again.[9]

❦

As the *Overland Monthly* spiraled into bankruptcy, one of the de Youngs' rival newspapers, the *Evening Bulletin*, offered Muir a job as roving correspondent, paid by the piece. The paper soon became his chief means of financial support, beginning with his first submission, in June 1874, of an appreciation of the paintings of William Keith.

Keith, who arrived in San Francisco a decade before Muir, in 1859 from Aberdeen, Scotland, was a man whom Muir inevitably was bound to love. They were the same age, spoke with a common Scottish burr, and shared a love for nature in the Sierra. Where Muir was embarking on a career of writing about that landscape, Keith was learning to paint it, with warm, romantic colors suggested by German and French influences and John Ruskin's writings. Muir described Keith as a "poet-painter" and his painting "The California Alps" an "inspired *bible* of mountains." They had met at Muir's Yosemite cabin in 1872 and now were neighbors in the city, where Keith maintained

William Keith, the San Francisco painter who was Muir's close friend and frequent hiking companion. (H-A, JMP)

his studio to which wealthy buyers were beginning to flock. In later years as the painter's style became more subjective and impressionistic, Muir became more critical, charging that Keith was not seeing nature true but overemphasizing his private moods, that he was drifting away from art based on scientific reality to a gauzy, self-absorbed attitude. Muir the scientist increasingly preferred what seemed to be the verisimilitude of photography, while Keith seemed increasingly interested in painting a personal vision of color and mood. Yet in the early years of their friendship Muir applauded unreservedly Keith's "devout truthfulness to nature."[10]

But art criticism was only a minor part of Muir's newspaper writing career. He would supply a steady stream of articles, five or more per year, down to the early 1880s and then add a few more in later years—almost eighty articles in all—and nearly all of those pieces took readers to the great western outdoors. He taught himself the art of travel writing, sending back breezy dispatches that often made the front page, sandwiched among the daily news columns. He sent pieces from the more unfamiliar regions of California that he wanted to explore and from a greater West that lay beyond—the huge wilderness lying at the headwaters of the Kings and Kern rivers in the southern Sierra, the stark grandeur of the Owens Valley, the azure skies reflected in Lake Tahoe, the sun-filled plain of Pasadena and the San Gabriel mountains, the temperate rain forests around Puget Sound, the vast austerity of Nevada and Utah—culminating in a set of dispatches from the cold, mysterious Alaskan coast.

The headlines affixed to those articles tell what the newspaper wanted from his pen: "Summering in the Sierra," "John Muir Gives Some Curious Facts about Sierra Snow," "John Muir's Description of a Wonderful Region," "John Muir Shakes the Dust of the Town from His Feet and Flees to the Mountains," "Rattlesnakes and Bear Tracks," "A Graphic Description of Salt Lake City." The paper wanted stories of physical adventure told with the author situated prominently in the foreground; it wanted him to explain the practicalities of nature travel to office-bound readers and to conjure up a vision of beauty that would relieve all the cares of urban life. Conspicuously missing in his instructions was any mention of religion; no Christian God was to be sought in the alpine glow, nor even that post-Christian spiritual force that for Muir suffused the rocks and trees. This paper was a secular institution for a secular audience. Understanding those requirements, Muir learned to write, and write marvelously, for the local market.

"The regular tourist, ever on the flow, is one of the most characteristic productions of the present century." On the whole, Muir continued, and sounding more positive than he had been in Yosemite Valley, "they are a most hopeful and significant sign of the times, indicating at least the beginning of our return to nature." If he had a moral purpose in writing for the newspaper, it was to encourage people to become a better kind of tourist and make that primordial return for at least a part of every year. "We work too much and rest too little," he declared. "You cannot leave your business? Yes, but you *will* leave it." Killed by overwork, you will end up in the hearse of "the jolly undertaker." Work hard at your urban job, Muir was telling his readers, but allow time each year—as he was doing—for "Nature's rest cure." He even advocated a "law of rest," forcing people to lay down their pens and ledgers as he was doing for weeks and months at a time. "Compulsory education may be good; compulsory recreation may be better." In the year 1876, which marked the nation's one-hundredth birthday, he proposed a new kind of "Centennial freedom." Set free the many urban slaves who are "duty bound, business bound." Give every person enough leisure to go into nature: "men, women and children of every creed and color, from every nation under the sun," farmers, businessmen, lawyers, scientists, even "wealthy and elegant loafers trying to escape from themselves."[11]

A fear of danger, however, haunted the urbanite whenever he or she contemplated going into the wilder parts of the country. If the city was seething with violence and crime, and people were dying there from overwork as well as gunshots, nature was even more likely a place where one might get killed. Popular fears included wild ravenous animals, avalanches, and windstorms, but the biggest fear of all was of vengeful Indians still at liberty, armed with guns and a determination to defend their lands from invaders. The fear of marauding Indians was a staple of American popular culture going back to colonial times.

Muir went to extreme lengths to assure himself and his readers that the violence nature seemed to threaten was in truth rather harmless. Any careful, observant person might easily survive the most dreadful events, he promised, and even find them thrilling. As proof he recalled a tumultuous day he spent, in December 1874, along a tributary of the Yuba River, above the old mining town of Grass Valley. All that day the wind roared, and trees cracked off or were uprooted at the rate of one every two or three minutes. Far from running to shelter, he ventured out gleefully to feel the force of the wind and watch the dance of green conifer branches swaying and waving in the gale. "Then it occurred to me," he wrote, "that it would be a fine thing to climb one of the trees to obtain a wider outlook and get my ear close to the Aeolian music of its topmost branches." He climbed one of the tallest and swung there "like a bobolink on a reed." The top of the tree lashed back and forth in an arc of twenty or thirty degrees, yet he kept his high perch for hours, closing his eyes and enjoying the "music" and the "delicious fragrance that was streaming past."[12]

There was no real danger, he argued, because he knew his tree species—knew which were brittle and which had fibers of iron, which snapped in two and which were more resilient. He had picked his tree with considerable caution, avoiding the shallow rooted and widely spaced Ponderosa pines that were knocked down easily in high wind and choosing a tall clump of Douglas "spruces" (firs) that stood like a tuft of grass. Knowledge gave him confidence, and the forest gave him a ride like no other. What may have seemed like a lunatic act to a timid, uninformed novice was, in fact, hardly any risk. Or so he implied. Probably most of his readers were happier reading about such adventures, imagining what it must have been like, than going out immediately to find their own tree in a storm.

Indians were a somewhat different threat, harder for a naturalist to read than a forest and out of his range of experience. Aside from a band or two of nomadic Monos encountered in the high country and the few Indians who survived as peaceful, permanent residents in Yosemite Valley, Muir had met almost no indigenous people, and those he had met he had not really known. He had argued against Indian genocide and recognized the legitimacy of Indian land claims, but he shared some of the fear of Indian violence floating irrationally throughout white society.

In one of his first newspaper articles, published in December 1874, he reported from a recent Indian-white battleground on the Oregon border. Perhaps he had been sent there by the paper with the assignment of writing a rousing story. A Modoc band chief, Keintpoos (or Captain Jack), and his people had taken refuge in the dark pitted landscape of the Lava Beds, refusing confinement on a reservation as agreed to by most Modocs in a treaty. From November 1872 to April 1873 the U.S. Army laid siege to the resisters, until they captured Keintpoos and hanged him for the killing of a white peace commissioner. Come on the scene months later, Muir's sympathies went out to the white soldiers who had lost their lives in this tragic campaign. "Modocs, like most other Indians," he wrote in a sweeping and uncharacteristic racial stereotype, "are about as unknightly as possible. The quantity of the moral sentiment developed in them seems infinitely small."[13] Perhaps he was telling the paper's readers what they wanted to hear, but more likely he was expressing his own ambivalent views. Defend vigorously the Indian's right to survive he did, but like so many other Americans he wanted a pacified land, where no one carried guns or knives and where city folk were safe to go, even if that safety required a military conquest over the natives.

A few years later, in early May 1877, Muir ventured into another bloody place that many Americans feared, the federal territory of Utah, and did not leave until mid-June. He came to write four articles for the *Bulletin*, which were published on 22 and 25 May and on 14 and 19 June; after his death, they were reprinted, along with other newspaper essays, in the book *Steep Trails*.

Whether the newspaper sent him to Utah on assignment or he went on his own initiative is, again, not clear. Other papers were sending reporters at this time to cover what outsiders feared would be a war between the Mormons' Nauvoo Legion and federal troops. On 30 April, only days before Muir arrived, a New York *Herald* journalist had been granted an interview with the head of the Latter-Day Saints, Brigham Young, and his counselors down in Cedar City, where the main subject was the execution a few months earlier of John D. Lee for the Mountain Meadows Massacre (in which a night band of Mormons and Indians had killed men, women, and children traveling from Missouri). Lee's confession was made public in April, and it accused Young of being an accessory to the crime. Young told the reporter that he did not approve of violence and could not be held responsible for the evil that others did. But the "Gentile," or non-Mormon, press was not convinced of his innocence. According to the anti-Church Salt Lake *Tribune* of 13 May, "sedition is being preached from every Mormon pulpit, and the followers of the crime-stained and imperiled Prophet are preparing themselves for open rebellion."[14] The federal troops at Fort Douglas were put on alert. Thus, the atmosphere was tense and charged when Muir arrived. It seems plausible that the paper hoped he would turn in an exciting story about a war between Mormons and the U.S. government.

If, in fact, the paper expected him to send back an account of bloodshed and uproar, it was disappointed. Muir was not interested in becoming a battlefield reporter. His four submissions avoided all mention of brutality in man or nature and focused instead on hikes through gentle snowstorms, baths in the Great Salt Lake, and rock climbs in the Oquirrhs. He had, in fact, a very pleasant stay. "As for the Mormons one meets," he wrote, "however their doctrines be regarded, they will be found as rich in human kindness as any people in all our broad land."[15]

The first article, entitled "The City of the Saints," presented a picture of life in their capital city, while admitting it was hard to pay attention to the social scene when the mountains were so grand. Muir strolled about Salt Lake City admiring its leafiness, its gurgling irrigation channels (polluted, he observed), its profusion of lilacs and tulips, its plain-style homes. The women he met on the streets, however, seemed "weary, repressed," overburdened with hard work, and the men seemed even more overwhelmed by the institution of plural wives. He complained about exclusiveness: "A more withdrawn, compact, sealed-up body of people could hardly be found on the face of the earth than is gathered here, notwithstanding railroads, telegraphs, and the penetrating lights that go sifting through society everywhere in this revolutionary, question-asking century." The Mormons seemed to defy the tides of progress, resisting the outside forces of technology and cultural change. Everywhere he encountered a defensive attitude toward outsiders: "We are as glad as you are that Lee was punished," he was told; "we Saints are not as bad as we are called." Muir did not want to hear such apologies; he had not come to indict or to praise, but to see the country.[16]

Besides writing articles for his paper, Muir also kept, as he often did on his travels, a private journal. This one contained some of his worst handwriting, which may explain why so few have given it any attention. But it reveals an acutely observant mind. Privately, Muir took a more complicated view of this much-abused religious minority (as he did the Indians), liking and disliking them in about equal measure. It demonstrates too his background reading in Mormon history and theology.

On 21 May he arrived in the village of Nephi, lying about ninety miles south of Salt Lake City in the shadow of one of the territory's largest peaks, Mt. Nebo, which he had come to climb. Muir liked Nephi so much that he neglected to describe his climbing and instead wrote extensively about the village and its people. He stayed with a seventy-three-year old bishop, a Welshman named Evans, who told of the persecutions he had endured in New York, Ohio, Missouri, and Illinois before fleeing to Utah. Evans now lived safely and contentedly with his five wives and forty-one children.[17]

Muir admired their new prosperity—"the best fed best clad happiest & most self respecting poor people I ever saw." He attributed their success to a strong work ethic and practical approach to life. "There is a method," he wrote, "in all their madness call it fanaticism or what you will they keep their feet on the ground." For all their "extraordinary extravagance concerning angels & god & heaven," they never become so excited "as to forget their cows & crops[,] their children's bread." What a contrast, he added, to the "swoomy contortions screaming such as occur in camp meetings" of Protestant fundamentalists he had known.[18]

Expressing a sense of practicality were the many clocks Muir found in this Mormon's house—one ticking in every room. For an erstwhile inventor who had obsessively hand-carved a lot of wooden clocks and had crafted many machines of his own, this emphasis on time-work discipline, on machine-like rationality, was a positive sign. Yet the goal of that work seemed unjustifiable. Muir found his Mormon hosts acquisitive to a fault. Life was almost all labor and thrift for the sake of accumulation. He complained that they tirelessly drove their shovels and picks into the flowery soil, blind to the beauty of the earth.[19]

Mormons, according to Muir, had set themselves up as superior to all other beings. To call oneself a "saint" and dismiss everybody and everything else as heathen was abhorrent. "The sun is a saint," he wrote in his notebook, "so is the snow & the gl[acier]s & every virgin river."[20] Divine love spreads through all of nature equally and indiscriminately. To dismiss anything in nature as unsaintly or fallen, or treat it merely as raw material for making farms and money was, according to his thinking, an act of illiberality and sacrilege.

Muir copied in his journal a section of Mormon leader Parley Pratt's *Key to Theology* on the "three resurrections," the last of which is supposed to usher in a thousand-year millennium of peace and prosperity on earth. But first, Parley said, the earth must undergo a radical transformation. Its mountains must be leveled, its valleys plowed, its swamps drained, its deserts redeemed. The entire globe must be turned into a great productive farm criss-crossed by steam locomotives and telegraph lines. All the hidden minerals must be dug out of the earth and turned into useful commodities. Wives too must become "more fruitful than ever," bearing large numbers of children.[21]

For the California lover of wilderness and a close friend of many women, this had to be an appalling vision. Leveling those sublime mountains? Plowing up every square rood of land? Women endlessly pregnant? Humans proliferating everywhere, destroying all nature and all possibility of solitude?

For Muir the best thing about Mormons was not their attitudes toward nature or women but their attitudes toward children. Their babies, he wrote, "are petted & loved & left to grow like wildfl[ow]ers."[22] Remembering his own childhood with its heavy doses of physical punishment, he marveled at how much his hosts doted on their offspring. Anyone who treated children well won his respect, and in this regard the Mormons rated high. "The production of babies is the darling pursuit industry of Mormons." Later he wryly calls it "baby farming."[23] The village of Nephi was mainly raising children—they were its biggest crop.

Muir observes how nature and climate must eventually constrain that human fertility. "There is a limit to this crop as to every other," he writes. "It is control[l]ed by the quantity of water available for irrigation." Wherever a stream issues from the mountains and forms a delta, there also develops "a delta of babies . . . as if like the boulders they had been washed down in floods." Just as farmers could not cultivate crops above a certain elevation, so babies could not thrive there either. "The height of the baby line in Utah," he estimates, is about six thousand feet. Above this line one could find only "babyless, barren miners gold seekers." Utah's elevation and climate, in other words, must put a check on its agricultural and population growth. This was a land of severe limits.[24]

The pressure placed on women to increase Mormon numbers disturbed Muir repeatedly. "Every woman," he writes, here became "a factory." In another strange but strikingly ecological metaphor, he describes the childbearing wife as a tree in an eastern forest where huge flights of migrating passenger pigeons come out of the sky and alight, breaking and bending her branches, sending up a din of cooing and covering the ground with their droppings.[25]

While in Nephi, Muir went to hear one of the Mormon founder Joseph Smith's widows speak at a "women's industrial meeting." Women, she argued against feminists, should pursue "the right" to bear children, nurture them, and practice virtue (and not, she implied, the right to be free of patriarchy).[26] Muir was skeptical about her narrow definition of rights; he could not see that producing huge families was good for women's health or that it was either a right or a duty. Polygamy he said little about, but the fact that those five Evans wives had borne forty-one children bothered him. Such overproduction seemed harmful to women's health and unsustainable in the arid environment.

Muir, to be sure, was himself the product of a large family, eight children in all, exactly the same ratio per woman as in the Evans household. And, truth to tell, he had loved growing up with that big brood of siblings elbowing around the table. Visiting the villagers of

Nephi brought home what he had missed in his solitary mountain days: children, domesticity, and the presence of women. He felt with new intensity that his life had been too driven by a need for personal spiritual discovery and renewal while his other compelling need for family ties had gone unsatisfied.

In one of the most poignant passages in all of Muir's writings, he confesses (probably after climbing Mt. Nebo) that "coming down from the mountains to men I always feel . . . out of place. . . . I am always glad to touch the living rock again & dip my head in high mountain sky. In Mormon baby thickets I feel more than ever insignificant."[27] But those baby thickets appealed to his heart. He was caught in an excruciating tension between a desire to connect with nature and a desire to connect with people.

The first question that village women commonly asked him when he entered their houses was, how many children do you have? Before they took his hat or offered a chair, they wanted to know whether he was a family man or not. "I say Ive not had baby opportunities . . . I have been in the woods gathering fl[owe]rs & studying nature birds & [squirrels] & wild sheep are my own children." His unnamed hiking companion bragged to the women that he had eight little ones at home. And then the good wives turned their full gaze on Muir, wondering how many children he had. "I look out the door to the [mountains] instinctively and fortunately there are [mountains] before every Utah door—and say Ive not got any."[28] For a man who loved children and needed a family, the admission did not come easily.

⚬━━✦━━⚬

That the West, fabled for its endless riches, was actually a land of environmental limits became a regular new theme for Muir the peripatetic reporter. What he saw in Utah of humans dangerously pushing against those limits he had already begun to see in California and elsewhere. Turning to more political matters, he added his voice to a conservation movement that in the post–Civil War era was emerging across the nation.

His first published comments on the need for conservation came in 1874, following a trip to a fish hatchery in northern California. In an article for the *Evening Bulletin* on the hatchery's salmon breeding project Muir took note of a turning point in American thinking.

> When the New England pilgrims began to fish and build, it seemed incredible that any species of destruction could ever be made to tell upon forests and fisheries, apparently so boundless in extent; but neither our "illimitable" forests or ocean, lake, or river fisheries are now regarded as inexhaustible.

Three years earlier the U.S. government had established a Fish Commission to stave off the precipitous decline of salmon and other edible fish stocks. Biologist Livingston Stone was sent to California to set up a station for collecting salmon eggs on the McCloud River, flowing down from Mt. Shasta. Stone hired Wintu natives to strip fish of their roe and milt and raise the manually fertilized eggs in a hatchery. The year of Muir's visit the McCloud hatchery shipped 1.5 million eggs to points as diverse as Bangor, Maine, Niles, Michigan, and New Zealand to restock depleted streams. That this conservation project was organized for profit did not bother him. "Nature's method" of reproduction and regeneration was too slow and inefficient, so man must intervene and speed the recovery of a declining resource.[29]

A few months after his visit to the McCloud hatchery Muir discovered the reason that salmon had died—because rivers had died. "*I have seen a dead river*," he wrote to Jeanne Carr from Yuba County, "a sight worth going round the world to see." On eastern rivers like the Connecticut an intrusion of mill dams and "those strangely complicated filths for which our civilization is peculiar" were killing fish or driving them away. In California, however, the threat came mainly from hydraulic mining in the Sierra foothills. To extract the last traces of gold the miners had created powerful water-cannons to wash away the sedimentary layers. Oblivious to the consequences, they had clogged rivers with mud and gravel, flooded agricultural fields, and filled in part of San Francisco Bay. Salmon, which depended on clear water for spawning, had lost their habitat to this destructive technique, which was freely pursued until halted by a federal court in 1884.[30]

The destruction of California forests added to hydraulic mining's impact on rivers. Muir threw his support to a growing protest against deforestation with an article entitled "God's First Temples: How Shall We Preserve Our Forests?" which appeared in the Sacramento *Record-Union* on 5 February 1876.[31] Some months earlier he had set off on a north-south line along the giant sequoia belt, huffing up and down ravines cutting across his path and looking for new groves of the great trees. One popular theory argued that *Sequoiadendron giganteum* was a species out of time, doomed to natural extinction; lumbermen, therefore, might as well cut them before they died a natural death. Muir was intent on showing that the giant tree was, in fact, still thriving in all the habitats where it was well adapted. He located plenty of groves along his route, culminating in the southern Sierra (where stood the largest tree on earth by volume, the General Sherman Tree, nearly three hundred feet high and over thirty feet thick at its base). Timber capitalists, not nature, threatened to send such healthy living giants to the grave.

In November 1875 Muir wrote to state senator William C. Hendricks, cousin of the governor of Indiana and friend of Muir's Indianapolis friends, about what he had discovered. "I wish something could be done this session by your law builders for the preservation of our magnificent forests. No part of the resources of our young state is so little appreciated, & so ruthlessly destroyed." He pressed the same point in his Sacramento newspaper piece, warning that deforestation would allow soil erosion "to a vastly more destructive degree than all the washings from hydraulic mines concerning which we now hear so much." The most destructive forces among the mountain forests were fire and ax. Sheep men, in order to make more pasture for their flocks, deliberately set raging fires. Lumbermen added to the onslaught. A single sawmill had cut two million board feet of sequoias in a single season, and more such mills were appearing rapidly.[32]

"In European countries," Muir wrote, "especially in France, Germany, Italy and Austria, the economies of forestry have been carefully studied under the auspices of Government with the most

Muir drawing of sequoias scorched by fire, Mariposa Grove, 1875. (H–A, Shone)

beneficial results. Whether our loose jointed Government is really able or willing to do anything in the matter remains to be seen." Nothing came of his appeal for governmental action. The politicians in Sacramento had no control over the federally owned Sierra forests and little interest in stopping the destruction, while politicians in

Washington remained indifferent. Muir would have to wait another fifteen years before the federal government protected any public lands from unregulated timber cutting or burning.

He did not come to these views on forest conservation unaided or alone. His old teacher Ezra Carr was there before him, with an 1874 essay on "Forestry: Its Relation to Civilization," which Muir undoubtedly read. After surveying the pace of deforestation in the East and warning that California was plunging down the same sad road, Carr proposed a progressive agriculturist's solution: learn to treat forests as a renewable and profitable crop, which scientific management could enhance. Individuals should replant whatever they cut down. Government should establish tree plantations on its lands—not monocultures of imported eucalyptus from Australia but diversified native species, which was the recommended practice in Europe. To encourage forest conservation Carr proposed teaching a course at the state university on best practices, using the Berkeley campus grounds as a laboratory.[33]

Besides European policies, Professor Carr owed an intellectual debt to conservation ideas stirring in the eastern states. He quoted Franklin Hough, the upstate New York physician who, at the 1873 meeting of the American Association for the Advancement of Science, urged Congress and the states to protect the country's surviving forests. Carr also quoted the Vermont-born advocate of forest conservation, George Perkins Marsh, author of *Man and Nature; or, Physical Geography as Modified by Human Action,* first published in 1864 and reprinted frequently during the 1870s. Echoing Marsh, Carr declared that careful husbandry of the earth's resources was the mark of advanced civilization, whereas environmental destruction was a road to ruin. But unlike Marsh, he emphasized, besides their economic significance, the "higher" value of trees as moral and aesthetic reflections of "the Infinite, Beneficent Creator."[34]

That vision, balanced between the practical and the ideal, resonated with Muir's views. Like others in the early conservation movement he went into the forests with a deep religious feeling, but at the same time he accepted the economic logic that lay behind practical fish and forest management. Civilization had its hooks in him all right, not only the hooks of urban society but also the hooks of a new political reform movement.

c━━◆━━o

For Ezra and Jeanne Carr life in California brought a promising new start, a few disappointments, and one great tragedy. They embraced the far-western state and its landscape and people more enthusiastically than Wisconsin. Ezra's scheme to develop an ambitious agricultural and forestry institute at the university in Berkeley, however, failed to get support, and once again he lost his academic position. Driven into politics, he proved more successful, winning election as state superintendent of instruction (Swett's former position). The Carrs moved to Sacramento, where they bought a farm and threw their spare energy into organizing farmers for the Grange, a national agrarian reform movement. Preoccupied in those battles, they had less and less time for Muir, who teased that they were too embroiled in "conventions elections womens rights & fights—& buried beneath many a load of musty granger hay."[35] Buried they were, for many of their causes ended in defeat. Then in 1875 came tragic news that put an abrupt end to all their political activism: their son John was murdered.

Exhausted by these sad events, the Carrs retired to a forty-two-acre parcel of land in Pasadena in 1880. They joined a group calling itself the Indiana Colony, headed by the physician Orville Conger of Madison, Wisconsin, which had bought a large property for subdivision into rural estates here at the base of the San Gabriels and east of Los Angeles. They called their estate "Carmelita," or little orchard garden, for they meant to create out of the dusty fields an oasis of orange, lime, and palm trees and beds of showy flowers, complete with a large Victorian house overlooking the Arroyo Seco. Whatever was left of Jeanne's New England communitarianism, her "village improvement" idealism, would have its last expression here.[36]

Muir came down to visit his friends' new home and write a newspaper article on what kind of opportunity "this aristocratic little colony" offered. Conger, who had been his advisor in Madison, showed off the new irrigated orange groves and urged Muir to buy a five-acre plot and become his neighbor: "By the time your last mountain is climbed their fruit will be your fortune." Muir was mildly impressed by the economic possibilities and more impressed by the chance to overcome here "the bad effects of homelessness, developed to so destructive an extent in California.... When a man plants a tree, he plants himself." He was sorely tempted to join the aspiring colony, but then decided it was better suited for more "travel-worn pioneers" like the Carrs, seeking rest in "a terrestrial heaven." For his readers he warned that the high cost of land, at a hundred dollars an acre, put Pasadena out of the reach of poor people, while those who, suffering from bad lungs, came here hoping for a health cure would be helped more by spending their summers in the Sierra forests.[37]

Muir's thoughts were increasingly filled with dreams of "planting himself," of acquiring a home of his own, surrounded by trees that he had planted and by a wife and children. He envied the companionate marriages enjoyed by his friends the Swetts and Carrs. Among his male siblings he was the only one still unwed. David, supported by his Portage haberdashery, was a husband and father; Daniel, a medical doctor in Lincoln, Nebraska, was also married; and soon also would be all but one of the sisters. To Sarah he wrote wistfully, "I, who am fonder of domestic life than any of my bros., remain a bachelor."[38]

Jeanne Carr, who understood him so well, may have been even more concerned about his unmarried status than he, and before she moved south into retirement she was determined to see him wed. In July 1874, she introduced him to "my dearest friends in California," a family named Strentzel whom she had met at Grange affairs. There was the father John, a bearded doctor of Polish origin, his stout wife Louisiana, and their only daughter, Louisa (or "Louie"), age twenty-seven and unmarried. Jeanne had decided that Louie was the best available woman Muir could find for a helpmeet.

The Strentzel family told a classic California story of pluck and courage, of perilous pioneering that had ended happily in a state of comfortable affluence. John, born in Lublin, Poland, to a wealthy Lutheran family, had fled his country after serving in a rebel uprising against Russian control; in Hungary he learned the arts of vini-culture and winemaking and completed a medical degree at the university in Budapest. Immigrating to Texas, he met and married Louisiana, who bore him two children: Louisa Elizabeth Wanda (1846) and John Erwin Burcham (1848). Packing up their goods and babies, the Strentzels set out with a large wagon train to cross the har-rowing southwestern deserts and join the gold rush into California. Miraculously, they survived the crossing and set up a general store on the lower Merced River, where they made money supplying flour, milk, and tools to miners. But then a terrifying flood washed away all their possessions. In 1853 they resettled on twenty acres of land near Martinez in Contra Costa County. By the time they met Muir, they had expanded their holdings into a more substantial ranch of orchards and vineyards nestled among the green coastal mountains. Dr. Strentzel carried on a limited medical practice but made most of his income through horticulture. The early death of their son John left Louie the sole heir.[39]

What Jeanne Carr saw in Louie, making her a suitable wife for Muir, were many qualities that were hers as well. Much as Jeanne was for Ezra, Louie was a strong right arm to her father, helping him run the ranch and going with him faithfully to Grange meetings. She had been educated across the Carquinez Straits in Benicia at a private all-girl academy, was well read and an accomplished pianist; like Jeanne she loved nature, par-ticularly in its gentler, softer, botanical moods. She was a liberal-minded Christian, in regular attendance with her mother at the local Methodist Episcopal Church. Like Jeanne, she supported women's suffrage. She was, in other words, the daughter Jeanne never had and seemed the perfect match for the protégé whom Jeanne had loved and championed since his student days.

A single daguerreotype survives of the Louie that Muir first encountered. It shows a fine-featured and well-dressed woman of dark hair and eyes staring impassively at the camera. Her letters reveal glimpses of a passionate self beneath that careful outward reserve. On 2 March 1875 a letter from Louie came to Jeanne that she promptly showed to Muir, who agreed that it was "a marvellous piece of scribery almost fairy in fineness & daintiness." In small, elegant penmanship

Daguerreotype of MRS. LOUIE STRENZEL MUIR, *wife of John Muir*

*Daguerreotype of young Louie Strentzel. (Linnie Marsh
Wolfe,* Son of the Wilderness*)*

Louie expressed a feeling of kinship linking nature to human life,
a feeling that could only endear her to his heart. She went on that
she could not accept the "vivisectionist theory that insects and animals
suffer no pain but rather enjoy the processes of being cooked, eaten,
or tortured alive. So if Mr. Muir should write for the Horticulturist
[magazine] a description of that 'carnivorous Darlingtonia,' I must
beg you to see that he makes the account no more dreadful than is
actually necessary." Despite the letter's mincing tone, she was no
shrinking violet. In the same letter where she brought up vivisection
she congratulated Jeanne for escaping from the clutches of those male
politicians "who deny even a woman's eligibility to vote and [hold]
offices!"[40]

All three of the Strentzels, following Jeanne's introduction,
began to follow attentively the growing literary reputation of their new
acquaintance and to regard him, as Jeanne did, as an uncommonly
talented man of science and letters. They read his magazine and newspaper pieces, applauded his views on forest conservation, and collected

reports that his "wonderful eloquence," as Mrs. Strentzel put it, was winning him acclaim on the lecture circuit. Muir, with his long auburn hair and beard, his clear blue eyes, and his sinewy, self-confident manner, charmed the whole trio immensely. That he was becoming a figure of state and national fame made him all the more desirable as a family friend, although whether Louie or Muir immediately saw each other as a possible marriage partner is impossible to say.

Late in 1875 Muir published his first article in *Harper's New Monthly Magazine*, on "Living Glaciers of California." It was his first appearance in a journal of national circulation, and three more pieces for that magazine would follow, and then another ten for *Scribner's Monthly*, published from 1878 to 1881, and two more for its successor, the *Century Magazine*, published in 1882.[41] All but one were on subjects drawn from the California mountains—a Shasta snowstorm, the water ouzel, the wild sheep, the coniferous forests. A sole exception, "The Bee Pastures of California," recalled the Central Valley in flower as Muir had first seen it in 1868.

Nature's wildness was invading not only the literary world of San Francisco but also that of New York City, as urban readers from coast to coast felt a need to connect with the outdoors. Backed by major publishing houses, the editors of elite magazines—Richard Watson Gilder and Robert Underwood Johnson of *Scribner's* and the *Century* in particular—aimed at reconciling a still divided nation, uplifting the civilized virtues (including nature appreciation), and freeing the American mind of narrow utilitarianism. "The quality of your work," wrote editor Johnson to Muir, "is in keeping with the tone we are aiming to give ... We desire to see everything you write." By 1880 *Scribner's* had raised its circulation to over 100,000, and Muir's outdoor essays explain part of that success. "You are one of the *true* poets," wrote an admirer from Chicago's grain commission offices; "I would there were more such in our world. In this [heavy?] material age we are too often blind and deaf to the sights and sounds of nature. Her harmonies seem to be recognized by the few."[42]

Muir's network of admiring friends was spreading throughout California as well, as far north as Chico, where John and Annie Bidwell made their capacious home open to him as an honored guest.

The appeal of nature writing was not merely felt in the city but here too among the rural gentry. Like the Strentzels, the Bidwells were members of the pioneering generation, but John Bidwell arrived with the Bartleson-Bidwell party back in 1841, the first group of Americans to reach California overland by wagon. He worked for John Sutter, on whose land gold was first discovered, and he fought alongside Captain Frémont to wrest control away from Mexico. With money earned in the diggings, he bought a 22,000-acre Spanish land grant and created a vast agricultural business, Rancho Chico, with orchards, vineyards, wheat, and cattle. Briefly he served in Congress and, in 1875, ran unsuccessfully for governor on an antimonopoly ticket. With his wife Annie, he fought for women's suffrage, the prohibition of alcohol, an end to political corruption, fair treatment for the native Indians and the Chinese, and protection of the state's natural beauty.[43]

The childless Bidwells opened to Muir a huge fund of generous friendship. He first met them during his travels through the Shasta area with Asa Gray and Joseph Hooker in September 1877, after which he spent five weeks at the Bidwell farm, petted and stroked like a literary lion. Their twenty-six-room, ornate Italian villa, furnished in plush carpets and massive dark furniture gleaming with polish, offered comfort on a level Muir had never experienced before. He found it difficult to leave, or to turn down their invitation to move in as a permanent guest. But leave at last he did in a boat he threw together and called the "Snag Jumper," baling his way down the Sacramento River and then floating in another jury-rigged vessel down the San Joaquin, arriving finally at Martinez harbor. There waited the patient Strentzels, whose amenities were not quite as grand as the Bidwells' but who presented a highly eligible daughter eager to welcome him.

"These poor legs in their weariness do enjoy a soft bed at times & plenty of nourishment," Muir wrote to sister Sarah, explaining why he had spent Thanksgiving dining sumptuously at the Strentzels. For two whole days they had stuffed him with turkey, chicken, beef, fruits, and jellies and begged him to stay a month. Such domestic bliss was getting irresistible, but once more he tore himself away, hiking over to Mt. Diablo before heading back to a winter of work in the city. It was reassuring that Martinez lay not far away—a short ride by steamboat, and then in 1878 an even shorter ride by rail from the Bay area—almost suburban in its nearness and yet countrified in its distance.

By springtime he was eating again at the Strentzels' table and telling them about a late summer-fall expedition he was planning to Nevada. In 1876 he had traveled as the invited guest of Captain A. F. Rodgers of the U.S. Coast and Geodetic Survey, who was spearheading the western part of an effort to survey the entire nation along the 39th Parallel. Rodgers and his team worked by triangulation: setting up a baseline, then projecting from its ends a triangle whose point could be plotted on a map. Done over and over, the method yielded a set of exact measurements and more detailed knowledge of western topography. When offered a second opportunity to see the Great Basin with these government scientists, Muir readily accepted. Mrs. Strentzel tried to pull him back. "Why do you go away and risk your life among those murderous Indians," she asked, "when you might just as well remain at home in peace and comfort with your many friends. At least wait awhile until there is good prospect of the war troubles being ended." Ignoring her fears, he left for Genoa, Nevada, but wrote to reassure her, "If an explorer of Gods fine wilderness should wait until every danger be removed then he would wait until the sun set. The war country lies to the north of our line of work some two or three hundred miles." The survey party would never be far from a railroad and would travel well armed.[44]

Muir rode with the survey group from July to September, crossing the Great Basin with its parched mountains, and on this trip discovered how much the desert intrigued him, even on days of extreme heat. Now that the Carrs were far away and fading from his inner circle, he sent his glowing reports to the Strentzels and insisted repeatedly that he was safe from all human or nonhuman dangers. "There is something perfectly enchanting to me in this young desert with its stranded island ranges. . . . All the Indians we meet are harmless as sage-bushes though perhaps about as bitter at heart." In early July he wrote to Dr. Strentzel:

> How hot I was riding in the solemn silent glare, shadeless—waterless. Here is what the early emigrants called the 40 mile desert well marked with bones &

broken wagons. Strange how the very sunshine may become dreary. How strange a spell this region casts over poor mortals accustomed to shade & coolness & green fertility. Yet there is not real cause that I could see for reasonable beings losing their wits & becoming frightened.

He bragged repeatedly about his tough constitution. While others in the party nearly died of thirst and exhaustion, "I never for a moment lost my will & wits."[45]

Lest Muir forget the generous table they spread, the Strentzels sent him a box of their newly harvested grapes by rail. The box missed him once, then twice—"the lost grape expression" of their kindness, Muir lamented—but the grapes finally caught up with him in Ward, Nevada, in late September, in far from edible condition. There the party had encamped in a well-used horse corral. Even Muir, who had "a horror of sleeping upon any trodden ground near human settlements not to say amoniacal pens," bedded down next to Captain Rodgers and awoke the next morning to find his face and blankets well dusted with dried manure blown about by the wind. Undoubtedly, the spoiled grapes reminded him of folks in that cleaner, greener valley waiting for his return.[46]

As the season ended Muir felt that he had learned a great deal about the ancient glaciers that, in wetter times, had covered this inland region, about the various pines and their distribution, and above all about the frenzied pursuit of wealth that had left behind such a sad set of spent mining ruins. "The healthful ministry of wealth is blessed," he wrote, but there was nothing healthful about this kind of wealth-seeking. Greed had come to Nevada as a "fever," a violent storm, a locust-like plague devouring everything before it. Far from being picturesque like the ruins of Europe, the busted Nevada mining towns lay like "the bones of cattle that have died of thirst. . . . They are monuments of fraud and ignorance—sins against science . . . not in harmony with nature." Perhaps as he wrote those words for the *Evening Bulletin*, he was thinking of the more pleasing kind of wealth represented by the estates of Bidwell and Strentzel, where profit was also the motive but a profit that did not seem to disturb the peace of nature.[47]

Returned to his writing desk in Upham's house in San Francisco and working on his "Bee Pastures" essay, Muir complained to the Strentzels how exiled he felt "out here on the outermost ragged edge of this howling metropolis of dwelling boxes." Stoically, he was enduring it all until he could escape once more to . . . well, he did not list any names or places. Come spring, however, he headed straight to their valley, and this time it was all for Louie's sake. On returning home, in a private letter he confessed how much he missed her and that somehow he had carried away in his pocket "that slippery fuzzy mesh you wear round your neck." It had taken almost five years for the tentative lovers to reach that moment of intimacy. The next step, engagement and marriage, was as fated and unresisted as a rock rolling down the mountain.[48]

Mrs. Strentzel scribbled in her diary for 17 June that "yesterday evening Louie and Mr. Muir became engaged for life." The Doctor and she had gone to bed soon after dinner when Louie came into their room, quivering with emotion; she threw her arms around Louisiana's neck and cried, "O Mother all is well, all is well." Next morning the three Strentzels and Muir sat beaming at each other across the breakfast service. Mrs. Strentzel felt that "my own Son, my *Johnnie* had been given back to me." He seemed not only a good match for their daughter but also a substitute for their dead son. Muir had been "the only man" that the elder Strentzels had ever felt that they could take into their family "as one of us, and he is the only one that Louie has ever loved, altho' she has had many offers of marriage."[49] After breakfast the betrothed couple went for a stroll in the orchard until it was time for Muir to return to the city. Still a restless, inveterate traveler, he had now set his foot on a path that led to marriage, and at its end stood not only a radiant wife but two jubilant parents and a permanent home in the world.

CHAPTER 9

The Shores of Alaska

On a drizzling October day in 1879 a wooden canoe left the scraggly frontier village of Fort Wrangell, in the panhandle of Alaska, bound for the icy north. More than two hundred miles of salt water lay ahead, a challenge for the canoe's simple oars and sails. The crewmembers were anxious because of the lateness of the season and height of the waves. All were members of the Tlingit tribe, with no reported last names: Toyatte (senior and leader), Kadichan, Stickeen John, and Sitka Charley. Amidships sat Samuel Hall Young, a Presbyterian minister newly arrived in the Alaskan territory to establish the white man's civilization. "I had very many things to learn and many more to unlearn," he confessed. In the bow rode the recently engaged Muir, his sharp eyes scanning the sinuous channel, the towering slopes, and the lush islands. In such a densely forested country their vessel carved from a tall cedar was hardly more than another stick of driftwood floating on the water. They disturbed the deep silence no more than the patter of rain.

Within days of his betrothal, Muir set forth on that expedition, the first of many he would make to Alaska and his first sea voyage since coming to California. It was an abrupt departure that left his fiancée and her parents anxious, far more than his Nevada excursion had done, about his safety and perhaps raising the question of whether he was ready for marriage and settled life after all. He was plunging back into the cold, and plunging with undomesticated enthusiasm. To the Bidwells he wrote tellingly, "I am going home. Going to the mountains, to the ice & forests & flowers."

Alaska, however, was a "home" he had just learned about, and a long way from the home he was planning with Louie in the Alhambra Valley. While lecturing to a Sunday School convention in Yosemite

Valley, he had met the Reverend Sheldon Jackson, a pint-sized minister with a big commitment to Christian justice, who had established the first Presbyterian mission in that northern territory, at Fort Wrangell. Jackson talked passionately about the north's wild beauty; after the convention, he announced that he was heading straight back to address the spiritual needs of its native people. Acting on an impulse, Muir followed aboard the steamship *Dakota*, bound for Puget Sound, where he would try to get passage to Fort Wrangell. "I will probably visit Alaska," he wrote to the Bidwells, "ere I return in the fall." Presumably, he said the same to the Strentzels about where he was going and how long he would be gone, but Alaska was more than a probable destination—it was suddenly irresistible.[1]

In his own mind the anxieties of the Strentzels about his ramblings were overwrought; of course he would come back safely and of course he would become a husband and son-in-law in due time. But now he had an itch to see a nature wilder than anything he had experienced and add to his knowledge of earth history. Part of that knowledge would come from native guides and their families, for whom he developed considerable respect and affection. Their familiarity with land and sea proved impressive, and their skill was essential to any outsider, even one as adept in the outdoors as Muir. But he went to Alaska to make a scientific kind of investigation that they neither valued nor quite understood: he wanted to observe the power of nature to remake the world through glaciation, which was displayed there on a grand scale. The north would help him understand how climate had changed, how landscapes had been shaped, how plants succeeded one another over time, and how humans adapted to extreme places.

Twelve years before he arrived, in 1867, the U.S. government had purchased nearly 600,000 square miles of Russian America, an area two-thirds the size of the Louisiana Purchase—thereafter known as Alaska Territory, or the Great Land. The native inhabitants, numbering in the tens of thousands, had abruptly become subjects of the rising American empire. Divided into many distinct cultures, ranging from the Inupiats (or Eskimos, as they were then called) of the treeless Arctic to the Tlingits and Haidas of the panhandle's temperate forests, they were all swept into the nation's maw.

Only a few whites ventured into Alaska's immense interior in those early years. Then, and for decades to come, the part that Americans knew best was limited to the coast—an interminable shoreline that was half-again as long as all the coasts of the United States. Along this shore lived most of the territory's people, native or white, and this was the country that Muir came to see and understand.

Until the Klondike gold rush of 1897, the Alaskan economy was based mainly on exploiting and killing animals. Fish, seals, walruses, whales, bears, dogs, and caribou were the key economic resources, all susceptible to abuse and depletion. Those animal bodies had long furnished shelter, clothing, fuel, transportation, and food for the natives. Now white Americans came to join the hunt, albeit on a more intensive scale. In 1878 they opened their first salmon canneries. Sealers from the United States took over from the Russians in the Pribiloffs, and whaling ships from New England combed the Arctic Sea for whale oil and baleen. In exchange for supplying carcasses, the natives received rifles, calico, tobacco, and the molasses that they used in making alcohol, or "hootch." Whites and natives were thus linked in an economy of bloodshed.

A few thousand U.S. citizens had already arrived in hot pursuit of wealth, legal or illegal, but at the moment Muir arrived, there still was no government in Alaska. Troops had built a fort or two, and then left after Washington legislators cut their budgets. Fear of a native uprising and massacre of whites was agitating the villages of Sitka and Fort Wrangell, bringing a naval officer and his armed ship to restore the peace. The officer, Captain L. A. Beardslee, reported that the Indians despised many of the whites, seeing them as a band of renegades and outlaws. While Beardslee was trying to create a citizen's peacekeeping council among the white settlers, one of them shot his wife with a revolver and another beat his mistress and turned her onto the streets. A flood of illicit alcohol was inflaming old differences among the tribes, stirring them to bouts of violence. When Muir walked blithely off the boat at Fort Wrangell, only a few weeks after Beardslee, he was walking unaware into a cauldron of racial tension and aggression.

That first trip Muir made to Alaska was hardly a luxury cruise. Many nights were spent under a canvas lean-to, trying to keep warm by a log fire or lying on a sled wrapped in a bearskin robe. The trip had to be financed by his meager journalistic earnings, including a series of travel letters he sent back to the San Francisco *Daily Evening Bulletin*. What he got for his hard-earned dollars were not only memories of incomparable mountains and seas but also plenty of chances to suffer privation and even risk death.

He did not come to take possession in the name of imperial America, or to exploit natural resources for personal gain, or even to promote a nascent tourist industry. He came because an insatiable hunger for natural beauty and the knowledge of how that beauty had been achieved drove him relentlessly, farther and farther north.

On 14 July he trailed the Rev. Jackson and two other divines down the gangplank at Fort Wrangell, where another missionary, S. Hall Young, formed a reception committee. Young was surprised and overwhelmed. He felt his hand gripped by "a lean, sinewy man of forty, with waving, reddish-brown hair and beard, his shoulders slightly stooped," wearing a Scottish cap, a long, gray tweed ulster, and an irresistible smile. The pious missionary took to the famous California naturalist like a hungry man to a cook, for Young was a nature lover as much as a soul saver. Muir, he wrote, "was esteemed and welcomed by the doctors of divinity, but little appreciated by any of them. He lived in a different world." Instantly, Young felt his loyalty to Jackson weaken and his wanderlust intensify.[2]

Muir's appreciation of the churchmen's mission was decidedly mixed. He granted that the Indians needed help in confronting the invading culture, particularly in avoiding the devastating consequences of drink, which so often produced a "whiskey howl" when inebriated men and women became loud and dangerous to themselves and everyone else. They needed better examples of modern civilization than the gold miners who came down the Stickeen (Stikine) River from British Columbia gold fields to spend the winter on the coast, most of whom were "struggling blindly for gold enough to make them indefinitely rich to spend their lives in aimless affluence, honor, and ease." The churchmen offered better values, a fact the natives seemed to appreciate. But in Muir's eyes the Indians, when they were not undone by alcohol, already possessed a strong ethical compass, exemplified in their kindness toward children and strangers, and were in some respects less superstitious than "many of the lower classes of whites." And, he was soon complaining, some of the missionaries, far from showing compassion, "seem to be devoting themselves to themselves."[3]

Mixed feelings about the churchmen would soon tilt toward contempt. Eager to see more than the "moist dragglement of unpretentious wooden huts and houses" around the fort, he eagerly joined a couple of trips the missionaries organized into wilder country. In each case he came back disgusted with their company. First they sailed up the Stikine River, where more than a hundred glaciers could be seen, remnants of the great ice sheet that had recently carved a deep Yosemite-like canyon. Chunks of ice floated around their boat as they continued on to the old Hudson's Bay trading post of Glenora. Here, ignoring the churchmen's warnings, Muir and Young set off to climb a nearby mountain and gain a grand view of the coastal range. Near sunset Young, struggling to keep up with his nimble companion, slipped on loose rock and slid over the edge. He saved himself from a fatal plunge by clutching at an outcropping, but the effort dislocated both shoulders, leaving him hanging in severe pain over a glacier a thousand feet below. Muir, whistling old Scots songs to cheer him up, managed to get below on a narrow ledge and then to swing his companion to safety. Carrying the injured man down to the level surface of the ice, Muir worked until midnight to reset his shoulders and bind his arms tight to his body with a torn-up shirt. "All that night," Young later wrote, "this man of steel and lightning worked, never resting a minute, doing the work of three men. . . . My eyes brim with tears even now when I think of his utter self-abandon as he ministered to my infirmities." When they got back to the boat around dawn, the disapproving ministerial party upbraided Young for his foolishness in going off on a wild goose-chase with Muir. "Oh, hell," roared Muir. "Can't you see the man's hurt?"[4]

The ministers and their wives also seemed insufficiently sensitive to the Indians and to the beauty of their surroundings. In late July they organized another boat excursion, this one north to the Chilkat tribe living along the Lynn Channel in hope of establishing a church among them. For a while the ministerial faces glowed with delight as they looked on the "glorious page of Nature's Bible," forgetting "the whole system of seminary and pulpit theology." But as the boat moved too slowly and the cost of the voyage mounted, the group decided to return home, their mission to the Indians postponed and their enthusiasm for nature quickly exhausted. Muir was disappointed and irritated by the limits of their piety.[5]

On the way back they stopped at a deserted Indian village where native builders and artists had left traces of their craft in cedar houses and totem poles. Muir, who knew something about woodworking, was impressed: "With the same tools not one in a thousand of our skilled mechanics could do as good a work." But while he was sketching away, one of the divines sawed off a totem pole and hauled it aboard ship— "a sacrilege," Muir lamented. The Indians in their party complained about the outrage but were willing to accept a few presents in compensation. Muir left no doubt about whose side he was on in the episode.[6]

Determined to complete the aborted voyage and see the "ice mountains" to the north that both miners and Tlingits had described, Muir induced Young to join him on a canoe trip. Native rowers would do all the hard work, sparing the healing shoulders. They left on 9 October, camping most of the time but on one occasion sleeping under an Indian roof ("I never felt more at home," Muir reported). Their route took them up the western side of Admiralty Island and around the top of Chichagof Island, where they stopped to preach a sermon to the Hoonah, emphasizing their common origins and urging a policy of peace and harmony. Rumors of conflict among the Chilkats revised their destination; instead of making for the Lynn Channel, they decided to cross the Icy Strait and drift along the shoreline, seeking glaciers.

On their laps they spread out the British sea captain George Vancouver's chart of 1794, but as the Hoonah warned, it proved badly out of date. Over the intervening eighty-five years the coastal wall of

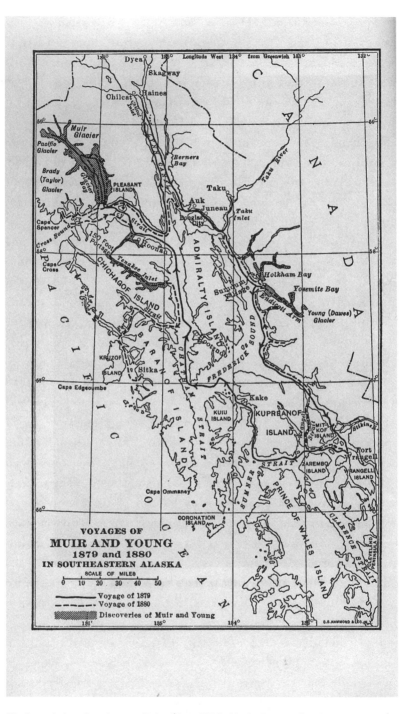

Muir's travels through southeastern Alaska. (Samuel Hall, Alaska Days with John Muir, *1915*)

glaciers had cracked and retreated, opening up a fjord some twenty miles long, which would become known as Glacier Bay. Energized by the prospects of discovery, they plunged straight into that opening, paddling down the middle, looking left and right at land that was as new as any in the world. Here was a wilderness as unexplored as Muir could want. Here was an incomparable laboratory for studying the making and remaking of the natural world.

Only recently had the Hoonah entered the bay, appearing along with the willow and alders in the wake of the glaciers, establishing summer camps on the newly exposed shore where they hunted harbor seals and game. Muir's party surprised one such hunting party, who brandished their guns before getting reassurance that no harm was meant. Two years before Muir arrived, Lieutenant Charles Erskine Scott Wood of the U.S. Navy had been here, palavering with the native hunters and hiking into the Fairweather Mountains, but he produced no written record of his explorations until 1882, and then they were vague and unscientific. Thus, Muir was the first man to write about this austere landscape, to understand the physical processes in motion, and to suggest names for some of the more prominent features—the Geikie and Hugh Miller inlets, for example, named in honor of some of Scotland's great contributors to geology.[7] The largest of the inlets and glaciers others would name after Muir. Such names did not suggest that any man owned this fresh, rugged face of nature, but only that those who helped reveal its story to science deserved special recognition.

The Indians in the canoe party, not much interested in geology and worried about the approaching winter and the distance between them and their families, grew impatient with Muir's insatiable curiosity. Their leader Toyatte called him a witch for his relentless pushing into dangerous places, while the others could see no sense in braving sleety rain or canoe-crunching ice to get more views. Yet one morning, for a long moment, they stood together in silent awe as the dawn rose, turning the high peaks to a deep redness like "molten metal fresh from a furnace." Differences of knowledge or creed fell away as they shared a "holy vision" of divine power at work on earth. Later Muir credited his Indian companions with an "eager, childlike attention" to nature akin to his own, so different from "the deathlike apathy of weary town-dwellers" beaten down by "toil and care and poor shallow comfort."[8]

The earnest minister Young felt assured that Muir, in exploring Glacier Bay, was "a devout theist," giving credit to "the immanence of God in nature and His management of all the affairs of the universe." Despite a week of nearly ceaseless rain, the naturalist was in a constant state of high ecstasy, praising the Creator repeatedly for showering the earth with love and beauty. Under Muir's instruction the minister was led to see how the seemingly ruthless force behind volcanic upheavals, the burying of granite peaks under deep blankets of ice and snow, or rubbly moraines dumping into the sea were all expressions of a divine plan. And if nature was ever being renewed and improved, then surely nature could produce also a nobler race of human beings. "All things," Young concluded, "work together for good." Through Muir's optimistic influence the minister gained confidence that, even in this seemingly godforsaken Glacier Bay, nature gave reason for hope.[9]

Muir's fiancée in Alhambra Valley had been left at home struggling with her misgivings about the risks that he was taking. It was hard for Louie to appreciate the impulses that took her lover away from their warm, pleasant nest and drove him back into a lonely and dangerous life in the wild. Did his writing, she wondered, require him to go so far away as Alaska? They corresponded regularly, sending letters by slow-moving boats, Louie always fretting about the dangers posed by nature, and he trying to bolster her courage by telling her that God was everywhere, even in the far north, always looking out for him. "Surely you would not have me away from this work," he asked, "dawdling in a weak willed way on your lounge." But why did he have to go so far to find God? "I shiver," she wrote, "with every thought of the dark cruel winter drifting down, down—and never a beam of sunshine on all that wide land of mists. . . . O John, John, do not stay too long."[10]

Muir did not tell her everything that happened on the voyage; he left out details that might heighten her anxiety or offend her sensibilities. He described his adoption into the Tlingit tribe and the bestowal of an Indian name, but did not mention that he was offered an Indian wife. He omitted Young's near fatal accident on the mountainside and the often lawless condition of this intercultural frontier, the physical dangers to which he was exposed. But he tried her patience sorely by delaying his return, stopping over for a full month in Portland where he got entangled in "a snarl of lectures" that lasted into the next year. It was late January 1880 when Louie discovered, through reading the shipping news, that he had reached San Francisco.[11]

When finally they were reunited, Muir soothed away all the Strentzel family concerns. He indicated a readiness to give up his wandering ways and settle down to married life on the ranch. They fixed their wedding date for 14 April in Martinez, one week before his forty-second birthday. He was nine years older than his bride. The Rev. I. E. Dwinelle of Sacramento would perform the marriage ceremony, and Muir found a tailor to make him a proper suit. Writing offers continued to roll in during those months of planning for the ceremony, Scribner's Magazine wanting several articles on Alaska, while his newspaper asked for "a bunch of facts on lack of government" in the territory. But his final bachelor days were too packed with social demands to permit any serious work. With a former mayor of San Francisco he inspected the new Golden Gate Park emerging from the city's western sand dunes. He dined at the Bohemian Club with bookseller Upham and attended a play at the Baldwin Theatre, finding "no healthy sentiment in it" and the atmosphere badly polluted by the gaslights. With another friend, the real-estate agent Thomas Magee, he went skiing and tramping around Lake Tahoe and talking future land investments. None of those distractions was very satisfying; to Louie he complained, "I am drifting, and unsettled, and lonesome, in this big trodden wilderness of tameness." Their wedding could not come soon enough, now that he had seen Alaska.[12]

The couple insisted on a small, quiet ceremony, but afterward their news quickly went out over the state and country. No one in Portage even knew the event was coming, nor did the Bidwells or many other friends. Likewise in Indianapolis, Muir's marriage came as a shock: Janet Moores, who as a small girl had comforted him as he lay blinded in his boarding house, wondered how he could have deserted her: "You were our sweetheart since we were little things." Who is this bride, she wondered—"a bird or a flower, a fairy, a nymph, a disguised princess, or simply a woman after Wordsworth's heart and your own?" Only Jeanne Carr, down in Pasadena, knew about and approved the match since she had done so much to arrange it. To Mrs. Strentzel, she wrote, "Above fame, and far stronger than any wish to see his genius acknowledged by his peers, I have desired for him the completeness which can only come in living for others, in perfected home relations." Louie, she declared, "is the *only* woman that I ever knew, who seemed a mate for John." A male friend took a more jocular view of Muir's choice of bride and in-laws: "Dr is a Millionaire and the daughter is the only child! Now our dear little Johnny is in clover. . . . How soon do you start upon the circuit of the globe?"[13]

That full round-the-earth circuit would have to wait for a quarter century. The immediate reality was little clover and a lot of work, as the groom moved his trunks and books to the ranch and undertook to learn the orchard business. He did not intend to be an idle son-in-law but a willing volunteer for the job of agricultural manager of the whole Strentzel estate. For three months after the wedding he devoted himself to family life and business, getting initiated into the needs of the various crops and the challenges of fruit marketing. But his friends knew how hard it would be for him to settle down in such a fixed life for very long. And true to their predictions, late in July he put all that husband and ranch business aside as the traveling itch came over him again. He would not go around the world, but he would go back north once again to Alaska. After packing his bags and saying goodbye, he sailed on the steamer *California*. He left Louie pregnant but promising to be back in time for the fall grape harvest and well in advance of the birth of their first child.

❦

Muir's sudden reappearance at Fort Wrangell in July 1880 surprised the Rev. Young, now married to a fellow missionary and running a training academy for Indian youth. "When can you be ready," were Muir's first words when they met, "get your canoe and crew and let us be off."[14] He was keen to see Glacier Bay once more, this time in a summer mood. Once again he would send field dispatches to the San Francisco newspaper and would fill a notebook with journal entries and pencil sketches of the landscape. Wild Alaska had begun to displace the Sierra Nevada in his passions. Its glaciated mountains, forests, roiling seas, bears, wolves, whales, and migrating salmon were all on a scale far exceeding California's grandeur, making his pulse pound with excitement. Young was instantly caught up in the spirit and ran off to pack his clothes.

They would need a new set of Indian oarsmen for this second journey, for good Toyatte had been shot in the forehead by a drunken member of another tribe. "Thus died for his people," Muir mourned, "the noblest old Roman of them all."[15] In place of the first crew they recruited Captain Tyeen, Hunter Joe, and Smart Billy. On an impulse the minister brought along his wife's longhaired dog Stickeen, a small brown and black mongrel, over the protests of the rest of the party. On a bright, calm mid-August day they pushed off, heading for Cape Fanshawe, Sum Dum (Holkam) Bay, and the new gold-mining town of Juneau.

The *Evening Bulletin* sent along instructions that Muir should turn in a thrilling report from the gold diggings, but he would not cooperate. "These men must think I am a fool like the rest of this crowd [of miners]," Young remembered him saying, "asking me to leave my nature study and join that mob!" In one of his columns, printed on the paper's front page, he addressed the mining prospects but with little enthusiasm: "This country will be found moderately rich in the precious metals, but owing to obstacles in the way of their development, all the other resources—fish, furs, timber, etc.—will be brought into the market of the world long before any considerable quantity of mineral wealth has been uncovered." That was as far as he would go in economic analysis or booster rhetoric.[16]

American-style materialism had entered the heads of the Indians too, often deadening their traditional values and making them no better than the whites in destructiveness. Hunter Joe, for example, while the sails were carrying the canoe forward and leaving him little to do, casually shot a seagull flying overhead. Muir severely reprimanded him for such pointless cruelty, and Captain Tyreen warned that the deed would bring bad luck. Joe blamed the invading whites for causing him to forget that animals, like humans, have souls and must be respected. It was a defense with which Muir sympathized, but not if it meant falling back into a superstitious belief that human illness or misfortune came from vengeful animals. He would not abandon scientific explanation, which could not find any such linkage. For him, religion and ethics must be compatible with modern science. On the other hand, modern science was compatible with moral consideration for all creatures. At the other end of the canoe sat Indian men who were caught in a conflict between their ancient shamanistic beliefs and the thoughtless cruelty and money-obsession of a frontier society.[17]

Briefly, they entered and explored Glacier Bay, little changed from the previous year, but then moved on west to the shallow new fjord named Taylor Bay, left behind by the retreat of the massive Taylor (now Brady) glacier, which lies like a gleaming breastplate on the flanks of Mt. Crillon. Struggling for a foothold on the dull slate-gray mud and gravel left behind by the retreating ice were bright garden spots of grasses, yellow moss, saxiphrage, epilobium, and sedges, while along the glacial edges could be seen the remains of ancient forests crushed by the ice. Scattered everywhere were pulverized chips and splinters of wood. The crew gathered salmon berries and strawberries and hunted grizzlies, but Muir was hungry for ice.

Rising early one wet, blustery morning he set out alone to walk across the great glacier—seven miles wide at a point near camp. He took along an ice axe and a chunk of bread, but despite the gathering storm, carried no blankets or gun or matches. Even then he felt encumbered and soon shed his heavy rubber boots and overcoat, letting the rain thoroughly soak him from head to toe. In his steps trotted the minister's little dog Stickeen, refusing to go back to the tent and gamely following wherever Muir would go. The surface of a glacier is not glassy smooth and level but heaves into sharp crusts and is pitted with deep holes and crevasses, a rough place for both human and canine feet. All day they labored across this "prairie of ice" and then down its lateral moraine, until darkness began to gather and the danger of spending an unsheltered night far from camp began to loom. Belatedly, they set out to make a quick return.

The way back was more daunting than Muir expected, for in his path yawned more and more crevasses, gaping like black chambers of death. Again and again man and dog had to leap those cracks in the ice, until they came to one that was forty feet across, too wide to jump. Retracing their path in the waning light to find another route was no option. Eight feet down the sides of the crevasse, however, stretched a bridge of ice from wall to wall—a fragile sliver above the chasm. With his axe Muir cut steps down to the bridge and then inched his way across. More cutting of footholds brought him precariously up the other side.

He had left the dog behind. Stickeen was painfully aware of its predicament and, frantic with fear of being abandoned, began to howl and whine. Muir coaxed it to follow his lead. Screwing up its courage, the dog flew down the steps, over the bridge, and up to safety. Its whole body was shaking with nervous tension and a rush of adrenaline; the little mutt whirled, danced, and moaned with relief. Muir too was shaken by their close call with death. "The joy of deliverance burned in us like fire, and we ran without fatigue, every muscle with immense rebound glorying in its strength." By ten p.m. they were back in camp, drying out before a crackling fire but too exhausted to eat.[18]

The journal entry for that day did not mention the nearly fatal ordeal, perhaps because he was still too mentally exhausted to want to relive the awful moment. The only record came in a passage he wrote years later—capturing a still vivid memory, as he could never forget the dog's tumult of emotions. Stickeen's fear, he believed, was as real and painful as any ever felt by a human being, and the dog's bravery as impressive as a man's. Mutual peril had joined man and dog in an intense comradeship, erasing hierarchical distinctions between the species. Returning to Fort Wrangell, Muir had to take leave of his small companion, never to see him again. But he went away realizing, more than ever, that being kind to animals, avoiding needless cruelty to them, was only the first step toward a new ethic. A fuller respect on the part of humans for all the ways in which they were bound together in feeling and intelligence with other animals was also required. Animals were not alien to the human consciousness; they shared the same emotions and felt the same vulnerability to death as humankind, bonding them to humans in an ancient kinship. Three decades later he could still say, "Nothing in after years has dimmed that Alaska storm-day."[19]

Telling of the dog's bravery came to be the most popular story in Muir's abundant repertory. He told it over and over in elegant parlors, in railroad smoking cars or aboard ship, on hiking trails, and as he did so, it expanded in length and dramatic effect. In 1897 the *Century* published a version under what he thought was a trivializing title, "An Adventure with a Dog and a Glacier." The magazine editor omitted much of the story's radical moral content, including lines that criticized human prejudice and discrimination against other creatures: "The more we learn of them the nearer to ourselves we find them," he had written in the original draft. "We throw our heavens open to every vertical mammal but close them against the horizontal ones.... I believe that there is a hereafter for some of God's other people as well as for Jews & Gentiles, & that measured by love some dogs may be great even in heaven." Then in 1909 Houghton Mifflin brought out a thin volume titled *Stickeen*, which became one of Muir's best-selling books. Not only did it appeal to a nation of pet lovers but also to an age that had become fascinated by the psychology and intelligence of nonhuman beings. The spread of evolutionary thinking, animal-welfare legislation, bird-watching, and other challenges to homocentrism all gave this story of an ordinary-looking but brave little dog a deeper significance, exactly as Muir hoped.[20]

More than promoting an inclusive system of ethics motivated Muir. He was also haunted by guilt, for it had been his thoughtlessness that put a fellow creature's life in danger, as it did his own. Just as he had carelessly led Stickeen's "master," the Rev. Young, on a nearly fatal hike, he had failed to consider the dog's physical limitations in their trek over the ice. In both cases he had expected his companion to be as strong, agile, and impervious to the elements as he; after nearly killing them both, his heart softened and he felt remorse. Stickeen's story revealed not only a richness of personality and character in the animal world but also shortsightedness bordering on incompetence in the outdoors.

Most of Muir's admirers, listening to his story of Stickeen and other tales, did not doubt for an instant his survival skills in the outdoors. But a few saw him in a different light. "In spite of his having spent a large part of his life in the wilderness," wrote one of his good friends, the naturalist C. Hart Merriam, Muir "knew less about camping than almost any man I have ever camped with."[21] At times he seemed foolishly indifferent to cold, discomfort, lack of sleep, or threats to life and limb. Often he set off into the backcountry without sufficient gear or left too late in the day for common sense. He had to endure long periods with little food. All his life he gave little thought to hypothermia or a new bout of malaria or a crippling fall a long way from help. While many assumed that he was a master of survival techniques, someone always to be depended on, Merriam found him to be a negligent hiker who too often let his passion overcome his judgment. He trusted too much in the constant benevolence of nature or in the prevision of others.

Such may have been all right in his innocent youth, but now he was a middle-aged married man, and others depended on his taking greater care. They included the ever-trustful Young and his dog Stickeen, both of whom he let down in his sometimes careless way. Then there was Louie waiting anxiously in California, who would have been devastated by any mishap to him. And then there was the child waiting to be born. All of them he had put at risk that nearly final day on the Taylor glacier.

⚬━✦━⚬

True to his promise, he was back on the Strentzel ranch by late September and ready to minister to the needs of Louie, who was going through a difficult pregnancy. News came that his father Daniel was ailing too. The old man was now very lame and living with his daughter Joanna, while mother Ann continued to live independently in Portage. Daniel seemed to have mellowed with age, losing some of his harsh intolerance: "I think he has a kindlier feeling toward the whole world," Joanna reported. "I believe he will yet spend his last days with us." But Muir, although an inveterate traveler who had run away twice to Alaska, was not ready to go see his father or any of his midwestern kinfolk. He had not seen any of the Muirs since the fall of 1867. Through the fall and winter after his second Alaska trip he chose to stay by Louie's side and ignore the pleadings from Joanna and others to come on a visit. Annie Bidwell wondered whether he had finally and permanently settled down: "Have you found there is some happiness in this world outside of glaciers and other glories of nature?"[22]

Early the next spring, on 25 March, Louie gave birth to a baby girl, whom they named Annie Wanda. She had many namesakes—mother Ann Gilrye Muir, the spinster-sister Annie in Portage, Annie Bidwell in Chico. Perhaps to avoid the confusion of names, she became simply Wanda, and for her father she was the very perfection of nature. "A tiny healthy happy daintily featured lassie," he gushed, "not at all dull & lumpish like most of the baby garblings that I have seen . . . How beautiful the world is, & how beautiful is the time of the coming of our little love." She came precisely at "bloom time" in the orchards, brightening their interior space as the fruit trees brightened the ranch. "Never since the Glacial Period or the Baby Period began," he wrote to Mrs. Bidwell, "were happier people."[23]

The once-solitary man of the mountains was now not only husband and son-in-law but also the world's most enthusiastic father. Little girls were always his favorites, and he would be blessed with two of his own. He would choose their clothes, supervise their education, introduce them to the outdoors, hover over them too protectively, and spoil them shamelessly. Never once would he raise a hand to punish them, so determined he was to avoid the harsh disciplining that he had experienced as a lad. How he would have behaved in the role of father had he faced the different challenge of raising a son or two would never be known. Daughters were what he wanted, and daughters were what he got. Now surrounded by baby Wanda, wife Louie, and the doting grandparents under a common roof, he was as passionately domesticated as he once had been passionately alone in the wild.

Domesticated, that is, for a while—until 4 May 1881, when once more a chance to travel appeared and he boarded a ship that would take him away from family warmth and off to cold Alaskan shores again. This time he joined the government's Revenue Marine vessel *Thomas Corwin*, a coal-burning steamship captained by Calvin L. Hooper of the Navy, bound for the Aleutians, the Bering Strait, and the Arctic Ocean. An invitation came to join the crew as ship's naturalist, along with the physician and anthropologist Irving Rosse and the ornithologist E. W. Nelson, and Muir felt he could not refuse the opportunity. They would be gone until October, a period of nearly six months during which he would produce still more letters to the *Evening Bulletin*, more entries and sketches for his journals, and, posthumously, through the editorial compiling of his literary executor William Badè, a book entitled *The Cruise of the Corwin*. That book would bring together some of the most engaging pieces of writing that Muir ever produced. It would capture a profound change going on in nature and in the condition of the northern territory's human inhabitants.

A predecessor of the U.S. Coast Guard, the Marine Service was responsible for preventing smuggling and assisting mariners in distress. Three ships had disappeared in the Arctic Sea—two whaling vessels, the *Vigilant* and *Mount Wollaston*, and the scientific expeditionary steamer *Jeannette*. Commanded by Lt. George W. DeLong (U.S.N.), the *Jeannette* was sent out to explore the mysterious Wrangel Land (not to be confused with Fort Wrangell), which some thought might be a large island that touched the North Pole, or even another Antarctica. The ship had left San Francisco nearly two years earlier but then, it was assumed, had been caught in the Arctic ice pack and the crew stranded on land or sea. The *Corwin*, outfitted with a reinforced hull and substantial provisions, was to rescue them, or at least bring back a report on their fate.

The rescue mission was a bust. No survivors, no wreckage, nor much reliable information could be found for any of the lost vessels. While the *Corwin* was refueling with coal in Plover Bay, at the extreme eastern end of Siberia's Chukchi Peninsula, the *Jeannette* was being crushed in the ice five hundred miles to the northeast. The ship quickly sank, and Capt. DeLong put his men in three small boats that they pulled over the ice until they could row through open water to the Lena Delta. Only two of the boats made it, and then they came ashore at widely separated points. DeLong's group died soon after their landing, at the end of October 1881, from starvation and exposure. The party headed by chief engineer George Melville, although badly frostbitten, survived on tea and pemmican until local Yakuts saved them. Revived and rested, they managed to find their comrades' bodies frozen in the snow, along with a pathetic last note in DeLong's journal. Then they made their mournful way back to the United States via St. Petersburg, arriving in New York "one year from the day when our three boats were separated in that fatal gale."[24]

Muir's expedition, in contrast, was almost idyllic, at least in the eyes of one who could be thrilled by the experience of summering in the Arctic. Summer, to be sure, was a relative term. Although days were extraordinarily long, the sky was overcast almost the entire voyage, and snow and sleet were daily in the air. In those northern latitudes the temperate rain forests were left far behind, and in their place loomed bleak, brown coastal mountains lapped by iron-gray seas. Yet there was richness of life—a complex ecosystem of human hunters, pelagic mammals, and colonies of birds whitening the islands with their guano. Confined behind a ship's rail much of the time, going ashore only where the captain permitted, Muir devoted much of his attention to the native peoples he met. Many came on board, smiling and joking, and others he visited in their settlements. He took notes on everything, but especially on their way of life in this most difficult of environments.

After a tumultuous crossing of the North Pacific, the ship came into what is now Dutch Harbor, Unalaska. Glaciers, Muir noted, had given this island and others in the Aleutian chain a sharp, forbidding profile, but then blankets of moss and lichen had softened their edges. Warmed by ocean currents, the place allowed the growing of a few vegetables and grains and offered pasture for livestock. Civilization here seemed surprisingly advanced for so remote a location. The Alaska Commercial Company, whose agent entertained them in his snug parlor, had organized the native men into a well-paid workforce for killing seals or otters for their furs. Their earnings, however, were spent on western-style clothing, "not so good as their own furs," on household trinkets for their crowded, fetid cottages, and on "kvass," a kind of beer that sent them into "hoggish dissipation, hair-pulling, wife-beating, etc." The Russian Orthodox Church was still present, trying to save their souls, but that seemed a futile effort against the Aleuts' descent into a poisonous mix of savagery and civilization.[25]

Next on the itinerary were the Pribiloffs, where a hundred thousand seals were harvested every year out of a population of some three to four million, plus another forty thousand taken in trade with the Russians. Six thousand sea otters died annually too. Only the native peoples, and whites married to native women, could, by law, do the killing. In the face of such organized mass slaughter, Muir's distress over a sailor's shooting of a single seal floating on a cake of ice may seem disproportionate. But in this instance he was eyewitness to a brutal killing. "It seemed cruel to kill it, and most wonderful to us, as we shivered in our overcoats, that it could live happily" in water that hovered around the freezing point, with "wet sludge for its bed."[26]

He condemned the ubiquitous supply of alcohol but was not ready to condemn the selling of rifles to the natives, for they could survive only by the hunt, and in that hunt a rifle was superior to a harpoon. Overall, those natives who remained more or less independent of the white man's economy, apart from buying a few guns and ammunition, seemed better off than those who had become company employees. In late May they landed at a self-reliant village on St. Lawrence Island, where Muir first encountered the Inupiats, to him a distinctive and attractive people. "Dressed in their roomy furs, tied at the waist, they seem better-dressed than any other Indians I have seen." Although short of cash, they avoided the squalor and misery of more U.S.-trade dependent villages.[27]

On the Siberian coast he had an opportunity to examine how one might contrive a boat or house in a land without many trees. Each was made of animal skins stretched over a few sticks of driftwood; protected by such thin membranes the natives were able to survive the elements. Inside the huts it was cold, Muir recorded, for they had little firewood and ate their meals uncooked. But inside also was a set of clean, fur-lined bedrooms into which whole families piled and where they slept comfortably nude through the severest weather.

Through June and July the *Corwin* crisscrossed the Bering Strait repeatedly, dodging the winter ice pack and waiting for it to recede enough to allow them access to the Arctic. They put a party ashore in Siberia to search by dogsled for traces of the missing vessels, and Muir got an opportunity to ride behind "two rows of tails" across the frozen ground before returning to his ship. Two days later they broke their oaken rudder against a piece of ice and had to put into shallow water to make repairs. Often they saw whalers and smelled their burn-ing try-works, by which they reduced blubber to oil. The Inupiats showed them how to eat the raw, rubbery whale skin, with the blubber still attached, their knives and fingers flying but their manners sur-prisingly polite and temperate. So the gloomy, depressing, but often interesting days passed, while they waited for an opening.

Muir filled his long hours by gathering evidence of glaciation wherever they touched land. Plover Bay, for example, proved to be a fjord, with walls two thousand feet high. Along their route he noted an abundance of volcanic cones, many of them forming distinct islands, but the ice had swept over them too and in some cases made islands where once there had been a solid mass of land. The whole of Bering Strait, so clearly a land bridge between continents at one time, had been gouged by ice. "While the crystal glaciers were creating Yosemite Valley," he wrote to Louie, "a thousand were uniting here to make Behring Strait & Behring Sea. The south side of the Aleutian chain of islands was the boundary of the continent & the ocean."[28]

But the grand events of ancient times kept receding before the liv-ing drama in the here and now: shipwrecks, lost souls, death in many forms. One of the most melancholy stops was made on their return to St. Lawrence Island, lying athwart the strait in American waters. In early July, some two months from home, Muir penned reports to Louie and the newspaper of what he had seen there—dead bodies scattered across a surface of black lava. His fellow naturalist Nelson, "a zealous collector for the Smithsonian Institution," as Muir described him, gathered a hundred human skulls, "throwing them together in heaps to take on board, just as when a boy in Wisconsin I used to gather pumpkins in the fall after the corn was shocked. The boxfuls on deck looked just about as unlike a cargo of cherries as possible, but I will not oppress you with grim details."[29]

Earlier a population of 1,500 natives had lived on the island, but then during the winter of 1877–78 two-thirds had died of starvation. Seven villages were completely depopulated, the last to die remaining in their beds or piled like firewood in a corner. Newspaper reports of the tragedy had been published in Honolulu and New Bedford, blaming the deaths on the commercial over-hunting of walruses on which the people subsisted. While some argued that liquor had left them too drunk to hunt, Muir merely noted that the village inhabitants had not frozen to death nor lacked hunting weapons; they had plenty of warm skins and ammunition, which seemed to support the argument that it was commercial hunters who were indirectly responsible.[30]

All around the grim scene other forms of life continued to thrive. On that midsummer day nature seemed especially abundant and full of beautiful possibilities, presenting a bright contrast to the human charnel.

> Gulls, plovers, and ducks were swimming and flying about in happy life, the pure salt sea was dabbling white against the shore, the blooming tundra swept back to the snow-clad volcanoes, and the wide azure sky bent kindly over all—nature intensely fresh and sweet, the village lying in the foulest and most glaring death. The shrunken bodies, with rotting furs on them, or white, bleaching skeletons, picked bare by the crows, were lying mixed with kitchen-midden rubbish where they had been cast out by surviving relatives while they yet had strength to carry them.

The bodies and skeletons of a thousand men, women, and children challenged any easy optimism about nature's benevolence toward humankind. One of the survivors, who led them on a grim tour, summed up the grisly scene: "Dead, yes, all dead, all mucky, all gone!"[31]

Muir concluded that the people had died not merely because of white over-hunting of the walrus but also from too much reliance on the white man's goods and technology, sapping their traditional skills of survival. He warned that "unless some aid be extended by the government," all of the native peoples might die off. Washington must intervene to conserve the natives' food resource and protect them from an alien economy. "They seem easily susceptible of civilization, and well deserve the attention of our government."[32]

In fact native as well as white hunters had decimated the walrus population. The Inupiats possessed guns as well as whiskey, and with guns they could satisfy their seemingly insatiable hunger for trade goods. Days after visiting St. Lawrence, while coasting the shores of Alaska's Kotzebue Sound, Muir reported that traders there had been illegally exchanging repeating rifles for ivory, whalebone, and furs and that, far from avoiding the exchange, the local inhabitants protested any government effort to interfere. Tribes wanted the rifles to compete against one another in getting hides rather than meat. They destroyed "large amounts of game which they do not need. The reindeer [caribou] has in this manner been well-nigh exterminated within the last few years." Later he noted that the natives "make it a rule to kill every animal that comes within reach, without a thought of future scarcity," a behavior that made sense in a time of stone-tipped spears but made no sense in a time of guns. Perhaps the starvation on St. Lawrence Island was a sign of increasing maladaptation. If so, Muir believed that government must do more to protect those vulnerable people from outmoded habits as well as insidious new ways.[33]

The white hunters did not get off easily in Muir's moral accounting. The casual shooting of walruses by his own captain and messmates shocked him. It was a complete waste as the dead bodies immediately sank into the cold water. Near Icy Cape he watched commercial tusk hunters make quick work of any animals they found lounging innocently on the ice. Like the plains bison that was shot only for its tongue, the Pacific walrus (weighing twice as much) was shot only for its tusks, or for mere sport. The rest of the carcass was left to rot or feed wolves. It was a sad commentary on American morals. "From the shepherd with his lambs to the red-handed hunter, it is the same; no recognition of rights—only murder in one form or another."[34]

Sometimes the white hunters themselves died, or nearly so, of their cupidity. Late in the whaling season of 1871 thirty-three ships were trapped in the ice near Port Belcher on Alaska's Arctic coast, causing a catastrophic economic loss to their homeport of New Bedford, Massachusetts, although all lives were spared. By 1876 only twenty vessels comprised the Arctic whaling fleet, and half of them miscalculated the ice pack and got caught, most of their crews disappearing. Five years later, when Muir came on the scene, there were only a few last whaling ships still prowling those treacherous waters, still endangering men's lives to squeeze out a last return on investments. Two of the final casualties were the *Mount Wollaston* and the *Vigilant*. The only traces they left behind were tales told by Chukchi natives of going out to scavenge a ghostly ship and the lone pair of spectacles they found.[35]

Finally the pack ice retreated and the Arctic opened for traffic. After many failed attempts, Capt. Hooper was able to turn his bow toward Herald Island and, looming beyond, Wrangel Land. A British ship had discovered Herald in 1849, while Wrangel Land had likely never felt a human presence, unless the ill-fated *Jeannette* had reached it. Hooper put a fresh load of bituminous coal down into the hold, dug out of the cliffs at Cape Lisburne, and prepared his crew for spending, if necessary, the next winter immobilized in a frozen sea. It was by no means certain that they would be able to return from this excursion any time soon.

Muir described their historic landing on Herald Island for his San Francisco readers, proudly emphasizing his own role as intrepid pathfinder. A wide rampart of ice—breaking up, melting fast, but still difficult to pass through—defended the island, which was a solid chunk of granite some six miles across and as much as 1,200 feet high. It took the ship nine hours of effort and the coal-fired power of its engine to get close enough for a landing, and then they were still some two or three hundred yards from shore. They anchored in the midst of ice blocks sixty-five feet thick. While many of the crew dashed pell-mell to the snowy cliffs and made a futile effort to climb, Muir carefully chose the most suitable place for making an ascent and, with his ice axe, cut out steps and easily made his way up. At midnight he reached the high center of the island where he spent "one of the most impressive hours of my life." The sun was a red blur on the horizon, and the silent frozen ocean stretched indefinitely northward.[36]

On his way back to the ship, he made a quick collection of yellow poppies, mustard, dwarf willow, and other plants growing on this hard land. He spotted an Arctic fox and, clambering down the cliffs, passed thousands of gulls and murres standing on narrow ledges "like bottles on a grocer's shelf." A curious polar bear came swimming toward the ship, until the captain killed it with a bullet in the neck. No traces of the *Jeannette* appeared, although it was here that the ship was caught fast in the ice and for nearly two years was carried far to the west/northwest before sinking.

Fog moved in as the *Corwin* neared Wrangel Land.[37] A "land of mystery," it seemed likely to remain mysterious, as the ship sailed to and fro for nearly a week, unable to make a landing. Here again an armor of sea ice protected the land from any human invaders. But at last, on 12 August, they found a lead in the pack that brought them, with engine roaring, to a dry gravel bar that lay before the mouth of

Muir drawing with the caption: "First landing on Wrangel Land by a party from the steamer Corwin, while searching for the Jeanette Expedition." (H–A, JMP)

a wide, deep river. At last they could come ashore on the southeast corner of the island. All they found of human traces was scattered beach detritus: a bowhead whale with the baleen removed (the horn-like material found in the upper jawbone of certain species, used for corset stays), an oak barrel-stave, part of a boat's mast, a broken kayak paddle, and a fragment of a biscuit-box.

They named the river Clark and followed it a short distance into the snow-free, unglaciated interior, where the highest peaks jutted up more than 3,600 feet. Muir and his fellows could get only a glimpse of this large treeless island, some seventy miles long and forty miles wide. Despite its inaccessibility to sailors, its lowland lakes, tundra, and wetlands provided a well-populated nesting ground for birds, ranging from snowy owls and eider ducks to kittiwakes and sandpipers. Somehow ground squirrels had found their way to this isolated habitat, perhaps by a long-vanished land bridge, and polar bears were so numerous that Muir called Wrangel "the land of the white bear." Here too, if the party had stayed longer and looked harder, could be found the tusks and bones of the hairy mammoth, which had survived on the island for thousands of years after it went extinct on the Asian and North American continents.

Because of the condition of the ice, the *Corwin's* crew could allow themselves only two hours ashore on Wrangel Land. Muir waved a reluctant farewell to its stark beauty: "A land more severely solitary could hardly be found anywhere on the face of the globe." Ship's physician Rosse sounded more nationalistic and imperial. In commemoration of their visit, he recorded,

> a flag, placed on a pole of driftwood, was erected on a
> cliff, and to the staff was secured a wide-mouthed bot-
> tle and a tin cylinder, in which I enclosed information
> of our landing, etc. On raising the flag three cheers
> were given, and a salute was fired from the cutter in
> honor of our newly acquired territory. . . . [I]t may be
> remarked with pardonable pride that the acquisition
> of this remote island, though of no political or com-
> mercial value, will serve the higher and nobler pur-
> pose of a perpetual reminder of American enterprise,
> courage and maritime skill.[38]

Giving up on the *Jeannette* and the lost whalers, they sailed aimlessly around for a few more weeks, hoping for another chance at Wrangel Land but spending most of their time inspecting a reindeer domestication project among the Chukchi people and tacking through the Bering Strait.

By late October Muir was safely back home on the Strentzel ranch, unpacking his plant specimens and getting reacquainted with his baby daughter. When he had departed the orchards still had a few blooms glowing on their branches; now the growing season was over, Wanda was seven months old, and he was ready to put his rambling days behind him for a long while. He would have to wait a full decade before returning to Alaska, but he would never erase the images of that land, sea, and people from his mind's eye.

Far from a timeless dream world lying outside of history, Alaska presented a story of endless change—the oldest, most fundamental kind of change on the planet, caused by the forces of nature. Muir's ancestors had supposed that nature is always the same, following an ancient cycle of seasons established at the moment of Creation. Muir saw the nature of Alaska differently; he looked on it as a historian, discerning "ages" and "periods" while trying to explain why change occurred and what it produced. Alaska and the whole polar region that it bordered was everywhere a new, emergent, unfinished land, and that was its wonder. Daily it shifted with the flow of ice, now opening, now closing, now advancing, now receding in ways that humans could neither control nor predict.

Too often people looked on those natural changes as simply destructive. They saw the motion of land and ice as a threat to life, stability, and prosperity, which from a limited view was undeniably true. Forests disappeared under the glaciers, while expensive ships got crushed at sea. But people failed to see, Muir felt, that every change in the natural world prepares the ground for new life to flourish. Without the shifting ice there would be no polar bears, walruses, seals, nor the mosses and lichens that found an inviting foothold on fresh morainal soils. "What we in our faithless ignorance and fear call destruction," he wrote, "is creation finer and finer."[39] The moment of creation, he insisted, is now. Change is constant, change is good.

All the shores of Alaska, and of Siberia and Wrangel Land, told a story of earthly progress.

But there was a second kind of change going on in that northern country that troubled Muir—changes that humans brought to other forms of life and to each other. Those changes came as a consequence of the annexation of Alaska by an aggressive, modernizing nation that destroyed so much of what it touched. Suddenly an age-old relationship between native societies and the animals that supported them had been disrupted. A stable balance between predator and prey had begun to fall apart. Guns were the source of that disequilibrium, but the deeper problem was a new casualness about the taking of life that Muir witnessed among the Indians and Inupiats as well as whites.

Exactly how the two kinds of change differed, or why one was hopeful and the other distressing, Muir did not try to probe philosophically. For him, the geological forces making the natural world seemed to follow a divine plan that was forever creating beauty, like an artist painting over and over on the same canvas. In contrast, the forces of civilization loosed on the far north were murderous, not artistic. Armed with deadly technology, men shed the blood of innocent creatures with no remorse and little purpose. "One cannot but help feel sympathy with and be proud of these brave neighbors," Muir confessed, "fellow citizens in the commonwealth of the world."[40] He was thinking about whales and porpoises when he wrote those words, but they applied equally to all the creatures he met on his travels. He came home distressed by the slaughter he had witnessed—genocidal, he might have said, because his definition of "people" included all the plant and animal species that civilized man regarded as inferior or expendable.

That call for a new moral inclusiveness was not limited to plants and animals; Muir worried also about the fate of the indigenous peoples of Alaska and Siberia, whether they had already sunk into a debased dependency or were struggling to keep their economic freedom. He had discovered much in the "so-called savages" to admire: the quiet, competent dignity of Toyatte; the tears of a wife telling her husband good-bye; the laughing eyes of children raised without fear in a hard land; the shrewd negotiations of native traders who met the whites on equal terms.

As he moved farther away from the frontier settlements, where whites and natives lived intermingled, the natives became more and more attractive in their moral character. Inupiats, he decided, "are better behaved than white men, not half so greedy, shameless, or dishonest." Acknowledging how little he had come to know them in his travels, he was nonetheless strongly drawn to them: "These people interest me greatly, and it is worth coming far to know them, however slightly. . . . There was a response in their eyes which made you feel that they are your very brothers."[41]

Many have missed that humane, openhearted side of Muir who, for all his criticism of man's foibles, responded warmly to almost everyone he met, as a fellow citizen in nature's great commonwealth. Even Capt. Hooper of the *Corwin*, whom he criticized for mindlessly slaughtering walruses and polar bears, remained a friend; months after their cruise, Hooper brought along some of his crew on a cordial visit to Alhambra Valley. Muir made many friends among the whites invading Alaska for commercial or evangelical gain, as he did among the native peoples. He was not indiscriminant—rather, he was sympathetic. When he declared that he had found a home in the north, he meant that he had both touched its wild harmony and been touched by its all too human story, where change so often meant injustice, suffering, or death.

His friend the Rev. Young recalled a moment in their travels when Muir's empathy for the native Alaskans kept him up all night, nursing a sick child. Following their first excursion into Glacier Bay, they paid a visit to the Chilcat village of Yindestukki, whose chief man was Donnawuk. Worn out after much travel and tribal oratory, the explorers could not sleep because of the feeble whimpering of a very small baby whose mother had died. No nursing mothers in the village could provide any milk for the infant, and he was dying of starvation. Muir brought a can of milk from their canoe, diluted it with warm water, and began an all-night vigil of feeding and care. He bathed the child and walked with him in his arms for five or six hours, until he fell asleep. The next day they left their whole supply of canned milk with the chief's household, with instructions on feeding. Donnawuk was so moved that he offered to give the baby, if he survived, to Muir. Seven years later Young returned to the village and found that the baby had lived and grown into a healthy boy, whom he named John.[42]

So those passages along the Alaska coast in 1879–81 would be memorialized twice over: first in the naming of the Muir Glacier and then in the naming of an Indian boy whose life Muir had saved. The glacier stood as an exemplar of the great natural force that had sculpted a land of such compelling beauty and grandeur. The boy's recovery and development, on the other hand, represented a hope that western civilization might prove a blessing, rather than a curse, to the endangered peoples of the north.

CHAPTER 10

Husbandry

Since ancient times, poets have celebrated agriculture as a wooing of the earth, but Muir was not one of them. While he agreed that the earth is alive and fertile, he did not confuse plowing it with marriage. The farmer he cast into a more antagonistic relationship with the natural world. That realism came from enduring too much drudgery in his youth and from reading the Bible, which offered a harsh view of the origins of agriculture. According to the Book of Genesis, farming began as punishment for disobedience—Adam and Eve's eating the forbidden fruit. Agriculture lies outside the Garden of Eden in a fallen world where the farmer must wage unending war against a hostile array of thorns, thistles, and other impediments.

He had entered California's still-wild environment dreaming of how he might throw aside the plow and live on native flowers, sequoia sap, and pine needles. But the practical, hardheaded side of his character told him that he could not escape the burdens of physical labor; sooner or later he must live by the sweat of his brow. When he needed bread, he would have to work for it. Although he found in writing a way to escape that kind of labor, he understood nonetheless that society could not live without farming.

But if California offered Americans no escape from the necessity of agriculture, it did offer hope that agriculture might become a more attractive way of life than his father's pessimistic Old Testament allowed. "Farming," Muir wrote to his brother two years after arriving on the West Coast, "was a grim, material, debasing pursuit under father's generalship, but I think much more favorably of it now."[1] After a decade of sorting through his options, agriculture had so improved in his mind that he happily agreed to become a farmer again.

Such was implied in his decision to marry Louie Strentzel and, in effect, her family's rural estate. In becoming her spouse he acquired an acreage of his own, given as a kind of dowry at marriage, along with managerial responsibilities for the adjoining Strentzel property. For a while, it was an appealing job and, for the rest of his life, the Strentzel-Muir ranch was an appealing place to live. He would stay there more than thirty years and eventually be buried in the Alhambra Valley.

In deciding to marry Muir had decided to become a good husband *and* a good husbandman. The good husband is one who "husbands" the family resources, prudently managing the money and expenses of a household. The good husbandman, in the language of ancient rural tradition, is one skilled in the arts of husbandry, or farming. He applies knowledge and intelligence to the cultivating of plants and the raising of livestock. He manages the earth for long-term productivity and makes careful use of natural resources. Practical, intelligent management and a sense of responsibility were virtues deeply engrained in Muir's temperament, the legacy of his parents and grandparents and of his self-image as a native Scot—virtues that he now put into practice.

Later generations would tend to ignore this side of Muir's temperament and what it implied for his relationship to nature. Through his published writings Muir the solitary mountaineer, the devoted worshipper who found in nature a divine and perfect order, would inspire readers, but too often they would miss the significance of his years as a farmer whose goal was to reorder the earth's resources. They would not appreciate that much of his life, boy and man, was devoted to making the earth yield crops. Muir said little about that agricultural side or about the satisfactions or pains it brought. A few hints in his letters and unpublished journals are all we have to reveal what husbandry meant to him: a few glimpses of how he used the land, how he regarded the results, and how his practices compared to those of other farmers. Scanty though they are, those glimpses are enough to make Muir a more complicated figure in the landscape than a simple lover of the wild.

Muir the agriculturalist accepted that nature must, to some extent, be transformed by technology and labor into farms, food, money, and family security. Not whether that transformation should occur at all, but how far he or society ought to go in that direction became the persistent question of his later years.

His father-in-law John Strentzel had chosen well the site of his estate—a sun-filled valley flanked by miles of rolling hills. Native live oaks, Pacific madrone, and laurel dotted the hillsides. Extensive plantations of imported eucalyptus trees were also beginning to take root, adding a sharper tang to the air. Cattle grazed on the grassy flanks, which turned brilliantly green in the rainy winters and tawny gold in the rainless summers. A creek coursed down the valley floor to merge with the broad Sacramento River, where it passed through the Carquinez Straits before rounding into San Pablo and San Francisco bays. Fog flowing in from the Pacific Ocean often submerged San Francisco and the coastal hills circling the bay, but fog was a less frequent visitor to this interior valley. Here temperatures were warmer than on the coast while the summer heat was less intense than in the

John Strentzel standing on his ranch, with the old adobe house in the background. (John Muir Historic Site, National Park Service)

Central Valley, making a sheltered, temperate place ideal for growing things. Strentzel saw immediately that "here I can realize my long cherished dream of a home surrounded by orange groves, and all kinds of fruits and flowers, [where] I can literally recline under my own vine and fig-tree."[2]

Mexican soldiers, disappointed by the lack of game, had dubbed this valley the Arroyo el Hambre, or valley of hunger. Despite that discouraging name, the commander of the Presidio in San Francisco, Don Ignacio Martinez, had been pleased to receive from the government of Mexico a grant of 17,000 acres in and near the valley. He called his part of the valley the Rancho el Pinole and, on his retirement, settled here and built an adobe house for his family.[3]

In April 1853, the Strentzels began acquiring lands of the deceased Don Martinez, until they owned a main ranch covering 856 acres in the valley and surrounding hills and an extended estate of 2,665 acres, including rangelands in the nearby Briones Hills. Louisiana Strentzel renamed the Arroyo el Hambre the Alhambra Valley, after the sumptuous citadel of the Moorish kings of Spain. They changed more than the name. According to the *California Farmer* in 1864, "Dr. Strentzel found this valley a wild and has converted it into a Paradise, . . . one of the beauty spots of California. . . . The scenery around is worthy of the pencil of our best artists, the grouping of the lofty hills is truly grand, light and shade, clear mountainside and shady nook, groups of trees, cattle ranches, and here and there a cottage, make it picturesque."[4]

The Strentzels did not follow the Moorish style in making their architectural embellishments. They put up a Dutch Colonial house, with broad gambrel roof and a row of dormer windows, which later became the home of Muir and his bride. Farther up the valley, on a low knoll, the older couple erected in 1882 an imposing gray-painted residence in the Italianate style—three stories high surmounted by a windowed cupola from which one could see all the way to the harbor. The new house featured twin front parlors with brick fireplaces and lofty ceilings, a formal dining room and a large kitchen in the rear, several bedrooms and a study on the second floor, with a great open storeroom on the third floor. No mere farmhouse, it was a veritable mansion exuding genteel respectability, a harbinger of a new era in California agriculture.

Stretching away from the great house, up and down the valley where Don Martinez's cattle had once grazed, now marched the serried rows of Strentzel's orchards and vineyards. The immigrant physician turned gentleman farmer looked on this scene with more than quick profit in mind; he was a social visionary, a reformer, and an agricultural experimentalist. He dreamed of creating a more sustainable rural community, one based not on the casual beef and hide trade of the past, or on the immense wheat and barley fields that had characterized much of California farming since statehood, but rather on the more steady investments of the horticulturist. Grain production, Strentzel warned repeatedly, depleted the soil and, because of its volatile markets and industrial scale, was an unstable foundation for the cultivator. "The soil," he warned, "is rapidly failing in productivity owing to the rapacious system of American agriculture."[5]

The completion of the transcontinental railroad opened a better, more long-term alternative of raising fruit and shipping it to eastern cities. American consumers were eager to put more fruit on their tables, and California was the best place ever to produce it. Horticulture would encourage soil conservation and social stability. Thus a new era of farming—an era of tending permanent trees and vines heavily laden with fruit—would put more money into the pockets of the rural producer, would encourage people to put down roots, and would fill their senses with beauty and fragrance.

Strentzel gained considerable credibility for his vision by winning many state fair ribbons for his red and white wines. At the 1863 fair he first showed off his sweet white Muscat raisins, a variety that would one day become the basis of a major state crop. He tried growing not only new kinds of grapes for wine and raisin making but also thirty-six varieties of apples, thirty-five varieties of pears, fifty varieties of peaches, along with quinces, plums, figs, olives, and almonds. The Alhambra Valley would grow almost anything, he believed, and he spent most of his remaining days trying out the possibilities. He became renowned across the state not only for his picturesque home but also for the practical promise of his plantings.[6]

Others shared Strentzel's dream of creating a horticultural utopia on the West Coast. The most famous was another Forty-Niner, the Hungarian immigrant Agostan Harazthy, who planted the first wine grapes in Sonoma County and in 1859 published his influential *Report on Grapes and Wine in California*. Two years later he brought back from Europe 200,000 cuttings and rooted vines of every variety, which helped turn fruit into a new bonanza. By 1880 the state was annually producing over three million pounds of fresh fruit and four hundred thousand pounds of dried fruit. Five years later the fresh fruit crop totaled forty-five million pounds, along with nearly six million pounds of dried fruit and seventeen million gallons of wine. Those boom years were precisely the time when Muir moved onto the Strentzel estate, and he too caught the fever of a better kind of agriculture that would redeem the state from its destructive past of gold mining and wheat speculating.[7]

Historian Steven Stoll has characterized those investors in California fruit as orchard capitalists. Many, he notes, preferred to call themselves growers rather than farmers, aligning themselves with the capitalist logic of specialization, economic efficiency, and entrepreneurialism rather than older yeoman ideals of security, sufficiency, and community. Certainly, it took capital to get started in this business, more than many dirt farmers could scratch together; a mere twenty-acre vineyard could cost $7,500 for land, buildings, drying trays for turning grapes into raisins, and packing boxes. The profits were not quick to roll in, although eventually they could be substantial. A single acre could yield five or six tons of grapes and the net gain could run over $100 a ton. For patient investors there were substantial fortunes to be made in fruit growing, and the prospect attracted many men and women who looked on their properties as lucrative factories for making sweet returns.[8]

But capitalism is not the whole story. The appeal of horticulture was for many Californians not simply a matter of industrial or capitalistic economics but of social and moral reform. They envisioned the breaking up of huge landed estates and the emergence of a smaller-scale husbandry accessible to people of middling means. A future of twenty-acre homesteads devoted to vineyards meant more

opportunity for people to live on the land, in contrast to the thousand-acre farms of the wheat kings or the ten thousand-acre ranches
of the cattle kings. Horticulture promised flourishing market towns,
rural schools, and close-knit neighborhoods. The era of fruit growing, they hoped, would bring a turn toward denser settlement and a
spirit of mutual aid.[9]

For all his land acquisitiveness, which often put him at odds with
his neighbors over boundary lines, Strentzel believed wholeheartedly
in that ideal of rural commonwealth. In an 1855 letter to an agricultural paper he called on farmers to congregate "in villages or close communities."[10] Twenty years later he had joined a national organization
to promote that ideal: the Patrons of Husbandry, popularly known as
the Grange. It was an organization that tried to defend older rural values against the industrial capitalist invasion and at the same time help
farmers survive in the new competitive order. Enlightened self-interest
rather than selfishness was its guiding ethos. "In essentials, unity," read
the Grange motto; "in non-essentials, liberty; in all things, charity."

Founded in 1867, the Grange movement spread quickly until
there were thousands of local branches across the nation, 250 of them
in California alone. They tried to defend farmers against a growing
class of middlemen, including most notoriously the railroads that
increasingly, through variable rates and oligopolistic concentration,
controlled their marketing. The Grangers were not opposed to the
market economy or private property. "In our noble Order," they
declared, "there is no communism, no agrarianism. We are opposed to
such spirit and management of any corporation or enterprise as tends
to oppress the people and rob them of their just profits. We are not
enemies to capital, but we oppose the tyranny of monopolies. . . . We
desire only self-protection and the protection of every true interest
of our land by legitimate transactions, legitimate trade, and legitimate profits."[11] Toward that end they pooled their capital to establish
their own banks, insurance companies, cooperative stores, gristmills
and canneries, machine works, and even utilities. John Strentzel, for
example, who served as leader (or "master") of the Alhambra Grange,
formed an association to build a shipping wharf and a gas and electric
company in the town of Martinez.

Ezra Carr, author of a history entitled *The Patrons of Husbandry on the Pacific Coast*, explicitly linked the Grange movement to the San Francisco social critic Henry George and his campaign against land monopoly. Concentrated ownership, Carr echoed, was creating "a nation of landlords and tenants, of great capitalists and poverty-stricken employees."[12] The remedy for that growing inequality lay not only in challenging the power of the middlemen but also in changing the mode of taxation, imposing heavier levies on the vast estates and encouraging their owners to sell off to smallholders. Land should be viewed as the gift of nature to all, Carr argued, and it should be as widely distributed as possible. Again, he was not calling for a return to primitive or subsistence farming, but for a more progressive agriculture devoted to market production, affordable lands for all who wanted them, and a belief that the fruits of the earth ultimately belonged to everyone.

Muir gravitated toward idealistic people like the Strentzels, Carrs, and Bidwells who shared his disapproval of the naked pursuit of money. They also shared his passion for the outdoors, loved the beauty of natural things, and found spiritual value in them. As John Strentzel described himself, they were "worshippers of nature."[13] They believed in protecting forests and were thrilled like Muir by mountain vistas.

At the same time these were people who loved to grow plants on an agricultural scale. They had left the city to seek a rural residence where they could produce food in association with like-minded neighbors. Even the San Francisco educator John Swett and his wife Mary, with whom Muir had boarded for many years, eventually moved out to the countryside, buying property adjacent to the Strentzel ranch farther up the Alhambra Valley and going into grape and wine production. All were committed to developing an agricultural economy in California that was cooperative, liberal, and democratic. Muir clearly preferred the company of such people to that of gold miners, city merchants, unrestrained lumbermen or sheepherders, or anyone without conscience or scruple.

Yet he sometimes cast a sardonic eye on his friends' enthusiasms. He lived within their Grange circle, attended Grange meetings, but did not always support the Grange movement. Compared to the others, he was less inclined to idealize rural life. He was never fully convinced that building a cooperative utopia among farmers could succeed on a practical level. Organizations and institutions never held much attraction, for like his father Daniel he was independent and nonconformist. He was a passionate reformer, but the focus of his reform was more personal, inward looking, and spiritual than outward or social. Farming, like everything else for him, must be first and foremost an individual way of life. One pursued it according to one's talents constrained by one's conscience.

When he looked into the eyes of most California farmers Muir did not find much talent or conscience. On the whole they suffered, he wrote in the San Francisco *Evening Bulletin*, from "dry rot." Farmers were too often poor, shiftless men lacking any enthusiasm for work. One happy exception was a group of "gentle grangers" he discovered trying to create farms in the flat, droughty Mussel Slough area at the southern end of the Central Valley. After years of playing at farming "as at cards, speculating and gambling," they dug an irrigation ditch from the Kings River to their fields. Now they were able to raise more reliable crops of corn and alfalfa, and an infectious happiness abounded. He had come upon them as he was tracing the lowland effects of glaciations in the mountains and observed that they had found good sediments to work with and had captured a good supply of melt water. The glaciers were producing a bountiful harvest. To one who had often been hungry in his travels, longing for a loaf of bread, the prospect of those healthy crops and prosperous farms was no trivial matter. "Cheerless shanties, sifted through and through with dry winds, are being displaced by true homes embowered in trees and lovingly broidered with flowers; and contentment, which in California is perhaps the very rarest of the virtues, is now beginning to take root. Irrigous [irrigation] revivals are breaking out all over the glad plains, and wildcat farming is dead."[14]

In an unpublished journal covering that visit to the Tulare farmers Muir sounded even more the agrarian visionary. An irrigated Central

Valley, he calculated, could support a million farms of ten or twenty acres each, a prospect that he did not try to discourage. "The snow-fountains of the Sierra," he wrote, "are sufficient to water every rod of this vast valley & make it yield crops of every clime in unsurpassed abundance & with the advantages of good climate & sublime scenery." The only obstacles to that pleasing prospect were the private corporations racing to get control of the water and sell it dearly to the farmers, "thus making the independence that naturally belongs to husbandry impossible." A better policy, he believed, would make it possible for the farmers to own the water themselves and dig their own ditches, which would allow them to keep the gains in their pockets and keep agriculture open to as many people as possible.[15]

Yet in another journal entry of the same period, Muir distanced himself from agrarian reformism. He found such thinking too focused on matters of human economy and human society, and he challenged himself and others to take a broader view of man's place in nature. Humans should learn to cherish their wilder plant and animal companions as well as their domesticated, moneymaking crops. In doing so they would come to see themselves as fellow creatures whose moral obligations transcended work and production for mere human consumption.

> Be Grangers if you will but in Heavens name be more than Grangers...see what other brothers of the All Father are doing. see other flocks. see Gods forestry Gods horticulture. Do not make a festisch [sic] of a grapevine or a Bartlett pear or Japanese persimmon Man is more than meat—& the body than raiment....Vineyards were made for man not man for vineyards...The stormy rushing semifrantic industry of Cal farmers & fruit growers bear about the same relation to rational bread winning that a throbbing delerious fever does to calm health.

In that more critical mood Muir could poke fun even at the Carrs and their zealous efforts to reform the political economy and could even disagree with the Strentzels and their friends over the Grange movement. Save yourself, he once admonished Jeanne Carr, from "the hawks and the big ugly buzzards and cormorants—grangeal, political, right and wrongical."[16]

After his marriage, he did not try to conceal his skepticism about some of the proposed agricultural reforms. His mother-in-law recorded in her diary a confrontation in the family parlor when a neighbor and fellow Grange member Henry Raap joined them for the evening. "He and John had a spirited argument about the Grange institution. John is very much opposed to it."[17] The grounds for that evening's opposition are obscure, but presumably Muir objected, as he had in his journal, to the narrow anthropocentrism of the movement. The Grangers focused too much on what humans should do to the earth, too little on what nature should mean to humans—a broader life beyond their vanity, arrogance, and narrow economism.

In a culture that had long exalted "those who labor in the earth," that had identified them, in Thomas Jefferson's famous words, as "the chosen people of God," Muir was inclined to dissent. Far from being divinely appointed stewards of the earth, farmers were not even a chosen people. In his most thorough critique of the agricultural mind, the essay "Wild Wool," published in the *Overland Monthly* of 1875, Muir charged that farming was shot through with the dogma that "the world was made especially for the uses of men." Modern science, he pointed out, demonstrated that such was not true: every plant and animal had evolved as part of the greater whole of nature, "married to every other" species but expressing "the most intense individuality." No species existed primarily for the welfare of other species, including humans. It was an "enormous conceit" to think otherwise, and it led to a false celebration of human greatness.[18]

The opening words of that 1875 essay might have been addressed to Ezra Carr or other Grangers and horticulturalists. "I have a friend," writes Muir, "who has a call to plow, and woe to the daisy sod or azalea thicket that falls under the savage redemption of his keen steel shares."

> Not content with the so-called subjugation of every terrestrial bog, rock or moor-land, he would fain discover some method of reclamation applicable to the

ocean and the sky; that in due calendar time they might be made to bud and blossom as the rose. Our efforts are of no avail when we seek to turn his attention to wild roses, or to the fact that both ocean and sky are already about as rosy as possible—the one with stars, the other with dulse, and foam, and wild light. The practical developments of his culture are orchards and clover-fields that wear a smiling, benevolent aspect, and are very excellent in their way, though a near view discloses something barbarous in them all. Wildness charms not my friend, charm it never so wisely; and whatsoever may be the character of his heaven, his earth seems only a chaos of agricultural possibilities calling for grubbing-hoes and manures.

The friend could appreciate "azure skies and crystal waters" and was opposed to laying an axe to the mountain pines. But even this professed nature lover and forest conservationist found "something essentially coarse" in nature that "must be eradicated by human culture."[19]

Muir's agricultural friend, so embedded in human chauvinism, made an odious distinction: "Culture is an orchard; nature is a crab." Muir retorted that, in terms of flavor or beauty, the wild crab apple was in fact superior to the domesticated fruit of the orchard. It was inferior only in *quantity*; the wild apple trees could not yield enough to satisfy human demand. So the agriculturist must take that tree from the wilderness into his orchard, pruning, grafting, and manuring until it produced many more bushels of fruit. The new tree derived by human ingenuity was necessary, and was even admirable in its way, but it was not absolutely superior to the natural one. "Orchard apples are to me the most eloquent words that culture has ever spoken," Muir went on, "but they reflect no imperfection upon nature's spicy crab."[20] Each had its own place on earth. People needed the orchard apple to feed their bodies, but they needed to preserve the wild apple to feed their spirits.

Actually, Muir's brief career as a sheepherder in the California hills had left him with a lasting conviction that domesticated plants and animals were inferior to their wild ancestors. Months of trailing flocks of sheep into the high meadows, watching them devour

the vegetation and then sadly die in large numbers from bear preda-
tion or cold weather, soured him forever on raising livestock or even
allowing them on the open range. In contrast, the wild native sheep of
the Sierra were larger, tougher, smarter animals; even their fleece was
superior for fineness and depth. Domestication had turned the wild
animal into "a round bundle of something only half alive."[21]

Following Charles Darwin's theory of evolution, Muir asserted that
natural selection was similar to but better than artificial selection by a
human breeder. Both processes produced change in organisms over
time. In artificial selection, or domestication, it was human whim or
need that determined which individual variations in a plant or animal
species would be encouraged. Such selection had been going on since
a very early period, until the natural ancestor of modern breeds of
animals or varieties of fruit was often hard to identify. Nature oper-
ated in the same way that the animal breeder did, except that the cri-
teria for selection were far more diverse, complex, and attuned to
natural forces. The effect of adaptive pressures on organisms over
immense stretches of time produced, in Darwin's words, "beautiful
co-adaptations everywhere and in every part of the organic world."[22]
Muir agreed about the beauty as well as functionality of natural selection, adding that men were now engaged in a massive destruction of
that beauty, replacing the wonderful achievements of natural selection with the inferior works of artificial selection.

Realistically, Muir knew that agriculture would continue to turn
wild things into cultural artifacts better suited to human need. At the
same time the varieties created by agriculture were seriously flawed.
"We still seem to be as far from definite and satisfactory results as we
ever were." Among sheep, for example, while one breed produced
wool that was "apt to wither and crinkle like hay on a sun-beaten hillside," another produced wool that was "lodged and matted together
like the lush tangled grass of a manured meadow." All the farmer's
stock, mongrels and purebreds alike, suffered from instability and
proneness to disease. "Would it not be well, therefore, for some one
to go back as far as possible and take a fresh start?"[23]

Muir was suggesting a radical approach to agriculture based on
Darwinian biology. The farmer and breeder should turn to nature for

inspiration and use the wild species of plants and animals as a standard to be emulated rather than a blunder to be corrected. They should preserve the processes of natural selection in their unspoiled settings—that is, the wild places of earth. Agriculturists needed that wildness for making "a fresh start." Rather than merely collecting dozens of varieties of the domesticated sheep or apple or grape, as men like Strentzel were doing, they should preserve the wild ancestors and incorporate them into their husbandry. They should diversify their breeding stock and reintroduce the complexity and fitness of those ancestors into the domesticated lines of farm and ranch. "A little pure wildness," Muir argued, "is the one great present want, both of men and sheep."[24]

California agriculture, for all its amazing diversity, from low-intensive cattle grazing to high-intensive fruit and vegetable cultivation, from haphazard backcountry methods to the Grange's integrated program of cooperative producing and marketing, lacked a deep respect for the natural world. Agriculturists had not taken Darwin's new theory of evolution seriously. They still prided themselves on their conquest over nature and natural selection. Muir was not calling for a return to a pre-agricultural existence when humans supposedly lived in close harmony with nature. What he sought, and did not find among his reform-minded friends, was an approach to growing food that was more daringly experimental, more aware of human failures, and more open to nature's wisdom.

In the months immediately following his marriage to Louie, from April to July 1880, Muir set about learning the techniques of orchard and vineyard management. After his third trip to Alaska, around the time of the fall grape harvest in 1881, he began to take over from his father-in-law the daily supervision of the whole estate. That work would require his full energies over the next seven years and would never be wholly absent until late in his life.

Surprisingly, under his management the Muir-Strentzel ranch did not become the site of a radical experiment in breaking down the walls that separated agriculture from wilderness. Muir did not try to introduce wild fruits and graft them on to the many varieties that Strentzel had collected. It would seem that he was in an especially favorable place to do so, for he had a father-in-law who admired him greatly, was impressed by science, and was convinced of the need for agricultural innovation. Yet Muir followed closely in the track laid down by the older man. It may seem an astonishing capitulation for one who had been so critical of others' failure to think in more revolutionary terms. The reason for his conservatism was that the property provided a substantial income for the family that he would not put in jeopardy through an unusual breeding program. He proved to be a cautious businessman rather than an agronomic revolutionary.

As ranch manager Muir continued the Strentzel pattern of cultivating a wide array of fruits, not specializing in one or two crops, as did more capitalist-minded growers who followed industrial mass-production methods, but still seeking a substantial return. Grapes (especially the Muscat), quinces, walnuts, peaches, pears, plums, oranges, lemons, and apricots all remained part of the ranch's output. Each crop required different kinds of knowledge and technique, each put demands on Muir's time and expertise, and each turned a profit.[25]

We can get some idea of the chores he had to do by consulting the leading contemporary guidebook for orchardists, Edward J. Wickson's *The California Fruits and How to Grow Them*, first published in 1889 and reissued in many editions. The annual production cycle varied from fruit to fruit but followed a common general pattern. Winter was the season for clearing land for new plantings, growing seedlings in nurseries, laying out the new stock in straight lines and geometrical squares, grafting fruit trees, and pruning trees and vines. Grape picking usually began around the first of September, after the fruit and nut trees had stopped bearing. The grapes earmarked for raisins were placed on flat trays exposed to the sun and turned over several times, until they were ready for the tedious work of sorting and grading. Whether fresh or dried, all the fruit went into wooden boxes cut from redwoods and sugar pines that grew in the mountains, taking a substantial toll on the native forests, and was shipped in heavily laden wagons down to the Martinez waterfront.[26]

Muir in a pear orchard on the Strentzel-Muir ranch. (H-A, JMP)

Winter and summer alike, the threat of mildew was always present in the orchard, requiring repeated dusting of the plants with powdered sulfur compounds. During the growing season the orchard manager was constantly on guard against insects, ground squirrels, and birds preying on the crops. Cut worms, borers, tent caterpillars, leaf lice, cottony cushion scale, and vine hoppers were constant threats, which the orchardist must fight with poisoned baits of bran, molasses, and arsenic. Other remedies included various emulsions of kerosene, fish oil, soap, tobacco, carbolic lime, lead arsenate, or Paris green. Small insects of the genus *Phylloxera* had devastated the vineyards of France and, by the 1850s, were showing up in California, sending panic through horticultural ranks. The worry continued for decades, leading Muir to sign a petition requiring all growers to kill any insects by boiling their packing boxes at wharf side.

Birds he was less inclined to destroy than insects, despite their many depredations; after all, he was widely celebrated as one of the nation's leading advocates for wild birds. But the California ground squirrel was another matter. Growing to a foot in length and a pound or two in weight, *Citellus beecheyi* was a persistent terror to the orchard grower—nibbling on new plant growth, digging holes around roots. The standard treatment for this pest, which Muir probably followed to save his crops, was to smoke them out of their holes or poison them. Poison consisted of a concoction of strychnine, cyanide of potassium, honey, eggs, and vinegar mixed with wheat or barley and pushed down the holes. Or orchard workers pumped carbon bisulfide gas into their dens, closing the openings and suffocating the rodents within.

All of this production and protection required plenty of labor; even a small twenty-acre vineyard exceeded the work capacity of a single individual. Typically, horticulture demanded an army of full-time or itinerant orchard workers, most of whom in the early years were immigrant men from China. Coming to the Sierra in the gold-rush years from the impoverished Pearl River (Xi Jiang) valley and delta of South China, they often turned to agriculture when the gold was gone, becoming tenant farmers or fruit pickers. Anti-immigration groups in the state persuaded Congress, in 1882, to impose a moratorium on Chinese manual workers seeking entry to the country, cutting off the cheap labor supply. Still, there were 75,000 Chinese already in the state, almost ten percent of the population, and they were heavily concentrated in a few places, including Contra Costa County, where there were plenty of jobs in the canning plants and on farms and ranches.

Behind the Strentzel mansion stood the "China house," a segregated dormitory for the estate's hired hands. Managing that work force became one of Muir's most common, and vexing, duties. On a January day in 1882, for example, he worked all day with ten Chinese workers to make, bind, and label 12,000 cuttings for the vineyard. Those men were intelligent, knowledgeable, at times quarrelsome, and far from docile. Like the white landowners for whom they labored, they had, in the words of historian Sucheng Chan, "great entrepreneurial drive." Muir was forced into constant negotiation with them to keep the place running and, at critical moments, found himself short of workers, as they left for better opportunities. He said little about his problems, but even his family back in Wisconsin sensed that labor troubles were making his life one of gnawing anxiety. Sister Sarah Galloway sent her sympathy, hoping that the "care and oversight of those Chinamen will not upset you again."[27]

In many ways Muir improved the family business, partly by improving the efficiency of the work force and partly by eliminating a few of the less profitable crops that Strentzel had introduced. This winnowing for improved productivity was still going on after Muir succeeded in hiring others, mainly his relatives from Wisconsin, to take over daily management in the late 1880s. On one occasion after retirement he went into the field to oversee a worker who was pulling out, with two stout Norman horses, the old Mission grapes dating back to the Spanish-Mexican era. Although a good table grape, the variety was "but a poor wine grape & brings a very low price for either table or wine. The padres ought to have known better, such good judges as they are in most things relating to the stomach." Muir always accepted, perhaps more than his father-in-law did, that the modern farm must bow to market pressures if it means to make money.[28]

Yet during his most intense, full-time years of farm management, Muir had often been frustrated by the daily grind of responsibilities that he bore without aid of an assistant or overseer. He did not want to live or work elsewhere but only to get back some of his freedom and get back to his nature studies and writing. Early on, he wrote to the editor of the *Overland Monthly*:

> I am lost & choked in agricultural needs & am almost beyond the memory even of literary work so that much as I should like to give you the article you want I am not

able or nearly able to do so. Work is coming upon me from near & far & at present I cannot see how I am to escape its degrading vicious effects. Get some one to write an article on the vice of overindustry, it is greatly needed in these times of horticultural storms.

Later he complained to brother David that the ranches were "an eternal fountain of work. Cant you send me out a half dozen good steady young men (or women) to work"?

Louie understood completely what her husband had sacrificed to join the Strentzel family and tried, with some success, to impress her parents with the toll that the estate was taking on him. "A ranch that needs and takes the sacrifice of a noble life or work," she declared, "ought to be flung away beyond all reach and power for harm."[29] Eventually, after Dr. Strentzel's death, they resolved to put up large sections of the estate for lease or sale and hired a manager for the rest.

Enjoying the more genial aspects of life on the estate waited until after Muir had retired from the pressures of daily management and could stroll casually about the place, observing and taking pleasure from the bucolic scene. In 1895 he kept a short-lived journal of eighty-six pages on "Ranch Life." In it he extols the springtime beauty of the vineyards alive with new growth: "Lovely balmy morning. What a stir there is in every living leaf—every cell a busy factory & how enormously fertile are the kingdoms of insects—the air is all swirling & thril[l]ing with singing wings—especially of the ephemera. They rejoice & play in large assemblies & keep time in a wonderful way going round & round in giddy whirls & spirals mostly from left to right with the sun into which they are geared in some mysterious way." Gophers, however, are in "destructive abundance." In May, while the men are loading boxes of cherries for the market, he stops to watch a pair of wrens feeding their babies in a woodpile nest and herons roosting in the sycamores. June finds him in San Francisco selling cherries and pears and in the river-port of Valona, where he signs leases with tenants of the Strentzel-owned warehouses and wharf. In June the weather turns hot and the "Chinamen" make the first shipment of apricots, which are small and scarce this year.[30]

Why did Muir throw himself into a career of fruit ranching, and why did he devote so much care to making that business profitable for a full decade? Just as he was acquiring a national reputation as a visionary naturalist going into the wild and seeking the natural life, he made an abrupt detour into agriculture. In part he did so because he was weary of the crowded, denaturalized city, where he lived most of the year and depended on finding work as a writer; he was drawn to rural quiet and the farmer's life on the land. Farming had long been imprinted on his sense of identity, from those occasional walks in the East Lothian countryside with his grandfather Gilrye to his adolescent years of planting and harvesting in frontier Wisconsin. Even when he sought to leave farming behind, he remained a man with a farming past that he could not shake off.

Agriculture also appealed to a powerful side of his personality—the desire to make things work and work more efficiently, to create as well as discover order in the world. All his early obsession with machines, saw mills, power dams, and factories now found an outlet in producing and boxing raisins or cherries for the marketplace. An example of that deep-seated trait appeared in Mother Strentzel's diary: "John has made for each man a little machine, his own invention, which facilitates the work very much, and greatly aids them in planting the vines perfectly strait."[31] As he had done at the Trout mill in Ontario, where he had discovered through long, feverish days how to turn out thousands of rakes and brooms, he drove himself obsessively to produce fruit. Perhaps he was still intent, as he had been in Indianapolis, on showing the world that "the Scotch are the salt of the earth—and the salt of *machines*." Being a good manager, whether of factories or farms, was part of the Scotsman's cultural heritage, his claim to the world's respect and respectability. Always it had clashed with Muir's strong yearning to escape into the wild and lose himself in its beauty and wholeness.

But now he had still another, even more compelling reason to saddle himself with the responsibility of husbandry. He had become a loving and conscientious husband, a family man, and a breadwinner. His wife, baby, and the older couple all depended on him for their comfort and the security of their assets. Like any husband, he had become the subject of others' expectations. A married man was expected to be fully engaged in the business of earning a living, and Muir, despite traveling off to Alaska, tried hard to live up to those expectations. Aware that his writing for newspapers and magazines had never made much money, not enough to support Louie and her kin in their accustomed way of life, he took on the challenge of commercial agriculture. He did so out of affection as much as duty.

⚬━╍━⚬

For several years into their marriage John and Louie were always together, neither venturing far from home. Louie would always be the more rooted of the pair; she would spend her entire adult life on the Strentzel estate, resisting almost all travel. A trip to San Francisco was a long one for her; consequently, much of her home state she never saw. The baby Wanda grew up to resemble her mother in being rooted to the home place; eventually, she too settled as a married woman right there on the Strentzel estate. The Alhambra Valley was their sanctuary from the world.

On one occasion, to be sure, the parents did leave the nest for a few weeks, putting the grandparents in charge of Wanda. In early July 1884 Muir took his wife to see the Yosemite Valley that had meant so much to him. They stayed at Black's Hotel, making happy reunion with its owners, but as a restorative the trip was not a great success. Both parents worried constantly about the baby and the house, despite reassurances from Grandma that "your home is ok. Ah Jung feeds the chickens and milks the cow, Tim waters flowers. . . . Have brought John's papers and your most valuable things over here, kept house locked up. None of the locks is very safe." Louie hoped that the journey would be good for Muir—"he looks thin and pale and tired." He did improve enough to send home a comical sketch of the figure that Mamma cut in the outdoors: her rotund body in a tent-like dress and broad-brimmed hat plodding up the trail, with him pushing from behind with walking stick, until the stick began to hurt Mamma's back. Another sketch shows her riding sidesaddle on a horse, looming nearly as large as her mount.

Clearly the wild Sierra country was better suited to Muir's than Louie's physical condition or interests, and never again would they go on an excursion together.[32]

Louie's desire to stay close to home, surrounded by familiar flowerbeds and household servants, prevented any meeting with her husband's parents. She never saw them or Wisconsin, even though she had the financial means to go. For a while, the same unwillingness to travel east could be seen in Muir too. He had severed nearly all connection with his family circle, aside from an occasional letter. The last time he saw his parents or brothers and sisters was fourteen years before his marriage. Promises to go were easy to give, but those promises went unfulfilled.

To his sister "Highland Mary" he explained his reluctance to make the long journey back: "I begin to fear your winters zero. Both my feet were frozen on Mt Shasta & I am troubled with cold feet . . . my bones are rather bare . . . & I'm apt to cough at times. You might hear me coughing now on a good telephone." None of those ailments, however, had kept him from going to Alaska or walking on glaciers. His main reason for staying put was the weight of the estate and family on his shoulders. Those burdens took a lot out of his thin carcass. Despite the abundant food he provided for the Strentzel table, he personally ate little—a few crackers, a glass of claret, a "bird picking" of fruit, and, "going back to the faith of my fathers, a poke of oatmeal a luggie of porritch & bicker of brose."[33] Apparently, he did not derive enough energy from that scanty diet both to run an orchard and to travel back to cold Wisconsin.

Curious about their brother's married life in that far-off balmy valley, Sarah Galloway and Maggie Reid, the oldest sisters, came on a visit in October 1882, with Muir paying their fares. The New Year found them still present as houseguests, enjoying the rest and change of climate but getting grumpy letters from their husbands. Mary too wanted to come and see John's home, so "delightfully romantic from what you write," but could not leave her lawyer husband. "Oh that we could be all together once more," she lamented. "Do you suppose that will ever be? We seem to be getting more and more scattered, instead of anything else." Muir did not see much chance for a family reunion:

"One strikes root more or less deeply wherever we chance to stop any length of time & in the case of a large family like ours growing on different kinds of soil & with varying pursuits etc death is about the only harvester that can bring us together."[34]

The visiting sisters brought news of the Muir family, much of it sad and distressing. One of the twins, Annie, had taught school for a while but was now suffering from tuberculosis. Brother David had lost his beloved wife Katie, and his haberdashery in Portage had never been a commercial success. Daniel had become a medical doctor, but his practice in Racine had not prospered, leading him and his wife to move to Lincoln, Nebraska; he had stopped communicating with John and had never repaid the money he owed him. Joanna, the youngest sibling, had finally found a husband, Walter Brown, who proceeded to plunge them into one financial mishap after another; she lost an infant daughter to cholera and lost a little boy a few years later.

Then the aging Muir parents, who were still living apart, had each descended into a state of melancholy. Mother Ann survived in Portage on a small rental income from Daniel's property investments and an annuity from her deceased father in Dunbar; she pined endlessly for the old country, the Kirk on the hill where her family was buried, and her faraway sister and niece. Daniel, who had abandoned the family to evangelize in Canada, was now lame and wasting away, living with Joanna in the piney woods of Arkansas and occasionally preaching to ex-slaves. As Joanna wrote: "He will not listen to reason.... he must have his own way about *every* thing or he is unhappy."[35]

A fear that his parents were dying finally moved Muir to take leave of his agricultural and domestic responsibilities and make a long overdue journey to the Midwest. In the summer of 1885, when Louie was pregnant with their second child, he boarded a northbound stagecoach to begin three months of travel. "I feel tired already," he wrote Louie, "and dread the whole trip. Still I feel that unless I see my mother now I never shall in this world." On 12 August he arrived at Sissons Station near Mt. Shasta, the old beloved mountain pulling at his heart. "I still feel a strong draw to the wilderness," he confessed, "impelling me to leave all and linger here. But I will not—putting away the temptation as a drunkard would whiskey."[36]

His next destination was the Yellowstone National Park, which he could not resist swinging out of his way to see. The Northern Pacific railroad took him from Portland, Oregon, to Gardiner, Montana, where he descended from the cars bone-weary and, for the first time since his malarial days on the Florida coast, doubting his powers of endurance. The nearby Mammoth Hot Springs, where water bubbles through soft limestone, forming multihued terraces and shallow pools, did not appeal to him, nor did the gray sagebrush plains. He vomited his hotel lunch along the trail. The next day he met an agreeable couple, Alfred and Fay Sellers from Chicago, and they set out together on horseback to see the park's other celebrated wonders. This first "national park" was only thirteen years old, and accommodations inside its boundaries were little different from those the Indians had used—tents and campfires—before being driven out. Their camp cook, serving up aged beef and vegetables from tin cans, did nothing for Muir's indigestion. As Old Faithful began to spout, "my organ began spouting vast quantities of hot acid water in close accord."[37]

Yet somehow despite his temporary bout of stomach distress, a daily drubbing by hail and cold rain, and falling off his horse, he managed to scribble an article for the San Francisco *Evening Bulletin*. He extolled the rich, wild beauty of the park, the canyons, the remnant population of bison, the trout-filled Yellowstone Lake, and the many thermal springs. Above all it was the park's geographical position as headwaters for three major rivers—the Yellowstone/Missouri, the Green, and the Snake—that excited his imagination. The park was like a great fountain of water, he wrote, gushing out of the ground and flowing in all directions. "Through all its forms," he ended the article, "forever and forever water is beautiful."[38]

After a single week's camping in Yellowstone, he was back on the rails, heading eastward to Portage, where he arrived at the end of August. Nearly two decades had gone by since he had last seen this place. The countryside seemed flatter and smaller after his high-country ramblings, yet his mother seemed little changed. For weeks they reminisced about Dunbar and family, and he revisited the old homestead, the surviving neighbors, the boyhood pleasures of Fountain Lake and Observatory Hill. He packed up his plant specimens from Florida and his first hand-whittled machines to ship back to California. There were also matters of business that had to be attended to. David's shop, the Parry and Muir company, which was heading toward bankruptcy, owed him $800 on an old loan, plus interest at ten percent per annum; he renegotiated the debt by reducing the interest to zero on David's half of the loan (because, he explained in a rare slur, "I had not the conscience of a Jewish banker"). To Louie he explained, "I feel that I have been quite generous & at a very moderate expense, while actually getting rich in the middle of the generosity." Meanwhile, he ate heartily for the first time on the trip, adding to his weight (he bragged that it was up to 138 pounds) and losing the persistent stomachache.[39]

Rested and more pleased with himself, Muir set off for Kansas City, Missouri, where Joanna had recently moved with her family and her added charge, Daniel. Potentially, it threatened to be a tense, quarrelsome encounter between father and son. Yet he found Daniel in a feeble, emaciated state, confined to bed. "He does not know me," Muir wrote home, "and I am very sorry." He tried talking "broad Scotch," which stirred the old man some. Over and over Muir repeated that he was his son, until at last Daniel responded vaguely, "O yes my dear wanderer." Earlier, before his decline into dementia, Daniel had confessed to Joanna that he had made terrible mistakes in raising his children, regretting especially the "cruel things" he had said to John, and advised her to treat her children with more generosity and love. Now his end was near. The son lay down beside the father, holding his hand for long spells, closer than they had been over most of their lifetime and yet farther away. In early October Daniel died, with the tearful son standing at his bedside.[40]

Muir sent a tribute home that was full of hard-won, sympathetic understanding of Daniel's long-agitated mind, the difficult course he had run from orphaned child to old man. "Few lives that I know [were] more restless & eventful than his," he wrote, "few more toilsome & full of enthusiastic endeavor . . . in the midst of the devils of terrestrial strife & darkness & faithless misunderstanding that well nigh overpowered him at times & made bitter burdens for us all to bear." He had been "a member of nearly every church in succession under the sun," yet remained "youthful & enthusiastic to the end, his mind active & glowing with a fire beneath all his burden of years and pains." Everyone in the clan (except Dan, busy with his patients in Lincoln; Sarah, now sick and depressed by the recent loss of her husband and a child; and Mother Ann, over seventy years old) came to the funeral. "In all our devious ways & wanderings," Muir said of his siblings, "we have loved one another."[41]

It was time to get back to running the ranch. All during his travels Muir had felt guilty about leaving so much work in the hands of Louie and Dr. Strentzel, although he tried to do a little compensatory business along the way. Passing through Chicago, he interviewed fruit importers about selling the estate's crop directly to them in the future. From Portage he confessed, "I cannot shut my eyes to the fact that the main vintage will soon be on and requires my presence, to say nothing of your uncertain state of health." Yet by waiting for Daniel to die, he had missed the fall grape harvest. Louie reported that "the squirrels, gophers, rats and mice are mightier than ever. The quail

The Strentzel-Muir ranch after the building of the railroad trestle in 1897. The manse sits on a knoll in the left-center of the picture, while the old adobe house is on the extreme right. (H-A, JMP)

are attending to the Zinfandels, but they, the birds, will be all the better-flavored for our dinners by and by."[42] Despite her cheery tone, she was in no shape to manage the work; heavily laden with child, a short walk or buggy ride left her breathless. Muir, with his invalid, unmarried sister Annie in tow, came rushing home via Santa Fe, the Southwest, and the Central Valley.

Shortly after his return to Alhambra Valley, Louie gave birth to their second daughter, Helen, on 23 January 1886. Small and frail from the beginning, Helen was often sick and once or twice came close to dying. More than ever, Muir cooed and fretted and lost sleep over the children. Helen was one more huge responsibility, a burden on his heart, and he worked harder than ever to give her the prospect of growing up well and secure.

He could no more escape his growing responsibilities as son and brother than father and husband. All his siblings seemed to depend on him for guidance and for regular infusions of cash. The trip to the Midwest, coinciding with his father's death, had thrust Muir into the center of family affairs. He was now effectively the head of the Muir clan, increasingly responsible for the welfare of his mother and siblings. They looked to him as the family's greatest success and leader. Sisters turned to him with their physical, financial, or emotional problems. Under pressure, he had agreed to join the other Muir children in a syndicate to invest their money, he contributing more than anyone else to the pool. The widowed Sarah came in, bringing her meager savings, along with brothers David and Daniel, Margaret and her husband John, who were buying land and raising horses in Nebraska and Kansas, and the city-dwelling Browns. Together they invested in the prairie ranching business, in "Muir's Addition" (a housing development in Lincoln), and in Walter Brown's land and building speculations in Kansas City. Muir put thousands of dollars into those enterprises, primarily to enhance his siblings' prospects but perhaps hoping again to get "rich in the middle of the generosity."

Little came of those ventures, although they went on for several years. Their main effect was not to enrich Muir's pocketbook but rather to elevate him to the status of family banker and last resort for those in trouble. The Reids soon fell into that category as their crops failed and their livestock died for lack of good pastures. "Thanks for your money order," wrote Maggie; "husband John lies awake nights worrying about our affairs."[43]

Muir had gone through a profound transformation in the eyes of his siblings. Earlier, in taking leave of home he had seemed a maverick with independent or even self-destructive ideas, an irresponsible boy with few worldly cares. But after he married, made some money, and became their emotional and financial mainstay, he stood like a pillar of strength in contrast to their own lives. Joanna in particular exemplified that transformation in her attitudes toward him. Before his marriage she upbraided him for his unorthodox views, his failure to support Protestant Christianity:

> I can readily see how with God's great glorious book of nature, which has become so intelligible to you, continually spread out before you and continually yielding you some grant [great], fresh truth, that religious denominationalism with all it carries in its train, must seem insignificant and useless; and yet, you naughty bad boy! What could the world in general do without churches and Sunday schools? You know that they who are not pure in heart cannot see God in his works they see only sheep pastures and firewood, and unless the truths of God be shouted into their ears will never know Him at all until perhaps when they have slunk away into the spirit world there to find that they have never learned to live. So you must be good and not talk like that anymore.

Like others, she had trouble figuring out his newfound faith: what did he mean by "God" and where was his "church"? She was more indulgent toward other aspects of his free-spiritedness. He had always seemed wonderfully free of anxiety or overtaxed nerves: "For so long a time we considered you the grand exception to the curse, standing as you do on a higher plane, cooling your brow in the pure mountain air and feasting your soul on the absorbing study of sweet soothing nature, untrammeled by either the love, or the fear of society and its folly." But with his successful marriage and business enterprise, so much more impressive than her own, she began to look on him, not with reproof or envy, but with awe. He now seemed to work harder than any of them and to achieve more. She mixed a growing admiration with genuine solicitude: "You are doing [something noble] for the whole family. . . . Can you stand the pressure?"[44]

Apparently he could stand it as long as necessary. Through the 1880s he drove himself to make money on his own acreage and that of his father-in-law, amassing a large personal savings account and improving the Strentzels' worth considerably. In the terms set by his society he proved that he was a worthy husband through his adept husbandry. He tied himself to a staggering set of obligations, all driven by genuine and grateful affection. Some of those obligations would never end, but the daily obligation to make crops and make money did gradually ease off. No one could find fault when he declared that he had fulfilled his loving duties as husband, father, son, and brother. He was now ready to take on other responsibilities.

CHAPTER 11

A Call to Lead

During the 1880s, while Muir was turning into "a proper cultivated plant," his contemporary Mark Twain was publishing some of his greatest, most subversive, works: *The Prince and the Pauper, Life on the Mississippi, Huckleberry Finn*, and *A Connecticut Yankee in King Arthur's Court*. The two men were only three years apart in age; both had made their way west after the Gold Rush and, after exploring the mountains, had taken up residence in San Francisco and begun writing careers. Twain had left California just before Muir arrived. One man's experience there made him a lifelong satirist who poked fun at moral improvers, while the other's made him a conservationist.

It was Twain who gave the last part of the nineteenth century its enduring cognomen—the Gilded Age. His novel of that title, co-authored with Charles Dudley and published in 1873, lampooned frontier confidence men and corrupt Washington politicians. Under the shiny surface of a confident, prosperous nation, the novel suggested, lay a cheap, tawdry reality. Bribery, opportunism, trickery, and hypocrisy had become the leading national traits. Only a century old, America's noble experiment in liberal democracy had become a farce. Twain and Dudley poked wicked fun at the something-for-nothing attitude that seemed to have driven out all virtue and sincerity.[1]

In a newspaper essay, Twain contrasted his age's lack of reverence and moral purpose with the ancient Westminster catechism that Muir had learned at his grandfather's knee. The old religious creed asked, "What is the chief end of man?" The proper answer was that man's purpose is "to glorify God, and fully enjoy him forever." But now the pervasive goal had become simply "to get rich." In what way? "Dishonestly if we can; honestly if we must." Who or what, asked Twain, is our God? "Money is God. Gold and greenbacks and stock—father, son, and the ghost of the same—three persons in one: these are the true and only God, mighty and supreme."[2]

Like the famous humorist, Muir no longer believed in the Westminster catechism of his ancestors, but unlike Twain he still believed in the possibility of moral progress. After achieving a sufficiency of wealth, he wanted to spend the remainder of his days teaching Americans to take a new attitude toward nature. He hoped to bring greed under the control of ethics, aesthetics, and enlightened self-interest, and his strategy for doing that was to join the movement to conserve nature and natural resources, one of the great reform efforts of the so-called "Gilded Age" that Twain neither acknowledged nor appreciated.

Plenty of other reformers appeared on the scene during the period 1870-1900, most of them interested in distributing the nation's affluence more equitably rather than checking the assault on nature. The Knights of Labor, Henry George, Edward Bellamy, the Populists, and an assortment of socialists and anarchists all protested the rising plutocracy and called for economic justice. The conservation movement both shared their critique and tried to transcend it. Conservationists were as appalled as other reformers by ruthless self-aggrandizement that made a few men incredibly rich while leaving large numbers of their fellow citizens in abject circumstances. But in contrast to the economic redistributionists, they worried that the unchecked exploitation of nature would leave later generations of Americans with an impoverished environment, affording neither wealth nor beauty for anyone. They protested the slaughter of wildlife, the devastation of forests, the pollution of cities, and the desiccation of waterways as threats to the well-being of all Americans, present and future.

Another characteristic distinguished the conservationists from other contemporary progressive reform movements: they were usually silent on traditional Christian beliefs. Unlike the Social Gospellers, who tried to apply Jesus' message to problems like poverty, inequality, and poor health, conservationists seldom invoked His name. Instead, they appealed to distinctly human needs in the present and future and did so in a language usually devoid of religious content. Or they appealed, as Muir did, to a post-Christian religion of nature where mountains and forests were the source of human redemption.

Contrast the conservationists to the popular agrarian reformer William Jennings Bryan, who, in his 1896 speech to the Democratic national convention, thundered against the moneychangers: "You shall not press down upon the brow of labor this crown of thorns. You shall not crucify mankind upon a cross of gold." Other advocates of social justice likewise drew on evangelical Protestantism to inspire their hearers, blurring the lines between social reform and traditional religious crusading.[3] In doing so, they hearkened back to such antebellum reformers as the abolitionists, who had seen themselves as Christian soldiers marching against the evil power of slave-owners. But typically that was not the spirit behind the conservation movement. Conservationists did not see saving nature as doing the work of a Christian God.

In their preference for a more secular and scientific outlook, the conservationists had much in common with the school of philosophy known as pragmatism, which took form during the Gilded Age. The pragmatists, including Chauncey Wright, Charles Peirce, William James, and Oliver Wendell Holmes, Jr., were a herd of unruly steers, but commonly they turned away from evangelical religious certainties and looked to natural science. They took Darwin's theory of evolution seriously, with all that it implied for the origin of life, social customs, and ethics. For them, questions of right and wrong had to be approached, not as divinely ordained truths, but as ideas shaped by circumstances, as tools crafted for human survival and happiness. True ideas were those that effectively solved a problem. They saw society as part of nature, changing as nature changed, and therefore its ideas or principles should be selected through trial and error in response to a changing environment.[4]

Muir was a naturalist and reformer, not a philosopher, but as a reformer he shared much of the pragmatists' outlook. Darwinism and science had transformed his thinking too, and like the pragmatists he had abandoned the strait-laced dogmas of traditional Christianity. He had no trouble accepting that our knowledge is partial and uncertain, or that humankind must make up rules by which it lives. He shared the pragmatists' devotion to liberal values—freedom of thought, encouragement of individuality, and openness to experience. The tendency of pragmatism to subject all beliefs to the acids of skepticism, to insist that all notions of truth and all perceptions of harmony in the universe must be appraised for their social utility, ran hard against his faith in the harmony of nature. In that regard, he was a pragmatist more in the style of the tender-minded William James than the tough-minded Chauncey Wright, who looked on nature as mere "cosmical weather," offering humans little guidance.[5] But in the end a persistent religiosity did not stop Muir from becoming a pragmatic, not absolutist, reformer.

For example, he did not argue that humans must always put nature's welfare above that of human beings. On the contrary, he promoted conservation as a means to improved happiness for people. Human health—mental, physical, and economic—depended on access to the natural world. To be prosperous a society must use its natural resources rationally and carefully; to be happy and fulfilled a society must be in contact with the natural beauty around it. A sharp distinction between conservation (or wise use of resources) and preservation (the non-use of resources) does not really apply to him. Privately, he was still convinced that man should not be the measure of all value, that justice must extend to all creatures, and that accumulating money should not become the chief end of living. Publicly, however, he defined the goal of conservation as fuller human development.

Had that decade of marriage, fatherhood, and the ranch made him less radical? Had he abandoned revolutionary ideas about the rights of other creatures and adopted a more anthropocentric way of thinking? According to historian Roderick Nash, the older Muir "camouflaged his radical egalitarianism in more acceptable rhetoric centered on the benefits of nature for people," a deceptiveness that Nash blames on Muir's turn to politics.[6] It should be said that Muir had never seen any contradiction between his emphasis on the rights of animals, plants, and even rocks and his conviction that nature offered people important material and moral benefits. He had never proposed to wall off *all* of wild nature from human use. Always he had been a man of complex attitudes, mixing spirituality and utility, nature's rights and humankind's pleasures, and he would continue to try to balance those attitudes to the end of his days. But Nash is right:

as a more successful and worldly Muir began to push for conservation, he tried to avoid sounding doctrinaire and to come up with acceptable, practical proposals.

❦

In spring 1887, while he was still actively managing the ranch, Muir agreed to take on the editing of a lavish book of essays and engravings, *Picturesque California,* a forerunner of the modern travel magazine.[7] Sold by subscription, the many sections of the book dribbled out piecemeal, the full array of twenty-six essays and accompanying pictures, many of them full-page scenes, taking years to complete. Besides serving as general editor, Muir wrote six of the essays (recycling newspaper writings he had done more than a decade earlier and including two essays on the Pacific Northwest simply because he wanted an excuse to go there). The other authors included Joaquin Miller, John P. Irish, Charles Howard Shinn, and old friend Jeanne Carr, whose contribution was entitled "The Heart of Southern California." The pictures were engravings from the canvases of William Keith, Thomas Hill, Frederick Remington, Charles D. Robinson, Julian Rix, and others. Although undertaken for profit, the book aimed to show that the West Coast offered more than opportunities for gain; here was abundant beauty, natural and man-made, worthy of celebration.

The most important consequence of the project for Muir was that it allowed him to escape the vineyards and, after so long a period of pent-up domestication, find a way back to the wild. During the summer of 1888 he went on a camping trip to gather impressions of Lake Tahoe and then, with Keith and his paint box, traveled to Shasta, the Columbia River, Mt. Rainier, and Puget Sound. Along the way he found not only plenty of beauty to extol but also evidence of increasing environmental destruction. "The wedges of development," he wrote, "are being driven hard and none of the obstacles or defenses of nature can long withstand the onset of this immeasurable industry."[8] The wild forests around the harbors and rivers were nearly gone: they were too accessible to resist a voracious civilization. In contrast

Rainier, which he climbed with local guides, remained pristine; its yawning crevasses, icy slopes, and summit endured because they were so forbidding to people.

Muir's essays, like the book as a whole, were supposed to show that progress had not ruined America's natural grandeur or corrupted its people. But in contrast to the other authors, he found much to criticize. Most travelers, he complained, cling to the "battered highways like a drowning sailor to a life-raft." They conjure up terrifying images of ravenous animals, war-like Indians, fevers, and starvation lurking in the wilderness. The Indians, he reassured, were either "buried" or "civilized into comparative innocence, industry, or harmless laziness." That was not an outcome he applauded, but such was the reality. Bears too posed little danger; they were nearly all gone, along with other large animals, killed through settlers' irrational fear. Relax, he recommended, and learn to love rather than fear this land. The West may once have seemed (although never in his own mind) a place of "darkness and death," of crushing ice and volcanic eruptions, but the region had "emerged to the kindly warmth and life of today."[9]

The next summer, June 1889, found Muir entertaining a guest who would change his life. Through much cajoling and driving, he would turn Muir's criticism into activism and recruit him to be a leader in the burgeoning conservation movement. The guest was Robert Underwood Johnson, associate editor of *The Century*, a New York magazine that boasted a million readers and an influential role in American thought and taste. Johnson had come to recruit articles on the Gold Rush era but also to get Muir writing for them again. They met in San Francisco's Palace Hotel, Muir playing the country innocent lost in confusing hallways until Johnson rescued him. Johnson would show him around urban corridors of power too. He quickly seized on Muir as the ideal prophet for the age: "a slender figure of medium height, with longish, shaggy beard just beginning to turn gray, and the kindliest gray eyes."[10] Muir provided the charisma, Johnson the movement.

The editor was then thirty-six, fifteen years younger than Muir. A large, imposing man sporting a pince-nez and well-trimmed whiskers, Johnson had grown up in rural Indiana, in a Republican family of mixed Presbyterian-Quaker roots, and graduated from Earlham

College. He had worked briefly for the Civil Service Commission in Washington, learning the ways of politics, before he entered the magazine business. Moving to New York, he came under the tutelage of Richard Watson Gilder, the brains behind *The Century*'s success. The slender, soft-eyed Gilder thought the country needed a higher standard in art, literature, music, and politics—a genuinely gold instead of gilt standard. He instilled in his protégé a taste for the finer things in life. Both men were traditionalists in aesthetics and progressives in politics. Religion they took for granted, but it was conspicuously marginal to their ideal of a higher civilization. Social reform, however, was not marginal; the editors campaigned against squalid tenement houses, the abuse of patronage, and female inequality. Nor was nature marginal; *The Century* became an important voice for conserving the natural beauty and wealth of the continent.[11]

Muir led Johnson away from the city and into Yosemite Valley and then up to Soda Springs, in the Tuolumne Meadows, where they camped under a star-filled sky. The sight and smell of the

Robert Underwood Johnson. (Library of Congress)

tourist-dominated valley had left both men in a disturbed, complicated mood. Below, they had taken rooms in the new Stoneman Hotel, but its commodious elegance and the surrounding granite walls of the valley stood in stark contrast to most of the valley floor, marred by a repulsive saloon, the repugnant odor of a pig sty, fields plowed up for crops or fenced for cattle, acres upon acres of tree stumps, overall a tacky commercialization. "The treatment of the floor of the valley," wrote Johnson, "should have been put in the hands of the very best experts" to "preserve and enhance the composition, unity, and natural charm of the pictures presented to the eye."[12] Instead, the state-appointed Yosemite Commission had allowed the extraordinary place to deteriorate into an overgrazed, overcut, overbuilt shamble.

Outside the park, in the high country where the tourist seldom ventured, they escaped that degradation and drank in the alpenglow of the surrounding peaks. But here too, Muir pointed out, was a damaged landscape, the vegetation devastated by too many seasons of too many sheep. It had been twenty years since he had trailed Pat Delaney's flocks through this country—twenty summers of intense grazing, free of charge and with no stocking limits except those the sheep owners imposed on themselves. The result was diminished tree and wildflower richness, trampled meadows, and muddied water.

Johnson argued that so beautiful but fragile a place should be protected in a new Yosemite National Park, like a second Yellowstone but with a spectacular hole carved out of the center. The valley, despite its bad management, would likely remain under state control, although neither man had any confidence in the state commissioners and preferred that the valley revert to the federal government and become part of the projected national park.

As their campfire threw sparks into the air, Johnson tried to fire up his companion for the hard work ahead. Muir, he insisted, was the essential man to lead the effort to create a new park here. His first task should be to write a couple of articles for *The Century*, including a map suggesting the outlines of the proposed park. As for rescuing the valley, they should lobby to bring Frederick Law Olmsted back to California and put him in charge of cleaning up the mess. Olmsted alone had the skilled eye to eliminate the ugly and restore the beautiful. As it turned out, the state commissioners were adamantly against bringing Olmsted in, which would have been an admission of their failure, while Olmsted seemed uninterested in taking command. That left Johnson and Muir to lead the fight to save what the latter called "our grand 'Central Park' in the Sierra."[13]

Overwhelmed by so much responsibility, Muir checked into a city hotel after they came down from the Sierra. By staying away from ranch duties for a few weeks, he hoped to finish *Picturesque California* and do some preliminary writing on Yosemite. Some of those tasks he managed to complete, including three short articles for the San Francisco *Evening Bulletin*; but by fall, he had still made little progress on the magazine pieces. His home desk, he whined, was covered by "a scrawny orderless mass of fragments." Johnson did not relent; in letter after letter he laid on the whip. "Why don't you start an association for preserving California's monuments & natural wonders—or at least Yosemite?" he demanded. "It would be a good influence if you guarded carefully the membership. You'd have to face obloquy but *you personally* are the one to do it and decent people would help. How timid you Californians are anyhow." Then came another lash: "Knowing you as a gentle hermit, I do not expect propagandism from you; but I should think with little effort you could interest some influential people to organize quietly so as to make themselves felt."[14]

Muir dawdled and resisted, pleading his unsuitability for the role of leader. "I would gladly do anything in my power to preserve Natures sayings & doings here or elsewhere," he replied, "but have no genius for managing societies." It was hard enough to find the time or discipline to write those articles. While he dithered, *The Century* went to press with letters from other critics of the Yosemite Commission—a hard-drinking attorney from California, George McKenzie, a Connecticut judge named Lucius Deming, who had visited the park, and Johnson himself—letters that stirred up many newspapers to complain too. "There are places in the valley," McKenzie wrote, "where one is forced to wonder why the axes themselves did not turn and smite the men who were putting them to such base uses."[15]

"It makes me feel silly," Muir confessed, "that Mackensie [sic] turbid with smoke & alcohol should be able to do so well in an hour what I have been unable to do on a theme I love so well in a whole month of effort." He warned that "Mack" was a shill for certain railroad, hotel, and stagecoach interests who were seeking a change in management that would give them an unequivocal monopoly over the tourist business.[16] Another Johnson recruit to the cause was George Robinson, a disgruntled landscape painter whose studio in the valley had been closed down by the Yosemite Commission, and he too, said Muir, was not to be fully trusted. Those men, nonetheless, had leaped into the fray while he was struggling to strike a tone that would be more temperate and persuasive.

Muir was cautious in part because he had low hopes for success; he had already surrendered much of the battle to the enemy. "The love of Nature among Californians is desperately moderate," he wrote to justify his laggardness. "Long ago I gave up the floor of Yosemite as a garden, & looked only to the rough taluses & inaccessible or hidden benches & recesses of the walls. All the flowers are wall-flowers now, not only in Yosemite but to a great extent through the length & breadth of the Sierra. Still the Sierra flora is not yet beyond redemption & much may be done by the movement you are making." The battle, he was saying, was Johnson's; he would assist but not expect any great triumph.[17]

In March 1890 a congressman from Los Angeles, William Vandever, introduced a bill to reserve from private ownership some two hundred square miles of land adjacent to the Yosemite Valley. He was following the recommendation of state engineer William Hammond Hall that all the tributaries flowing into the Merced River needed protection. That proposal fell far short of the grand new park that Johnson and Muir had envisioned around the campfire; it omitted not only Tenaya Lake but also the separate Tuolumne watershed, including Hetch Hetchy Valley. McKenzie came out hard against the proposal, but Muir decided to support it in the hope that, later on, they could enlarge the boundaries and revamp the Commission, replacing the governor's political appointees with the president of the University of California, the president of the state board of agriculture, the president of the Mechanics' Institute, and perhaps an army officer.[18]

He did not give up wholly on the idea of a large-scale national park in California, however, and finally, late in the spring, managed to finish his *Century* pieces, "The Treasures of the Yosemite" and "Features of the Proposed Yosemite National Park." The first would be published in August 1890, the second in September. Both were worth waiting for—beautifully illustrated, authoritative but lyrical guides to the much-disputed landscape that ended with a quiet plea for its conservation. He opened by recalling his first sighting of the Sierra, so "gloriously colored and so radiant that it seemed not clothed with light, but wholly composed of it, like the wall of some celestial city." Then he grasped the reader by the hand and went flying over towering forests and plunging waterfalls, flower-strewn meadows, deep glaciated valleys, the granite rocks of ancient origins. Only in the last paragraph of the second article did he make his pitch that the nation should reserve some of this grandeur "for the use and recreation of the people." "All that is accessible and destructible is being rapidly destroyed," he warned, "and by far the greater part of this destruction of the fineness of wildness is of a kind that can claim no right relationship with that which necessarily follows use."[19]

Muir had found the balanced tone and the pragmatic argument that would mark his conservation philosophy for years to come. He was calling for a more enlightened utilitarianism. Use should not mean destruction. Use should be wise, humane, and broad in concept. Use should include more than material consumption. The highest use of the Sierra was to feed men's spirits and satisfy their hunger for beauty.

The first article on saving Yosemite included a map of the proposed national park, and it was far more sweeping than Vandever's. It included the entire upper watersheds of both the Merced and Tuolumne rivers, forming a great square on three sides with the Sierra divide providing a long eastern boundary. Water, liquid or frozen, had carved these twin masterpieces out of rock and made them one, he suggested, and that same flow of water should define the shape of preservation. But of course boundary making would not be that simple.

His articles deposited in the mail, Muir beat a temporary retreat from the battle over parks and reservations. He gave his editor permission to cut up both pieces as he liked and return the unwanted stuff. "I can't learn to skip well from point to point like a linnet in a cherry orchard pecking here & there at the best clusters."[20] It was not back to the orchards he was turning, however; on 14 June he went aboard the steamship *City of Pueblo*, bound for Glacier Bay, Alaska. Over the summer season, while others continued wrangling over Yosemite's condition and while Johnson journeyed to Washington to speak before Congressional committees, Muir would be hiking across "crystalline prairies" of ice, far away from the heat and smoke of politics.

This would be his fourth trip to Alaska, his third to Glacier Bay—but his first in nearly a decade. In the interim, a multitude of photographers, journalists, scientists, and tourists had discovered the bay, hundreds of them showing up every summer. At Port Townsend, Washington, Muir changed to the steamer *Queen*, which ran regular excursions into Glacier Bay. Travelers came to hear the crack and boom of the glacier collapsing into the tidewater, to marvel at the translucent blue and emerald icebergs floating around their ship, and to gather pictures, rounded pebbles, and shreds of ancient cedars left behind by the melting ice. Muir's companion was Henry Loomis, with whom he had climbed Mt. Rainier, but everyone aboard seemed his friend and admirer. He wrote home that "a report is going the rounds among the passengers that Muir, the discoverer of the M[uir] glacier is on board and is going up to see that it is not running away or being damaged."[21] Now he was one of the tourist attractions, giving lectures and pointing out what was most important to see.

The Muir Glacier had indeed "run away" to the extent of five miles since he had first encountered it, the melting of the ice opening up an inlet, or fjord, of that length. The ship went as far as it could up the inlet and as close to the glacial wall as the captain dared. Muir and Loomis disembarked there with a load of lumber and food, intent on staying for the summer months. At first they slept in a wood-floored tent, but eventually they built near the east end of the Muir Glacier a windowless hut with stone chimney. Rain fell much of the time, but they disregarded the dark and gloomy skies and went hiking, measuring, and geologizing to their hearts' content. Muir had left California with a severe case of bronchitis, coughing up globs of phlegm and eating little. Now, disregarding medical advice that he stay home and stay warm, he began to recover. The cough disappeared, his lungs cleared, and his appetite came roaring back. To little Helen he described his typical breakfast menu: beans, mush, bacon, a whole quart of coffee, hard tack, dried peaches, cheese, pancakes, and yeast powder bread. As ever, his body as well as mind thrived on cold temperatures.

Other boatloads of tourists appeared in the inlet, including more long-term company. On 1 July Professor Harry Fielding Reid of the Case School of Applied Sciences in Cleveland arrived on the *Glen W. Elder* with a party of students to make a scientific survey of the Muir Glacier. They too had heard of the famous "Professor Muir" and happily joined his "village."[22]

While they unpacked their instruments, Muir hammered together a wooden sled with iron runners for longer field trips on his own. He had acquired a bearskin, which he stitched into a sleeping bag; thus outfitted, he crossed the inlet and took off across the ice on a nine-day journey. Through the lonely nights a pack of wolves kept up an ominous howling; his only weapon was an alpenstock, but he was not really worried so long as they had mountain goats for prey. A more serious threat might be a bad fall with no one to help him. One day such a catastrophe almost happened; he skidded on a steep bank of snow and plunged to a pile of slate at the bottom. Nary a scratch, he bragged. But when a pair of ravens came swooping down, croaking scornfully and looking for a meal, he resolved to be more careful and to preserve his dignity—and his flesh. "Not yet," he shouted to the scavenging birds, "not yet."[23]

Soon after he got back to camp, the *Queen* reappeared with two hundred more tourists hanging over the rail with their Kodaks ready for snapshots. The captain had brought along a pile of lumber and an oil burning stove for Muir's hut, which would do much to counteract

Muir drawing of the Howling Valley near the Muir Glacier, Glacier Bay, Alaska. (H-A, JMP)

the cold wind whistling across the open terrain. There were also letters from home, reporting Louie's efforts at ranch management in his
absence. Wind had ripped through the grapevines, ground squirrels
were doing their usual damage, but apples and pears were growing
well, and fruit prices were high. She had only four Chinese laborers
on hand to do the work. A fire had destroyed several warehouses in
Martinez. Helen had two rotting teeth extracted, and the girls were
now brushing more diligently. As always fearful and wanting him
home, she sent a prayer that "the good Father above will not fail to
lead you, His own dear child, in safety through all the darkness of
Alaskan storms."[24]

That summer, however, it was luck more than divine intervention
that repeatedly saved Muir from a fatal mishap and his wife from wid-
owhood. Away from camp, he ran many risks that he did not reveal in
his letters. In addition to his slide down the snow bank, he narrowly
escaped being crushed by floating icebergs. Nervously, he crossed many
ice-sliver bridges, on one occasion falling into a hidden crevasse and
getting a frigid bath, and when the sun finally came out he was severely
blinded by the glare. For days he lay with a snow poultice on his inflamed

eyes and staggered around seeing double, with no one to guide him back to the hut. Louie had more to worry about than she knew.

Compensation for those risks included a front-row view of the most spectacular glaciated mountains on the continent: the Fairweathers (despite the name, they were often shrouded in clouds) and, behind them, the St. Elias range. On cold clear nights brilliant purple and green auroras pulsed across the skies. Then there were lessons in plant succession for the botanist. Ancient stumps six and ten feet tall indicated where immense forests had once flourished, before being broken off by the ice, and yet there were also new spruce groves taking root, and green patches of *Cassiopeia*, alder bushes, and fireweed, wild gardens on which butterflies fed. Nature was in a state of perpetual change and recovery. Willow ptarmigans ran chucking through his camp, and red-billed oystercatchers scurried along the shore. Humpback whales, harbor seals, and king salmon swam in the inlet. And at odd moments some great jewel of ice would break from the crystalline wall and plunge noisily into the sea, sending spray hundreds of feet high. Here was danger, but here also was knowledge and radiance enough to satisfy Muir's insatiable appetite.

"There is love of wild Nature in everybody," he wrote in his journal, "an ancient mother-love ever showing itself whether recognized or no, and however covered by cares and duties." And he added (stealing shamelessly from Henry David Thoreau), "In God's wildness lies the hope of the world—the great fresh unblighted, unredeemed wilderness."[25]

Whether there was enough "love in everybody" to save the California Sierra was about to be tested, and the test would prove positive and encouraging. When Muir got home in September, in time to supervise the grape harvest and nurse a sick daughter, the state and nation alike were afire with passion to preserve the outdoors. It was hard to keep one's mind on family matters. In an intense period of mere weeks Congress would establish not one but three national parks in California, setting in motion a broad, comprehensive policy of wild land conservation unprecedented in American or world history. Building on that precedent the country would create a whole new system of national parks—making Yellowstone no longer *the* national park but the first of many parks—and also a system of national forests. From that beginning would grow one of the most ambitious and influential government conservation efforts on the planet. It would rank as one of American democracy's finest hours. Muir had returned just in time to witness and participate in that creative burst, when the nation seemed to awaken miraculously to the significance of nature and confute Mark Twain's charge of a meretricious age motivated by selfishness.

Robert Underwood Johnson deserved much of the credit for setting the nation on a new course. As Louie enthused, "Many good Californians are rejoicing over the beginning of success for your noble effort to save our Sierra woods and gardens from the hands of manifold destroyers."[26] Johnson, however, could not have had a full sense of what was afoot. Countless others were playing a part, often obscurely, as the tide began to turn from an ethos of private appropriation and unrestrained exploitation of resources to one of public ownership and protection.

On the last day of September 1890 Vandever's bill for Yosemite came up for vote in Congress, but it was no longer the same bill. The House Committee on Public Lands had enlarged it considerably into a proposed "Yosemite National Park" consisting of nearly two million acres and including everything that Muir had suggested in his *Century* article that appeared earlier that same month. Committee members had gathered the support of the entire California delegation, the state's governor, and the U.S. Department of the Interior, along with newspapers across the land. The committee report declared: "The preservation by the Government in all its original beauty of a region like this seems to the committee to be a duty to the present and future generations. The rapid increase of population and the resulting destruction of natural objects make it incumbent on the Government in so far as may be to preserve the wonders and beauties of our country from injury and destruction, in order that they may afford pleasure as well as instruction to the people."[27] The bill passed both houses of Congress, and on 1 October President Benjamin Harrison signed it into law.

Unexpectedly, Yosemite became not the nation's second but its third park. Just days before protecting the Yosemite watersheds, Congress created a park in the southern Sierra—later named Sequoia National Park—which was approved by the president on 27 September. Muir, although he knew that region well through numerous expeditions, had little to do with this act, while Johnson, who supported the proposal in his congressional lobbying, had never even seen the place. Again, it was William Vandever who introduced a bill "to set apart a certain tract of land," and it was others who enlarged that proposal into national parkhood.

George W. Stewart, a child of the gold camps and editor of the backcountry newspaper the Visalia *Delta,* was the nature lover who worked hardest to save the southern Sierra range. He first became worried about the giant sequoias there, which were threatened by lumbermen, and kept up a barrage of editorials on the matter. Like Muir, he had explored the headwaters of the Kings, Kaweah, and San Joaquin rivers, all flowing out of immense wild canyons and watering the great valley below, and he wanted them saved too. A few scientists, hiking the region in the wake of the Whitney Survey, added that the high peaks should be preserved. A state senator drew lines on a map to designate a large park stretching from the General Grant grove of big trees clear to Mt. Whitney, a prescient idea that the legislature in Sacramento failed to act on. Then a lobbyist for the Southern Pacific Railroad, Daniel Zumwalt, an ardent mountaineer who was in Washington to represent his employers' interests, lobbied for a larger park that would save a beautiful wilderness while affording better watershed protection for the railroad's agricultural holdings in the Central Valley. Meanwhile, low-country farmers grew anxious about the security of their irrigation water and its sources in forest cover and added their support for preservation. Finally, the commissioner of the General Land Office in Washington, William Sparks, suspended all land claims in eighteen Sierra townships, on evidence of fraudulent entries, giving the conservationists a chance to seek permanent security for the still pristine uplands.[28]

Once again, a conservation impulse began as a little acorn and sprouted into a mighty oak. Vandever had wanted to set aside a single township on which remnant groves of sequoia trees stood; Congress doubled that amount to a total of seventy-two square miles. Then in the same bill that established Yosemite National Park legislators thought again and added five more townships to their southern Sierra park, including the famous Giant Forest. Thinking further, they created still another park named after the General Grant big tree—some local socialists had called it the Karl Marx tree, but the name did not stick—and a grove of fellow sequoias.

Did the politicians know precisely what they were doing? Nobody in Congress had examined the lay of the land for himself or was very familiar with what those township boxes on the map contained in the way of natural features. All they knew was what they had heard from locals, that here were some of the greatest trees on earth and protecting them would benefit everybody except a few lumbermen and sheepherders who would be kept out of the reserves. Safeguarding natural beauty, the politicians suddenly decided, should be their responsibility.[29]

Muir had little role in setting up those other parks, aside from the general effect his writings had on creating a climate for conservation. But the new Yosemite National Park was indeed the result, Johnson wrote, "of your very outspoken reference to the depredations of that region, and practically to your sketch of the limits, which I think are identical with those of the bill."[30] Once a few private claims within the reserved territory could be quieted, the reservation would match the scale of Yellowstone. But as predicted the valley had been left under state management, although Congress authorized an investigation into whether the Yosemite Commission had done its job well. The criticism made of the valley's appearance had not been kind to the state's reputation for stewardship. In particular, Muir's criticisms, carefully restrained though they had been in public venues, had cut deep—so deep that he had made a few serious enemies. He now became the target of attacks by the secretary-treasurer of the Yosemite Commission, John P. Irish, an Oakland newspaper editor, a Democratic political hopeful, and one of Muir's authors for *Picturesque California*.

When he returned from Alaska, Muir found a letter from Irish demanding proof that pigs, cattle, plows, and axes had harmed the valley's scenery. In newspaper letters and in the *Biennial Report of the*

Commissioners, Irish called Muir a liar, a libeler, and a rascal. He pointed an accusatory finger at Muir's own record of depredations:

> The only organized destruction of the valley's forest was attempted many years ago, when the State's primacy was disputed by squatters and John Muir helped run a sawmill, using Yosemite Falls as water power. Muir logged and sawed the trees of the valley for commercial purposes, and the mill was finally suppressed by the State, which he now falsely accuses of "rapidly destroying all that is accessible and destructible in the valley."

What the commission had been trying to do, Irish explained, was to restore the "original" condition, "as it came from the hand of Nature and the Indians, who had long been its guardians." When the Indians owned the place, the valley floor had been open and "park-like," due to regular burning of the underbrush. But then the white man took possession, suppressed the burning, and allowed too much vegetation to accumulate. The commission, by cutting trees and brush more responsibly than Muir had ever done, was trying to bring back that Indian openness. That is, if one ignored the non-Indian pigpen, the saloon, the rickety fences, and the hayfield, they were improving the view.[31]

In his defense, Muir answered simply, "I never cut down a single tree in the Yosemite, nor sawed a tree cut down by any other person there. Furthermore, I never held, or tried to hold any sort of claim in the valley, or sold a foot of lumber there or elsewhere." To Johnson he sent a more detailed but private explanation of his early days in the valley, his employment by Hutchings, and the source of the lumber he had sawed in that man's mill. "A tremendous windstorm blew down a considerable number of the large yellow pines & it was from these fallen trees that the mill logs were obtained." He refused to be drawn further into defending his character against Irish, whose "moral sense seems to have given way & sloughed off in utter ruin and rottenness like a stranded jellyfish trampled & decomposed. To argue with a dead man would be more hopeful than with John P."[32]

Johnson commiserated but had more serious tasks for Muir's pen than controversy with a braying politico. They must get Congress to create still another national park, this one around Kings Canyon, located on the Middle Fork of the Kings River. A letter written on 28 August indicates that over the summer Johnson had planned a campaign to preserve this spectacular gem of the southern Sierra.[33] It was the deepest canyon in North America, plunging some 8,000 feet, forming another Yosemite-like valley ten miles long and a half-mile wide, this one created by water and ice flowing down the slopes of Mt. Tyndall and Mt. Whitney. Aboriginal tribes, gold prospectors, and Whitney Survey scientists Clarence King (it was not his name affixed to the place but that of the kings of Spain) and William Brewer had passed through or near the canyon well before Muir arrived in the mid-1870s, but few had reported on its splendor. There still was no easy way into its innermost depths. Inexplicably, Congress had left the canyon out of the new Sequoia and General Grant parks, and Johnson was determined to see that it was reserved from exploitation too.

The General Land Office had recommended a massive park stretching from Kings Canyon across the Owens Valley all the way to the Nevada border, but Congress had dismissed that suggestion as too grandiose. The Johnson-Muir team was, therefore, determined to be more cautious and pragmatic. They would draw the boundary no farther east than the Sierra divide to prevent criticism and defeat by mining interests. Preparing that more conservative map required a ground reconnaissance by Muir that would freshen his memory and provide material for an article in *The Century*. Johnson kept urging him to get it done as soon as possible. Just as the grape harvest was winding down, however, and he was packing to go, John Strentzel, who had been sick for some time, died. The reconnaissance had to be postponed until June of the following year, and the magazine article would not appear in print until November.

Dr. Strentzel left his wife and daughter an estate worth more than $235,000. Some of that inheritance was surely due to Muir's skilled, businesslike management, but now the two intertwined acreages, and all of the doctor's far-flung property investments, were more than ever the son-in-law's responsibility. He was the sole male in the household, answerable in society's view for its four female dependents—his wife, two daughters, and mother-in-law. Five years later, in 1895 Louisiana died, leaving Louie dependent solely on her husband and daughters for family ties and companionship.

Following John Strentzel's death and as a sign of enlarged responsibility, Muir moved his family out of their Dutch Colonial house and into the Strentzel manse, with its house servants, spacious bedrooms, and fine views of the Alhambra Valley. In doing so he gained new prominence among the area's landowning elite. The bigger house offered him a second-floor study with fireplace where he intended to take refuge from the ranch—he called it his "scribbling den"—and settle down to write. But to dedicate himself more than ever to a career of writing was to take up an even greater role in the conservation movement. He might now be head of the whole estate, but he also ranked as America's leading voice for the conservation of nature. The demands had only gotten bigger and more complicated.

The following spring, 1891, John and Maggie Reid arrived from the Great Plains, their horse-raising business a financial bust, and Muir assigned his brother-in-law the job of ranch foreman. Reid had not seen much success in agriculture so far, but Muir needed someone he knew and trusted as friend and manager, and he wanted to help his sister out of her family's difficulties. The hiring freed him from the daily burden of fruit and orchard oversight. By the end of May he was prepared at last to make that reconnaissance into the southern Sierra, in the company of the artist George Robinson. Muir wanted to get more accurate data for his Kings Canyon park proposal, to see what changes had occurred to one of his most beloved areas, and to get "the scales & burrs of business rubbed off in the brush & rocks & winds of that glorious wilderness."[34] For the next three weeks they tramped the high country, with map, journal, camera, and easel in hand.

What they found was not all glorious: a lot of bear hunters were prowling the forests, and a greatly increased number of sawmills were disturbing the silence. The mills took every species of tree they could reach, including sequoia. Felling the giant trees shattered them into many pieces, and what their fall did not break up, a stick of dynamite could—anything to get manageable fragments for the mills. Those sites of screeching blades cutting through logs would have to be eliminated from the park proposal.

Muir's article, finished in mid-August, got a grateful but scolding acceptance from Johnson—it was so late in arriving—and a modest check for $185. The editor entitled the piece, "A Rival of the Yosemite," which indicated the strategy that he proposed to follow in persuading Congress and the Secretary of the Interior, John W. Noble, to set it aside as parkland. Nature had been lavish in providing more than one Yosemite for humans to enjoy, and humans should be no less generous in conserving that abundance. Muir's article described the outstanding features of the place, ticked off the growing assaults around its edges, and lamented the extermination of grizzly and black bears underway by sport hunters and the ubiquitous sheepherders. Robinson's accompanying pictures left no doubt that here was indeed a counterpart to the more familiar valley to the north—

Muir drawing of the "Yosemite-like" Kings Canyon on the South Fork of the Kings River, California. (H–A, JMP)

equally sublime, far less well known. Muir's map proposed a wedge-shaped addition that would add Kings Canyon to Sequoia National Park, carefully drawn to exclude any substantial economic interests. "This region," he concluded, "contains no mines of consequence, it is too high and too rocky for agriculture, and even the lumber industry need suffer no unreasonable restriction. Let our law-givers then make haste before it is too late to set apart this surpassingly glorious region for the recreation and well-being of humanity, and all the world will rise up and call them blessed."[35]

This time Congress, perhaps feeling that it had set aside enough parkland for the moment, failed to act on the proposal. Secretary Noble supported the extension, but legislators had temporarily lost their will. Fortunately, they had set up another avenue for protection that proved almost as efficacious. On 2 March 1891, a few days before adjourning, Congress had passed the General Revision Act, aimed at preventing fraudulent land entries and repealing a few misguided homesteading policies. The conference committeemen, in reconciling the conflicting House and Senate bills, had taken it upon themselves to insert a clause that would allow the president to set aside forest reserves in the West. It was still another sharp break with precedent, this time marking the beginnings of a national forest system.

The purpose of inserting that forest-reserve clause was never explained fully to other legislators, nor perhaps did the whole Congress, in voting approval, understand altogether what it was doing. Was the goal to protect vulnerable watersheds for the sake of western irrigators? Or prevent large timber companies from monopolizing a valuable resource? Or save lovely forests from spoliation? The act did not say. It was left up to President Harrison to decide the ruling purpose of the new reserves. Weeks later, he used his new authority to designate the nation's first forest reserve, a remote area around Yellowstone National Park that was in no imminent danger from loggers or near irrigation interests—a choice that unmistakably made aesthetics the first and dominant rationale of forest conservation.[36]

During the next two years Harrison, a Republican from Indianapolis and hitherto not known to be a visionary conservationist, set aside reserves covering thirteen million acres. Among them was a Sierra forest reserve (1893), covering some four million acres—and including Kings Canyon. The reserve ran along the western slope of the Sierra divide, spanning the gap between Yosemite and Sequoia parks. Its designation did not close that space to all future economic use, but it did prevent any further privatization of the "Range of Light," and it made the federal government its protector in perpetuity.

The English political philosopher Lord James Bryce later declared that national parks were the best idea that Americans ever had. If so, then the national forests might rank as the second best idea. Together, the two kinds of federal conservation would eventually protect nearly three hundred million acres, reaching from the Everglades of Florida to the Brooks Range in northern Alaska. The birthing of those ideas occurred in the Yellowstone and Sierra regions during the infamous Gilded Age, but especially during the 1890–93 period when it became clear that land conservation had become a legitimate and necessary part of American democracy.

⊙━✦━⊙

As the full magnitude of what had been achieved began to sink in, people talked about the need for a nongovernmental organization to play watchdog over the public park and forestlands. Few trusted the politicians to be constant or clear-headed. Naturally, John Muir must be recruited to support or even lead such an organization. He had ducked Johnson's suggestion that he form an "association" to watch over the Sierra, but it came back to ensnare him. This time the idea of a citizens' watchdog group originated among a few professors and students at the University of California who, like Muir, looked to the mountains for enlightenment as well as pleasure. Joachim Senger, professor of German, had suggested as early as 1886 that a library of mountaineering books be established in Yosemite Valley, providing a place where enthusiasts could come together and share experiences. In spring 1891 another faculty member, William Armes, a lecturer in English, wrote Muir about forming a "Sierra Club," modeled after the Alpine Club of Portland, Oregon, and the Appalachian Mountain Club of Boston.

"Count me in as a hearty worker," Muir replied. To Johnson he dubbed the proposed organization "the Defense Association," indicating that it would be more than a hiking club; its purpose would be to defend conservation achievements in the Sierra.[37]

One year later the professors, after much milling around, had gathered support from nonacademic circles and finally set a time and place for their first organizational meeting—28 May 1892, at the law office of Warren Olney in San Francisco's First National Bank building. Muir agreed to preside, hoping "to do something for wildness and make the mountains glad." More prosaically, the articles of incorporation specified "preserving forests and other natural features of the Sierra Nevada Mountains" as their goal but, beyond the politics of conservation, they aimed to "explore, enjoy and render accessible the mountain regions of the Pacific Coast."[38]

Muir was the unanimous choice to serve as president of the Sierra Club, a position he would hold for the rest of his life. He accepted the office not because his "genius" had changed from private to public, but because he expected that he would serve mainly as a figurehead for the organization. In the initial years that was so; most of the driving energy came from the Bay Area academic and scientific community, particularly the two Berkeley humanists Senger and Armes, who were elected the first secretaries of the Club. An undergraduate student, Robert Price, was also named a founding director, along with Mark Kerr and Willard Johnson, employees of the U.S. Geological Survey. Lawyer Olney became vice-president, while the remaining members of the early leadership core came from the newly established Leland Stanford University in Palo Alto: geologist John Branner and university president David Starr Jordan.[39]

For the first open meeting, held on 16 September at the California Academy of Sciences, 250 members and friends showed up, with the professions far more represented than business or politics. Muir was not present, but he did make it to the second meeting, by which time the attendance had doubled, and introduced the evening speaker, Major John Wesley Powell, director of the Geological Survey, who spoke on his historic exploration of the Grand Canyon in 1869.[40] For the third meeting, when many prominent men of science, literature, and government from around the nation were elected honorary members, including Powell and Robert Underwood Johnson, Muir was once again absent.

Ranch duties and family misfortunes may explain part of that absenteeism. Reports had come that David's dry goods business was going bankrupt, and Muir traveled east to save his brother's livelihood and reputation. The best remedy seemed to be to bring David and his wife Etta back to California and put him, with brother-in-law John Reid, in charge of daily operations on the ranch. After visiting his old landlord in Indianapolis, Mrs. Sutherland, in whose house he had lain blind for so many depressing weeks, Muir roared through Nebraska, briefly visiting his siblings there. He made it back home with David and Etta in tow just in time for the monthly meeting of the Grange. His whirlwind trip had done a lot of good, wrote sister Annie in Portage: "He cheered us up beyond what seemed possible."[41] Even so, she, Sarah, and their mother were all that remained of the Muirs in Wisconsin, and none of them was faring well. Nor were Muir's headaches on the ranch over. Despite recruiting more help, he was still plagued by too much land to oversee, too many meetings to attend, and too little time for the work he had to do. He knew he had to cut back either on the family business or on conservation. Soon portions of the ranch property went on the market for sale or lease.

The laird of the Alhambra Valley had been thrust into a national leadership role in the conservation movement, but it was a role full of irony. His long, unkempt beard reminded people of a figure out of the Old Testament—a visionary speaking of higher values needed by an age of materialistic excess. His eyes shone with generosity, humor, shrewdness, and enthusiasm; such a man could show Americans how to see beauty in the world, beyond the factory and sawmill, the farm and city. But at the same time he was a leader who tried to avoid stirring up the money interests unnecessarily, hoping to enlist them on his side. This seer did not come dressed in sackcloth and ashes; rather, he appeared in a well-tailored suit of broadcloth, signifying a man of worldly accomplishment, a prosperous businessman. He lived and entertained in an impressive manor house, with flowers and fresh fruit, a bottle of wine and a box of cigars on the dining table. Editors, agriculturalists, businessmen, professors, poets, scientists, and humanists all looked on him as one of them. He seemed to harmonize the cultural and social contradictions of his time—uniting vision and achievement, simplicity and wealth, spirituality and pragmatism. For that reason the Gilded Age made him one of its prophetic voices.

Muir would henceforth be identified as the greatest founder of the conservation movement, even though others preceded him, others showed up at critical moments, and others contributed important ideas. He was always a reluctant leader, diffident and inclined to head for the hills when he heard the call to arms. What he gave the movement was, nonetheless, indispensable: the compelling image and words of a prophet standing before unsullied nature in a posture of unabashed love. That love of nature was both rhapsodical and worldly, a love that knew no bounds but knew how to compromise. He inspired Americans to believe that nature deserved higher consideration. Plenty of others shared that belief, but no one articulated it better.

CHAPTER 12

The Company of Green Men

On the first of May 1893, the World's Columbian Exposition opened its gates to celebrate the four-hundredth anniversary of Christopher Columbus's discovery of the New World. This most fabulous of "world's fairs" rose like a dream on the shores of Lake Michigan near Chicago: a gleaming white city of Venetian lagoons and canals, of Roman classical domes and columns that proudly declared, "Here is the new seat of empire for the earth." Over the spring and summer tens of millions of visitors came to gape at the splendid buildings designed by the nation's leading architects. They strolled through leafy grounds laid out by Frederick Law Olmsted and marveled at exhibits from states and countries competing to display the wonders of modern industry, science, and civilization. On the adjoining Midway Plaisance, an avenue of popular amusements, they rode on the first Ferris wheel, watched Little Egypt dance the "hootchy-kootchy," and ate a foreign sandwich called a hamburger.

Nowhere in the great temples labeled Agriculture, Manufactures, Mines, and Machinery did the fair address the ecological toll that four centuries of European settlement had taken on the North American continent. By 1893 all the larger species of predators and herbivores had suffered drastic declines, as had birds, forests, and fur-bearing mammals. Some of the planet's best soils had been depleted or lost to erosion. Waterways ran polluted across the land, and the air over many cities had become polluted by the burning of coal. Most of this damage came from the pursuit of unfettered capitalism in a cultural climate that made economic growth the dominant value. But even backwoods communities of white Euro-Americans, located far from urban markets or capitalists, only occasionally practiced restraint or conservation. None of this darker outcome, however, was on display in Chicago.

Muir arrived alone at the fair on 25 May and stayed several days, as captivated as everyone else by the glittering spectacle. He lodged with Alfred and Fay Sellers, a wealthy business couple whom he had met on his Yellowstone camping trip. Together, they went to see the paintings of William Keith, Thomas Hill, and others in the California exhibit—marvelous examples of landscape art that told only a half-truth about the western environment. Keith and Muir were supposed to meet here and then travel together to New York and Scotland, but Keith had already left and would prove frustratingly elusive until the two men made it home four months later. So Muir glanced over his absent friend's paintings on display, sniffed that they were not his best, and trailed his hosts on to other exhibits. "I wandered & gazed," he wrote Louie, "until I was ready to fall down with utter exhaustion."[1]

He complained that the fair was "a cosmopolitan rat's nest"—and then laughed when he discovered a real nest in a glass case with stuffed wood rats. All the bric-a-brac of mass production was jammed inside those buildings, mixed among high art and museum-dead nature. But outside, the effect was magical, especially at night when tens of thousands of electric lights flashed on. The twentieth-century revolution that electricity would make possible was one of the fair's shining promises. George Westinghouse and Thomas Edison had invented those light bulbs, but it was the Croatian immigrant Nikola Tesla who invented the alternating current transmission system that powered the fair. Muir was impressed: "It was all fairyland on a colossal scale & would have made the Queen of Sheba & poor Solomon in all their glory feel sick with helpless envy."[2]

A few days later he would leave Chicago, meet Tesla in his New York City laboratory, and write an enthusiastic report to Louie. Neither wife nor husband had any doubts about the social worth of Tesla or other inventors or about the coming age of electricity, telecommunications, typewriters, or other manifestations of mechanical progress. They were more skeptical about modern cities and more critical of the quality of life they offered. Yet places like San Francisco, Chicago, and New York had an irresistible appeal, for here were found those amazing expressions of the new. Muir would meet in those great metropolises some of the most talented people in the world, and he would find them highly agreeable, for they graciously treated him as one of them.

"I had no idea that I was so well known considering how little I have written." On 12 June he penned a long letter to Louie, giving a full account of his flattering reception in the East's urban centers. First he had visited *The Century* offices in New York with the notion of saying a brief hello before holing up in a hotel room to finish an article on Glacier Bay. The editor Robert Johnson, however, gave him little chance to write. First he was introduced to the celebrated naturalist John Burroughs, who journeyed down from his hemlock-shaded retreat near the Hudson River, and the two Johns were instantly mated for life. Muir went on to a sparkling dinner at Richard Gilder's in Washington Square. He dined at the Gramercy Park mansion of the lumber merchant James Pinchot, whose twenty-seven-year-old son Gifford was home from his job as consulting forester to the Biltmore Estate in North Carolina and eager to meet a man "so well known to the friends of the forest in this country." He was then received as pampered houseguest at the West Point estate of Henry Fairfield and Loulu Perry Osborn. The son of a wealthy railroad promoter, Osborn had taught at Princeton and Columbia and was in charge of mammalian paleontology at the American Museum of Natural History (where he would later serve as president).[3]

For a few moments Muir managed to steal away to see Central Park and reported to his wife on the glacial scoring he found on its exposed rocks. And through it all he suffered from the city's intense summer heat that drove most of the upper bourgeoisie away: "It has been very hot here & I felt all the time as if somebody had rubbed the inside of my undercloths with very sticky molasses."[4]

Johnson insisted that they add Bostonians to Muir's circle of acquaintances, and off they rattled on the night train. There they were received at the palatial suburban estate of Harvard professor of botany Charles Sprague Sargent—a manor house surrounded by eighty acres of exquisite gardens and pond. Sargent, like Osborn, had inherited considerable wealth and made a career in natural science as a forest expert and director of the Arnold Arboretum. After an audience with the mayor, Muir also met historian Francis Parkman, philosopher Josiah Royce, and the popular Maine author Sarah Orne Jewett.

But the highlight of what had become pilgrimage as much as lionization was a jaunt to Concord, where they toured Ralph Waldo Emerson's house and study, visited the Sleepy Hollow gravesites of Emerson and Thoreau, and then rode out of the village to that Mecca for America's literary naturalists, Walden Pond. Muir had not expected to be so moved by the sight of the "resting places of these grand men," and he imagined "how glad I would be to feel sure that I would also rest here," although he supposed he would be buried next to his mother in Portage. Walden he described as "a beautiful lake about half a mile long fairly embosomed like a bright day eye in wooded hills. . . . No wonder Thoreau lived here two years. I could have enjoyed living here 200 years or 2000." Most fortifying to his sense of belonging was the warm reception he got from Emerson's son, who declared that his name was a household word. The day quickly passed: Muir spent less time in Concord than Emerson had in Yosemite and then, like his renowned visitor thirty years earlier, a traveling companion shuffled him off. But he felt a distinct laying on of hands in this Concord-Boston center of Transcendentalism, distinguished publishing houses, and outstanding universities.[5]

Everywhere he dined Muir was asked to tell the story of little dog Stickeen edging nervously across that Alaskan ice bridge. While liveried servants listened behind the parlor door, his hosts passed around the champagne and declared him a wonderful tale-spinner. They hailed him as a powerful voice for forest and nature conservation. They welcomed him as a fellow member of America's cultural elite who were trying to bring intelligence, virtue, and grace to the exercise of political and economic power. Muir could aid their mission with his aura of moral authenticity, his intimate knowledge of the western side of the continent, and his eye for natural beauty. Just as Emerson had called him "one of my men," the New York and Boston intelligentsia declared he was "their man" too. With so much effusive praise billowing his sails, he set off in high confidence to take on Europe.

Muir's first priority in making an Atlantic crossing, his first since boyhood, was not to see the famous sights of Europe but to restore his sense of Scottish identity. Landing at Liverpool, he went straight to Edinburgh and Dunbar in search of roots. Johnson had given him a letter of introduction to the publisher David Douglas (no relation to the famed Scots explorer-botanist whose name is honored in the Douglas fir). They talked long into the night, exchanging tales of Sir Walter Scott, Hugh Miller, and Alaskan ice, and the next day toured the dark, imposing Castle, the Royal Mile, and Arthur's Seat. "Feeling lonely & a stranger in my own native land," Muir wrote that he was deeply grateful to Douglas, who "brought me back into quick & living context with it & now I am a Scotchman & at home again." The stately dignity of Edinburgh overcame his generic distaste for urban noise and squalor; it was "far the most beautiful town I ever saw."[6]

The small city of Dunbar lit an even warmer spark in his heart—his native place! What had once been the Muir family home was now the Lorne Temperance Hotel, but he dossed down at the rival St. George. A few school chums were still around and were astounded to see him again after nearly fifty years' absence. They worked in the High Street shops that he might have inherited had he stayed. The only relative still living there was his cousin Margaret Hay Lunum and her daughter, and he moved in with them for ten days of reminiscing, sightseeing, and adulation. Remarkably, some of the locals had read his articles in *The Century* and followed his career in America. From Dunbar he traveled to Dumfries, where his beloved Robert Burns had died, then on to Glasgow, Loch Lomond, Oban, and through the Western Isles. The overcast skies, the cold sea, and the heather in bloom all reminded him of Alaska, though nowhere so grand.[7]

On 6 August he completed his return to cultural roots with a pilgrimage to Wordsworth's grave in Grasmere. His notes on the scene were brief and simple, his emotions deep but inexpressible. He took in the surrounding ice-sculpted mountains, "remarkably massive"; the maple, yew, pine, and ash trees of the graveyard; the plain gray headstones shining in the drizzle. "I stood with damp eyes and a lump in my throat," he wrote, as he felt the powerful influence that the poet had wrought in his life as in so many others. Then he went out as he had come in, on the Kendal and Windermere Railway, whose construction Wordsworth had denounced as a sacrilegious attack on the

"temples of Nature," fearing that it would bring in "swarms of plea-
sure-hunters, most of them thinking that they do not fly fast enough
through the country which they have come to see." Muir was flying
fast along with the rest, but he paused long enough to pay homage at
the gravesite, a pilgrim more than pleasure seeker, and to acknowledge a man and landscape that had helped shape his own passion for
nature.[8]

Beyond remembering who he was and where he came from, the
main justification for the European trip was to observe and compare glaciers, and now Muir settled down to "his studies," with notebooks and sketching tools in hand. He voyaged among the fjords of
Norway, as far north as Trondheim, then turned south to the Alps of
Switzerland and Italy. His mountain agenda included Louis Agassiz's
hometown of Chamonix in the Rhone valley, where the theory of the
Ice Age originated, as well as Mt. Blanc and the rugged area around
Chiavenna and Lake Como. In such rocky, wooded places he found
a remarkable degree of wildness surviving in the heart of Europe and
a growing feeling for nature among the citizenry, who were out hiking the trails as he was. "I am delighted with my Swiss trip," he wrote
home. "I was able to read the main features [of glaciation] easily."[9]
What he learned of scientific value was that, in Western Europe as
in western North America, glaciers were retreating as the climate
warmed. But he also wanted Louie to know that he had a serious purpose in his rambles and was gaining useful insights as well as spending
a lot of money and seeing a lot of magnificent scenery. The old idea
of writing a comprehensive book on glaciation had been left behind;
the insights were all for his personal edification.

Zurich, Geneva, and Basel were resting points on the way back,
but he zipped past the French cities, for their language that he had
studied as a schoolboy had nearly vanished from memory and it was
hard to find anyone who spoke English. Even the dogs did not understand his accent or vocabulary, refusing "to wag their tails to my 'bon
chien.'" Soon he was back in London, where he could understand the
lingo, although he did not feel much at home in that vast imperial
city. He complained about getting lost in its "canyons," a synthetic
wilderness of intricate streets, clubs, and social classes that he could

not read or navigate. The botanical wonders of Kew Gardens he found green and sympathetic enough, and its director Joseph Hooker (who had camped with him and Asa Gray on Mt. Shasta) a kindred spirit. He made his way to Westminster Abbey and the House of Parliament, leaving his card for James Bryce, the famous politician of the Liberal Party, mountaineer, and author of *The American Commonwealth*, published in 1888. But traveling alone, feeling like an inferior provincial in the seat of world empire, a Scots-American who belonged on the margins of civilization, Muir was eager to leave the place behind.[10]

On landing in New York, Johnson snared him for a quick tutorial in national politicking. They went to Washington, D.C., where they interviewed anyone likely to be influential in protecting the parks and forest reserves. Muir made key contacts that would prove useful for future conservationist work. The U.S. capital seemed less overwhelming than the Victorian metropolis he had just visited, and, sounding like a man happy to be home and among his own kind, he allowed that the White House was "a rather nice dwelling, but not at all awfully so."[11]

⊙═╾╋╼═⊙

Back in the Alhambra Valley in time for fall harvest, he confronted one of the most difficult challenges of his life—not getting in the grapes but writing his first book. All of his youthful book-making ambitions had come to naught. He had lacked discipline and resolve. Could he succeed at last in putting together a full volume rather than scattered articles for magazines and newspapers? He was now fifty-five years old, supported by a loving wife and daughters twelve and seven years old, resident in a grand house that ran by the labor of others, and was left alone for long periods with his growing library, unpublished journals, and published articles gathered around him. He had come home with a book contract from the Century Company. The ever-demanding Johnson was driving him to produce. So was the memory of the many influential people he had met, all of them impressed by his early writings but all expecting even greater things of him. The moment had come to write in earnest, and the stakes were high.

Johnson had made book writing seem easy: select some of those previously printed articles and assemble them into a coherent whole. Months flew by as he sorted through the pile, selecting and discarding, changing a word here and there, and playing with their order in the table of contents. In the end he came up with sixteen chapters, two of them new essays, the rest drawn from back issues (1875–1882) of *Scribner's, The Century, Overland Monthly, Harper's,* and the San Francisco *Evening Bulletin.* He called the book *The Mountains of California* and published it in August 1894. It would be the first of several books he would write, most of them assembled in the same fashion from his bachelor archives, his early intense scribbling, but *Mountains* would be the best of the bunch, an enduring classic in American nature writing.[12]

The patchwork nature of the book was hard to deny, but the pieces somehow held together like the complexly diversified landscape they portrayed. Although the introductory essay, "Sierra Nevada," began with a regionalist argument that mountains gave Californians their peculiar cultural identity—mountains always in sight, always working on people's imagination—Muir did not mean to provide an environmental interpretation of the state's character. He ignored those ranges near most of the state's population: the Coast Range, the San Gabriels, the San Bernadinos. Instead, he wandered wherever ice still glistened, even beyond California to Mt. Fairweather, Mt. Blanc, the Rockies, the Wasatch Range of Utah. He ended the book low down in the "bee pastures" of the Central Valley, that flowery plain that had once greeted his hungry eyes. But mainly he focused on the central uplands, the High Sierra wilderness, his totem place on earth. From a distance "no mark of man is visible on it, nor anything to suggest the richness of the life it cherishes, or the depth and grandeur of its sculpture."[13] The book was meant to be a guide into that unknown grandeur, an interpretation of a landscape where culture had barely penetrated and did not rule as it did in New York or London.

Old, familiar themes echoed in the book. Muir recalled his discovery of the persistence and significance of glaciers in the Sierra, the amazing power of tiny crystals of snow to transform themselves into giant plows and chisels. The ancient ice sheets, so forbidding to the human mind, were necessary to carve beauty, make soil, replenish rivers, and irrigate the greatest forests in the world and the most inviting meadows. If the cold hardness of ice could produce so much goodness, so much beauty and life, then why should humans be afraid of anything in the nonhuman world? Why worry about passing windstorms, floods, earthquakes, or other forms of natural violence? Muir reiterated his view that it was only fear that made people avoid the wilderness and blindness that drove them to try to control and dominate it. Learn to bend with the trees in the wind. Plunge into whitewater rapids like the cheerful little ouzel. Observe the chattering confidence of squirrels that they will survive.

In the chapter on "Glacial Lakes" he speaks of the wilderness as "a beautiful system" in which the parts are harmoniously related to one another. To appreciate that system required rigorous knowledge of geology, botany, and zoology, but also it required a capacity for "joy" and "love." Emotional responsiveness was perfectly compatible with cool judgment and careful observation. Elsewhere in the book he speaks of acquiring a "loving conception" of the forest—and the word "loving" was one of the few additions he made to the original text.[14] More emphatically than ever, he believed that feeling and fact were not opposed; they enriched one another, and together they opened human eyes to the deeper harmony that gave nature meaning and coherence.

The longest chapter, placed at the book's center, was a composite piece entitled "The Forest." It may stand as the core of Muir's approach to the natural world of the Sierra. Seventeen tree species, ranging from the Digger pine (*Pinus sabiniana*) to the incense cedar (*Libocedrus decurrens*) and single leaf pinyon (*Pinus monophylla*), appear here in a brief mountain silva. Each tree is meticulously described in taxonomic and ecological terms and also appraised for its aesthetic qualities. "Most beautiful of all" is the "exquisitely delicate and feminine" hemlock spruce (or mountain hemlock, *Tsuga mertseniana*), which can stop the heart of the most hardened prospector "seeking only game or gold." Nobler than any other tree, and more endangered, is the *Sequoia gigantea*, the giant redwood that had proved nearly indestructible in the long history of North America but now is "rapidly vanishing before the fire and steel of man."[15]

The Mountains of California, on the whole, was not a conservation tract, nor did his editor Johnson pressure him to make it one, although the book's promotion of nature appreciation certainly had political and ethical implications. Seeing beyond politics as well as culture, the book was meant to be an interpretation of a world that humans had not made—its development over time and its relationships over space. Such a world where people were not dominant, Muir was saying, still exists and is worth knowing for its own sake. Understanding that world should induce a greater sense of humility among humankind. Thoreau had preached a similar message in Walden, but he could not avoid putting a lot of himself into his books or dwelling on his alienation from society, his search for an alternative way of living. Muir, in contrast, tried to erase himself and indeed all humans from his pages. Not completely or ruthlessly: he dredged up childhood memories when he made fun of Christianity by contrasting the mournful hymn "Old Hundredth" to Scottish folk ballads, the latter sounding so much more pleasing and congruous in the woods. He acknowledged the presence of people in the mountains in a sketch of Indians he met on the trail, of the Latino immigrant he had met in Eaton Canyon, and of an old gold mining camp and its gnarly denizens. But generally humans and their extractive activities were not the center of attention here, nor was theology or philosophy. Nor was his own personality or his conservation views.

Muir piled on the scientific facts. His essays were not only devoid of politics but also of popular entertainment; they offered advanced natural history, requiring patience and a thirst for knowledge on the part of his readers. He satisfied what literary scholar Lawrence Buell calls a "taste for detail" that characterized the late nineteenth century, an age of "realism" in which readers wanted to experience the material world and know it thoroughly and factually.[16] They also wanted the rhetorical excesses of preceding ages pruned back, leaving the facts to speak more for themselves. To meet that matter-of-fact standard, Muir avowed that he had succeeded in "killing adjectives and adverbs of redundant growth—the verys, intenses, gloriouses, ands and buts—by the score."[17]

Fewer romantic flights and more cold, hard facts did not mean a view of nature that was nothing but materialist. When he came to nature, he was still the idealist, and the tension in his writing remained one of science versus religion. Not only did Muir hope to instill a "loving conception" of the natural world through a presentation of facts; he also maintained that "love," or an underlying benevolent order, informed the facts. As to the ultimate source of that love, Muir remained as vague and ambivalent as ever. He speaks of "God's love" flowing through the natural world, suggesting a conventional theist belief that nature had been designed by a superior being. But more often in the book he speaks of "Nature's love" or "Nature's methods," as though Nature was itself the ultimate source of benevolence, or as though Nature and God were one. However hazy his vision into the deeper truths, such was a message that the age of realism wanted. People demanded not only a fuller understanding of reality but also plenty of reassurance that they were not standing on the edge of nihilism. The mountains must offer a glimpse of essential goodness and harmony in the universe.

In May 1894, as Muir's book was going into production, fifty thousand workers went on strike at the Pullman factory south of Chicago. The company president, George Pullman, who had invented the Palace sleeping car for rail travelers, had forced them into a desperate situation by cutting wages but keeping rents high on the houses he required his employees to live in and keeping the prices high in his company store. The strike against wage cutting spread among railroad workers across the nation, shutting down the country's transportation lines. A severe economic depression the previous year had left many working-class Americans impoverished and ready to join hands against the growing power of corporations. Some of the angriest set fire to the World's Fair grounds. At Pullman the striking workers found an impassioned leader in Eugene Debs who, after President Grover Cleveland sent in the U.S. Army to end the strike and imprisoned him for stopping the delivery of mail, became an implacable foe of capitalists and their lackey politicians.

Muir's family and friends expressed concern over the strike, fearing a breakdown of law and order across the country, but they seemed ambivalent about who was more to blame, labor or capital. Mother Ann wrote: "What a great deal of trouble these *strikes* are making all through the country from what we read about in the Papers we hardly know what to expect next." Sister Joanna declared, "No more Democratic administration for me. . . . I believe I am on a strike too." She was primarily upset with President Cleveland and his party for leaving the country in such a mess. Robert Johnson denounced the "*annus terroribus*" that was tearing society apart. Muir's book, he wrote, "ought to be a success—if these stupid strikers in and out of Congress would let business revive!" Muir, acknowledging that he had rushed his book into print and that his timing was bad, responded, "In a sad democratic year I make no complaint." "Everybody here," he added, "is talking strikes, wages, & capital corporations." Contrary to the mountains, American society was not characterized by an underlying goodness or harmony.[18]

In his Indianapolis and early California days Muir had sweated alongside workers who were little different from those at Pullman. He understood firsthand their struggles to survive, their sense of brotherhood, and their ethos of mutual aid. More recently, however, he had become a property-owner, an employer of often unruly, undependable laborers largely of Chinese origin. There is no evidence that he exploited them, but he was now on the other side of an economic relationship. Perhaps because of his shifting, ambiguous class status, he chose not to join one side or the other in the ongoing battle between labor and capital to control American industry. Nor did he align himself with the Democrats or Republicans. In fact he left no record of voting in an election or of his political affiliations during this tumultuous decade of the 1890s. Divided in his national identity, a Scotsman *and* an American, he had also become more divided in his class and political sympathies.

Conservation of nature was the program of reform he most believed in, a reform that neither capital nor labor, Democrats nor

Republicans, owned or made their priority. Debs and his railway workers were thoroughly blind to the importance of nature; their lives were too often circumscribed by the heat and din of blast furnaces, by polluted skies, and by crowded streets to care about a world beyond the paycheck. A few may have spent their Sundays, as Muir had done while working for Osgood, Smith, and Company, looking for green forests and quiet solitude beyond the city limits, but rank and file workers tended to be more concerned about hanging on to their skimpy income than conserving the beauty or long-term survival of America's land and water resources. Likewise, George Pullman and his fellow factory owners usually put profits over the beauty, health, or longevity of the green world.

Committed conservationists like Muir, therefore, tended to stand apart from the industrial battleground, leading to harsh charges of elitism, indifference, or obstructionism from the polar extremes. They denounced business greed over and over but did not throw much support to workers trying to organize themselves into labor unions, although unionization offered significant hope for economic democracy and, potentially, a powerful check on the corporate assault on nature. Although critical of capitalists, conservationists did not trust radicals like Debs to care about a nonhuman world beyond the factory or railway yard. Thus, two separate movements, one to reform relations with nature and the other to reform the distribution of power within a capitalist system, grew up in the late nineteenth century. Independently, they attacked different sides of an impregnable citadel. Both armies fought for reform, both worried about the incorporation of America, both believed in democracy, but they could not agree on a common strategy of attack.

Class loyalties or conflict did not easily define the conservationists. They could be found in many walks of life, some poor, some rich, some rural, some urban, although most probably came from the middling classes, identifying with neither the plutocracy nor the proletariat. A diverse group, they were united by opposition to laissez-faire economic attitudes; they called on individuals to practice a new conservation ethic and on the federal government to help preserve and manage natural resources. They were, above all, wildlife and plant lovers—the company of green men. Their leaders may have included gentrified folk like Johnson, Sargent, and Pinchot, who were wealthy or well-educated or both, but those leaders were not necessarily representative of all conservationists; they were simply the most powerful and influential. All green men, leaders and followers, saw their cause as a fight for the welfare of present and future generations, a battle to redeem a society poisoned by self-interest and class divisions.

Conservationists, whatever their social origins as individuals, agreed that the greatest threat facing American democracy was the continuing grab for resources by selfish, unregulated individuals. Grabbers showed little concern for the greater good and little obedience to the few laws that existed. They might include a corporation stealing timber from the public lands, a sheepherder invading the national parks or forests, or a market hunter killing birds or game wholesale. Excessive shooting should be illegal, along with cutting down trees without permission or exterminating the last few bison, whether for subsistence or marketplace gain. Such selfishness cut across lines of income and ethnicity. There was no difference between rich and poor when it came to stealing from the public domain, or leaving behind a trail of devastation, or resisting all rules and restraints. Laissez faire could not be forbidden to one class and permitted to another. All citizens must be equal before the law, conservationists believed, and all individuals must respect the rights of others.

Not every one in the green company was male, for many women too were calling for an ethic of environmental restraint. They included Mary Hemenway, Celia Thaxter, and Olive Thorne Miller, leaders in the Audubon Society for protecting birds, and Helen Gompertz, Katharine Hittell, and Eliza Campbell, charter members of the Sierra Club. At the National Geographical Society there was Elizah Scidmore, an explorer of the Alaskan coast and a strong voice for forest conservation. The most prominent of those women undoubtedly belonged, like their male counterparts, to the more economically secure ranks of society, but no more so than the men were all women conservationists rich. They too tended to avoid the industrial confrontation going on between labor and capital, but like the men they believed they were fighting for the well-being of all people for all time.[19]

Muir exchanged letters of mutual admiration with a number of women who shared his green hopes. Among them was Olive Thorne Miller, who came on a visit to the home of "our greatest Nature lover" and praised him for the leadership he gave to bird protection. His essay on the water ouzel, reprinted in *The Mountains of California*, did enormous good for the cause, she wrote, and "all bird lovers must acknowledge him their head."[20] What Miller perhaps did not realize was how important women, particularly Jeanne Carr, had been in forming Muir's moral imagination at an earlier stage. He had become a conservationist in part because of female influence.

Muir had not forgotten that debt, and he carried many of his early friendships with women into later years. Jeanne Carr, however, had nearly dropped out of sight. Once she had married him off to Louie Strentzel she could put him out of her mind, and he tended to forget her as well. He did send her a copy of his first book, with an apology for its long delay in appearing. It was their first communication in years. In reply she said nothing about the book or about Muir's new prominence in conservation circles; her mind was preoccupied with the recent death of her husband Ezra and with glimpses of her own mortality. In a few years she would fall victim to dementia, sell her beloved home Carmelita, and end her years sadly in the Kings' Daughters Home near San Francisco. Muir would write her a few more times and see that she was made comfortable in the nursing home. He could hardly recognize the woman who had once befriended, taught, loved, and inspired him. His first book should have been dedicated to her (he made no dedication), for more than anyone else she had encouraged him to write down his thoughts and share his passion for nature with the public.[21]

Despite those common bonds across gender lines, at this stage of his life Muir turned for his closest friendships and associations to the company of forest-loving men. Against the fierce clamor of strikers clashing with their bosses, the conservationists tried to get attention for the plight of the nation's forests. Following the depletion of the eastern forests, most recently around the Great Lakes, timber companies were moving south and west, seeking fresh supplies of wood for railroad ties and city housing. Behind them, they left dry, dead piles of slash that fed forest fires, bare hillsides that eroded into creeks and rivers, and impoverished habitat for many nonhuman species and human communities. Out west, where most of the land was still owned by the federal government, the dangers of deforestation were increasing: a loss of forest cover meant also a loss of stream flow in a land where water was a scarce resource, where irrigation was necessary for agriculture. A bleak future of timber, water, and wildlife depletion seemed to be the fate of the nation, unless conservationists could seize the day.[22]

Two national magazines crusaded for a change of policy: *The Century* and *Garden and Forest*, the latter established in 1888 by Charles Sprague Sargent and edited by William A. Stiles.[23] From its inception Sargent's journal had called for the reservation of all forested public lands from sale and settlement and their protection, along with that of the national parks, from thieves and vandals by the U.S. military. He envisioned making forestry part of the training program at West Point, much as the military academy had taken on surveying, mapping, and civil engineering at a time when there was little foreign threat. Some of the brightest cadets should be assigned to study forestry principles on the academy grounds, Sargent argued, and officers and their men should be stationed to protect and manage the western reserves.

Early in 1895, Robert Johnson organized for his magazine a roundtable of commentary on the Sargent plan. The respondents, who included some of the most prominent figures in the conservation movement, agreed on the need for more government-owned reservations. Where they could not agree with Sargent was on putting the army in charge of management. Most wanted some mix of military and civilian responsibility. "A military officer," warned Frederick Law Olmsted, "ought not to be a Jack-of-all-trades." The Prussian-born Bernhard Fernow, head of the Forestry Division in the Department of Agriculture, did not think that placing the military in complete charge was a permanent solution, while Gifford Pinchot, trained like Fernow in European ways, insisted that the country needed a rigorously educated cadre of civilian professionals at the top, but allowed that soldiers might serve as patrols. Muir, in contrast, seconded the Sargent plan as "a complete solution of all our problems." But in tune with the others, he pointed out that "it is impossible . . . to stop at preservation. The forests must be, and will be, not only preserved, but used." Following the experience of all "civilized countries," the public forests, "like perennial fountains, may be made to yield a sure harvest of timber, while at the same time all their far-reaching beneficent uses may be maintained unimpaired."[24]

That was what he said and believed, as part of his pragmatic conservation philosophy, and he marshaled all the utilitarian reasons he could find. Lumbering had to be allowed, and irrigation of the lowlands, even though it meant losing native vegetation in the valleys, had to be accepted as a justification for forest protection. Despite this embrace of utilitarianism, however, he was more often than not thinking about the best way to preserve rather than use the forests for material ends.

Soldiers seemed to him the best guardians in an age when so many civilians in government rotated in and out of office and were susceptible to corruption. He had watched the army come into the new national parks, Yosemite especially, which they faithfully defended against trespassing sheepherders and timber cutters. The first soldiers, a troop of cavalry, appeared in Yellowstone in 1886, followed by troops dispatched to the Sierra parks in 1891 under the command of Abram "Jug" Wood and Joe Dorst. One of their most effective strategies was to evict sheepherders from one side of the parks, their flocks from the other—requiring a lot of tough, hot riding on the part of the soldiers but highly discouraging to the intruders. They dared to evict even state legislators out for a lawless hunt. A few of the soldiers joined the Sierra Club, and its antiwar, pacifist president came to regard them as comrades in arms. "Our thanks are due these quiet soldiers for unweariedly facing and overcoming every difficulty in the way of duty," he told Club members. "And always it is refreshing to know that in our changeful Government there is one arm that is permanent and ever to be depended on."[25]

So effective were the military patrols in Yosemite that local economic interests pushed their congressman, Anthony Caminetti, a Democrat from Amador County, to introduce legislation that would diminish that park by half, opening it to privatization. Muir was willing to see a few of its acres eliminated, trying as ever to be a compromiser, but on the whole the Caminetti bill seemed "villainous" for it would turn over to lumbermen one of the finest forests in the entire Sierra. The Club debated the bill vigorously before deciding, somewhat gingerly, to take their first political stance and oppose it as their president wished. Caminetti was defeated for re-election, and the park's boundaries remained intact for another decade.[26]

In the next national election year, 1896, Secretary of the Interior Hoke Smith asked the National Academy of Sciences to recommend policies for all the public forests in the West. The Academy's president, retired Harvard chemist Wolcott Gibbs, willingly took charge of organizing an official commission, "for no other economic problem" surpassed forest conditions as a social issue.[27] Gibbs asked his colleague Sargent to chair the commission, in effect reprising his work on the *Report on the Forests of North America* (1884), a volume for the Census Bureau. Thick in girth and severe in manner, lacking in the eyes of many people much broad human sympathy, Sargent was deeply passionate about trees. Generally, he had little faith in government, but as a conservation reformer he allowed that government must hold on to its remaining forests for the public good. The other members of the commission were Gibbs (ex officio); William H. Brewer, Yale botanist and former member of the Whitney Survey in California; General Henry Abbott of the Army Corps of Engineers; Alexander Agassiz, Harvard zoologist and son of Louis Agassiz; Arnold Hague, representing the U.S. Geological Survey and an untiring advocate of the Yellowstone park; and young Gifford Pinchot, listed simply as "practical forester."

Muir was not a regular member of the commission, but he agreed to join the others as an advisor on a grand summer tour of western forests. That had not been his preferred itinerary: he had longed to go to Alaska's Cook Inlet and Prince William Sound, but Sargent's request led him to rearrange all travel plans. He would go along with the distinguished commissioners to inspect the public lands and recommend new conservation measures. That is, he would go *after* he received his first college diploma. Harvard University invited him to come and receive an honorary A.M. degree at its June commencement.

Johnson, who had a hand in the invitation along with Sargent, asked Louie to persuade her husband to accept, for it would do him and the cause of conservation good. Muir grumbled and fretted, but he went to receive what he called his "Harvard baptism," staying with the Sargents and preening himself over his first academic degree and his splendid ceremonial robes.[28]

But if the academic honor was recognition of his growing national stature and made him more than ever valuable for the commission's political purposes, it came at a moment of unexpected pain and loss. On his way east to get his degree Muir stopped to see his mother and found her heart failing and death approaching. He told old Scots stories to cheer her, and then departed for Cambridge, worried that he might not talk to her again; the day before commencement, he received a telegram saying that she had died. After the ceremonies, he sped to Portage for her funeral. "Mother was beautiful in life & death," he wrote Johnson.[29] Family business matters detained him briefly, as he sorted out the modest inheritance with his sisters and brothers, and then with many sad embraces he said good-bye to Wisconsin for the last time. Sargent was waiting in Chicago, and together they would go inspecting forests.

Coming from opposite ends of America, the two men formed a friendship that summer that would blossom and then fade over the years. Sargent showed an unsuspected capacity for fraternity and was uncharacteristically effusive in his praise for *The Mountains of California*: "I have never read descriptions of trees that so pictured them to the mind as yours do. No fellow who was at once a poet, naturalist, and a keen observer has to my knowledge ever written about trees before and I believe you are the man who ought to have written a Silva of North America. Your book is one of the great productions of its kind and I congratulate you on it." As it happened, Sargent had his own *Silva of North America* in the works (published 1891–1902), and he would dedicate one of its fourteen volumes, on the pines, to Muir. They made an odd couple—one heavy, reserved, and patrician; the other thin, enthusiastic, and egalitarian—but they exemplified the kind of unexpected alliances that the conservation movement forged.

The forest commission pursued its investigations far from the patriotic bunting and florid oratory of that year's presidential race, one of the most hard-fought in American history, pitting the conservative Republican William McKinley against the Democratic-Populist fusion candidate William Jennings Bryan. The high cost of money, the plight of hard-pressed farmers, the bitter conflict between unions and corporations, not nature or conservation, dominated newspaper headlines. But the commission saw itself occupied with more momentous, nonpartisan matters than those of the political campaign. As Bryan was ripping away from the rear of railroad cars and McKinley was staying home nonchalantly in Ohio, they put themselves through three months of strenuous travel—sleepless nights in Pullman cars jolting along the rails; long aching days on bumpy wagon roads; small, stifling rooms in bad hotels; poorly cooked food.

The great prairies offered the commission nothing of relevance. In passing over it Muir marveled at the lush, fertile beauty of Iowa, but Nebraska was, as ever, monotonous to his eyes, and South Dakota too dry and dusty—until they reached the Black Hills, where the cool green islands that dot the West began. Spirits were high as Hague led them through his beloved Yellowstone. They marched relentlessly on to Montana's Lake MacDonald (soon to become part of Glacier National Park), the Pacific Northwest, the high forests of California, the reserve surrounding the Grand Canyon, until the party ended their tour in Colorado. Fellow traveler Muir had not stayed the course; he went home after Arizona, worn out by "the rapidest mountaineering I ever did."[30]

Everyone marched quickstep under Sargent's command, until Gifford Pinchot joined the party and drew Muir into small boyish rebellions. They sneaked off to go fishing, cut up behind the dignified backs of the others, and plotted to skip away to Alaska, before Pinchot was sentenced to making a solitary reconnaissance in the Bitterroots.[31] Muir, who had no official standing, was free to come and go as he liked, but Pinchot had assumed the duty of coordinating the commission's travels and should have been more attentive to his job. As a practical, commercial-minded forester he often clashed with their chairman Sargent, the academic botanist, over questions of purpose and authority. Muir, caught in the tension between the two men, found both antagonists to be good traveling companions. "I enjoyed Sargent," he wrote Johnson,

Gifford Pinchot. (Library of Congress)

"the only one of the Com. that knew & loved trees as I loved them."
On the other hand, he was charmed by Pinchot's smooth manners, tall
handsome bearing, and macho stunts like sleeping outdoors even in
pouring rain.[32]

Near the end of the commission's grand tour Muir and Pinchot
camped together on the rim of the Grand Canyon, while the others bedded down indoors. For both men, this was their first time to
experience the West's grandest, most riotously multicolored landscape of stone and light. Muir rattled on until midnight, brimming
over with exuberance, as their campfire burned like a tiny point of
light against the darkening canyon void. Pinchot wrote in his autobiography, *Breaking New Ground*, how unforgettable his companion was
on the occasion, "a storyteller in a million." But perhaps the most
telling moment of all occurred when the two men disagreed over killing wild things. "When we came across a tarantula," Pinchot recalled,
"he wouldn't let me kill it. He said it has as much right there as we
did." They would soon discover even bigger differences in values and

ambitions, differences that would split conservationists into separate, sometimes contending, camps.[33]

The forest commissioners returned east in time for Election Day, when McKinley handily won over Bryan. Likely most of the green men approved the country's choice, for the populist from Nebraska seemed more interested in inflating the price of corn than keeping the dollar sound. "I am rejoiced that California is all right in the election," Sargent wrote to Muir after hearing that the state had gone for McKinley.[34] In a bipartisan spirit, all the same, the commission decided to recommend to outgoing President Cleveland that he set aside, by executive order, thirteen new reserves aggregating over twenty million acres, more than doubling the national forests. Cleveland did precisely that and touched off a firestorm of protest from many western congressmen of both parties. They had not been consulted, they fumed, the proposed reserves were poorly drafted, and their establishment would lock up resources vital to economic development. The Democratic president left office with the reserves still in limbo, turning the controversy over to his Republican successor, McKinley, who was not known for any conservation inclinations.[35]

On 1 May 1897 the forest commission submitted its final report, written by Sargent after many concessions to Hague and Pinchot. Much of it might have been written by George Perkins Marsh, the Vermont-born foreign diplomat who had warned about deforestation three decades earlier and so profoundly influenced Sargent and the others. The report added to Marsh's warnings that "forest administration is now regarded as an important Government duty throughout the civilized world, [but] it has been wholly neglected by the United States." Reserves had been made, though not enough of them, and all those lands "must be made to perform their part in the economy of the nation." Doing so required some form of government administration. The commission proposed a system that would both earn a profit and protect vital watersheds and timber supply, that would include Sargent's army guardians and Pinchot's civilian managers. Soldiers, the report suggested, should take charge of the public forests temporarily, but eventually a permanent bureau should be established in the Department of Interior, with a director who would preside over a series of regional departments spread over the West, each with trained foresters and civilian rangers to enforce the law, protect against devastating fires, and sell mature trees to private lumbermen. Everyone on the commission signed the much-amended report. Pinchot, after so much distrusting of Sargent's judgment, had gotten everything he wanted.[36]

Well, *almost* everything. Most of all Pinchot wanted a job within the Washington bureaucracy and, eventually, he wanted personal control over the public forests. As the commission's report was beginning to circulate, he went to see the new president and his designated Secretary of the Interior, Cornelius Bliss, a dry-goods merchant from New York. Bliss offered him the post of special forest advisor to his department, disregarding the rival presence of Bernhard Fernow in the Department of Agriculture. The price exacted for that job was that Pinchot must support McKinley's decision to suspend the new reserves for a year, to try to placate the irate western legislators, and in effect to ignore the commission's recommendations for a while—maybe forever, as rumors floated that the Geological Survey wanted to take over the national forests and that Pinchot had good friends there who might put him in charge.[37]

Sargent felt betrayed by the ambitious young whippersnapper and persuaded Muir that Pinchot had played a devious game. The Harvard professor observed that "the most trying sort of a person to deal with is a fool and in the last year I have had my share of them to manage." Pinchot was, however, no fool but a serious rival, maneuvering himself into a position of power and influence. Neither Gen. Abbott nor he wanted anything more to do with him. Muir, after congratulating Pinchot on his appointment, changed his mind and seconded their estimate of Pinchot's character. "That Mr. Pinchot would accept such an appointment I would never have believed. . . . When the time comes for letting in light on this dry goods forestry," he would be ready to help expose the double-dealing. Muir's shift in attitude was not due only, or even primarily, to Sargent's influence on political matters of administration; rather, he began to realize that Bliss's new man and his western camp mate, Pinchot, intended to support limited sheep grazing in the Oregon and Washington reserves if doing so would win those states' acceptance of conservation. That was a price Muir was not willing to pay. On the surface he continued to greet the aspiring forester cordially but privately had come to regard him as shallow, opportunistic, and undependable. "I still look for lots of good work from Pinchot," he wrote, "but his giving way like snow in thaw to the sheep owners & political agents of forest robbers is mighty discouraging."[38]

Politics, however, is the art of taking what you can get. Muir, more than the imperious Sargent, was learning that even small victories might require compromise and persistent effort. Facing what he called "a bad lot" of powerful western senators allied to "corporations with their shady millions" that seemed invincible, he realized how fragile were the parks and reserves. Everything that had been achieved could be undone in the new administration. He would not race breathlessly into the conservative Republican president McKinley's camp as Pinchot was doing, but he would try to rally conservationists to defend their gains and keep the momentum alive. For example, on a camping trip to Yosemite he had met a Pasadena banker and amateur photographer, Theodore Lukens, whom he recruited to the Sierra Club as a new green man. Write to the politicians, he urged him, and "make their lives wretched until they do what is right by the woods. Only thus by making public opinion can they be made to mind." Muir had no more enthusiasm for politicking than Sargent, but he was willing to engage in that kind of grassroots recruiting and democratic persuasion.[39]

While he would not accept any sheep on the reserved land, he granted that some changes needed to be made in the regulations and rules governing the parks and forest reservations. One of his greatest concessions (for an advocate of animal rights) would allow "hunting at certain seasons for food."

> We are all natural hunters like cats with killing instincts derived from hunting ancestors & I suppose only in heaven is there no bloodshed. Still, I can't help feeling that there should be a good big wild place set apart in each park or reservation as a safe refuge for the wild birds & beasts in which no gun should ever be fired— sort of wild beast paradise.

He detested the taking of animal life for sport, but not being a vegetarian he felt compelled to accept the legitimacy of some degree of subsistence hunting, even apparently in Yosemite or Yellowstone.[40]

Harvesting trees on a sustained-yield basis was also a legitimate use of the public lands that he endorsed from his first days as a conservationist to the end of his life, always with the proviso that people needed wildness along with economic commodities. A policy of forest multiple-use that included the protection of wild beauty became his principal theme in a series of magazine and newspaper articles undertaken in the first year of the McKinley presidency to shore up public support for conservation. Putting aside the goal of nature appreciation, he wrote as a political activist, preaching a policy of moderation and reason, but one based on a vision of nature ever renewing and self-restoring even in the face of industrial civilization.

Through the intervention of Sargent, offers had come from the editors of *Harper's Weekly* and the *Atlantic Monthly* to publish Muir's account of the forest commission's work and proposals. He accepted the call, even though writing was always hard, unnatural work, like "a cowboy dragging steers with a rope."[41] In June 1897 a piece defending the national parks and reservations appeared in the first magazine, while in August a piece entitled "The American Forests" came out in the second, followed the next January by still another essay for the *Atlantic*. Together, the powerful effect of these articles helped turn the tide in McKinley's Washington back to conservation.[42]

Muir told about the commission's strenuous travels, the extraordinary richness and beauty they had discovered everywhere they stopped, the enthusiasm they had found among western locals for the government reserves (more than ninety percent of the people they had met had declared their approval). "Complaints are made in the name of poor settlers and miners," but the real opponents of public ownership were "the wealthy corporations" keeping themselves "hidden in the background." They mouthed the egalitarian slogan, "the greatest good for the greatest number," but "the greatest is too often found to be number one."[43]

Muir accepted that environmental change and economic development were inevitable, and to a point even desirable. "I suppose we need not go mourning the buffaloes," he wrote. "In the nature of things they had to give place to better cattle, though the change might have been made without barbarous wickedness." Some forests and grasslands had to give way to "orchards and cornfields," for the people needed to eat and live. Like the national forest commission or green men in general, he did not come out against all growth in the nation's population or consumption. America was still the land of abundance, rich in potential wealth as in beauty, and that abundance could continue if selfish people did not destroy the land's capacity for regeneration. The son of immigrants, Muir was grateful for the blessings he had found in the New World, and he wanted to share them with others, including the hordes of new immigrants crowding the receiving halls of Ellis Island.

> The United States government has always been proud of the welcome it has extended to good men of every nation, seeking freedom and homes and bread. Let them be welcomed still as nature welcomes them, to the woods well as to the prairies and plains. No place is too good for good men, and still there is room. They are invited to heaven, and may well be allowed in America. Every place is made better by them.

But *using* nature's resources for human betterment had degenerated into *destroying* nature's capacity for renewal. The promise of America the Beautiful, providing a rich, wild, productive home for millions, was being spoiled by the actions of a few.[44]

For thousands of years God had cared for the great American forests, "the best he ever planted," saving them from cycles of drought, fire, disease, avalanches, and floods. Indians had burned the forests repeatedly without doing permanent damage. But among the white men were fools who knew no environmental limits or imposed any self-restraint on their appetite for money. While the rich, "sleepy with wealth," and the poor, "sleepy with poverty," remained silent, greed and robbery ran rampant across the continent. Only Uncle Sam could control that monstrous egoism and put in its place a new conservation ethic.

e⊶o

One spring afternoon in 1899 a special train of Pullman cars pulled out of New York City bound for Seattle. Aboard were scientists from elite universities, museums, and government bureaus—two botanists, two zoologists, two geologists, etc.—a Noah's ark of natural history. They were on their way to the Alaska coast to survey its resources for a nation that still knew little about its northern territory acquired three decades earlier. The most knowledgeable among the scientists was William Dall of the Geological Survey, author of the wonderful travel book *Alaska and Its Resources,* published in 1870, just after the territory had passed from Russian to American hands. Other experts included William Brewer, Bernhard Fernow, Grove Karl Gilbert, Robert Ridgeway, Henry Gannett, and the group's foreman, C. Hart Merriam, director of the Biological Survey in Washington, which catalogued the nation's flora and fauna and their economic potential. Most of the men were at least moderate conservationists in their views.

The Noah in charge of this brain-filled ark was Edward Harriman, a short man with large ginger moustache and shrewd, penetrating eyes. Under the pressure of family poverty, he had dropped out of grade school at age fourteen to take a lowly office job in New York's financial district. Extraordinarily talented and determined, he had risen to become the most powerful railroad capitalist in the country. Following the '93 depression he had wriggled his way into the incompetent Union Pacific's hierarchy and was now chairman of its board. Eventually, he would also control the Southern Pacific, the Illinois Central, assorted other railroads, the Pacific Mail Steamship Company, and the Wells Fargo Express Company. Feared as a power-hungry "colossus of roads," he was also widely celebrated for turning a jerrybuilt, national transportation system into a model of efficiency.[45]

The struggle to bring order and profitability to that system had left him exhausted, and now he sought recuperation by going to

Alaska to hunt. He was after the famed Kodiak Island grizzly bear, the fierce brown giant that drove big-game hunters wild with desire. Harriman would take along his whole family—wife, five children, relatives, and friends—in the elegant coastal steamer the *Glen W. Elder*, with its crew of sixty-five officers and men, plus a gang of hunters and packers to handle the bears. The ship still not full, Harriman invited the scientists along at his expense to expand the voyage into a quest for greater knowledge of the territory. Was it an empty icebox of no future value, or was it a fabulous frontier offering a wealth of new resources, from timber and fisheries to coal and gold and unspoiled natural beauty?[46]

And still there was room on the ship. Merriam asked John Burroughs to go and provide a narrative account of the expedition, which would introduce a projected multivolume set of scientific papers. He recruited artists Louis Fuertes and Fred Dellenbaugh (who had been a member of John Wesley Powell's second Colorado River exploring trip) and photographer Edward Curtis. Then an invitation went out to John Muir, the famed conservationist and author of two recent *Century* articles, "The Alaska Trip" and "An Adventure with a Dog and a Glacier." It took some coaxing and explaining, but Muir agreed to join the party as a glacial expert. Not at all certain about Harriman or the scientists as agreeable traveling companions, he wrote to Sargent, "Pray for me. . . . I wish I were going to those leafy woods instead of Icy Alaska."[47]

The previous summer Muir had not gone north but had decided to ramble all over the "leafy" east, revisiting his hiking adventures as a poor but free young man. Twice he had passed through Canada, retracing some of his Civil War draft dodger's trail, and visited northern New England and the Berkshires. Twice he had followed Sargent on a botanizing tour of the South; retracing some of his 1867 trek to the Gulf, he went back to Cedar Key, found Sarah Hodgson who had nursed him during his bout with malaria, and sailed to Key West, less than a hundred miles from Cuba. This time, however, he did not cross the watery gap with Humboldtian visions dancing in his mind, for a fierce war was on to free that island-nation from Spanish rule. The United States, ostensibly in support of Cuban independence, had declared war against Spain, and Theodore Roosevelt was leading a troop of volunteer Rough Riders in the name of freedom. Muir, bemoaning the "darkness of the Cuban war clouds" and "this Cuba din," skedaddled back to California. Forty years earlier his adopted nation was just coming out of a devastating civil war; now it was united, muscular, and ready to make its might felt beyond its borders.[48]

Despite longing to travel through eastern America again with Sargent, Muir could not resist the invitation to go on the Harriman expedition to Alaska. Whichever direction he went, the old wanderlust stirred within him, as it seemed to do every few months, encouraging him to leave home and family responsibilities behind, including the dreaded work of writing, and to ramble in whatever direction lay forests or wildness. He was as greedy to experience that wildness as others were to accumulate money. Ever since he had left the family farm in Wisconsin, he had been a rambler, unable to stay in one place for long. Marriage and family had not succeeded in killing that inner desire to go and see. Alaska had long laid a hold on his imagination, so despite misgivings about the purpose of the expedition, he was soon packing his trunk for the north. If Harriman had to bag a bear, Muir had to bag a few more bracing, aurora-filled nights.

He joined up with the expeditionary force at Seattle and went aboard their commodious vessel, sharing a stateroom with Charles Keeler of the California Academy of Sciences. Up the familiar Inland Passage they sailed. For two months the ship was their home, while a constantly moving picture of green and white splendor unrolled before their eyes. They had a barnyard of animals mooing and cackling below decks in case the hunting proved bad. They had a full wine cellar and plenty of cigars and cigarettes, a passel of fascinating lecturers for the evenings, and lots of canoes, tents, and sleeping bags for onshore fieldwork. Unlike his previous travels to Alaska, this one would be quite genteel in its accommodations and company.

Muir soon became fast friends with many of the scientists, especially Merriam and Gannett, and he became a regular in the smoking room, where puffing away on a cigar or cigarette with the rest he spun stories, gave opinions, and played the wise old veteran. The Harriman children quickly took to him. His worries about being trapped among

John Burroughs and John Muir in the Catskills. (H-A, JMP)

a group of pompous old fogies proved groundless. If anything, it was Muir who got on other people's nerves, particularly those of his friend and fellow literary naturalist Burroughs.

Burroughs and Muir had formed a mutual admiration society from their first meeting in New York, but now they were competing for the title of nature's truest lover. The former was at a disadvantage on the voyage: he was so attached to his home in the Catskills that he could not live or love anywhere else so well. This was his first trip to Alaska, and first trip west of his home state. Muir, in contrast, carried his passion for nature to many ports, like an amorous sailor, and every new onshore scene brought him to his feet in wonder. As they cruised toward Wrangell, Juneau, Glacier Bay, Yakutat Bay, Cook's Inlet, Kodiak, the Aleutian Islands, and the Bering Sea, Burroughs felt more and more homesick and then positively seasick. Too many glaciers, dark towering forests, barren islands, and gray choppy seas left him moaning and wondering why he had come so far. Muir, on the other hand, proved to be an unsympathetic, even scornful, companion, for he could not fathom how someone might find the rugged northern climes less than alluring. The two men remained bonded in name—"the twa [two] Johnnies," they were called—and in cause, but Muir was openly disparaging toward Burroughs and his insufficient ardor for the wild.[49]

Nor was he reticent about criticizing the founder and benefactor of the party, Harriman, for his avidity for money and blood sport. The most sarcastic comments went silently into his journal. At Yakutat, where the great hunter went ashore with his beaters and failed to find anything to shoot, Muir penned, "No bears no bears oh Lord no bears shot what has thy servants done."[50] They reached Kodiak on the Fourth of July, and this time the railroad man was successful in bringing back two trophies (aka "specimens"), a mother grizzly and her little cub. Muir was appalled by the slaughter. He let even the Harriman children know that he had a low opinion of that sort of killing, until he had them vowing that they would personally never shoot another living thing.

Then he added an even more irreverent note about his big-businessman host. One evening the sycophantic scientists were praising the "blessed ministry of wealth" that had brought them on such a noble cruise, was feeding them so well, and was looking after all their personal and research needs. "When these wealth laudations were sounding loudest," Muir teasingly interrupted to say, "I don't think Harriman is very rich. He has not as much money as I have. I have all I want and Mr. Harriman has not." Someone passed the quasi-criticism to their host, who came over to Muir after dinner to explain his motives in acquiring wealth. "I never cared for money except as power for work," Harriman said. "What I most enjoy is the power of creation, getting into partnership with Nature in doing good, helping to feed man and beast, and making everybody and everything a little better and happier." His apparent earnestness blunted Muir's lance. The businessman did not accept the notion that there should be a limit to acquisitiveness, but he gave capitalism a moral purpose—promoting the welfare of both nature and humanity. His expanding railroad network, in his eyes, was intended to enhance the earth as well as make the nation bigger and better. Muir sensed that his host was quite sincere, and from that moment on, bear hunter though he might be, Harriman was seen as a well-meaning friend and potential ally of the conservation movement.[51]

Home again in Martinez, Muir received a warm, admiring letter from the four girls in the Harriman entourage, which he answered at length. Despite his forebodings, the trip had turned out to be "the grandest" he had ever taken. "Nearly all my life I have wandered and studied alone. On the Elder, I found not only the fields I liked best to study, but a hotel, a club, and a home, together with a floating university in which I enjoyed the instruction and companionship of a lot of the best fellows imaginable." He had formed a new set of alliances, young and old, that would last for years. After the voyage, he reported that he had gone with C. Hart Merriam and Gifford Pinchot to try to save the Calaveras grove of redwoods from logging. Captain Doran had paid him a visit, and Gilbert was coming too, as were Gannett and others. His shipmate Charlie Keeler was contemplating moving to the Strentzel-Muir estate so that they could carry on their shipboard conversations about the enchantment of poetry, the pleasures of science, and the hideousness of killing and war. "Remember your penitential promises," the letter to the girls ended. "Kill as few of your fellow beings as possible and pursue some branch of natural history at least far enough to see Nature's harmony."[52]

Those parting words were inadequate to express Muir's personal philosophy as a naturalist and conservationist, but they came close. They can serve as a brief summary of his guiding principles as he passed the age of sixty and as the nineteenth century came to a close. Because he was the most widely recognized leader in the company of green men, the words may also suggest an important part of what many in that company also believed. Nature, particularly its forests, offered an ideal of harmony to a nation torn apart by conflict between capital and labor, country and city, imperialists and anti-imperialists. That harmony was first and foremost one of beauty; nothing in nature was ugly or discordant, a lesson that could be learned by hiking a trail into the Sierra or standing at the rail of a steamer along the Alaskan coast. The challenge was how to help American society achieve that same degree of moral and aesthetic unity.

Violent confrontation was not the way to achieve ecological harmony, a beautiful landscape, or a decent civilization. One must start by resolving to conserve the natural world for the sake of human beings and other forms of life. Conservation offered both an economic and aesthetic program of social reform—learning to use natural resources more carefully, for long-term renewability, and learning to preserve wild places where humans could go to learn about how nature constructs harmony. Muir tried, as other green men did, to push conservation in both directions. Achieve those reforms, he believed, and a truer, better democracy would evolve in which people of diverse origins, abilities, and needs would live in greater peace and mutuality, just as all the elements of nature did. If a forest could thrill the senses and still the troubled heart with its harmonies, then society could become like that forest. Such was the hope of the green men.

For all his dour Calvinist background and his frequent regression to pessimistic feelings, Muir struggled to stay optimistic about people, progress, and the future of human-nature relations. Nature, he told himself and his audience, still offered plenty of wild beauty to enjoy and learn from, and plenty of opportunity for good homes for good people. The challenge of the age was to hold on to that promise. Doing so required both love and intelligent understanding of nature. Much had been achieved in the last ten years in park, forest, and wildlife conservation and in public awareness of the natural resources of the nation. Other nations were taking similar steps. A new generation was coming to maturity and showing signs of better thinking. Where in his youth he had often walked alone and apart, Muir now felt he had many companions.

Conservation, of course, had its naïve side, just as did the labor radicalism of Debs or the prairie populism of Bryan or the capitalist dreams of Harriman. All reforms and revolutions live on hope and fail when they lack sufficient honesty or realism. No ethic constructed by a flawed species could ever prove wholly reliable. No institution devised by the mind of man could be forever dependable. Muir was no simpleton about such matters. But he started with an idealization of nature, a tendency to look beyond its surface cruelties and hazards, and he tried hard to be similarly generous in his assessment of people. He counted, as other green men did, on the federal government to lead the way toward reform, through public ownership of natural resources, and on the civic virtue of the government's military and civilian stewards. Perhaps he was too naïve in believing that a man like Harriman, however enlightened he might be about the uses of wealth, would always use his vast fortune for the common good. Perhaps he missed the darkness that lies within all men and women, capitalists and noncapitalists alike, and the darkness that lies within the forest. If so, it was blindness he shared with other reformers of his day. All reformers, then and later, were idealists about nature, society, or humanity.

"Don't despair," he counseled a morose Sargent. Have faith that even a weak reed like Pinchot can be counted on to do good work. Selfishness will be overcome, and harmony will prevail. Such hopefulness had directed Muir's steps from youth. "I am always happy at the center," he had told others back in his Wisconsin days, and that attitude had carried him a long way. It had brought him to the head of the conservation movement in America. Rich and poor, women and men, now looked to him for inspiration. He was their prophet of a new and better world coming.

CHAPTER 13

Earthquakes

G lacier Point looms like a strong gray shield over the secluded but vulnerable Yosemite Valley. A famous photograph taken there in May 1903 shows Muir standing shoulder to shoulder with President Theodore Roosevelt. They seem confident of their position, though poised on the edge of a 3,200-foot cliff, their backs to a great abyss. Muir is dressed in baggy denim trousers, a shapeless coat with a flowery sprig in his lapel, a necktie and collar, and a creased hat on his head. He looks under-nourished but erect—a man at the peak of his career as a writer and conservationist. Roosevelt wears military jodhpurs with puttees, a heavy sweater showing beneath his open field jacket, a jaunty bandana around his neck, and a Stetson on his square head. He is broad chested and self-assured—relishing his immense popularity as occupant of the White House. They have just agreed that ownership of the much-abused valley below should revert to the federal government and become part of Yosemite Park. Politically, they have forged a formidable alliance on behalf of nature.

In early March of that year, a few days after arranging with Professor Sargent to go botanizing through Europe and Russia, Muir had received indirect word that "an influential man from Wash[ington] wants to make a trip into the Sierra with me." Could they change the date of sailing? "I might be able to do some forest good in talking freely around the campfire." The "influential man" was President Roosevelt, who then sent a more direct and irresistible invitation: on my upcoming trip through the Yosemite region, "I do not want anyone with me but you, and I want to drop politics absolutely for four days and just be out in the open with you." Sargent agreed to postpone their date of departure, and Muir agreed to meet the president immediately after his appearance in Berkeley and San Francisco.[1]

Muir and Theodore Roosevelt at Glacier Point, Yosemite, 1903. (Library of Congress)

Several dignitaries were in the Roosevelt party that greeted Muir at the Raymond train station, but the president and the naturalist soon left them behind, riding their horses toward the rim with a couple of park rangers and a packer trailing behind. Five feet of winter snow still lay on the ground, and more snow fell on their campsite, as Roosevelt and Muir talked long into the night about glaciers, sequoias, and conservation. Both men, reported one of the rangers, wanted to do all the talking. Coming down into the valley after their photo at Glacier Point, they rode past the crowd gathered at Camp Curry, ignoring the banquet and fireworks show prepared in Roosevelt's honor, and on to the meadow at the foot of Bridalveil Fall, where they camped and palavered for another night. Never before, Muir wrote his wife, had he enjoyed "so interesting[,] hearty & manly a companion." To friends he wrote, "Camping with the President was a remarkable experience. I fairly fell in love with him."[2]

Years later Roosevelt, recalling their outing with pleasure, praised Muir's sense of citizenship, his devotion to the cause of nature preservation, his wonderful gift of conversation. As a nature writer, he ranked Muir "second only to John Burroughs, and in some respects ahead" of that rival. Muir exuded a "delightful innocence and good will," an "inability to imagine that any one could either take or give offense." To illustrate, Roosevelt told about a letter Muir showed him from Sargent, suggesting that the president might furnish personal introductions to foreign potentates, which would be helpful on their travels. Muir had forgotten the harsh appraisal of the president included at the end of the letter: "He takes a sloppy, unintelligent interest in forests," wrote Sargent, "altogether he is too much under the influence of that creature Pinchot." The president laughed over Muir's absent-mindedness. He poked fun too at his guide's gaps in outdoor expertise. Roosevelt figured himself to be a pretty good field naturalist and was astonished that Muir could not identify some of the birds they heard. It seemed that Muir was interested only in "unusually conspicuous" scenery, not in the small things that Burroughs (and he) so carefully observed. What he failed to realize was that Muir was mainly a botanist and geologist, not an ornithologist, although by no means indifferent to the smallest of plants or the faintest striations on rock.[3]

No previous American president had been so well informed and so avid a wildlife lover as Roosevelt. He looked on Muir as a kindred spirit who could help him find the true value of Yosemite away from society. All the same the outing was arranged for political impact. The president wanted to capture some of Muir's prophetic aura to bolster his own image and policies. He had tried to do the same with Burroughs. On his way to California Roosevelt had stopped over at the

Yellowstone Park, accompanied this time by Burroughs, who predictably testified to the president's hardy spirit and outdoor aptitude.

Burroughs was famous for woodsy rambles around his Catskills cabin, for rural images of robins, old pastures returning to birch trees, and woodchucks. Yellowstone was hardly his territory, no more than the coast of Alaska had been. On the other hand, he was credited with stimulating a back-to-nature sentiment in the late nineteenth and early twentieth century. And in contrast to others who shared that feeling, he was ready to defend Roosevelt's controversial reputation as a big-game hunter. Burroughs even professed himself ready to take up a gun to kill game or any varmint; "the fewer [varmints] there are," he avowed, "the better for the useful and beautiful game." He was, for all his nature-loving philosophy, no conservationist or animal-rights activist, nor indeed a reformer of any kind. But he appealed to a circle of out-of-doors enthusiasts whom Roosevelt wanted to attract to his side politically.[4]

Muir's audience and connections were somewhat different. Unlike Burroughs, he was a western mountain man, at ease in the saddle or climbing a rock, images that reinforced Roosevelt's zest for the strenuous, manly life. Yet Muir also appealed intensely to women and men opposed to sport killing and other displays of super-masculinity in nature. When Daniel Beard wrote to get his support for a society of boys called the Sons of Daniel Boone (a precursor to the Boy Scouts), Muir replied that the society should encourage boys to grow out of "natural hunting blood-loving savagery into natural sympathy with all our fellow mortals—plants and animals as well as men." Similarly, he lamented to Henry Osborn that "the murder business & sport by saint & sinner alike has been pushed ruthlessly," until there was little wildlife left to slaughter; it was time, he hoped, for a "glimmering recognition of the rights of animals & their kinship to ourselves." Those feminine-sounding, ethical sentiments were not fully shared by Roosevelt or Burroughs, both of whom looked on hunting and fishing as ideal training for manhood and believed that a more vigorous manhood was needed to save the nation.[5]

Theodore Roosevelt had not been elected to the presidency. A violent anarchist had thrust him into office by assassinating William

McKinley less than a year after his re-election to a second term, with Roosevelt sharing the ticket. Suddenly with that tragic death, decades of presidential lethargy and a weak federal government came to an end (so much for the cause of anarchism). The robust young vice-president from an elite New York City family believed in a strong nation-state, and he came charging into the White House determined to turn the country around. He would use presidential power to end corruption, civilize the corporations and trusts, and restore harmony between economic classes and races. Abroad, he would seek to turn America into a decisive force for liberal ideals by building a world-class navy, creating a fortified canal across the Isthmus of Panama, and bearding the savage European imperialists. That entire program required muscle as well as morality, a fusion that Roosevelt called "the new nationalism."

High on Roosevelt's domestic agenda was a vigorous commitment to conservation of nature and natural resources. In his first annual message to Congress, he spoke for nearly half an hour about expanding the forest reserves and making the government responsible for developing the arid West through dam and reservoir construction. "The creation and maintenance of the national wealth" was his first concern in natural resource policy—making nature yield long-term, permanent economic benefits that could grow the nation—but he was also sensitive to "the ever-increasing numbers of men and women who have learned to find rest, health, and recreation in the splendid forests and flower-clad meadows of our mountains. The forest reserves," he believed, "should be set apart forever for the use and benefit of our people as a whole and not sacrificed to the shortsighted greed of a few."[6]

Just weeks before meeting Muir, Roosevelt established by executive order the first federal bird reserve at Pelican Island off the coast of Florida. He signed the National Reclamation Act that promised to develop the water resources of the West for the benefit of all. And in 1905 he transferred the forest reserves (but conspicuously not the parks) to the Department of Agriculture, putting them under the control of his chief conservation advisor Gifford Pinchot. During his administration Roosevelt extended federal protection to 230 million acres of land, an area larger than California and Texas combined.

The Gilded-Age conservation movement had become the Roosevelt-Progressive conservation movement.[7]

That entire program Muir supported, especially the new forest reserves. He was relieved to hear that, despite Pinchot's advisory role in the White House, Roosevelt was opposed to letting sheep and cattle loose in the reserves. For years Muir had gone along with utilitarian conservation, provided that "wise use" included spiritual and aesthetic values, and he was confident that Roosevelt shared his thinking that those values were as important as economic benefits. He could overlook the president's passion for killing things, his exaggerated masculinity, even his love of war and weapons because he thought that the president loved nature as he did. In 1904 he voted (the only presidential vote we can be sure he ever made) for Roosevelt over his Democratic opponent Alton Parker, a colorless, conservative judge, and sent his camping friend a telegram of congratulation after his landslide victory.[8]

A shrewder observer of the political landscape might have noticed, however, dangerous fault lines in the rock on which the two allies stood. What looked solid was in fact prone to fractures and quakes. Soon after Roosevelt's electoral triumph, the cracks began to appear. Conservationists began to quarrel among themselves, and the harmony that seemed so perfect at Glacier Point in 1903 did not last. The president would prove to be a less solid hope than he once had seemed. Muir would increasingly find himself struggling to keep his footing next to the most powerful but also most calculating man in the nation.

In the interim between the Harriman expedition and the camping trip with Roosevelt, Muir had mostly stayed home, tending to his family's needs, lobbying to save the Calaveras grove of redwoods, and writing. William Randolph Hearst's paper, the San Francisco *Examiner*, commissioned him to write a few articles, and *The Century* persuaded him to return to the Grand Canyon and take its measure in words.

His chief project was to complete a series of articles for the *Atlantic Monthly*, most of them revisions of his Yosemite pieces published a quarter century earlier in newspapers. When the series was complete, Houghton Mifflin brought them together in Muir's second book, *Our National Parks*, published in 1902.[9]

The book's brief preface makes Muir's conservation intentions clear: "to show forth the beauty, grandeur, and all-embracing usefulness of our wild mountain forest reservations and parks" so that people will come and enjoy and protect them, "so that their right use might be made sure." The opening and closing chapters were those magazine articles inspired by Muir's travels with the National Forest Commission. He had returned home from that survey more convinced than ever that "wildness is a necessity." Even the "scenery habit" at its shallowest, pursued by tourists decked out in "silly" plumage and cameras, expressed a genuine need to escape "the vice of over-industry and the deadly apathy of luxury." The western parks and reserves offered healing to a nation cursed by too much work. "Few in these hot, dim, strenuous times are quite sane or free; choked with care like clocks full of dust, laboriously doing so much good and making so much money,—or so little,—they are no longer good for themselves." For businessmen or for their workers, for the moguls or the underclass, nature was useful for restoring mental health.[10]

Muir's notion of therapy was not to sit gazing idly at a distant forest or mountain range or to take a few snapshots and move on to the next overlook. Until late in life he never carried a camera himself. Rather than collecting mere pictures, he urged people to collect a better understanding of how nature works—how it is always creating and recreating patterns of order and beauty, how it can stimulate the mind and elevate the feelings. Every wild place, he wanted readers to see, is a "grand old palimpsest" that science can decipher.[11]

Yellowstone Park, for example, he described as an ever-changing mosaic formed by volcanism, geysers and flowing water, fires raging through resinous pines, animal communities struggling to survive. Nature, here as elsewhere in Muir's experience, is deeply historical, not fixed for all time as in a picture; always it undergoes transformation, incorporating the new into the old. We cannot find in nature any soothing escape from history, impermanence, strife, or death.

But learning how nature manages that change and how it generates a unified complexity is good tonic for the troubled, careworn human mind. That mental stimulation is why preserving wilderness is necessary and useful.

Muir was one of America's first and best park naturalists, a consummate guide to the outdoors who led his readers, as he had led so many visitors to Yosemite in his early years, on enthralling hikes, stopping here and there to point out the big and the small things of nature, identifying species but also explaining their ecological connectedness. He was intrigued by system and relationship, by the role that each piece plays in the whole, as well as the dynamics of change. *Our National Parks* was written for a nation that was moving to the city, forgetting the experience of a world that humans had not made, but also living in an age that had accumulated new knowledge of how the earth works, far more scientific knowledge than any other generation had possessed. Bringing that new understanding to the intelligent but uncomprehending public was Muir's purpose in writing, and no places were better suited to that purpose than the great parks of the West, where nature could be viewed on a grand scale and yet closely observed at any point along the trail.

The single most dramatic moment of environmental change in Muir's memory was an earthquake experienced in Yosemite Valley back in March 1872, when he was living in a cabin behind Black's Hotel. He had reported the event to the Boston Society of Natural History and then incorporated that report into his second book. At two o'clock in the morning he was awakened by a deep-throated rumbling in the earth and, "both glad and frightened," had run outside to see whether the valley walls were going to topple down on his head. Eagle Rock, a short distance away, did break loose and fall two thousand feet in a shower of boulders, clouds of dust, and deafening noise, crushing tall Douglas firs like weeds. Both the Indians and whites living in the valley were shaken by the disaster. Muir recalled telling them to cheer up, for no one was injured and Mother Earth was merely "trotting us on her knee to amuse us and make us good." The event helped him see how the valley had been formed, and it demonstrated that even a terrifying catastrophe could "enrich" the landscape with beautiful new taluses and rock faces. "Storms of every sort . . . are only harmonious notes in the song of creation, varied expressions of God's love."[12]

Surprisingly little (in view of Muir's intense spiritual feelings) of *Our National Parks*, like *The Mountains of California*, ventures beyond science into the realm of religion or philosophy. A mere handful of phrases scattered over more than three hundred pages try to point the reader beyond the natural world and the explanations of science. The most extensive comment on religion comes at the end of the Yellowstone chapter, where Muir seems to fall back on Emerson's more extreme Transcendental immaterialism that he had avoided in the past.

> A multitude of still, small voices may be heard directing you to look through all this transient, shifting show of things called "substantial" into the truly substantial, spiritual world whose forms flesh and wood, rock and water, air and sunshine, only veil and conceal, and to learn that here is heaven and the dwelling-place of the angels.[13]

Here he seems to dismiss as a mere "show" the nature that he has spent so much time trying to understand, while the real world, the world that truly counts, he locates beyond earth in some empyrean realm. That higher world is where God and his fellow spirits live, removed from the impermanence of the western forests, mountains, and prairies.

When the essay "The Yellowstone National Park" first appeared in 1898, Muir was sixty years old. As he aged and became more prosperous and prominent, with a national following to lead, he became more traditional in his beliefs—by no means reverting to a conservative, evangelical Christianity, but sounding more and more like a typical theist or Transcendentalist seeking beyond nature a God in Heaven, a Creator of the world's material forms, or a great Spirit hovering over the earth. In a 1903 interview the journalist Ray Stannard Baker quoted Muir on evolution: "Some scientists think that because they know how a thing is made, that therefore the Lord had nothing to do with it. They have proved the chain of development, but the Lord made the chain and is making it."[14] His earlier pantheistic tendencies, which celebrated every nodding flower, every zephyr, as divine in itself, became more muted. "All is beauty, all is God," he had once maintained. Now he was more careful to reassure his more conventional readers that beauty is *made by* God. To be sure, even in old age he was careful not to push nature or science aside. He confined his personal beliefs to the margins, dropping only a few casual reassurances to his readers that he believed in a Supreme Being.

Contrast such theistic expressions, however brief or casual, to the more radical views that became characteristic of John Burroughs in his later years. In 1900 Burroughs published his book *The Light of Day: Religious Discussions and Criticisms from the Naturalist's Point of View*, in which he took a stand against all traditional theistic creeds. More politically conservative than Muir, he was nonetheless more consistently radical in theology and remained so to the end. "In the light of modern astronomy," he wrote, "one finds himself looking in vain for the God of his fathers, the magnified man who ruled the ancient world." Humans had always invented gods to serve their needs, he pointed out, but now science had made all of those inventions obsolete. "We must recognize only Nature, the All; call it God if we will, but divest it of all anthropological conceptions." Nature was neither good nor bad, nor designed with humans in mind. It was simply that "vast congeries of vital forces" that gives rise to all life and will outlast all forms and beings. A religious impulse may be part of human nature, but people should put Nature, not a heaven-dwelling Father, at the center of their faith.[15]

So Muir had tended to think in his youthful, Wordsworthian years. And unlike Burroughs he was always sure, young or old, that the natural world exemplifies love and goodness, never evil or danger or indifference. But money and fame had made him more of a conformist than he seems to have realized, just as they had done for Wordsworth. In later years, he dressed in a better grade of cloth and traveled in a more comfortable style; likewise, he drifted back toward the more traditional view, shared by Louie and most of his friends, that nature is a book where we read about God. By protecting wilderness Americans were protecting those pages from the mind of the Creator, pages that were an ever changing "show."

The greatest show on earth, the Grand Canyon and its surrounding forest reserve, puts in a rushed appearance in *Our National Parks*. Not yet officially a park, it was initially set aside as one of a new round of forest reservations, covering two million acres, by President Cleveland and, after much delay, ratified by McKinley. In January 1902, Muir set off for the Canyon, hoping to catch it dressed in a mantle of winter snow and to learn more about it for a magazine piece. A new spur of the Santa Fe Railroad had just been completed to the canyon rim (and just before Muir arrived, a steam-powered automobile, a Toledo Eight-horse, had also arrived). He deplored the "belts of desolation" that railroads always brought to such wild places, even while he marveled at the swift, comfortable travel they made possible. No technology, however, could ever spoil the Grand Canyon, he was sure, any more than the oceans or the Polar Regions.

Here he found no sheltering domesticity as in Yosemite but a vast, impersonal, rocky metropolis made by eons of erosion—"nature's own capital city." It was filled with wondrous light and shadow, color and form, layer upon layer of sediments carved by the most simple of tools, water and wind, over immensities of time. White people who came here from "corn and cattle and wheat-field countries" often saw only desolation in this city, only dead empty temples, but the native people had found plenty of life here in sheltered niches scattered along its pathways. The Indians that Muir met in walks along the rim or on the trail to the Colorado River far below were "able, erect men," whose eyes expressed patience, persistence, and understanding. Over thousands of years they had survived, along with the cactuses, lizards, and mountain pines, by a spirit of accommodation. The Canyon seemed a familiar and comfortable home to them.[16]

It was July before Muir finished the Canyon piece, complaining to Johnson that it was "the toughest job I ever tackled." His stay had not provided any deep knowledge of the place, and he floundered as a mere painter of words. A couple of books had helped inform his understanding: John Wesley Powell's *Exploration of the Colorado River* (1875) and Clarence Dutton's *Tertiary History of the Grand Cañon District* (1882), with its stunning atlas of maps and plates by William Henry Holmes. But Muir realized that he wrote about the Canyon as a passing tourist, not as a guide steeped in knowledge and experience, that all he could offer others was an inducement to come and see for themselves this most ancient of landscapes, this extraordinary geological record of "a past infinitely remote." By "studying this old, old life in the light of the life beating warmly about us," he promised his readers, "we enrich and lengthen our own."[17]

One definition of a tourist is a person traveling for pleasure. That would cover every excursion Muir made throughout his life; in the broadest sense, he was always traveling for pleasure. But the level of pleasure he derived from his travels was very uneven: the best trips brought glimpses of the sublime, the next best improved his understanding of nature's mechanisms, and the least pleasurable meant wearily shuffling past an array of "important," man-made monuments. In his later years, as he wandered farther from home and moved more rapidly through a lot of places, the pleasures became more shallow and the pains more pronounced.

The worst trip of his life was, in some respects, the one he made with Charles Sargent in 1903–04, which threw him halfway around the globe before he could split off on his own. Only then did the trip become more deeply pleasurable, but even then none of it could compare with that ecstatic first summer in the Sierra. Although the purpose of the expedition was to collect rare Asian plants for the Arnold Arboretum and to study world forests, the trip had elements of the gentleman's Grand Tour upgraded for an age of steamers and railroads. Its pace and ambitions nearly killed him. No book or even article came from it, only a few letters and an unpublished journal. Afterward, he could say that he had seen the round world, but in fact he had not, by his own ideal of seeing into the fullness of things, really seen much at all.

Leaving his bear-hug intimacy with Roosevelt, he went straight to New York, without returning home, and met Sargent and his son Robeson, a landscape architect, who were waiting to commence their expedition to Europe and Russia. Going to Russia required a passport, and Muir had one in hand, proof that he was a naturalized U.S. citizen. In his application he had put down his occupation as "botanist" and described himself as five-feet ten-inches tall, with gray eyes ("slight defect in the right eye"), gray hair, Roman nose, and long thin face. While in New York he rushed to see Edward Harriman, who though stricken by appendicitis generously sent out letters of introduction across his global network of railroad and steamship lines. The Sargent-Muir party left on 29 May aboard the *S.S. Celtic*. After a dull voyage they docked in Liverpool and headed toward a posh London hotel. Sargent, who had taken command of the passports (and everything else), discovered that those documents were missing; most likely, he thought, they had been stolen aboard ship. In fact, they had slipped into the lining of his suitcase and would not be discovered until he was back in Boston. That mishap was only the first of many bad experiences.

Because the three travelers were forced to wait for new travel documents, Muir had to cancel a side trip he had hoped to make to Scotland to see family and friends. A special invitation had come from the world's richest man, his fellow Scots-American Andrew Carnegie, to visit Skibo Castle, his newly acquired baronial mansion near Dornoch Firth. Muir had to decline but added an admiring note: "Though living most of my life in the American wildernesses, I have not been an uninterested spectator of your career as one of the most influential of Scotchmen."[18]

Soon, with new passports in hand, the Sargent-Muir triad was roaring through Paris, Amsterdam, Berlin, and St. Petersburg, feeding on a rich diet of museums, botanical gardens, private mansions, and restaurants. In all those countries Muir was impressed by the wealth of paintings, the trappings of aristocratic life, and "the great gardeners" who had turned the collecting and growing of plants into a form of art. After a month of viewing such achievements, the artifacts of high civilization, his pleasure wore thin. He was especially glad to escape the Russian capital, a "huge semi-dismal old town, of huge yellow public buildings, war monuments[,] barbaric colored churches & cathedrals & palaces full of armor jewelry & some fine paintings."

What he most wanted to see, what he thought he had come to see, was more of the world's native trees.[19]

On the Fourth of July he found bliss in the Raivola forest on the Karelian isthmus north of St. Petersburg. Long a part of Finland, the flat, boggy, glaciated area, covered with an old plantation of pine, spruce, and larch trees intermixed with potato and rye fields, had been annexed by Russia. "It is the tallest & most uniform patch of manufactured forest I have seen," Muir wrote in his journal, but at least they were genuine trees far from a manicured urban garden. Around noon the travelers came upon a log cabin whose inhabitants cordially greeted them and laid out a plain lunch of brown bread, boiled eggs, and fresh wild strawberries and huckleberries floating in milk. "This little visit to a Finland farm house is one of the most delightful experiences of our journey so far. I could live at that home always, & I could not help thinking that if ever I was very weary & required a long calm rest I would like best to go to a Finland farm. No pleasure so fine is to be found in all Petersburg palaces."[20] In the months ahead, when he would often grow weary and out of sorts, he would think longingly back on that idyllic spot in the woods and its simple, wholesome people and food.

Sargent, having paid his respects to the European scientific establishment and taken in the great art galleries, proposed a rail journey down to the borders of the Black Sea—stopping at Sebastopol, Yalta, Batumi—and the Caucasus region, where they might find virgin ground for discoveries. Wild flowers they found in abundance, especially on the slopes of Mount Kazbek overlooking Chechnya, but also they found bad hotels and bad food. Muir fell sick from the "acid grey soup" they were served and took to his bed, unable on some days to accompany Sargent into the field. He lay in agony, trying to read long books of history and travel or gazing through train windows on the filthy, crowded Georgian villages they passed through, where the people seemed beaten down by their burdens. Back in Moscow he noted that the past three weeks had been "very hard, very hot, very dirty. . . . Must be tough or w[ou]ld probably have died."[21]

Even worse conditions lay ahead. Buying tickets on the still incomplete Trans-Siberian Railroad, they crossed six thousand miles of wheat fields, birch forests, and piney mountains, passing over the Volga and the Urals, skirting Lake Baikal's southern tip, and plunging relentlessly on to Vladivostok. Everywhere, Russia seemed agriculturally underdeveloped, compared to the United States, and yet plagued by famine, most recently in the preceding year. "Yankee enterprise sadly wanting or adventurous builders of homes. The whole country seems a government camp."[22] But it was not the unplowed, unharvested monotony of the Siberian wilderness that Muir found so objectionable—his journals are full of eager description of woodland scenes passing before their gaze. Rather, he was sick of his tedious imprisonment on a train. For eight days they slept in the same fetid clothes, sometimes with no hotel rooms available at their stops. Their only chance to get out and experience the country was an invitation to visit an American mining claim in the Altai foothills, and Sargent nixed it to save time. Wild, mysterious forests flashed before their eyes, and then were gone, untasted and unexplored.

As soon as they arrived on the Pacific Coast, on 18 August, Sargent proposed more heavy railroading through Manchuria to Beijing and Shanghai in quest of foreign plants. Muir, however, offered resistance— he preferred to go to sea, clear his head, and get his digestion back in order. His abdominal pains had grown acute, not helped by the morphine and brandy he was taking as a remedy. His body weight fell to one hundred pounds. Yet Sargent, he confided to his journal, "never seemed to think of me sick or well or of my studies only of his own until he feared I might die on his hands & thus bother him."[23] Fortunately for the sick man, the railroad links through Manchuria were not yet finished, and they were forced to sail to Shanghai via the Sea of Japan.

Once aboard ship Muir's persistent illness miraculously vanished within a day or two. Undoubtedly, his decision to resist the Sargents and set his own course was the medicine he most needed. He was as sick of them as he was sickened by the crowds, oppressive heat, indigestible food, and endless clacking of wheels on rails. After some friendly wrangling, they parted company on the Bund, the Sargents heading into China's interior and Muir leaving the country altogether.[24]

Shanghai afforded a first exposure to the Chinese in their native land, amidst their ancient, complex civilization. Heretofore on his ranch he had known mainly poor, illiterate peasants who spoke little English and were hard to manage. A scribbled note from this part of the trip shows him struggling to sort out his thoughts on race, immigration, and assimilation:

> Some of the best people in the world are Chinese, and we must not hate them. Hatred of any race of human beings is both foolish and wicked. We should live in Christian sympathy and charity with our Chinese neighbors, while living reasonably and naturally apart from them. Birds of a feather flock together, and it is right that we should thus flock together with nations, even with those that at first may be a little differently spotted and speckled from our own, like the Irish and Scotch and even Japanese. But we should not try to flock together too closely with the Chinese, for they are birds with feathers so unlike our own they seem to have been hatched on some other planet. America can make Americans out of almost any people, but Chinese though . . . [25]

Then he broke off his sentence, as his new ship, the *S.S. Bayern*, pulled out of the harbor, bound for Singapore and the dark, teeming nations of India and Egypt.

Like most middle-class whites of his time, Muir conceived of the United States as a melting pot in which profound cultural differences would disappear over time, leaving only superficial flavors of older national identities. Immigration would, and must, be followed by a high degree of assimilation if a new, unified nation was to emerge. Naturally, he assumed that Anglo-Celtic-Yankees should define the norms for the nation: an enterprising spirit, a morality derived from Judeo-Christian religion, a commitment to liberal democracy. Yet he also acknowledged the common humanity of people, their shared love of nature, and their universal capacity for generosity as well as meanness. Touring other nations did not alter substantially his uncertainty about how deep ethnic differences went, but it did stimulate more awareness of human variety and similarity. There, for example, stood

China in its antique grandeur, there stood individual Chinese he had met—intelligent, educated, as decent as himself—and then there were all those Chinese immigrants in California, so seemingly alien, always living poorly on the margins of society.

India might have been, for a man with a weakened constitution, a cause of further turmoil and discomfort. But Muir spent three weeks there, from late September to mid-October, in an open-minded, ecstatic mood, captivated by banyans, prowling monkeys, gilded temples, streets filled with half-naked bodies, the botanical gardens of Calcutta, the Taj Mahal, and the famed pilgrimage site of Benares, where he observed younger women helping older ones "down the stone steps into the brown muddy flood" of the holy Ganges.

Darjeeling, Mount Everest, and the whole Himalayan range were, predictably, "the most interesting part of my trip," he wrote to Louie, although they had not been part of his original plan of travel. Traveling by horse cart to the hill station of Simla, he passed humped cattle and camels on the road and, at the end, reached the elevation of the deodar (*Cedrus deodara*, "timber of the gods"), a tree of drooping foliage widely planted in the West as an ornamental but here forming a vast native forest. Through the trees in the early mornings he had clear glimpses of the lofty white mountains, until around midmorning "mist like clds grew from small beginnings & gradually wreathed each pk & its long slopes with ravishing effects."[26]

Not a single letter from home had yet reached him since he had left the United States four and a half months earlier—he was moving too fast and erratically for any to catch up—but he regularly poured out his impressions in letters and picture-post cards. From Simla he reported hiking six miles up a wooded hill without a bit of fatigue. His appetite was back, he was regaining weight, and he was a free man.[27]

Having come so far out of his expected way, Muir proposed to add Egypt and Palestine to his wanderings and headed up the Suez Canal to see the Pyramids. (The Holy Land he had to bypass because of a cholera epidemic.) From a boat's rail on the great Mother Nile he could see a narrow green ribbon of irrigated fields, water wheels, mud houses, and camels, with the desert sands blowing not far off in the distance. Back in Cairo in the dining room at famed Shepheard's Hotel, he met the "three Bells," young, wealthy siblings from Philadelphia who found his company lively and amusing. An elderly Englishwoman overheard him describing the giant sequoias of the Sierra and broke into his rhapsody to ask whether they would make nice furniture. Turning fiercely on her, Muir demanded, "Would you murder your own children"? The "stolid dame," Emily Bell remembered, "fairly jumped with fright, evidently thinking she had addressed a madman." She quickly finished her meal and left the room, with furtive glances backward.[28]

Turning eastward again, Muir determined to add those two other strongholds of Britain's empire, Australia and New Zealand, to his itinerary before heading home. Landing in Perth, he got busy collecting the outlandish-looking plants and seeds growing in Kings Park, the sprawling reserve of bush land and gardens overlooking the city. Nothing in Eurasia had been as unique or colorful as these, and he had collected nothing to this point. The botanizing continued in Melbourne's famed gardens and in the Blue Mountains behind Sydney, where the new year of 1904 found him in the company of fellow scientists he had met. Australia's eucalypts were familiar to him, for a few species had been introduced into California. Some members of the genus were reputed to rank as the tallest trees in the world, but Muir was delighted to learn that they were not quite up to the height of his own redwoods. Altogether, he spent four months "down under," much of it in the company of plant enthusiasts like himself, united by a common language, cultural heritage, and commitment to saving native vegetation from their fellow colonizers.[29]

Sheep ran everywhere in those antipodal landscapes, along with exogenous rabbits and people, creating even more damage than in North America. Settlers burned the forests heavily to make way for pastures. Large parts of the North and South islands of New Zealand, like Australia, were covered with the white man's sheep, corrugating the green hillsides, chewing on the fragile bush. Muir took note of those impacts as he traveled from Auckland south to the thermal mud pots of Rotorua, across broad Lake Taupo and the lava plain of Tongariro, established as a national park in 1894. Following a well-organized tourist route, he floated down the muddy Whanganui River, which flows through soft eroding hills dotted with tree ferns and Maori settlements, and arrived in the capital Wellington, "a good substantial looking town." He crossed to the South Island, and on 3 February the Christchurch Press listed him among new arrivals. A week later he was back in that intensely English city on the Avon River, after taking another long stagecoach ride, this one across the Canterbury Plains to Mount Cook Hermitage, which had already become a popular destination for glaciologists and mountaineers.[30]

"The strange & rich vegetation has compelled me," he wrote Louie, "to begin my botanical studies over again." More than a hundred species now filled his newly acquired plant press. He felt rejuvenated, back in his "early morning days," like marching through Georgia again. Lonely too, for the only word he had had from home were a few telegrams reassuring him that all was well with his wife and daughters.[31]

Another long voyage returned him to Sydney, from which he took passage along the Queensland coast to Darwin, to the Moluccas and the Philippines, to Hong Kong, Canton, Nagasaki, Yokohama. In those last two cities he encountered not only the renowned Japanese gardens (displaying a "wonderful liking for the grotesque & the minutely fine & curious") but also their formidable battleships charging into war. While he had been down in Australia, a war had broken out between Japan and Russia and was raging along the very coastal region where he and the Sargents had recently passed. Despite the war and the fearful beginnings of Japan's imperial thrust into the Asian mainland, his voyage homeward turned out uneventful, made in the company of jabbering workers recruited for the sugar plantations of Hawaii. In that newest acquisition of the American empire, he met the Cornell-trained forester Ralph Hosmer, visited Honolulu's Bishop Museum filled with Polynesian artifacts, reunited with one of the Graydon girls who had cheered him in his Indianapolis days of blindness, and rode over the fluted Pali cliffs to the windward shore.

By late May he was home on the ranch once more, chipper in spirit and fatter in frame, weighing nearly 150 pounds. He had been gone for over a year, counting his days spent with Roosevelt in Yosemite. Only a few Americans had seen as much of the world as he; only a few had the money and leisure to travel so far. The very possibility of so ambitious a trip testified that the world was becoming linked together into one economy, English was becoming a global language, and western (and now eastern) imperialists were entering into ever more deadly competition armed with steel-clad ships and long-range guns. Those contesting empires were supplanting the local and autonomous, leaving wounded cultures as well as dead bodies and disrupted ecosystems in their wake. Yet at the same time they were laying down modes of transportation that drew all peoples and all natural resources together into a single global flow.

An era of world tourism had emerged. Many of those tourists were not as self-reliant or well read or experienced as Muir. Yet even for him the challenges and dangers of travel could be daunting. He might easily have died along the way. The rigorous trip, moreover, had offered more than he could fully absorb into his thinking or convert into general ideas. Age had made him not only more susceptible to physical ailments but also more settled in his opinions. Faced with so much complexity, so many bewildering sights, he tended to stay focused on the daily schedule and on the plants and scenery directly in front of him, avoiding larger questions about modern war, the clash of cultures, or the environmental impact of the global economy. Wars he had always preferred to oppose more by shunning than protesting. But as an active conservationist he had forced himself to take public stands and propose policies. Such did not happen during or after his world tour. Neither he nor the Sargents nor any of the acquaintances he had made along the way was prepared to take up the huge and difficult question of what this increasingly global civilization, this modern ease of movement for labor or commodities, meant for mankind's relations with nature.

Going around the world had not changed Muir's thinking substantially. He had added to his herbarium, his stock of impressions, his long list of friends and colleagues, but he came home with no large new insights into nature or society. Nothing in his journal suggests that travel had helped him see the world, himself, or his adopted country more profoundly. Had he walked the whole distance, it might have been different.

⚬════╪════⚬

For the past quarter century the Alhambra Valley had been Muir's comfortable, stable base from which he went in and out like a wandering star. Always and reliably, his wife was there—manager, homebody, his center of gravity. Her support could easily be taken for granted, for she never criticized him for long absences. Their marriage had been thoroughly happy and secure, if never erotic or hot-blooded. In letters home he signed his name rather stiffly—"Yours, John Muir"—while to him she was always simply "Louie." Although he was not indifferent to her feelings or welfare and was never unfaithful, he hungered constantly for a wider, more diverse realm of companions and conversations. He needed more stimuli than she or the family estate could provide. Yet he also needed her more than anyone else he had ever known.

When they were little children, Wanda and Helen, in contrast to Louie's seeming invulnerability, were "my darlings," small fragile things that required his constant solicitude. He fretted over them like a mother bird trying to shield her fledglings from a cold, cruel existence outside the nest. Whenever he was home, he nursed, petted, and played with them, and they called him "dear Papa." They went on walks together in the nearby hills, but the girls were never allowed to go far from home. Remembering his own hard life as a child, he idealized children (as he did nature) and enveloped his daughters in unstinting affection, never punishing them and always smothering them in protectiveness. Unfortunately, they grew up faster than he wanted and began to show signs of wanting to escape the sanctuary he had provided for them.

Wanda eventually became a student at the state university in Berkeley, an active sorority girl, while Helen stayed under his protection longer, getting her education at home and never going to college. Both of them he dearly loved, but Wanda he looked on more with

Wanda, Helen, Louie, and John Muir at home in Martinez, California, circa 1905. (H-A, JMP)

affection than intense rapport, as he did the mother she so closely resembled: "a faithful steady scholar," he described her, "quiet, womanly, not in the least odd or brilliant, but strong-willed, earnest, and unstoppable as an avalanche."[32] Helen (or "Midge") was his favorite: petite, amusing, smart, daring, and unconventional. He had vague dreams of her carrying on his spiritual mission and becoming a great writer on the outdoors, but he had trouble setting her free as he had been to explore the more rugged and remote wild areas. On returning from his world tour, much to his chagrin, he found his little Helen a grown woman, self-reliant and increasingly interested in life outside the valley, but not so inclined to follow his lead.

Getting to that outside world became more enticing for the girls when, back in 1897, Muir sold for a nominal ten dollars a right-of-way to the Santa Fe Railroad through the ranch lands. The company erected an imposing viaduct spanning the vineyards and connecting through a tunnel to Oakland. Trains ran to and fro several times a day, stopping at "Muir Station," just a few minutes' walk from the family manse. At this small depot the ranch's produce could be conveniently loaded on to boxcars, saving a long wagon ride down to the Martinez harbor. Wanda could commute from the university on weekends. Helen, still confined to the home and her tutors, loved to wave from her window to the passing locomotive engineers and, watching them coming and going several times a day, developed a yearning to be free.[33]

The aesthetic impact of the railroad on the Alhambra Valley was, of course, considerable; the once secluded orchards and vineyards had become polluted by the smoke and thunder of the machine age. But Muir did not seem to mind. For all his love of wilderness, he was always comfortable with new technology. He made the Santa Fe deal thinking shrewdly as a practical businessman, a frequent traveler, and a host eager for company coming down the rails. Within two hours, a brief time compared to the old days of boat travel, he could reach the city to lunch with William Keith or attend a Sierra Club meeting, and then return home the same day to sleep in his own bed. In turn, an increased stream of passengers arrived on the Muir doorstep—Stanford and Berkeley professors, government scientists, writers, journalists, men of commerce, and fellow Club members.

The Sierra Club had never required much attention or presence from its president, for so far it had not become active in public campaigns for conservation. In the summer of 1901 it launched what would become its most popular activity, an annual summer outing to the mountains for its members. On the first outing, to Tuolumne Meadows, Muir went along and shared camp with over a hundred people, including cooks and packers. For the first time he allowed his daughters to accompany him to the high country. "Wanda & Helen take to this life in the rocks & woods like ducks to water, as if born to it," he was pleased to report to Louie, who as usual stayed home. "No one could guess that this was their first mountaineering." Given that their meals were prepared and their baggage handled by others, and that dozens of jolly young men and women were in the party, playing guitars and singing around the big fire, they were hardly roughing it. Muir himself took his ease in camp; he slept long hours, gorged on trout, gave a talk or two to the adoring crowd, and pronounced the outing

Muir with a Sierra Club group on the trail to Hetch Hetchy, 1909. (H-A, JMP)

"a great success." His daughters, with or without him, would become regulars on future outings up and down the California range.[34]

One tragic note dampened the general delight of that first Sierra Club outing: Joseph LeConte, long-time professor of science in the state university, beloved mentor to students, one-time hiking companion to Muir, and charter member of the Club, died of a heart attack while in camp. Muir, shaken by the death of his old friend, returned home and, dressed in a new black Prince Albert coat, represented the Club at the funeral in Berkeley. Human death was supposed to be a benign, wholesome part of nature, or so he had argued since his near-delirious sojourn in the Bonaventure Cemetery over three decades earlier. Now, however, death became all too familiar and all too final, and far less easy to look on with philosophical abstractness. Catharine Merrill, who had been his motherly confidante in Indianapolis days, died in 1900. His forty-niner friend in Chico, John Bidwell, "the greatest farmer in the West," died in 1901. Jeanne Carr died in December 1903. And sister Annie, unwed and alone, also died that year, the last of the Muir breed in Wisconsin.

Fortunately, many other friends survived, many new ones came into his life, and some old ones even reappeared after a long absence. Out of the distant past came letters from William Trout of Meaford, Ontario, paying that long overdue salary for winter millwork. Another letter came from Harry Randall, the motherless boy whom Muir had taken along to work at the Hutchings hotel. Never a very apt student, Randall was now a grocery clerk in Worcester, Massachusetts. "I can see you now," he wrote Muir, "leaned back in your home made chair covered with old sheep skins reading Humboldt but just the same John I gained a great deal of knowledge from you which has been a lot of help to me."[35] Other letters of remembrance came from classmates in Madison, from acquaintances in Prairie du Chien, and even from a former student at the Oak School in Oregon, Wisconsin. Such lasting friendship and loyalty were gifts Muir had always gathered easily and given away in abundance.

Yet undeniably the foundations of his social world were quaking and fracturing. David and his wife, tiring of orchard work, left the Alhambra Valley, resettling at Pacific Grove, California. The Reids, whom Muir had done so much to assist, were itching to be independent landowners. Maggie alone among the kinfolk remained gratefully planted on the place, often Louie's sole female companion, for Wanda and Helen had decided it was time to begin venturing out more in their father's footsteps.

Within days of returning from his world tour, Wanda and Helen were insisting that he take them to the Grand Canyon. "The girls are already pulling me off into the wilderness," he wrote to a friend, "and as I like both them and the wilderness I let 'em."[36] The family could get free passes on the Santa Fe Railroad, thanks to the right-of-way deal, and off father and daughters went to the Colorado Plateau, leaving Louie tending her rose beds and oleander. They were not gone long—ten days of strolling the Canyon rim, watching the grand sunset show, and discovering to the southeast another vividly painted desert where ancient petrified trees lay scattered and broken on the ground.

The winter season of 1904–05 wrecked any plans Muir made for a quiet, contemplative stretch at home. He had expected to be ensconced in his "scribble den," thinking over which book projects he ought to take up next, answering the scores of letters that had piled up during his world tour, and getting back to never-ending conservation issues, including the recession of Yosemite Valley to the federal government. But then illness interfered—a wave of influenza (or "grippe"), bronchitis, and pneumonia. Everyone but Wanda was hit, Helen worst of all. When she came down with a seriously inflamed lung, infected by *Mycobacterium tuberculosis*, Muir was compelled to put everything else aside to save her life.

Pneumonia and tuberculosis were among the most common causes of death in the pre-antibiotic age. Typically, the bacteria attacked the lungs, generating heavy mucus, racking coughs, chest pains, fever, and shortness of breath. Often victims, especially the old, died through suffocation. Despite his unusual fitness from so much climbing and hiking, despite his large vital capacity, Muir was increasingly plagued with such infections in his later years. He sniffled and wheezed through the rainy seasons and could get little done. Helen too had a history of pulmonary illness, often rendering her pale and breathless, justifying much of the protectiveness with which Muir had enveloped her.

For those who could afford it, doctors recommended going to a warm, dry place where their lungs might recover. So the father and his daughters decided to spend the summer of 1905 in Arizona, letting its dry air heal their bodies as so many other consumptives (i.e., tuberculars), asthmatics, and pneumonia-prone Americans were beginning to do. Helen would thrive in that setting, so much that she lived to an old age, but at the cost of never again living in the Alhambra Valley. Long stays in the Southwestern mountains and deserts, mainly to be with his daughter but also to allow his own vulnerable lungs to mend, would occupy much of the rest of Muir's life too, forcing him away from his high piney forests into barren, brown lands that he could never love so well.

The great awakening to nature that was sweeping through urban civilization, a movement in which Muir was a popular international leader, was now pulling people—pulling him—into the Southwest.

That region had long been "the epitome of ugliness and emptiness" to earlier white travelers, or to those who looked to Switzerland or Italy for models of landscape beauty. John Wesley Powell and Clarence Dutton had forced some change in that negative attitude, encouraging a more positive appraisal of the desert's stark beauty. The shift was furthered by such works as John Van Dyke's *The Desert* (1901) and Mary Austin's *The Land of Little Rain* (1903). Another important figure in the growing love of deserts was Charles Lummis, a former newspaper reporter in Los Angeles who founded the magazine *Out West*, through which he promoted desert appreciation and a respect for Indian and Latino cultures and civil rights. Muir and Lummis had struck up a friendship, with the former sending money to the editor's Native American welfare projects, and the latter, always ribbing and wise-cracking but still supporting nature conservation. To some extent, Muir learned through such influences to find beauty far away from ice-carved mountains and moraines.[37]

Following Lummis's advice the three Muirs headed down to the homeland of the Cahuilla Indians, called by the white man *Agua Caliente*, or Palm Springs. "The first night," Muir wrote Lummis, "we lay down under an olive tree in the sandy orchard, and the heat of the sand along our spines brought vividly to mind Milton's unlucky angels lying on the burning marl." Nonetheless, they loved the cool nights and the days hot enough "to evaporate every disease and all one's flesh." A few weeks later they showed up as guests on the Sierra Bonita ranch near Mount Graham in southeastern Arizona. Here, Henry ("Don Pedro") Hooker, who ran cattle and horses on his 400,000-acre spread in what was still Apache country, received his guests at his adobe hacienda with an open-handed generosity. "I never breathed air more distinctly, palpably good," Muir noted in a journal; "it is clean, fresh, and pure as the icy Arctic air."[38]

Then came word that Louie was critically sick with pneumonia and calling them home. Muir and Wanda left Helen behind to continue recuperating, sparing her the exposure to northern California fogs and family distress, and rushed to Louie's aid. For six weeks they lingered at her bedside, watching her suffer from what turned out to be an advancing tumor and listening to her labored breathing. On

6 August she died with her husband nearby. Devastated and feeling guilty for his many self-indulgent absences, he buried her in a wooded grove a short distance up the Alhambra Valley.

Condolences poured in from all over the country, including a note from President Roosevelt (who early in his career had suffered a shattering loss of both wife and mother), advising Muir to "get out among the mountains and the trees, friend, as soon as you can. They will do more for you than either man or woman can."[39] Instead of going to the Sierra, however, the bereaved husband returned to the Southwestern desert, seeking the emotional support of his daughters and the dry heat that might evaporate sorrow as well as sickness. This time they put up near the Petrified Forest region of eastern Arizona, where the Santa Fe Railroad had established a coaling and watering station named Adamana, an isolated spot along the tracks where the only hostelry was the low-slung Forest Hotel and the social demands were as minimal as the landscape.

"I have been overburdened & overworked in every way during the last two eventful months & am almost dead tired." In such a state, Muir confided to his Pasadena friend Theodore Lukens, he had turned for sympathy to "our Heavenly Father." But it would appear that nature was as important as prayer in his recovery; each day he drove a buckboard wagon along the dry bed of the Puerco River and through the yellow bunchgrass to study the fossilized forest that lay exposed over the heavily eroded surface, testifying to a time in the Late Triassic when Arizona was a wet, subtropical habitat. He had found great trees even in the desert. There were also reptilian bones and Indian ruins to explore, and petroglyphs to decipher. In the evenings the Muirs sat on the hotel's long veranda, talking to the guests who stopped for a night or two or to the occasional hobo, before retiring to their cabin (and Helen to her all-weather tent, where she slept to strengthen her constitution).[40]

Come January, father and daughters were still in residence when Alice Cotton and her parents arrived to inspect the brilliantly hued remnants of the ancient forest. They sat down next to the famous naturalist John Muir, who claimed to be making a study of the Petrified Forest for a magazine. He struck Alice as an extraordinary figure, "interested in everything." While other tourists came and went, he

Muir examining a petrified log in Arizona, circa 1905. (H-A, Muiriana)

had hunkered down to excavate a large house-ruin built by vanished peoples, studying their pottery and the large ant hills nearby sparkling with glittering rock gems, and to theorize about what species the old trees represented. Some six miles from the hotel he discovered, in an area of dark, furrowed mudstone, an overlooked stretch of the ancient preserved trees, which he dubbed the Blue Forest (today's Blue Mesa).

Although he misdated the age of the trees and made errors in their identification, he filled a notebook with close observations, buttressed by scientific reports he consulted in the Bay Area libraries.[41]

Muir and Wanda left their Adamana sanatorium for good in August 1906, after a year of off-and-on residence. A few months earlier Congress passed the American Antiquities Act, which allowed the president to set aside national "monuments"—pointedly not large scenic "parks," which would meet with local resistance, but rather "historic landmarks, historic and prehistoric structures, and other objects of historic or scientific interest." President Roosevelt seized on the new legislation to preserve such places as Mesa Verde, Devil's Tower, the Grand Canyon, and the Petrified Forest National Monument, the last covering some 60,000 acres. Muir had little to do with passing the act or making any of those designations, but he provided both the railroad and the federal government with sketch maps of possible boundaries for the Petrified Forest monument. He also tried to defend the site from vandals and commercial interests, some of whom wanted to pulverize the ancient stone logs for industrial abrasives. On the other hand, he saw nothing wrong with picking up a few pieces of the mineralized wood and the Indian artifacts for his own purposes, including an earthen pitcher he gave to Alice.[42]

Home again in the "dismal old" Strentzel manse, Muir had to confront a future without Louie or his maturing daughters, with only his Chinese house man Ah Fong for company. "No matter what friends or husbands you may be blessed with or bothered with," he wrote to Wanda and Helen, "you will never have so devoted & devout lover as I am because I know you best. . . . O dear these lonely days!! I must either get into consuming hard work or go up a canon."[43] He fell to the melancholy task of sorting out Louie's estate, selling and leasing her properties, administering her will that gave almost everything, including the house, to her daughters, and setting up bank accounts that would allow Helen to live permanently in the desert environment. All that he owned was his large vineyard (leased to others), a part-interest in some rangelands in the Briones hills (inherited from his father-in-law), his books and royalties, and his bank savings (money he had earned for himself in the first years of his marriage). The girls allowed him to go on living free of charge in the Strentzel manse. On these assets he could easily get by.

In June 1906, less than a year after Louie's death, Wanda married Thomas Hanna, a civil engineer interested in irrigation and water-supply work whom she had met at the university. She did not consult her father about the choice, and from his point of view it was not a happy one. For one thing it removed her from his household and left him more alone than ever. The couple moved into Don Ignacio Martinez's old adobe a short walk away from the big gray house on the knoll. Tom shifted careers and took over the ranch management from all the departing Muir kin, running the place to suit his own ideas. Although still close at hand, Wanda had unmistakably moved out of her father's household and into her own, separate orbit.

Abruptly, too, the guests stopped arriving at Muir Station. Daily meals in the manse were served to a solitary diner. Left alone to think and brood, Muir still felt pangs of guilt over having ignored his wife's weakened condition while he had looked after the girls. "Up to her last day," he wrote his cousin in Dunbar, "my noble wife was not aware of the hopelessness of recovery, nor indeed were any of us though warned by the doctors a month before." He had failed to heed the danger signals and had lost her. The past year spent largely in the desert, absorbed in sand, rock, and sun, had temporarily helped assuage his grief, "bringing back something of the old free life with Mother Nature." But that life would never altogether return; long ago he had given it up for the sake of Louie and a family existence, and it was not clear now what would fill his sense of emptiness.[44]

<hr />

"The earth tremors increased in violence, and rose and took possession of all walls, shaking them so that masonry and timbers crunched and creaked and groaned. There was a sickening sensation as if everything were toppling.... After forty-eight tumultuous seconds, every one of which was packed with sensations of destruction, followed a bewildering calm." Charles Keeler, one of Muir's good friends in San Francisco, thus remembered waking up to the massive earthquake that struck the city a little after five a.m. on 18 April 1906. He rushed with others still in their nightdress into the streets, which were covered with rubble and choking with dust. A few steel-ribbed buildings stood tall against the general desolation, but nearly 30,000 buildings had been destroyed, the "worst havoc" wrought "in the poor, crowded districts south of Market Street."[45]

One of the worst urban disasters in American history, the 1906 earthquake affected more than San Francisco; it was felt from southern Oregon to south of Los Angeles and east into the Great Basin, and even seismographs in Germany recorded the movement. The rupture in the earth's crust stretched three hundred miles along the California coast. The total toll in human life and property is still hard to estimate; at least 700–800, but perhaps as many as 3,000, died. Nature delivered a hammer blow to humankind. But, as writer Philip Fradkin has argued, San Francisco suffered more from human stupidity and mismanagement, before and during the quake, than from a treacherous nature. The real crisis began when fires started and raged out of control, and when the mayor issued a shoot-to-kill order to stop looting. Madness and incompetence among the local elite turned a natural disaster into a holocaust.[46]

The city's water supply system broke apart, as cast-iron pipes cracked at the joints and the water jetted uselessly into the air. Thousands of distribution mains and connecting pipes were fractured, mostly where decades of ill-advised building on landfill and reclaimed marshes had occurred. Muir's old neighborhood of Valencia Street was one of the worst hit: once a deep swamp, the area had been filled with dirt and even garbage to make a building foundation, and with the quake that soil turned to liquid and the surface collapsed four to five feet. Water, gas, and electrical lines snapped. Fires broke out, and residents who were trapped in the wreckage burned to death.[47]

Damage in the Alhambra Valley was less catastrophic but still severe. The town of Martinez was left "in ruins," reported Wanda, though fortunately spared an aftershock of fires. Aunt Margaret's house shifted eight inches off its foundation. The Strentzel manse lost all five of its chimneys and the plaster ceilings collapsed, although no books or pictures were damaged. Only the old adobe went unscathed.[48]

Coming a few months after Louie's death and Helen's illness, the California earthquake further shook Muir's sense of security and peace. He did not turn against nature as a false goddess or lose his faith in divine benevolence, but he realized more than ever how much misfortune and sorrow lurk in the world, and he was clear about who bears the cost when societies take nature too much for granted. Two months after the quake he rode a streetcar up Market Street to Valencia to inspect the damage. "It is wonderful how rapidly new temporary buildings are going up," he reported to Helen, "many are already furnished & look as if meant to be permanent." City leaders vowed that they would create a grand new San Francisco out of the ashes and dust, which would rank among the finest metropolises of the world. Muir echoed their optimism, but added that "the losses of thousands of poor labor people will be felt all their lifetime."[49]

The homecoming years after the illness-plagued 1903–04 world tour, contrary to all expectations, had been shaken by more illness and by bouts of loss and adversity. As he wrote to Katharine Graydon in Honolulu, "the last three years have been full of change and trouble and anxious care. . . . As for books I haven't written a word for the press in the last three years."[50] Since camping with President Roosevelt he had not spent any time in Yosemite or the Sierra. All the once-giddy days traveling with his impressive East Coast friends—Johnson, Burroughs, Sargent, Harriman, Osborn, Merriam, Gannett—seemed far away, back in the "auld lang syne," overshadowed by the recent family, community, and personal misfortunes.

While he was trying to cope with those crises, the conservation movement scored an important victory: the incorporation of Yosemite Valley into the surrounding national park. Despite a long, strenuous effort by the state's commissioners to defend their stewardship, the politicians in Sacramento had voted, in February 1905, to turn the valley back to the federal government for safekeeping. Muir had made nine trips to Sacramento to lobby for that outcome, but most of the burden had fallen on Will Colby, secretary of the Sierra Club. William Randolph Hearst's newspaper had opposed the recession and in its pages vilified Muir, one of their own contributors; on the other side of the business divide stood the supportive Southern Pacific Railroad, now under the control of Edward Harriman. Colby encouraged Muir to ask his powerful friend for help, which he did, and Harriman's word to the railroad's legal counsel William Herrin was sufficient to bring the biggest economic interest in the state over to the side of the recessionists. When the smoke had cleared, Muir wryly noted, "the [Southern Pacific] is regarded as the great power (at times benign) behind the awful Sacramento throne. Sacramento! What a name for the place so beset with scrawny political thorns and briars and poison oak. . . . Now, thank Heaven, I'm out of it. My political education commenced a month or two ago and is now complete in all its branches."[51]

Harriman intervened again when the U.S. Congress took up the matter, by persuading the powerful Speaker of the House Joseph Cannon to set aside his penny-wise scruples and endorse the legislation. California's Senator George C. Perkins, a charter member of the Sierra Club, pushed hard in the other legislative chamber to accept the California offer, and President Roosevelt threw in his support. In the closing moments Muir, although far from the scene of action, followed the outcome closely. When the bill successfully passed Congress in July, he sent congratulations to Robert Underwood Johnson, who had played a pivotal role: "The fight you planned by that famous Tuolumne campfire seventeen years ago is at last fairly gloriously won, every enemy down derry down." Above all, he gave credit to Colby, "the only one of all the club who stood by me in downright effective fighting."[52]

Granting Yosemite Valley national park status was one of the great triumphs of the Roosevelt conservation era. Hard choices would always have to be made between accessibility to and protection of the enlarged park, between commerce and constraint, and it would take another ten years before Congress established a national park office that would develop uniform principles to guide those decisions. But a move that had begun in Civil War days to set aside areas of outstanding natural beauty from private acquisition and development had become fully established as public policy. Although he had not been there in the beginning of the movement to save the valley, nor present for the final showdown in Washington, Muir was widely recognized as the greatest advocate of the park, of the whole Sierra range, and indeed of all the remaining wild places in America—a role that he had understood and accepted as his life's purpose and was bearing impressive fruit. Coming after so many tearful, terrible events, that triumph for Yosemite had to be a shining hour.

On the horizon, however, another small, deep tremor was beginning to be felt, one that should have been an omen to Muir of bad things to come. During the Congressional debate, several proposals had surprised and nearly sidetracked the recessionists –proposals to reduce park boundaries, run railroads into the valley, or allow water-storage reservoirs. All were defeated, but all would live another day. Six weeks after the San Francisco earthquake the nation's chief forester Gifford Pinchot wrote city engineer Marsden Manson: "I hope sincerely that in the regeneration of San Francisco its people may be able to make provision for a water supply from the Yosemite National Park." In November he urged the engineer to approach the secretary of the Department of Interior, James R. Garfield, for permission to secure water from within the park.[53] Both Manson and Pinchot were members of the Sierra Club, the latter made an honorary member as the government's director of forest reserves. They did not, however, share Muir's or Colby's view that a national park was not a proper place for producing an economic commodity, including a water supply.

To this point the Club had shied from taking political stands, perhaps wisely in view of the disagreements lurking within its membership over the meaning of conservation. Within and beyond the Club the conservation movement was not unified or single-minded. A fracture ran through it like the San Andreas fault line running through California. Although no one in those days had introduced the theory of plate tectonics or understood well how earthquakes happen, they were in fact standing on an unstable political surface under which two plates were beginning to grind against one another. When the rupture came, it would be wider and more devastating than anyone had foreseen, wider even than the president of the United States could straddle. That quake would irrevocably separate Muir not only from Pinchot but also from the "bully" president with whom he had once stood at Glacier Point in cheerful comradeship. Muir could repair the shattered chimneys on his house, but how could he fix the emptiness inside that dwelling, the horrible loss of his wife and the absence of his daughters? And how could he prevent the breaking apart into opposing camps of a movement he had worked so hard to promote?

CHAPTER 14

The Troubled Nature of Wealth

The day Muir counted seventy rings on his lean, upright trunk he spent alone in the Strentzel manse. No friends or relatives gathered round to wish him many happy returns or to drink to his lifetime achievement. Except for ailing Margaret, none of his siblings now lived nearby, and his daughters were preoccupied with their own lives and pointedly assertive of their independence. The day after his milestone birthday, he described himself plaintively to the distant and neglectful Helen as a "venerable old child (of Nature), . . . pegging away here in my den practicing my old skill in cooking as well as scribbling. Wis[h] my den could be transported to the desert beside you. . . . Ever your lover. J.M."[1]

That was the role he had imagined for himself: the father-lover who stood first in his daughters' affections, whose advice they still sought and heeded. But such was not to be. Wanda was temporarily down in Berkeley giving birth to her second son (she would have five sons and one daughter in all) and was now the wife of a man whom Muir did not much like, probably because of his indifference to the old man's wishes. Helen was even farther away, riding her pony with cowboys and miners around desolate, flyblown Daggett, a ramshackle town in the Mohave Desert, a long way from her father's world of high moral principles, nature conservation, and civic virtue. She was married to a handsome spendthrift whom he distrusted. Perhaps Muir never wanted her to marry anyone but always to remain his little Midge for the rest of her life. Instead, she fell in love with Buell Funk and, without seeking her father's blessing or counsel, eloped with him. She would bear four sons and never return to the home place. His favorite child had joined a community of frontier scoundrels and would never realize the literary career he had imagined for her.[2]

As much as he could Muir tried to ignore those disappointments of parenthood. From his upstairs study window, deliberately kept free of curtains, he could look between twin Washington palm trees down the valley and down on the blooming gardens and orchards that encircled the house. Here was Louie's legacy of graceful, genteel domesticity that had drawn him from a peripatetic bachelorhood and helped make him a success in the eyes of the world. These days, however, his own eyes were usually focused on what he called the glacial moraines of notebooks and journals that lay across the floor. His mind moved through them with barely perceptible progress, trying to discern what unwritten books they might contain. Were there a dozen or a hundred volumes to be extracted? Much of his past life lay hidden in those weathered bundles of field jottings, bringing back memories rich in wild places, in ecstatic wandering, a life now behind him.

Whenever he took up his pen these days, it was usually to defend his beloved Yosemite country from economic development. Pushing all else aside, including his anxieties about his daughters and his strong inclination to linger over happier memories, he turned his den into a war room, adding telegrams, correspondence, and drafts of pamphlets to the moraines. On his seventieth birthday he wrote to President Roosevelt:

> I am anxious that the Yosemite National Park may be saved from all sorts of commercialism & marks of man's work other than the roads, hotels, etc., required to make its wonders & blessings available for mankind. For as far as I have seen there is not in all the wonderful Sierra, or indeed in the world, another so grand & wonderful & useful a block of Nature's mountain handwork.

He may never have sent that letter; hours later, he wrote another and more bitter one, criticizing the "miserable dollarish" motives of the "capitalists" who plagued his old age with schemes to turn the park into profitable commodity. Roosevelt protested, "Do not run down those men too much." But Muir had seen into their hearts and feared that the only reverence to be found there was for money and the things that money could buy.[3]

The battle to preserve Yosemite Park began to heat up again in the fall of 1907 and remained hot for the next six years. It absorbed most of old man Muir's energies. At stake was not only the park itself but the question of what conservation meant—merely another definition of "development" or a movement to set limits to growth and the pursuit of wealth?

During the Roosevelt administration the United States became the world's leading industrial nation, outpacing Great Britain and Germany in production and consumption. Business was turning the whole continent into an immense factory for producing oil, wheat, automobiles, skyscrapers, sprawling suburbs, grandiose estates with manicured gardens, elite universities, and sumptuous galleries of art. This irrepressible giant was beginning to need the whole earth to satisfy its appetite. Muir had learned not to pick any big quarrel with the giant; beyond the borders of Yosemite, he had learned to accept much and question little.

He was no Luddite. Directly behind his dwelling stood the silver railroad trestle that he had welcomed; inside the house he had installed a telephone, electric lights, and a typewriter. But he worried that no place might be sacrosanct from the giant's maw, no sense of the sacred might survive. Saving the American soul from a total surrender to materialism was the cause for which he fought. The Sierra Nevada had been his first and would be his last stand.

Congress had set aside the Yosemite Valley as a state park in 1864, established a national park around it in 1890, and then reclaimed the valley as part of the national park in 1903. Now San Francisco wanted to dam one of the two principal watersheds in the park, the Hetch Hetchy valley through which ran the Tuolumne River, to create a reservoir for its water supply. In the sum of American economic expansion the intrusion might have seemed a minor, obscure matter, but to Muir immense issues were involved: why had the nation preserved that "pure wildness" in the first place? What part should mountains, rivers, natural meadows, or wild creatures play in American life? If the nation set aside some natural places as especially sacred, how far beyond their borders should a sense of the sacred extend? What should be the fate of prairies, wetlands, or coastal marshes? Would there be any room in an acquisitive society for wildness, or for nonmaterial, spiritual values?

Tough questions for anyone, they were especially hard for an ailing and wearied man thrust into political activity for which he had little enthusiasm. He felt tethered by illness that often kept him indoors and vexed by his social responsibilities. To sister Mary he confessed that he was doing a lot of sulking and growling these days. "Impossible," she replied, "you who are ever remembered as placid—peaceful and patient—and living in the higher—the most beautiful in the realm of thought." She was thinking of a much younger man, unhurried and untroubled. The septuagenarian was a different sort, mixing wonderful memories with a more urgent need to settle a few last matters. A battle to win, several books to write, perhaps a last excursion or two to make— he had to get "something worth while off my hands before dark."[4]

❦

Cool, rainy winters in the Alhambra Valley were hard on his aging lungs; staying at home, he went through bouts of the influenza virus. Recurrent waves of high fever, sore throat, aching muscles, and extreme tiredness prostrated him, threatening pneumonia.[5] Helen had shown the same susceptibility; exile in the desert was the only way they knew to save her life. But Muir himself would not follow that remedy. He had become too attached to the old place, to his high-ceilinged den and accumulated books and papers. Although ever the self-styled "wanderer" who claimed the mountains as his only true home, he was in fact a firmly rooted man. When Helen proposed selling the manse, he decided to buy it and five surrounding acres, confessing, "I hate the idea of ever parting with it."[6]

But cough-wracked and lonely winters could drive him out of the home place from time to time, down to southern California where he found sunshine, dry air, and companionship among a group of generous friends. Many of them were indubitably capitalists but of an enlightened, sympathetic sort. They included such residents of upscale Pasadena as Theodore Lukens, banker, real-estate developer, and forester, and Alfred Sellers, retired from a Chicago title abstract company; while in Los Angeles, there were John and Katharine Hooker, whose fortune came from manufacturing steel pipe, much of it used in irrigation.

Not all of Muir's California friends, in the south or north, were from the well-to-do class. The Calkinses, retired from newspaper work in Iowa, were not rich, nor was Charles Lummis, editor, litterateur, and Indian rights activist, with his picturesque home in the Arroyo Seco; nor were such Stanford professors as Vernon Kellogg and Melville Anderson, who welcomed Muir into their bookish lives; nor were old intimates like the artist Keith or the educational reformer Swett. When Muir needed a warm place to recoup his strength, however, he would migrate to affluent friends like the Hookers, who lived in a buff-colored Spanish-colonial mansion on West Adams Avenue—locally known as millionaires' row—in Los Angeles. Here he could forget for a while his abstemious habits, his family troubles, his littered study, and sleep on luxuriant white sheets, wear a fresh garden rose in his buttonhole, eat and drink rich foods and wines, and be chauffeured around town in a new automobile.

What those diverse friends had most in common was not an interest in protecting any privileged positions but an openness to nature as an aesthetic and spiritual resource. Muir entered their homes as an oracle on what the natural world offered beyond an opportunity to make money. All his friends had broken free as he had done from traditional religion and were drawn to California's desert and mountain landscapes as sources of modern piety. The Hookers, for example, were children of the New England intelligentsia who had turned from biblical doctrine to science, art, and the outdoors for inspiration. John Hooker, a descendant of the Puritan founder of Connecticut, had retired early from business to devote himself to various philanthropies, including the installation of a state-of-the-art telescope on

Mount Wilson. Katharine, who was related to the academic Whitneys of Yale and Harvard, was a hiker, craftsman, traveler, and the author of *Wayfarers in Italy*, illustrated by her daughter Marion's photographs. Their mansion was a high-minded salon where Muir could meet writers and artists, just as he had done in the homes of Jeanne and Ezra Carr. Once more he became the occasional lodger, working in a third-floor garret during the days and conversing with his hosts long into the evenings.[7]

He amused them with his humorous stories, his lapses into Scottish brogue, or his disregard for appearances. His wardrobe included a good three-piece suit, but sometimes he wore whatever felt most comfortable. One morning as he came down the stairs, packed to leave, the Sellers and their guests laughed to see a long gray nightgown trailing out of his satchel. There was something simple, casual, unassuming, and altogether natural about his character that they adored, and they would do whatever they could to protect him from the burdens of old age and the obstacles to his writing.[8]

All Muir's friends were worried that he might never get another book in print. His last major work, *Our National Parks*, had appeared in 1901 and nothing more seemed forthcoming. His story of man, dog, and glacier, *Stickeen*, came out in 1909, but only after much procrastination; although it sold well, it was little more than a short story. But what larger lessons had Muir learned in the course of his extraordinary life—what big insights into the cosmos? The pressing need was to get his memoirs written, in one or several volumes, where he could describe the experiences that had made him famous, the path that had led from obscurity to international acclaim, the central role of nature in his life, and what he had gained from so much sauntering into wild places.

"I usually finish what I begin," Muir wrote, "but in the last four years every literary plan has been interrupted about as soon as work on it was fairly under way & no friend however kind is able to help in such troubles." He felt "barren and useless." Friends tried repeatedly to overcome his lassitude. The Calkinses offered to move into his house as live-in aides and help him organize his material. The

Hookers offered a paid secretary in addition to their garret. Others simply sent words of encouragement. William Kent, who had made a fortune in Chicago real estate and livestock trading before retiring to Marin County, California, and was one of his most ardent admirers, wrote, "Your life has been so interesting and so entirely unique that an account of it should not be lost to the world." Self-described as a "pugnacious, meat-eating barbarian," Kent looked to his mentor to show the way to "philosophical balance which is a matter of course to you [but] comes very hard to me." So, to gratify such friends and disciples, Muir put an autobiography at the head of his list of writing projects, hoping that he could find the wellness and peace of mind to produce the reflective account of his life that everybody seemed to want.[9]

A potential roadblock to that memoir showed up in the form of an ex-minister and popular writer on southwestern themes, George Wharton James. He had persuaded Jeanne Carr, in her sad last years, to turn over to him all her letters from Muir, including letters discussing his relationship with Elvira Hutchings. There was nothing morally devastating in them, but Muir was persuaded by his friends that he must get them into his possession, for they were rightfully his property. Not only might James use them to forward his own projected biography, but also he might publish them as they were, giving Muir no opportunity to decide what should be published and what should be cut or omitted. Katharine Hooker denounced "that unspeakable man who robbed you and the dead to make money for himself. Really there should be some adequate punishment for such as he." James resisted all their censoring efforts, repeatedly proclaiming his innocence: "I love you with too deep a reverence to allow a line to be issued . . . that does not honor and glorify you." Under pressure, he negotiated with Sellers to allow the letters to be typed and Muir to decide what he did not want published. In the end it hardly mattered what the letters revealed about Muir's feelings about Carr or Hutchings, since later generations would be less puritanical in judging his private life.[10]

Los Angeles proved a better sanitarium for congested lungs than a paralyzed writing hand. Still not a word of autobiography had been composed when an invitation came from Edward Harriman for Muir to spend part of the summer of 1908 at his summer camp on Upper Klamath Lake's Pelican Bay, midway between the California-Oregon border and Crater Lake. Here would be no distracting salon atmosphere or strolls among the garden statuary. Surprisingly, in view of its owner's financial power, the camp consisted of a simple two-story log house (the "Lodge") with shaded verandas, set in a grassy clearing near the lake shore: a bucolic setting far away from cities, chauffeurs, and chattering society. Unlike Hooker or Sellers, E. H. Harriman was not the retired-gentleman type who sought highbrow leisure and self-culture. Relentlessly he drove himself, he drove everyone who worked for him, and now he was ready to drive Muir to get his inspiring story on paper for America's edification.

During the Harriman expedition to Alaska, the two men had come to a mutual understanding, disagreeing on how far any man's life should be devoted to making money and on the ethics of shooting animals for pleasure, but agreeing on the value of an efficient railroad system and on the wisdom of establishing national parks. They had formed an improbable bond. Harriman had won plaudits by rushing aid to a flooded Imperial Valley and a shattered, burning San Francisco. More recently, however, he had come under fierce attack by an even more powerful Muir friend, President Roosevelt, for acting as feudal lord over the nation's transportation network, defying public control or accountability. In Roosevelt's mind Harriman symbolized the evil side of American business, impeding the country's moral and economic progress. Caught between two loyalties, Muir chose to ignore their dispute as an unseemly wrangle over power and to see in Harriman only a well-meaning benefactor. "You have done a giant's work in the past years," Muir assured his friend in the midst of his political troubles, "making the country's ways straighter, smoother, stronger, safe, bettering and befriending most everybody."[11]

Muir went to Pelican Bay prepared to be rescued from his long spell of writer's block. Harriman, he hoped, would spur him to better results than any of his other friends had done, and he fell to work. A male secretary followed him everywhere he went, whether walking in

Newspaper cartoon of the railroad kingpin Edward H. Harriman, bestriding the continent. (George Kennan, E. H. Harriman)

the Ponderosa pine forests, sailing in a boat from their private dock, or sitting on the veranda with a cup of tea, jotting down whatever Muir remembered from his childhood days in Scotland and Wisconsin.

"I'm fairly dizzy, most of the time," he wrote to Helen, "& I cant get out of it for there's no withstanding Harriman's stenographer under orders[.] I intended stopping only a day or two but H. wouldn't hear of it ordered me to stay until he showed me 'how to write books' I've never been so task-driven in a literary way before. I don't know when Ill get away & get free from this beneficent bondage." He stayed for three intense weeks. "What a time I had so kind & hearty & full of work. I dictated over a thousand pages of M.S. mostly a hard rough confused mass judging by what I have examined in type-written copy. Most is still in short hand & will be typed & forwarded from N.Y." The miracle was that he was not merely cutting and pasting from the notebooks, nor touching up old magazine articles. Disorganized he may have been, but he was producing new material, more than he had produced in a long while.[12]

Another three years would pass before that flood of memories would take shape as *My Boyhood and Youth,* published in 1912 by Houghton Mifflin. Harriman would be dead by that time; even his phenomenal model of self-discipline could not move the writer along as fast as he had hoped. Yet without Harriman's intervention, or the moral support of so many other well-meaning and well-to-do friends, Muir could never have shaken off his torpor and melancholy, or gotten his writing back on track.

<hr/>

Despite his doctor's advice to slow down, Harriman would not tolerate much idleness. He would go bear hunting with his boys or catch fish with his daughters but all the while continue scheming to improve the country's railroad infrastructure. Originally, he had come to Upper Klamath Lake to look over possible routes for a new connecting line from the Sacramento Valley to Portland, Oregon. At the other end of the lake from his camp sat the frontier town of Klamath Falls, and from its outskirts stretched a high, cold desert, the Klamath Basin. Here water collected in vast, shallow wetlands and chains of lakes, providing one of the most critical habitats for migrating waterfowl in the West. Through this stark but biotically rich landscape Harriman contemplated building his line, but first he needed to assess its potential to generate passengers and freight.

In 1905 Congress authorized a federal reclamation project in the basin that would convert lakes and marshes to agricultural lands. The U.S. Reclamation Service, established just three years earlier under director Frederick Haynes Newell, a hydraulic engineer, made the area one of its top priorities, although some experts warned that the Klamath Basin's high elevation and peaty, alkaline soils could not support a profitable farm economy. The government disregarded the warnings and promised to build dams, canals, and drainage ditches that would open up 200,000 new acres for settlement. Harriman was drawn to the neighborhood because of that promise. During the month before Muir arrived, he summoned to his camp a succession of railroad underlings, including Muir's friend William Herrin, vice president of the Southern Pacific, along with irrigation advocates, to assess how much agricultural production the reclamation project might yield and how much revenue it might add to the railroad's coffers.[13]

In that same year, 1908, President Roosevelt, learning of the abundant biota in the basin (some six million birds breeding or passing through seasonally), declared that Lower Klamath Lake would become a federal wildlife sanctuary.[14] It was the country's first large waterfowl refuge, established to protect such native species as the white pelican, the western grebe, the pintail and mallard duck, the white-faced ibis, the tri-colored blackbird, and such predators and scavengers as the peregrine falcon and bald eagle. Originally, the refuge covered 80,000 acres, but a later president, Woodrow Wilson, would cut it nearly in half to please the farmers. Thus, in this remote place clashed two opposing ideas: irrigation by federal agents to develop the West and add to the nation's farm product versus the protection of wild species and their habitat from invasion and extinction. The struggle between those ideas would continue through the rest of the twentieth century, during which the birds and fish would consistently lose, their numbers plummeting to a fraction of their original levels. The Indian tribes of southern Oregon, so dependent on hunting and fishing for their subsistence, would lose too, as their claims on the water were ignored.[15]

When he answered Harriman's invitation, Muir was naively stepping into an environmental controversy of long-lasting significance. He came and went away without taking any notice of it in his transcripts, letters, or journals. While a massive destruction of critical bird habitat was beginning not far from Pelican Lake, he was absorbed in his memories of Wisconsin's early "paradise of birds." He seemed to be, and perhaps was, unaware of Oregon's avifaunal significance, uncritical of the dubious project of federal reclamation, and indifferent to Roosevelt's new program for a series of wildlife refuges to set alongside the national parks.

Muir felt free to criticize his host's shooting at trophy bears but seldom questioned the broader ecological toll that followed in the wake of railroad expansion. That he had come to love the good-hearted builder and his sweet tempered family explains part of the silence. Naturally, he was grateful for Harriman's behind-the-scenes lobbying that had saved Yosemite and for the good works his friend achieved in other settings. He had visited the man's private estate, Arden House, with its 8,000 acres of dense forest in the Ramapo highlands north of New York City, and he knew how much Harriman loved that forest and its creatures, how he had saved that beautiful woodland from timber speculators, how nature was for him, as it was for Muir, a realm to revere and conserve. Compared to his Wall Street contemporaries, Harriman seemed devoted to letting nature alone, at least in select places. All the same, he was in the business of bringing change to the country's environment, of carrying commodities to market, of introducing "improvements" in the form of farms, crops, and mail-order consumption to the farthest corners of the continent. The Klamath Basin, much of it a treeless desert lacking any spectacular scenery, was a promising candidate for such improvement. Muir, who could not have been ignorant of Harriman's intentions, by his silence concurred in the scheme.[16]

One year after Muir's sojourn at Pelican Bay, in early September 1909, Harriman died of stomach cancer. After the news rocked the nation, the widow Mary Harriman beseeched Muir, pointedly not any of his business associates, to write a eulogy that would defend his moral character. Published privately, it was one of the most touching tributes Muir ever penned, and deeply revealing of his often tolerant, hopeful attitude toward men of wealth. His friend, he wrote, had moved across the landscape like an immensely powerful glacier,

> cutting canyons through ridges, carrying off hills, laying rails and bridges over lakes and rivers, over mountains and plains, making the nation's ways straight and smooth and safe, bringing everybody nearer to one another. He seemed to regard the whole continent as his farm and all the people as his partners. . . . Nothing he had was allowed to lie idle. A great maker and harvester of crops of wealth . . . fortunes grew along his railroads like natural fruit. Almost everything he touched sprang up into new forms, changing the face of the whole country.

Muir repeated what Harriman had told him along the Alaskan shore, that he cared little for money except as a tool with which to create and thus to get into "partnership with Nature in doing good." Beneath a brusque, domineering manner, the eulogist assured the public, beat a warm heart and a love of humanity as well as nature. "In almost every way," Muir cryptically added, "he was a man to admire," without specifying in what ways he was not.[17]

What is remarkable is Muir's willingness to go beyond the normal praise of character to celebrate Harriman's role "in developing the country and laying broad and deep foundations of prosperity." Just as the Ice Age had destroyed an older world to bring about a newer and finer landscape, so the capitalist carved, eroded, and pushed rock and soil into new and better configurations. Harriman the capitalist became a natural force, and like nature worked toward a higher harmony and beauty. The comparison left no room for disapproval, protest, or opposition. Capitalism and nature, according to Muir, worked as allies in the shaping of earth's destiny.

Most social and political reformers of the early twentieth century, including Roosevelt and his Progressive and liberal Republican followers, and including Muir, accepted the growing concentration of affluence as the price exacted by modern technology. They dared not question whether a meaningful democracy could survive in an age in which the massing of capital intensified, in which the domination of nature required the domination of some men over others.

Roosevelt's remedy was to elect people like himself—intelligent, forceful, and public-minded—to political office and give them the power to regulate or break up the trusts or monopolies. This was a large part of what contemporaries called "Progressivism," a strategy of bringing moral purpose back into the economy. It was a reform movement aimed at "giving justice from above." William Kent, another so-called Progressive, argued that no progress could come from below; it could only come when natural leaders like him chose to serve the people rather than pursue their own self-interest. Such reform-minded politicians countered power with more power—the power of the good man who should be given authority to intervene.[18]

Muir pursued a somewhat different strategy as a social reformer: encouraging the rich and powerful to heed their feelings for nature, to live for more than money, to set aside areas of great natural beauty that could liberate their better selves. He too supported the ideal of good government as a counterweight to the private sector, but he feared that politicians were no more to be trusted than businessmen to revere and protect God's creation. Thus, he would work with the Harrimans as well as the Roosevelts. He would work with anyone, those in power as well as those on the bottom of society, who appreciated nature.

What needed to be changed, he declared to John Burroughs, was the whole mentality of "our dollar-seeking, dollar-sick nation," a devilish materialism that ran through all levels and into all corners of society.[19] Capitalism, or what he often called "commercialism," was originally responsible for that sickness, but it had spread so far as to infect even social reformers as well as corporate executives, Democrats as well as Republicans, women as well as men. He denounced a "money madness" that had distorted the country's judgment and corrupted its virtue, taking possession of people's heads so that they could not think clearly about the ends of life or accept any restraint on their appetite. Instead of proposing some new ideal of political leadership, a turn to the "best people" to rule over capitalism, he tried to lead his fellow citizens toward new ideas and values in their personal lives that could contain that widespread materialistic virus. He taught them to cultivate leisure instead of endless work. He argued that they should be content with what they had and respect and revere something greater than humankind. To some extent and with some people he felt he was succeeding. With the likes of the Lukens or the Hookers or the Harrimans, he sensed an awakening to that post-materialist way of life. Rich though they were, those people were not yet dead spiritually.

Muir's mission of reform crossed lines of class, gender, and education, but mainly the people who looked to him for guidance were those who had grown up in but given up on traditional Protestant Christianity. They had ceased going to church or looking to the established ministry for answers. Typically, they lived in the northeastern part of the country, the upper Midwest, or the West Coast—people like the Hookers, who had separated themselves from religious orthodoxy by the influence of science, Transcendentalism, or other liberalizing influences. Whether they went into business or education, law or the arts, they commonly hungered for a faith to replace the one they had known as children.

Here, for example, is one of Muir's converts to the religion of nature, a desk-bound Charles Elliott writing from Portland, Oregon: "We, who are not able to keep in constant communion with the great out-doors, need some-one to bring that vast domain to our desks and our evening lamp, and to keep alive in us that, too often smothered, natural impulse to get close to Mother Earth at every opportunity." Compelled by the pressures of a business career to live in the city, Elliott found that "writings such as yours bring into my life the sparkling, invigorating ozone of the snow-purified mountain-tops, which goes far toward expelling the dust and smoke with which the City fills my lungs. Books such as yours, and the distant view I have daily of snow capped Hood make my days at least endurable." In an earlier time Elliott might have been content to kneel in a pew every Sunday, but now he sought the mountains, where Mother Earth or Nature's God could be touched and felt.[20]

Traditional Protestantism, with its ethos of hard work, postponement of gratification, and self-reliance, had helped create an economic powerhouse in the United States as it had in northern Europe. It had energized men like Harriman better than any legislation or natural instinct could have done to build a nation of rails, banks, steel mills, and productive farms. But among some Americans, the work ethic, along with the old Christian theology, was weakening its hold; and Muir was one of those cutting away its roots. He wanted to free others, and free himself, from the kind of workaholic temperament that he had seen in his father or on the Indianapolis factory floor. All his adult life he had been seeking a new era devoted to deliberate, health- and spirit-enhancing leisure in the presence of nature.[21]

His post-Protestant ethic was never intended to encourage frivolous cafe society or cheap amusements but rather to send more people hiking and camping in God's wilderness. Nature was the best tonic for the nation's diseased way of thinking—more efficacious than any high-minded president or any government regulation at encouraging a spirit of generosity and philanthropy among the rich and more useful than a settlement house or a union card in restoring the mental and physical health of the poor. He did not criticize market regulations, unions, or reform politics but found them all inadequate. The best remedy for the ills of an industrial, class-divided society was popular access to nature and a shared vision of nature's divine harmony.

Yet in his religious teaching Muir allowed a telling distinction between ordinary and extraordinary nature. Ordinary nature, represented by places like Klamath Basin, could be turned over to developers like the railroad men or reclamationists; extraordinary nature, on the other hand, represented by spectacular Yosemite Valley or

Mt. Rainier, must be saved from the blight of development. Thus, the religion of nature came to be focused on setting aside showy temples and cathedrals, not protecting more commonplace wayside chapels—on preserving forested, mountainous places far away from human population centers and inaccessible to many Americans. Thus, they offered little directly to the poor urban dweller, who could not afford a ticket or time to visit them. Politically, the distinction between ordinary and extraordinary nature would be difficult to make and easily susceptible to economic influence.

Proposing a new religion to cure America's obsession with riches was by no means an unprecedented project, for from his youth Muir had sought such a faith for himself and his contemporaries. But as Muir had grown older, more celebrated, and more befriended by the rich and powerful, his faith had changed in subtle ways. It became more permissive in the latitude it allowed to wealth and progress.

The young Muir had gone into nature without much money, wearing rough-and-tumble clothes, camping with anyone he met, regardless of their skin color or social standing. He loved mountains but also prairies, marshes, and every tree or flower, humble or grand. Then he had been on fire with the rising spirit of liberal democracy, exemplified by Burns and Wordsworth, Emerson and Thoreau, Humboldt and Rousseau, and felt deeply the connections between a radical social vision of equality and a vision of nature's divine harmony.

The old Muir, in contrast, kept company with a "better" sort of people and often traveled in luxuriant style. His old love of conversation and thirst for friendship did not disappear, but now when he talked and talked to those he met it was, ironically, to those whom he had scorned in his thousand-mile walk to the Gulf of Mexico: "civilized, law-abiding gentlemen in favor either of a republican form of government or of a limited monarchy."[22]

It would misleading to call the old Muir a conservative, for the label would imply that he defended the propertied classes and resisted reform or revolution. He never repudiated his youthful ideals nor tried to emulate the rich in his private life nor defended them as a class. He continued to oppose the concentration of power in monopolies or social elites. He used the word "capitalist" as a term of reproach. He denounced laissez-faire ideology as the "gobble gobble school of economics." Those persistent critical attitudes, on the other hand, did not make him a dangerous or imminent threat to privilege, for he took little interest in politics or economics, seemed indifferent or helpless about the growing inequality in society, and never questioned whether religion could be a sufficient answer to capitalism. Consequently, his message to the elite classes could be easily misinterpreted as a license to pursue money six days a week, while on the seventh they should go to the mountains.

⚬━✦━⚬

One of the wealthiest men in San Francisco, James Phelan, never went to the mountains on any day nor evinced any feeling for wild nature. Son of an Irish Catholic immigrant who had come to California in 1849 and made a fortune in banking, Phelan had grown up in the city and made its aggrandizement his ruling passion—not merely the concentrated settlement at the tip of the peninsula but the future metropolis that he imagined growing up around the entire Bay, absorbing even the Santa Clara Valley far to the south. He was a man of considerable property interests; private profit and public good always intermingled in his schemes. Mainly he dreamed of a city to rival Chicago, Paris, or Rome in size and global influence. In 1902 he heard about the Hetch Hetchy Valley in Yosemite National Park and immediately coveted it for his imperial design.

Phelan became mayor of San Francisco in 1897 and proceeded, illegally the courts said, to dismiss a majority of the Board of Supervisors on a charge of corruption. During the rest of his three terms he would try to run city affairs with an iron fist and a big thirst, showing little regard for his opponents. Reports came to him from various engineers in the federal government and the city's public works department that a deep, easily dammed valley lay high on the Sierra flanks, one hundred fifty miles from the city and nearly a mile above sea level, with an abundance of pure, clear water flowing through it from a melting snow pack. Disregarding its location within Yosemite Park, the U.S. Geological Survey had identified it as a prime reservoir site. The mayor rushed to secure it for the city before any competing interests could get there. An employee of the USGS, Joseph Lippincott, secretly drew up cost estimates for a dam at Hetch Hetchy and another at Lake Eleanor, also within the park, and an aqueduct to bring the water to San Francisco. The estimated price would be $38 million, or about what it would cost to buy out the privately owned, monopolistic Spring Valley Water Company, which had furnished a local supply for decades. Then Lippincott filed a claim, in Phelan's name but for the sake of the city, on a reservoir site in the national park. Thus began a decade-long assault on the park that would involve three U.S. presidents, various secretaries of the Department of Interior, the Congress, the press, the Sierra Club, and Muir.[23]

Photograph of Hetch Hetchy Valley before it was dammed for San Francisco's water supply. (H-A, JMP)

Even cold-eyed engineers extolled Hetch Hetchy's natural beauty as gem-like and regretted that it might one day have to be flooded. But for Phelan nature had little emotional appeal and only one purpose: to enrich his and other human beings' lives. In an article entitled, "Hetch Hetchy for the Wealth-Producer," he dismissed the nature lovers as self-indulgent, pleasure seeking "fox hunters," descendants of the English aristocracy who would deny the "toiling masses," or the real wealth producers, access to resources. Happiness lies in "unobstructed prosperity," he argued, not only for the present inhabitants of San Francisco but also for all those to come—and he hoped they would be multitudes. Some day, he predicted, the state would count fifty million residents, all wanting water, homes, and jobs. Anyone who would protect the park was denying those future residents and "obstructing the wheels of progress." Switching epithets, he lumped the nature lovers with primitive white or Indian hunters. "The hunter is the forerunner of the pioneer," he wrote, "but we cannot maintain the conditions of the wilderness when the pioneer wants to build a home."[24]

In 1900 San Francisco consumed 25 million gallons of water a day. The Spring Valley Company could furnish no more than 35 million gallons, so the city was already approaching the limits of local supply. In another half century per capita consumption, the city's boosters predicted, would nearly double, and with population growth, the demand would total 180 million gallons a day. Half of that current consumption, according to a Stanford professor of engineering, was wasted, and much of the projected increase in consumption would likewise be wasted. Phelan, however, was not interested in achieving wise or careful use of a limited resource; he was not a conservationist, he was a cornucopian. He wanted the city's cup filled and running over—water not merely for pioneer homes but for luscious green lawns, ornate fountains, and a feeling of unlimited abundance. His creed was exactly that of the legendary William Mulholland, head of the Los Angeles Department of Water and Power: "If we don't get the water, we won't need it."[25]

A plentitude of fresh water ran off the California highlands, and the techniques of capturing it for urban real-estate development were not difficult. The big problems were mainly legal and economic: water flowed through an elaborate system of rights, claims, and human desires established by various levels of government and a slew of private interests, including rural irrigators, mining companies, electric power utilities, and, increasingly, conservationists.

An example of the latter's growing agency in the waterscape came in 1905 when Muir's affluent disciple William Kent purchased 611 acres covered with coastal redwood forest in Marin County, across the Golden Gate from San Francisco. Through the ancient forest ran limpid Redwood Creek, from Mt. Tamalpais down to the Pacific shore, a stream as attractive to the water seekers (there were rumors of a dam and reservoir to follow deforestation) as the trees were to the lumbermen. By saving "this beautiful and restful wilderness" from exploiters "who for a few dirty dollars would have deprived millions of their birthright," Kent wrote, he was acting on Muir's philosophy—conserving both forest beauty and health-giving watershed.[26]

A few years later Kent deeded half of that purchase to the federal government for a national monument, under the terms of the 1906 Antiquities Act, which had protected the Petrified Forest. Gifford Pinchot oversaw the document of transfer, and the President received it enthusiastically. Kent named the new monument Muir Woods in tribute to his teacher's vision. Others had named after the naturalist several plant species, an Alaskan glacier, a mountain, and many young trees planted in schoolyards ("Muir Trees," the students called them), but this was the finest recognition ever given him, bringing a gush of gratitude.

> Saving these woods from the axe & saw, from money-changers & water changers, & giving them to our country & the world is in many ways the most notable service to God & man I've heard of since my forest wanderings began—a much needed lesson & blessing to saint & sinner alike. That so fine divine a thing should have come out of money-mad Chicago! Wha wad a' thocht it! Immortal sequoia life to you.

How such deeds shine, Muir wrote right after the announcement in January 1908, "amid the mean commercialism & apathy so destructively prevalent these days."[27]

Other watersheds, however, did not have charismatic redwoods or philanthropic angels to defend them from the politics of grab, negotiate, buy and sell. San Francisco was, like all other cities, including Los Angeles and Oakland, required to purchase water from private companies or purchase land and water rights to create a municipally owned supply. In the Sierra highlands Mayor Phelan and his staff of engineers and lawyers were blessed with an abundance of possible rivers to divert and lakes to drain. But the only site that offered perfect conditions for their project and was miraculously free of all encumbrance and private ownership was the Hetch Hetchy Valley. Here they might dam and flood completely free of any charge. They could claim California's finest *and* cheapest water. The great Yosemite Valley might have served even better for a reservoir, but then it had many worshipful fans who would fight to preserve it. Hetch Hetchy, in contrast, was almost unknown to the public. No well-off nature lover like William Kent stood in the way, no speculators had staked out a prior claim, none but a few politicians in Washington controlled the resource and they could be easily persuaded to give the water away for free.

A complaisant congressman from Stockton persuaded his fellow legislators to pass the Right of Way Act (1901), giving the Secretary of the Interior the power to permit canals, pipe lines, tunnels, or other water conduits through California's national parks. Neither Muir nor the Sierra Club raised any protest; they simply were unaware of what was going on. Had they been paying attention, they still might not have objected because the act did not contemplate any large water reservoirs and it did stipulate that the Secretary must honor the purposes for which the parks had been established by safeguarding their beauty and natural wonders. On 20 January 1903 Secretary of the Interior Ethan Hitchcock, a conservative Republican and holdover from the McKinley administration, denied a permit for reservoir rights at Lake Eleanor and Hetch Hetchy as a violation of Yosemite Park's purposes.

He denied repeat petitions from San Francisco again on 22 December 1903 and once again on 20 February 1905.[28]

Phelan and his fellow boosters, including City Attorney Franklin Lane and Chief Engineer Marsden Manson, were outraged by this unexpected impediment to their scheme. Worse, Phelan was now out of office, although still a power behind the scene, and the new mayor, Eugene Schmitz, had decided that any further pursuit of a Hetch Hetchy water supply was futile. San Francisco, concluded the Schmitz faction, must follow the lead of Oakland across the bay and begin looking seriously at other, somewhat more expensive sources.[29]

Hitchcock's stubbornness proved only a temporary setback. Events over the next few years gave the Phelan scheme new life. First, the city's anti-Phelan and anti-Hetch Hetchy mayor discredited his position by accepting a bribe from a rival water scheme. Then the San Francisco earthquake and fire evoked sympathy throughout the nation for the embattled city and awareness of its inadequate plumbing, although no amount of water could have prevented the breaking of pipes and hydrants. Then, in spring 1907 Secretary Hitchcock resigned from office and was quickly replaced by an Ohio lawyer and U.S. senator, James R. Garfield, son of an assassinated president. A liberal Republican and staunch ally of Roosevelt and Gifford Pinchot, Secretary Garfield signaled that he might reopen hearings on a permit to build a dam in Hetch Hetchy Valley.

Garfield's sudden revival of the permit question awakened Muir from wheezy old age, family anxieties, and inward-looking memories. Could it be true that the president he had so trusted, and had camped with in Yosemite, might after all betray him? Would his administration, which had done so much for forests, wildlife, and national parks and monuments, now allow the invasion of an unspoiled valley? On 2 September he wrote to Robert Underwood Johnson that, incredibly, they were in a fight once more, and this one "promises to be the worst ever."[30] The first phase of that fight would last another nine months, ending in May 1908, a few weeks after his seventieth birthday, a frantic and fearful time that left Muir feeling bitter, exhausted, disappointed, but still clinging to hope.

To remind himself of what he was fighting for, he led artist Keith on a pack trip into Hetch Hetchy, with the idea of producing a magazine article that would tell Americans what was at stake there. "After my first visit in the autumn of 1871," he wrote, "I have always called it the Tuolumne Yosemite, for it is a wonderfully exact counterpart of the great Yosemite, not only in its crystal river and sublime rocks and waterfalls, but in the gardens, groves, and meadows of its flowery, park-like floor."[31] Standing waist-deep in the grass among aromatic pines, one felt humbled by encircling stone monoliths like Kolana, nearly 2,000 feet high, and plunging falls like Tueeulala. The walled valley was only three miles long, half the length of its more famous counterpart, but blessedly free of hotels and dusty wagon roads.

The magazine article, published in November (with, unfortunately, not a single illustration from Keith) reminded people of why parks had been created in the first place—to satisfy "a natural beauty hunger" in poor and rich alike, "for everybody needs beauty as well as bread, places to play in and pray in where Nature may heal and cheer and give strength to body and soul alike." This therapeutic place, he warned, so little known to the outside world, was threatened by

> robbers of every degree from Satan to Senators, city supervisors, lumbermen, cattlemen, farmers, etc., trying to make everything dollarable, oftentimes disguised in smiles and philanthropy, calling their plundering "utilization of natural beneficent resources," that man and beast may be fed and the Nation allowed to grow great. Thus the Lord's garden in Eden and the first forest reservation, including only one tree, was spoiled. And so to some extent have all our reservations and parks.

The schemers counted on public ignorance and gullibility to get their way, but Muir was confident that ninety percent of San Franciscans, if they saw the valley, would oppose its damming. "The voice of the San Francisco Board of Supervisors is not the voice of California nor of the Nation."[32]

A revised version of the article appeared in the *Sierra Club Bulletin*, illustrated with dazzling photographs by Club members and refuting the arguments made by dam proponents. San Francisco could satiate even a Phelan-sized thirst by tapping a long list of other watersheds; they might have to pay a few million dollars to do so, but the cost would be amortized over a long period. Almost none of the proponents had actually visited the valley, yet they denigrated its qualities and extolled the "improvements" they would introduce. Far from making a splendid natural-looking lake in the mountains, as promised, they would make only a rough imitation of nature at best and, in times when the water level was lowered by urban demand, an ugly man-made storage tank with slimy sides and exposed rotted stumps.

Muir could no longer contain his anger over such deception masking base greed: "These temple-destroyers, devotees of ravaging commercialism," expressed a "perfect contempt for Nature, and instead of lifting their eyes to the mountains, lift them to dams and town skyscrapers. Dam Hetch-Hetchy! As well dam for water-tanks the people's cathedrals and churches, for no holier temple has ever been consecrated by the hand of man."[33]

In Muir's eyes, Americans in establishing the national park had done nothing less than create a sacred place. He could still see the past effects of sheep and cattle grazing in the valley, but nature was quickly recovering from those profane traces—"rewilding," as later preservationists would say—and restoring itself to an Eden-like state as holy as any the Bible ever described. Throughout the coming ages the public would cherish it as a place to "play," to camp or hike in pursuit of physical or mental health, but also to "pray," for this would be more than a mere sporting field. Its highest and best use would be religious.

Muir did not claim any special revelation or a mantle of priesthood for himself in that new religion. Anyone could see and read Hetch Hetchy's spiritual truth, so that his role was merely to draw attention, describing and explaining what he saw, encouraging others to come to this consecrated ground and experience it on their own—and to defend it against the blind infidel. Among those enemies, he feared, were bad influences around the president, most dangerously the president's conservation advisor, Gifford Pinchot.

Pinchot, whom Muir had regarded warily ever since Sargent had complained about his political opportunism, had been encouraging Phelan's scheme for years and may have had something to do with Hitchcock's replacement by Garfield. He professed to be open minded, but open to whose desires? In late summer 1907 Pinchot attended an irrigation congress in Sacramento and, as an honorary member of the Sierra Club, came to the directors' meeting where Hetch Hetchy was the subject. He confessed that he had never seen the valley, was not even aware that it lay within the park, and then eased himself out of the room by recommending that the Club seek from the secretary a balanced hearing. Muir took his advice and began writing letters to Roosevelt and Garfield, but also to the Appalachian Mountain Club in Boston, the Alpine Club in New York, and anyone else he knew on the East Coast—editors, bureaucrats, old friends—who might persuade Garfield to turn down the permit.[34]

His underlings, President Roosevelt wrote, "are rather favorable to the Hetch Hetchy plan, but not definitely so." He was likewise ambivalent—mixed in loyalties, divided in sentiments, and watching which way the wind might blow. "I will do everything in my power," he wrote, "to protect not only the Yosemite, which we have already protected, but other similar great natural beauties of this country." Then he added a telling qualification: protection must have the support of California's citizens or it would fail. If people disagreed with park protection, if they saw it as an interference "with the permanent material development of the State instead of helping the permanent material development, the result will be bad." So far he had heard little support for Hetch Hetchy's preservation, which put him in "the disagreeable position" of protecting a valley that "apparently hardly anyone wanted to have kept, under national control."[35]

Muir interpreted Roosevelt's ambivalence as a lack of presidential leadership and a disregard for strict interpretation of the law, for national commitments made long ago, and for the principles of true conservation. After all, if Hitchcock had had no fear of turning the

Phelan party down, on the basis that he had no legal authority to permit an intrusion that would radically change the park's natural features, Roosevelt could have instructed Garfield to do the same. He was, after all, celebrated as a conservation-minded president, and he was in his final months in the White House. He could at least leave it to Congress to decide whether the people wanted the valley handed over or not. Taking either stance, however, risked offending powerful men in the West's largest city, and that was a consideration always looming in the politician's mind.

Some have argued that the Hetch Hetchy controversy symbolized a clash between the utilitarian doctrine of the "greatest good of the greatest number of people for the longest time" and a "sentimental" aesthetic and spiritual yearning for wild country. Roosevelt, however, was not arguing philosophical principles but a greater sensitivity to public attitudes and the necessity of accommodating them. Muir, in contrast, thought most Americans, including Californians, were on his side, that the administration was too timid in reading the popular will; it was not listening to the voice of the people but to the rumble of money and political clout, looking forward to future elections, including perhaps a Pinchot run for the White House.

The utilitarian doctrine of "wise use" of natural resources, which Pinchot especially championed within the administration, was an ill-defined concept that had little scientific or economic foundation. What did "wise use" or "the greatest good" mean and who decided that meaning? Who did the counting up of the "greatest number of people"? Pinchot gave few answers; his notion of "wise use" was more a slogan than a well-grounded philosophy, one loose enough to allow ambitious politicians to gain control over natural resources while satisfying the business community that they were not anti-business. Often the doctrine focused on determining not what "the people" wanted but on what the most powerful people wanted, or would support. "Wise use" may have hinted at some principled interference with free-market forces, the tempering of exploitation with wisdom, but in practice that interference was nonsystematic and nonadversarial, and was advanced as a way to achieve a more "business-like" outcome.[36]

Muir, whose life had long demonstrated considerable prudence and economic rationality, had never opposed "wise use" as part of conservation, including the selective harvesting of trees, the damming of waterways for irrigation, and even the destruction of wildlife habitat for economic development. He had allowed such use, private or public, all over the map. But the creation of a national park, in his view, was not about using natural resources more efficiently or protecting consumers from monopoly prices, but of consecrating a small part of nature, through liberal democratic processes, to higher ends. No cabal of capitalists and bureaucrats, with extravagant dreams of urban or national grandeur, should be permitted to overturn that expression of natural piety. To give the capitalists whatever they wanted, as the Roosevelt administration apparently was leaning toward doing, was not principled compromise but surrender.

On 11 May 1908 Garfield announced he was reversing his predecessor's decision and allowing San Francisco to build reservoirs at Lake Eleanor and Hetch Hetchy. In his long months of deliberation he had deliberately disregarded all arguments that there were good, affordable alternatives; "it is sufficient that after careful and competent study the officials of the city insist . . . that this is the only practicable and reasonable source of water supply for the city." He refused to scrutinize the city leaders' claims or question that their self-interest was in the nation's best interest. But he did impose, under Roosevelt's pressure, a few conditions on the permit, including a requirement that the voters of San Francisco approve, by a two-thirds majority, the expenditure of funds for dam construction, and, most important, that the city fully utilize the waters of Lake Eleanor first and build a reservoir in Hetch Hetchy only after it had reached the limit of the Eleanor supply.[37]

That staggered order of development Garfield and his boss regarded as a reasonable compromise between city needs and nature protection. Muir reluctantly went along, allowing that turning Lake Eleanor into a reservoir "would do but little harm to the park." A letter from the president that he shared with Sierra Club secretary William Colby, marking it "strictly private & confidential," acknowledged Muir as the source of the Solomonic solution. Roosevelt wrote, "I am trying to see if we can not leave the things on the line that you indicate—that is, damming Lake Eleanor & letting San Francisco depend for a generation or so upon that & the Tuolumne tributaries. But of course I must see that S.F. has an adequate water supply."[38]

Muir was not pleased to have been pushed so close to the wall, but he had indeed yielded. Angry though he was at Pinchot's "false twaddle" and conniving ways, his readiness to give "everything to politicians & rich schemers," the old man tried to find some bright lining to the cloud hovering over his beloved park. He tried not to look on the Garfield decision as a defeat but instead as a reprieve, after which another generation would have to reconsider the valley's fate. To Helen he wrote: "Hetch Hetchy is safe for at least a generation or so & we hope forever. In the meantime S.F. is to have Lake Eleanor for a reservoir under many restrictions, & in no case is H.H. to be touched until Eleanor & Cherry Creek sources are developed to utmost capacity. Which will not be in our days."[39]

Forty-eight hours after the Garfield decision was handed down—the timing was not incidental, for the secretary was rushing to bury a divisive issue—President Roosevelt stood before a gathering of all the nation's governors and many special guests to sell conservation as necessary for national survival. The protection of nonhuman life or of natural beauty, or even of outdoor recreational opportunity, had vanished from the agenda; a more material strategy of avoiding resource depletion and national decline was all that mattered. The idea for calling the governors together came from Robert Underwood Johnson, but the message he heard was not exactly what he had in mind. Johnson was in the crowd, as a member of the periodical press, along with J. Horace McFarland of the American Civic Association, but they were the sole representatives of the nature aesthetes. All the politicians, manufacturers, engineers, public health advocates, and bureaucrats, who were the designated audience, overwhelmed them, and that audience helped narrow the meaning of conservation down to a road map leading toward long-term economic prosperity.

Roosevelt rose to greet his powerful guests and to warn what lay ahead if the nation continued on a path of wasteful production and consumption:

> The conservation of our natural resources and their proper use constitute the fundamental problem which underlies almost every other problem of our National life. Unless we maintain an adequate material basis for our civilization, we can not maintain the institutions in which we take so great and so just a pride; and to waste and destroy our natural resources means to undermine these material bases.

"We have become great in a material sense," he argued, "because of the lavish use of our resources, and we have just reason to be proud of our growth. But the time has come to inquire seriously what will happen when our forests are gone, when the coal, the iron, the oil, and the gas are exhausted, when the soils shall have been still further impoverished and washed into the streams, polluting the rivers, denuding the fields, and obstructing navigation." The impending collapse of the American empire was Roosevelt's theme. A state planned and managed economy was his remedy. The conference of governors offered a technocrat's response to Armageddon.[40]

Muir was not invited to the conference nor would his views have been well received in such a political gathering, for he would have questioned the very materialism that Roosevelt appealed to, along with his message of impending doom. The United States was in no danger of economic collapse, Muir would have scoffed, only of losing its soul. The White House was attempting to redefine and popularize conservation and did not want any competing views, even if it meant excluding some of the nation's most widely known conservationists. The Sierra Club sent a letter to the delegates reminding them of "the paramount value of scenic beauty among our natural resources." Muir praised the event as "novel & notable" and continued to admire Roosevelt. But he could not praise Pinchot's self-inflating role in orchestrating the conference or trying to seize control of the conservation movement, for "he never hesitates to sacrifice anything or anyone in his way."[41]

Less than a year later Roosevelt was out of office, and his Secretary of War William Howard Taft was elected president. Pinchot was still head of the Forest Service, but a Seattle lawyer and former General Land Office commissioner, Richard Ballinger, had replaced Garfield. If anyone assumed that the Hetch Hetchy issue had been resolved, they were mistaken. Phelan's men were not willing to wait another generation or two to build their dam in the valley; they wanted it badly and they wanted it now. Even before Roosevelt was packed up and out of town, they were back knocking at the Department of Interior's door, asking for a new ruling, while simultaneously lobbying Congress for a legislative decision that would give them what they wanted. Throughout Taft's entire term, they would tirelessly knock and knock, refusing to take the Garfield decision as final. After all, they could be patient; the water supply they sought was not to quench an immediate need but to realize a distant rose-colored dream.

Disgusted and incredulous, Muir girded up for a more prolonged battle, this one far more expensive for it would require sending lobbyists to Washington to persuade legislators to deny a permit. Much of the cost of the campaign would have to come out of his own pocket and those of a few friends, none of them truly rich, while San Francisco had a public treasury to draw on—bundles of money to pay the salaries of lawyers and engineers, to fund the gathering of data, to commission beguiling pictures of a made-over valley. Most of the front-line defense against that juggernaut would fall on the shoulders of three men: William Colby, secretary of the Sierra Club and a junior lawyer in a firm headed by one of the dam's key supporters; Edward Parsons, talented San Francisco writer and photographer and member of the Club's executive committee; and William Badè, professor of Old

Testament literature and Semitic languages at the Pacific Theological Seminary, Berkeley, and editor of the *Sierra Club Bulletin*. Muir met with them often, but mainly he sat at home wielding his pen, generating a Sierra-like blizzard of letters to politicians and opinion makers.

Remarkably, after losing ground while his old camping friends Roosevelt and Pinchot were in office, Muir and his lieutenants began to regain ground with a new administration in Washington that seemed to care little about camping or conservation. With Taft in office, Muir's star rose, while Pinchot's fell. The friends of Hetch Hetchy worked to mobilize support across the whole nation, from Los Angeles to Boston, creating one of the first grassroots environmental campaigns in American history. Women, although still unable to vote in national elections, joined the cause and became vital players. Muir sometimes misunderstood the strategy he helped to devise, as when he told Colby, "If the great corporations are with us we will win."[42] In the end it was not those corporations, not concentrated, or even individual, wealth that gave their movement strength, but the zeal and devotion they awakened among the intelligent, middling classes, both men and women.

In February and March 1909, as the nation's capital was preparing for Taft's inauguration, Muir traveled southward to dry out his lungs and lobby friends and newspapers. At the Petrified Forest he met John Burroughs and journeyed with him to the south rim of the Grand Canyon and to southern California. In an interview with editor Harrison Gray Otis, Muir won support from the powerful *Los Angeles Times*. He came home convinced that the farther he went from San Francisco, the less enthusiasm for its schemes he could find either in elite or popular opinion. Burroughs proved a harder case to persuade. The two Johnnies saw Yosemite together later that spring, where they spatted over who loved nature more and whether Burroughs would aid Hetch Hetchy's cause. Adamantly he would not, partly because he was indifferent to its fate, partly because he was irritated by Muir's relentless argumentativeness. "I love you," said Burroughs, "though at times I want to punch you or thrash the ground with you."[43]

A few members of the Sierra Club proved just as hard to persuade and took San Francisco's side in the dispute. The city's engineer and chief Phelan mouthpiece, Marsden Manson, a member of the Club, started a revolt from within, taking with him Warren Olney, one of the founding directors, David Starr Jordan, president of Stanford, and a few others. The Club's hikes and outings were becoming more fractious, to the delight of papers like the San Francisco *Call,* which gleefully trumpeted a major schism in the organization. The Club's leaders were cruel to mothers and babies, Manson charged, and yet they were soft and effeminate, "admirers of verbal lingerie and frills." They did not reflect the members' more robust views. But in a club referendum on the matter, 589 (a clear majority of the total membership) favored keeping Hetch Hetchy in its natural state, while only 161 voted to turn it into a reservoir. Still, to avoid tearing the Club apart, Muir and other dam opponents decided to create another organization, the Society for the Preservation of the National Parks, and to remove the Sierra Club from the lobbying business.[44]

Taking a cue from Manson and his attacks on dam opponents as "short-haired women and long-haired men," an editorial cartoon in the *Call* portrayed Muir as a stout old woman in a dress, apron, and bonnet, trying to sweep back the Hetch Hetchy project with a straw broom. In the cartoon a torrent of water pours out of the rock-girded mouth of a valley, not dammed by modern technology but wildly raging out of control and threatening to destroy everything in its path. Muir, weak and futile as a woman, cannot stop the masculine force of the current. So all the nature lovers, all the flower-loving "sentimentalists," will be swept away by the irresistible force of urban development.

As the conservation movement began to attract many women as well as men to its ranks, some male conservationists began to feel anxious about their role as reformers and their place in society as a whole. Worried that defending birds, plants, or beauty in the landscape might make them appear less than masculine, they began to make a distinction between grassroots activists (a suspect category where most women belonged) and professional environmental managers (hard-headed, practical-minded men like themselves). Muir, according to that categorization, fell into the first group. Nobody had ever questioned his

Sweeping Back the Flood

San Francisco Call *cartoon lampooning Muir as an effeminate "nature lover."*
(*Holway Jones,* John Muir and the Sierra Club)

strength, bravery, or fortitude in the face of lashing storms or daunting rock climbs. He had been a man's man who nonetheless looked
on women as equal partners in understanding and who believed that
a passion for all things natural slumbered in everyone, regardless of
gender. Such passion was now suspect.[45]

As the Hetch Hetchy debate entered a new phase of widened controversy, requiring a nation-wide mobilization of nature lovers, Muir
wisely paid no attention to that campaign of denigration. He welcomed
the assistance of many women, within the Club and beyond. Perhaps
the most effective among his female allies was the Chicago scholar and

editor, Harriet Monroe, who founded the magazine *Poetry* in 1912. Over the preceding two decades she had discovered the wilderness of Arizona and California and had joined the Sierra Club after trekking with its members through Hetch Hetchy valley. Muir recruited her for the Society for the Preservation of National Parks' advisory board, and on its behalf she testified before congressional committees that were beginning to take up the question of damming the valley. She proved one of the Society's most effective spokespersons. "It is for you," she instructed senators at their first hearing on the subject, "to keep this treasure intact for the future, to pass it on, like a crown jewel to the generations who shall know and love it." The highest use to which the valley could be put was to inspire "a nation's art."[46]

To the surprise and discomfiture of the gender-baiting dam proponents, the most important men in the Taft administration—the president himself and his Interior secretary Ballinger—proved friendly to preservation. In contrast to their predecessors, these politicians were not inclined to give the city everything it wanted and certainly not to give it Hetch Hetchy. In February 1910 Secretary Ballinger asked San Francisco to demonstrate why the valley should not be deleted altogether from the Garfield permit, forcing the city for the first time to prove a need for this particular site.

Signs were looking favorable for such a tilt toward preservation months earlier, but it took intense lobbying in Washington by Johnson of the *Century* and important face-to-face conversations with Muir in the setting of the park to persuade the new administration to reexamine the compromise that Roosevelt had forged. Johnson argued to the president and his secretary that it was illegal for any cabinet officer to overturn a law passed by Congress, which is what the Hetch Hetchy grant amounted to. Then he showed photographs of the valley to Ballinger, who was astonished by its beauty and wanted to see the place. Taft jumped in ahead, writing to Muir that he wanted his company on a trip to Yosemite Valley and another to Alaska. Muir gladly accepted the new president's overture, adding that "giving the slightest hold on Hetch Hetchy to the San Francisco schemers was the one great mistake of the Roosevelt administration." Taft and Muir met in Yosemite Valley in

October 1909, and a few weeks later Ballinger showed up for a guided tour of Hetch Hetchy, never before seen by a high federal official.[47]

Taft would have looked more at home among the walruses of Alaska—he was a round mustachioed giant of a man—than on the steep trails around Yosemite. In many ways, though, he was a man of contradictions and surprises: a Protestant who did not believe in the divinity of Christ, a pro-business trust-buster, a former minister of war who was a pacifist, a strict constructionist of the law, and despite his girth an energetic hiker. He spent three days reveling in the valley's famed sights. Despite a good deal of ribbing he gave Muir for his anti-commercialism, the president seemed committed to protecting the national parks against exploiters. "The merriest man I ever saw," Muir wrote, "& he made all his company merry. The birds & squirrels & deer were half charmed & frightened. Ballinger I also liked & the H.H. scheme seems doomed." As proof of that conclusion Muir offered the president's own published words: Within the parks "all wild things should be protected & the scenery kept wholly unmarred."[48]

How to make such intentions legally sound and binding, not whether conserving nature in the parks against developers was right or not, was Taft and Ballinger's main concern—after all, they were trained lawyers. San Francisco must be given its day in court to make a case for retaining rights to Hetch Hetchy, even if it took years to do so. Further studies were needed, experts must be assembled. Muir and friends, with no particular standing in this hearing and no means to hire their own experts, were forced to wait while the wheels of justice slowly turned.

Then came a bombshell. In the fall of 1909 a Department of the Interior agent, Louis Glavis, charged his boss Ballinger with approving mining claims on public coal-bearing lands in interior Alaska without thorough investigation. Glavis thought he had uncovered a shady deal and took his charges to Pinchot, who went straight to the president. Taft, after a thorough investigation, exonerated his secretary, but Pinchot, dissatisfied with that decision, took the charges to the press. Looking back on the episode forty years later, he was still sure that Taft had whitewashed a crime. A later secretary of Interior, Harold Ickes, disagreed; Ballinger, he concluded after his own investigation, had been the victim of Pinchot's machinations to discredit the Taft administration for political ends. Whatever the truth of those charges and countercharges, Pinchot found himself out of a job—fired for insubordination—by March 1910.[49]

The Pinchot-Ballinger squabble divided the Republican Party into warring factions and eventually brought Theodore Roosevelt back into politics to run against Taft in the next general election. For Muir on the other side of the continent it was a reminder of why he disliked "faithless politics." Yet he took sides in the dispute, fiercely supporting Ballinger and reflecting that "Pinchot seems to have lost his head in coal and timber conservation & forgotten God and his handiwork. He has been our worst enemy in the park fight." Months later he was sorry to see "poor Pinchot running amuck after doing so much good hopeful work—from sound conservation going pell mell to destruction on the wings of crazy inordinate ambition." He was even sorrier to see a burnt-out Ballinger resign from office, in March 1911, and go back to his Seattle law practice, leaving the park's fate once more uncertain.[50]

The Hetch Hetchy hearings dragged on and on in Congress, with San Francisco unable to secure immediate administrative rights to the contested valley or to get legislative approval but opponents unable to stop it decisively. Congressional committees split over the proposed dam, and neither the House nor Senate could produce a positive vote for the city. To counter the city's advantages of money and staff, the preservationists kept on organizing their national movement. To legislators, newspapers, and women's clubs they mailed an illustrated pamphlet entitled "Everyone Help to Save the Famous Hetch-Hetchy Valley," explaining how a dam would, in Muir's words, defraud "ninety millions of people for the sake of saving San Francisco dollars." The pamphlet asked for contributions and provided a form letter to send to key legislators—setting a pattern for future campaigns. The city answered with slickly produced, expert "reports" by hired professionals. In this prolonged trench warfare both sides fired off as many arguments as possible, hoping that some of them would find their target.

Proponents and opponents agreed that the valley should serve some human need but had trouble agreeing even among themselves on what that need was. The city heralded the proposed dam as part of a nationwide liberation from the oppressive hand of monopoly, in this case the private utility Spring Valley Water Company. Yet by 1910 the city had gained the power to regulate the company's water prices, and always it could have exercised the power of eminent domain to secure the company's properties. Monopoly was a specious argument dragged in for effect, concealing the real motive of getting a marvelous source of water (and electric power) for free. Then the city pleaded that, without the dam, its poorer residents might perish from thirst, when in truth the consumers it had in mind had not yet been born. Their arguments were not completely insincere, but they were reluctant to admit that they wanted the dam simply to grow the city.

The park defenders, on the other hand, offered an unstable, incompatible mix of recreation and religion that they called "scenery." Americans, they argued, needed scenic beauty, but they could not really say why a pristine valley was more scenic than one occupied by man-made structures. While Muir may have spoken of conserving the "pure wildness" of the valley, many of his fellow activists seemed not interested in wildness at all. Rather than a reservoir they called for tourist development—hotels, riding stables, and trails like those that Yosemite Valley offered.[51] These defenders wanted to make the place over into an all-season resort, a "playground," while they repeated Muir's notion that this was a consecrated "temple." That twinned vision of outdoor recreation and outdoor religion was an unholy mix; it addressed different needs that potentially were in conflict with each other.

No use of the valley, to be sure, even as a religious sanctuary, could occur without improved public awareness and access. The dam builders promised to cut new roads in and around the valley, and so did their opponents. Even Muir was compelled, if he wanted to defend Hetch Hetchy, to put forth a program of better roads and trails to bring people into its hidden recesses and make its beauty accessible. In fact, he proposed nothing less than "a grand circular drive," comparable to the one in Yellowstone, that would allow travelers to make an easy circuit of all the Yosemite Park's main features. His friend Henry Osborn explained the idea to the publisher of *Collier's Weekly*: the drive would go up the Yosemite Valley and cross the high country to Tuolumne Meadows, then come down the spectacular Tuolumne Canyon into Hetch Hetchy, making "one of the grandest drives" in the world. Muir, he reported, was trying to raise money to build it, "a trifling sum in comparison with the glorious scenery which it will open up to the American people."[52] The proposal shows how far Muir and other defenders would go to save their park. If the park was now "consecrated" ground, not to be despoiled for commercial purposes, they were nonetheless willing to plow a road through it. Far from being a fanatical preservationist or a rigid noncompromiser, Muir showed once again that he, like the scene-stealing Pinchot, could practice the politics of pragmatism, even at the cost of moral clarity.

⚬━✦━⚬

The winter of 1911 found Muir residing in Los Angeles with the Hookers, trying to stitch together a guide book on Yosemite for Johnson's Century Company, and from time to time visiting Helen and her family living out among the vultures and ruffians, the creosote bushes and borax hills. In Pasadena he dined with Theodore Roosevelt, just back from a hunting trip to Africa (now he was hunting for campaign support), and John Burroughs. Remarkably, Muir harbored no hard feelings toward the ex-president, despite his dithering expediency while in office, and lobbied him once more to help save Hetch Hetchy, which Roosevelt promised to do but never would. Muir had his own plans to travel far and wide, to make the last big trip of his life, first going back east and then to South America and Africa. "You know I never like to travel," he professed to Helen, who knew better, "and somehow I feel less and less inclined to leave home than ever."[53] Yet the wandering itch was on him again. When he said fare-well in April, around the time of his seventy-third birthday, he was setting out all alone, on a ramble that would last almost a year.

William Keith died on the eve of departure, leaving a large gap in Muir's most intimate circle. The two Scots immigrants had long shared a love of the outdoors, tramping and disputing up and down the mountains together. Keith had been one of the last of the romantic landscape painters, while Muir preferred black-and-white photographs of the same scenes, which he saw as closer to the objectivity of science; yet they did not disagree that going out to seek the beauty of nature was an act of worship. Keith's death would be followed by the unexpected and simultaneous deaths of John Hooker and Alfred Sellers, whose homes Muir had just left. "I wonder if leaves feel lonely," he asked his daughter, "when they see their neighbors falling."[54]

Once more he climbed aboard a fast continental train, this time riding in the private car of a high-level executive of the Southern Pacific Railroad. They roared through Nebraska, with Muir throwing a kiss at sister Mary as they passed her home, and on to Washington, D.C., where he set out to lobby on behalf of the valley. He met with President Taft, the new secretary of the interior Walter Fisher, Speaker of the House Champ Clark, and "smoked & talked over the whole H.H. history with immortal Joe Cannon in his private room in the capital." Old friends in the federal science agencies, C. Hart Merriam at the Bureau of Biological Survey and Robert Marshall at the Geological Survey, received him warmly, while pleading that their government-funded positions did not allow them to join his crusade—they might lose their jobs or endanger their budgets. At a late-night dinner of the Boone and Crockett Club, an influential group of affluent, conservation-minded big-game hunters, he spoke for an hour and a half on the national parks. It was a marathon performance by the old man, reclaiming his authority as one of America's leading conservationists, whatever his rivals may have done to marginalize him.[55]

In New York he was a literary lion once again, as he had been seven years earlier. Johnson had arranged his election to the American Academy of Arts and Letters, whose highly select roster included

Samuel Clemens (Mark Twain), Winslow Homer, Woodrow Wilson, Henry Adams, and Charles Eliot Norton. The American Alpine Club, which had made him its president, a figurehead job, gave a sumptuous dinner garnished with many accolades. Such a heady reception started a flow of ink from his pen. He hurriedly finished the Yosemite guide-book at the Osborns' spacious summer home on the Hudson and at Mary Harriman's townhouse in the City, secluding himself for days on end. The Century editors took it hot from his hands and rushed it into production, along with a new edition of *The Mountains of California*, with a dedication to his late wife Louie. Also on the swing east he contracted with Houghton Mifflin to bring out his autobiography, extracting a hefty twenty percent royalty on each copy sold along with magazine serial rights; and the Boston firm published, in June, his youthful journal *My First Summer in the Sierra*.

At June commencement time the college dropout accepted another honorary degree, this one a doctorate of letters from Yale University, with full pomp and ceremony and an afternoon baseball game. "When my name was called," he reported to Katherine Hooker, "I arose with a grand air, shook my massive academic plumes into finest fluting folds, . . . stepped forward in awful majesty and stood rigid & solemn like an ancient sequoia . . . while the orator poured praise on the hon-ored wanderer's head—, and in this heroic attitude I think I had better leave him."[56] All these honors he read not merely as evidence of per-sonal fame but also as support for his efforts to save Hetch Hetchy.

Then, with that flurry of books newly in print or soon to be in print, and his stamina and digestion severely tested, Muir left for an extended holiday abroad. On the twelfth of August (far later than planned) he sailed for the coast of Brazil. He was fleeing the political trenches, the social whirligig, and the pressures of being a popular author. Over a long span of years he had done all he could to save the embattled valley; now he planned to "vanish in the wilderness of the other America." Helen had fretted over his traveling so far without a guardian, offering to send her husband Buell to watch over him. His friend at the Geological Survey Robert Marshall had also urged that he needed a younger companion: "I would not let a man who means so much to the world, and especially to these United States, go alone." But Muir shrugged off their worries, for he was feeling rejuvenated by the prospect of global adventure. He would be picking up the trail he had abandoned in 1867 when malaria had prevented his following Alexander von Humboldt. He would be seeing where his life might have led if fate had allowed.[57]

The coal-burning steamer was at sea for two weeks, during which the passengers had little to do but watch the waves and stare at the clouds. Muir had a fresh journal on his knee, but he did not intend to fill it with introspective jottings or assessments of all that had happened in the forty-four years that had passed since he had sailed the Caribbean. This was an opportunity to forget everything on which he had been working and to concentrate on the new, especially on new plants. The amateur botanist yearned to discover a fresh world of Southern Hemisphere vegetation, particularly a few species that he had read about but never seen, and to know them in their native habitat.[58]

Landfall was the city of Pará (later known as Belém), a transshipment point for vessels going up the Amazon River. Once ashore, Muir began scribbling down notes on the wild tropical forests that edged the city and on its fascinating botanical garden, his first stop. Among the unusual plants there was a giant water lily, *Victoria amazonica,* whose leaves could reach eight feet across. Where did it call home, he wondered, and how far away was that? Soon he was heading up river, his boat a mere dot on the Amazon's immense surface, brushing along a tangled bank, fending off droning mosquitoes, sleeping at night under a net with an electric fan stirring the heavy air. Manaus was as far upriver as he got; it sat in the middle of "the greatest forest wilderness in the world," near where the Rio Negro mixes its black water with the tawny Amazon. He never found the water lily in that wild hinterland, but he touched the green world that Humboldt had described so vividly decades earlier.

Speaking no Portuguese, Muir had to depend on the generosity of English-speaking friends, mostly expatriate Americans, whom he met along the way. They were usually in the backcountry to exploit its resources, which mainly meant tapping the *Hevea* rubber trees and exporting the rubber to make tires for the wagon and automobile industry of North America. To connect their remote plantations to the river's currents, they were building a railroad at enormous cost in capital and human lives. Muir's hosts included a young rubber exporter as well as the head of the railroad company, both of whom opened their homes and libraries to him. What they did not know, nor could their guest imagine, was that within a year sales of Brazilian rubber on the world market would collapse, due to competition from Sumatra and Malaya. Muir went away delighted with his explorations and charmed by his hosts (he had met "the best citizens," he wrote to Helen), but learning little about how the Humboldtian paradise was vanishing and how vulnerable the forest was to northern appetites.[59]

The golden fleece of Muir's travels, however, was not to be found in the Amazonian basin. He was looking for a genus of evergreen coniferous trees, the *Araucaria*, that were living fossils dating back to the Mesozoic age. South America boasted only two species; all the rest were native to New Caledonia. One of the American species, *A. angustifolia* (formerly *braziliensis*), grew in southern Brazil and had become the dominant timber tree of the country. The other species, *A. araucana*, popularly known as the monkey-puzzle tree, grew in the Andean foothills of Chile and Argentina. Both looked like immense umbrellas turned inside out. Their long bare stems, rising as high as a hundred feet, terminated in a thick tuft of horizontal, spreading branches. Muir devoted October and November to tracking these species down, passing through such big cities as Rio de Janeiro, São Paulo, Montevideo, and Buenos Aires but paying little attention to them beyond their botanical gardens and consular offices.

The *angustifolia* tree, now one of the world's critically endangered species, then could be found growing by the thousands on the grassy tableland of the state of Paraná. To get there Muir traveled by railroad through a heavily glaciated landscape that reminded him of California and Alaska, before arriving at an intense scene of timber harvesting and milling. He filled his journal with measurements and sketches of the trees. It was, he wrote, the "most interesting forest I have seen in my whole life. Formal, yet variable, and always impressive with auld-lang-syne Sequoia-like physiognomy."[60] He might have been back in Yosemite, he exulted, so similar were the trees and rocks, but here in Brazil there was no protection afforded such beauty at all.

The other species, *Araucaria araucana*, required a long train ride across the Argentine pampas, "one vast, rich, green, grass sod" fenced with barbed wire and grazed by millions of cattle, sheep, and horses. On 11 November he arrived at Santiago, Chile, where the U.S. minister plenipotentiary, who had instructions from President Taft to give him V.I.P. treatment, met him at the station and offered lodging. From his bedroom window at the legation he could see the snowy Andes, but he had come neither for mountain gazing or dinner parties. Instead, he quickly put himself in the hands of a knowledgeable American lumberman who took him hundreds of miles south to show him the unusual forest he sought. From the host's ranch they rode horseback across ridge after ridge, until they spied a long line of the

Muir drawing of an Araucaria *forest on the pages of his South American travel journal, 1911. (H-A, JMP)*

strikingly shaped trees silhouetted against the sky. On the banks of a cold, brawling stream they camped beneath a grove. "A glorious and novel sight," Muir scribbled, "beyond all I had hoped for. Yet I had so long dreamed of it, it seemed familiar. My three companions slept under tarpaulin tents, strangely fearing the blessed mountain air and dew." Despite being the oldest and frailest of the party, he stayed out in the open where he could gaze upward at the trees.[61]

One continent down, another to go. There was no direct passenger service from Montevideo to Capetown, South Africa, so he was forced to sail north to the Canary Islands, where he could book passage southward along the West African coast on the Dutch steamship *Windhuk*. The clouds were often more interesting than his single-minded fellow passengers, most of them headed to the diamond and gold mines. Arriving in Cape Town, he checked into a hotel that stood at the foot of cloud-drenched Table Mountain and headed immediately to the botanical gardens.

With that beguiling introduction to Africa, he took the train to Bulawayo, passing the Kimberley diamond mines and skirting the Kalahari Desert, and then rushed on to the famed Victoria Falls on the Zambezi River. The drifting, smoke-like spray from that thundering cataract created a brilliantly green microhabitat that contrasted strikingly to the tawny desiccated landscape he had been seeing. A native boy led him a mile away from the falls, back into the dry savanna, where he finally came upon the baobab tree, *Adansonia digitata*. That day turned out to be "one of the great tree days of my lucky life."[62]

The baobab represented for him the essence of the African continent's vegetative soul. Before humans intervened, it had been widely dispersed across Africa and India. It can live for thousands of years, giving sustenance to many types of creatures around it—a tree that is also an ecosystem. The massive trunk, which is exceeded only by the sequoia in girth, supports a comparatively scanty tangle of branches, which are leafless most of the year; the ensemble resembles a fat tree that got planted wrong side up, with the bare roots waving in the air. "Strange tree," Muir wrote, "in bark like the skin of an elephant. Corrugated and wrinkled like the skin of hippopotamus." Its natural companions on the savanna included the mopane tree and the myriad varieties of acacia, along with such iconic animals as the lion, giraffe, and wildebeest. Muir had penetrated straight to the warm, brown heart of Africa—and, in contrast to many tourists, including Roosevelt, he did so without firing a shot.[63]

What he did not stop to investigate along the way was the full human story of this continent, so drenched in war and killing, so riven by the forces of tribal competition, age-old slavery, and European imperialism. He did pause to see one of the rockiest places on earth, the Matopos hills near Bulawayo, where the British-born founder of the DeBeers diamond company and colonizer of Rhodesia (now Zimbabwe), Cecil Rhodes, had been buried less than a decade earlier. Although Muir read many books on the human as well as natural history of the regions he was visiting, he discussed in his journal little of what he saw of conflict or abuse. He did not put down any thoughts of a political nature. Only in the picturesque city of Zanzibar did he add a brief note about its "woeful, slave-ful history." He said nothing about the recent English–Afrikaner war in southern Africa or the relentless expansion of the British Empire, which had started with his own native Scotland and was now laying a large hand on Africa. He had only trees in mind.

Nairobi, Kilimanjaro, Lake Victoria, the headwaters of the Nile, the Red Sea, and the Suez Canal all passed before his gaze, until on 9 March 1912, he reached the Italian port city of Naples. The ancient ruins of Pompeii were the last of his tourist stops, before he turned toward America and home. Earlier he had sent off a letter to the Osborns from East Africa, proclaiming, "I've had the most fruitful time of my life on this pair of hot continents." It was a heartfelt phrase that he repeated in letters to Helen, the Hookers, and his Sierra Club comrade Will Colby. But what exactly was the fruit he had collected? "Fain I would write about it," he added, "but it's utterly unletterable."[64]

Whatever the swing through the Southern Hemisphere had done for his mental health or fund of pleasure, it did not provide good material for Muir the author. Back in New York, he had offers to publish something about his travels and began to search for appropriate illustrations to accompany an article or two. He had taken photographs along the way, but he wanted better works of art or scientific description to make his thin journal entries seem more substantive. Eventually he gave up and decided to leave his encounter with the "hot continents" unlettered and unpublished.

After pausing to pick up a copy of his new book, *The Yosemite,* which he dedicated to Robert Underwood Johnson, "originator of the Yosemite National Park," Muir went home to California. Instead of proceeding to the ranch, he settled into his daughter Helen's new home on Formosa Avenue in Hollywood, just months after the first moving picture studio opened down the street. Buel was seeking a fortune in the advertising business, which would fail like all his other misbegotten schemes. Here in a town that would soon become the epitome of American decadence Muir rested from his strenuous travels through the spring and summer and mailed copies of his book, with apologies for the many typographical errors that had crept in during his absence, to friends on several continents. At last in October he motored north toward home, stopping to attend a conference at Yosemite convened by the Interior Department to discuss the management and protection of the national parks.

The leading question at the conference was whether automobiles should be allowed to enter Yosemite. Advocates of the new transportation argued that there would be fewer accidents on the steep grades with autos than with the "pre-historic wagon way." All signs, Muir reported, pointed to a victory for the automobile enthusiasts. "Under certain precautionary restrictions," he supposed, "these useful, progressive, blunt-nosed mechanical beetles will hereafter be allowed to puff their way into all the parks and mingle their gas-breath with the breath of the pines and water-falls, and, from the mountaineer's standpoint, with but little harm or good." Once more he was ceding ground to an intrusive civilization, recommending that nature lovers flee to the higher elevations to escape the unstoppable machines. He even promoted the invasion by repeating his proposed loop road linking all the park's scenic features, to be designed by "landscape gardeners." Surely he realized that such a road would soon be open to automobiles as well as carriages, fouling the air all the way to Tuolumne Meadows. If an automobile or a landscaped road could be tolerated, why not a dam? Or a reservoir circled by good roads and picnic grounds, expressing mankind's harmony with nature, as cleverly proposed by San Francisco?[65]

"The Yosemite Park," wrote Muir, "was lost sight of" during the conference, as delegates wrestled with seeking more visitors and yet professing to safeguard the attraction. Muir, like the others, accepted that the public must be enticed and then accommodated; he knew that they would insist on being "rolled on wheels with blankets and kitchen arrangements." Giving people what they wanted was the price that conservationists had to pay to generate support for the park. They must remember, however, that the "highest value of wild parks" was not to satisfy a yen for comfort and speed but as places of "recreation, Nature's cathedrals, where all may gain inspiration and strength and get nearer to God."[66]

Like the conference, Muir's guidebook to the park, *The Yosemite*, was aimed both at drawing visitors in and keeping some of their inventions out or under control, but it offered little guidance for doing that. Admittedly, it was not a book into which he had put much effort; he warned a friend "there was but little available good in it for busy strangers."[67] Every one of its fifteen chapters had been published earlier as magazine articles, and in turn those articles had drawn on memories that went even farther back to some of his first journals. Delightful as they were, they gave little indication of how much had changed since Muir had first arrived almost a half century earlier. Mainly, the book was an evocation of a state of wilderness that he had known as a young man, when the tourists were few. Only the final chapter on the proposed Hetch Hetchy dam addressed any current controversy, and then his message was simply, "Not here."

Yet the book, flawed though it was as a philosophical guide to the ethics and aesthetics of nature preservation, quickly became a weapon in the interminable struggle to prevent San Francisco's dam from taking over that undeveloped valley. The struggle began to heat up soon after Muir returned home from his foreign travels. The long stalemate of the Roosevelt and Taft administrations was about to come to an end. A final solution was fast approaching.

Muir had returned to a country in the throes of a bitter, pivotal race for the presidency. The contest ended in November 1912 with the election of Woodrow Wilson, a Democrat, to the White House and a Democratic majority to Congress. Wilson won because the Republican party, which with few exceptions had ruled the country since the Civil War, was badly split between Taft's supporters, the Old Guard establishment, and Roosevelt's army, who bolted with him to form a new Progressive, or Bull Moose, Party. Taft carried only two states, Utah and Vermont; Roosevelt won California, Pennsylvania, and a few others, but finished well behind Wilson in the popular vote and the Electoral College. The campaign was more than fervently fought; it was almost deadly to one of the candidates. Weeks before the election, Roosevelt took a bullet in his chest from an assassin's gun. His life was narrowly spared, but his formidable energy was sapped and his national political career finished, along with that of his ever-present advisor Pinchot.

"The killing of presidents," Muir asked of a friend, "is this never to end?" The best loved and most useful of rulers seemed to be the ones "selected for murder." But however much he was horrified by his old campfire friend's brush with death, he stopped short of endorsing Roosevelt in the election. Perhaps he did not vote at all. Politics meant little to him beyond the struggle over Hetch Hetchy, which was hardly an issue in the campaign. Months after the election, he wrote to Johnson, who had supported Wilson, "I always had faith in Taft. . . . Now we must plan for the coming Congress battle [over Hetch Hetchy]. Do you know the new Secy of the Interior or our good new President?"[68] It was a naïve or disingenuous question. Muir already knew that Wilson had chosen for his secretary none other than Phelan's personal friend, fellow Democrat, and San Francisco's attorney in the pursuit of Hetch Hetchy, Franklin Lane. Suddenly, the fate of the valley, any realist would have said, was all but sealed.

In mid-1913, while the University of California at Berkeley honored Muir and his long-time friend and neighbor John Swett with LL.D. degrees, some fellow Californians were preparing a lynching. Congressman John Raker, a Democrat from the isolated northeastern region of the state, introduced a bill that would give San Francisco all that it sought, not only dams and aqueduct rights but also a permit to generate electricity. Pinchot, although now on the political sidelines, would not fade away; he brought his disagreement with Muir into the open when he testified in congressional hearings: "The fundamental principle of the whole conservation policy is that of use," he declared, "to take every part of the land and its resources and put it to that use in which it will best serve the most people." Hetchy Hetchy should be put to the highest use, as a domestic water supply, although oddly Pinchot would not support any other economic use of the park like the harvesting of trees.[69]

William Kent, once a disillusioned businessman seeking moral direction but now sitting in the House of Representatives, abruptly went over to the anti-Muir faction. Although he had saved the Redwood Creek watershed from destruction (an area adjoining his own property), he now supported the city's flooding of the national park and patronized Muir before his fellow congressmen. "I hope you will not take my friend, Muir, seriously," he wrote, "for he is a man entirely without social sense. With him it is me and God and the rock where God put it, and that is the end of the story. I know him well, and so far as this proposition is concerned, he is mistaken." That characterization was hardly fair to the Muir who had accommodated automobiles, roads, reclamation, and railroads in his "Godful" wilderness. The newborn "socialist" Kent was fearful that California's large private utility company, Pacific Gas and Electric, might grab the Hetch Hetchy site for generating power if San Francisco did not get it first. It was a needless worry, since the federal government could just as easily deny a permit to a private utility as to a municipality.[70]

Clearly, the "wise use" arguments for damming the valley had not become more consistent or coherent. In response, Muir managed to rally an imposing list of dam opponents, men and women with plenty of "social sense" and unquestioned humanitarian impulses. They included such notable academics as Joseph N. LeConte, professor of engineering at Berkeley, Charles Eliot, former president of Harvard, the nature writer Enos Mills, the photographer Herbert Gleason, and the landscape architect Frederick Law Olmsted, Jr. Newspaper endorsements came from the New York *Times,* Boston *Transcript,* Louisville *Courier-Journal,* and Denver's *Rocky Mountain News.* California's Senator John D. Works opposed the dam, as did Helen Elliot, the president of the California Federation of Women's Clubs. Muir's own state was divided over the issue, although the dam's enemies seemed to be more visible and vocal the further east one went, where a preservation ethos was stronger than development mania.[71]

The preservationists' cause, nonetheless, had been lost in the last election. Congress quickly approved the Raker bill, and on 19 December President Wilson signed his name to the legislation, handing over the valley to Phelan and friends. At last a glittering future was securely in their hands. As a kind of personal celebration the ex-mayor had under construction a baronial estate overlooking the city of San Jose, which he named the Villa Montalvo, with extensive grounds laid out by Muir's friend John McLaren, the designer of the Golden Gate Park. No dam would be built for another decade, but Phelan would stand ready for that day when gardens and commerce would be lavished with Yosemite water.

Muir was, of course, devastated and exhausted by the long ordeal. To the Kelloggs at Stanford he confessed, "It is hard to bear" the loss of the valley—"it goes to my very heart. But in spite of Satan & Co. some sort of compensation must surely come out of even this dark damn-dam-damnation." The friends responded with a note of condolence and yet of congratulation: "The work you have done has had a *big* moral effect on the nation."[72] Without his inspiration and leadership there would have been little debate or struggle over a remote valley that hardly anyone ever visited. However compromised, his passion for nature had ignited a conservation movement across the country that was political, religious, aesthetic, and moral in scope, one that would fight on against the hydra-headed developers for generations to come. "I have done my best," Muir wrote to Helen, "and am now free to go on with my own work." But conservation was also his work, and that effort, however outgunned at Hetch Hetchy, would endure as long as any of his science or books.

The production of wealth had been the dominant issue in the struggle over the mysterious valley with the strange-sounding Indian name: where such production should be allowed and where not, whether other human values should be given priority, or what limits Americans would accept on turning nature into cash. The sad lesson staring Muir in the face was that those who already had plenty of wealth could be weak, undependable allies in the struggle. His millionaire friends more often than not failed or betrayed him when they were up against so powerful a force as the San Francisco boosters. Harriman, Hooker, and Sellers had all died without contributing any financial aid, and their spouses stayed out of the fray. Kent proved to be an unstable mix of impulses. Henry Osborn could spare no time from his country retreat or his museum work on extinct mammals. Roosevelt and Pinchot, both men of considerable wealth who had been much lauded for their conservation work, embraced or gave way to political pressures. Andrew Carnegie, friend and fellow immigrant, told a San Francisco newspaper: "John Muir is a fine Scotchman. . . . but for all that it is too foolish to say that the imperative needs of a city to a full and pure water supply should be thwarted for the sake of a few trees or for scenery, no matter how beautiful it might be."[73] In fact, no one of substantial fortune came to the valley's rescue. All of Muir's moneyed friends either stayed indifferent or went over to the other side.

Muir never believed that mere affluence makes people care more about preserving nature or stimulated a faith in nature's goodness that the poor man did not share. But he was hopeful that the rich might agree that affluence is a limited good and would join in his mission of saving a few wild remnants. He looked hopefully among the privileged classes for some openness to nature, some capacity for reverence in a secular, materialistic age. Openness was there, but it was not strong or widespread enough to contest the power of the growth ideology in

America. Even the self-styled Progressives, eager to put the economy under government oversight, when put to the test insisted on economic growth, national expansion, and material values above everything else.

All along Muir persisted in believing that not only the affluent classes but also the masses of men and women would rally to his cause, and many did in fact do so across the nation. Perhaps they felt, as he did, some spiritual yearning that only the cathedral-like national parks could satisfy. But there were not enough of them raising their voices, for the common people, like the wealthier classes, were driven by a quest for jobs, land, and upward mobility more than they were drawn to the religion of nature.

Thus, Hetch Hetchy's fate was settled. A decade after Congress's authorization, the O'Shaughnessy dam would be dedicated and would drown the valley to a depth of three hundred feet. This remote site in the mountains would thereafter be as quiet as a tomb. During the next century hardly anyone would ever visit it. No scenic roads would ever get built around or through it, despite all the promises San Francisco had made, and the tourists would seldom see its diminished granite cliffs and waterfalls reflected on the reservoir's cold, gray waters. Had they come, the message of this place would have been unmistakable: nature must always be open to the pursuit of wealth and growth, and even so magnificent a site as this must not escape.

"Slight Progress Heavenward"

Defeat over Hetch Hetchy left Muir weary of political battles and pining for long-lost days in the wild. "With the New Year comes new work. I am now writing on Alaska," he wrote. "A fine change from faithless politics to crystal ice and snow."[1] America's cities and capitalists had barely laid their hands on that far northern territory. Altogether he had made seven trips there, the longest of them the cruise of the Corwin, and poring over his extensive journals allowed him to revisit in his mind that great littoral. Once more he was leaping over dangerous crevasses and listening to glaciers cracking and falling into the sea. Once more he was a young man, fired with a passion for life that no frigid gale could ever daunt.

While reading those fading pages of his notebooks he may have felt a morning vigor, but in truth the sundown of his life was fast approaching. The "New Year" was 1914, the last he would know. His final days would be plagued by a return of the influenza virus, which eventually advanced to a fatal case of pneumonia. In January he had to miss a meeting of the Sierra Club directors because of "severe grippe cold," and for months to come he would be confined to home, traveling little and keeping close to a log fire.[2]

It had been two years since he had last sought the dry climate of southern California. In that time he had not seen Helen or her desert home, while several of his former Los Angeles–Pasadena hosts, who once had offered refuge from the northern clime, had either died or moved away. One of those wealthy friends, Katharine Hooker, after her husband's death tried to establish a more intimate relationship with Muir, pressuring him to become her traveling companion or partner. She moved to Berkeley, where her daughter lived (and perhaps to be nearer to Martinez). She kept asking him to use her personal name, to become more familiar: Why do you always call me Mrs. Hooker, she asked, "why not Katharine?" When he inscribed a book to her, she complained, "Very nice, but not as affectionate as it might be." Fending off all her overtures, he clung to his lonely, self-reliant privacy. When she asked him to join her on a Mediterranean cruise, he declined, although the change of climate might have improved his health. "I would like to see Athens and Rome," he admitted, "& a few of the Greenland and Antarctic ice-floods; then I'd willingly let my legs rest." She was suggesting, however, a long boat cruise rather than a glacier saunter, and offering a closer kind of companionship than he wanted.[3]

So he stayed home, choosing to suffer through the damp winter and seldom seeking company. Much of the Strentzel manse stood unused, except for his "scribble den" and his bedroom across the upstairs hall. Aside from breakfast, he took his meals at Wanda's house, the old Mexican adobe, spending a few hours each day there with his rambunctious grandsons before returning to solitude. Most of the time, despite his poor health, he devoted to trying to patch his Alaska journals into a coherent narrative. When the book was finished, he promised himself, when he had sacrificed most of his flesh by a lack of food and exercise, he would "rattle up a mountain for reincarnation."[4]

After the death of her husband Edward, one of Muir's staunchest allies in the Hetch Hetchy campaign, Marion Randall Parsons offered to come to his home one or two days a week to serve as his secretary and typist. "No one unacquainted with Mr. Muir's habits of work and living could appreciate the difficulty," she later wrote, "nor, indeed the humorous nature of the task.... Confusion was no word for the state of his manuscripts." Tattered journals had been repeatedly revised or amended, so that as many as five different versions of the same text existed. He had randomly penciled notes on paper bags or on the margins of newspapers, fiercely saving every scrap and preventing anyone from cleaning up the mess. Like a starved bear looking for ripe raspberries, he rambled erratically among the old manuscripts, plucking here and there a juicy passage to savor and leaving a littered trail behind him. Finally, Parsons hit on the strategy of hiding copied and rejected sheets inside a roll of papers bound with red ribbons and labeled—in huge capitals—"Copied!" It was the only way she could keep him from backtracking or wandering off the path.[5]

"This business of writing books," he complained, "is a long, tiresome, endless job." It had always been hard for him; he sweated over every sentence, phrase, and paragraph, trying to bring to the page the spontaneous enthusiasm that animated his conversation while carefully keeping himself on the margins. Despite his slow, tangled method, Parsons was amazed at how sharp his critical faculty remained to the end. "No trace of pessimism or despondency, even in the defeat of his most deeply cherished hopes," darkened his positive philosophy of life, she reported, and "only in the intense physical fatigue brought on by his long working hours was there any hint of failing powers." He was up at dawn each morning, and he was still poring over his manuscripts at ten o'clock each night.[6]

In June he wrote his publisher, "the Alaska book will be only notes of travel." His grander ambition was to write "several volumes" of autobiography, only the first of which had so far been published. *My Boyhood and Youth* attracted many readers and stirred up much favorable comment. The story appeared serially, in abridged form, in four issues of *The Atlantic Monthly* (November 1912–February 1913), before Houghton Mifflin made it a book in the spring of 1913. A teacher in Boston was so impressed that she assigned it to her foreign-born students to inspire them with the story of an immigrant boy who had risen to success and showed them how to embrace America's natural beauty. Andrew Carnegie was also a fan, congratulating his fellow Scot and sending along a copy of his own rags-to-riches story, "How I Served My Apprenticeship as a Business Man."[7]

Others were more struck by the Old Testament harshness of father Daniel depicted in the book, the beatings that Muir had endured, and how, miraculously, they had not made him hard or unforgiving. "It shows what can be accomplished against frightful odds," wrote a forester whom Muir met in the Philippines. His surviving sisters, Sarah, Mary, and Joanna (brothers David and Daniel staying silent), were disturbed by the stern picture of their father, although none of them had suffered as much as Muir. A former resident of Marquette County, James

Whitehead, who knew the whole family, charged that the book exaggerated Daniel's severity. "I lived in that neighborhood for 30 years," he recollected, and "no one thought or dreamed of Mr. Muir's punishing his children as John afterwards claimed he did." He remembered a man of unusual honesty and rectitude, not the ogre who appeared in the son's writings.[8]

A more serious charge was that Muir had "mercilessly pilloried" Whitehead's father, accused in the magazine articles of abusing his half-wit brother Charlie and driving him to suicide. "I never knew my father to strike him or inflict physical punishment of any kind upon his brother," Whitehead protested. The criticism struck home, and Muir offered to soften the indictment in the forthcoming book version. He regretted that his "life-long hatred of cruelty" had, in this case, led him to an unfair characterization that had brought pain. "I never did intentional injustice to any human being or animal," he offered in self-defense; but in this case his own suffering from child abuse had left him highly sensitive to any act of cruelty or injustice, to the point of distorting the facts and blinding him to the virtues of the elder Whitehead.

> Your father, like my own, was, I devoutly believe, a sincere Christian, abounding in noble qualities, preaching the Gospel without money or price while working hard for a living.... and from youth to death never abating one jot of his glorious foundational religious enthusiasm. I revere his memory....

Perhaps so, but criticism of a repressive home environment was more the message of *My Boyhood and Youth* than reverence for ancestors. Yet privately, in his twilight months, he had to admit how closely his own life had followed his father's path.[9]

Take away the disciplining rod and change the specific doctrines they preached, and the life stories of son and father bore a near resemblance. Like Daniel, John had disregarded conventional teaching and sought his own gospel to preach; once he found that gospel, he never lost his "glorious foundational religious enthusiasm." But the differences in the two men's doctrines were significant. Instead of depicting a fallen world, which in turn had corrupted humans, and calling on them to repent of their sins before an angry God, the son's gospel depicted a morally pure, benign, and gentle Nature. Love was the ruling principle of that natural world, a world from which humans could derive cleansing and salvation. Liberality, receptivity to science, tolerance of individuality, and openness to beauty were the qualities needed for that redemption. Sin was no longer a violation of God's commands but an inability to see or appreciate the harmony that flowed through the natural world.

The liberal son had turned out to be a far more famous and successful evangelist than his conservative father. His "enthusiasm" had fired many minds, of high and low estate, and helped spread a new religion. He had not altogether overcome "faithless politics," but he had come close, in one supremely beautiful place, to defeating the dominant American cult—a competing religion in fact—of money and economic growth. As he wrote to Johnson, "the long drawn-out battle work for nature's gardens has not been thrown away. The conscience of the whole country has been aroused from sleep, and from outrageous evil compensating good in some form must surely come."[10] That was a more promising outcome than Daniel could have claimed in his last, feeble days.

Buried in the piles of old letters Muir had received was one from New York publisher and editor Walter Hines Page, now Ambassador to Great Britain. "California and Alaska," Page wrote, "will be here a long time after we are all gone; but your books must be got ready for the long life that awaits them, for they must live as long as the country remains safe from the final clash of things. . . . I will say to my sons, 'When you are in doubt[,] here, here is American literature by a man who is Nature and whom you have seen and talked with.'"[11] Not merely to write about the natural world, but to "be Nature" was Muir's public role. To touch him or to read his words was, for many people, tantamount to experiencing that liberating and hopeful order suffusing the universe.

Yet a dark cloud loomed over Muir's last moments as it did over all of western civilization. In the summer of 1914 a Bosnian Serb freedom fighter shot and killed the heir to the Austro-Hungarian

Portrait of Muir by W. E. Dassonville, San Francisco, circa 1910. (H-A, JMP)

throne, and within weeks the major European powers were at war. In early August German troops invaded Belgium, massacring women and children and sacking towns and farms; ten days later the British Expeditionary Force landed in France to give fight. The rumble and stench of giant cannons, airplanes, armored cars, and poison gas filled the air and would make this war the most deadly to date in world history. They called it the Great War—but it was great in carnage, not in ideals. Eight million people died. Neither side could claim to be defending profound moral principles from attack, but only shifting alliances of power.[12]

The old homeport of Dunbar, where Daniel had once recruited soldiers for the British Army, was now a mobilization center and frontline of defense. By the end of August, a local reported, over three thousand recruits had passed through the town on their way to the deadly battlefields. A volunteer guard was watching for German U-boats along the Firth of Forth. Muir had been a steady contributor to Dunbar's poor fund; now he added to his list of charities the Red Cross campaign for British and Belgian war relief. Although far away, the violence of war invaded his study and distracted him from his cherished memories while bringing up long-forgotten scenes from America's Civil War when he had first announced that he was a pacifist.[13]

Construction of the dam at Hetch Hetchy commenced about the same time as the European war. The valley, he lamented to Johnson, "is dead," as an army of men were busy "doing desolation work." Shifting to those other armies battling in Europe and his friend's recent round of editorials against the "Kaiser's war work," he tried to summon up some optimism for home and abroad: "Civilization has not gone very deep as yet, but we are making some slight progress heavenward."[14]

Such optimism on either front—the defense of nature or of peace and civilization—would become harder than ever to sustain in the decades ahead. The First World War marked for many an end to the "age of liberal principles" that Muir had described back on the Yosemite trail in the early 1870s. That age had opened with the French and American revolutions. A century and a half later it threatened to collapse. Liberal ideals lay knocked down and trampled by boots and tanks. After the war the spirit of reform died in country after country, leaving behind a fearful, cynical, and anxious mood. Writers began talking of a "lost generation," a sense of alienation, or the end of innocence. That post-war mood would be followed by a worldwide depression, another world war, the rise of fascism and totalitarianism, the invention of weapons of mass destruction, the spread of human misery, and the degradation of the global environment, all further challenging the ideals of liberal democracy.

Muir would never know the full violence and destructiveness of the twentieth century. In November 1914 his persistent lung ailments became more serious, slowing his work habits. Facing another rainy season, he began to think of going south for relief. An invitation came to join Sierra Club members at their annual Christmas holiday outing in southern California, held at the Muir Lodge dedicated just a year earlier.[15] Declining their invitation because of poor health, he found it nonetheless irresistible. Then a week before Christmas he abruptly packed up and left for the southern part of the state, hoping to breathe deeply of the desert air and restore frayed ties with his adored Helen. Perhaps too he expected to join those fellow club members gathered in his honor at the lodge. But none of this was to happen. The Mohave Desert did not bring a cure. His pneumonia quickly became worse, his lungs filled with fluids, shutting off the flow of oxygen through his body.

A worried Helen sent him off, resisting and complaining, with Buell to the California Hospital on South Hope Street in Los Angeles. Early on the day before Christmas, alone in his room, Muir died. Neither of his daughters was even in the same city, nor were his son-in-law or any friends at his bedside when the end came. Few people even knew how sick he was. The unfinished Alaska manuscript lay scattered on his blankets, so he may have been thinking in his last moments of tall green forests and ice creeping down steep mountainsides. On 26 December a stricken Sierra Club held at Muir Lodge a memorial service for their absent and fallen leader. His body was shipped home to Alhambra Valley, where he was buried next to Louie.

Newspapers far and wide carried his obituary, telling admirers around the world that the incomparable Muir was dead. Often they tried to sum up his achievement—to define his place in history. The *New York Times*, for example, credited him with setting aside the "great natural parks in the Far West."[16] Eleven of them had so far been established, along with several national monuments. Others saw him as the main force behind the country's unique system of national forest reserves. Still others looked on him as the fountainhead of the conservation movement in the United States, which taught not only the preservation of special places but also a more caring and careful relationship with nature in all her guises.

"Although he was not a maker of many books," the *Times* continued, "John Muir achieved for himself an enviable place in our prose literature....Simplicity and elegance are admirably mingled in his descriptions of the scenery that he loved." He helped establish a new genre of writing, building on the innovations of the English parson-naturalist Gilbert White, Concord's Henry David Thoreau, and John Burroughs.[17] That new genre of the writer's craft was focused more on nature and its workings or meanings than on the trials and triumphs, the works and days, of humankind. It would be a long time before connoisseurs of good writing accepted the genre into their canon, but already observers like the *Times* recognized something new in the literary world, for which Muir deserved considerable credit.

At the time of his death he had produced five book-length classics for nature lovers: *The Mountains of California* (1894), *Our National Parks* (1901), *My First Summer in the Sierra* (1911), *The Yosemite* (1912), and *The Story of My Boyhood and Youth* (1913). Marion Parsons finished, to the best of her ability, the manuscript on which he was still laboring at the end, and it was published posthumously as *Travels in Alaska* (1915). At the request of Muir's daughters, William Badè became literary executor and assembled three more books from the unpublished journals and magazine articles: *A Thousand-Mile Walk to the Gulf* (1916), *The Cruise of the Corwin* (1917), and *Steep Trails* (1918). All of those titles were brought together by Houghton Mifflin, between 1916 and 1924, in *The Writings of John Muir*, along with Badè's two-volume *Life and Letters*.

Among the many encomiums pouring in was that of James Bryce, distinguished historian and professor of civil law at Oxford University, peer of the realm, ambassador to the United States from 1907 to 1913, member of the Liberal Party, and admirer of the American national park system. His words may stand as a summary of what Muir's friends and admirers saw in their hero. In the *Sierra Club Bulletin* Bryce called him the patriarch of American lovers of mountains, one who had not only a passion for the splendours of Nature, but a wonderful power of interpreting her to men. The very air of the granite peaks, the very fragrance of the deep and solemn forest, seem to breathe round us and soothe our sense as we read the descriptions of his lonely wanderings in the Sierras when their majesty was first revealed. . . . You of the Club will cherish the memory of a singularly pure and simple character, who was in his life all that a worshipper of nature ought to be.[18]

The San Francisco daily press, in contrast, seemed more interested in the large sum of money that Muir left behind, a possible taint on his saintly reputation. Three weeks after his death the *Chronicle* reported that his estate was worth $241,137 (or more than four million in today's dollars). The sum included a half-interest, shared with Helen and Buell, in a 1,300-acre ranch near Valona, other agricultural lands, and the Strentzel home. Astonishingly, over $180,000 of that wealth came from savings accounts in San Francisco and Martinez banks. No one imagined that he had been so rich. As one reporter put it, "A large sum of money did not seem to fit somehow with the popular conception of the naturalist passing months idealistically in the mountains."[19]

Wanda explained how the money had accumulated following the hard, shrewd work her father had done years ago on the Strentzel estate, making the ranch more productive and profitable than it had been before. He had enhanced his father-in-law's wealth and earned money for himself as well, clearing some $5,000 per year over a decade, all of which he had put away and saved. Martinez old-timers remembered him coming to the local bank with large cloth bags labeled "laundry," containing his earnings from the fruit and vine business. The daughters found a list of his bank deposits pasted on the wall, faded and partially washed away by rain coming in the open window. It took some effort to decipher the largest deposit.

The casualness of his record keeping indicated how little the money meant to him. Assiduous though he may have been in carrying out his family duties and thrifty to the point of self-denial, Muir had hardly been a man focused on making money. Compared to the great fortune makers of his day—Rockefeller, Harriman, J. P. Morgan, Vanderbilt, Carnegie—his estate was rather modest. He had barely managed his wealth, earning far less than he could have done by careful, attentive investment; his bank deposits drew only a modest four percent interest. As a farm manager, millwright, and efficiency expert in an Indianapolis factory, he had been driven to succeed, cutting costs and pursuing markets with uncommon skill. As a capitalist, however, in the handling of money for maximum increase, he was lackadaisical, even indifferent. According to his personal ethos, accumulating dollars should not be the chief aim of life; at best dollars were a means to independence, at worst a base distraction from the higher purposes of life.[20]

Ignoring those newspaper revelations, most Californians remembered not his accumulated wealth but his love of the outdoors, and in honor of that love they made his the most famous and ubiquitous name in their state's history. The Muir name began to appear on signs, buildings, and natural features all over the place—from schools to real-estate companies to parklands. In 1915 the state legislature appropriated an initial $10,000 to construct the John Muir Trail through one of the most spectacular mountain vistas in the nation. Finished in 1938, the centenary of his birth, the trail ran over two hundred miles long, from Yosemite Valley to Mt. Whitney. Another honor came nearly seventy years later when the state of California chose for its commemorative quarter design the picture of an enraptured Muir standing with walking staff in hand and gazing at Half Dome to symbolize its cultural and natural heritage.

Other memorials created throughout the United States and Scotland suggest that Muir's vision of nature survived the onslaughts of modern war, violence, cynicism, and money-madness. His vision managed even to increase in popularity, so that today the Sierra Club counts nearly one million members across the North American continent, while many other environmental organizations, inspired by him, have grown up as well, including the Nature Conservancy, Restore Hetch Hetchy, Scotland's John Muir Trust, the Canadian

Friends of John Muir, and various plant and animal protective societies all over the planet.[21]

America's National Wilderness System, established in 1964 and preserving more than one hundred million acres of land in pristine condition, partly owes its existence to him. Inspired by his example, Americans also expanded their national park system to nearly four hundred sites, and over time radically enlarged their sense of what nature is worth preserving. Many of those sites added during the twentieth century are rather ordinary places without mountains or other scenic grandeur or charismatic mega-fauna. They include state parks, city and county parks, open spaces, river walks, and wildlife refuges. Most radically, legislators voted to protect every endangered species, even the lowliest and most unprepossessing—the Furbish lousewort, the snail darter, the desert pupfish, the spotted owl.

All those efforts at nature preservation, protecting the high and the mighty, the extraordinary and the ordinary, the obscure and the beloved, flow out of the worldview of liberal democracy. Modern societies have not only sought to preserve Nature in all her forms but also to open those preserved places to any and all human beings, regardless of class or ethnicity, far more so than our universities, country clubs, or gated communities. In that preservation effort they have acknowledged a moral obligation beyond the human species. Americans, like other peoples, have followed Muir's youthful trail of passion toward a more comprehensive egalitarianism in our relations with the earth.

Through knowing John Muir better, we can see how the modern love of nature began as an integral part of the great modern movement toward freedom and social equality, which has led to the pulling down of so many oppressive hierarchies that once plagued the world. We come to realize that fighting to save the great whales, the tropical rain forests, or even a single acre of prairie has been a logical outcome of that movement, along with all efforts to decrease the human footprint on the planet, to use resources more justly and responsibly, and to achieve a greener society.

The ultimate destination of the conservation (or environmental) movement that Muir helped found is to transform the United States and other nations into "green" societies where pollution and waste of natural resources will have diminished significantly, where nature will become more than a ruthlessly exploited or even prudently managed "economic resource." Nature will be granted a higher emotional, spiritual, and aesthetic value—a value in itself. No one in nineteenth-century America was more important than Muir in persuading people to move toward such a vision.

Despite the persistent power of the Muir legacy, however, there is still much working against it. Conservative forces that would take us back to biblical fundamentalism or other religious orthodoxies of the past are still potent; for such orthodox believers, a Muir-like turn to nature for spiritual inspiration represents a fearful step toward paganism, excessive freedom of interpretation, and denial of established authority. Another religious-like orthodoxy that continues to contest Muir's legacy is the belief that nature exists solely to benefit humankind. "Nature loves man, beetles, and birds with the same love," was the core of Muir's philosophy. But succeeding generations have made only limited progress toward adopting that outlook. From Mao Zedong and Joseph Stalin to the captains of American, British, or East Asian industry, the opposite view has often prevailed, in which the earth exists to serve the material demands of *Homo sapiens*, regardless of the ecological consequences. Thus, an overpopulated and overconsuming human race is threatening the greatest loss of biodiversity since a meteor wiped out the dinosaurs.

Whether Muir's deep faith in nature is still possible in our own time is a question that his admirers must continue to ask themselves and to find answers of their own. Can contact with nature inspire people to a higher ethic, a greater decency? Or is the human species by and large incapable of reverence, restraint, generosity, or vision? Have we truly learned to respect a nature that we did not create, a world independent of us, or do we see only the hand of humankind wherever we look? Muir was a man who tried to find the essential goodness of the world, an optimist about people and nature, an eloquent prophet of a new world that looked to nature for its standard and inspiration. Looking back at the trail he blazed, we must wonder how far we have yet to go.

Notes

PROLOGUE

1. JMW (John Muir Writings), I (*My Boyhood and Youth*):4. See bibliography for the edition used.
2. Edward O. Wilson, *Biophilia* (Cambridge: Harvard Univ. Pr., 1984), prologue. See also Stephen R. Kellert and Edward O. Wilson, eds., *The Biophilia Hypothesis* (Washington, D.C.: Island Press, 1993); and Dan Flores, *The Natural West* (Norman: Univ. of Oklahoma Press, 2001), 9–28.
3. M, "Bears," JMP (John Muir Papers), 34:2018. In these notes, "M" always indicates John Muir.
4. *Oxford English Dictionary*, 2d ed. (Oxford: Clarendon Press, 1989), vol. 8, p. 882.
5. JMW, I (*A Thousand-Mile Walk to the Gulf*):358.
6. "Reminiscences of Helen Muir," Linnie Marsh Wolfe papers, JMP, 51:113.
7. Tocqueville, *Democracy in America*, 451–52.
8. Tocqueville, *Democracy in America*, 555–58.

CHAPTER 1

1. Thomas Carlyle, *Oliver Cromwell's Letters and Speeches*, vol. 8 of *The Works of Thomas Carlyle* (London: Chapman and Hall, 1902), 197–98.
2. Miller, *History of Dunbar*, 313. For full citation of shortened titles, see "Select Bibliography."
3. Smout, *History of the Scottish People, 1830–1950*, 135.
4. JMW, I (*My Boyhood and Youth*):16.
5. Smout, *History of the Scottish People, 1560–1830*, 36.
6. Herman, *How the Scots Invented the Modern World*, 273.
7. Smout, *History of the Scottish People, 1560–1830*, 8–9, 22–23, 29–31.
8. M, "Obituary," *Wisconsin State Register*, 31 Oct. 1883, p. 3.
9. After 1700 the Muir clan, which had long been independent, was absorbed as a "sept," or affiliate, into several larger Scottish clans—Gordon, Campbell, Donald, and others.
10. M, "Obituary."
11. According to William Frederic Badè [in JMW, IX (*Life and Letters of John Muir*):15], Daniel had a child by his first wife, although there is no evidence in local records to support that claim or to establish the date of the marriage or of Helen's death. Muir always spelled Ann's name with an "e," but in the parish records it is given as "Ann" (Register of Birth & Baptisms, Parish Register of Dunbar, 1798–1819, microfilm

reel 4; Register of Marriages, 1833, microfilm reel 8, International Genealogical Index, British Isles).

12. Town Clerk's Letter Books, Dunbar, B.18/15/3, National Archives of Scotland. Daniel was first elected to the council on 23 May 1846 with 29 votes.

13. Daniel J. Withrington and Ian R. Grant, eds. *The Statistical Account of Scotland. Vol. II: The Lothians* (1791–99; East Ardsley, Wakefield, England: EP Publishing Co., 1975), 497; Smout, *History of the Scottish People, 1830–1950*, 14–15.

14. William Cobbett, *Cobbett's Tour in Scotland*, ed. Daniel Green (Aberdeen: Aberdeen Univ. Press, 1984), 14.

15. JMW, I:37.

16. JMW, I:36.

17. JMW, I:11–12.

18. JMW, I:36.

19. JMW, I:13, 15.

20. JMW, I:24–25.

21. JMW, I:28. For a favorable portrait of Dominie Lyon, see Heather I. Lyon, "The Silver Tea Pot," unpublished manuscript (1985), Haddington Local History Centre, East Lothian, 57–72. Lyon's troubles with town leaders are discussed in *Minute Books of Magistrates and Committees*, National Archives of Scotland, B.18/14/1.

22. JMW, I:4, 23, 36.

23. M, Pasadena [Calif.] *Evening Star*, 26 Jan. 1907, pp. 6–7.

24. Burns, I, 137–45, 193–94, 126–28.

25. See, for example, the poem "The Tree of Liberty" (1794), in Burns, *Poems and Songs of Robert Burns*, II, 910–13, where the title itself suggests a connection between new liberal ideals and nature.

26. Wordsworth, *Prelude*, 78–79, 96–101.

27. Wordsworth, *Prelude*, 99, 201.

28. Dick, *Christian Philosopher*, 87. The classic work in this body of literature is William Paley, *Natural Theology: Or, Evidences of the Existence and Attributes of the Deity, Collected from the Appearances of Nature*, first published in London in 1802.

29. Wordsworth, *Prelude*, 333–53.

30. Dunbar Council Minutes, National Archives of Scotland, B. 18/13/10 (1841–59); JMW, I: 43–45.

31. See Thomas Chalmers, *Alexander Campbell's Tour in Scotland* (Louisville, KY: Guide Printing Co., 1892).

32. West, *Alexander Campbell and Natural Religion*, 4–7. See also D. M. Thompson's entries on Thomas and Alexander Campbell, *Dictionary of Scottish Church History & Theology* (Edinburgh: T & T Clark, 1993), 125, 130.

33. West, *Alexander Campbell and Natural Religion*, 4–7.

34. *Memoirs of Alexander Campbell*, ed. R. R. Richardson (Cincinnati: Standard Publishing Co., 1897), II, 571–72.

35. JMW, I:45–47.

36. Smout, *History of the Scottish People, 1830–1950*, 23–31.

37. Livesay, *Andrew Carnegie and the Rise of Big Business*, 3–15; Brander, *Emigrant Scots*, chap. 6. On government attitudes toward immigration, see Mackenzie, *Scotland in Modern Times*, 174.

38. John Simpson has tracked down the details of the Muirs' voyage in *Yearning for the Land*, 49–54. It lasted thirty-eight days, plus a week aboard ship during the loading of cargo.

CHAPTER 2

1. Cited in Nesbit and Thompson, *Wisconsin*, 150.
2. JMW, I (*My Boyhood and Youth*):51.
3. Nesbit and Thompson, *Wisconsin*, 201–3; Wyman, *The Wisconsin Frontier*, 157–84.
4. Stanley, *Heart of John Muir's World*, 22–28. Fountain Lake came to be known as Muir Lake, but when the family sold out and left, it became Ennis Lake.
5. Daniel Muir, "Declaration of Intent for Citizenship," JMP, 51:158.
6. JMW, I:52–53.
7. JMW, I:52, 128.
8. JMW, I:145.
9. JMW, I:56, 62.
10. David Muir to M and sisters, 17 Dec. 1882, JMP, 4:2241. See also Waltraud A. R. Brinkmann, "Challenges of Wisconsin's Weather and Climate," in *Wisconsin Land and Life*, ed. Robert C. Ostergren and Thomas R. Vale (Madison: Univ. of Wisconsin Press, 1997), 49–64.
11. JMW, I:163–64.
12. JMW, I:63, 159–82.
13. JMW, I:179–80.
14. JMW, I:181–86.
15. JMW, I:68–69, 74–75, 83, 89.
16. Turner, "The Significance of the Frontier," *Frontier and Section: Selected Essays of Frederick Jackson Turner* (Englewood Cliffs: Prentice-Hall, 1961), 56.
17. Joseph Schaefer, *Wisconsin Domesday Book*, Vol. I: *A History of Agriculture in Wisconsin* (Madison: State Historical Society of Wisconsin, 1922), 55; JMW, I:168–69.
18. JMW, I:173–74. For sketches of Muir's neighbors, see Stanley, *Heart of John Muir's World*, 16–37; and Wolfe, *Son of the Wilderness*, 45–51. Wolfe's material was heavily derived from personal interviews that she did in the 1940s, of which there remains no written record, and which often seems embellished for dramatic effect.
19. JMW, I:174–75.
20. Park, *Travels in the Interior Districts of Africa*, ed. Kate Ferguson Masters (Durham: Duke Univ. Press, 2000); Humboldt and Bonpland, *Personal Narrative of Travels to the Equinoctial Regions of America during the Years 1799–1804*, 3 vols. (London: Henry G. Bohn, 1852).
21. JMW, I:207–8.
22. Charles Reid to M, 9 Feb. 1858, JMP, 1:27.
23. M to a friend, ca. 1856, JMP, 1:20, 37.
24. JMW, I:194.
25. JMW, I:201.
26. Muir Papers, no. 4145, Wisconsin State Historical Society Archives.

CHAPTER 3

1. *Wisconsin State Journal*, 25 Sept. 1860, p. 2; *Wisconsin Evening Patriot*, 25 Sept. 1860, p. 3. JMW, I (*My Boyhood and Youth*):216.
2. M to S. Galloway, Sept. 1860, JMP, 1:48.
3. M to Daniel H. Muir, 19 Nov. [1860], JMP, 1:465. No year appears on this letter, but the content clearly shows that it was written in Prairie du Chien while Daniel was still living at home.

4. M to S. Galloway, 1 Dec. 1860, JMP, 1:72.

5. M to Frances Pelton, ca. 1861, JMP, 1:151.

6. JMW, I (*My Boyhood and Youth*):218–19.

7. Daniel Muir to M, 17 Apr. 1861, JMP, 1:111.

8. School costs are given in *Catalogue of the Officers and Students of the University of Wisconsin* (Madison: Atwood & Rublee, 1862).

9. M to Mary, Anna [Annie], and Joanna Muir, May 1861, JMP, 1:117.

10. JMW, I:223–25; "Reminiscences of Milton Griswold," JMP, 51:1018.

11. M to Galloways, fall 1861, JMP, 1:146.

12. Ezra Carr, "The Claims of the Natural Sciences, To Enlarged Consideration in Our Systems of Education" (Madison: Calkins & Proudfit, 1856). See also Ezra Carr file, University Archives, University of Wisconsin Memorial Library.

13. Curti and Carstensen, *University of Wisconsin*, I, 93–94.

14. M, "Principles of Physics and Natural Philosophy," JMP, 31:36.

15. Jeanne Carr, "Notes on John Muir," Jeanne and Ezra Carr papers, Huntington Library, CA 40, box 2. One version has Jeanne Carr serving as the head judge in the state fair competition where Muir got a prize, but she does not mention this event in her memoirs.

16. Jeanne Carr, "My Own Story," Jeanne and Ezra Carr papers, Huntington Library, CA 40, box 2.

17. Curti and Carstensen; JMP, 1:290. Butler's *Index Rerum* can be found in the State Historical Society of Wisconsin Archives.

18. M to Galloways, 9 Feb. 1862, JMP, 1:186.

19. M to Galloways, 9 Feb. 1862, JMP, 1:186.

20. M, "Old Log Schoolhouse," JMP, 31:27.

21. Charles E. Vroman, "John Muir at the University," *Wisconsin Alumni Magazine* 16 (June 1915): 560.

22. Vroman, "John Muir at the University," 557, 560, 564.

23. *Catalogue of the Officers and Students of the University of Wisconsin for the Year Closing June 24, 1853* (Madison: Atwood & Rublee, 1863), 7.

24. Ann Muir to M, 1 Mar. 1862, JMP, 1:188.

25. M to Galloways, 1862, JMP 1:250.

26. M to Frances Pelton, 1861, JMP, 1:167.

27. M to Galloways, 1 June 1863, JMP 1:290; to Mr. and Mrs. Ambrose Newton, 2 Aug. 1863; 1:308. Muir also joined the Athaenean Society, a student literary organization, and became an active debater.

28. M to Mrs. Pelton, 28 Sept. 1862, JMP, 1:222.

29. M to Daniel H. Muir, 20 Dec. 1863, JMP, 1:323.

30. M to Emily Pelton, 27 Feb.–1 Mar. 1864, JMP, 1:337. This letter incorporated texts composed during the excursion of the preceding summer. While passing through Prairie du Chien, Muir stopped to visit the graves of Frances Pelton and her infant daughter Fannie, both of whom had died during the previous year. Apparently, he did not see Emily, despite calling twice at her house, for her uncle and Frances's husband intervened and sent him away. See Wolfe, *Son of the Wilderness*, 87; and M to Emily Pelton, 27 Feb. 1864, Muiriana Collection, Univ. of the Pacific.

31. M to Daniel H. Muir, 20 Dec. 1863, JMP, 1:323.

32. M to Emily Pelton, 27 Feb.–1 Mar. 1864, JMP, 1:337.

CHAPTER 4

1. Robin Winks, *Canada and the United States: The Civil War Years* (Baltimore: Johns Hopkins Univ. Press, 1960), 3, 209–10.

2. This route is largely conjectural, based on the memories of Peter Trout, who admitted he was "not very sure" of it (Trout, "What I Know about John Muir," undated typescript, Meaford Museum, Meaford, Ontario).

3. Traill, *The Backwoods of Canada* (1836; Toronto: McClelland & Stewart, 1989), 56.

4. Muir's description of this discovery, originally sent to Jeanne Carr, was taken without her permission by James Butler and published in the Boston *Recorder*, 21 Dec. 1866; reprinted in Gisel, *Kindred and Related Spirits*, 40–42. It was Muir's first publication.

5. M to Annie Muir, 23 Oct. 1864, JMP, 1:356.

6. Trout, *Trout Family History*, 121–28; William Sherwood Fox, *The Bruce Beckons: The Story of Lake Huron's Great Peninsula* (Toronto: Toronto Univ. Press, 1952), 135–43.

7. M to Mary Muir, 23 Oct. 1864, JMP, 1:359.

8. M to Mary, Anna, and Joanna Muir, 24 Dec. 1865, JMP, 1:393.

9. M to Emily Pelton, 23 May 1865, JMP, 1:368.

10. M to J. Carr, 13 Sept. 1865, JMP, 1:376. According to Linnie Marsh Wolfe, Muir carried a volume of Humboldt's with him into Canada (*Son of the Wilderness*, 83).

11. M to J. Carr, 13 Sept. 1865, JMP, 1:376.

12. See Holmes, *Young John Muir*, 125–29.

13. J. Carr to M, 24 Sept. 1865, JMP, 1:382.

14. M to J. Carr, 21 Jan. 1866, JMP, 1:407; M to David Muir, 28 Feb. 1866, 1:414.

15. Daniel Muir to M, 24 Feb. 1866, JMP, 1:411.

16. Trout, *Trout Family History*, 123. Years later the debt was finally paid.

17. W. H. Holloway, *Indianapolis: A Historical and Statistical Sketch of the Railroad City* (Indianapolis: Indianapolis Journal Print, 1870), 381.

18. M to S. Galloway, May 1866, JMP, 1:442.

19. M to Daniel H. Muir, 7 May 1866, JMP, 1:431.

20. M to Daniel H. Muir, 7 May 1866, JMP, 1:431; 12 Aug. 1866, 1:453.

21. Muir papers, no. 26655, Wisconsin State Historical Society Archives.

22. Muir's letters to Harriet Trout, July 1866 and January 1867, Meaford Museum, Meaford, Ontario; Celustus Sutherland to M, 14 Aug. 1866, JMP, 1:451.

23. J. Carr to M, 12 Oct. 1866, JMP, 1:461.

24. M to Mary and Anna Muir, 11 Feb. 1867, JMP, 1:488; M to Mary Muir, 22 Apr. 1867, 1:538.

25. See the Merrill-Graydon family papers, Indiana Historical Society, esp. box 1, folder 30, and box 3, folder 29. Muir's tribute was published in Catharine Merrill, *The Man Shakespeare and Other Essays* (Indianapolis: Bowen-Merrill, 1902), 32–38.

26. Merrill Moores, "Recollections of John Muir As a Young Man," JMP, 51:384.

27. M to Daniel H. Muir, 27 Sept. 1866, JMP, 1:459.

28. M, "Beltology," Muir papers, no. 4145, Wisconsin State Historical Society Archives.

29. Muir recalls his accident in his manuscript autobiography, JMP, 45:11020–11022.

30. Indianapolis *Daily Journal*, 9 March 1867, p. 8.

31. M to Merrills, 4 Mar. 1867, JMP, 1:492.

32. J. Carr to M, 6 Apr. 1867, JMP, 1:519.

33. M to J. Carr, 3 Apr. 1867, JMP, 1:511.
34. J. Carr to M, 15 Apr. 1867, JMP, 1:535.
35. M to J. Carr, 2 May 1867, JMP, 1:549. The likely source of Carr's and Muir's interest was J. L. Wiseley's article, "The Yosemite Valley, California," *Harper's New Monthly Magazine* 32 (May 1866): 697–708.
36. Muir to the Trouts, 4 April 1867, Meaford Museum, Ontario.
37. Moores, "Recollections," JMP, 51:391–92. Daniel's mean-spirited demand of payment appears in Wolfe, *Son of the Wilderness*, 107, but the story nowhere appears in Muir's own accounts.
38. Moores, "Recollections," JMP, 51:392; M to Galloways, July 1863, JMP, 1:306.
39. M to J. Carr, 30 Aug. 1867, JMP, 1:587; M to Daniel H. Muir, 1 Sept. 1867, 1:589.

CHAPTER 5

1. Charles Darwin, *The Voyage of the Beagle* (1839; Garden City, N.Y.: Doubleday, 1962), 500. See also Sachs, *Humboldt Current*, 98–101.
2. Alexander von Humboldt, *Personal Narrative*, trans. Thomasina Ross (1805; London: Henry G. Bohn, 1852), vol. II, 371.
3. M, "Florida and Cuba Trip," JMP, 23:64. For an example of a "practical man," see JMW, I (*A Thousand-Mile Walk to the Gulf*):254.
4. On the first page of his journal, later cut from the published version, Muir quotes those lines from Julius Caesar, Act IV, Scene iii.
5. M, "Florida and Cuba Trip," 23:64.
6. Henry Thoreau's essay, "Walking," published in *Atlantic Monthly* (9 [June 1862]: 657–74) while Muir was a college student in Madison, might well have served as Muir's philosophical guide on his trek southward. It seems likely, given his friendship with James Butler and the Carrs, who were all products of New England intellectual life, that Muir would have discovered, read, and been thrilled by Thoreau's words: "I wish to speak a word for Nature, for absolute freedom and wildness, as contrasted with a freedom and culture merely civil,—to regard man as an inhabitant, or a part and parcel of Nature, rather than a member of society." But there is no evidence that Muir had done so, or that Thoreau, who had died a few months before his "Walking" manifesto was published, exercised any direct influence over Muir at this point.
7. Muir may echo here the last great work of Alexander von Humboldt, *Cosmos: A Sketch of a Physical Description of the Universe*, originally published in German in 1845–47, which declares in its opening pages: "Nature considered rationally, that is to say, submitted to the process of thought, is a unity in diversity of phenomena; a harmony, blending together all created things, however dissimilar in form and attribute; one great whole . . . animated by the breath of life" (London: George Bell & Sons, 1893, vol. I, 2–3).
8. JMW, I:258.
9. M to J. Carr, 9 Sept 1867, JMP, 1:591.
10. JMW, I:277.
11. JMW, I:262, 270, 272.
12. JMW, I:276.
13. M, "Florida and Cuba Trip," JMP, 23:39.
14. See Lisa Brady, "The Wilderness of War: Nature and Strategy in the American Civil War," *Environmental History* 10 (2005): 435–39.
15. M, "Florida and Cuba Trip," JMP, 23:43; JMW, I:287.

16. JMW, I:288.
17. On Savannah's sullen mood, see "Carl Schurz's Letter from the South," *Georgia Historical Quarterly* 35 (1951): 243–49. For the postwar turmoil over Reconstruction, see E. Merton Coulter, *Georgia: A Short History* (Chapel Hill: Univ. of North Carolina Press, 1960), ch. 26.
18. Muir did not mention, for example, a controversy over whether blacks should be allowed to organize a torchlight procession that was raging while he was there; see the Savannah *Daily News and Herald*, 8–11 October 1867.
19. M, "Florida and Cuba Trip," JMP, 23:63.
20. M, "Florida and Cuba Trip," JMP, 23:55.
21. M, "Florida and Cuba Trip," JMP, 23:58–59.
22. M, "Florida and Cuba Trip," JMP, 23:58; JMW, I:303.
23. M, "Florida and Cuba Trip," JMP, 23:58.
24. M to David Muir, 15 Oct. 1867, JMP, 1:595.
25. JMW, I:319.
26. JMW, I:329–31.
27. JMW, I:324.
28. JMW, I:325.
29. In a letter to his brother, Muir identified his illness as "coast fever and dropsy," but there can be no doubt that it was malaria that struck him. M to Daniel H. Muir, 7 Jan. 1868, JMP, 1:611. For the etiology of the illness, see the U.S. Center for Disease Control's Website, http://www.cdc.gov/malaria.
30. JMW, I:354–56. The original version in the journal is only marginally different; instead of "heathen idols," for example, Muir wrote, "idol institutions of the Hindoos." M, "Florida and Cuba Trip," JMP, 23:110–11.
31. Alphonso Wood, *Class-Book of Botany* (New York: A. S. Barnes, 1866), 10, 12.
32. JMW, I:333.
33. M to Merrills and Mooreses, 6 Jan. 1868, JMP, 1:610.
34. JMW, I:356–57.
35. M to David Muir, 13 Dec. 1867, JMP, 1:601.
36. M, "Florida and Cuba Trip," JMP, 23:119.
37. JMW, I:370–71.
38. JMW, I:389, 391.

CHAPTER 6

1. M, "Rambles of a Botanist among the Plants and Climates of California," *Old and New* 5 (June 1872): 768–69.
2. M to Catherine Merrill, 19 July 1868, JMP, 1:635.
3. The lines quoted are from "Paradise Regained," in *The Portable Milton* (New York: Viking Press, 1949), 549. Also see Merchant, *Reinventing Eden*, and Wyatt, *The Fall into Eden*.
4. M, "Autobiography," JMP, 45:11033–36.
5. M, "20 Hill Hollow," JMP, 23:171, 181.
6. M, "20 Hill Hollow," JMP, 23:154, 162.
7. M to David Muir, 14 July 1868, JMP, 1:632; M to John & Margaret Reid, 13 Jan. 1869, 2:692.
8. Olmsted, *California Frontier*, 659.
9. J. Carr to M, 31 Aug. 1868, JMP, 1:647, M to J. Carr, 24 Feb. 1869, 2:694.

10. According to Gisel (*Kindred Spirits*, 159), Muir's relationship with Jeanne Carr was one of pupil and teacher, and her role in shaping his career "cannot be overemphasized."

11. J. Carr to M, 28 Mar. 1869, JMP, 2:711. On Jeanne's interest in the Reverend Brooks's natural theology, see Williams, *God's Wilds*, 47–51.

12. M to J. Carr, 29 July 1870, JMP, 2:858.

13. That there were extensive differences between the two versions can be gathered by comparing an excerpt of the original he sent Jeanne Carr on 3 October 1869 with the 1887 revision. Muir sent her a copy of his 2 September journal entry (mistakenly identified in the letter as 2 August), which can be found in JMP, 2:755 (M to J. Carr, 3 Oct. 1869). For the later revised version, see Muir, "Sierra Journal Summer of 1869," JMP, 31:514–16.

14. JMW, II (*My First Summer in the Sierra*):157.

15. JMW, II:16.

16. JMW, II:250.

17. JMW, II:147.

18. The phrase "hoofed locusts" first appeared in print in Muir's article, "The Mountain Lakes of California," *Scribner's Monthly* 17 (Jan. 1879): 416, but was misprinted as "hooped locusts." For a sympathetic history of the sheep men, see James Snyder, in "Putting 'Hoofed Locusts' Out to Pasture."

19. JMW, II:22–24.

20. JMW, II:54–55, 58–59.

21. JMW, II:226.

22. JMW, II:220. He was quoting Burns's poem, "For A' That and A' That," stanza 5 (1795).

23. M to Daniel H. Muir, 5 Dec. 1869, JMP, 2:776; M to David Muir, 20 Mar. 1870, JMP, 2:792.

24. Greene, *Historic Resource Study*, 27; Gibbens and Heady, *Influence of Modern Man*, 4–10.

25. See Sanborn, *Yosemite*, 59–60.

26. M, "Yosemite Year Book," JMP, 23:200. A federal law in 1841 gave squatters a "preemption right" to settle on nonsurveyed and nonappropriated public lands and later buy at minimum price without competition.

27. M to J. Carr, 5 Apr. 1870, JMP, 2:805; Whitney, *Yosemite Book*, 20.

28. See Runte, *Yosemite*, 28–44.

29. M to Daniel H. Muir, 5 Dec. 1869, JMP, 2:776; M to J. Carr, 6 Dec. 1869, JMP, 2:778.

30. On Yosemite artists, see Ogden, "Sublime Vistas and Scenic Backdrops," in Orsi et al., *Yosemite and Sequoia*, 49–68; Sanborn, 158–83; and Solnit, *River of Shadows*. Other important painters include Thomas Hill and William Keith. On photographers, see Sandweiss, *Print the Legend*, 276–78.

31. M to Trouts and Jays, 2 Jan. 1870, and to Duncan Sterling, 30 Jan. 1870, in the Meaford Museum, Meaford, Ontario; Sarah Hodgson to M, 10 Apr. 1869, JMP, 2:716; M to Emily Pelton, 29 Jan. 1870, JMP, 2:784; 15 May, 2:817; 2 Apr. 1872, 2:1085. Pelton relocated to California in 1870 and later married.

32. M to J. Carr, fall 1870, JMP, 2:883.

33. M to J. Carr, 29 May 1870, JMP, 2:826.

34. M to Daniel H. Muir, 21 June 1870, JMP, 2:852. Barnum was among 150 tourists ("the rich and great," as Muir described them) in the valley on 21 June 1870. See also Demars, *Tourist in Yosemite*; Peter Blodgett, "Visiting 'The Realm of Wonder':

Yosemite and the Business of Tourism, 1855–1916," in Orsi et al., *Yosemite and Sequoia*, 33–48.

35. M to Mrs. James Butler, Aug. 1869, JMP, 2:745. See also the nearly full chapter devoted to this episode in JMW, II:178–90.

36. See Yelverton's travel narrative, *Teresina in America*, II:58–90, for her stay in Yosemite Valley.

37. Yelverton, *Zanita*, 6, 208.

38. M to Galloways, 25 Apr. 1872, JMP, 2:1102.

39. For Elvira Hutchings and Jeanne Carr's correspondence, see Frank Buske, "To Love Is Painful," *John Muir Newsletter*, spring 1997.

40. Gisel, *Kindred Spirits*, 381.

41. M to J. Carr, 8 Sept. 1871, JMP, 2:958.

42. J. Carr to M, 2 Oct. 1870, JMP, 2:876; M to J. Carr, 22 Dec. 1870, JMP, 2:881.

43. M to J. Carr, 8 Sept. 1871, JMP, 2:958.

44. M to J. Carr, 8 Sept. 1871, JMP, 2:958.

CHAPTER 7

1. M to J. Carr, 7 Oct. 1874, JMP, 3:1445.

2. M to J. Carr, 3 Apr. 1871, JMP, 2:906; M to S. Galloway, 5 Apr. 1871, 2:916.

3. Muir wrote an account of this event for *Scribner's Monthly* (1880) and reprinted it as a chapter in *The Mountains of California* (1894). The most extensive analysis of Muir's thinking during his high-mountain days is Cohen's *Pathless Way*, who calls the experience on Mt. Ritter (pp. 67–71) a decisive moment in Muir's awakening to the fused oneness of matter and spirit—a Zen Buddhist–like "satori," when he gained an insight into the very essence of nature.

4. M, "Studies in the Sierra, VII," 70; JMP, 24:846–47; M, "Mount Whitney," San Francisco *Daily Evening Bulletin*, 24 August 1875, p. 1.

5. M to Alice McChesney, 8 Nov. 1874, JMP, 3:1449. See M, "Shasta in Winter," San Francisco *Daily Evening Bulletin*, 2 Dec. 1874, p. 1.

6. Ullman, *Age of Mountaineering*, 24–65.

7. Whitney, *Yosemite Book*, 80–82.

8. Ruskin, *Modern Painters*, in *Works*, VI, 108.

9. Ruskin, *Modern Painters*, in *Works*, VI, 360–61, 367, 376.

10. M to J. Carr, 3 Apr. 1871, JMP, 2:906; J. Carr to M, 3 Feb. 1872, JMP, 2:1237.

11. M to J. Carr, 14 Oct. 1872, JMP, 2:1190.

12. M, "Torreya; Merced Canyon," JMP, 24:878–79; "Flood-Storm in the Sierra," *Overland Monthly*. 14 (June 1875): 496.

13. King, *Mountaineering in the Sierra Nevada*, 252–53.

14. Tyndall, *Glaciers of the Alps*, 13.

15. Whitney, "The Geological Survey of California," 7, 9.

16. Worster, *River Running West*, 203–8.

17. LeConte, *Journal of Rambles*, cited in Stephens, *Joseph LeConte*, 123. LeConte wrote his wife from the field that Muir was "of great service to us." LeConte Papers, Bancroft Library, University of California at Berkeley, box 1.

18. Agassiz published his landmark *Études sur les glaciers* in 1840 and accepted a professorship at Harvard eight years later.

19. M, "Living Glaciers of California," *Harper's New Monthly Magazine* 51 (Nov. 1875): 547–48. This article was reprinted in the prestigious *Silliman's Journal of Science and Arts*

5 (Jan. 1873), under the title, "On Actual Glaciers in California." Earlier, in 1871, Clarence King had discovered a glacier on Mt. Shasta and published an account in the *American Journal of Science and Arts*. See Sachs, *Humboldt Current*, 225.

20. M to J. Carr, 8 Oct. 1872, JMP, 2:1176; J. Carr to M, 24 Sept. 1872, 2:1163.

21. M, "Yosemite Glaciers," New York *Tribune*, 5 Dec. 1871, p. 8. Editor Greeley had been among the earliest visitors to Yosemite Valley, which may explain why he found Muir's piece so appealing.

22. Whitney, *Yosemite Book*, 77–79.

23. See Dean, "John Muir and the Origin of Yosemite Valley," and Samuel Kneeland, *The Wonders of the Yosemite Valley and of California*, 2d ed. (Boston: A. Moore, 1872), 90–91.

24. Matthes, "John Muir and the Glacial Theory of Yosemite," 10.

25. M, "Hetch Hetchy Valley," Boston *Weekly Transcript*, 25 Mar. 1873, p. 2.

26. M to Daniel H. Muir, 1 Nov. 1871, JMP, 2:989; 5 Mar. 1872, 2:1063; M to James Cross, 25 Apr. 1872, 2:1099.

27. M to J. Carr, 14 July 1872, JMP, 2:1129.

28. M, "Studies in the Sierra, VII," 65.

29. M, "Studies in the Sierra, I," 393.

30. M, "Studies in the Sierra, I," 403.

31. Worster, *River Running West*, 313–16. The opposing theory of "catastrophism," which pointed to such violent events as Noah's flood and volcanic explosions to explain geological development, seemed at the time more in keeping with religious orthodoxy. More recent scientists have tended to combine the two theories into a composite of natural events, some slow and steady, others sudden and disruptive.

32. M, "Studies in the Sierra, IV," 183; "Studies in the Sierra, V," 400.

33. M, "Studies in the Sierra, VI," 539–40.

34. M to J. Carr, 12 May 1872, JMP, 2:1115; 11 Dec. 1871, 2:1008.

35. "Mrs. Carr's Lecture on the Big Tuolumne Cañon, before the Oakland Farming Club," Oct. 1873, Jeanne Carr Papers, Huntington Library, box 2.

36. M to S. Galloway, 3 Sept. 1873, JMP, 2:1294.

37. Daniel Muir to M, 19 Mar. 1874, JMP, 3:1364.

38. M, "Studies in the Sierra, II," 495–96.

39. M, "Tuolumne," JMP, 23:426.

40. Darwin cited in Dupree, *Asa Gray*, 244–45.

41. Asa Gray to M, 4 Jan. 1872, JMP, 2:1020.

42. M to J. Carr, 14 July 1872, JMP, 2:1129.

43. M to S. Galloway, 16 July 1872, JMP, 2:1131; M to J. Carr, 27 July 1872, 2:1132.

44. M to S. Galloway, 29 Nov. 1877, JMP, 3:1654. The Gray-Hooker quote comes from Annie Bidwell's reminiscences, cited in Wolfe, *Son of the Wilderness*, 194.

45. The books surviving from Muir's personal library are in Special Collections, University of the Pacific, and include copies of both *The Journal of Researches* and the two-volume *Life and Letters of Darwin*. Muir marked passages in the former on the horrors of slavery, the puzzling varieties of finches found among the Galápagos Islands, and the enormous height of Australia's kauri trees, and in the latter on Darwin's rejection of biblical revelation and the theistic argument from design. Muir made a special note of the agnostic Darwin's view on ultimate matters, expressed in a letter to Asa Gray: "Let each man hope and believe what he can."

46. Published by W. R. Keen Cooke in Chicago, 1871.

47. M to A. Bidwell, 1 Feb. 1878, JMP, 3:1689; 13 Feb., 3:1703; 28 Mar., 3:1720.

48. M to A. Bidwell, 1 Feb. 1878, JMP, 3:1689. In the end papers of his personal copy of John Ruskin's *Time and Tide*, which is preserved in the University of the Pacific's Special Collections, Muir jotted this caustic note: "Don't turn up yr nose at Darwin. He loved truth as devoutedly as you & with even more self-denial."

49. M, "Wind Storm," JMP, 23:528.

50. Cited in Wolfe, *John of the Mountains*, 93.

51. M, "Tuolumne 1872," JMP, 23:361.

52. Michael Branch ("Angel Guiding Gently," 133) puts the critical difference thus: "Emerson understood nonhuman nature to be ultimately valuable in its capacity to minister to man," while Muir believed that the natural world "exists only to serve its own ends."

53. On Thoreau's ecological thinking, see Worster, *Nature's Economy*, 57–112.

54. M to R. W. Emerson, 8 May 1871, JMP, 2:924; JMW, VI (*Our National Parks*):145.

55. M to R. W. Emerson, 6 July 1871, JMP, 2:940; 18 Mar. 1872, 2:1068; 27 Feb. 1872, 2:1074.

56. M to R. W. Emerson, 3 Apr. 1872, JMP, 2:1087.

57. M to J. Carr, 29 May 1870, JMP, 2:826; M, "Hetch Hetchy Valley," Boston *Weekly Transcript*, p. 2. Muir's annotated copy of *The Maine Woods* shows many marginal markings but little comment.

58. Woolson's book *Dress Reform* (1874) was a modest contribution to the women's rights movement after the Civil War. See Huber, *Wanderer All My Days*, 149–53.

59. Thoreau, *Walden*, ed. J. Lyndon Shanley (Princeton: Princeton Univ. Press, 1971), 75. See also what remains of Muir's library, University of the Pacific Special Collections.

60. Abba Woolson to M, 23 Mar. 1873, JMP, 2:1252.

61. M, "Sequoia Studies," 24:1205, 1231, 1203; "Owens Valley," JMP, 24:1179.

62. M to J. Carr, 28 Aug. 1872, JMP, 2:1148.

63. M to R. W. Emerson, 18 Mar. 1872, JMP, 2:1068.

64. M to J. Carr, 1872, JMP, 2:1122.

CHAPTER 8

1. Background on the Swetts comes from Nicholas Polos, "The Neo-Californians," in Miller, ed., *John Muir in Historical Perspective*, 63–82; and the *Dictionary of American Biography*.

2. Anne Cheney to M, 4 Apr. 1877, JMP, 3:1602; Mary Louise Swett to Louie Strentzel, 8 Apr. 1880, in JMW, IX (*Life and Letters of John Muir*):132–33.

3. M to S. Galloway, 23 Apr. 1877, JMP, 3:1607.

4. Walker, *San Francisco's Literary Frontier*, 256–83. Muir gets put into the category of "practical literature" (pp. 290–93).

5. M to S. Galloway, 12 Jan. 1877, JMP, 3:1582.

6. M, "Flood-Storm in the Sierra," *Overland Monthly* 14 (June 1875): 494.

7. Starr, *Americans and the California Dream*, 132. See also Brechin, *Imperial San Francisco*, 174–75.

8. Henry George, *Progress and Poverty* (1879; reprint, New York: Modern Library), 10.

9. M to J. Carr, 31 July 1875, JMP, 3:1502; M to Strentzels, 28 Jan. 1879, JMP, 4:1835. At this time Golden Gate Park was just beginning to emerge out of sand dunes on the far western edge of the city under the guidance of engineer William

Hammond Hall; its most influential architect, John McLaren, a native of Scotland, would become park commissioner in 1887.

10. "Art Notes," San Francisco *Evening Bulletin*, 20 June 1874, p. 3; *Overland Monthly* 14 (May 1875): 481. See also Cornelius, *Keith: Old Master of California*, chaps. IV–VI.

11. M, "Summering in the Sierra," San Francisco *Evening Bulletin*, 20 July 1876, p. 1; 24 Aug., p. 1.

12. M, "A Wind Storm in the Forests of the Yuba," *Scribner's Monthly* 17 (Nov. 1878): 55–59.

13. M, "Modoc Memories," San Francisco *Evening Bulletin*, 28 Dec., 1874, p. 1. For an account of the Modoc War, see Isenberg, *Mining California*, 131–37.

14. Salt Lake *Tribune*, 13 May 1877, pp. 1, 2, 3. For background, see Will Bagley, *Blood of the Prophets: Brigham Young and the Massacre at Mountain Meadows* (Norman: Univ. of Oklahoma Press, 2002).

15. Muir, JMW, VIII (*Steep Trails*):125.

16. For a portrait of the city in this period, see John S. McCormick, "Salt Lake City," *Utah History Encyclopedia*, ed. Allan Kent Powell (Salt Lake City: Univ. of Utah Press, 1994).

17. Nephi had been founded in 1851. See Keith N. Worthington, Sadie H. Green, and Fred J. Chapman, *They Left a Record: A Comprehensive History of Nephi, Utah, 1851–1978* (Provo: Community Press, 1979); and H. L. A. Culmer, *Utah Directory and Gazetteer for 1879–80* (Salt Lake City: Culmer, 1879), 355.

18. M, "Travels in Utah," JMP, 25:1324, 1327.

19. M, "Travels in Utah," JMP, 25:1321, 1344, 1368.

20. M, "Travels in Utah," JMP, 25:1321.

21. M, "Travels in Utah," JMP, 25:1362.

22. M, "Travels in Utah," JMP, 25:1318.

23. M, "Travels in Utah," JMP, 25:1318, 1322.

24. M, "Travels in Utah," JMP, 25:1323, 1324.

25. M, "Travels in Utah," JMP, 25:1321, 1322.

26. Utah's territorial legislature granted women the right to vote in 1870, but Congress revoked the right to discourage polygamy and Mormon ballot stuffing. It was restored in 1895 when Utah became a state.

27. M, "Travels in Utah," JMP, 25:1329.

28. M, "Travels in Utah," JMP, 25:1329, 1330.

29. San Francisco *Evening Bulletin*, 29 Oct. 1874. See also McEvoy, *The Fisherman's Problem*, 48–51.

30. M to J. Carr, 10 Jan. 1875, JMP, 3:1475. See also Isenberg, *Mining California*, 23–51; and Merchant, *Green versus Gold*, 113–16.

31. The editor of the paper, William H. Mills, a longtime land agent for the Southern Pacific Railroad and a friend of the Carrs, was "a staunch defender of farm interests and one of the West's early conservation leaders." He crusaded against hydraulic mining and for mountain watershed protection. See Orsi, *Sunset Limited*, 360.

32. M to William Hendricks, 20 Nov. 1875, JMP, 3:1515; Sacramento *Record-Union*, 5 Feb. 1876. See also M, "On the Post-Glacial History of Sequoia Gigantea," *Proceedings of the American Association for Advancement of Science* 25 (May 1875): 242–53.

33. Carr, "Forestry: Its Relation to Civilization," manuscript, Jeanne and Ezra Carr papers, box 1, CA 12, Huntington Library.

34. Following Franklin Hough's address, the AAAS persuaded Congress to establish a commission to report on forest conditions and the nation's future wood supply, with Hough at its head. Following the commission's *Report upon Forestry* (1878–1884), Hough became chief of the Division of Forestry in the Department of Agriculture.

George Perkins Marsh served as American ambassador to Turkey and Italy until his death in 1882 in the mountains east of Florence. See Lowenthal, *George Perkins Marsh*.

35. M to J. Carr, 3 June 1875, JMP, 3:1498.

36. Orville Conger to Carrs, 27 Nov. 1876, Jeanne and Ezra Carr papers, box 4. For a description of Carmelita and its famous guests, including the novelist Helen Hunt Jackson (who wrote much of her novel *Ramona* at Carmelita), see Albert Carr, "The Genesis and Development of 'Carmelita,'" Carr papers, box 5, CA 14. Today the Carr property is the site of the Norton Simon Museum and highway I–210.

37. JMW, VIII:138, 140–44.

38. M to S. Galloway, 12 Jan. 1877, JMP, 3:1582.

39. "Biography of John Strentzel," Strentzel papers, Bancroft Library.

40. Louie Strentzel to J. Carr, 21 Mar. 1875, JMP, 3:1482.

41. For background on these magazines, see Frank Luther Mott, *A History of American Magazines* (Cambridge: Harvard Univ. Press, 1938–68), III, 457–80.

42. R. U. Johnson to M, 13 Dec. 1877, JMP, 3:1669; John McLandburgh to M, 11 Feb. 1878, 3:1700. An essay that they could not get Muir to write was on western farm life. Johnson hoped to have that essay illustrated by one of their favorites, Mary Hallock Foote, a native of New York now living with her husband Arthur, a mining engineer, in New Almaden, California.

43. See Gillis and Magliari, *John Bidwell and California*.

44. Louisiana Strentzel to M, 18 June 1878, JMP, 3:1763; M to Louisiana Strentzel, 20 June, 3:1765.

45. M to John Strentzel, 5 Aug. 1878, JMP, 3:1777; to Strentzels, 28 Aug., 3:1785.

46. M to Strentzels, 11 Sept. 1878, JMP, 3:1796; to John Strentzel, 28 Sept., 3:1806.

47. M, "Nevada's Dead Towns," San Francisco *Evening Bulletin*, 15 Jan. 1879, p. 1.

48. M to Strentzels, 28 Jan. 1879, JMP, 3:1835; M to Louie Strentzel, 18 Apr., 3:1868.

49. This passage from Louisiana Strentzel's diary, dated 17 June 1879, is missing from the fragments preserved in the Bancroft Library, but a copy may be found in the library of the John Muir National Historical Site, Martinez, California.

CHAPTER 9

1. M to Bidwells, 19 June 1879, JMP, 3:1886.

2. Young, *Alaska Days*, 12; Young, *Hall Young of Alaska*, 172. Born in western Pennsylvania in 1847, Young came to Alaska a year earlier than Muir and worked to improve Indian education. See Ted C. Hinckley, "The Early Alaskan Ministry of S. Hall Young, 1878–1888," *Journal of Presbyterian History* 46 (Sept. 1968): 175–96.

3. JMW, III (*Travels in Alaska*):107, 154–55; M, "Notes of a Naturalist," San Francisco *Evening Bulletin*, 6 Sept. 1879. Muir began, in the last years of his life, to assemble from his journals and magazine and newspaper articles a coherent book on Alaska, which was published posthumously in 1915 as *Travels in Alaska*. The differences among these various written texts are trivial.

4. Young, *Alaska Days*, 37–56. Muir's account of the mountain rescue appears in JMW, III:50–55.

5. JMW, III:71; M, "Alaska Glaciers," San Francisco *Evening Bulletin*, 23 Sept. 1879, p. 4.

6. JMW, III:90, 93.

7. Archibald Geikie (1835–1924) was director of Scotland's Geological Survey and professor at the University of Edinburgh; his younger brother James (1839–1915) was the author of *The Great Ice Age and Its Relation to the Antiquity of Man*, published in 1874.

Hugh Miller (1802–1856) was a self-taught geologist, widely admired for such vividly written books as *The Old Red Sandstone* (1841) and *Footprints of the Creator* (1850).

8. JMW, III:178, 186–87, 191.

9. Young, *Alaska Days*, 97, 111.

10. M to Louie, 9 Oct. 1879, JMP, 3:1927; Louie to M, 24 Oct., 3:1930.

11. M to Louie, 6 Jan. 1880, JMP, 4:1973.

12. M to Louie, Feb. 1880, JMP, 4:1986.

13. Janet Moores to M, 5 May 1880, JMP, 4:2041; J. Carr to Louisiana Strentzel, [no date], 4:2054; J. Carr to M and Louie, 3 June, 4:2057; John Lemmon, 4 June, 4:2059.

14. Young, *Alaska Days*, 126.

15. JMW, III:248. For an account of Toyatte's death, as he was attempting to pacify an angry mob, see Young, *Alaska Days*, 127–29. Muir named one of the Stikine canyon glaciers after this chief and in his journal wrote, "As servants, friends, fellow-travelers," such native men "were far superior to the average American or European" ("Transcript of 1st Alaska Trip," JMP, 26:2107). To Louie he wrote, "I felt a singular interest in the Thlinket Indians I met & something like a missionary spirit came over me. Poor fellows I wish I could serve them" (3 Aug. 1880, JMP, 4:2096).

16. Engberg and Merrell, *John Muir: Letters from Alaska*, 78.

17. JMW, III:284–85.

18. M, "An Adventure with a Dog and a Glacier," *Century* 54 (Aug. 1897): 776.

19. M, *Stickeen*, 71. The Muirs later gave the name "Stickeen" to a family pet they kept on the ranch.

20. Quotations from the original draft can be found in Limbaugh, *John Muir's "Stickeen,"* 107–8. Limbaugh shows how widely Muir read to prepare this manuscript—drawing on over one hundred volumes from his library, but most importantly from George Romanes's *Animal Intelligence* (1883). For the popularity of the animal-story genre during this period, see Lutts, *The Wild Animal Story*, 1–21; and Mighetto, *Muir among the Animals*, xi–xxviii.

21. C. Hart Merriam, "To the Memory of John Muir," *Sierra Club Bulletin* 10 (Jan. 1917): 148–50.

22. Joanna Brown to Louie, 23 Oct. 1881, JMP, 4:2244; Annie Bidwell to M, 8 Apr., 4:2202.

23. M to Ann Muir, 27 Mar. 1881, JMP, 4:2192; M to Annie Bidwell, 29 Mar., 4:2198.

24. George W. Melville, *In the Lena Delta* (Boston: Houghton Mifflin, 1885), 413. See also Sachs, *Humboldt Current*, 273–332.

25. JMW, VII (*Cruise of the Corwin*):15–16.

26. JMW, VII:20–25.

27. JMW, VII:27–31.

28. M to Louie, 16 June 1881, JMP, 4:2270. See also his report, "On the Glaciation of the Arctic and Subarctic Regions Visited by the United States Steamer Corwin in the Year 1881," *Report of the Cruise of the U.S. Revenue Steamer Thomas Corwin, in the Arctic Ocean, 1881*, by Capt. C. L. Hooper, 48th Cong., 1st sess., 1884, Senate Exec. Doc. 204, 135–47. Muir also published a report, "Botanical Notes," in *Cruise of the Revenue Steamer Corwin in Alaska and the N.W. Arctic Ocean in 1881* (Washington: Government Printing Office, 1883), 47–53.

29. M to Louie, 4 July 1881, JMP, 4:2287.

30. Bockstoce, *Whales, Ice, and Men*, 137–41. Not until 1908 did the federal government prohibit the commercial killing of walruses.

31. JMW, VII:118–22.

32. JMW, VII:122.

33. JMW, VII:133–34, 139.

34. JMW, VII:156.

35. Bockstoce, *Whales, Ice, and Men*, 143–79.

36. JMW, VII:166–68.

37. The island, like Fort Wrangell, was named after the Russian admiral Baron Ferdinand Petrovich von Wrangell (1796–1870), who had ventured into the Arctic but never sighted nor landed on the island. So rich is the undisturbed biological diversity here that the Russian-owned island is now a UNESCO World Heritage Site.

38. Irving Rosse, "The First Landing on Wrangel Island," electronic book edition, Project Gutenberg, www.gutenberg.org/etext/18643.

39. JMW, III:323.

40. JMW, III:5.

41. JMW, VII:76–77.

42. Young, *Hall Young of Alaska*, 212.

CHAPTER 10

1. M to David Muir, May 1870, JMP, 2:828.

2. Anon., "Biography of John Theophil Strentzel," Strentzel papers, Bancroft Library.

3. *History of Contra Costa County, California* (1882; reprint, Martinez, CA: Contra Costa County Historical Society, 2000), 40; Anon., *Martinez: A California Town* (Martinez: RSI Publications, 1986).

4. *California Farmer and Journal of Useful Sciences* 22 (11 Nov. 1864): 121.

5. Strentzel to Samuel Erwin, 25 Mar. 1860, Strentzel papers. See also Strentzel's review of local agricultural development in *Illustrations of Contra Costa California with Historical Sketches* (1879; reprint, Oakland: Smith & Elliott, 1952), 13–15. Also, E. W. Hilgard, *Report on the Physical and Agricultural Features of the State of California* (Washington: GPO, 1884), 45–46, 110–111.

6. Edward J. Wickson, *The California Fruits and How To Grow Them*, 6th ed. (San Francisco: Pacific Rural Press, 1912), 54–55.

7. N. P. Chipman, *Report on the Fruit Industry of California* (Sacramento: State Board of Trade, 1889), 10.

8. Stoll, *Fruits of Natural Advantage*, 32–62.

9. Tyrell, *True Gardens of the Gods*, 36–55; Vaught, *Cultivating California*, 53.

10. Strentzel to Col. James L. L. Warren, 12 Feb. 1855, Warren papers, Bancroft Library, C-B 418, box 1.

11. Carr, *Patrons of Husbandry*, 109. The first president of the California Farmers' Union, a predecessor of the Grange, was Muir's friend from Chico, the highly successful rancher and orchardist John Bidwell, while Louie Strentzel had been a frequent attendee of Grange meetings with her parents and was often called on to play a medley of tunes from the Grange songbook on the piano.

12. Carr, *Patrons of Husbandry*, 290–303.

13. Strentzel, *Illustrations of Contra Costa California*, 13.

14. M, "Tulare Levels," San Francisco *Evening Bulletin*, 17 Nov. 1875, p. 1.

15. M, "California Agriculture," JMP, 39:6670–76.

16. M, "Sequoia Studies from Yosemite," JMP, 24:1210; M to J. Carr, 31 July 1875, JMP, 3:1502.

17. Louisiana Strentzel diary, 27 Jan. 1882, Strentzel papers, CF 16, folder 11.

18. M, "Wild Wool," *Overland Monthly* 4 (April 1875): 364.

19. M, "Wild Wool," 361.

20. M, "Wild Wool," 365.

21. M, "The Wild Sheep of California," *Overland Monthly* 12 (April 1874): 359.

22. Charles Darwin, *The Origin of Species by Means of Natural Selection* (1859; reprint, New York: Modern Library, n.d.), 51.

23. M, "Wild Wool," 365.

24. M, "Wild Wool," 366.

25. Muir contributed a new variety of peach to the ranch's production, which became one of the recommended varieties for California orchards. Originating as a "chance seedling," the Muir peach boasted the following qualities: "Fruit large to very large; perfect freestone; flesh clear yellow, very dense, rich and sweet; pit small; tree a good bearer and strong grower, if on rich soil, to which it is best adapted; . . . fruit a good shipper and canner, and particularly adapted to drying because of exceptional sweetness and density of flesh; yield, one pound dry from less than five pounds fresh." Wickson, *California Fruits*, 288.

26. Wickson, *California Fruits*, esp. pp. 570–73 on insecticides. See also T. Hart Hyatt, *Hyatt's Hand-book of Grape Culture* (San Francisco: H. H. Bancroft and Co., 1867); Gustave Eisen, *The Raisin Industry* (San Francisco: H. S. Crocker and Co., 1890).

27. Chan, *This Bitter-Sweet Soil*, 406; S. Galloway to M, 20 Nov. 1885, JMP, 5:2842. See also Vaught, *Cultivating California*, 69–73.

28. M, "Ranch Life," JMP, 28:3226. Richard Orsi ["'Wilderness Saint' and 'Robber Baron,'" 138] miscasts the Strentzel-Muir ranch as "a modern, scientifically managed factory of green gold," but he accurately notes the ties that Muir developed to some figures in California's business community.

29. M to Milicent Shinn, 18 Apr. 1883, JMP, 4:2492; M to David Muir, 26 Dec. 1887, 5:3028; Louie to M, 9 August 1888, 5:3138.

30. M, "Ranch Life," JMP, 28:3222–65. On one occasion, while planting buckeyes along the valley stream, Muir "got fearfully poisoned with poison oak" and had to be confined to his room for several days, with a badly swollen face. Louisiana Strentzel diary, 16 Jan. 1881.

31. Louisiana Strentzel diary, 21 Feb. 1882.

32. Louisiana Strentzel to Louie, 14 July 1884, JMP, 5:2623; Louie to Strentzels, 6 July, 5:2615; M to Wanda, July 10 and 16, 5:2618, 2625.

33. M to Mary Hand, 31 Dec. 1884, JMP, 5:2658.

34. Mary Muir Hand to her sisters, 19 Dec. 1882, JMP, 4:2447; M to Hands, 1 Jan. 1883, 4:2461.

35. Joanna Brown to M, 22 Apr. 1882, JMP, 4:2371.

36. M to Louie, 11 and 12 Aug. 1885, JMP, 5:2742, 2745.

37. M to Louie, 20 Aug. 1885, JMP, 5:2754; 30 Aug., 5:2764.

38. M, "The Yellowstone Park," San Francisco *Evening Bulletin*, 27 Oct. 1885, p. 4.

39. M to Louie, 19 Sept. 1885, JMP, 5:2794.

40. M to Louie, 3 and 4 Oct. 1885, JMP, 5:2807, 2810.

41. M to Louie, 6 Oct. 1885, JMP, 5:2815.

42. M to Louie, 10 Sept. 1885, JMP, 5:2784; Louie to M, 12 Sept. 1885, 5:2786.

43. Margaret Reid to M, 15 Feb. 1888, JMP, 5:3068.

44. Joanna Brown to M, 12 Feb. 1880, JMP, 4:1979; 8 Dec.? 1889, 6:3357; 23 June 1889, 6:3261.

1. For Muir's contacts with Twain and Warner, see Huber, *Wanderer All My Days*, 79–81. Muir may have met Twain at the offices of the *Century Magazine* in late September 1893.
2. Mark Twain, letter to the New York *Tribune*, 27 Sept. 1871, p. 6.
3. See Kazin, *Godly Hero*, xiv–xviii.
4. The best guides to this philosophical school are Weiner, *Evolution and the Founders of Pragmatism*, and Menand, *Metaphysical Club*.
5. Menand, *Metaphysical Club*, 209–14.
6. Nash, *Rights of Nature*, 41.
7. The book was inspired by the success of William Cullen Bryant's *Picturesque America; or, The Land We Live In* (New York: D. Appleton, 1872), which extolled the country's scenic beauty.
8. M, "Washington and Puget Sound," *Picturesque California*, 427.
9. M, "The Basin of the Columbia River," *Picturesque California*, 480–98.
10. Johnson, *Remembered Yesterdays*, 279.
11. McFarland (*Mugwumps, Morals & Politics*, 188–89) lists both Gilder and Johnson among the New York Mugwumps who in 1884 bolted the Republican Party to vote for the reform-minded Democrat Grover Cleveland. He sees them as, on the whole, progressives who expressed a healthy ambivalence about urban-industrial society.
12. Johnson, "Open Letters," *Century* 39 (Jan. 1890): 478.
13. M to R. U. Johnson, 13 Jan. 1890, JMP, 6:3377.
14. M to R. U. Johnson, 29 Oct. 1889, JMP, 6:3342; R. U. Johnson to M, 21 Nov. 1889, 6:3350; R. U. Johnson to M, 20 Feb. 1890, 6:3388.
15. M to R. U. Johnson, 6 Dec. 1889, JMP, 6:3353; McKenzie, "Open Letters," *Century* 39 (Jan. 1890): 476.
16. M to R. U. Johnson, 6 Dec. 1889, JMP, 6:3353; 20 Apr. 1890, 6:3431.
17. M to R. U. Johnson, 4 Mar. 1890, JMP, 6:3400.
18. M to R. U. Johnson, 4 Mar. 1890, JMP, 6:3400. See also Runte, *Yosemite*, 54–55.
19. M, "The Treasures of the Yosemite," *Century* 40 (Aug. 1890): 483; "Features of the Proposed Yosemite National Park," *Century* 40 (Sept. 1890): 667.
20. M to R. U. Johnson, 4 Mar. 1890, JMP, 6:3400.
21. M to Louie, 18 June 1890, JMP, 6:3470.
22. Bohn, *Glacier Bay*, 62.
23. Muir, "Alaskan Sled Trip" journal, JMP, 28:3042; JMW, III (*Travels in Alaska*):362–63.
24. Louie to M, 12 and 17 July 1890, JMP, 6:3492, 3499.
25. M, "Alaska," JMP, 40:7739, 7743.
26. Louie to R. U. Johnson, 27 Aug. 1890, JMP, 6:3519.
27. 30 Sept. 1890, *Congressional Record*, 51st Congress, 1st session, 10752.
28. See Dilsaver and Tweed, *Challenge of the Big Trees*, chap. 4.
29. See Orsi, *Sunset Limited*, 363–64. The railroad's was only one voice among many, but as Orsi argues, its voice was one of the most persuasive.
30. R. U. Johnson to M, 3 Oct. 1890, JMP, 6:3537.
31. Yosemite Commission, *Biennial Report, 1889–90*, 8–9, 15. See also Irish's letter to the Oakland *Evening Tribune*, 8 and 12 Sept. 1890, and the editor's response, 10 Sept. 1890, which was sympathetic to Muir and went on to advocate the preservation of "the whole region comprising the backbone of the Sierra from the American river south to the Kern."

32. M, letter to Oakland *Evening Tribune*, 16 Sept. 1890; M to R. U. Johnson, 24 Oct. 1890, JMP, 6:3552.

33. R. U. Johnson to M, 28 Aug. 1890, JMP, 6:3521.

34. M to R. U. Johnson, 13 May 1891, JMP, 7:3715.

35. M, "A Rival of the Yosemite," *Century* 43 (Nov. 1891): 97.

36. See Steen, *Origins of the National Forests*, 3–9. The crucial role in writing the final version of the bill may have been played by Preston Plumb of Kansas, a key member of the Senate Committee on Public Lands. See William Elsey Connolley, *The Life of Preston Plumb* (Chicago: Browne & Howell, 1913), 361–62.

37. William Armes to M, 15 May 1891, JMP, 7:3717; M to Armes, 26 May, 7:3729; Muir to R. U. Johnson, 13 May, 7:3715. See Jones, *John Muir and the Sierra Club*, 4–5; and Cohen, *History of the Sierra Club*, 8–12. Two organizations to defend America's wildlife had appeared in 1887: the Boone and Crockett Club for big-game animals and the Audubon Society for birds.

38. M to Henry Senger, 22 May 1892, reprinted in *Sierra Club Bulletin* 19 (Jan. 1917): 138.

39. Michael Smith calculates that 14% of the 182 charters members of the club were earth or life scientists (*Pacific Visions*, p. 144), a percentage that went down as the membership rose. Other prominent scientists in the early group include Joseph LeConte, George Davidson, William Dudley, Gustav Eisen, and Alice Eastwood.

40. Two years later congressional enemies, unhappy with Powell's directorship and his cautious views on how irrigation and land development should proceed, forced him out of the Geological Survey. See Worster, *River Running West*, 494–507, 534.

41. Annie Muir to Louie, 27 Apr. 1892, JMP, 7:3917.

CHAPTER 12

1. M to Louie, 29 May 1893, JMP, 7:4149.

2. M to Louie, 29 May 1893, JMP, 7:4149.

3. M to Louie, 12 June 1893, JMP, 7:4176; Gifford Pinchot to M, 19 June 1893, 7:4200.

4. M to Wanda, 7 June 1893, JMP, 7:4169.

5. M to Louie, 12 June 1893, JMP, 7:4176. See also Huber, *Wanderer All My Days*, 2–82, for a full account of Muir's first trip to New England.

6. M to Louie, 6 July 1893, JMP, 7:4240.

7. M to Louie, 12 and 22 July 1893, JMP, 7:4249, 4252; M to Helen and Wanda, 13 July 1893, 7:4250.

8. JMP, 27:2938–39. The Wordsworth quotation is from Winter, *Secure from Rash Assault*, 107–8. The Lake District was finally protected under the National Parks and Access to the Countryside Act of 1949.

9. M to Louie, 28 Aug. 1893, JMP, 7:4301.

10. M to Wanda, 25 Aug. 1893, JMP, 7:4300; James Bryce to R. U. Johnson, 9 Nov. 1895, 8:5044.

11. M to Louie, 30 Sept. 1893, JMP, 7:4338.

12. Muir distributed free copies of the book to friends all over the United States and Europe. After two years it had sold 3,000 copies. R. U. Johnson to M, 14 Dec. 1897, JMP, 9:5688.

13. JMW, IV (*The Mountains of California*):5–6. A closer view, however, would reveal many marks and disturbances.

14. JMW, IV:162.

15. JMW, IV:222, 231.

16. Buell, *Environmental Imagination*, 415–16.

17. M to R. U. Johnson, 3 Apr. 1894, JMP, 8:4492.

18. Ann Muir to Daniel H. Muir, 9 July 1894, JMP, 8:4566; Joanna Brown to M, 28 July 1894, 8:4574; R. U. Johnson to M, 3 Aug. 1894, 8:4577; 18 July, 8:4571; 7 Nov., 8:4650; 21 July, 8:4572.

19. Scidmore, "The New National Forest Reserves," *Century* 46 (Sept. 1893): 792–97. See also Price, *Flight Maps*, 62–73.

20. Miller, "Reminiscences of a Visit to Muir Home," JMP, 5:377.

21. M to J. Carr, 5 Nov. 1894, JMP, 8:4647; Carr to M, 18 Dec., 8:4719. On her confinement, see M to B. O. Kendall, Jan. 1902, 12:6958. A mutual friend realized the size of Muir's debt to Carr and thought it should justify a book dedication; see Galen Clark to J. Carr, 3 Dec. 1894, 8:4683.

22. The standard account remains Samuel Hays, *Conservation and the Gospel of Progress*, which, for all its many strengths, defines the conservation movement too narrowly and leaves Muir on the margins.

23. Following the death of Stiles, the weekly *Garden and Forest* ceased publication after 29 Dec. 1897. Another important conservation magazine was George Bird Grinnell's *Field and Stream*.

24. M, "A Plan to Save the Forests," *Century* 49 (Feb. 1895): 626–34.

25. M, "The National Parks and Forest Reservations," *Sierra Club Bulletin* 1 (Jan. 1896): 275. A thorough analysis of the military's early role in the national parks and of "Old Army virtue" as grounding for conservation is Meyerson, *Nature's Army*.

26. M to R. U. Johnson, 13 Dec. 1894, JMP, 8:4713. For a fuller discussion of the Caminetti bill and the politics of the Sierra Club in this period, see Jones, *John Muir and the Sierra Club*, 11–18.

27. Wolcott Gibbs in "A Model Forestry Commission," *Century* 52 (May 1896): 157.

28. R. U. Johnson to Louie, 27 May 1896, JMP, 9:5174; M to R. U. Johnson, 3 June 1896, 9:5179.

29. M to R. U. Johnson, 28 June 1896, JMP, 9:5222.

30. Muir to Louie, 21 Sept. 1896, JMP, 9:5297.

31. Muir interrupted his advisory role to tour southeastern Alaska with Professor Osborn and his Columbia students for two weeks in August—his fifth trip to the territory. In summer 1897, he accompanied Sargent and Edward Canby to the Yukon gold fields.

32. M to R. U. Johnson, 30 July 1896, JMP, 9:5270. Pinchot to M, 21 Oct. 1896, JMP, 9:5315. See also Miller, *Gifford Pinchot*, 129–30, 133–34; and Steen, *Conservation Diaries of Gifford Pinchot*, 68–77. After returning home, Pinchot proudly sent Muir a copy of his book *The White Pine* (1896), co-authored with Henry S. Graves—a dull little manual for determining board feet and timber growth rates.

33. Pinchot, *Breaking New Ground*, 103.

34. Charles Sargent to M, 5 Nov. 1896, JMP, 9:5331.

35. Dana and Fairfax, *Forest and Range Policy*, 59–64. McKinley suspended the reserves temporarily but eventually made them permanent.

36. National Forest Commission, "Report of the Committee," 55th Cong., 1st sess., 1897, Senate Doc. 105, vol. 5. In addition to new forest reserves, the commission recommended establishing new national parks at the Grand Canyon and Mt. Rainier.

37. Charles Sargent to M, 6 Apr. 1897, JMP, 9:5501; 8 June, 9:5544. By this point John Wesley Powell had retired; it was his successor Charles Walcott who was

rumored to be angling for the forest reserves. Fernow would leave office in 1898 and go on to establish and direct the first professional school of forestry in the United States at Cornell University.

38. Charles Sargent to M, 19 Apr. 1897, JMP, 9:5517; 3 May, 9:5519; M to Sargent, 28 Oct., 9:5652; M to R. U. Johnson, 27 Mar. 1898, 10:5887. Miller (*Gifford Pinchot*, pp. 119–23) has effectively demolished the myth that Muir and Pinchot had an angry confrontation in a Seattle hotel lobby over sheep grazing.

39. M to R. U. Johnson, 18 June 1897, JMP, 9:5551; M to Lukens, 18 Apr. 1897, 9:5513. The camping trip was a five-week outing in summer 1895.

40. M to Lukens, 18 Apr. 1897, JMP, 9:5516. For a defense of those hunters, see Reiger, *American Sportsmen and the Origins of Conservation*.

41. M to Walter Hines Page, 16 Apr. 1897, JMP, 9:5511.

42. These articles caused tension with Johnson, who feared that his publishing rival William Hines Page was luring Muir away. Warned the confident and exacting author, "You will have to pay well" for anything submitted in the future (M to R. U. Johnson, 7 Jan. 1898, JMP, 10:5739).

43. M, "The National Parks and Forest Reservations," *Harper's Weekly* 41 (5 June 1897): 566. See also M, "The Wild Parks and Forest Reservations of the West," *Atlantic Monthly* 81 (Jan. 1898): 15–28.

44. M, "American Forests," *Atlantic Monthly* 80 (Aug. 1897): 145–57. The nation's population was approaching seventy-four million at the time Muir was writing.

45. See Klein, *The Life & Legend of E. H. Harriman*. On the Harriman expedition, see Kennan, *E. H. Harriman*, vol. 1, 185–213; Goetzmann and Sloan, *Looking Far North*; and Sachs, *Humboldt Current*, 333–37.

46. Harriman "was beginning to visualize the most grandiose railroad scheme of all: a line that would circle the world," connecting Alaska and Siberia (Goetzmann and Sloan, *Looking Far North*, 8). Such a railroad was never built, and Harriman's expedition stuck to the coast rather than going into the interior where most of the line would have to be constructed.

47. C. Hart Merriam to M, 1 Apr. 1899, JMP, 10:6088; M to Sargent, 30 Apr., 10:6112. See also M to Merriam, 10 Apr., 10:6098; Merriam to M, 19 Apr., 10:6100.

48. M to R. U. Johnson, 7 Jan. and 25 Apr. 1898, JMP, 10:5739, 5806. See also the travel letters he sent to family members: 10:5892, 5897, 5907, 5930, 5977, and 5975. As the war evolved into American empire building in the Pacific, Muir grew more critical; he speaks of "the miserable Manilla [*sic*] war" (M to R. U. Johnson, 27 Mar. 1899, JMP, 10:6082).

49. After the hunters returned empty-handed from a place Muir had described enticingly, Burroughs cattily remarked, "there might not be any bears in Howling Valley after all—Muir's imagination may have done all the howling." Burroughs, "Narrative of the Expedition," *Harriman Alaska Series, vol. 1: Alaska*, 40.

50. M, "Harriman Expedition," JMP, 29:3707.

51. M, *Edward Henry Harriman*, 35–36.

52. M to Mary Harriman et al., 30 Aug. 1899, JMP, 10:6195.

CHAPTER 13

1. M to Charles Sargent, 12 Mar. 1903, JMP, 13:7503; Theodore Roosevelt to M, 14 Mar., 13:7516. For a glowing anticipation of Muir's upcoming trip to "Cold Siberia," see Bailey Millard in the San Francisco *Examiner*, 29 Mar. 1903.

2. "Charlie Leidig's Report on President Roosevelt's Visit in May, 1903," typescript, Yosemite National Park Research Library; M to Louie, 19 May 1903, JMP, 13:7647; M to Merriams and Baileys, 1 Jan. 1904, 14:7876.

3. Roosevelt, "John Muir," 27–28. Roosevelt's approach to wildlife usually involved killing; he would capture an unfamiliar species with his hat or shoot it with a gun and take it home for identification.

4. Burroughs, *Camping and Tramping with Roosevelt*, 7. See also Renehan, *John Burroughs*, 246–49, 253; and Schmitt, *Back to Nature*, 23–25. Burroughs and Roosevelt were allies in a campaign to discredit "nature fakers," popular writers who told stories about heroic, ethical wild animals. See Schmitt, 45–55; and Dunlap, *Saving America's Wildlife*, 27–31.

5. M to Daniel Beard, Apr. 1907, JMP, 16:9133; M to Henry Osborn, 16 July 1904, 14:8053.

6. *The State Papers as Governor and President, 1899–1909*, vol. 15, *The Works of Theodore Roosevelt* (New York: Charles Scribner's Sons, 1926), 102, 104.

7. See Dalton, *Theodore Roosevelt*, 239–48; Cutwright, *Theodore Roosevelt*, 210–27.

8. Theodore Roosevelt to M, 11 Nov. 1904, JMP, 14:8198.

9. The book was Muir's most popular in his lifetime, selling about 8,000 copies in its first decade (sales and royalties list, JMP, 47:12731).

10. JMW, VI (*Our National Parks*):4–5.

11. JMW, VI:73.

12. JMW, VI:283–89. For the original report, see *Proceedings of the Boston Society of Natural History* 15 (1873): 185–86.

13. JMW, VI:82.

14. Ray Stannard Baker, "John Muir," *Outlook* 74 (June 1903): 376.

15. Burroughs, "God and Nature," *Writings of John Burroughs*, vol. 11: *The Light of Day*, 181–90.

16. M, "The Grand-Cañon of the Colorado," *Century* 65 (Nov. 1902): 109, 114–15.

17. M to R. U. Johnson, 9 July 1902, JMP, 12:7131; M, "The Grand-Cañon," 116.

18. M to Andrew Carnegie, no date, JMP, 12:7691. Carnegie made his great fortune through manufacturing steel in Pittsburgh, Pennsylvania. In 1900, after a career marred by industrial violence against striking workers, he began giving away his money to humanitarian causes. He moved back to Scotland and became particularly focused on building an International Peace Palace in the Netherlands.

19. M, "World Tour," JMP, 29:3941. For a more detailed account of Muir's Russian travels, see William H. Brennan, "John Muir in Russia," *John Muir Newsletter*, Fall 1993, Winter 1994, Summer 1994.

20. M, "World Trip," JMP, 29:3934–37. Muir refers to the Lindula (or Lintula) region, but Mikko Saikku of the University of Helsinki has identified it as the Raivola forest, which was planted in the early eighteenth century (personal communication, 16 Mar. 2002).

21. M, "World Tour," 29:3978–79.

22. M, "World Tour," 29:4026–27.

23. M, "World Tour," 29:4028.

24. The two Sargents continued on to Java and Korea, collecting in all eight thousand bulbs, seeds, and roots, before returning home late in the year. For a summary of their travels, see the Boston *Evening Record*, 29 Dec. 1903.

25. M, "World Trip: The Chinese," JMP, 45:10931.

26. M to Louie, 3 Oct. 1903, JMP, 13:7786; 29:4051.

27. M to Louie, 18 Oct. 1903, JMP, 13:7797.

28. "Reminiscences by Emily Bell," 13 Oct. 1915, JMP, 51:3.

29. The karri (*Eucalyptus diversicolor*) of western Australia, which ranges up to 300 feet tall, came closest to the American redwoods, which in exceptional cases can reach 350 feet.

30. A survey of newspapers during Muir's six-week stay yielded no other mention of his presence. He might have found a better reception in Dunedin, the major Scots settlement in New Zealand, but he did not go there or to the wild fjord land of Milford Sound. See "World Tour," JMP, 30:4175–4210; Hall, "John Muir in New Zealand"; and Paul Star and Lynne Lochhead, "Children of the Burnt Bush: New Zealanders and the Indigenous Remnant, 1880–1930," in *Environmental Histories of New Zealand*, ed. Eric Pawson and Tom Brooking (Melbourne: Oxford Univ. Press, 2002), 119–35.

31. M to Louie, 27 Jan. 1904, JMP, 14:7888.

32. M to Katharine Graydon, 22 Oct. 1900, JMP, 11:6492.

33. See John Keibel, *Alhambra Valley Trestle Then and Now* (Concord, Calif.: n.p., 1999).

34. M to Louie, 20 July 1901, JMP, 11:6683.

35. William Trout to M, 2 Aug. 1904, JMP, 14:8096; Henry Randall to M, 29 Mar. 1902, 12:7041.

36. M to C. Hart Merriam, 4 June 1904, JMP, 14:7967.

37. Pomeroy, *In Search of the Golden West*, 158–59. See also Limerick, *Desert Passages*.

38. Muir to Lummis, 13 June 1905, JMP, 15:8565; M, "Arizona," 45:10936–39, and "Henry Clay Hooker Tribute," 45:10967–68.

39. Theodore Roosevelt to M, 17 Aug. 1905, JMP, 15:8653.

40. M to Theodore Lukens, 27 Aug. 1905, JMP, 15:8663. See Wild, "Months of Sorrow and Renewal."

41. Alice Cotton Fletcher, "Along the Way I Met John Muir," JMP, 57:405. For the fossil tree journals, see JMP, 30:4347–4358; 33:1772–1844. Muir mistakenly thought that the giant club mosses *Sigillaria* and *Lepidodendron*, dating back to the Carboniferous, were the most common species in the Petrified Forest, but the dominant species were conifers.

42. Lubrick, *Petrified Forest National Park*, 76; Rothman, *America's National Monuments*, 56–58. For Muir's role in mapping the monument, see M to John Byrne, 12 Sept. 1906, JMP, 16:8945; M to Frank Bond, 15 Jan. 1907, 16:9050; M to William Colby, 15 Jan. 1907, 16:9052.

43. M to Helen and Wanda, 15 Jan. 1906, JMP, 16:8783. Records show at least three different names for a Chinese servant in the Strentzel manse: Ah Jung, Ah Sun, and Ah Fong.

44. M to Margaret Lunam, 13 Oct. 1905, JMP, 15:8709; M to J. E. Calkins, 8 Apr. 1906, 16:8840

45. Keeler, *San Francisco through Earthquake and Fire* (San Francisco: Paul Elmer, 1906), 1–3.

46. Fradkin, *Great Earthquake*, xi. A modern scientific assessment of the earthquake can be found at www.quake.usgs.gov/info/1906.

47. Fradkin, *Great Earthquake*, 72–73. Edward Harriman sent the city $200,000 in relief funds and mobilized his railroad empire to help the city and its refugees. See Fradkin, 202–4, for an account of his tussle with James D. Phelan, Jr., local banker and politico, over who was in charge of the relief effort. For the business community's campaign to play down the bad publicity of the earthquake, see Theodore Steinberg, *Acts of God: The Unnatural History of Natural Disaster in America* (New York: Oxford Univ. Press, 2000), 26–34.

48. Wanda to M, 18 Apr. 1906, JMP, 16:8859. Muir was temporarily away in Arizona when the quake hit; straightaway he came home to oversee repairs.

49. M to Helen, 10 June 1906, JMP, 16:8909; M to Margaret Lunum, 13 May, 16:8881. The Sierra Club lost all of its records in the fire; and William Keith, who had become one of the wealthiest artists in America, lost 2,000 paintings (16:8883).

50. M to Katharine Graydon, 15 Dec. 1906, JMP, 16:8985.

51. M to E. H. Harriman, 4 Jan. 1905, JMP, 15:8305; M to William Herrin, 26 Feb., 15:8413. Muir gave credit to Harriman for the victory in a letter to R. U. Johnson, 24 Feb., 15:8406. For a first-hand account of the political maneuvering in Sacramento and Washington, see "Remembering Will Colby," *Sierra Club Bulletin* 50 (Dec. 1965): 71–73. Also, Orsi, *Sunset Limited*, 364–70.

52. M to R. U. Johnson, 16 July 1906, JMP, 16:8937.

53. Gifford Pinchot to Marsden Manson, 28 May 1906, JMP, 16:8895; 15 Nov., 16:8972.

CHAPTER 14

1. M to Helen, 22 Apr. 1908, JMP, 17:9689.

2. For a more detailed but highly colored account of Helen's life in Daggett, and Muir's anxiety over her seedy companions, see Wild, *Fantasy and Reality in Daggett*, 11–41.

3. M to Theodore Roosevelt, 21 Apr. 1908, JMP, 17:9664; Roosevelt to M, 27 Apr. 1908, 17:9686.

4. M to J. E. Calkins, 15 Sept. 1908, JMP, 17:9887.

5. In 1918, an especially virulent strain of influenza killed 600,000 Americans, the worst epidemic in the nation's history, and millions more people overseas. See Alfred Crosby, *Epidemic and Peace 1918: America's Forgotten Pandemic* (New York: Cambridge Univ. Press, 1976).

6. M to Helen, 4 June 1908, JMP, 17:9783.

7. See Samuel Marshall Ilsley, "Katharine Hooker: A Memoir" (Santa Barbara: Schauer Printing Studio, 1935); and Jennifer Watts, "Wayfarer in Italy: The Photography of Marion Osgood Hooker," *Southern California Quarterly* 85 (spring 2003): 83–100.

8. "Reminiscences of J. E. Calkins," JMP, 51:77.

9. M to J. E. Calkins, 7 March 1908, JMP, 17:9588; M to Theodore Lukens, 11 March 1908, 17:9602; William Kent to M, 16 October 1908, 17:9918; 3 Nov., 17:9940.

10. Katharine Hooker to M, 3 Aug. 1907, JMP, 16:9194; George Wharton James to M, 16 July 1908, 17:9826. A thorough account of the James controversy appears in Bonnie Giesel, *Kindred Spirits*, which reprints the extant Carr-Muir letters and lists all those that have disappeared. It is impossible to know what Muir did not want published. After his death Wanda Muir Hanna successfully took James to court to stop his publishing plans, and in 1915 Houghton Mifflin brought out a family-approved selection, *Letters to a Friend*.

11. Klein, *Life and Legend of E. H. Harriman*, 400–401; M to Harriman, Jan. 1907, JMP, 16:9074.

12. M to Helen, 21 Aug. 1908, JMP, 17:9873; 10 Sept., 17:9882.

13. Langston, *Where Land and Water Meet*, 83–87; Blake, *Balancing Water*, 52–57.

14. Roosevelt was proud of the steps he had taken "to preserve from destruction beautiful and wonderful wild creatures." They included fifty-one bird refuges (starting with Pelican Island off the Florida coast), four big-game refuges, five national

parks or monuments, and protection of wildlife in Alaska. See *Theodore Roosevelt: An Autobiography* (New York: Macmillan, 1916), 434–35.

15. Frank Graham, Jr., *The Audubon Ark: A History of the National Audubon Society* (New York: Alfred Knopf, 1990), 43–45; Blake, 90–95.

16. Klein, 68–70. Arden's forested acres became, in 1910, the Bear Mountain–Harriman State Park. The family also acquired and donated another Harriman State Park, in northwestern Idaho near Yellowstone National Park.

17. M, *Edward Henry Harriman*, 3–5, 7, 36.

18. George E. Mowry, *The Era of Theodore Roosevelt*, 89.

19. M to Burroughs, 9 Nov. 1909, JMP, 18:10534.

20. Charles Elliott to M, 17 May and 9 July 1912, JMP, 20:11675, 11726.

21. See Daniel Rodgers, *The Work Ethic in Industrial America, 1850–1920* (Chicago: Univ. of Chicago Press, 1978).

22. M, *A Thousand Mile Walk*, 136–37.

23. For a more detailed history of the controversy over damming Hetch Hetchy, see Righter, *Battle over Hetch Hetchy*; Simpson, *Dam!*; Jones, *John Muir and the Sierra Club*; Runte, *Yosemite*; Nash, *Wilderness and the American Mind*, chap. 10; Hundley, *The Great Thirst*; Clements, "Politics and the Park"; and Richardson, "The Struggle for the Valley."

24. Phelan, "Hetch Hetchy and the Wealth-Producers," *California Weekly* 18 (26 March 1909): 283–84.

25. C. D. Marx, "Water Supply for San Francisco," *Transactions of the Commonwealth Club of California* 2 (June 1907): 272–81; William Kahrl, *Water and Power: The Conflict over Los Angeles's Water Supply in the Owens Valley* (Berkeley: Univ. of California Press, 1982), 156.

26. Kent to M, 16 and 17 Jan. 1908, JMP, 17:9495, 9500.

27. M to Kent, 14 Jan. and 6 Feb. 1908, JMP, 17:9487, 9527.

28. Jones, 89–91; Righter, 27–28.

29. Will Tevis, owner of the Bay Cities Water Company, which had water to sell from the American and Consumnes rivers, tendered the bribe. A grand jury removed the entire Schmitz administration from office following the 1906 earthquake. See Brechin, 107–8.

30. M to R. U. Johnson, 2 Sept. 1907, JMP, 16:9241.

31. M, "The Tuolumne Yosemite in Danger," *Outlook* 87 (2 Nov. 1907): 486.

32. M, "The Tuolumne Yosemite in Danger," 488–89.

33. M, "The Hetch-Hetchy Valley," *Sierra Club Bulletin* 6 (Jan. 1908): 219–20.

34. Theodore Roosevelt to M, 16 Sept. 1907, JMP, 16:9269; M to James R. Garfield, 6 Sept. 1907, 16:9246.

35. Theodore Roosevelt to M, 16 Sept. 1907, JMP, 16:9269.

36. On Pinchot's effort to apply "the rhetoric of the market" to conservation, see Brian Balogh, "Scientific Forestry and the Roots of the Modern American State," *Environmental History* 7 (Apr. 2002): 198–225.

37. The Garfield decision was printed in House Committee on Public Lands, *Use of Lake Eleanor and Hetch Hetchy Valleys to San Francisco, Cal.*, 60th Cong., 2d Sess., 1909, H. Rept. 2085, Appendix A, 5–9.

38. M to Theodore Roosevelt, 21 Apr. 1908, JMP, 51:203; Roosevelt to M, 27 Apr. 1908, JMP, 17:9686; M to William Colby, 23 May 1908, 17:9750. Muir had suggested giving the city Lake Eleanor, but he never offered that Hetch Hetchy should follow at some future date.

39. M to Helen, 24 May 1908, JMP, 17:9753.

40. *Proceedings of Conference of Governors, May 13–15, 1908* (Washington: GPO, 1909), VI, 8.

41. M et al. to Theodore Roosevelt, 2 May 1908, JMP, 17:9702; M to R. U. Johnson, 2 June, 17:9778.

42. M to William Colby, 31 Dec. 1908, JMP, 17:10020.

43. M to R. U. Johnson, 7 Feb. 1909, JMP, 18:10157; Burroughs to M, 28 Dec. 1910, 19:11146. In a review of *Yosemite*, Burroughs disagreed with the religious message Muir found in nature: "Whatever else wild nature is, she certainly is not pious, and has never been trained in the Sunday-school. But, as reflected in Mr. Muir's pages, she very often seems on her way to or from the kirk" (*Literary Digest* 44 [1 June 1912]: 1165).

44. Marsden Manson, "Hetch-Hetchy: The Law and the Facts," *California Weekly* 1 (18 June 1909): 475–76. On the split within the Club, see Jones, 108–17. Muir became president of the SPSN and Badè its vice president; the national advisory council included former Secretary of the Interior John Noble, Robert Underwood Johnson, J. Horace McFarland, Harriet Monroe, Alden Sampson, and Edmund Whitman.

45. See Rome, " 'Political Hermaphrodites' "; Merchant, "Women of the Progressive Conservation Movement"; and Smith, *Pacific Visions*, 177–80.

46. Monroe testimony, Senate Committee on Public Lands, *Hetch Hetchy Reservoir Site, Hearing on Joint Resolution 123*, 60th Congress, 2d sess., 1909, 31. See also Robin Schulze, "Harriet Monroe's Pioneer Modernism: Nature, National Identity, and *Poetry: A Magazine of Verse*." The author kindly shared this unpublished manuscript.

47. M to William Taft, Sept. 1909, JMP, 18:10484.

48. M to Katherine and Marian Hooker, 20 Oct. 1909, JMP, 18:10501; M to Colby, 1 Nov.? 1909, 18:10526.

49. Pinchot, *Breaking New Ground*, 501; Ickes, "Not Guilty! Richard A. Ballinger—An American Dreyfus," *Saturday Evening Post* 212 (25 May 1940): 9–11, 123 ff. See also Miller, *Gifford Pinchot*, 206–26.

50. Henry Osborn to M, 25 Jan. 1910, JMP, 19:10692; M to Osborn, 8 Feb., 19:10705; M to R. U. Johnson, 3 Sept., 19:11046.

51. Nash (*Wilderness and the American Mind*, 181) interpreted the Hetch Hetchy fight as a pivotal moment in the effort to preserve "wilderness," while Robert Righter argues (*Battle over Hetch Hetchy*, 5–6) that both sides advocated development—for water storage or tourism. Muir's view that the valley was consecrated ground should not, however, be confused with any form of economic development.

52. Henry Osborn to Robert Collier, 6 Apr. 1910, JMP, 19:10788.

53. M to Helen Funk, 31 Mar. 1911, JMP, 20:11283.

54. M to Helen Funk, 30 May 1911, JMP, 20:11347.

55. M to Mary Hand, 30 Apr. 1911, JMP, 20:11315; M to Colby, 8 May 1911, 20:11323. Robert Underwood Johnson was at work on a history of conservation that would restore Muir to the head of the movement, along with John Wesley Powell and Bernard Fernow, all marginalized by Pinchot's self-promotion.

56. M to Katharine Hooker, 26 June 1911, JMP, 20:11384.

57. Helen Funk to M, 3 Aug. 1911, JMP, 20:11459; Robert Marshall to M, 28 June, 20:11397.

58. For a reprint of the journal and travel correspondence, see Branch, *John Muir's Last Journey*.

59. M to Helen Funk, 18 Sept. 1911, JMP, 20:11489. On the rubber speculators, see Richard P. Tucker, *Insatiable Appetites: The United States and the Ecological Degradation of the*

Tropical World (Berkeley: Univ. of California Press, 2000), 229–33; and Warren Dean, *Brazil and the Struggle for Rubber: A Study in Environmental History* (New York: Cambridge Univ. Press, 1987).

60. Branch, *John Muir's Last Journey*, 88.
61. Branch, *John Muir's Last Journey*, 115.
62. Branch, *John Muir's Last Journey*, 147.
63. Branch, *John Muir's Last Journey*, 149. In contrast to Muir's bloodless expedition, Roosevelt's safari party to Africa, just three years earlier, killed or trapped over 11,000 animals, 500 of them big-game animals like elephants and white rhinos. The carcasses were offered to the Smithsonian Institution and the American Museum of Natural History.
64. Branch, *John Muir's Last Journey*, 159–60.
65. M to Howard Palmer, 12 Dec. 1912, JMP, 20:11913. John Freeman, a contract engineer hired by the city, tried to appease nature lovers by arguing that, "by care in the designs, the use for water supply can be made to add greatly to the scenic value, and the large expenditure which ordinary water rates permit upon development work, can bring the scenic beauties of the Hetch Hetchy Valley within reach of a hundred-fold more people than would otherwise find it possible to enjoy them during the next quarter or half century." *On the Proposed Use of a Portion of the Hetch Hetchy, Eleanor and Cherry Valleys* (San Francisco: Rincon Publishing Co., 1912), 151.
66. M to Howard Palmer, 12 Dec. 1912, JMP, 20:11913.
67. M to Katharine Hooker, 3 Apr. 1913, JMP, 1:12136.
68. M to Anna Dickey, 30 Oct. 1912, JMP, 20:11868; M to R. U. Johnson, 23 Mar. 1913, 21:12106.
69. House Committee on Public Lands, *Hetch Hetchy Grant to San Francisco*, 63d Congress, 1st sess., H. Rpt. 21, 1913, 26–27. Thirty years later, in his autobiography *Breaking New Ground*, Pinchot never mentioned the Hetch Hetchy episode or his role in it. Perhaps he was ashamed of how political motives had, on that occasion, led him to distort his ideals.
70. William Kent quoted in Nash, "John Muir, William Kent, and the Conservation Schism," 132.
71. Charles W. Eliot to M, 7 Nov. 1913, JMP, 21:12480; R. U. Johnson to M, 30 July, 21:12316; Helen Elliot to M, 13 Oct., 21:12433. See Righter, 129.
72. M to Kelloggs, 27 Dec. 1913, JMP, 21:12542; Charlotte Kellogg to M, no date, 21:12572; M to Helen, 13 Dec. 1913, 21:12528.
73. The quote from Carnegie, originally appearing in the San Francisco *Chronicle*, had been saved by Muir in a marked envelope and was reprinted in *John Muir Newsletter*, spring 1991.

EPILOGUE

1. M to R. U. Johnson, 1 Jan. 1914, JMP, 22:12613.
2. M to Edward Parsons, 19 Jan. 1914, JMP, 22:12642.
3. M to Katharine Hooker, 3 Apr. 1913, JMP, 21:12136.
4. M to Katharine Hooker, no date, JMP, 21:12554.
5. Parsons, "John Muir and the Alaska Book," 33–35.
6. Parsons, "John Muir and the Alaska Book," 35.
7. M to Houghton Mifflin Co., 12 June 1914, JMP, 22:12802; Mrs. E. B. Harvey to M, 17 Jan., 22:12640; Andrew Carnegie to M, 6 Nov. 1913, 21:12477. Muir praised

Carnegie in turn for "coming forth out of that tremendous titanic iron and dollar work with a heart in sympathy with all humanity." M to Carnegie, 22 Jan. 1914, 22:12648.

8. "Reminiscences of James Whitehead," William Frederic Badè papers, JMP, 51:00015.

9. James Whitehead to M, 30 Jan. 1913, JMP, 21:12041; M to Whitehead, 13 Feb., 21:12061. The slightly revised story of Charlie Whitehead's death appears in *My Boyhood and Youth*, 170–73, where it becomes an indictment of the stoicism and repression of natural affection that the old Scots religion forced on people.

10. M to R. U. Johnson, 1 Jan. 1914, JMP, 22:12613.

11. Walter Hines Page to M, 25 Nov. 1901, Walter Hines Page papers, Houghton Library, Harvard University.

12. The United States entered the war in 1917, three years after it began, on the side of Great Britain, and on 11 November 1918 the war ended with Germany's surrender.

13. Thomas Bisset to M, 31 Aug. 1914, JMP, 22:12906; Isabel Wilder to M, 22 Nov., 22:12999.

14. M to R. U. Johnson, 17 Sept. 1914, JMP, 22:12932.

15. The Muir Lodge was located in Big Santa Anita Canyon above Sierra Madre and Pasadena. For historic photos of the rustic building, before rampaging floods washed it away, see http://angeles.sierraclub.org/about/MuirLodge.asp.

16. New York *Times*, 25 Dec. 1914.

17. New York *Times*, 3 Jan. 1915.

18. Bryce, "A Message and Appreciation," *Sierra Club Bulletin* 10 (Jan. 1916): preface. Other tributes in this issue came from Robert Underwood Johnson, Charles Keeler, Henry Osborn, Marion Randall Parsons, William Badè, and William Colby.

19. San Francisco *Chronicle*, 19 Jan. 1915; Arno Dosch, "The Mystery of John Muir's Money," 21. The latter article was sarcastically subtitled, "A Simple Naturalist's Studies in the Temple of Mammon."

20. The daughters divided their father's inheritance, and Helen used her portion to build a showy home in Daggett and generally allowed Buell to squander it. They gave the Strentzel manse to the Sierra Club, which soon sold it to a private owner. In 1964 the National Park Service acquired the house and nine attached acres as the John Muir National Historic Site. More recently, Dunbar, Scotland, has transformed Muir's birthplace into a first-class museum.

21. Among his Asian followers was the late Ryoza Azuma of Japan, author of *The Life of John Muir: Father of Nature Conservation* (1973).

Bibliography

The most valuable resource for this book has been the *Microfilm Edition of the John Muir Papers*, edited by Ronald H. Limbaugh and Kirsten E. Lewis, 55 reels (Chadwyck-Healey, 1986), herein cited as JMP, followed by reel number and frame number. Muir's sixty-plus journals have now been digitized and are available at the University of the Pacific's Holt-Atherton Library Website: http://library.pacific.edu/ha/digital/index.asp.

Many of the illustrations in this book are also taken from the Holt-Atherton Special Collections, University of the Pacific Library (copyright 1984 Muir-Hanna Trust) and are published here, along with the letters and journals, by permission. The illustrations are identified as H-A, followed by the collection name.

An outstanding guide to Muir's published writing is William F. and Maymie B. Kimes, *John Muir: A Reading Bibliography* (Palo Alto: William P. Wreden, 1977). For citations of Muir's books, I have generally used *The Writings of John Muir*, Sierra edition (Boston: Houghton Mifflin, 1916–1924), in 10 volumes, herein cited as JMW, followed by volume and page numbers.

For those interested in reading Muir's own words the Sierra Club has provided electronic texts of all his writings in the John Muir Exhibit (http://www.sierraclub. org/), while the University of Georgia has made available a full digital facsimile edition of Houghton Mifflin's *The Writings of John Muir* at its Website (http://fax.libs.uga.edu/ PS2447xM5/). Many other editions of individual volumes or collections have been published in Scotland as well as the United States, including William Cronon's *John Muir: Nature Writings* (New York: Library of America, 1997).

The following bibliography is a selected list of archival collections and published works dealing with Muir's life and times that have been important in the writing of this book.

MANUSCRIPT COLLECTIONS

Arnold Arboretum, Harvard University
　　Charles Sprague Sargent papers
Bancroft Library, University of California, Berkeley
　　William F. Badè papers
　　John Bidwell papers
　　William Colby papers
　　Robert Underwood Johnson papers
　　Sierra Club papers
　　John Strentzel papers
　　John Swett papers
Houghton Library, Harvard University
　　Walter Hines Page papers

Huntington Library
  Ezra and Jeanne Carr papers
  Charles Keeler papers
  Theodore P. Lukens papers
  John Muir papers
John Muir National Historic Site, Martinez, CA
  Newman Collection
National Archives of Scotland
  Dunbar Council Minutes
  Minute Books of Magistrates and Committees
  Town Clerk's Minute Books, Dunbar
State Historical Society of Wisconsin
  John Muir papers and drawings
University of the Pacific
  William Frederic Badè papers
  John Muir papers
  Muiriana collection
  Shone collection
  Linnie Marsh Wolfe papers
Yosemite National Park Research Library
  James Mason Hutchings diary

BOOKS

Albanese, Catherine L. *Nature Religion in America from the Algonkian Indians to the New Age.* Chicago: Univ. of Chicago Press, 1990.

Anderson, David, et al. *John Muir's Dunbar.* North Berwick: Tantallion, 1998.

Badè, William Frederic. *The Life and Letters of John Muir.* 2 vols. Boston: Houghton Mifflin, 1928.

Bate, Jonathan. *Romantic Ecology: Wordsworth and the Environmental Tradition.* London: Routledge, 1991.

Bederman, Gail. *Manliness & Civilization: A Cultural History of Gender and Race in the United States, 1880–1917.* Chicago: Univ. of Chicago Press, 1995.

Bidwell, John. *A Journey to California, 1841: The Journey of John Bidwell.* 1843; reprint, Berkeley: Friends of the Bancroft Library, 1964.

Blackburn, Thomas C., and Kat Anderson, eds. *Before the Wilderness: Environmental Management by Native Californians.* Menlo Park, CA: Ballena, 1993.

Blake, Tupper Ansel, Madeline Graham Blake, and William Kittredge. *Balancing Water: Restoring the Klamath Basin.* Berkeley: Univ. of California Press, 2000.

Bockstoce, John R. *Whales, Ice, & Men: The History of Whaling in the Western Arctic.* Seattle: Univ. of Washington Press, 1986.

Bohn, Dave. *Glacier Bay: The Land and the Silence.* Gustavus: Alaska National Parks and Monuments Association, 1967.

Branch, Michael P. *John Muir's Last Journey: South to the Amazon and East to Africa.* Washington: Island, 2001.

Brander, Michael. *The Emigrant Scots.* London: Constable, 1982.

Brechin, Gray. *Imperial San Francisco: Urban Power, Earthly Ruin.* Berkeley: Univ. of California Press, 1999.

Brewer, William H. *Up and Down in California in 1860–1864.* Reprint, Berkeley: Univ. of California Press, 1966.

Buell, Lawrence. *The Environmental Imagination: Thoreau, Nature Writing, and the Formation of American Culture*. Cambridge: Harvard Univ. Press, 1995.

———. *Writing for an Endangered World: Literature, Culture, and Environment in the U.S. and Beyond*. Cambridge: Harvard Univ. Press, 2001.

———. *Emerson*. Cambridge: Harvard Univ. Press, 2003.

Bunnell, Lafayette Houghton. *Discovery of the Yosemite. And the Indian War of 1851, Which Led to that Event*. Chicago: Fleming Revell, 1880.

Burns, Robert. *The Poems and Songs of Robert Burns*. 3 vols. Ed. James Kinsley. Oxford: Clarendon, 1968.

Burroughs, John. *The Writings of John Burroughs*. 23 vols. Boston: Houghton Mifflin, 1904–23.

———. *Camping & Tramping with Roosevelt*. Boston: Houghton Mifflin, 1906.

Carosso, Vincent P. *The California Wine Industry: A Study of the Formative Years, 1830–1895*. Berkeley: Univ. of California Press, 1951.

Carr, Ezra S. *The Patrons of Husbandry on the Pacific Coast*. San Francisco: A. L. Bancroft, 1875.

Chan, Sucheng. *This Bittersweet Soil: The Chinese in California Agriculture, 1860–1910*. Berkeley: Univ. of California Press, 1986.

Clark, Jean Hanna, and Shirley Sargent, eds. *Dear Papa: Letters between John Muir and His Daughter Wanda*. Fresno: Panorama Books, 1985.

Clark, Ronald. *The Victorian Mountaineers*. London: B. T. Batsford, 1953.

Clarke, James Mitchell. *The Life and Adventures of John Muir*. San Diego: Word Shop, 1979.

Coates, Peter. *Nature: Western Attitudes Since Ancient Times*. Berkeley: Univ. of California Press, 1998.

Cohen, Michael P. *The Pathless Way: John Muir and American Wilderness*. Madison: Univ. of Wisconsin Press, 1984.

———. *History of the Sierra Club, 1892–1970*. San Francisco: Sierra Club Books, 1988.

Cohen, Nancy. *The Reconstruction of American Liberalism, 1865–1914*. Chapel Hill: Univ. of North Carolina Press, 2002.

Cornelius, Brother. *Keith, Old Master of California*. 2 vols. New York: Putnam, 1942–57.

Curti, Merle, and Vernon Carstensen. *The University of Wisconsin, 1848–1925*. 4 vols. Madison: Univ. of Wisconsin Press, 1949–94.

Dalton, Kathleen. *Theodore Roosevelt: A Strenuous Life*. New York: Knopf, 2002.

Dana, Samuel Trask, and Sally K. Fairfax. *Forest and Range Policy: Its Development in the United States*. New York: McGraw-Hill, 1980.

Demars, Stanford E. *The Tourist in Yosemite, 1855–1985*. Salt Lake City: Univ. of Utah Press, 1991.

Deverell, William. *Railroad Crossing: Californians and the Railroad, 1850–1910*. Berkeley: Univ. of California Press, 1994.

Dick, Thomas. *The Christian Philosopher*. Philadelphia: Key, Mielke & Biddle, 1832.

Dillenberger, John. *Protestant Thought and Natural Science: A Historical Interpretation*. Garden City: Doubleday, 1960.

Dilsaver, Lary M., and William C. Tweed. *Challenge of the Big Trees: A Resource History of Sequoia and Kings Canyon National Parks*. Three Rivers, CA: Sequoia Natural History Association, 1990.

Dorman, Robert L. *A Word for Nature: Four Pioneering Environmental Advocates, 1845–1913*. Chapel Hill: Univ. of North Carolina Press, 1998.

Dunaway, Finis. *Natural Visions: The Power of Images in American Environmental Reform*. Chicago: Univ. of Chicago Press, 2005.

Dunlap, Thomas R. *Saving America's Wildlife*. Princeton: Princeton Univ. Press, 1988.

———. *Faith in Nature: Environmentalism as Religious Quest*. Seattle: Univ. of Washington Press, 2004.

Earl, John. *John Muir's Longest Walk*. Garden City, NY: Doubleday, 1975.

Edwards, Rebecca. *New Spirits: Americans in the Gilded Age, 1864–1905*. New York: Oxford Univ. Press, 2006.

Ehrlich, Gretel. *John Muir: Nature's Visionary*. Washington, D.C.: National Geographic Society, 2000.

Engberg, Robert, and Donald Wesling, eds. *John Muir: To Yosemite and Beyond, Writings from the Years 1863 to 1875*. Madison: Univ. of Wisconsin Press, 1980.

———, and Bruce Merrell, eds. *John Muir: Letters from Alaska*. Madison: Univ. of Wisconsin Press, 1993.

Farnsworth, R. W. C. *A Southern California Paradise (in the Suburbs of Los Angeles)*. Pasadena: R. W. C. Farnsworth, 1883.

Farquhar, Francis P. *History of the Sierra Nevada*. Berkeley: Univ. of California Press, 1966.

Fishburne, Charles Jr. *The Cedar Keys in the Civil War and Reconstruction, 1861–1876*. Cedar Key, FL: n.p., 1982.

Fiske, Turbese, and Keith Lummis. *Charles E. Lummis: The Man and His West*. Norman: Univ. of Oklahoma Press, 1975.

Flanagan, Maureen A. *America Reformed: Progressives and Progressivisms, 1890–1920s*. New York: Oxford Univ. Press, 2007.

Fleck, Richard F. *Henry Thoreau and John Muir among the Indians*, Hamden, CT: Archon Books, 1985.

Fox, Stephen. *The American Conservation Movement: John Muir and His Legacy*. Madison: Univ. of Wisconsin Press, 1985.

Fradkin, Philip L. *The Great Earthquake and Firestorms of 1906: How San Francisco Nearly Destroyed Itself*. Berkeley: Univ. of California Press, 2005.

Gatta, John. *Making Nature Sacred: Literature, Religion, and Environment in America from the Puritans to the Present*. Oxford: Oxford Univ. Press, 2004.

Gibbens, Robert P., and Harold F. Heady. *The Influence of Modern Man on the Vegetation of Yosemite Valley*. Berkeley: Univ. of California Division of Agricultural Sciences, 1964.

Gifford, Terry. *Reconnecting with John Muir: Essays in Post-Pastoral Literature*. Athens: Univ. of Georgia Press, 2006.

Gillis, Michael J., and Michael F. Magliari. *John Bidwell and California: The Life and Writings of a Pioneer, 1841–1900*. Spokane: Arthur H. Clark, 2003.

Gisel, Bonnie Johanna, ed. *Kindred and Related Spirits: The Letters of John Muir and Jeanne C. Carr*. Salt Lake City: Univ. of Utah Press, 2001.

Goetzmann, William, and Kay Sloan. *Looking Far North: The Harriman Expedition to Alaska, 1899*. New York: Viking, 1982.

Greene, Linda Wedel. *Historic Resource Study: Yosemite National Park, California*. 3 vols. Washington, D.C.: National Park Service, 1987.

Guha, Ramachandra. *Environmentalism: A Global History*. New York: Longman, 2000.

Hampton, H. Duane. *How the U.S. Cavalry Saved Our National Parks*. Bloomington: Indiana Univ. Press, 1971.

Harrison, Robert Pogue. *Forests: The Shadow of Civilization*. Chicago: Univ. of Chicago Press, 1992.

Hays, Samuel P. *Conservation and the Gospel of Efficiency: The Progressive Conservation Movement, 1890–1920*. Cambridge: Harvard Univ. Press, 1959.

Henderson, George L. *California and the Fictions of Capital*. New York: Oxford Univ. Press, 1999.

Herman, Arthur. *How the Scots Invented the Modern World*. New York: Crown, 2001.

Holmes, Steven J. *The Young John Muir: An Environmental Biography*. Madison: Univ. of Wisconsin Press, 1999.

Huber, J. Parker. *A Wanderer All My Days: John Muir in New England*. Sheffield, VT: Green Frigate Books, 2006.

Hutchings, James Mason. *In the Heart of the Sierras. Yo Semite Valley and the Big Tree Groves*. Reprint, Lafayette, CA: Great West Books, 1990.

Hyatt, T. Hart. *Hyatt's Handbook of Grape Culture*. San Francisco: H. H. Bancroft, 1867.

Ise, John. *The United States Forest Policy*. New Haven: Yale Univ. Press, 1920.

——. *Our National Park Policy: A Critical History*. Baltimore: Johns Hopkins Univ. Press, 1961.

Isenberg, Andrew C. *Mining California: An Ecological History*. New York: Hill & Wang, 2005.

Issel, William, and Robert W. Cherny. *San Francisco, 1865–1932: Politics, Power, and Urban Development*. Berkeley: Univ. of California Press, 1986.

Jacoby, Karl. *Crimes against Nature: Squatters, Poachers, Thieves, and the Hidden History of American Conservation*. Berkeley: Univ. of California Press, 2001.

Johnson, Robert Underwood. *Remembered Yesterdays*. Boston: Little, Brown, 1923.

Johnston, Hank. *The Yosemite Grant, 1864–1906*. Yosemite National Park: Yosemite Association, 1995.

Jones, Holway R. *John Muir and the Sierra Club: The Battle for Yosemite*. San Francisco: Sierra Club, 1964.

Kazin, Michael. *A Godly Hero: The Life of William Jennings Bryan*. New York: Knopf, 2006.

Keeler, Charles Augustus. *San Francisco through Earthquake and Fire*. San Francisco: P. Elder, 1906.

Kennan, George. *E. H. Harriman: A Biography*. Boston: Houghton Mifflin, 1922.

King, Clarence. *Mountaineering in the Sierra Nevada*. Ed. William Howarth. Reprint, New York: Penguin, 1989.

King, Thomas Starr. *A Vacation among the Sierras: Yosemite in 1860*. San Francisco: Book Club of California, 1962.

Klein, Maury. *The Life and Legend of E. H. Harriman*. Chapel Hill: Univ. of North Carolina Press, 2000.

Kneeland, Samuel. *The Wonders of the Yosemite Valley and of California*. 2d ed. Boston: A. Moore, 1872.

Knoepflmacher, Ulrich Camillus, and Georg Bernhard Tennyson, eds. *Nature and the Victorian Imagination*. Berkeley: Univ. of California Press, 1977.

Kollin, Susan. *Nature's State: Imagining Alaska as the Last Frontier*. Chapel Hill: Univ. of North Carolina Press, 2001.

Landow, George P. *The Aesthetic and Critical Theories of John Ruskin*. Princeton: Princeton Univ. Press, 1971.

Langston, Nancy. *Where Land and Water Meet: A Western Landscape Transformed*. Seattle: Univ. of Washington Press, 2003.

Larson, Roger Keith. *Controversial James: An Essay on the Life and Work of George Wharton James*. San Francisco: Book Club of California, 1991.

Le Conte, Joseph. *A Journal of Ramblings through the High Sierra of California*. Reprint, New York: Ballantine, 1971.

Limbaugh, Ronald H. *John Muir's "Stickeen" and the Lessons of Nature*. Fairbanks: Univ. of Alaska Press, 1996.

Limerick, Patricia. *Desert Passages: Encounters with the American Deserts*. Albuquerque: Univ. of New Mexico Press, 1985.

Livesay, Harold C. *Andrew Carnegie and the Rise of Big Business*. 2d ed. New York: Longmans, 2000.

Lockmann, Ronald F. *Guarding the Forests of Southern California: Evolving Attitudes toward Conservation of Watershed, Woodlands, and Wilderness*. Glendale, CA: Arthur H. Clark, 1981.

Lowenthal, David. *George Perkins Marsh: Prophet of Conservation*. Seattle: Univ. of Washington Press, 2000.

Lubick, George M. *Petrified Forest National Park: A Wilderness Bound in Time*. Tucson: Univ. of Arizona Press, 1996.

Lutts, Ralph H. *The Nature Fakers: Wildlife, Science & Sentiment*. Golden, CO: Fulcrum, 1990.

——, ed. *The Wild Animal Story*. Philadelphia: Temple Univ. Press, 1998.

Lyon, Thomas J. *John Muir*. Boise, ID: Boise State College, 1972.

Mackenzie, Agnes Mure. *Scotland in Modern Times, 1720–1939*. London: W. & R. Chambers, 1941.

Marsh, George Perkins. *Man and Nature*. 1864; reprint, Seattle: Univ. of Washington Press, 2003.

Matthes, Francois E. *The Incomparable Valley: A Geologic Interpretation of the Yosemite*. Berkeley: Univ. of California Press, 1950.

McEvoy, Arthur F. *The Fisherman's Problem: Ecology and Law in the California Fisheries, 1850–1890*. New York: Cambridge Univ. Press, 1986.

McFarland, Gerald. *Mugwumps, Morals & Politics, 1884–1820*. Amherst: Univ. of Massachusetts Press, 1975.

Melham, Tom, and Ferrell Grehan. *John Muir's Wild America*. Washington: National Geographic Society, 1976.

Menand, Louis. *The Metaphysical Club: A Story of Ideas in America*. New York: Farrar, Straus & Giroux, 2001.

Merchant, Carolyn. *Green versus Gold: Sources in California's Environmental History*, edited by Carolyn Merchant. Washington, D.C.: Island Press, 1998.

——. *Reinventing Eden: The Fate of Nature in Western Culture*. New York: Routledge, 2003.

Merriam, C. Hart, ed. *Harriman Alaska Expedition*. 12 vols. Washington: Smithsonian, 1910–1914.

Meyerson, Harvey. *Nature's Army: When Soldiers Fought for Yosemite*. Lawrence: Univ. Press of Kansas, 2001.

Mighetto, Lisa. *Muir among the Animals: The Wildlife Writings of John Muir*. San Francisco: Sierra Club Books, 1986.

——. *Wild Animals and American Environmental Ethics*. Tucson: Univ. of Arizona Press, 1991.

Miller, Char. *Gifford Pinchot and the Making of Modern Environmentalism*. Washington: Island, 2001.

Miller, James. *The History of Dunbar*. Dunbar: James Downie, 1859.

Miller, Sally M., ed. *John Muir: Life and Work*. Albuquerque: Univ. of New Mexico Press, 1993.

——, ed. *John Muir in Historical Perspective*. New York: Peter Lang, 1999.

——, and Daryl Morrison, eds. *John Muir: Family, Friends, and Adventures*. Albuquerque: Univ. of New Mexico Press, 2005.

Moore, James R. *The Post-Darwinian Controversies: A Study of the Protestant Struggle To Come to Terms with Darwin in Great Britain and America, 1870–1900*. Cambridge: Cambridge Univ. Press, 1979.

Morrison, Ernest. *J. Horace McFarland: A Thorn for Beauty*. Harrisburg: Pennsylvania History and Museum Commission, 1995.

Mowry, George E. *The California Progressives*. Berkeley: Univ. of California Press, 1951.

Muir, John. *Edward Henry Harriman*. New York: Doubleday, Page, 1911.

——. *Stickeen: The Story of a Dog*. 1909; reprint, Boston: Houghton Mifflin, 1912.

——. *Rambles of a Botanist among the Plants and Climates of California*. Los Angeles: Dawson's Book Shop, 1974.

Nash, Roderick F. *The Rights of Nature: A History of Environmental Ethics*. Madison: Univ. of Wisconsin Press, 1989.

——. *Wilderness and the American Mind*. 4th ed. New Haven: Yale Univ. Press, 2001.

Nesbitt, Robert C., and William F. Thompson. *Wisconsin: A History*. 2nd ed. Madison: Univ. of Wisconsin Press, 1989.

Nicholson, Marjorie Hope. *Mountain Gloom and Mountain Glory: The Development of the Aesthetics of the Infinite*. Reprint, Seattle: Univ. of Washington Press, 1997.

O'Grady, John P. *Pilgrims to the Wild: Everett Ruess, Henry David Thoreau, John Muir, Clarence King, Mary Austin*. Salt Lake City: Univ. of Utah Press, 1993.

Olmsted, Frederick Law. *The Papers of Frederick Law Olmsted: Vol. 5: The California Frontier, 1863–1865*. Ed. Victoria Post Ranney, Gerard J. Rauluk, and Carolyn F. Hoffman. Baltimore: Johns Hopkins Univ. Press, 1990.

Orsi, Richard J. *Sunset Limited: The Southern Pacific Railroad and the Development of the American West, 1850–1930*. Berkeley: Univ. of California Press, 2005.

——, Alfred Runte, and Marlene Smith-Baranzini, eds. *Yosemite and Sequoia: A Century of California National Parks*. Berkeley: Univ. of California Press, 1993.

Parsons, Marion Randall. *Old California Houses: Portraits and Stories*. Berkeley: Univ. of California Press, 1952.

Philippon, Daniel J. *Conserving Words: How American Nature Writers Shaped the Environmental Movement*. Athens: Univ. of Georgia Press, 2004.

Pinchot, Gifford. *The Fight for Conservation*. New York: Doubleday, Page, 1910.

——. *Breaking New Ground*. New York: Harcourt, Brace, 1947.

Piper, H. W. *The Active Universe: Pantheism and the Concept of Imagination in the English Romantic Poets*. London: Univ. of London/Athlone Press, 1962.

Pomeroy, Earl. *In Search of the Golden West: The Tourist in Western America*. Reprint, Lincoln: Univ. of Nebraska Press, 1957.

Pomeroy, Elizabeth. *John Muir: A Naturalist in Southern California*. Pasadena: Many Moons, 2001.

Price, Jennifer. *Flight Maps: Adventures with Nature in Modern America*. New York: Basic Books, 1999.

Reiger, John F. *American Sportsmen and the Origins of Conservation*. Rev. ed. Corvallis: Oregon State Univ. Press, 2001.

Renehan, Edward J., Jr. *John Burroughs: An American Naturalist*. Post Mills, VT: Chelsea Green, 1992.

Richardson, Elmo R. *The Politics of Conservation: Crusade and Controversies, 1897–1913*. Berkeley: Univ. of California Press, 1962.

Richardson, Robert D., Jr. *Emerson: The Mind on Fire*. Berkeley: Univ. of California Press, 1995.

Righter, Robert W. *The Battle over Hetch Hetchy: America's Most Controversial Dam and the Birth of Modern Environmentalism*. New York: Oxford Univ. Press, 2005.

Rothman, Hal. *America's National Monuments: The Politics of Preservation*. Reprint, Lawrence: Univ. Press of Kansas, 1989.

Runte, Alfred. *Yosemite: The Embattled Wilderness*. Lincoln: Univ. of Nebraska Press, 1990.

——. *National Parks: The American Experience*. 3d ed. Lincoln: Univ. of Nebraska Press, 1997.

Sachs, Aaron. *The Humboldt Current: Nineteenth-Century Exploration and the Roots of American Environmentalism*. New York: Viking, 2006.

Sanborn, Margaret. *Yosemite: Its Discovery, Its Wonders, and Its People*. Yosemite, CA: Yosemite Association, 1989.

Sandweiss, Martha A. *Print the Legend: Photography and the American West*. New Haven: Yale Univ. Press, 2002.

Sargent, Shirley. *Theodore Parker Lukens: Father of Forestry*. Los Angeles: Dawson's Book Shop, 1969.

———. *John Muir in Yosemite*. Yosemite, CA: Flying Spur, 1971.

———. *Solomons of the Sierras: The Pioneer of the John Muir Trail*. Yosemite, CA: Flying Spur, 1989.

Scharff, Virginia J., ed. *Seeing Nature through Gender*. Lawrence: Univ. Press of Kansas, 2003.

Schmitt, Peter J. *Back to Nature: The Arcadian Myth in Urban America*. Reprint, Baltimore: Johns Hopkins Univ. Press, 1990.

Schrepfer, Susan. *Nature's Altars: Mountains, Gender, and American Environmentalism*. Lawrence: Univ. Press of Kansas, 2005.

Sellars, Richard West. *Preserving Nature in the National Parks: A History*. New Haven: Yale Univ. Press., 1997.

Simpson, John Warfield. *Yearning for the Land: A Search for the Importance of Place*. New York: Pantheon, 2002.

———. *Dam! Water, Power, Politics, and Preservation in Hetch Hetchy Valley and Yosemite National Park*. New York: Pantheon, 2005.

Smith, Herbert F. *John Muir*. New York: Twayne, 1965.

Smith, Michael L. *Pacific Visions: California Scientists and the Environment, 1850–1915*. New Haven: Yale Univ. Press, 1987.

Smout, Thomas C. *A History of the Scottish People, 1560–1830*. London: Collins, 1969.

———. *A Century of the Scottish People, 1830–1950*. London: Collins, 1986.

Solnit, Rebecca. *Savage Dreams: A Journey into the Landscape Wars of the American West*. New York: Vintage, 1994.

———. *River of Shadows: Eadweard Muybridge and the Technological Wild West*. New York: Viking, 2003.

Spence, Mark D. *Dispossessing the Wilderness: Indian Removal and the Making of the National Parks*. New York: Oxford Univ. Press, 1999.

Spring Valley Water Co. *The Future Water Supply of San Francisco: A Report to the Honorable Secretary of Interior and Advisory Board of Engineers of the United States Army*. San Francisco: Rincon Publishing Co., 1912.

Stallnecht, Newton P. *Strange Seas of Thought: Studies in William Wordsworth's Philosophy of Nature*. Bloomington: Indiana Univ. Press, 1958.

Stanley, Millie. *The Heart of John Muir's World: Wisconsin, Family, and Wilderness Discovery*. Madison: Prairie Oaks, 1995.

Starr, Kevin. *Americans and the California Dream, 1850–1915*. New York: Oxford Univ. Press, 1973.

———. *Inventing the Dream: California through the Progressive Era*. New York: Oxford Univ. Press, 1985.

———. *Material Dreams: Southern California through the 1920s*. New York: Oxford Univ. Press, 1990.

Steen, Harold K., ed. *Origins of the National Forests: A Centennial Symposium*. Durham, NC: Forest History Society, 1992.

———. *The Conservation Diaries of Gifford Pinchot*. Durham, NC: Forest History Society, 2001.

Stephens, Lester D. *Joseph Le Conte, Gentle Prophet of Evolution*. Baton Rouge: Louisiana State Univ. Press, 1982.

Stoll, Mark. *Protestantism, Capitalism, and Nature in America*. Albuquerque: Univ. of New Mexico Press, 1997.

Stoll, Steven. *The Fruits of Natural Advantage: Making the Industrial Countryside in California*. Berkeley: Univ. of California Press, 1998.

Strong, Douglas H. *Tahoe: An Environmental History*. Lincoln: Univ. of Nebraska Press, 1984.

———. *Dreamers and Defenders: American Conservationists*. Reprint, Lincoln: Univ. of Nebraska Press, 1988.

Sutton, S. B. *Charles Sprague Sargent and the Arnold Arboretum*. Cambridge: Harvard Univ. Press, 1970.

Szasz, Ferenc Morton. *The Divided Mind of Protestant America, 1880–1930*. University: Univ. of Alabama Press, 1982.

Taylor, Ray W. *Hetch Hetchy: The Story of San Francisco's Struggle to Provide a Water Supply for Her Future Needs*. San Francisco: Ricardo Orozco, 1926.

Taylor, Bob Pepperman. *Our Limits Transgressed: Environmental Political Thought in America*. Lawrence: Univ. Press of Kansas, 1992.

Thomas, Keith. *Man and the Natural World: A History of the Modern Sensibility*. London: Allan Lane, Penguin, 1983.

Tocqueville, Alexis de. *Democracy in America*. Ed. J. P. Mayer, trans. George Lawrence. Garden City, NY: Anchor Books, 1969.

Trout, W. H. *Trout Family History*. Milwaukee: n.p., 1916.

Turner, Frederick. *Rediscovering America: John Muir in His Time and Ours*. New York: Viking, 1985.

Turner, Tom. *Sierra Club: 100 Years of Protecting Nature*. New York: Abrams, 1991.

Tyndall, John. *Hours of Exercise in the Alps*. New York: D. Appleton, 1875.

———. *The Glaciers of the Alps & Mountaineering in 1861*. New York: E. P. Dutton, 1906.

Tyrrell, Ian. *True Gardens of the Gods: California-Australian Environmental Reform, 1860–1930*. Berkeley: Univ. of California Press, 1999.

Ullman, James Ramsey. *The Age of Mountaineering*. London: Collins, 1956.

Vale, Thomas R., and Geraldine R. Vale. *Walking with Muir across Yosemite*. Madison: Univ. of Wisconsin Press, 1998.

Vaught, David. *Cultivating California: Growers, Specialty Crops, and Labor, 1875–1920*. Baltimore: Johns Hopkins Univ. Press, 1999.

Walker, Charlotte Zoe, ed. *Sharp Eyes: John Burroughs and American Nature Writing*. Syracuse, NY: Syracuse Univ. Press, 2000.

Walker, Franklin. *San Francisco's Literary Frontier*. New York: Knopf, 1939.

Walls, Laura Dassow. *Emerson's Life in Science: The Culture of Truth*. Ithaca: Cornell Univ. Press, 2003.

———. *Seeing New Worlds: Henry David Thoreau and Nineteenth-Century Natural Science*. Madison: Univ. of Wisconsin Press, 1995.

Watkins, T. H. *John Muir's America*. New York: Crown, 1976.

Weiner, Philip P. *Evolution and the Founders of Pragmatism*. Cambridge: Harvard Univ. Press, 1949.

West, Robert Frederick. *Alexander Campbell and Natural Religion*. New Haven: Yale Univ. Press, 1948.

Whitney, Josiah D. *The Yosemite Book*. New York: Julius Bien, 1868.

———. *The Yosemite Book*. New York: Julius Bien, 1868.

Wild, Peter, ed. *Fantasy and Reality in Daggett: John Muir's Desert Correspondence*. Johannesburg, CA: Shady Myrick Research Project, 2007.

Wilkins, Thurman, and Caroline Lawson Hinkley. *Clarence King: A Biography*. Rev. ed. Albuquerque: Univ. of New Mexico Press, 1988.

———. *John Muir: Apostle of Nature*. Norman: Univ. of Oklahoma Press, 1995.

Williams, Dennis C. *God's Wilds: John Muir's Vision of Nature*. College Station: Texas A & M Univ. Press, 2002.

Winter, James. *Secure from Rash Assault: Sustaining the Victorian Environment*. Berkeley: Univ. of California Press, 1999.

Wolfe, Linnie Marsh. *Son of the Wilderness: The Life of John Muir*. Reprint, Madison: Univ. of Wisconsin Press, 1978.

———, ed. *John of the Mountains: The Unpublished Journals of John Muir*. Reprint, Madison: Univ. of Wisconsin Press, 1966.

Wood, J. W. *Pasadena, California, Historical and Personal*. Pasadena, n.p., 1917.

Wordsworth, William. *The Prelude: Selected Poems and Sonnets*. New York: Holt, Rinehart, & Winston, 1954.

Worster, Donald. *Nature's Economy: A History of Ecological Ideas*. 2d ed. New York: Cambridge Univ. Press, 1994.

———. *A River Running West: The Life of John Wesley Powell*. New York: Oxford Univ. Press, 2001.

Wyatt, David. *The Fall into Eden: Landscape and Imagination in California*. Cambridge: Cambridge Univ. Press, 1986.

Wyman, Mark. *The Wisconsin Frontier*. Bloomington: Indiana Univ. Press, 1998.

Yelverton, Theresa. *Teresina in America*. 2 vols. 1875; reprint, New York: Arno, 1974.

———. *Zanita, a Tale of the Yo-semite*. 1872; reprint, Berkeley: Ten Speed, 1991.

Yosemite Commission. *Biennial Reports*. Sacramento: State Printer, 1867–1902.

Young, Samuel Hall. *Alaska Days with John Muir*. 1915; reprint, Salt Lake City: Peregrine Smith, 1990.

———. *Hall Young of Alaska*. Chicago: Fleming Revell, 1927.

ARTICLES AND CHAPTERS

Anderson, Melville B. "The Conversation of John Muir." *American Museum Journal* 15 (1915): 116–21.

Badè, William Frederic. "John Muir." *Science* 41 (1915): 353–54.

———. "John Muir." In *Dictionary of American Biography*. Vol. 8, 314–17. New York: Scribner's, 1943.

Barrus, Clara. "With John O'Birds and John O'Mountains in the Southwest." *Century* 80 (1910): 521–28.

———. "In the Yosemite with John Muir." *Craftsman* 23 (Dec. 1912): 324–35.

Beesley, David. "The Opening of the Sierra Nevada and the Beginnings of Conservation in California 1827–1900." *California History* 75 (1996–97): 322–37, 383–85.

Bland, Henry Meade. "John Muir." *Overland Monthly* 47 (1906): 517–25.

Blodgett, Peter J. "Visiting 'The Realm of Wonder': Yosemite and the Business of Tourism, 1855–1916." *California History* 69 (1990): 118–33.

Branch, Michael P. "'Angel Guiding Gently': The Yosemite Meeting of Ralph Waldo Emerson and John Muir, 1871." *Western American Literature* 32 (1997): 126–49.

Buell, Lawrence. "The Thoreauvian Pilgrimage: The Structure of an American Cult." *American Literature* 61 (1989): 175–99.

Buske, Frank E. "John Muir: 'Go to Alaska. Go and See.'" *Alaska Journal* 9 (1979): 32–37.

———. "John Muir and the Alaska Gold Rush." *Pacific Historian* 25 (1981): 37–49.

———. "John Muir's Alaska Experience." *Pacific Historian* 29 (1985): 113–23.

Carr, Jeanne C. "John Muir." *California Illustrated Magazine* 2 (1892): 88–94.

Clarken, George Gerard. "At Home with Muir." *Overland Monthly* 52 (1908): 125–28.

Clements, Kendrick A. "Engineers and Conservationists in the Progressive Era." *California History* 58 (1979–80): 282–303.

———. "Politics and the Park: San Francisco's Fight for Hetch Hetchy, 1890–1913." *Pacific Historical Review* 48 (1979): 184–215.

Coates, Peter. "In Nature's Defence: Americans and Conservation." Keele University, Staffordshire: British Association for American Studies Pamphlet Series, 1993.

———. "John Muir." In *Reader's Guide to American History*. Ed. Peter Parish, 470–72. London: Fitzroy Dearborn, 1997.

Cohen, Michael P. "John Muir's Public Voice." *Western American Literature* 10 (1975): 177–87.

———. "Stormy Sermons." *Pacific Historian* 265 (1981): 21–36.

Colby, William E. "John Muir—President of the Sierra Club." *Sierra Club Bulletin* 10 (1916): 2–7.

———. "Yosemite and the Sierra Club." *Sierra Club Bulletin* 23 (1938): 11–19.

Crimmel, Hal. "No Place for 'Little Children and Tender, Pulpy People': John Muir in Alaska." *Pacific Northwest Quarterly* 92 (2001): 171–80.

Cronon, William. "Landscape and Home: Environmental Traditions in Wisconsin." *Wisconsin Magazine of History* 74 (1990–91): 83–105.

Dannenbaum, Jed. "John Muir and Alaska." *Alaska Journal* 2 (1972): 14–20.

Dean, Dennis R. "John Muir and the Origin of Yosemite Valley." *Annals of Science* 48 (1991): 453–85.

DeLuca, Kevin, and Anne Demo. "Imagining Nature and Erasing Class and Race: Carleton Watkins, John Muir, and the Construction of Wilderness." *Environmental History* 6 (2001): 541–60.

Devall, Bill. "John Muir As Deep Ecologist." *Environmental Review* 6 (1982): 63–86.

Dixon, Elizabeth I. "Some New John Muir Letters." *Southern California Quarterly* 46 (1964): 239–58.

Dosch, Arno. "Mystery of John Muir's Money." *Sunset* 36 (1916): 20–22, 61–63.

Engberg, Robert. "John Muir: from Poetry to Politics, 1871–1876." *Pacific Historian* 25 (1981): 11–19.

———. "John Muir, the Geologist of the Yosemite." *Pacific Historian* 27 (1983): 47–51.

Fleck, Richard F. "John Muir's Evolving Attitudes toward Native American Cultures." *American Indian Quarterly* 4 (1978): 19–31.

———. "John Muir's Homage to Henry David Thoreau." *Pacific Historian* 29 (1985): 54–64.

Hall, Colin Michael. "John Muir in New Zealand." *New Zealand Geographer* 43 (1987): 99–103.

Holliday, J. S. "The Politics of John Muir." *California History* 63 (1984): 135–39.

Holmes, Steven J. "John Muir, Jeanne Carr, and Ralph Waldo Emerson: A Case-Study of the Varieties of Transcendentalist Influence." *Journal of Unitarian Universalist History* 25 (1998): 1–25.

Hyde, Anne Farrar. "Temples and Playgrounds: The Sierra Club in the Wilderness, 1901–1922." *California History* 66 (1987): 208–19.

———. "William Kent: The Puzzle of a Progressive Conservationist." In *California Progressivism Revisited*. Ed. William Deverell and Tom Sitton, 34–56. Berkeley: Univ. of California Press, 1994.

James, George Wharton. "John Muir: Geologist, Explorer, Naturalist." *Craftsman* 7 (1905): 637–54.

John Muir Newsletter 1– (1981–present).

Johnson, Robert U. "John Muir As I Knew Him." *Sierra Club Bulletin* 10 (1916): 9–15.

Keeler, Charles. "Recollections of John Muir." *Sierra Club Bulletin* 10 (1916): 16–19.

Kelley, Robert L. "The Mining Debris Controversy in the Sacramento Valley." *Pacific Historical Review* 25 (1956): 331–44.

Kimes, William F. "Honors Come to John Muir from the Land of His Birth." *Pacific Historian* 25 (1981): 86–91.

Leighley, John. "John Muir's Image of the West." *Annals of Association of American Geographers* 48 (1958): 309–18.

Limbaugh, Ronald H. "The Nature of John Muir's Religion." *Pacific Historian* 29 (1985): 16–29.

———. "Stickeen and the Moral Education of John Muir." *Environmental Historical Review* 15 (1991): 25–45.

———. "John Muir and Modern Environmental Education." *California History* 72 (1992): 170–77.

Lockmann, Ronald F. "Improving Nature in Southern California: Early Attempts to Ameliorate the Forest Resources in the Transverse Ranges." *Southern California Quarterly* 58 (1976): 485–98.

———. "Forests and Watershed in the Environmental Philosophy of Theodore P. Lukens." *Journal of Forest History* 32 (1979): 82–91.

Long, David R. "Pipe Dreams: Hetch Hetchy, the Urban West, and the Hydraulic Society Revisited." *Journal of the West* 34 (1995): 19–31.

Lowitt, Richard. "The Hetch Hetchy Controversy, Phase II: The 1913 Senate Debate." *California History* 74 (1995): 190–203.

Lundberg, Ann. "John Muir and Yosemite's 'Castaway Book': The Troubling Geology of Native America." *Western American Literature* 36 (2001): 25–55.

Lynch, Ann T. "Bibliography of Works by and about John Muir, 1869–1978." *Bulletin of Bibliography* 36 (1979): 71–80.

Lyon, Thomas J. "John Muir's Enlightenment." *Pacific Historian* 25 (1981): 50–57.

Merchant, Carolyn. "Women of the Progressive Conservation Movement: 1900–1916." *Environmental Review* 8 (1984): 57–85.

Merrell, Bruce. "'A Wild, Discouraging Mess': John Muir Reports on the Klondike Gold Rush." *Alaska History* 7 (1992): 30–39.

Merritt, J. I. "Turning Point: John Muir in the Sierra, 1871." *American West* 16 (1979): 4–15, 62–63.

Meyer, John M. "Gifford Pinchot, John Muir, and the Boundaries of Politics in American Thought." *Polity* 39 (1997): 267–84.

Mighetto, Lisa. "John Muir and the Rights of Animals." *Pacific Historian* 29 (1985): 103–12.

Miller, Char. "The Greening of Gifford Pinchot." *Environmental Historical Review* 16 (1992): 1–20.

———. "What Happened in the Rainier Grand's Lobby? A Question of Sources." *Journal of American History* 86 (2000): 1709–14.

Morris, David Copland. "A Dog's Life: Anthropomorphism, Sentimentality, and Ideology in John Muir's Stickeen." *Western American Literature* 31 (1996): 139–57.

Nash, Roderick. "John Muir, William Kent, and the Conservation Schism." *Pacific Historical Review* 36 (1967): 423–33.

Novak, Barbara. "American Landscape: Changing Concepts of the Sublime." *American Art Journal* 4 (1972): 42.

O'Brien, Bart. "Earthquakes or Snowflowers: The Controversy over the Formation of Yosemite Valley." *Pacific Historian* 29 (1985): 30–41.

Ogden, Kate Nearpass. "God's Great Plow and the Scripture of Nature: Art and Geology at Yosemite." *California History* 71 (1992): 88–109.

——— "Sublime Vistas and Scenic Backdrops." In *Yosemite and Sequoia: A Century of California National Parks*. Ed. Richard J. Orsi, Alfred Runte, and Marlene Smith-Baranzini, 33–49. Berkeley: Univ. of California Press, 1993.

Olney, Warren. "Water Supply for the Cities about the Bay of San Francisco." *Out West* 31 (July 1909): 599–605.

Orsi, Richard J. "'Wilderness Saint' and 'Robber Baron': The Anomalous Partnership of John Muir and the Southern Pacific Company for Preservation of Yosemite National Park." *Pacific Historian* 29 (1985): 136–56.

Osborn, Henry Fairfield. "John Muir." *Sierra Club Bulletin* 10 (1916): 33–36.

Parsons, E. T. "Proposed Destruction of Hetch-Hetchy." *Out West* 31 (1909): 607–27.

Parsons, Marion R. "John Muir and the Alaska Book." *Sierra Club Bulletin* 10 (1916): 29–32.

Penick, James L., Jr. "The Age of the Bureaucrat: Another View of the Ballinger-Pinchot Controversy." *Journal of Forest History* (1963): 15–20.

Pisani, Donald J. "Forests and Conservation, 1865–1890." *Journal of American History* 72 (1985): 340–59.

———. "Forests and Reclamation, 1891–1911." *Forest & Conservation History* 37 (1993): 68–79.

Polos, Nicholas C. "John Muir, a Stranger in the Southland." *Pacific Historian* 18 (1974): 1–12, 18.

———. "The Educational Philosophy of John Swett and John Muir." *Pacific Historian* 26 (1982): 58–69.

Prescott, Gerald. "Farm Gentry vs. the Grangers: Conflict in Rural California." *California Historical Quarterly* 56 (1977–78): 328–45.

Proffitt, Merrilee. "The Sierra Club and Environmental History: A Selected Bibliography." *California History* 71 (1992): 270–75.

Rakestraw, Lawrence. "Sheep Grazing in the Cascade Range: John Minto vs. John Muir." *Pacific Historical Review* 27 (1958): 371–82.

Rice, William B. "A Synthesis of Muir Criticism." *Sierra Club Bulletin* 28 (1943): 79–95.

Richardson, Elmo R. "The Struggle for the Valley: California's Hetch Hetchy Controversy, 1905–1913." *California Historical Society Quarterly* 8 (1959): 249–58.

Riley, Glenda. "'Wimmin is Everywhere': Conserving and Feminizing Western Landscapes, 1870 to 1940." *Western Historical Quarterly* 29 (1998): 4–23.

———. "Victorian Ladies Outdoors: Women in the Early Western Conservation Movement, 1870–1920." *Southern California Quarterly* 83 (2001): 59–80.

Robinson, John W. "A Fine Shaggy Excursion: John Muir in the San Gabriels." *Pacific Historian* 23 (1979): 90–100.

———. "The Creation of Yosemite Valley: A Scientific Controversy from the Nineteenth Century." *Pacific Historian* 24 (1980): 376–85.

Rome, Adam. "'Political Hermaphrodites': Gender and Environmental Reform in Progressive America." *Environmental History* 11 (2006): 440–63.

Roorbach, Eloise. "John Muir." *Craftsman* 27 (1915): 479–80.

Roosevelt, Theodore. "John Muir: An Appreciation." *Outlook* 109 (6 Jan. 1915): 27–28.

Ryan, P. J. "The Martinez Years: The Family Life and Letters of John Muir." *Pacific Historian* 25 (1981): 79–85.

———. "John Muir and the Tall Trees of Australia." *Pacific Historian* 29 (1985): 124–35.

Sackman, Douglas C. "'Nature's Workshop': The Work Environment and Workers' Bodies in California's Citrus Industry, 1900–1940." *Environmental History* 5 (2000): 27–53.

Sargent, Charles S. "John Muir." *Sierra Club Bulletin* 10 (1916): 37.

Schofield, Edmund A. "John Muir's Yankee Friends and Mentors: The New England Connection." *Pacific Historian* 29 (1985): 65–89.

Schrepfer, Susan R. "Conflict in Preservation: The Sierra Club, Save-The-Redwoods League, and Redwood National Park." *Journal of Forest History* 24 (1980): 60–77.

Sheats, Paul D. "John Muir's Glacial Gospel." *Pacific Historian* 29 (1985): 42–53.

Shields, Scott A. "California 1900...on the Threshold of a New Century: Turn-of-the-century Art, Artifacts, and Photographs from around the State." *California History* 79 (2000): 102–10.

Simonson, Harold P. "The Tempered Romanticism of John Muir." *Western American Literature* 13 (1978): 227–41.

Smith, Michael L. "The Value of a Tree: Public Debates of John Muir and Gifford Pinchot." *Historian* 60 (1998): 757–78.

Snyder, James B. "Putting 'Hoofed Locusts' Out to Pasture." *Nevada Historical Society Quarterly* 46 (2003): 139–72.

Stanley, Millie. "John Muir in Wisconsin." *Pacific Historian* 29 (1985): 7–15.

Stoll, Mark. "God and John Muir: A Psychological Interpretation of Muir's Life and Religion." In *John Muir: Life and Work*. Ed. Sally M. Miller, 64–81. Albuquerque: Univ. of New Mexico Press, 1993.

Strong, Douglas H. "The History of Sequoia National Park, 1876–1926: Part I: The Movement to Establish a Park." *Southern California Quarterly* 48 (1966): 103–28.

———. "The Sierra Forest Reserve: The Movement to Preserve the San Joaquin Valley Watershed." *California Historical Society Quarterly* 46 (1967): 3–17.

———. "The Sierra Club—A History." *Sierra Club Bulletin* 62 (1977): 10–14, 16–20.

Swett, John. "John Muir." *Century* 46 (1893): 120–23.

Terrie, Philip G. "John Muir on Mount Ritter: A New Wilderness Aesthetic." *Pacific Historian* 31 (1987): 34–44.

Turner, Frederick. "Toward Future Muir Biographies: Problems and Prospects." *Pacific Historian* 29 (1985): 157–66.

Van Hise, Charles R. "John Muir." *Science* 45 (1917): 103–9.

Vroman, Charles E. "John Muir in College." *Scientific American Supplement* 80 (1915): 103.

Wadden, Kathleen Anne. "John Muir and the Community of Nature." *Pacific Historian* 29 (1985): 94–102.

Walker, Richard A. "California's Golden Road to Riches: Natural Resources and Regional Capitalism, 1848–1940." *Annals of Association of American Geographers* 91 (2000): 167–99.

Watkins, T. H., and Dewitt Jones. "Conversations with John Muir: An Experiment in the Bridging of Time." *American West* 13 (1976): 30–41.

Weber, Daniel B. "The Transcendental Wilderness Aesthetics of John Muir." *Pacific Historian* 25 (1981): 1–10.

Wesling, Donald. "John Muir and the Human Part of the Mountain's Destiny." *Pacific Historian* 25 (1981): 58–63.

Wild, Peter. "Months of Sorrow and Renewal: John Muir in Arizona, 1905–1906." *Journal of the Southwest* 29 (1987): 20–40.

Williams, Dennis. "John Muir and an Evangelical Vision for Western Natural Resources Management." *Journal of the West* 35 (1996): 53–60.

Witschi, Nicolas. "John of the Mines: Muir's Picturesque Rewrite of the Gold Rush." *Western American Literature* 34 (1999): 316–43.

Worster, Donald. "John Muir and the Roots of American Environmentalism." In *The Wealth of Nature: Environmental History and the Ecological Imagination*, 184–202. New York: Oxford Univ. Press, 1993.

Wyatt, Edith. "John Muir." *New Republic* 2 (1915): 69–71.

Acknowledgments

My obligations in putting this book together are too numerous to remember or properly acknowledge. They include many fine scholars who have written on John Muir's life, above all Michael Cohen and Steven Holmes, from whom I have learned far more than I could indicate here, along with all the librarians who have given generously of their time and expertise. Foremost among the latter are the staff in Special Collections at the Holt-Atherton Library of the University of the Pacific, which has the finest holdings of Muiriana anywhere: Shan Sutton, Trish Richards, and Michael Wurz. Other librarians at the Bancroft Library, the California State Library, the Huntington Library, the Shaw Historical Library of the Oregon Institute of Technology, the Spencer and Watson libraries at the University of Kansas, and the Wisconsin State Historical Society have furnished invaluable assistance. Pam Woolner of the Meaford Museum, Ontario, Thaddeus Shay of the John Muir Historic Site, National Park Service, in Martinez, California, and Linda Eade and Jim Snyder of Yosemite National Park have also been helpful.

Several Muir enthusiasts in Dunbar, Scotland, have provided important background information, photographs, and walking tours. They include David Anderson, Dan Cairney, and Jim Thompson, along with a visiting American scholar, John Warfield Simpson. Peter Coates of the University of Bristol has added to my knowledge of Scottish history and culture, as well as of Muir's growing reputation in his native country.

My graduate research assistants, Shen Hou and Daniel Kerr, have been indispensable, and I am grateful to the University of Kansas for supporting them and for all its generous assistance to me over nearly two decades. I owe a big debt to Steve Anderson, Marco Armiero,

Stefania Barca, Karl Brooks, Kent Curtis, Brian Donahue, Greg Cushman, William Deverell, Deborah Fitzgerald, Eric Freyfogle, Sara Gregg, James Hunt, Karl Jacoby, Nancy Langston, Peter Mancall, Mary Mackey, Leo Marx, Curt Meine, Carolyn Merchant, Eve Munson, Timo Myllyntaus, Viv Nelles, Robert Righter, Harriet Ritvo, Mikko Saikku, Marni Sandweiss, Mark Stoll, Ed Schofield, Theodore Steinberg, William Swagerty, Dorothy Zeisler-Vralsted, Angus Wright, and above all my wife Beverley Worster, who either shared their research with me, commented on portions of the manuscript, arranged public lectures, or otherwise eased my way and deepened my thinking.

Three talented historians went through the entire manuscript carefully and offered many valuable suggestions: Beth LaDow, Adam Rome, and Paul Sutter. All are former students, and I am very proud of their scholarly accomplishments. They, and many more like them whom I have had the privilege of teaching at several universities, have enriched my life in innumerable ways, and I have dedicated this book to all my students, past, present, and future.

At Oxford University Press, I have had the pleasure of working with executive editor Susan Ferber, whose shrewd advice immeasurably improved the book, and I thank her and others now and formerly at the press, along with my loyal agent Gerry McCauley, for their continuing support and interest over the years.

Index

Page numbers in *italics* refer to illustrations

American Association for the
    Advancement of Science, 197,
    236, 478 n.34
American Civic Association, 429
American Commonwealth, The (Bryce), 338
American frontier. *See* frontier
    settlements
American Museum of Natural History,
    334, 492 n.63
"An Adventure with a Dog and a Glacier"
    (Muir), 260
Anderson, Melville, 405
animals:
    anthropocentric view of, 143
    egalitarian views of, 8, 56, 137–38,
        144–45, 352, 369
    emotional life of, 259–61
    JM's empathy for, 6–7, 51, 56, 146,
        154, 265, 268, 273
    See also hunting
*An Inquiry into the Nature and Causes of the Wealth
    of Nations* (Smith), 18, 19
Appalachian Mountain Club, 328, 426
Appalachian Mountains, 38, 119, 125
Araucaria, 443–45
Arctic, 258, 263, 264
Argentina, 443, 444–45
"A Rival of the Yosemite" (Muir),
    326–27
Arizona, 391–92
Armes, William, 328, 329
Arnold Arboretum, 334, 377
Athens, Ga., 128
Atlantic Monthly, 356, 372, 456
Audubon, John, 36
Audubon Society, 345, 484 n.37
Australia, 383, 384, 488 n.29

Badè, William, 263, 431–32, 462,
    491 n.44, 493 n.18
Baker, Ray Stannard, 374
Ballinger, Richard, 431, 435, 436–37
Ball, John, 185
baobab tree, 445–46
Barnum, Phineas T., 174
Bartleson-Bidwell party, 242
Beard, Daniel, 369
Beardslee, L.A., 248
Belgium, 459

Bellamy, Edward, 306
Bell, Emily, 383
Bering Sea, 361
Bering Strait, 263, 266
Berkeley, Calif., 236, 237, 386
Bidwell, Annie, 241–42, 246, 247, 255,
    262
Bidwell, John:
    death of, 389
    friendship with JM, 241–42, 246,
        247, 255
    prosperity of, 242, 389, 481 n.11
Bierce, Ambrose, 219
Bierstadt, Albert, 172
Billy (shepherd), 159, 161–62
biological surveys, 190
"biophilia," 5–6
Black's Hotel, 168, 169, 180, 296, 373
Blakley (Blackley), Hamilton, 20
Blakley, Mary Muir (aunt), 20, 59
Blanc, Mount, 185, 339
Bliss, Cornelius, 354
Bloomington, Ill., 115
Blue Forest (Blue Mesa), 394–95
Boling, John, 167
Bonaventure Cemetery, Ga., 130–33,
    140, 389
Bonpland, Aimé, 61
Book of Martyrs (Foxe), 115
Boone and Crockett Club, 440,
    484 n.37
Boston Academy of Science, 196
Boston Society of Natural History, 195,
    373
botany:
    and Asa Gray, 203–6
    JM's study of, 74–75
Bothwell, Earl of, 16
Boulton, Matthew, 18
Branch, George, 62
Branner, John, 329
Brazil, 61, 441, 443–44
Breaking New Ground (Pinchot), 352,
    492 n.69
Brewer, William, 190, 324, 349, 358
Bridalveil Falls, 165, *166*, 368
British Railway Company, 16
Brooks, Walter R., 158
Brown, Bradley, 62

industry:
    as dehumanizing environment, 106–7
    efficiency analysis by JM, 106–7
    and Pullman labor unrest, 342–43
    Scots as innovators in, 17–18, 63, 105,
        295
In Memoriam (Tennyson), 207
Inupiats (Eskimos), 247, 265–66, 274
invention and innovation:
    JM's talent for, 63–66, 209
    Scottish history of, 17–18, 63, 105,
        295
inventions by Muir, 63–66, 67
    as agriculturalist, 295
    alarm-clock bed, 64, 72, 74, 75, 82,
        97, 105
    drawings of, 64–66, *83*
    as schoolteacher, 82
    scythe-clock, 69, 70, 105
    self-setting sawmill, 63
    student desk clock, *83*, 84
    at Trout Hollow, 97–98, 295
Irish, John P., 309, 322–23
irrigation, 284–85, 411–12
Irving, Washington, 113
Italy, 446
Ivesia muirii (granite mousetail), 204

Jackson, Sheldon, 247, 249
James, George Wharton, 407, 489 n.10
James, William, 307, 308
Japan, 384
Jay, Charles, 96, 102, 117
Jeannette (ship), 263, 269, 270, 272
Jefferson, Thomas, 286
Jewett, Sarah Orne, 335
John Muir Birthplace Trust, *21*,
    493 n.20
John Muir Highway, 125
John Muir National Historic Site,
    493 n.20
John Muir Trail, 464
John Muir Trust, 464
Johnson, Andrew, 102
Johnson, Robert Underwood, *311*
    appearance, 310
    background, 310–11
    as conservation leader, 345
    correspondence with Louie Muir, 320

    as editor, 241, 310, 312, 326, 334,
        439, 486 n.42
    and Hetch Hetchy, 429, 435, 491 n.44
    and Kings Canyon, 324, 326
    political views, 343, 483 n.11
    relationship with JM, 310, 311–14,
        326, 328, 329, 338–39, 423, 439,
        447, 460, 486 n.42, 493 n.18
    and Sequoia National Park, 321
    and Sierra Club, 328, 329, 330,
        491 n.44
    and Yosemite, 312–14, 316, 320, 399,
        447
Johnson, Willard, 329
Jolliet, Louis, 47
Jordan, David Starr, 329, 433
*Journal of Researches, Naturalist's Voyage Round the
    World, The* (Darwin), 206, 476 n.45
Juneau, Alaska, 257, 361

Kadichan (Tlingit crew), 246
Kearney, Denis, 221
Keeler, Charles, 360, 363, 396–97,
    493 n.18
Keintpoos (Captain Jack), 227
Keith, William, 489 n.49
    death, 440
    exhibits, 333
    JM's friendship with, 183, 217,
        223–24, 333, 405
    painting style, 223, 224, 309
    trip to Hetch Hetchy, 424
Kellogg, Albert, 200
Kellogg, Vernon, 405, 451
Kennedy, Helen, 20
Kentucky, 123–25
Kent, William, 407, 414, 421, 450, 452
Kerr, Mark, 329
Kew Botanical Gardens, London, 205,
    338
Key to Theology (Pratt), 230
Key West, Fla., 359
King, Clarence, 183, 189–90, 191, 195,
    324
King, Mount, 190
Kings Canyon:
    drawing by JM, *326*
    exploration by JM, 325–26
    JM's advocacy for, 326–27

Muir, John: (*continued*)

THOUSAND MILE WALK: decision to see world, 114–17; as nonconformist, 119–21, 122, 123; satchel contents, 120–21, 122–23; journal-keeping, 122–23; through Kentucky and Tennessee, 123–27; through Georgia, 123, 127–33; through Florida, 123, 133–40; bout with malaria, 139–41, 146; religious concerns, 141–45; in Cuba, 145–47; travels to California, 147–48

YOSEMITE YEARS: arrives in California, 148, 149–50; first visit to Yosemite Valley, 150, 151–53; agricultural work, 153; sheep tending, 153–55, 158–59, 161–62; summer in the Sierras, 158–64; nature as religion, 160–61; Indian encounters, 162–64; winter work in Yosemite Valley, 164, 168–69, 171, 172–74; employed as naturalist-guide, 174–77; as character in novel, 176; relationship with Hutchings, 177–79; wants to become mountain naturalist, 179–82, 191–92; mountaineering, 182–85, 475 n.3; discovers glaciers in Sierras, 192–93; glacial origin theory, 194–99; Jeanne Carr visits, 200–201; embraces theory of evolution, 202–3, 204, 206, 208; friendship with Asa Gray, 204–6; friendship with Ralph W. Emerson, 209–12, 215, 335; friendship with Abba Woolson, 212–14

CITY LIFE: moves to San Francisco, 216–17, 222; lodges with Swetts, 217–18, 221; begins writing career, 218–20; becomes roving correspondent, 222–23; writes travel articles, 224–26; writes about Indians, 226–27; writes about Mormons, 227–32; hikes into San Gabriel Mountains, 3, 4, 11–12, 341; conservation theme in writing, 232–37, 233–37; visits Carrs in Pasadena, 237–38; friendship with Strentzels, 238–41, 242–44,

245; finds national audience, 241; friendship with Bidwells, 241–42; rides with 39th Parallel survey team, 243–44; engagement to Louie Strentzel, 245

ALASKA AND MARRIAGE: first expedition to Alaska, 246–55; canoe trip into Glacier Bay, 251–54; cares for hungry/starving Chilkat baby, 274–75; gets married, 255–56; learns orchard management, 256, 289; second expedition to Alaska, 256–58; on glacier with Stickeen, 258–61; birth of daughter Wanda, 262; third expedition to Alaska, 263–64; observations of Alaska cultures, 264–69, 273–74; explores Arctic islands, 269–72; returns to Strentzel ranch, 272; assumes management of ranch, 276–78, 289–96; travels with Louie to Yosemite, 296–97; Muir family relationships, 297–300; visits Yellowstone National Park, 299; death of father, 300–301; birth of daughter Helen, 302; as head of Muir clan, 302–4

CONSERVATION YEARS: as editor of *Picturesque California,* 309–10, 313; travels to Yosemite, 311–13; advocates for Yosemite park, 313–16, 322; fourth trip to Alaska, 316–19; Yosemite becomes national park, 320–22; conflict with Yosemite Commission, 322–24; father-in-law dies, 324–25; moves into Strentzel home, 325; hires brother-in-law as ranch foreman, 325; as advocate for Kings Canyon, 324–27; founding of Sierra Club, 328–30; elected president of Sierra Club, 329; hires brother to work on ranch, 330; as conservation leader, 330–31, 343–49; attends World's Columbian Exposition, 332–33; visits New York and Boston, 333–35; travels to Scotland, 335–37; glacier studies in Europe, 337; visits London and Washington,

Muir, John: (*continued*)
by Muir); as journal-keeper,
122–23, *131*, *135*, 160, 442–47,
444, 455–56; as millwright,
97–98, 101, 102, 139, 168–69, 172,
464; as mountain naturalist/
glaciologist, 89–90, 181–85,
191–202, 247; as reformer, 11, 284,
307–8; as Sierra Club president
(*See* Sierra Club); as writer, 3, 11,
218–220, 339–342, 406–407,
455–456, 462 (*See also* WRITINGS);
as Yosemite naturalist-guide,
174–77, 373
WRITINGS: "An Adventure with a
Dog and a Glacier," 260, 359; "A
Rival of the Yosemite," 326–27;
autobiography. See *My Boyhood and
Youth*; *Cruise of the Corwin, The* (1917),
263, 462; "Features of the Proposed Yosemite National Park," 315;
"God's First Temples: How Shall We
Preserve Our Forests?," 234; *Life
and Letters*, 462; "Living Glaciers of
California," 241; *My Boyhood and Youth*
(1913), 5, 13–14, 22, 50–51, 90,
406–10, 456–57, 462; *My First Summer in the Sierra* (1911), 160, 441, 462;
Our National Parks (1901), 372–77,
406, 462, 487 n.9; *Picturesque California*, 309, 310; poetry, 82, 108;
"Ranch Life," 294; *Steep Trails* (1918),
227, 462; *Stickeen*, 260, 406; "Studies in the Sierra," 197, 198–99, 219;
"The Alaska Trip," 359; "The Bee
Pastures of California," 241, 245;
"The City of the Saints," 228–29;
The Mountains of California (1894),
338–42, 346, 350, 374, 441, 462,
484 n.12; "The Treasures of the Yosemite," 315; *The Yosemite* (1912), 447,
448–49, 462; *Thousand-Mile Walk to the
Gulf, A* (1916), 122, 124, 462; *Travels
in Alaska* (1915), 462; "Wild Wool,"
286; *Writings of John Muir, The*, 462;
"Yellowstone National Park, The,"
374–75; "Yosemite Glaciers," 194;
"Yosemite Valley in Flood," 219
Muir, John (grandfather), 20

Muir, Katie (sister-in-law), 91, 238, 298
Muir Lodge, 461
Muir, Louie Strentzel (wife), *240*, *387*
appearance, 239
birth and childhood, 239
childhood, 239
correspondence with Jeanne Carr,
239–40
correspondence with JM, 254–55,
301–2, 318, 333, 334, 337, 382, 384
correspondence with Robert Johnson,
320
death, 392–93
engagement to JM, 245, 246, 254–55
and Grange movement, 239, 481 n.11
heirs of, 395
marital relationship, 296–97, 301–2,
318–19, 386, 441
marriage, 255–56
offspring, 262, 302
personal characteristics, 239–40
pre-engagement friendship with JM,
240–41, 242–44, 245
pregnancies, 256, 261, 298, 302
relationship with parents, 239, 245,
294, 324–25
unwillingness to travel, 296, 297
Muir, Margaret (sister). *See* Reid,
Margaret Muir
Muir, Mary (aunt). *See* Blakley, Mary
Muir
Muir, Mary (sister):
birth, 21
college, 82
relationship with JM, 74, 96, 297,
404, 440, 456
Muir, Sarah (sister). *See* Galloway, Sarah
Muir
Muir, Sarah Higgs (grandmother), 20
Muir, Wanda (daughter). *See* Hanna,
Wanda Muir
Muir Woods, 421–22
Mulholland, William, 420
Murphy, N.C., 138
Muybridge, Eadweard, 172
My Boyhood and Youth (Muir), 5, 13–14, 22,
50–51, 90, 406–10, 456–57, 462
My First Summer in the Sierra (Muir), 160,
441, 462

sheep:
    as destructive force on landscape, 161,
        162, 234, 312, 383
    domestication of, 287–89
    in pastoral traditions, 17, 161, 162
    on preserved lands, 348, 355
    as victim of man, 153–54, 287–88
Sherman, William Tecumseh, 127
Shiloh, Battle of, 85, 125
Shinn, Charles Howard, 309
Sierra Club:
    charter members of, 329, 345,
        484 n.39
    early female members of, 345, 435
    founding of, 328–30
    and Hetch Hetchy dam controversy,
        419, 425, 426, 432–33
    JM as president of, 3, 329, 388, 430
    Muir Lodge, 461
    and 1906 earthquake, 489 n.49
    receipt of Strentzel manse by,
        493 n.20
    and Roosevelt administration, 430
    summer outings by, 388–89, *389*
    as symbol of JM's legacy, 464
    and Yosemite Valley, 348–49, 398–99
Sierra Club Bulletin, 425, 432, 462,
        493 n.18
Sierra forest reserve, 328
Sierra Nevada:
    geology of, 185, 192–93
    observations by JM, 150, 160–61, 164,
        216–17, 339–41
    as tourist destination, 185, 186, 188
Silva of North America (Sargent), 350
Simla, India, 382
Sisson, Justin, 184–85
Sitka, Alaska, 248
Sitka Charley (Tlingit crew), 246
slavery, 43, 68–69, 85, 121
Smart Billy (Tlingit oarsman), 257
Smith, Adam, 18, 19
Smith, Hoke, 349
Smithsonian Institution, 191, 266,
        492 n.63
Smoky Jack (John Connel), 153, 158
Smout, T.C., 16, 23
Social Gospellers, 306
social reform:

after World War I, 460
nature as impetus for, 414–18
The Century as voice for, 241, 311
See also reform movements
Society for the Preservation of the
        National Parks, 433, 435, 491 n.44
Soda Springs, 159, 311
Sons of Daniel Boone, 369
South America:
    Darwin on, 118
    Humboldt on, 118–19
    JM's intent to visit as young man, 114,
        119, 164, 174
    visit by JM, 439–40, 441–45
Southern Pacific Railroad, 358, 398–99,
        411, 440
Spain, 359
Sparks, William, 321
Spring Valley Water Company, 419, 420,
        438
Stanley, John, 73
Starr, Kevin, 221
Staten Island, N.Y., 42
steam engines, 18, 23
Steep Trails (Muir), 227, 462
St. Elias range, 319
Stephen, Leslie, 185
Stevenson, Robert Louis, 14
Stewart, George W., 321
Stickeen (dog), 257, 258–61, 335,
        480 n.19
Stickeen (Muir), 260, 406, 480 n.20
Stickeen John (Tlingit crew), 246
Stikine River, 250
Stiles, William A., 347, 485 n.23
St. Joseph Island, 93
St. Lawrence Island, 265, 266–67
Stoddard, Charles Warren, 219
Stoll, Steven, 281
Stone, Livingston, 233
Stoneman Hotel, 312
St. Petersburg, Russia, 378
Strentzel, John (father-in-law), *278*
    appearance, 238
    birth/life in Europe, 238–39
    death, 324
    emigration to U.S., 239
    in Grange movement, 282, 283,
        285–86